LANDMARK ESSAYS ON TROPES AND FIGURES

Landmark Essays on Tropes and Figures offers a thorough overview of the most influential essays on rhetorical tropes and figures, providing a solid foundation for understanding this area of study. The book is divided into two parts. The first part deals with essays on the development of the concepts, their definitions, and their decline; the second part deals with applications: how figures and tropes have been used in various disciplinary domains, from literary criticism, to politics, science, advertising, and music.

This volume spans writing from the early 20th century to contemporary work, providing readers with a historically grounded base for study. It brings together book chapters and journal articles that would otherwise be difficult to locate, providing a ready-made collection of readings on the topic of tropes and figures.

Roberto Franzosi is Professor of Sociology and Linguistics at Emory University, Georgia, USA.

THE LANDMARK ESSAYS SERIES

Landmark Essays is a series of anthologies providing ready access to key rhetorical studies in a wide variety of fields. The classic articles and chapters that are fundamental to every subject are often the most difficult to obtain, and almost impossible to find arranged together for research or for classroom use. This series solves that problem.

Each book encompasses a dozen or more of the most significant published studies in a particular field, and includes an index and bibliography for further study.

Series Editors:
James J. Murphy
Krista Ratcliffe

Landmark Essays on Tropes and Figures
Edited by Roberto Franzosi

Landmark Essays on Historiographies of Rhetorics
Edited by Victor J. Vitanza

Landmark Essays on Archival Research
Edited by Lynée Lewis Gaillet, Diana Eidson, and Don Gammill Jr.

Landmark Essays on Rhetoric and Feminism: 1973–2000
Edited by Cheryl Glenn, Andrea Lunsford

Landmark Essays on Speech and Writing
Edited by Peter Elbow

Landmark Essays on Basic Writing
Edited by Kay Halasek, Nels P. Highberg

Landmark Essays on ESL Writing
Edited by Tony Silva, Paul Kei Matsuda

Landmark Essays on Rhetoric and Literature
Edited by Craig Kallendorf

Landmark Essays on Contemporary Rhetoric
Edited by Thomas B. Farrell

Landmark Essays on Aristotelian Rhetoric
Edited by Richard L. Enos, Lois P. Agnew

Landmark Essays on Bakhtin, Rhetoric, and Writing
Edited by Frank Farmer

Landmark Essays on Rhetoric and the Environment
Edited by Craig Waddell

Landmark Essays on Rhetoric of Science: Case Studies
Edited by Randy Allen Harris

Landmark Essays on Advanced Composition
Edited by Gary A. Olson, Julie Drew

Landmark Essays on Writing Centers
Edited by Christina Murphy, Joe Law

Landmark Essays on Rhetorical Invention in Writing
Edited by Richard E. Young, Yameng Liu

Landmark Essays on Writing Process
Edited by Sondra Perl

Landmark Essays on Writing Across the Curriculum
Edited by Charles Bazerman, David R. Russell

Landmark Essays on Rhetorical Criticism
Edited by Thomas W. Benson

Landmark Essays on Voice and Writing
Edited by Peter Elbow

Landmark Essays on Classical Greek Rhetoric
Edited by A. Edward Schiappa

Landmark Essays on Kenneth Burke
Edited by Barry Brummett

Landmark Essays on American Public Address
Edited by Martin Medhurst

LANDMARK
ESSAYS ON TROPES AND FIGURES

Edited by
ROBERTO FRANZOSI

Routledge
Taylor & Francis Group
NEW YORK AND LONDON

First published 2017
by Routledge
711 Third Avenue, New York, NY 10017

and by Routledge
2 Park Square, Milton Park, Abingdon, Oxon, OX14 4RN

Routledge is an imprint of the Taylor & Francis Group, an informa business

© 2017 Taylor & Francis

The right of the Robert Franzosi to be identified as the author of the editorial material, and of the authors for their individual chapters, has been asserted in accordance with sections 77 and 78 of the Copyright, Designs and Patents Act 1988.

All rights reserved. No part of this book may be reprinted or reproduced or utilised in any form or by any electronic, mechanical, or other means, now known or hereafter invented, including photocopying and recording, or in any information storage or retrieval system, without permission in writing from the publishers.

Trademark notice: Product or corporate names may be trademarks or registered trademarks, and are used only for identification and explanation without intent to infringe.

Library of Congress Cataloging in Publication Data
Landmark essays on tropes and figures / [edited by] Roberto Franzosi.
pages cm.—(The Landmark essays series)
Includes bibliographical references and index.
ISBN 978-1-138-92561-8 (hardback)—ISBN 978-1-138-92562-5 (pbk.)
1. Rhetoric. 2. Written communication. I. Franzosi, Roberto, editor. II. Title: Tropes and figures.
P301.L2935 2016
808—dc23
2015025880

ISBN: [978-1-138-92561-8] (hbk)
ISBN: [978-1-138-92562-5] (pbk)

Typeset in Minion
by Keystroke, Neville Lodge, Tettenhall, Wolverhampton

The cover displays plots based on data taken from the millions of books digitized by Google and made available through Google Books and displayable in Google Books Ngram Viewer. The upper plot shows the frequency of the words "rhetoric", "metaphor", "deconstruction", "linguistic turn", and "poststructuralism" between 1970 and 2008. The lower plot displays the frequency of the words "rhetoric" and "metaphor" between 1700 and 2008. The data show that rhetoric and metaphor have gone hand-in-hand not just in recent decades after "the great shipwreck of rhetoric", in Genette's expression, but through the centuries (plots of all other rhetorical figures would show these figures as very distant competitors of metaphor for book space). Only such late-twentieth century movements variously labeled deconstruction, linguistic turn, or poststructuralism rescued rhetoric from the "great shipwreck".

Jacobo Hieronymo Murphy consiliario atque amico
To Jerry Murphy, mentor and friend

CONTENTS

Acknowledgments   ix
Selected Works   xi

INTRODUCTION   1
James J. Murphy, Figures of Diction and of Thought from
Rhetorica ad Herennium, Book IV   17

PART I
THE CONCEPT OF TROPES AND FIGURES   25

1. James J. Murphy, *Topos* and *Figura*: Historical Cause and Effect?   27
2. Brian Vickers, The Functions of Rhetorical Figures   39
3. Sister Miriam Joseph, Elocution or Style   67
4. Peter Mack, Manuals of Tropes and Figures   75
5. Kenneth Burke, Four Master Tropes   91
6. Gérard Genette, Rhetoric Restrained   102
7. George Lakoff and Mark Johnson, Conceptual Metaphor in Everyday Language   111

PART II
APPLICATIONS: LITERARY CRITICISM   139

8. Herbert A. Wichelns, The Literary Criticism of Oratory   141
9. Sam Meyer, The Figures of Rhetoric in Spenser's *Colin Clout*   168
10. Paul de Man, Rhetoric of Tropes (Nietzsche)   187

POLITICS   198

11. Edward P. J. Corbett and Robert J. Connors, John F. Kennedy: Inaugural Address   198
12. Michael C. Leff and Gerald P. Mohrmann, Lincoln at Cooper Union: A Rhetorical Analysis of the Text   211
13. Charles N. Smiley, Lincoln and Gorgias   225
14. Richard P. Fulkerson, The Public Letter as a Rhetorical Form: Structure, Logic, and Style in King's "Letter from Birmingham Jail"   229
15. Jeanne Fahnestock, Introduction to Rhetorical Style: The Uses of Language in Persuasion   246

16	Jonathan Charteris-Black, Winston Churchill: Metaphor and Heroic Myth	250
17	Quentin Skinner, Paradiastole: Redescribing the Vices as Virtues	272

SCIENCE 287

18	Brian Vickers, The Royal Society and English Prose Style: A Reassessment	287
19	Jeanne Fahnestock, Ploche and Polyptoton	313

ADVERTISING 328

20	Edward F. McQuarrie and David Glen Mick, Figures of Rhetoric in Advertising Language	328
21	J. Anthony Blair, The Rhetoric of Visual Arguments	351

MUSIC 362

22	George J. Buelow, Rhetoric and Music	362

Index 389

ACKNOWLEDGMENTS

In the production of this book I have incurred debts to both individuals and institutions. Nicholas Crowe, Peter Mack, James Murphy, and Hanne Roer provided invaluable help. William Branson and Ingrid De Smet also provided suggestions. The seeds of this project were sown during a small conference on rhetoric I organized in 2012 at Emory during a fellowship year at the Fox Center for Humanistic Inquiry; James Murphy gently pushed me, not a rhetorician, to bring to fruition a topic I had explored for some years. I continued the work in the summer of 2013 at the Centre for Medieval & Renaissance Studies at Oxford and, in the Fall 2013, at the Italian Academy for Advanced Studies in America of Columbia University, where I held a fellowship. I completed the writing at Nuffield College, Oxford, with a fellowship in Hilary term 2014.

SELECTED WORKS

The collection brings together, under different headings, the most significant 20th century contributions to the study of tropes and figures. Exceptionally for the Landmark Essays series, the collection opens with Book IV of the anonymous *Rhetorica ad Herennium*, the seminal, first extant treatment of figures upon which all subsequent work would be based. Divided in two parts, the first part of the collection deals with essays on the development of the concepts, their definitions, and their decline; the second part deals with applications: how figures and tropes have been used in various disciplinary domains, from literary criticism, to politics, science, advertising, and music. Somewhat arbitrary, or personal, as these choices inevitably are, when it comes to figures the choices are made all more difficult by the relative scarcity of available work. To find sound theoretical work, I had to stretch back to the 1940s, particularly to Joseph's excellent classification of figures. As for applied work, weeks on end of reading turned up very few modern scholars who approach a text highlighting the gamut of rhetorical figures used in the text. Fahnestock is rare in that respect. Even in the field of literary criticism, textual analyses based on figures are surprisingly rare. More typical are analyses of a single figure (e.g., Booth's work on irony). In the Introduction, I depart from the standard approach to edited collections, where limited available pages are mostly or wholly spent on detailed descriptions of each selected work. Instead, I trace the historical development of figures and contextualize their role and place in the broader field of rhetoric. I leave to the readers some of the work but also the pleasure of finding out for themselves what each author has to say.

INTRODUCTION

Of Tropes and Figures and of Their Strange Career through the Centuries

Rhetorical figures were not born under propitious auspices. Gorgias, to whom we owe the first use of a handful of figures aimed at creating his symmetric style, did not fare well in his sparring with Socrates in Plato's dialogues.[1] His figures, though, not only survived, but grew and multiplied over the centuries.[2]

By the first century BC, figures had taken center stage in rhetoric. Cicero, like Aristotle, with little interest in rhetorical taxonomy, provides a simple list of figures without ever even naming them (e.g., *Orator* 39.135–139, *De Oratore* 3.201–205). But the anonymous author of the *Rhetorica ad Herennium*[3] dedicates the last book (Book 4) to the discussion of 64 figures, with definitions and examples of use. Quintilian similarly dedicates two books (8 and 9) of his *Institutio Oratoria* to figures, again defining each figure and providing examples of its use.

But what are tropes and figures?[4] Let Peacham answer that question for us. Tropes and schemes (or schemates or the Latin *figura*)[5] involve a change in the "forme of words, oration, or sentence, made new by art, differing from the vulgar maner and custome of writing or speaking."[6] But while tropes change the meaning of words or sentences, schemes only change the order of letters in a word, or words in a sentence, leaving meaning unaltered. Roman rhetoricians divided the figures into *figures of speech* (*verborum exornationes* or *figurae verborum*) related to verbal expression, and *figures of thought* (*sententiarum exornationes* or *figurae sententiarum*), related to ideas and arguments[7] (e.g., *Rhetorica ad Herennium* IV.13 and IV.46; Quintilian *Inst. Or.* 9.1.17).

We owe to medieval rhetoricians an increasing specialization of tropes and figures, in terms of both numbers of figures and specialized treatments (Faral 1924: 48–60; Murphy 1974: 32–37). Book IV of the popular *ad Herennium* started being circulated separately from the rest of the book. Some of the key medieval texts on rhetoric (and grammar) closely followed Book IV of the *ad Herennium*: from Donatus's *Ars Maior* (4th century AD), that introduces a distinction between tropes and schemate in the two brief sections *De tropis* and *De schematibus* (also circulated separately from the rest of the *Ars Maior*), to the Venerable Bede's *De schematibus et tropis* (written in 701).[8] Donatus, in his *Ars Maior,* states that there are many schemes, but that the most important ones are only 17 and provides definitions for each; similarly, he lists and defines 13 tropes. Later medieval grammarians and rhetoricians were more prolific in their lists. Alexander of Villa-Dei's *Doctrinale* (1199) treats 80 figures and Evrard of Béhune's *Graecismum* (1212) covers 103 figures.[9]

This trend continued well into the Renaissance with several new specialized treatises, from Petrus Mosellanus's *Tabulae de Schematibus et Tropis* (1516) to Johannes

Susenbrotus's *Epitome troporum ac schematum* (1540), Richard Sherry's *Treatise of Schemes and Tropes*, the first treatise in English vernacular (1550), Henry Peacham's *The Garden of Eloquence, Containing the Most Excellent Ornaments, Exornations, Lightes, Flowers, and Forms of Speech, Commonly Called the Figures of Rethorike* (1577, 1593), John Hoskins's *Directions for Speech and Style* (circa 1600).[10] The number of figures also kept climbing in the Renaissance, to 132 with Susenbrotus and nearly 200 with Peacham.[11] And even past rhetoric's Renaissance golden age, German Baroque rhetoricians extended to music the study of tropes and figures (Buelow 1980; Unger 1941; Vickers 1984; Bartel 1997). Later yet, French rhetoricians of the 18th and early 19th centuries continued to produce treatises specialized in tropes and figures (Dumarsais's *Traité des tropes*, 1730, Fontanier's *Commentaire raisonne des tropes*, 1818, and *Traite generate des figures du discours*, 1821–1827; Genette 1982: 103–126). And even general 18th century rhetorical treatises dedicate a great deal of space to elocution and figures. Half of Vico's *Institutiones oratoriae* (1711–1741) deals with elocution, "the most important part of this art [rhetoric] to the extent that eloquence has taken its very name from it."[12] The discussion of tropes and figures takes up much of Lamy's *La rhetorique ou l'arte de parler* (1741, revised edition) and of Blair's *Lectures on Rhetoric and Belles Lettres* (1783).

Rhetoric as an Organic Whole: The Function of Figures

"A figure has always a function," Vickers assures us. (1970:121). But what is that function? To "add strength to arguments and give them grace", would be Quintilian's answer (*Inst. Or.* 9.1.2). Still in the 16th century Sherry would write: "thys darre I saye, no eloquente wryter maye be perceiued as he shulde be, wythoute the knowledge of them [figures]" (*Treatise of Schemes and Tropes* 1550). "If style served only for pleasure," Melanchthon writes, "such pleasant music should still not be neglected" (La Fontaine 1968:222). But there is more to style, figures in particular, than just embellishment (*ornatus* or Peacham's *exornation*). For one thing, when there is no suitable word for a thing or concept, figures serve a practical function of allowing greater clarity of signification (Cicero *Orator* I.82; also Melanchthon/La Fontaine 1968: 232). Second, figures are fundamental tools for expressing in language both thoughts and emotions (logos and pathos) – tools that makes an orator "the emperour of mens minds & affections."[13] That much is clear from the very definition of figures found in the *Rhetorica ad Herennium*: "A figure of thought derives a certain distinction from the *idea*, not from the *words* [like figures of diction]" (IV.xii.18–xiii.19; emphasis added). Melanchthon correctly notes: "For the same expressions [figures], when applied for the purpose of confirming or confuting, are bases for argument and the sinews, as they are called. When applied for the purpose of adorning, they are called rhetorical ornaments" (Melanchthon, La Fontaine 1968: 264).

The inter-relationships among parts of rhetoric (e.g., means of persuasion, topics, branches of oratory, arrangement) are not always clearly spelled out, particularly in reference to figures. Aphthonius, in his *progymnasmata*, the rhetorical exercises that enjoyed centuries of continued use (Nadeau, 1952; Clark, 1952: 259), lists the *topics* to be used in each exercise, but there is no mention of figures. Roman rhetoricians only made passing references to the function of figures in relation to broader aspects of rhetoric (notably, means of persuasion). Cicero, at the end of his *Topica* and after a series of (rhetorical) questions, remarks (23.87): "Our next task is to consider what topics are suited to each question."[14] He goes on to list the topics most suitable for the different types of speeches (deliberative, judicial, epideictic) (24.91) and for the different parts of speech (e.g., introduction, narrative, conclusion) (26.97). But when it comes to "the figures' function ... Cicero is disappointing" (Vickers 1970: 98; see also Brennan 1960: 60). It is in the *Rhetorica ad Herennium* that we find occasional comments on the functions and pitfalls of certain figures (e.g., "*personification* may be applied to a variety of things... It is most useful in dealing with amplification and appeal to pity", IV.66). That practice continues in Quintilian's *Institutio Oratoria*,[15] with similar occasional comments on a figure's function and its relationship to means of persuasion (logos, pathos, ethos)[16] and parts of speech.[17]

In *ad Herennium* and *Institutio* we also find a fourfold classification of rhetorical operations, the *quadripartita ratio* – *adiectio* (addition), *detractio* (subtraction), *immutatio* (permutation), and *transmutatio* (transposition) – that provided rhetorical strategies for the manipulation and variation of discourse (*ad Herennium* IV.21.29; *Inst. Or.* 1.5.38; Lausberg, 1998: § 462). Medieval and Renaissance rhetoricians closely followed suit. But as they added more figures to the list, complete with definitions, examples, and sometime caveats,[18] they also started grouping the figures together in broader classifications that made explicit the relations between different parts and levels of rhetoric, in particular between figures and means of persuasive appeals and topics (Joseph 1947: 38–39).[19] [20] Indeed, "it would be a mistake to regard the treatises of the figurists as limited to a discussion of style in the narrow sense" (Joseph 1947: 34).[21]

Building on Quintilian's *quadripartita ratio*, Melanchthon, in his *Institutiones Rhetorices* (1521), classified figures in grammatical and rhetorical, further dividing the latter into three orders (Mack 2011: 216–217): a first order dealing with individual words but classified according to their function: repetition (e.g., *Epanaphora, Ploce, Paroemion*), omission (e.g., *Zeugma, Asyndeton*), conjunction (e.g., *Polysindeton, Homeoteleuton*), and separation (e.g., *Paranomasia, Membrum, Taxis*); a second order of figures of thought (e.g., question, exclamation, dubitation, prosopopeia, parrhesia) linked to pathos, and a third order of figures of amplification, "the highest peak of eloquence" (La Fontaine 1968: 261), (e.g., climax, synonyms, distribution, aitiology, antithesis) linked to logos. After all, "we shall provide amplifications in order to arouse people's *minds*" (Melanchthon/La Fontaine 1968: 202; emphasis added). In both *Elementa rhetorices* and *Elementorum rhetorices libri duo*, Melanchthon made explicit the link between figures and *topics of invention* when he subdivided the figures of amplification by topic (definition, division, cause, contraries, comparison and relationship, genus, circumstances and signs), as expressed in concrete instances of figures[22] (Joseph 1947: 38–39; La Fontaine 1968: 273–301).

Later 16th century rhetoricians adopted Melanchthon's three-order grouping of figures. Susenbrotus openly acknowledges Melanchthon's influence upon his three-order classification system (*Epitome* 1540 2.2.3). Both Melanchthon's and Susenbrotus's work served as the basis for Peacham's classification of figures.[23] In the second edition (1593) of his *The Garden of Eloquence*, Peacham divided his 193 figures into Melanchthon's three orders: a first order of "figures of words,"[24] further subdivided by their function – repetition, omission, conjunction, and separation – and a second and third order of "figures of sentences,"[25] with the second order figures being mainly of pathos (they "attend uppon affections," "the sundrie affections and passions") and the third of logos, especially amplification ("mighty to delight and perswade the *mindes* of men").[26] [27]

Yet, Melanchthon's and Peacham's broad classification of figures only begins to tell the tale of the complex relation between figures and other parts of rhetoric, from invention (through topics) to arrangement (different figures are more suitable for different parts of speech), from species of rhetoric (deliberative, judiciary, epideictic) to means of persuasion (pathos, logos, ethos). Several of Peacham's first-order figures are not just "ornament, pleasant to the eare," but also they "may serve to any affection," providing a function typical of second-order figures of pathos; that is particularly true for figures of repetition (e.g., symploce, epizeuxis, diacope), but also for those of separation (e.g., articulus). That is true also for some third-order figures of amplification/ *logos* (e.g., *auxesis*). When 19th century US southern newspapers refer to a lynched black man as "fiend," "brute," or "animal" they are not just amplifying via *auxesis* but arousing the readers' emotions. And although Peacham does not provide a specific grouping of figures of ethos, several of his second-order figures can be used by the speaker to deal with his own character (e.g., parrhesia, eucharistia, syngnome, threnos: see Joseph 1947: 272–286, 393–398). And the third-order figures of amplification are figures of logos, linked to topics.

Compared to Peacham, other 16th century English rhetoricians (e.g., Sherry, Puttenham, Hoskins) are much more traditional in their approach to figures. Yet, even these authors reveal a deep understanding of the close connection between figures and other parts of rhetoric. Sherry's *Treatise of Schemes and Tropes* (1550), along with the usual long list of names with definitions and examples of their use, includes a brief section on topics of invention (e.g., amplification through comparison and circumstances) and makes occasional remarks about the purpose of a figure, particularly in its relation to pathos (e.g., *pathopeia*). Hoskins's short treatise *Directions for Speech and Style* (circa 1600) similarly lists figures with definitions, examples, and caveats. But in grouping figures according to their function – varying, amplifying, and illustrating – Hoskins shows a keen awareness of the use of figures in relation to other parts of rhetoric to achieve specific purposes. Thus, for accumulation, a figure of amplification – the "heaping up of many terms of praise or accusing" (epideictic rhetoric): "I take the use of this amplification to be in anger, detestation, commiseration, and such passions as you, seeming thoroughly possessed with, would willingly stir in others" (pathos).

George Puttenham's *The Arte of English Poesie*, first published in 1589, is dedicated to the study of poetry, one third of the book dealing with ornament. Like all the other treatises, *The Arte of English Poesie* defines each ornamental figure, provides examples of its use, but unlike other treatises, is very explicit about what the reader should see in the example. After all, his audience is not the learned scholars, but the "Ladies and young Gentlewomen, or idle Courtiers, desirous to become skilful in their owne mother tongue,

Introduction 5

and for their priuate recreation to make now & then ditties of pleasure". Contrary to Peacham, Puttenham does not discuss figures' function. Yet, even in poetry, ornament is not simply for delight. There are, in fact, "two sortes" of ornament, "one to satisfie & delight th'eare onely by a goodly outward shew fet vpon the matter with wordes, and speaches smothly and tunably running: another by certaine intendments or sence of such wordes & speeches inwardly working a stirre to the mynde." Puttenham calls auricular the figures that "satisfie & delight th'eare onely" and sensable the ones that "geue it [speech] efficacie by sence." He would write: "a figure is euer vsed to a purpose, either of beautie or of efficacie."[28]

Post Renaissance: Rhetoric under Fire

By the end of the 16th century, the creative spree of rhetoric had run out of steam. The Renaissance, which had produced names such as Valla, Agricola, Melanchthon, Erasmus, Ramus, Suarez, Peacham, Puttenham and scores of others, came to an end. Rhetoric increasingly came under attack. Two lines in Samuel Butler's *Hudibras*, a satirical poem that has nothing to do with rhetoric,[29] are still popular today:

> For all a rhetorician's rules
> Teach nothing but name his tools.
> (Part I, lines 89–90)

Butlers' words echo in Thomas Sprat's *History of the Royal Society of London* published in 1667: "the Old [natural philosophy, including rhetoric and dialectic] could only bestow on us some barren Terms and Notions" (p. 438). It has become a common topic (*topos*, one of the rhetorician's named tools) in the modern history of rhetoric to hold Sprat's *History* responsible for delivering the fatal blow to rhetoric. A handful of quotes from the *History* are piled up as uncontroversial evidence of that blow – never mind that the *History* was largely ignored by contemporaries and "hardly quoted before the present century" (Vickers 1985: 4).

For Sprat, the New Science "prefers Works before Words" (p. 434) and achieves knowledge through the "tedious tryal of Experiments" (p. 12). The "*Art of Experiments* ... consists not in Topicks of reasoning, but of working ... proceeds on *Trials*, and not on *Arguments*." (p. 332) Galileo had said as much: "welcome are reasons and demonstrations, yours or Aristotle's, and not the texts and naked authorities, because our arguments ought to be around the empirical world, and not a paper world."[30] It is in the fight against this paper world that the men of the Royal Society have been "most solicitous," in "the manner of their *Discourse*," with "a constant Resolution, to reject all the amplifications, digressions, and swellings of style" (p. 113; also p. 40, 111). Closer to the topic of this collection, Sprat thundered: "Who can behold, without indignation, how many mists and uncertainties, these specious Tropes and Figures have brought on our Knowledg? ... of all the Studies of men, nothing may be sooner obtain'd, than this vicious abundance of *Phrase*, this trick of *Metaphors*, this volubility of *Tongue*" (p. 112). One of Sprat's men of the Royal Society, Francis Bacon, is similarly quoted for his views on the "excess" of rhetoric, tropes and figures in particular, on rhetoric's "hunt ... after words ... after the choiceness of the phrase, and the round and clean composition of the sentence, and the sweet falling of the clauses, and the varying and illustration of their works with *tropes and figures*, than after the weight of matter, worth of subject, soundness of argument, life of invention, or depth of judgement" (Bacon 1873: 29, emphasis added).

Yet, modern scholars may have been blinded by the common topic of their own creation of an anti-rhetoric stance of early scientists. In a masterful piece, Vickers (1985) convincingly debunks that topos, the Royal Society's anti-rhetorical stance being "the result of animus, or controversy, or Party politics, or religious dispute", rhetoric being just another weapon (1985: 23, 21, 41, 47, 61–63). Indeed, a brilliant use of rhetoric! And brilliant, no doubt, was the development by the Society of a new type of text: the scientific report. When fellows of the Royal Society substituted Aristotle's authority (*ipse dixit*) with the new authority of the experiment, not only did they invoke the topic of testimony to bolster their case (witnesses of various kinds, aristocrats better than commoners, testifying to the validity of the claims) but also that of circumstances (a narrative based on actors acting in time and space). The Society's fellows, in their research reports, chose narrative as the most appropriate rhetorical form to describe an event (the experiment), with detailed descriptions of even trivial details to provide rhetorical vividness (*enargeia*), a painting of the event, skillfully using a mixture of passive and active verbs to underscore realism (Dear 1985). Paradoxically, for the Royal Society's fellows, "style ... was more important than the substance" of their science (Dear 1985: 159).

For Bacon, "rhetoric, or art of eloquence [is] a science excellent, and excellently well laboured. For although in true value it is inferior to wisdom ... [its] duty and office ... is to apply reason to imagination for the better moving of the will." As Mack writes (2002: 294): "Bacon's work is evidently the product of the system he criticizes." That is also true for Sprat who repeatedly falls prey to his "specious Tropes and Figures", both those that "satisfie & delight th'eare" ("Works before Words", alliteration, "tedious trial") and of reasoning such as the rhetorical question or anthypophora, a figure linked to pathos. After all, these men, like other learned men for centuries before them and for several more centuries to come, at least until the late 19th century, if they learned anything they learned rhetoric.

Rhetoric had been the central pillar of the Liberal Arts curriculum of the *trivium*, based on grammar, rhetoric, and logic, since the early Middle Ages (Wagner 1983). From grammar schools to university, pupils learned rhetoric through a variety of pedagogical means, from reading of classical authors, to exercises[31] (the *progymnasmata*), letter writing, essays, orations, debates and disputations (taking both sides of an argument, *argumentum in contrarias partes* or *in utramque partem*), and commonplace books.[32] In a rare memoir by John of Salisbury we learn how Bernard de Chartres taught rhetoric (cited in Faral 1924: 99–100):

> in his reading of authors, he pointed out what was simple and according to the rules; he brought out the figures of grammar, the colors of rhetoric, the fine points of argumentation ... he forced us to reproduce what we had learned, using advice for some and the whip and

punishments for others. The next day, each of us had to bring in something of what he had learned that day . . . one day preparing the next.

Deeply steeped in the same culture, Renaissance humanists and scientists, philosophers and natural philosophers shared a common language in Latin and rhetoric. In the ever growing taxonomic complexity of rhetoric, mathematics, and the natural sciences, these scholars came to share the use of such symbols as graph parentheses for grouping and subdividing objects (e.g., Dee's *The Mathematicall Praeface to Elements of Geometrie of Euclid of Megara* of 1570, Gesner's various books on natural history of 1549, 1555, 1576, and Ramus's, Wilson's, Susenbrotus's, Melanchthon's, Erasmus's rhetorical treatises). They came to share a concern with method (e.g., Ramus and Bacon's discussion of both rhetorical and scientific methods in his *The Advancement of Learning* and *Novum Organum*; on method see Gilbert 1960: 39–66 and Ong 1958: 225–267). When Bacon, in his *De augmentis scientiarum* (1623), expanded to nineteen Melanchthon's five topical questions (La Fontaine 1968: 99) as a way to approach a scientific problem, he was using basic rhetorical topics to build knowledge in a specific scientific field: "1. Inquire what . . . 4. Inquire whether . . . 14. Inquire touching . . . ." And that truly Renaissance addition to the list of rhetorical exercises, the commonplace book,[33] may have contributed to the development of an inductive approach to science, as students grouped their notes in higher and higher categories (Blair 1992, Yeo 1996).

In any case, whether deeply trained in rhetoric or not, conscious or unconscious of the rhetorical underpinnings of one's writing, there is no escape from rhetoric. Thus, Sprat's "condemnation without appeal of rhetoric does not exclude its practice. One thing are the opinions about rhetoric, and another the practice of discourse" (Hallyn 1999: 620). As Frye aptly put it:

> Anything which makes a functional use of words will always be involved in all the technical problems of words, including rhetorical problems. The only road from grammar to logic, then, runs through the intermediate territory of rhetoric. . . . All structures in words are partly rhetorical, and hence literary, and that the notion of a scientific or philosophical verbal structure free of rhetorical elements is an illusion.
>
> (Frye 1957: 331, 350)

No doubt, as Dupriez says, "It is impossible to speak without figures. . . . Everything is rhetorical that relates to the speech act" (Dupriez 1980: 9; see also Bentham, cited in Vickers 1989).

Melanchthon best expressed these two ideas, of a critique of rhetoric that does not preclude its use, and of the inevitability of the use of rhetoric in any practice of writing, when he wrote: "Why, it is a fact that those who greatly condemn rhetoric, nevertheless admit praise of this art. For the nature of things compels them to try by means of words to make evident and amplify upon those things with which they are concerned" (La Fontaine 1968: 221). Not surprisingly, the pages of science are full of rhetoric, even of those metaphors so despised by Sprat (Gross 1990; Fahnestock 1999; on Bacon's and Society fellows' use of metaphor, see Vickers 1985: 11, 21). Galileo, who did not have much to say about rhetoric per se, but much (too much, to his chagrin) about Aristotelian (natural) philosophy and dialectics, was a master rhetorician.[34] Even science's choice of concrete language, of metonymic over metaphoric discourse *is* a rhetorical choice, a choice reflecting preferences of both individuals and historical periods (Jakobson 2002; Lodge 1977).

The Original Sin and the "Shipwreck of Rhetoric"

Elocutio had been "the hinge around which the whole of Renaissance moral and civic philosophy turned" (Vickers 1981: 129). But in the following centuries rhetoric came unhinged. Scholarly production waned. Rhetoric continued to be taught, even by names such as Vico who taught it in Naples for several decades in the first half of the 1700s or Adam Smith who taught it briefly at Edinburgh in the mid-1700s. Jesuit colleges[35] continued to expand in number throughout Catholic Europe, providing such excellent education (and just in rhetoric) with their *ratio studiorum*, a uniform and comprehensive curricular plan of studies, to deserve Bacon's repeated admiration in his *Dignity and Advancement of Learning*. The daily letters to his mother by George Chinnery, a student at Christ Church college at Oxford, testify that in the early 1800s the study of rhetoric occupied a great deal of a student's time, keeping young George from partying and drinking wine, or at least so he complains to his mother... (Wyland 2003).

If the new 17th century scientific culture had put elocution on trial, the rhetorical ornaments of tropes and figures in particular, 18th century philosophy mounted an attack on rhetoric tout court. At the heart of the attack was rhetoric's original sin, as first expressed by Socrates to Gorgias in Plato's dialogue *Gorgias*: rhetoric as a "foul thing," a "bad thing," the art of persuasion based not on truth (the realm of philosophy, according to Socrates) but on the "production of gratification and pleasure," with the appearance rather than reality of knowledge, a "flattery" "quick and clever" "with nothing fine about it."[36] Blair would openly acknowledge rhetoric's Janus faces, "as an Art which may be employed for persuading to ill, as well as to good. There is no doubt that it may" (pp. 158–9).

Philosophers never had anything nice to say about rhetoric, starting from Socrates and Plato ("a great injustice in Plato," according to Bacon p. 178). For Locke, rhetoric was "an art of deceit" "a perfect cheat." For Kant, "rhetoric... produced nothing but fraudulent discourse"; similarly, the English utilitarian philosopher Bentham saw "rhetoric as the very antithesis of rational discourse" (White 1997: 25, 26). And when the 19th century romantic era turned Blair's and Lamy's 18th century concern with *belles lettres* into literary criticism[37], the end result would be "the suppression of rhetoric" (White 1997). In delivering the first of six Mary Flexner lectures on rhetoric in February 1936 at Bryn Mawr College, I.A. Richards does not mince his words (1936: 3; emphasis added): "I need to spend no time, I think, in describing the *present state of Rhetoric*. Today it is the *dreariest and least profitable part of the waste* that the unfortunate travel through in Freshman English!" By 1970, with a rhetorical acknowledgement of *excusatio propter infirmitatem*, Roland Barthes would feel "obliged" to publish rudimentary notes on rhetoric, so "poorly known" was a field of knowledge that had all but disappeared (1970: 172).[38]

Ironic perhaps that the 1980s, in the wake of post-structuralism, deconstruction, and the "linguistic turn," should bring out a veritable explosion of scholarly work, from a wide range of disciplines, with "rhetoric" in the title, as confirmed by the data plot from Google Books Ngram Viewer reproduced in the cover jacket. Ironic also that a philosopher, Nietzsche, should be, for once, on the side of rhetoric: "What then is truth? A moveable host of metaphors, metonymies, and anthropomorphisms: in short, a sum of human relations which have been poetically and rhetorically intensified, transferred, and embellished." (2006: 117) Yet, you will be hard pressed to find in the vast late 20th century scholarly literature dealing with rhetoric an understanding of rhetoric as a complex organic whole. "Rhetoric as a whole network of relationships and procedures is now available only to those who reconstruct it by study" (Vickers 1989: 433).Rhetoric is now the domain of the expert. But when it comes to tropes and figures even expert rhetorical analyses are wanting: they rarely highlight the gamut of figures employed in a text (but then again, you will not find any mention of figures in any of Blair's lectures dedicated to a critical examination of the style of specific texts). After all, little by little, the Medieval and Renaissance emphasis on style which had translated into an emphasis on figures reversed course: figures shrunk down to the four master tropes (metaphor, metonymy, synecdoche, irony), and these to metaphor, metaphor taking over the field as the "'trope of tropes' (Sojcher), 'the figure of figures' (Deguy)."[39] As Genette (1982: 114) put it: "[A]t the beginning of the twentieth century, 'metaphor' was one of the rare terms to survive the great shipwreck of rhetoric."[40]

Learning Figures: Argumentum in utramque partem

And yet, it may have all been for the good this shipwreck of rhetoric. Is rhetoric a kind of knowledge worth acquiring in the modern world? What is the point of learning some 200 figures, at the high cost of daily drills (not to mention the whip, something even Melanchthon experienced from his teacher – Melanchthon, the *enfant prodige* who entered university at Heidelberg not yet thirteen and started teaching at Tubingen at age seventeen; from Melanchthon's writing as cited in La Fontaine 1968: 20)?

Let's address these questions as a rhetorical exercise, arguing our case from both sides, pro *and* con. Vickers would definitely fall on the pro side. He wrote a whole book *In Defence of Rhetoric* and that defense, as Sloane argues, is ultimately "an apology for figures and tropes" (Sloane, 1991: 124; for an impassioned defense of *elocutio*, see also Vickers 1981). Brandt stands on the opposite side. In his scathing review of Sonnino's *A Handbook to Sixteenth Century Rhetoric*, Brandt sees nothing defensible in this "moribund tradition" of a "taxonomic enterprise" "pedantic in its diligence and thoughtlessness." "[W]riting is a matter of ear. The language patterns available to me I have acquired by reading, not studying rhetoric. . . . Writing and classifying are two quite different activities." Nothing new here. Cicero, in the *Orator*, acknowledges "the two things that please the ear: sound and rhythm" (*Orator* 44–236; quote 163). But Cicero also knew that this music to the ear does not come out of thin air. It is the result of the careful application of different rhetorical figures. Cicero dedicates half of his *Orator* to the discussion of those (mostly grammatical) figures, albeit without specifically naming them.

Not surprisingly, Vickers assures us that "Cicero knew his trade" when it came to writing, and used a large number of rhetorical figures very effectively for his purposes, in spite of his cursory treatment of figures in his work on rhetoric (Vickers 1988: 312). Brandt concludes (1972: 125): "Am I supposed to learn this quantity of barbarous [rhetorical] terms and the definitions – often very imprecise ones – that go with them, and then apply a grid of that amplitude in an analysis of texts? I have better things to do with my time."

I am sure Brandt does. In any case, he also has a point. Does it matter that we should have picked up that Brandt has applied here the figure of rhetorical question or anthypophora (no doubt, a barbarous term)? Does it matter that Leff and Mohrmann refer to the generic figure of repetition in their analysis of Lincoln's speech at Cooper Union, rather than to specific figures of repetition, as Fahnestock does in the chapter on "Ploche and Polyptoton" of her *Rhetorical Figures in Science*? After all, even Melanchthon writes: "This (figure) [repetition] has many varieties and various names because sometimes the repetition comes at the beginning, sometimes at the end. *We shall be content with the general name for all these varieties*" (La Fontaine 1968: 249; emphasis added).

Of course, it does matter that we should recognize the figures in a text when doing critical rhetorical analysis (after all, much academic knowledge involves the pedantic mastery of esoteric knowledge for the insiders and the adepts). Or at least it matters that the analyst is aware of the range of rhetorical options the speaker/writer used. And does it matter that Lincoln or Darwin or Martin Luther King or Shakespeare or Sprat are aware of the name of each rhetorical figure they use? Probably even less so than the critic. What is important, however, is that they are aware of the effects of certain types of language use. And if they do use the figures with mastery, they probably are. And if they are, it probably means that they have paid attention to language, that they have spent a great deal of time figuring out how other masters have used language *effectively*. In any case, not all figures are about "sound and rhythm"; "figures of thoughts . . . do not soothe the ears but rather engage the mind," the deal with logic and forms of argumentation (Vico 1996: 173). Modern ignorance of these figures may lead to wrong interpretations of past authors, as Skinner masterfully shows about Machiavelli's use of paradiastole in *The Prince* (2002: 107–113).

So, let us bring this Introduction to a close with the words of Thomas Wilson, whose *The Arte of Rhetorique* contributed to Brandt's Renaissance rhetorical pedantry:

> a certain learned man and of much excellencie, being asked what was such a figure, and such a trope in Rhetorique: I can not tell (quoth he) but I am assured, if you looke in the booke of mine Orations, you shal not faile but find them. So that though he knewe not the name of such, and such figures, yet the Nature of them was so familiare to his knowledge, that he had the vse of them when soeuer he had neede.
>
> (1585: 160)[41]

Notes

1 Two of Plato's dialogues deal with rhetoric, the *Gorgias* and the *Phaedrus*, although Gorgias is involved in only one.

Introduction

2   A handful of rhetorical figures used by Gorgias of Leontini in his *Encomium of Helen* (fifth century BC), although not labeled them as such by him, are known as the "Gorgian figures": antithesis, isocolon, homoeoptoton, homoeoteleuton, and paronomasia (Murphy et al. 2003: 141). These figures were used to create the symmetric Gorgian style discussed by Cicero (e.g., *Orator* 92, 95, also 80–86).

3   It is not known how the handful of Gorgian figures (never named, in any case, by Gorgias, Murphy et al. 2003: 133) and Aristotle's emphasis on metaphor turned into the 64 *exornationes* of the *Rhetorica ad Herennium* (on this issue, see Murphy 1990: 242; on the handful of Aristotelian figures, see Vickers 1970: 93–94). For sure, neither Gorgias nor Aristotle were interested in the taxonomy of figures, the *Ad Herennium* being the first extant ancient rhetorical treatise to classify figures (Murphy et al. 2003: 133–34).

4   In modern rhetoric tropes and schemes have been generally subsumed under the term "figure", but in earlier periods the term figure was a synonym for scheme (Lausberg 1998: §§ 552–598, 600–910).

5   Bede, in his *De schematibus et tropis*, "On figures" writes: "The grammarians, using a Greek term, call this *schema*, we rightly call it a 'dressing,' 'form,' or 'figure,' because through it discourse is so to speak dressed up and ornamented" (in Copeland and Sluiter 2009: 267). For the equation of the two terms, see Susenbrotus (*Epitome troporum ac schematum*, 1540: 8).

6   Peacham (1593: 1). See also Melanchthon in his *Istitutiones Rhetoricae* (1529: 15), Susenbrotus in *Epitome troporum ac schematum* (1540: 8–9; for the exact same definitions, see also Donatus and Bede in Copeland and Sluiter 2009: 97, 268), Wilson in *The Arte of Rhetorike* (1585: 170–172).

7   And therefore, closely related to topics of invention.

8   In Halm (607–618); also partly translated in Copeland and Sluiter (2009: 267–271).

9   Camargo (1983: 106); on the number of figures in medieval rhetorical textbooks, see also Murphy (1974: 183, 185, 189, 190); see also the summary table in Faral (1924: 54).

10 On English style manuals, see Mack (2002: 84–95); see also Mack (2011: 208–227) for Renaissance manuals of tropes and figures.

11 See Corbett and Connors (1999: 378), Mack (2002: 85); for listings of Renaissance figures, see Taylor (1937), Dupriez (1984), Lanham (1991), Sonnino (1968); for a comparative table across 16 different authors from classical to Renaissance times, see Joseph (1947: 35).

12 Vico (p. 105); on the name, see Quintilian *Inst. Or.* 8, Pr.15; on the importance of eloquence, see Vickers (1981: 125).

13 Peacham (1593). For Quintilian, there is no "better way to induce emotions" than through the "judicious" use of figures (*Inst. Or.* 9.1.21). On the use of figures as means of expressing sentiments for Longinus and Peacham, see Vickers (1970: 102–108).

14 Cicero acknowledges that some topics are polysemically suited to deal with more questions, although probably better suited for specific questions. On the polysemic nature of figures (rather than topics) see the general discussion by Vickers (1988: 307–334, passim).

15 Quintilian, though, is mostly interested in general principles (Vickers 1970: 101).

16 For example, for pathos: *dissimulatio* induces laughter (Quintilian *Inst. Or.* 9.2.14); *asyndeton* "produce[s] outbursts of emotion" (9.3.50, 9.3.54); for logos: *praesumptio* is used to anticipate critiques to our arguments and usable anywhere in a speech but, particularly, in the introduction (9.2.16); *dubitatio* adds credibility to speech (9.2.19); "*enthymeme* is not [only] used to prove something but also to ornate the sentence" (8.5.9–10); "The other tropes left to describe are not used for meaning, but to embellish speech and to amplify it" (8.6.40). More generally, in reference to logos, Quintilian writes: "As far as proofs are concerned, the use of figures lends strengths to our arguments and makes them penetrate in the judges' souls without making them aware of this" (*Inst. Or.* 9.1.19). He also adds that figures are very effective for pathos, in moving the audience (9.1.21) and for ethos, in endearing a character (9.1.21).

17 At a general level, Quintilian, following Aristotle (*Rhetoric* 1414b), states: "The same ornaments are not suitable for demonstrative, deliberative, and judiciary causes" (Quintilian *Inst. Or.* 8.3.11 Italian; also 8.3.13–14). He also states: "we must clarify with which metaphors, which figures, which concepts, and finally with which collocation we can achieve our purposes" (*Inst. Or.* 8.3.41).

18 Peacham, for instance, in his *The Garden of Eloquence*, provides for each figure a brief section titled "The use of this figure" where he specifies what the figure should be used for, and in a subsequent section titled "The Caution" he also warns the reader about the pitfalls to avoid in the use of the figure.
19 Thus, for pathos, among the figures of exclamation, ecphonesis can be used "to express the greatness of our affections and passions, and thereby to move the like affection in our hearers" (Peacham 1593: 63) and mempsis can be similarly used "to move compassion" (1593: 66); and for logos, amplification "was first devised to increase causes" and parenthesis "serveth to confirme the saying by the interposition of a reason, and to confute the objection by the timely prevention of an answere" (1593: 198–99).
20 More generally, logos pathos, and ethos can be expressed by specific figures: enthymeme, sorites, or syllogismus for logos; adhortatio, adynaton, or cataplexis for pathos; anamnesis, litotes, or paronomasia for ethos.
21 On rhetoric as an organic whole, see Joseph (1947: 34, 36), Ragsdale (1965), Varga (1983: 88–89), Vickers (1988: 319); for modern classifications of figures that provide the user a way to go from function to figures, see Lanham (1991: 181–196), Sonnino (1968: 247–266), and Burton's Silva Rhetoricae website http://rhetoric.byu.edu/.
22 *Institutiones Rhetorices* (1523: b6r–b7v; c8v–d1r).
23 On this point, see Brennan (1960: 64–66); on Peacham's rhetoric, see also Joseph (1947: 38) and Vickers (1970: 106–108).
24 "The first order containeth those figures which do make the oration plaine, pleasant, and beautifull, pertaining rather to words then to sentences, and rather to harmonie and pleasant proportion, then to gravitie and dignitie" (pp. 40–41).
25 "The difference between the figures of words, and the figures of sentences is great, found both in their formes and effectes, for the figures of wordes are as it were effeminate, and musicall, the figures of sentences are manly, and martiall, those of words are as it were the colour and beautie, these of sentences are as the life and affection, which are divided into figures of affection [pathos], and figures of Amplication [logos]" (p. 91).
26 In Peacham's words: "The figures of this order be such, which for the most part do both amplifie" (1593: 119).
27 Contrary to Melanchthon, Peacham groups the figures of amplification into four broad *common topics: distributio*/division, *descriptio*/description, *comparatio*/comparison, *collectio*/collectives). Each group contains subgroups (e.g., *collectio* includes "proofes and conclusions", "Antecedent... [and] Consequent"; the figure of syllogismus contains references to circumstances).
28 That deep understanding of rhetoric as an organic whole between different levels and parts is there even among Ramists. Peter Ramus is often attributed with hastening the demise of rhetoric by relegating its domain to style, placing invention and arrangement under dialectic in his scheme. Yet, this separation was hardly relevant since Ramus strongly believed that dialectic and rhetoric should be studied together (Vickers 1981: 117; Mack 2011: 142–145; on the role of Agricola, Vives, Melanchthon, and Ramus in revolutionizing the field of rhetoric, see Mack 1992).
29 Published in three parts in 1663, 1664, and 1678.
30 *Dialogue Concerning the Two Chief Systems of the World – Ptolemaic and Copernican* 1632: 139, Vol. VII, also 57, 71, 80.
31 The very last words of the anonymous *Rhetorica ad Herennium* insist on this point: "All these faculties we shall attain if we supplement the precepts of theory with diligent practice" (IV.69). All Renaissance rhetoricians, from Agricola to Erasmus, Melanchthon and Suarez, drove the same point home: that learning required continuous exercise. Quintilian best expresses the purpose of these exercises: not learning by rote, where pupils mechanically apply a set of rhetorical rules, through which "they will only achieve dumb knowledge" (Quintilian, *Inst. Or.* 5.10.119), but repeated exercise so that the intelligent application of the rules most appropriate for a specific case becomes natural and unconscious (Quintilian, *Inst. Or.* 5.10.125; see Leff 1983: 34).
32 On the teaching of rhetoric at Jesuit colleges see Lang (1952: 288), Moss (1986: 138). On the teaching of rhetoric in Elizabethan times, see the chapter on English grammar schools in Mack

(2002: 11–47); for Oxford and Cambridge, see the following chapter, Mack (2002: 48–75); for an excellent brief summary of the teaching of rhetoric, see Vickers (1981: 116–125).
33 Collections of quotes on various topics (originally, moral issues, such as honor, virtue, vice, beauty, life, death, friendship, hate, but later expanded to include theological, philosophical, historical, and scientific issues) (Lechner 1962, Moss 1996).
34 On Galileo's rhetoric: Finocchiaro (1980), Hallyn (1999), Vickers (1983), Crombie (1996: 231–257).
35 Lang (1952: 288); Moss (1986: 138).
36 That original sin rendered rhetoric suspicious in the public eyes from the start (see also Cicero's doubts, *De inv.* I.1). As a result, rhetoricians insisted on the moral obligations of the orator who must be a "*vir bonus, dicendi peritus*", "a good man skilled in speaking" (Quintilian, *Inst. Or.* 12.1.1), a refrain repeated through the Middle Ages and the Renaissance. As Blair would put it: "There is no instrument of persuasion more powerful, than an opinion of probity and honor in the person who undertakes to persuade" (252).
37 On the transformation of rhetoric into literary criticism, see de Man (1983), Kennedy (1990), Wellbery (2000).
38 And yet, a blanket statement of a "disappearance" of rhetoric should be endorsed with some prudence. In 2013, Paolo Ardisson, not a scholar but a London businessman, could not only recite for me the definitions of all the main rhetorical figures he had learned decades earlier, in the mid-1970s, at the famous Liceo Classico Azuni in Sassari, Italy, but also recognize them in a text!
39 Genette (1982: 113). On the four master tropes, see also Burke (1941, 1945: 503–517). We find the reduction of all tropes to the four master tropes in Ramus (Mack 2011: 142–144) and Vico (Vickers 1988: 440). For a history of this progressive reduction, see Vickers (1988: 439–469).
40 Modern technology in the form Google Books Ngram Viewer both lends support to and qualifies Genette's statement. The time plots reproduced in the cover jacket of the frequency of the words "rhetoric" and "metaphor" found in the millions of books digitized by Google and made available through Google Books, show that rhetoric and metaphor do indeed go hand-in-hand, but not just in recent decades after "the great shipwreck of rhetoric", but through the centuries. Plots of all other rhetorical figures would show these figures as very distant competitors of metaphor for book space.
41 A similar comment is expressed in 1711 by Joseph Trapp, Professor of Poetry at Oxford (Vickers 1970: 56).

References

Bartel, Dietrich. 1997. *Musica Poetica. Musical-Rhetorical Figures in German Baroque Music.* Lincoln: University of Nebraska Press.

Barthes, Roland. 1970. "L'ancienne rhétorique." *Communications*, 16: 172–223.

Blair, Ann. 1992. "Humanist Methods in Natural Philosophy: The Commonplace Book." *Journal of the History of Ideas*, Vol. 53, No. 4, pp. 541–551.

Booth, Wayne C. 1974. *A Rhetoric of Irony*. Chicago: The University Of Chicago Press.

Brandt, William J. 1972. "Book review of Lee A. Sonnino, A Handbook to Sixteenth Century Rhetoric." *Foundations of Language* 9 (1): 123–25.

Brennan, Joseph X. 1960. "The Epitome Troporum Ac Schematum: The Genesis of a Renaissance Rhetorical Text." *Quarterly Journal of Speech* 46(1):59–71.

Buelow, George J. 1980. "Rhetoric and Music." In: pp. 793–-803, Stanley Sadie (ed.), *The New Grove Dictionary of Music and Musicians,* Vol. XV. London: MacMillan.

Burke, Kenneth. 1941. "Four Master Tropes." *The Kenyon Review* 3(4): 421–438.

Camargo, Martin. 1983. "Rhetoric." In: pp. 96–124, David L. Wagner (ed.), *The Seven Liberal Arts in the Middle Ages*. Bloomington: Indiana University Press.

Clark, Donald Lemen. 1952. "The Rise and Fall of Progymnasmata in Sixteenth and Seventeenth Century Grammar Schools." *Communication Monographs* 19 (4): 259–63.

Copeland, Rita and Ineke Sluiter (eds.). 2009. *Medieval Grammar and Rhetoric: Language Arts and Literary Theory, AD 300–1475*. Oxford: Oxford University Press.

Corbett, Edward P. J. and Robert J. Connors. 1999. *Classical Rhetoric for the Modern Student*. Oxford: Oxford University Press.

Crombie, Alistaire C. 1996. *Science, Art and Nature in Medieval and Modern Thought*. London: Hambledon Press.

Dear, Peter. 1985. "*Totius in Verba*: Rhetoric and Authority in the Early Royal Society." *Isis*, Vol. 76, No. 2, pp. 144–161.

de Man, Paul. 1983[1971]. "The Rhetoric of temporality." In: pp. 187–228, Paul de Man, *Blindness and Insight Essays in the Rhetoric of Contemporary Criticism. Introduction by Wlad Godzich, Theory and History of Literature, Volume 7, Second Edition, Revised*. Minneapolis: University of Minnesota Press.

Dupriez, Bernard. 1980. *Gradus: les procédés littéraires*. Paris: Union générale d'éditions.

Fahnestock, Jeanne. 1999. *Rhetorical Figures in Science*. Oxford: Oxford University Press.

Faral, Edmond. 1924. *Les arts poétiques du xiie et du xiiie siècle. Recherches et documents sur la technique littéraire du moyen age*. Paris: Librairie Ancienne Honore Champion.

Finocchiaro, Maurice A. 1980. *Galileo and the Art of Reasoning. Rhetorical Foundations of Logic and Scientific Method*. Dordrecht, Holland: D. Reidel Publishing Company.

Frye, Northrop. 1957. *Anatomy of Criticicism*. Harmondsworth: Penguin.

Genette, Gerard. 1982. "Rhetoric Restrained", Chapter 6, pp. 103–126, *Figures of Literary Discourse*, Translated by Alan Sheridan, Introduction by Marie-Rose Logan. New York: Columbia University Press.

Gilbert. 1960. *Renaissance Concepts of Method*. New York: Columbia University Press.

Gross, Alan G. 1990. *The Rhetoric of Science*. Cambridge, MA.: Harvard University Press.

Hallyn, Fernand. 1999. "Dialectique et rhétorique devant la nouvelle science du XVII siècle." In : pp. 601–28, Marc Fumaroli (ed.), *Histoire de la rhétorique dans l'Europe moderne, 1450–1950*. Paris: Presses Universitaires de France.

Halm, Karl. 1863. *Rhetores latini minores: Ex codicibus maximam partem primum adhibitis*. Lipsiae: B.G. Teubneri.

Jakobson, Roman. 2002. "The Metaphoric and Metonymic Poles." In: pp. 42–47, Rene Dirven Ralf Pörings (eds.), *Metaphor and Metonymy in Comparison and Contrast*. Berlin: Mouton de Gruyter.

Joseph, Sister Miriam. 1947. *Shakespeare's Use of the Arts of Language*. New York: Columbia University Press.

Kennedy, George A. 1990. "The Contributions of Rhetoric to Literary Criticism." In: pp. 349–364, George A. Kennedy (ed.), *The Cambridge History of Literary Criticism, Vol. 1, Classical Criticism*. Cambridge: Cambridge University Press.

La Fontaine, Sister Mary Joan. 1968. A Critical Translation of Philip Melanchthon's *Elementorum rhetorices libri duo*. [Latin Text with English Translation and Notes]. The University of Michigan, Ph.D. Dissertation. Ann Arbor, MI: University Microfilms, Inc.

Lang, Robert A. 1952. "The Teaching of Rhetoric in French Jesuit Colleges, 1556–1762." *Communication Monographs* 19(4):286–98.

Lanham, Richard A. 1991. *A Handlist of Rhetorical Terms*. 2nd edition. Los Angeles: University of California Press.

Lausberg, Heinrich. 1998. *Handbook of Literary Rhetoric: A Foundation or Literary Study*. Leiden: E. J. Brill.

Lechner, Joan M. 1962. *Renaissance Concepts of the Commonplaces*. New York: Pageant Press.

Leff, Michael C. 1983. "The Topics of Argumentative Invention in Latin Rhetorical Theory from Cicero to Boethius." *Rhetorica*, 1(1): 23–44.
Lodge, David. 1977. *The Modes of Modern Writing: Metaphor, Metonymy, and the Typology of Modern Literature*. Ithaca, NY: Cornell University Press.
Mack, Peter. 1992. "Agricola's Use of the Comparison between Writing and the Visual Arts." *Journal of the Warburg and Courtauld Institutes* 55: 169–179.
_____. 2002. *Elizabethan Rhetoric*. Cambridge: Cambridge University Press.
_____. 2011. *A History of Renaissance Rhetoric, 1380–1620*. Oxford: Oxford University Press.
Moss, Ann. 1996. *Printed Commonplace-Books and the Structuring of Renaissance Thought*. Oxford: Oxford University Press.
Moss, Jean Dietz. 1986. "The Rhetoric Course at the Collegio Romano in the Latter Half of the Sixteenth Century." *Rhetorica* 4 (2): 137–51.
Muir, Edward. 2007. *The Culture Wars of the Late Renaissance: Skeptics, Libertines, and Opera*. Cambridge, MA.: Harvard University Press.
Murphy, James Jerome. 1974. *Rhetoric in the Middle Ages. A History of Rhetorical Theory from St. Augustine to the Renaissance*. Berkeley, CA: University of California Press.
_____. 1990. "*Topos* and *Figura*: Historical Cause and Effect?" In: pp. G.L. Bursill-Hall, Sten Ebbesen, and Konrad Koerner (eds.), *De Ortu Grammaticae. Studies in Medieval Grammar and Linguistic Theory in Memory of Janpinborg*. Amsterdam: John Benjamins Publishing Company.
Murphy, James J. and Richard A. Katula, with Forbes I. Hill and Donovan J. Ochs. 2003. *A Synoptic History of Classical Rhetoric*. Third Edition. Mahwah, NJ: Lawrence Erlbaum Associates, Publishers.
Nadeau, Ray. 1952. "The Progymnasmata of Aphthonius in Translation." *Communication Monographs* 19 (4): 264–85.
Nietzsche, Friedrich. 2006[1873]. "On Truth and Lies in a Nonmoral Sense." In: pp. 115–23 Keith Ansell Pearson and Duncan Large (eds.), *The Nietzsche Reader*. Malden, MA: Blackwell.
Ong, Walter J. 1958. *Ramus. Method, and the Decay of Dialogue. From the Art of Discourse to the Art of Reason*. Chicago: The University of Chicago Press.
Perelman, Chaïm. 1982. *The Realm of Rhetoric*. Notre Dame: University of Notre Dame.
Richards, I.A. 1936. *The Philosophy of Rhetoric*. Oxford: Oxford University Press.
Skinner, Quentin. 2002. "Hobbes on Rhetoric and the Construction of Morality" In: pp. 87–141, Quentin Skinner, *Visions of Politics. Volume 3: Hobbes and Civil Science*. Cambridge: Cambridge University Press.
Sloane, Thomas O. 1991. "Schoolbooks and Rhetoric: Erasmus's 'Copia'." *Rhetorica* 9 (2): 113–129.
Sonnino, Lee A. 1968. *A Handbook to Sixteenth-Century Rhetoric*. London: Routledge & Kegan Paul.
Taylor, Warren. 1937. *Tudor Figures of Rhetoric*. University of Chicago Dissertation.
Unger, Hans-Heinrich. 1941. *Die Beziehungen zwischen Musik und Rhetoric im 16–18 Jahrhundert*. Würzburg: Triltsch.
Varga, A. Kibédi. 1983. "Rhetoric, a Story or a System? A Challenge to Historians of Renaissance Rhetoric." In: pp. 84–91, James. J. Murphy (ed.), *Renaissance Eloquence: Studies in the Theory and Practice of Renaissance Rhetoric*. Berkeley, CA: University of California Press.
Vickers, Brian. 1970. *Classical Rhetoric in English Poetry*. London: MacMillan.
_____. 1981. "Rhetorical and Anti-rhetorical Tropes: On Writing the History of *Elocutio*." In: pp. 105–132, E.S. Shaffer (ed.), *Comparative Criticism. A Yearbook*. Cambridge: Cambridge University Press.

_____. 1983. "Epideictic Rhetoric in Galileo's *Dialogo*." *Annali dell'Istituto e Museo di Storia della Scienza di Firenze*, VIII(2): 69–102.

_____. 1984. "Figures of Rhetoric/Figures of Music?" *Rhetorica*, 2(1):1–44

_____. 1985. "The Royal Society and English Prose Style: A Reassessment." In: pp. 3–76, Brian Vickers and Nancy S. Struever (eds.), *Rhetoric and the Pursuit of Truth. Language Change in the Seventeenth and Eighteenth Centuries*. Los Angeles: The William Andrews Clark Memorial Library, University of California.

_____. 1988. *In Defence of Rhetoric*. Oxford: Oxford University Press.

Yeo, Richard. 1996. "Ephraim Chambers's Cyclopaedia (1728) and the Tradition of Commonplaces." *Journal of the History of Ideas*, 57(1):157–175.

Wagner, David L. (ed.). 1983. *The Seven Liberal Arts in the Middle Ages*. Bloomington: Indiana University Press

Wellbery, David E. 2000. "The Transformation of Rhetoric." In: pp. 185–202, Marshall Brown (ed.), *The Cambridge History of Literary Criticism, Vol. 5, Romanticism*. Cambridge: Cambridge University Press.

White, Hayden. 1997. "The Suppression of Rhetoric in the Nineteenth Century." In: pp. 21–31, Brenda Deen Schildgen (ed.), *The Rhetoric Canon*. Detroit: Wayne State University Press.

Wyland, Russell M. 2003. "An Archival Study of Rhetoric Texts and Teaching at the University of Oxford." *Rhetorica* 21(3): 175–195.

FIGURES OF DICTION AND OF THOUGHT FROM RHETORICA AD HERENNIUM, BOOK IV

Figures of Diction

1. Epanaphora (*repetitio*) occurs when one and the same word forms successive beginnings for phrases expressing like and different ideas. This figure has much charm and also impressiveness and vigor in a high degree; therefore it ought to be used for both embellishment and amplification.

2. Antistrophe (*conversio*) occurs when we repeat, not the first word in successive phrases, but the last.

3. Interlacement (*complexio*) is the union of both figures, the combined use of Antistrophe and Epanaphora; we repeat both the first word and the last word in a series of phrases.

4. Transplacement (*traductio*) makes it possible for the same word to be frequently reintroduced, not only without offense to good taste, but even so as to render the style more elegant. To this kind of figure also belongs that which occurs when the same word is used first in one function and then in another.

5. Antithesis (*contentio*) occurs when the style is built on contraries.

6. Apostrophe (*exclamatio*) is the figure which expresses grief or indignation by means of an address to some man or city or place or object. If we use Apostrophe in the proper place, sparingly, and when the importance of the subject seems to demand it, we shall instill in our listener as much indignation as we desire. (Caplan: Quintilian, 9.3.97, assigns *exclamatio* to figures of thought.)

7. Interrogation (*interrogatio*) reinforces the argument that has just been delivered, after the case against the opponents has been summed up; but not all interrogation is impressive or elegant.

8. Reasoning by Question and Answer (*ratiocinatio*) occurs when we ask ourselves the reason for every statement we make, and seek the meaning of each successive affirmation. This figure is exceedingly well adapted to a conversational style, and both

---

Murphy, James J. "Figures of Diction and of Thought from *Rhetorica ad Herennium* Book IV." Appendix in: James Jerome Murphy, *Rhetoric in the Middle Ages: A History of Rhetorical Theory from St Augustine to the Renaissance*. Berkeley, Los Angeles, London: University of California Press, 1981 [1974]: 365–374.

by its stylistic grace and the anticipation of the reasons, holds the hearer's attention. (Caplan: Quintilian, 9.3.98, assigns it to figures of thought.) This figure is to be distinguished from *ratiocinatio,* the type of Issue which employs Reasoning from Analogy.

9. A Maxim (*sententia*) is a saying drawn from life, which shows concisely either what happens or ought to happen in life. Maxims may be either Simple or Double, and be presented either with or without reasons. We should insert maxims only rarely, that we may be looked upon as pleading the case, not preaching morals. When so interspersed, they will add much distinction. Furthermore, the hearer, when he perceives that an indisputable principle drawn from practical life is being applied to a cause, he must give it his tacit approval.

10. Reasoning by Contraries (*contrarium*) is the figure which, of two opposite statements, uses one so as neatly and directly to prove the other, as follows: "Now how should you expect one who has ever been hostile to his own interests to be friendly to another's?" (Caplan: Quintilian regards this as more a kind of argument than a figure of speech, and notes the similarity to Aristotle's *a fortiori* commonplace.)

11. Colon or Clause (*membrum*) is the name given to a sentence member, brief and complete, which does not express the entire thought, but is in turn supplemented by another colon. (Caplan: The doctrine of Colon, Comma, Period is Peripatetic in origin; Quintilian excluded Comma and Colon from the list of figures.)

12. Comma or Phrase (*articulus*) occurs when single words are set apart by pauses in staccato speech.

13. A Period (*continuatio*) is a close-packed and uninterrupted group of words embracing a complete thought. We shall best use it in three places: (1) Maxim, (2) Contrast, or (3) Conclusion.

14. Isocolon (*conpar*) is the figure comprised of cola which consist of a virtually equal number of syllables. (Caplan: Isocolon, Antithesis, and the next three figures—Homoeoptoton, Homoeoteleuton, and Paronomasia—are the so-called "Figures of Gorgias.")

15. Homoeoptoton (*similiter cadens*) occurs when in the same period two or more words appear in the same case, and with like terminations.

16. Homoeoteleuton (*similiter desinens*) occurs when the word endings are similar, although the words are indeclinable.

17. Paronomasia (*adnominatio*) is the figure in which, by means of a modification of sound, or change of letters, a close resemblance to a verb or noun is produced, so that similar words express dissimilar things. This is done in three ways:

    (1) through slight change or lengthening or transposition
        (a) by thinning or contracting the same letter
        (b) by the reverse

Ad Herennium: Figures of Diction and of Thought

      (c) by lengthening the same letter
      (d) by shortening the same letter
      (e) by adding letters
      (f) by omitting letters
      (g) by transposing letters
      (h) by changing letters
  (2) through greater changes
  (3) through a change of case in one of the nouns

(Caplan: The author knows only four parts of speech, so that "noun" would include "adjective.")

These last three figures are to be used very sparingly when we speak in an actual cause, because their invention seems impossible without labor and pains.

18. Hypophora (*subiectio*) occurs when we inquire of our adversary or ask ourselves what the adversaries can say in their favor, or what can be said against us. (Caplan: Quintilian, 9.3.98, assigns this to figures of thought.)

19. Climax (*gradatio*) is the figure in which the speaker passes to the following word only after advancing by steps to the preceding one. (Caplan: This figure joins with Epanaphora, Antistrophe, Interlacement, and Transplacement or Antanaklasis (*traductio*) to form a complete theory of Repetition.)

20. Definition (*definitio*) in brief and clear-cut fashion grasps the characteristic qualities of a thing. (*N.B.: Definitio* is also the subtype of "Legal Issue," i.11.19 of the *Rhetorica ad Herennium*.

21. Transition (*transitio*) is the name given to the figure which briefly recalls what has been said, and likewise briefly sets forth what is to follow next. (Caplan: This figure combines the functions of *enumeratio* and *propositio* used by the author in the Division and Conclusion.)

22. Correction (*correctio*) retracts what has been said and replaces it with what seems more suitable.

23. Paralipsis (*occultatio*) occurs when we say that we are passing by, or do not know, or refuse to say that which precisely now we are saying. (Caplan: Sometimes *praeteritio*. Quintilian, 9.3.98, puts this in figures of thought.)

24. Disjunction (*disjunctum*) is used when each of two or more clauses ends with a special verb. (Caplan: Quintilian, 9.3.64, says that devices like this and the two following are so common that they cannot lay claim to that art which figures involve.)

25. Conjunction (*conjunctio*) occurs when both the previous and the succeeding phrases are held together by placing the verb between them.

26. Adjunction (*adiunctio*) occurs when the verb holding the sentence together is not placed in the middle, but at the beginning or end.

27. Reduplication (*conduplicatio*) is the repetition of one or more words for the purpose of Amplification in Appeal to Pity. The reiteration of the same word makes a deep impression upon the hearer.

28. Synonymy or Interpretation (*interpretatio*) is the figure which does not duplicate the same word by repeating it, but replaces the word that has been used by another with the same meaning. The hearer cannot but be impressed when the force of the first expression is renewed by the explanatory synonym. (Caplan: Quintilian, 9.3.98, denies that this is a figure.)

29. Reciprocal Change (*commutatio*) occurs when two discrepant thoughts are so expressed by transposition that the latter follows from the former although contradictory to it, as follows: "You must eat to live, not live to eat."

30. Surrender (*permissio*) is used when we indicate in speaking that we yield and submit the whole matter to another's will. It is especially useful for evoking pity.

31. Indecision (*dubitatio*) occurs when the speaker seems to ask which of two or more words he had better use.

32. Elimination (*expeditio*) occurs when we have enumerated the several ways by which something could have been brought about, and all are then discarded except the one on which we are insisting. (Caplan: Cicero, Quintilian, and Aristotle all regard this as a form of argument, not a figure. It is known in modern argumentation as the Method of Residues.)

33. Asyndeton (*dissolutum*) is a presentation in separate parts, conjunctions being suppressed.

34. Aposiopesis (*praecisio*) occurs when something is said and then the rest of what the speaker had begun to say is left unfinished. (Also: *Interruptio*.)

35. Conclusion (*conclusio*) deduces, by means of a brief argument, the necessary consequences of what has been said or done before. (Caplan: Quintilian, 9.3.98, denies that this is a figure.)

There remain also ten Figures of Diction, which I have intentionally not scattered at random, but have separated from those above, because they all belong to one class. They indeed all have this in common, that the language departs from the ordinary meaning of the words, and is, with a certain grace, applied in another sense.

(Caplan: These ten figures of diction are *tropi*, a term which the author here does not employ. Quintilian, 8.6.1, defines a trope as "an artistic change of word or phrase from its proper signification to another." It is to be noted that tropes are not here separated from figures of diction.)

36. Onomatopoeia (*nominatio*) is a figure which suggests to us that we should ourselves designate with a suitable word, whether for the sake of imitation or for expressiveness, a thing which either lacks a name or has an inappropriate name.

37. Antonomasia or Pronominado (*pronominatio*) designates by a kind of adventitious epithet a thing that cannot be called by its proper name.

Ad Herennium: Figures of Diction and of Thought

38. Metonymy (*denominatio*) is a figure which draws from an object closely akin or associated an expression suggesting this object meant, but not called by its own name.

   (1) by substituting the name of the greater for that of the lesser
   (2) by substituting the name of the thing invented for the inventor
   (3) by substituting the instrument for the possessor
   (4) by substiuting the cause for the effect
   (5) by substituting the effect for the cause
   (6) by substituting the container for the content
   (7) by substituting the content for the container

39. Periphrasis (*circumitio*) is a manner of speech used to express a simple idea by means of a circumlocution.

40. Hyperbaton (*transgressio*) upsets the word order by means of either

   (1) Anastrophe (*perversio*), or reversal of natural order, or
   (2) Transposition (*transiectio*) changes the word order to gain more favorable rhythm.

41. Hyperbole (*superlatio*) is a manner of speech exaggerating the truth, whether for the sake of magnifying or minifying something. This is used either independently or by comparison.

42. Synecdoche (*intellectio*) occurs when the whole is known from a small part or a part from the whole.

   (1) The whole may be understood from the part, or part from the whole.
   (2) Singular may be understood from plural, and plural from singular.

43. Catechresis (*abusio*) is the inexact use of a like and kindred word in place of a more precise and proper one.

44. Metaphor (*translatio*) occurs when a word applying to one thing is transferred to another, because the similarity seems to justify tins transference. It is used

   (1) for vividness
   (2) for brevity
   (3) to avoid obscenity
   (4) for magnifying
   (5) for minifying
   (6) for embellishing

45. Allegory (*permutatio*) is a manner of speech denoting one thing by the letter of the words, but another by their meaning. It assumes three aspects:

   (1) Comparison, when a number of metaphors originating in a similarity in the mode of expression are set together.

(2) Argument, when a similitude is drawn from a person or place or object in order to magnify or minify.

(3) Contrast, when one mockingly calls a thing that which is its contrary.

Figures of Thought

1. Distribution (*distributio*) occurs when certain specified roles are assigned among a number of things or persons.

2. Frankness of Speech (*licentia*) occurs when, talking before those to whom we owe reverence or fear, we yet exercise our right to speak out, because we seem justified in reprehending them, or persons dear to them, for some fault. (Caplan: Quintilian, 9.2.27, denies that this is a figure.)

3. Understatement (*diminutio*) occurs when we say that by nature, fortune, or diligence, we or our clients possess some exceptional advantage, and in order to avoid the impression of arrogant display, we moderate or soften the statement of it.

4. Vivid Description (*descriptio*) is the name for the figure which contains a clear, lucid, and impressive exposition of the consequences of an act.

5. Division (*divisio*) separates the alternatives of a question and resolves each by means of a reason subjoined. There is this difference between the present kind of Division and that other which forms the third part of a discourse (in Book One): the former division operates through the Enumeration or Exposition of the topics to be discussed throughout the whole discourse, whereas here the division at once unfolds itself, and by briefly adding the reasons for the two or more parts, embellishes the style.

6. Accumulation (*frequentatio*) occurs when the points scattered throughout the whole cause are collected in one place so as to make the speech more impressive or sharp or accusatory.

7. Refining (*expolitio*) consists in dwelling on the same topic and yet seeming to say something ever new. It is accomplished in two ways:

   (1) by repeating the same idea
      (a) in equivalent words
      (b) in different styles of delivery as we change words
      (c) by the treatment
         (I) in dialogue form
         (II) in arousal form
   (2) by descanting upon the theme
      (a) by simple pronouncement
      (b) by reason
      (c) by a second expression in new form
      (d) by comparison

Ad Herennium: Figures of Diction and of Thought

    (e) by contrary
    (f) by example
    (g) by conclusion

8. Dwelling on the Point (*commoratio*) occurs when one remains rather long upon, and often returns to, the strongest topic on which the whole cause rests. There is no appropriate example of this figure, because this topic is not isolated from the whole cause like some limb, but like blood is spread through the whole body of discourse.

9. Antithesis (*contentio*) occurs when contraries meet. The Antithesis which is a Figure of Diction presents a rapid opposition of words, while in the Figure of Thought the opposing thoughts will meet in a comparison.

10. Comparison (*similitudo*) is a manner of speech that carries over an element of likeness from one thing to a different thing. It has four forms of presentation, each of which has a separate aim:

    (1) Contrast, whose purpose is embellishment
    (2) Negation, whose purpose is proof
    (3) Abridgment, whose purpose is clarity
    (4) Detailed Parallel, whose purpose is vividness

11. Exemplification (*exemplum*) is the citing of something done or said in the past, along with the definite naming of the doer or author. (Caplan: Examples are drawn from history.)

12. Simile (*imago*) is the comparison of one figure (*forma*) with another, implying a certain resemblance between them. It is used for either praise or censure.

13. Portrayal (*effictio*) consists in representing and depicting in words clearly enough for recognition the bodily form of some person.

14. Character Delineation (*notatio*) consists in describing a person's character by the definite signs which, like distinctive marks, are attributes of that character. (Caplan: Quintilian, 9.3.99, excludes this from the figures.) [Following this brief definition, the author supplies the longest single example of the book, portraying the character of a bragging beggar, iv.50.63–64.]

15. Dialogue (*sermocinatio*) consists in assigning to some person language which as set forth conforms with his character. (Caplan: Quintilian, 9.2.29, joins this figure and Personification as one.)

16. Personification (*conformatio*) consists in representing an absent person as present, or in making a mute thing or one lacking form articulate, and attributing to it a definite form and a language or a certain behavior appropriate to its character. (Caplan: This figure sometimes became a *progymnasma*, or composition exercise.)

17. Emphasis (*significatio*) is the figure which leaves more to be suspected than has actually been asserted. It is produced through:

   (1) Hyperbole
   (2) Ambiguity
   (3) Logical Consequence
   (4) Aposiopesis
   (5) Analogy

18. Conciseness (*brevitas*) is the expressing of an idea by the very minimum of essential words. (Caplan: Quintilian does not admit it as a figure, 9.3.99, but does treat it as a form of Asyndeton in 9.3.50.)

19. Ocular Demonstration (*demonstratio*) occurs when an event is so described in words that the business seems to be enacted and the subject to pass vividly before our eyes.

If you exercise yourself in these figures, Herennius, your speaking will possess impressiveness, distinction, and charm. As a result you will speak like a true orator, and the product of your invention will not be bare and inelegant, nor will it be expressed in commonplace language.

Remember always that you must combine both study and exercise to master the art.

If we follow these principles above, our Invention will be keen and prompt, our Arrangement clear and orderly, our Delivery impressive and graceful, our Memory sure and lasting, our Style brilliant and charming. In the art of rhetoric, then, there is no more.

Part 1:
The Concept of Tropes and Figures

1.
TOPOS AND *FIGURA*
Historical Cause and Effect?
James J. Murphy

This is an essay of proposal rather than one of conclusion. It proposes to identify a major issue which needs solution. The solution may require long and arduous historical study, but the issue is so central to language study that even the most difficult research will surely repay modern scholarship not only with new data but with a better understanding of how our own methods sometimes tend to defeat our efforts.

For instance stubborn reliance on definition is one of the anomalies to be seen in the history of language use, regardless of culture or of chronological period. Probably the best known linguistic example is the doctrine of *octo partes orationis*, popularized by the brief *Ars grammatica* of Aelius Donatus (c.350 A.D.), amplified by Priscian two centuries later in his own *Ars grammatica*, and then transmitted throughout Europe to be clamped down eventually on several emerging vernaculars — including English — to the confusion of struggling students and writers ever since. The efforts of 'Academies' to create linguistic orthodoxy through definition furnish another, continuing example.

Another type of definition that has proved to be specially pernicious throughout the history of language study has been that which decides which type of person should be allowed to study this or that aspect of language. Plato complained in several dialogues that the sophists were substituting language for thought, while Cicero in turn complained (*De oratore* III.xvi.6) that Socrates created a situation in which one set of teachers taught men how to think while another group taught them how to speak. By the end of the first Christian century Quintilian is found complaining in his *Institutio oratoria* (II.vi.6) that grammar teachers are threatening to take over the rhetorician's proper role. By the twelfth century John of Salisbury feels obligated to argue in his *Metalogicon* for a re-uniting of grammar, dialect, and rhetoric into a single subject for study; his argument was in vain, of course, and medieval university masters simply made grammar propaedeutic to the Aristotelian dialectic that shaped approaches to language for centuries to come. The concept of 'Faculty' in the European university has long reinforced this definitional tendency, just as the North American concept of 'Department' has verticalized studies in our own century.

There is nothing new about these observations, of course, but there is one historical phenomenon in our Western culture which seems to have escaped attention simply

---

Murphy, James J. "*Topos* and *Figura*: Historical Cause and Effect?" In: G.L. Bursill-Hall, Sten Ebbesen, and Konrad Koerner (eds.), *De Ortu Grammaticae. Studies in Medieval Grammar and Linguistic Theory in Memory of Janpinborg*. Amsterdam: John Benjamins Publishing Company, 1990: 239–253.

because of the way in which we study the history of language use. That is, what is the relation between *Topos* (Topic) and *Figura* (Figure)?

1. The Historical Background

The early historical data are clear enough. By the death of Aristotle in 322 B.C. he had introduced into his partially completed *Rhetoric* the concept of *Topos* as a 'class of enthymemes,' and includes in *Rhetoric* III.22–23 a sample listing of 28 such sources of arguments. Earlier, as part of his *Organon* or set of logical works, he had composed a separate work titled *Topics* which he says is devoted to analysing dialectical reasoning — reasoning which employs not premises known to be true but "probabilities that are generally accepted" (*Toipics* I.1). His *Rhetoric* alludes to this earlier work no less than nine times. Since later in the *Rhetoric* Aristotle introduces his discussion of *Lexis* or Style with the statement that "It is not enough to know what we ought to say; we must also say it as we ought" (*Rhetoric* III.l), the presumption is usually made that Aristotle makes a clear separation between the process of finding arguments and the process of putting them into words. When he does discuss style in the third book of the *Rhetoric*, though, Aristotle deals mainly in general terms with the desirable characteristics of effective language without constructing any specific system analogous to that of the *topoi*. His main recommendation for devising language that is 'clear but not mean' is the use of Metaphor, and even here he refers the reader to his *Poetics* for more detail. Aristotle writes at the level of broad principle, not of detail.

But a little more than two centuries later the first comprehensive Latin rhetorical treatise — the anonymous *Rhetorica ad Herennium* (c.86 B.C.) — does lay out a complete system of *figurae* based on assumptions which not only permeated ancient Roman thought about language but which dominated medieval and Renaissance thought as well and have had influence even into our own time. The tangled history of the *figurae* has yet to be written, but the ancient history of the devices (often termed *exornationes*) shows that grammarians as well as rhetoricians adopted them into their studies. Cicero takes them for granted, and Quintilian devotes two of the twelve books of his *Institutio oratoria* (A.D. 95) to a careful treatment of them; by Quintilian's time some of them are called 'tropes' (*tropi*). Donatus devotes the third book of his *Ars grammatica* (*Ars maior*) to *schemata* and *tropi*; this third book proved so popular in the Middle Ages that it often circulated as an independent work under the title *Barbarismus*. Encyclopedists like Martianus Capella, Isidore of Seville, and Cassiodorus Senator routinely include discussions of figures under both grammar and rhetoric. Medieval and Renaissance theorists take them for granted. Modern writers still wrestle with them (D'Angelo 1984),

In other words, the classificatory system of the *figurae* which first appears in the pseudonymous *Rhetorica ad Herennium* in the first century before Christ can be described accurately as a major tradition within Western theory and practice of language use. The problem for the language historian is that very little is known about the developments in rhetorical theory between the death of Aristotle and the appearance of a full-blown Roman rhetorical system a bit more than two centuries later. It is abundantly clear that both Cicero and the author of the *Rhetorica ad Herennium* have inherited — not invented — the ideas they describe in such detail. The author of the *ad Herennium*, in fact, refers constantly to 'my teacher' while Cicero (who wrote *De inventione* at age nineteen) simply states as already well-known a large number of precepts for which his text is the first extant evidence. George A. Kennedy has conjectured that both authors may have had a common teacher, though at different times; the somewhat different phrasings of the doctrines common to both these two early texts, then, may be due to each author's reliance on memory of oral teachings by their instructor (Kennedy 1972:116). This is an important point, because it confirms once more the well-established nature of Roman rhetorical theory by about 100 B.C.

The plain fact is that we do not know how the Roman rhetorical system arrived at the state of completion which is visible by 100 B.C. Some elements can be traced to particular sources — for instance many scholars credit Hermagoras of Temnos (second century B.C.) with the Doctrine of *Stasis* which plays a major part in both *De inventione* and *ad Herennium* — but we do not know what person or what school established the so-called "Five Canons" dividing rhetorical study into Invention, Arrangement, Style, Memory, and Delivery.[1] Some of the general ideas (e.g. Delivery having three elements) are seen as early as Aristotle, but others like the psychological progression of six steps in Arrangement of an oration appear only in the surviving Roman documents.[2]

Likewise we do not know how the comparatively generalized observations on Style found in Aristotle and his disciple Theophrastus later turned into the minutely detailed set of 64 *exornationes* found in the *ad Herennium*. What adds to the mystery is that this set of 64 appears virtually without explanation. All that the author says is that they add Distinction (*dignitas*):

> To confer distinction upon style is to render it ornate, embellishing it by variety. The divisions under Distinction are Figures of Diction and the Figures of Thought. It is a figure of diction if the adornment is comprised in the fine polish of the language itself. A figure of thought derives a certain distinction from the idea, not from the words.
>
> (*ad Herennium* IV.xii.18)

Then, abruptly, all the extant manuscripts begin the set with definitions and examples, starting with Epanaphora (*repetitio*) and ending with Ocular Demonstration (*demonstratio*). There is no further discussion of the nature of the figures, nor is there any discernible order in their presentation aside from the two major divisions noted above. Nevertheless this set, and its order of presentation, is petrified in the lengthy tradition which follows.

It is interesting to note that an analogous abruptness occurs in Aristotle, *Rhetoric* II.23, where he begins a set of 28 *topoi* (definitions and examples) without transition after noting that the *topoi* can be considered sources for enthymemes (see Appendix A). Aristotle's set, too, has no discernible order of presentation; but since elsewhere (his book *The Topics*) Aristotle identifies several hundred *topoi* altogether, it is clear that he intends the set of 28 in the *Rhetoric* merely as a sample to indicate potential uses of the method. It is not all clear from the text of the *ad Herennium*, however, whether the author regards his own set of 64 as a taxonomy or as a sample group; the tradition has tended to regard them as taxonomic, and their order as canonical,[3] but that in itself tells us little about the author's real intentions.

Meanwhile, it should be noted, the Romans also adopt the Greek principle that the *topos* (Latin: *locus,* or place) is a tool for finding ('inventing') arguments. Both the *De inventione* and the *ad Herennium* take it for granted that there exists a number of reliable 'places' or *loci* which can be developed into lines of proof for the assertions of a speaker. They are reliable in the sense that they occur naturally in controversy; and since they occur naturally, they can be analysed, brought into preceptive form, and then practiced. Thus both authors go to great lengths to spell out the most useful sub-*loci* for this or that type of argument. For example the Conjectural Issue (Question of Fact) in the *ad Herennium* (II.11.3) has six divisions: Probability, Comparison, Sign, Presumptive Proof, Subsequent Behavior, and Confirmatory Proof; each of these has sub-divisions. Each of these is what Aristotle would have called a *topos,* or source for a line of argument.

In fact Cicero wrote a separate book on the subject. He says in the preface to his *Topica* (44 B.C.) that he wrote it at the request of a friend who had asked him to explain the topical theory of Aristotle. He adds that he wrote the work from memory while on a sea voyage when he had no books available to him. Whether or not this is true, the *Topica* of Cicero provides a revealing insight into the Roman doctrine of topics as understood by a well-educated, practicing lawyer and politician of the first century before Christ. For Cicero, the topics are a part of Invention or finding of arguments:

> If we wish to track down some argument.... we must know the places or topics (*loci*) where arguments may be found; accordingly we may define a topic (*locus*) as the region of an argument, and an argument as a course of reasoning which firmly establishes a matter about which there is some doubt.
>
> Topics are either Intrinsic or Extrinsic. Extrinsic topics depend on testimony, and are brought in form outside the subject matter. Intrinsic topics, however, are inherent in the nature of the subject which is being investigated, such as arguments derived from the whole, from its parts, from its meaning, and from things which are in some way closely related with the subject which is being investigated.
>
> (*Topica* I.8)

Rhetoricians throughout Roman antiquity continue to discuss the doctrine of *loci* as a basic part of *inventio,* making it such an integral part of rhetoric that by the sixth Christian century Manilius Severinus Boethius (c.480–524) feels impelled to write a treatise explaining how the use of *loci* in rhetoric differs from its uses in logic and other fields. His *De differentiis topiciis* states that the topics can be used for both probable and necessary arguments, and can be employed in the four fields of dialectic, oratory, philosophy, and sophistry. But in all cases the topics are inventional in nature. What is important about this occurrence is not Boethius's fine distinctions, but the fact that he feels obliged to make them. The *loci* by this time have become such an important part of language use that their precise placement in the universe of discourse has to be delineated with great care. This is a further example of the way in which a widely-accepted tradition sooner or later forces its adherents to define terms which the tradition itself has accepted earlier without question. What the author of the *ad Herennium* accepted from his teacher without question in the first century before Christ is a major intellectual issue for Boethius seven centuries later. Yet Bede uses the *figurae* (not the *loci*) to illuminate scripture.

Historically, then, what we have seen so far is that in some fashion yet unclear to modern historians, the Romans inherited and taught a complicated and detailed set of *figurae* as a part of Style, while at the same time the concept of *topos* or *locus* as root of argument in Invention developed along a parallel but separate path.

Yet these distinct evolutions pose a major historical problem.

2. The Nature of the Problem

The basic problem is that on an intellectual level there is a close correspondence between many of the *topoi/loci* on the one hand, and many of the *figurae* on the other (see Appendix A, B, C). In the absence of clear historical data about the evolution of the two apparently separate systems, the modern observer is surely entitled to inquire whether the Greek *topoi* may in fact be the sources of the Roman *figurae*. In other words, did the classical Greek interest in the extrapolative powers of the *topoi* lead the more mechanistic Hellenistic redactors of the period 300–100 B.C. into applying to specific language usages the expansive capabilities which Aristotle and others had once reserved to the 'finding of arguments'? Or, to put it into Roman terms, did they apply to Style the methods once reserved for Invention?

It is one thing to say, as Eduard Norden does, that there are elements in artistic Greek style which can be identified by an observer — "die gorgianischen Redefiguren, die mit poetischen Worten ausgestattete Prosa, die rhythmische Prosa" (Norden 1958:16) — but it is quite another to discover how that which is describable but unsaid in Gorgias becomes for the Romans that which is explicit but unexplained. How does general Greek practice become specific Roman theory?

The nature of this problem becomes clear once an observer examines the various sets of ideas abstracted from their textual sources. There are some obvious, immediate parallels between the sets. 'Antithesis' occurs in both the Figures of Speech and the Figures of Thought of the *ad Herennium,* but also appears in Cicero's *Topica* as 'Contraries' and in Aristotle's sample *topoi* of *Rhetorica* II. 23 as 'Opposites.' Which is prior?

'Synecdoche' is defined in the *ad Herennium* as relating to a whole/part concept, but it also appears in Aristotle's *Topoi* set as "argument from parts to the whole" and in Cicero's *Topica* as "genus and species." Again, which is prior?

Comparison' is a Figure of Thought in the *ad Herennium,* while it is an Intrinsic Topic for Cicero's *Topica* and covers four of the 28 *topoi* which Aristotle includes in his *Rhetoric.* The *topos* of 'Inflection of Words' which is second on Aristotle's list also describes half a dozen of the *ad Herennium*'s Figures of Speech. Again, which is prior?

The *topoi* are prior in time. Did imaginative study of inventional processes over the centuries between Aristotle and Cicero spell out some new linguistic procedures which could be applied not only macroscopically to large conceptual units like the enthymeme but also microscopically to linguistic units as small as a word or a phrase? Abstractly speaking there is no reason to doubt this possibility. Currently we seem to lack the historical data to either prove or disprove this hypothesis. On the other hand it is possible that the evidence already exists, but that we as modern observers have been handicapped by our human tendency toward what I have earlier termed 'a stubborn reliance on definition.' Historians of logic look only to the *topoi*, while historians of grammar and rhetoric fasten only on the *figurae*. The cosmic intellectual forest may be hidden by the finite disciplinary trees.

For example a major historian of logic, Carl Prantl, devotes the bulk of his section in *Geschichte der Logik im Abendlande* on "Rhetorisch-logische Lehre bis zu den Römern" (Prantl 1927:505–27) to the delineation of Latin translations of Greek philosophical terms. He notes without comment, though, that the Greek term for 'conclusion' becomes in Cicero the Latin term *ratiocinatio* — without noting also that the term *ratiocinatio* is used for a Figure of Speech in *ad Herennium* IV.xv.23. Nor, when he lists the Latin terms *disiunctum* and *coniunctum* as translations of dilemmic terms from Greek dialectic,[4] does he note that these two terms occur consecutively as names of Figures of Speech in *ad Herennium* IV. xxvii. 37 and 38. Scarcely any other historians of logic deal with the matter at all.

On the other hand the marvelously detailed study of the figural tradition by Heinrich Lausberg in his *Handbuch der literarischen Rhetorik* is equally subject-narrowed. He devotes 314 pages of his second volume to a useful (alphabetically arranged) "Terminologisches Register" (Lausberg 1960 II, 639–957), which includes a four-page listing under the term *locus;* even here, though, the entries prove to be examples of particular citations throughout the first volume rather than any discussion of conceptual relations between *loci* and *figurae*. An equally well known study of the figural tradition is that of Leonid Arbusow, *Colores rhetorici; Eine Auswahl rhetorischer Figuren und Gemeinplätze als Hilfsmittel für akademische Übungen an mittelalterlichen Texten (1963)*. The title itself indicates the specialized direction of his investigation. While he does include a brief section (Arbusow 1963. 91–94) on "Topi (Gemeinplätze)," his effort is to indicate some large parallels between some Topics and some Figures — but only in the late classical and medieval periods rather than in the period of the origins of the figures. Even the influential work of Ernst Robert Curtius, *Latin Literature and the European Middle Ages* — which inspired a rash of topos-hunting literary studies after its first edition in 1961 — operates on a high level of abstraction in seeking broad parallels among ideas of writers from Homer to modern times; it is more suggestive than historical.

What seems to be needed now is a rigorous re-investigation of what we already think we know — but with this question in mind: did Greek *topos* lead to Roman *figurae*? It is far too early to advance even a cautious conjecture about the answer to that question, but the evident concordances between the two "systems," together with the chronological priority of the *topoi* (and the absence of contrary evidence), makes this topic for at least this writer a fascinating area of study which surely needs aggressive exploration. A solution to this historical problem would no doubt help us understand other modern problems of linguistic analogy.

Moreover, this historical problem may be more important than it might seem at first glance. Implicit in this question of the relation of *topos* to the *figura* is an even more fundamental question which strikes to the epistemological roots of our Western linguistic history. The question is so fundamental that its phrasing is critical: to put the question in the jargon of post-Roman rhetorical terminology, is Invention the same as Style? To put it in Aristotelian terms, does thought precede language? to put it into post-Saussurean terms, is languages the same as thought, or perhaps the creator of thought? To put it in post-Chomsky terms, is language capacity prior to thought and independent of it?

For whatever reasons, those second-century B.C. personages who taught the Romans had made a very clear judgement about the issue. By 100 B.C. it was standard doctrine that Invention (of ideas) was one human operation, and that Style (the application of words to ideas) was a separate operation; moreover, in this scheme Invention preceded Style in time during the process of composition either oral or written. No doubt the utter practicality of teaching young students to work this way was a reason for the universal acceptance of the 'theory' — it might better be described as the practice of a certain way of doing things. The Romans were notoriously quick to fasten on whatever worked even if they could not explain its workings — witness the arch — but the pervasive influence of Roman educational practices has lasted in some cases right down into our own century. The understanding of our own recent history might therefore be one more reason to pursue the matter.

Since this essay, as was pointed out at the outset, is one of inquiry rather than solution, the attention of the reader is now directed to the following appendices which list the three major 'sets' which may have a more direct relationship in the history of language study than we have heretofore been accustomed to recognize. Insofar as Definition is intended to be an aid rather than a barrier to scholarship, the reader is enjoined to seek parallel and concordance rather than disparity, among the sets. The need for further study may then be made clear.

Appendix A

Aristotle's Set of 28 Sample **Topoi (Rhetoric, II.23)**

There are twenty-eight specific lines of argument on which enthymemes, demonstrative and refutative, can be based.

1. opposites (from war to peace)
2. inflection (from justly to just)
3. correlation (e.g., if it is honorable to sell the tax contract it is honorable to buy it)
4. a fortiori (e.g., if the gods are not omniscient neither are men)
5. time
6. hoisting opponent with his own petard
7. definition

8. ambiguity
9. logical division (e.g., all crime comes from one of three motives and none of them applies to my case)
10. induction
11. appeal to precedent
12. argument from the parts to the whole
13. argument from consequences
14. argument from consequences of alternative cources of action (e.g., do not be a public speaker—if you speak honestly men will loathe you, if dishonestly, the gods will loathe you)
15. the contrast between appearance and reality
16. mathematical parallels
17. argument from identical consequences to identical antecedents
18. circumstances alter cases
19. isolating one possible motive as real
20. incentives and deterrents
21. incredible occurrences
22. inconsistencies in the opponent's case
23. meeting slander with fact (e.g., the woman kissing a lad was not his mistress but his mother)
24. argument from cause to effect
25. alternative proposal
26. inconsistency with past commitment
27. previous mistakes
28. play on names

Appendix B

Devices for Achieving Dignitas *in Style* Rhetorica ad Herennium, *Book IV*

Figures of Speech

1. repetitio (epanaphora)
2. conversio (antistrophe)
3. conplexio (interlacement)
4. traductio (transplacement)
5. contentio (antithesis)
6. exclamatio (apostrophe)
7. interrogatio (interrogation)
8. ratiocinatio (reasoning by question and answer)
9. sententia (maxim)
10. contrarium (reasoning by contraries)
11. membrum (colon)
12. articulus (phrase)
13. continuatio (period)

Topos *and* Figura: *Historical Cause and Effect?*

14. conpar (isocolon)
15. similiter cadens (homoeptoton)
16. similiter desinens (homoeteleuton)
17. adnominatio (paronomasia)
18. subiectio (hypophora)
19. gradatio (climax)
20. definitio (definition)
21. trasnsitio (transition)
22. correctio (correction)
23. occultatio (paralipsis)
24. disjunctum (disjunction)
25. coniunctio (conjunction)
26. adiunctio (adjunction)
27. conduplicatio (reduplication)
28. interpretatio (synonomy)
29. commutatio (reciprocal change)
30. permissio (surrender)
31. dubitatio (indecision)
32. expeditio (elimination)
33. dissolutum (asyndeton)
34. praecisio (aposiopesis)
35. conclusio (conclusion) (Special Figures of Speech: 'tropes')
36. nominatio (onomatopoeia)
37. pronominatio (antonomasia)
38. denominatio (metonymy)
39. circumitio (periphrasis)
40. transgressio (hyperbaton)
41. superlatio (hyperbole)
42. intellectio (synecdoche)
43. abusio (catechresis)
44. translatio (metaphor)
45. permutado (allegory)

Figures of Thought

1. distributio (distribution)
2. licentia (frankness of speech)
3. diminutio (understatement)
4. descriptio (vivid description)
5. divisio (division)
6. frequentatio (accumulation)
7. expolitio (refining)
8. commoratio (dwelling on the point)
9. contentio (antithesis)

10. similitudo (comparison)
11. exemplum (exemplification)
12. imago (simile)
13. effictio (portrayal)
14. notatio (character delineation)
15. sermocinatio (dialogue)
16. conformatio (personification)
17. significatie (emphasis)
18. brevitas (conciseness)
19. demonstratio (ocular demon stration)

Appendix C

Rhetorical Invention through Topics

(The Topica *of Cicero)*

In the century before Christ, Marcus Tullius Cicero composed a book for orators who wished to gather ideas for their speeches. This book, called *Topica,* deals with the *loci* or "places" in which a speaker can find ideas.

Following are some excerpts which may be of interest to a modern orator:

If we wish to track down some argument, we must know the places (*loci*) where arguments may be found; accordingly we may define a topic (*locus*) as the region of an argument, and an argument as a course of reasoning which firmly establishes a matter about which there is some doubt.

Topics are either Intrinsic or Extrinsic. Extrinsic topics depend on testimony, and are brought in from outside the subject matter.

Intrinsic topics, however, are inherent in the nature of the subject which is being investigated, such as arguments derived from the whole, from its parts, from its meaning, and from things which are in some way closely connected with the subject which is being investigated. Thus the Intrinsic topics are as follows:

1. Definition of the whole
2. Enumeration of the parts
3. Etymology or word meaning
4. Circumstances closely connected to the subject:
    a. Genus
    b. Species
    c. Similarity
    d. Difference
    e. Resemblances
    f. Contraries
    g. Corrolaries or adjuncts
    h. Antecedents
    i. Consequents

j. Contradictions
k. Cause
l. Effect
m. Degree or comparison.

"The topics are useful in all the parts of speech; some topics are proper to each part, of course, while aome are of use to all the parts alike."

Notes

1. Note the routine manner in which the author of the *Rhetorica ad Herennium* defines these five terms (Cicero's own definitions in the roughly contemporary *De inventione* being almost identical): "The speaker, then, should possess the faculties of Invention, Arrangement, Style, Memory, and Delivery. Invention is the devising of matter, true or plausible, that would make the case convincing. Arrangement is the ordering and distribution of the matter, making clear the place to which each thing is to be assigned. Style is the adaptation of suitable words and sentences to the matter devised. Memory is the firm retention in the mind of the matter, words, and arrangement. Delivery is the graceful regulation of voice, countenance, and gesture." (I.ii.3).
2. Again, the assumptive tone seems to indicate that these terms are already well established: "Invention is used for the six parts of a discourse: the Introduction, Statement of Facts, Division, Proof, Refutation, and Conclusion." *ad Herennium* I.iii.4. No Greek pattern of speech-parts gained universal acceptance, but beginning with Cicero and this author the six-part pattern becomes a standard for a millenium and a half.
3. Edmond Faral (*Les arts poétiques*, pp.52–54) has compiled an interesting chart of nine medieval treatises illustrating how these 64 tropes and figures and their order remain virtually intact in medieval poetic theory. For a general discussion of their medieval history see James J. Murphy, *Rhetoric in the Middle Ages*, especially pp.184–91.
4. Prantl does make one intriguing statement about the dialectical nature of figures, but abandons the subject immediately thereafter (1927 II, 423): "Alle Figuren stehen innerhalb der Parteiendialektik im Dienste der eigenen Partei-*Utilitas*." Yet he discusses only four figures briefly: *conciliatio, praeparatio, concessio,* and *permissio*.

References

Arbusow, Leonid. 1963. *Colores rhetorici: Eine Auswahl rhetorischer akademischer Figuren und Gemeinplätze als. Hilfsmittel für Übungen an mittelalterlichen Texten.* Zweite Auflage herausgegeben von Helmut Peter. Göttingen: Vandenhoeck & Ruprecht.

Aristotle. 1954. *The Rhetoric.* Transl. by W. Rhys Roberts. *Poetics.* Transl. by Ingram Bywater. New York: The Modern Library.

———. 1928. *Topics.* Transl. by W.A. Pickard-Cambridge. In *The Works of Aristotle* translated into English under the Editorship of W.D. Ross. Vol.1. Oxford: Clarendon Press.

Boethius, Manlius Severinus. 1882. *De differentiis topiciis libri quator. Patrologia Latina,* ed. by J.-P. Migne, vol. 64, cols. 1173–1216.

Bede, The Venerable. 1863. "De schematibus et tropis." *Rhetores latini minores,* ed. by Charles Halm, 227–60. Leipzig: B.G. Teubner. (Repr., Dubuque, Iowa: William C. Brown.)

Cicero, Marcus Tullius. 1949. *De inventione. De optimo genere oratorum. Topica.* Transl. by Harry M. Hubbell. Cambridge, Mass.: Harvard Univ. Press.

(Pseudo-Cicero). 1954. *Rhetorica ad Herrennium.* Ed. and transl. by Harry Caplan. Cambridge, Mass.: Harvard Univ. Press.

Curtius, Ernst Robert. 1953. *European Literature and the Latin Middle Ages.* Transl. by Willard R. Trask. New York: Pantheon Press.
D'Angelo, Frank J. 1984. "The Evolution of the Analytic *topoi*: A Speculative Inquiry." *Essays on Classical Rhetoric and Modern Discourse* ed. Robert J. Connors, Lisa S. Ede & Andrea A. Lunsford, 50–68. Carbondale, Ill.: Southern Illinois Univ. Press.
Ebbesen, Sten. 1981. "Commentators and Commentaries on Aristotle's Sophistici Elenchi." (= *Corpus Latinum Commentariorum in Aristotelem Graecorum* VII), I, 106ff. Leiden: Brill.
Faral, Edmond. 1924. *Les arts poétiques du XIIe et du XIIIe siècles.* (= Bibliothèque de l'École des hautes Etudes, fasc.238.) Paris: Champion. (Repr., 1958.)
Green-Pedersen, N.S. 1984. *The Tradition of the Topics in the Middle Ages.* Munich; Philosophia Verlag.
Grimaldi, William. 1958. "The Aristotelian Topics." *Traditio* 14. 1–14.
Holtz, Louis. 1979. "Grammariens et rhéteurs romains en concurrence pour l'enseignement des figures de rhétorique." *La rhétorique à Rome: Colloque des 10–11 décembre, 1977,* 207–20. Paris: Les Belles Lettres.
Kennedy, George A. 1963. *The Art of Persuasion in Greece.* Princeton, N.J.: Princeton Univ. Press.
———. 1972. *The Art of Rhetoric in the Roman World: 300 B.C.–A.D. 300.* Ibid.
———. 1980. *Classical Rhetoric and Its Christian and Secular Traditions from Ancient to Modern Times.* Chapel Hill, N.C.: Univ. of North Carolina Press.
———. 1983. *Greek Rhetoric under Christian Emperors.* Princeton, N.J.: Princeton Univ. Press.
Lanham, Richard A. 1968. *A Handlist of Rhetorical Terms.* Berkeley, Cal.: Univ. of California Press.
Lausberg, Heinrich. 1960. *Handbuch der literarischen Rhetorik: Eine Grundlegung der Literaturwissenschaft.* 2 vols. München: Max Huber.
Leff, Michael C. 1978. "The Logician's Rhetoric: Boethius' *De differentiis topicis,* Book IV." *Medieval Eloquence* ed. by James J. Murphy, 3–24. Berkeley, Cal.: Univ. of California Press.
Murphy, James J., ed. 1972. *A Synoptic History of Classical Rhetoric.* New York: Random House. (Repr., Davis, Cal.: Hermagoras Press, 1983.)
———. 1974. *Rhetoric in the Middle Ages: A history of rhetorical theory from Saint Augustine to the Renaissance.* Berkeley, Cal.: Univ. Of California Press.
Norden, Eduard. 1958. *Die antike Kunstprosa vom VI. Jahrhundert v. Chr. bis in die Zeit der Renaissance.* 2 vols. Stuttgart: B.G. Teubner.
Ochs, Donovan J. 1969. "Aristotle's Concept of Formal Topics." *Speech Monographs* 36.419–26.
Prantl, Carl. 1927. *Geschichte der Logik im Abendland.* Vols. I-II. Leipzig: Gustav Fock.
Quintilianus, Marcus Fabius. 1959–63. *Institutio oratoria.* Ed. and transl. by H.E. Butler. 4 vols. Cambridge, Mass.: Harvard Univ. Press.
Thurot, Charles. 1868. "Notices et extraits de divers manuscrits latins pour servir à l'histoire des doctrines grammaticales au moyen-âge," *Notices et extraits* 22.1–592. Paris: Impr. Nationale. (Repr., Frankfurt a.M.: Minerva, 1964.)

2.
THE FUNCTIONS OF RHETORICAL FIGURES
Brian Vickers

SINCE the beginning rhetoric has been thought to have an emotional and psychological influence. Homer's references to the power of eloquence form the earliest recognition of this potential, and it was soon perceived by the rhetoricians. G. M. Kennedy has written that 'In addition to logical argument Gorgias recognized the persuasive force of emotion. He regarded an orator as a *psychagôgos,* like a poet, a leader of souls through a kind of incantation.' He produced 'the serious passion which might be evoked by a speech' with the help of his rhetorical figures of symmetry and repetition, while in his speech on Helen Gorgias was the first to develop 'an analysis of psychological effects' (Kennedy, 63, 169). According to Plato, Thrasymachus also developed the appeal to the emotions *(Phaedrus,* 267c). From its earliest days onwards, whenever rhetoric is described in the abstract or personified, men always say that it has great power over the emotions, as a few quotations from our main periods will remind us. In the first century A.D. Plutarch writes (in North's translation), that the 'chiefest skill' of eloquence is 'to knowe howe to move passions and affections throughly, which are as stoppes and soundes of the soule, that would be played upon with a fine fingered hand of a conning master' (Craig, 173). As we have seen, Vives in 1531 described how man is ruled by his will, to which 'reason and judgment are assigned as counsellors, and the emotions are its torches. Moreover, the emotions of the mind are enflamed by the sparks of speech. So, too, the reason is impelled and moved by speech', and so rhetoric is the tyrant over all human activities (Vives, 180). In 1541 Nicholas Grimald, commenting on his tragi-comedy *Christus Redivivus,* described how poetry at its most intense, 'with marshalled words in battle array', can attack with the power of a winter snowstorm, and capture all who read it (Sweeting, 150). And in 1560 the Preface to Thomas Wilson's *Art of Rhetoric* has the descriptive title 'Eloquence first giuen by God, and after lost by man, and last repayred by God againe', which sets a Christian interpretation on to Isocrates' argument that eloquence is a civilizing force, and an irresistible one: 'such force hath the tongue, and such is the power of Eloquence and reason, that most men are forced, euen to yeeld in that which most standeth against their will' (Sig.A vii).

But the most vivid account of what Milton calls 'resistless eloquence' is that given by Martianus Capella in his encyclopedia, a description quoted by nearly all who write about rhetoric – and I would not want to be an exception, especially as it is very relevant here.

Vickers, Brian. "The Functions of Rhetorical Figures." *Classical Rhetoric in English Poetry*. Edinburgh: MacMillan. 1970: 83–121.

The work presents an allegorical marriage between Mercury and Philology, by which all who study literature are admitted to a divine presence. (As Ben Jonson wrote, refining on Isocrates: '*Speech* is the only benefit, man hath to expresse his excellencie of mind above other creatures. It is the Instrument of *Society*. Therefore *Mercury*, who is the President of Language, is called *Deorum hominumque interpres*' (*Timber; Works*, VIII.620–1). At this ceremony the seven liberal arts are present, and this is how rhetoric arrives:

> behold a woman of loftiest statute and great assurance, with countenance of radiant splendour, made her solemn entry. Helmeted and crowned with royal majesty, she held ready for defence or for attack weapons that gleamed with the flash of lightning. Beneath her armour the vesture draped Roman-wise about her shoulders glittered with the various light of all *figurae*, all *schemata*; and she was cinctured with most precious *colores* for jewels. The clatter of her weapons as she moved was as if thunder in the crash of a cloud aflame broke with leaping echoes. Nay, it seemed as if, like Jove, she herself could hurl the thunderbolt. For as queen in control of all things she has shown power to move men whither she pleased, or whence, to bow them to tears, to incite them to rage, to transform the mien and feeling as well of cities as of embattled armies and all the hosts of the people.
> (C. S. Baldwin, 93–4)

Some details of the allegory are forced, but the tremendous emotional power of rhetoric ('as if, like Jove, she herself could hurl the thunderbolt') is vividly presented. We notice that rhetoric has weapons, for attack and defence, and although the figures are partly described as ornaments, they clearly belong to the armoury. In the division of the styles Cicero's term for the Grand style was *vehemens*, and the tradition is preserved in Wilson's *Arte of Rhetorique:* in this kind we use 'vehement figures'. It is in the figures that the emotional force of rhetoric resides.

Classification of the Figures

So far I have been using the word 'figure' generally, to refer to all the devices of rhetoric, but properly it stands for one kind only. Classical rhetoric uses various systems to classify the figures, and there is much overlapping and confusion in terminology from which we still suffer. Indeed, the great desire to produce ever more comprehensive and logically arranged lists led to a plethora of classifications, and to an excessive enumeration. Theorists tried to account for every known phenomenon of language, with the result that a large proportion of the figures represent rare or extreme linguistic effects. I shall be adopting the simplest terminology, and shall be dealing only with major devices. All devices (or conventions) are divided, then, into 'tropes' or 'figures' (figures are sometimes called 'schemes'), and both groups were held to represent artistic deviation from the norms of language strictly conceived (thus begging such questions as whether language could exist without metaphor). Aristotle in his *Rhetoric* said that 'good style' was based on clear and appropriate language, but also on 'unfamiliar' or 'foreign' words, which because they differed from normal usage, were more striking (III.2; 1404 b9). The concept of rhetorical figures as representing an artistic transcendence of the ordinary or non-artistic resources of language was basic to rhetoric, from Quintilian: 'Ergo figura sit arte aliqua novata forma dicendi' (9.1.14) to Puttenham in 1589: 'Figurative speech is a noveltie of language evidently (and yet not absurdly) estranged from the ordinarie habite and manner of our dayly talke and writing' (159) to Henry Peacham in 1593: a figure is 'a forme of words . . . made new by Art' (1).

A trope (or 'turn') involves a change or transference of meaning and works on the conceptual level; a figure essentially works on the physical level of the shape or structure of language, and involves the disposition of words in a certain way. A trope affects the meaning of words; a figure only affects their placing or repetition. (The distinction between trope and figure is analogous to that in music between harmony and rhythm: a trope is like harmony, it exists vertically on various planes, while a figure is like rhythm, it exists horizontally, on one plane only.) Among tropes we include metaphor (or *translatio* in Latin), allegory (often described as an extended metaphor), litotes (understatement), irony, synecdoche (substituting the part for the whole), metonymy (substituting greater for lesser), hyperbole and so on. All tropes demand our recognition that ideas have been brought together on the conceptual or imaginative plane in a new and creative way, and the tropes have been the most popular and best understood of the rhetorical devices in all literature. Their application is so vast that it would be foolish to attempt here an outline of the history or function of any trope such as metaphor or irony. (Much of the best modern literary criticism has been produced in response to this challenge to reinterpret rhetoric, but some of it could benefit from a sharper historical sense. For instance, since rhetoric is a persuasive affective process, then metaphors should be regarded as persuasive, with an intention on the reader, not just as things of beauty in themselves.)

Since a history of any trope is impossible, and since the figures have by comparison received little attention in modern times, I shall devote myself mainly to them. The best classification known to me is that by Quintilian in book 9 of the *Institutes of Oratory*. He divides them first into 'figures of thought', which involve more general tactical processes in oratory (rhetorical question, apostrophe, dissimulation, insinuation), and then, more important, 'figures of speech', *figurae verborum*. (It is a sad proof of the decline of rhetoric that in modern colloquial English the phrase 'a figure of speech' has come to mean something fake, illusory or insincere: 'it was just a figure of speech' – 'he didn't mean it'; 'he was exaggerating'.) Quintilian groups figures of speech under four heads:

(*a*) variations of syntax, such as *hyperbaton* (departure from ordinary word-order, inversion), etc.
(*b*) modes of iteration: *polyptoton, ploce, epanodos, gradatio* (or *climax*), *anaphora, epanorthosis, epanalepsis, anadiplosis,* etc.
(*c*) word-play: *paronomasia, antanaclasis, syllepsis,* etc.
(*d*) balance and antithesis: *parison, isocolon, homoioteleuton,* etc.

Most of these figures will be defined and illustrated in this or the following chapter, but perhaps a word about terminology is in order here. To observe the names of the figures is not to suggest that writers always used them consciously or stiffly. As Abraham Fraunce pointed out in 1588, 'Neyther let any man thinke, that because in common meetings and assemblies the wordes and tearmes of Logike bee not named, therefore the force and operation of Logike is not therefore used & apparant. For, as in Grammar wee name neyther Noune, Pronoune, Verbe, nor any other parte of speech: and as in Rhetorike, wee make mention neyther of Metonymia, Synecdoche, Exclamatio, nor any other Rhetorical figure or trope: yet use in our speech the helpe of the one in speaking grammatically, and the direction of the other in talking eloquently', so in logic too the names become automatically transmuted into intellectual processes (Joseph, 31).

As we have seen, in classical schools and beyond every boy learned these and many more figures by heart over a number of years, and if the modern reader finds them strange at first sight you should not despair, for you will soon have a nodding acquaintance with them and nobody is going to test your memory. But it does seem important to give them the original Greek or Latin names which describes their function, and out of the many variations in terminology (best listed by Sonnino) I have chosen those I find most common. It seems equally important to use the right name rather than invent a new one, for the brave attempt by Puttenham to make them less forbidding to his audience by giving them English names descriptive of their effect ('Sillepsis or the double supply'; 'Parison, or the figure of even', 'Ploche or the doubler', 'Ironia the drie mock', 'Micterismus, or the fleering frumpe' – they seem like characters out of a lost canto of the *Faerie Queene*), although these descriptions are often apt, has resulted in many modern critics labelling them as 'quaint' and relegating them to that category of Elizabethan exuberance which doesn't need to be taken seriously. But chapter two of the third book of the *Arte of Poesie* has the ride '*How our writing and speaches ought to be figurative, and if they be not doe greatly disgrace the cause and purpose of the speaker and writer*' (Puttenham, 138), and Gascoigne says more bluntly that in writing anything, if you do not 'studie for some depth of devise in the Invention, and some figures also in the handlyng thereof, it will appeare to the skilfull Reader but a tale of a tub' (Smith, 1.48).

Modern Attacks on the Figures

If rhetoric is a great persuasive force, and if the figures are one of its chief weapons, then it might seem enough simply to accept this fact and pass on to the study of their literary functions. But although the importance of rhetoric in literary theory is recognized, and although modern criticism has shown us the presence of large-scale rhetorical processes and the influence of such constituent parts as the *topoi*, or decorum, or imitation, the rehabilitation of rhetoric has stopped short, abruptly, this side of the figures. Not only has it stopped there, but it has excused itself by ridiculing the figures; and not only has abuse come from the uninformed, as we might expect, but the very historians of rhetoric have been among the most authoritative and therefore influential mockers. Simply to limit illustration of this reaction to recent and useful surveys of rhetoric, in 1922 D. L. Clark, who later gave much valuable proof of the importance of rhetoric in education, dismissed the figures with a pointless bit of word-play: 'the glory of style to the classical rhetorician lay in its use of figures. Here rhetoric vindicated its practicality by a preoccupation with the impractical; and here, as in analysis, rhetoric bore the seeds of its own decay' (Clark [1], 29).

The Functions of Rhetorical Figures

In his *Art of Persuasion in Greece* (1963), the most enlightening study of Greek rhetoric yet made, George Kennedy's analyses of rhetorical theory often show how vital the figures were, yet he nowhere suggests that they might have had a literary function. Indeed, when he has to comment on the 'increasingly important role' played by figures it is in this tone: 'Theophrastus is probably responsible for elevating the subject to a level equal to diction and thus encouraging the process of identification of figures which led to the almost interminable lists in later rhetorical handbooks' (277). Like many writers unwilling to think about the figures in a creative way, Kennedy takes refuge in noting differences of terminology and 'confusion' (290), and he virtually dismisses the whole later development of the art as 'the dreary and trivial instruction of the rhetoricians' (321–2).

Historians of later periods have the same opinions. M. L. Clarke's *Rhetoric at Rome* (1953) reveals a dislike of 'technicalities' in his Preface (v–vi), which is confirmed when he comes to discuss the figures in his reconstruction of the *Ars Rhetorica*. Only two pages are given to this immense topic, and the rhetoricians' 'laborious thought' in classifying the schemes and tropes is brusquely dismissed: 'On the whole they shed little light for all their labours and wasted much effort on introducing confusing innovations of terminology and on discovering figures in modes of thought and speech which hardly deserve to be so called' (34). The second of these criticisms is familiar (justified, although exaggerated), and it will be another exit-line for unwilling readers of rhetoric. Clarke approves of the system of *Ad Herennium,* but would find it 'tedious and unprofitable to follow him through his list of figures', and is prepared to concede only that the subject should be studied 'however repellent or frivolous it may seem' (23). In a much slighter book on Renaissance rhetoric W. G. Crane points out that to analyse the rhetorical figures properly would need a large volume and comments: 'Its value would be doubtful' (59). Similar scornful dismissals of wasted effort are made by the most learned historian of Renaissance rhetoric, W. S. Howell, in his *Logic and Rhetoric in England,* 1500–1700 (1956):

> It may seem strange that human energy should be applied so diligently to this interminable enumeration of stylistic devices, when the subject of communication offers more philosophic and more humane approaches. [Such an interest is] more concerned with the husks than with the kernels of style.
>
> (33–4)

P. W. K. Stone's suggestion that the post-Romantic distrust of rhetoric is still with us can be illustrated here, for Howell shows a naïvely Wordsworthian concept of the proper language for poetry. Analysing the conventional definition of a trope given by a Tudor rhetorician he pronounces, with an air of discovery, that 'the implication is plain not only that tropes involve the use of words in some orbit outside of their usual ones, but also that, when these departures from the ordinary are made, the motive is often ornament rather than necessity' (130). Again, faced with Puttenham's perfectly conventional idea that prose is one step above ordinary conversation and that poetry is a step above prose, he observes with indignation that

> This view amounts to a denial that the language of ordinary life can be a medium for oratory or poetry. It also amounts to an affirmation that the medium for oratory and poetry can be found only by dressing-up the language of ordinary life with such violations of our daily speech as the tropes and figures represent.
>
> (328)

One could at least have expected a historian of rhetoric to remember his Aristotle and to see that the *Rhetoric's* approval of a 'foreign' air in some words (quoted above, p. 85) lies behind the persisting concept of the schemes and tropes as being language 'made new by art'. The more damaging fact revealed here is the naïve view of the relation between ordinary language and the materials of literature, a view which disables its holder from making any application of rhetoric to literature. It is perhaps the inevitable consequence of the situation so far prevailing in modern times whereby teachers of rhetoric have become professionals in that discipline, and have largely divorced it from literature (as in the American universities' departments of speech). And not many teachers of literature have been interested in rhetoric.

But in the field of English Renaissance literature several critics have made the bridge between rhetoric and drama with distinction: however, even these do not concede the figures much function. So Hardin Craig's distinguished survey of Elizabethan ideas, *The Enchanted Glass,* endorses Manly's judgement on medieval rhetoric. In the Renaissance rhetorics as in their predecessors, we are told, 'The elaborate system of technical devices was discussed only with reference to the form and structure of each device, never with reference to its emotional or aesthetic effects' (Craig, 162–3; Manly, 102). This may be true of the Middle Ages, but it is not of the Renaissance, and I shall quote ample evidence to refute it. Even Madeleine Doran, although so far enlightened as to realize 'The extraordinary vitality with which the dry formulae of rhetoric were converted into fruitful uses', still calls them 'dry formulae' and disputes 'whether formulated theory was ever quite adequate to the best literary practice. . . . Suggestions of a concept of style which recognizes it as organically functional appear occasionally in critical theory, but the decorative function is far more common' (43). Of course 'formulated theory' has never been 'quite adequate to the best literary practice', but with the figures the organic function is given much more stress by rhetoricians than her account would suggest. Rhetoric is often dismissed by modern critics even when it is under their noses. Thus M. M. Mahood, in her stimulating study of *Shakespeare's Wordplay,* though recognizing that word-play is an important topic 'in the whole line of rhetoricians' from Aristotle to Puttenham (9), abruptly dispatches Sister Joseph's account of the four types of pun by making an absolute disjunction between theory and practice. 'While the books of rhetoric can show us how the average Elizabethan was taught to embellish his Latin and English verses they tell us nothing of the poetic and dramatic function of these ornaments. Naming the parts does not show us what makes the gun go off' (19). This is, of course, a trivial objection concerning terminology, but in passing we might note that unless you know the parts and can manipulate them in the right order the gun will *not* go off! (I have already argued that one doesn't need to know all or indeed many of the names of the figures to appreciate their existence, for we use them in our everyday speech and writing; when Tristram Shandy's father went to enter his son's name 'at Jesus College in ****' the scholars were amazed at his natural abilities as a rhetorician, especially 'that a man who knew not so much as the names of his tools, should be able to work after that fashion with them'; book I, ch. 19.) And of course the important thing – to pursue this specious analogy a stage further – is to recognize that when the gun goes off it makes a bang and a bullet comes out – i.e. that the rhetorical figures have a strong emotional impact, as we shall see. We reject this view of rhetoric as being crude and merely ornamental, and must also reject. Miss Mahood's attempt to separate rhetoric from drama: 'When a pun is rhetorical in one of the mature plays, it is so because it is dramatically appropriate for the character to use rhetoric', or because Shakespeare's imagination works like that, or because the puns fit the world of the play (20–1). Of course this is all partly true, but rhetoric has precisely these functions among others. It is not 'anti-dramatic', nor is it really 'pre-dramatic', for the best writers absorb it into the living texture of their language. (One might also note that critics are sometimes prepared to discuss rhetoric as used by specific characters in Shakespeare and Milton, for example, but they are more embarrassed when it comes to considering the rhetoric used by the poets themselves. We are seeing only part of the truth.)

The dismissal of the figures of rhetoric comes from many scholars and critics who are evidently deeply acquainted with rhetoric, and we may be tempted to lament *Quis custodiet?* But there have been some defences, conducted mostly in general terms. Henri Marrou urged that the art of oratory creates an intimate bond between form and content. 'This is so because the effort to find the right expression demands and develops a sensitivity of thought.... "The right word is a sure sign of good thinking"' (90; Isocrates' dictum). Edmond Faral rightly pointed out that if the figures were only 'dry formulae', then a vast amount of pedagogic effort over two thousand years was wasted. 'One would be mistaken to believe that the teaching relative to tropes and their use is a simple theoreticians' exercise. It is not a game of abstractions: it is a teaching which aims at practical utility' (90). Elizabeth Salter has given a demonstration of the functional use of rhetoric in *Piers Plowman*, saying that it is used 'never for beautification, or as an end in itself, but always for the further enriching and clarifying of the sense' (37). All these observations are indeed perceptive, but they are concerned with the general relationship between form and content. The only critic who seems to have glimpsed the specific function of the figures is Rosemund Tuve, who in one chapter called 'The Criterion of Rhetorical Efficacy' (180–91) gives a forceful account of the whole rhetorical process of composition in Renaissance poetry. Writers work with a definite aim in view (180), a host of theorists argue that poetry is a super-rhetoric in its 'moving' power (181–4), imagery is especially effective in this functional aim (185–8), and particular rhetorical figures are said by Elizabethan rhetoricians to have emotional powers (184, 188). The novelty of Miss Tuve's argument is somewhat obscured here as elsewhere by her running battle with modem critics and modern poetry and by her constant juxtaposition of our attitudes with the Elizabethans', but it was a notable achievement: for the first time the figures were seen to have a literary function. Having reached the same position independently from an analysis of classical rhetoric, I now want to trace the development of this idea to the Elizabethans and beyond, developing its implications.

The Theory of Rhetorical Figures: Psychology and Emotion

In giving twelve chapters of his *Rhetoric* to the question of style, Aristotle indeed demonstrates his disagreement with Plato over the value of rhetoric (Wimsatt and Brooks, 68), but the space is mostly given to considering such things as clarity of style, weight, metaphor, vocabulary and prose-rhythm, and his detailed comments on rhetoric are not very illuminating. He refers to only a few figures (*antithesis, parison, paromoion*, 3.9.8–9) and sees their function in simple terms: *antithesis* is 'pleasing'. 'an *asyndeton* produces amplification' (3. 12.4). But in his remarks on the expression of emotion in speech (3.7) there are hints of both general and specific importance:

> Your language will be appropriate if it expresses emotion and character. . . . To express emotion, you will employ the language of anger in speaking of outrage; the language of disgust and discreet reluctance to utter a word when speaking of impiety or foulness; the language of exultation for a tale of glory, and that of humiliation for a tale of pity; and so in all other cases. This aptness of language is one thing that makes people believe in the truth of your story . . . Besides, an emotional speaker always makes his audience feel with him.

Here the listener is conceived of as responding directly to emotion, and especially by reflecting on the accuracy of its expression judged by how he has spoken when feeling similar emotions. Further, as Gerald Else has shown, in the terminology of this passage Aristotle points to 'the actual turns or "figures" of speech that characterize various feeling-states' (494). Aristotle is discussing such things as *aposiopesis, paralipsis, tapinosis*, and he actually identifies one figure with an emotional state: *hyperbole* is said to be a 'youthful or immature figure' and is therefore used by men in anger. To illustrate, Aristotle quotes Achilles' angry speech rejecting Agamemnon's offer of his daughter's hand: 'I will not marry Agamemnon's daughter, even if she rivalled golden Aphrodite in beauty and Athena in her handiwork' (*Iliad*, IX, 388–391), and Mr Else comments: 'The connection is evident. Homer, having observed how men speak in anger, has correctly (plausibly) put a hyperbole in Achilles' mouth', and the audience, having experienced both the emotion and its verbal expression, feels with Achilles (495). This is the first sight of a diagnosis which later theorists of rhetoric will repeat, that rhetorical figures are the conventional representation of verbal patterns expressed in states of extreme emotion.

Mr Else valuably connects this passage in the *Rhetoric* with the requirement in chapter 17 of the *Poetics* that the tragedian must work out the conflict in the events of his play in the 'patterns of speech' also. In Aristotle's words 'those who are in the grip of the emotions are most persuasive because they speak to the same natural tendencies in us, and it is the character who rages or expresses dejection in the most natural way who stirs us to anger or dejection' (486). The word here translated as 'patterns of speech' is related to *schemata* (the normal term for rhetorical figures), and in glossing it Mr Else makes an observation which is peculiarly relevant to the argument of this chapter:

> The forms or figures which the poet is to interpolate in the speech of his characters are 'figures of speech' not so much in the technical sense, i.e. manipulations of language *per se*, as in the broader sense of *modes of the expression of feeling* in language. Their appropriateness is not to be tested so much, therefore, by formal stylistic criteria as by the ear of the spectator

or reader, who says to himself, 'Yes, this is the way men do talk when they are angry or downcast or full of admiration; I have heard things said just that way many times'.

(495)

This is a perceptive comment on the psychological origin of rhetorical figures, but it will be my contention that all rhetorical figures are in fact 'modes of the expression of feeling in language'.

Aristotle was not over-explicit in his connection of rhetoric with feeling, but he gave some pregnant hints, and his followers developed several of his points. Theophrastus enlarged on the 'virtues' of style (Kennedy, 42, 212–84), and Demetrius, although following Aristotle in his manual *On Style*, written *c.* 270 B.C. (Demetrius, 32–8), far refined on him in sensitivity to the detail of language. Demetrius distinguishes four styles (the plain, the grand, the elegant and the forceful) and says that we 'must assign to each style the figures that are appropriate to it' (76). Repetition is one of the most useful devices, as in a speech by Ctesias, where it gives both vividness and a 'passionate tone' (109–10), and he distinguishes a whole category of 'Forceful figures'. These include *anadiplosis* (repeating a word from the end of one clause to the beginning of the next), *anaphora* (repeating a word at the beginning of subsequent clauses), and *gradatio* or *climax* (Greek for 'ladder') which he illustrates with a famous example from Demosthenes' speech *On the Crown*:

'I did not say these things and then refuse to move a proposal; I did not move a proposal and fail to go as an envoy; I did not go as an envoy and fail to persuade the Thebans.' This passage is like a man climbing higher and higher. If you were to put it like this: 'After my speech, after moving a proposal I went as an envoy, and persuaded the Thebans', he would be narrating facts, but saying nothing forceful.

(121)

The comment is acute, as is the rewriting of the idea to destroy the figure, and with it the effect. Demetrius notes quite subtle rhetorical effects. Within the forceful style, for example, repetition is not the only method: 'Brevity is so useful in this style that it is even more forceful *not* to say something, as when Demosthenes says: "Now I might remark – but I myself certainly do not wish to say anything offensive, and my accuser has the advantage in slandering me"' (117) – this is the figure *aposiopesis*, the sudden breaking-off of speech. Related to it is *paralipsis*, pretending to pass over topics while actually hinting at them, as in this example from Demosthenes: '"I make no mention of Olynthus, Methone, Apollonia, and the thirty-two cities in Thrace." With these words the orator has said all he wanted to say, and he says he will not mention them in order to give the impression that he has even more dreadful things to say' (120).

If that is a perceptive analysis of the figure's effect, still more so are those observations concerned with the dislocation of an expected linguistic sequence. The familiar theory that tropes and figures are artistic deviations from the norm of language is given a psychological rationale here. As language is the expression of thought and emotion, then a disturbance in the personality will be represented in a dislocation of the normal modes of syntax. Hence whenever we as orators or writers use fragmented expression it will be a sure sign of emotional disturbance, and the audience will regard the cause of that disturbance as a danger or an evil. So in general, the forceful style 'requires a vehement brevity, like men aiming blows in a close fight' (122), and in syntactical terms a 'lack of connectives, more than anything else, produces forcefulness' (121) – this is the figure *asyndeton*. This principle of dislocation also applies on a larger scale, for

> Just as we mentioned that the figure of omitted connective contributes to forcefulness, so does an altogether loose word-arrangement. A proof of this is found in Hipponax. When he wants to attack his enemies he breaks his rhythm, makes it halting instead of straightforward, less rhythmical, and this suits the forcefulness of his attack.
> (128)

The sensitivity to states of emotion as witnessed in syntax is seen again in Demetrius' awareness of the variety of effects possible from one figure. As Grube notes rather cautiously (27) Demetrius gives three separate examples of the figure *anaphora* (or initial repetition) and attributes three quite different results to them. The first is from the *Iliad,* the catalogue of ships in book II (671–4) where by repeating the name Nireus at the beginning of three consecutive lines Homer makes the act of leading only three ships to Troy (Nireus is never heard of again) seem very impressive, more so perhaps than it was (76). Secondly a poem by Sappho to the evening star opens with a list of its influences: 'all things you bring; you bring the sheep, you bring the goat, you bring the child to its mother', the repetition being said to produce an effect of charm (95): the charm lies in the meaning, of course, but the echoing structure certainly underlines it. The last example is from the speech of Aeschines against Demosthenes, an impassioned accusatory repetition (121), which gives the basic effect of intensity. Grube suggests that 'the fact that these effects are so different may raise doubts as to the soundness of Demetrius' basic categories', but surely it is a sign of Demetrius' recognition of the variable effect of a figure, and a very perceptive point.

The author of the *Ad Herennium* is not as sensitive to the functional qualities of style as Demetrius had been some two hundred years before him, and too often he merely says that a figure is 'charming' or 'impressive', but nevertheless we can find in his discussion in book 4 some definite indications of the relevant effects of figures. So he sums up the difference between *colon,* the brief clause which needs another to complete the sense, and *articulus,* which is similar to *asyndeton,* where the discourse is cut up by the force of expression (in his example: 'You have destroyed your enemies by jealousy, injuries, influence, perfidy') as being that while

> the former moves upon its object more slowly and less often, the latter strikes more quickly and frequently. Accordingly in the first figure it seems that the arm draws back and the hand whirls about to bring the sword to the adversary's body, while in the second his body is as it were pierced with quick and repeated thrusts.
> (4.19.26)

The image is repeated with variation in describing *conduplicatio* (or *ploce*), 'the repetition of one or more words for the purpose of Amplification or Appeal to Pity':

'The reiteration of the same word makes a deep impression upon the hearer and inflicts a major wound upon the opposition – as if a weapon should repeatedly pierce the same part of the body' (4.28.38). Though a simple explanation, it does bring out something of the effect of the figure. If weak on the emotional functions, he is perceptive in charting the figures' appeal to the reason, their union of logic, insinuation and probability. So he explains the function of Reasoning by Contraries (*contrarium* – denying the contrary of an idea before affirming it):

> it is not only agreeable to the ear on account of its brief and complete rounding-off, but by means of the contrary statement it alto forcibly proves what the speaker needs to prove; and from a statement which is not open to question it draws a thought which is in question, in such a way that the inference cannot be refuted, or can be refuted only with much the greatest difficulty.
>
> (4.18.26)

He gives the same forensic power to other large-scale figures of argument: *hypophora, similitudo, permissio,* which provokes pity, *aposiopesis* ('Here a suspicion, unexpressed, becomes more telling than a detailed explanation would have been'). He makes an acute comment on a figure later to be very popular with Renaissance writers, *correctio* (*epanorthosis*), which 'retracts what has been said and replaces it with what seems more suitable' ('O *eyes* – no eyes, but fountains fraught with tears'), writing that 'This figure makes an impression upon the hearer, for the idea when expressed by an ordinary word seems rather feebly stated, but after the speaker's own amendment it is made more striking by means of the more appropriate expression' (4.26.36). As well as other comments on the argumentative force of figures the author of the *Ad Herennium* stresses that rhetorical art should not draw attention to itself. Some elaborate figures 'are to be used very sparingly when we speak in an actual cause, because their invention seems impossible without labour and pains' (4.22.32). Most good rhetoricians from Aristotle on (*Rhetoric*, III.2; 1404 b18) urge that art must be concealed by nature.

From the point of view of the figures' function, as on other parts of rhetorical theory (Clarke, 51), Cicero is disappointing. Although adept at using the figures himself in a great range of emotional and forensic contexts, he does not seem inclined to stress their functional nature. The great practitioner does not need to explain the theoretical basis of his art: in Pascal's famous aphorism, 'La vraie éloquence se moque de l'éloquence.' Cicero 'is generally satisfied with an enumeration of the Figures' (D'Alton, 112), and when he does so it is in an off-hand, almost apologetic, way. In the *Orator* he simply lists the patterns which characterize figures without deigning to name them or discuss their function (39.135–9), and confines his comments to saying that the figures of thought are more important, and are frequently used by Demosthenes (l36). In his slightly fuller discussion in the *De Oratore* (3.201f) the same reluctance to indulge in definition and classification is seen, as the list is made as short and swift as possible. His only hint on function is that 'sometimes the repetition of words will produce an impression of force, at other times of grace'. The reader is naturally frustrated about Cicero's silence on this point, but at least we must concede that he has done the more difficult thing, using the figures in a way which provided later rhetoricians with vivid examples of their potential emotional and forensic power: he is quoted innumerable times by Quintilian.

The *Institutes of Oratory* is a much more satisfying work, combining the philosophical and historical approaches to rhetoric of Aristotle and Cicero with the technical detail of the *Ad Herennium* and with something of the psychological grasp of Longinus. Quintilian's advocacy of 'rhetorical ornament' starts from its practical effect on the audience. Though an orator's other gifts may appeal to the learned, 'this gift appeals to the enthusiastic approval of the world at large, and the speaker who possesses it fights not merely with effective, but with flashing weapons' (so reviving the *Ad Herennium's* sword-fighting metaphor, which was to have a long life). If properly used, as by Cicero in his defence of Cornelius, it can rouse an audience to an 'ecstasy of delight', and it is in any case very persuasive (8.3.2–5). When he comes to discuss the figures in detail, in book 9, Quintilian revives his metaphor from sword-fighting to stress the utility, of 'figures of thought' in terms of their intellectual penetration (the rapier not the cutlass), for as 'the task of the skilful swordsman is to give the impression that his design is quite other than it actually is, even so the oratory in which there is no guile fights by sheer weight and impetus alone' (9.1.19–20). He immediately stresses the figures' emotional function:

> Further, then is no more effective method of exciting the emotions than an apt use of figures. For if the expression of brow, *eyes* and hand has a powerful effect in stirring the panions, how much more effective must be the aspect of our style itself when composed to produce the result at which we aim?
>
> (9.1.21)

Here is a clear statement of the power of figures to be the channels of emotional as well as intellectual expression.

Quintilian's practical legal purpose assumes a wholly persuasive intent in the speaker, and does not go behind that to inquire into the psychological origins of the figures. But he does note their existence in common speech, and M. L. Clarke, drawing on a German study of spoken Latin, perceptively argues that 'there is a rhetorical element in any spoken language, if by rhetoric we mean speech designed to create an effect on the hearer. This is the function of much of ordinary speech, not least among the unsophisticated; even peasants and uneducated persons, observed Quintiltan, use hyperbole, "for no one is content with the plain truth"' (8.6.75). 'Everyday speech does not consist in the main of plain, straightforward, unimpassioned speech. There are certain modes of expression, rhetorical questions, exclamations, repetitions of words, which constantly recur in the emotional passages of Roman oratory.... Recognised and sanctioned as "figures" by the rhetoricians they were used with greater artistry by the professional orator, but they had their roots in popular speech' (39–40). As we will see, Longinus and Puttenham offer the same theory of the origins of the figures. But apart from this passing insight, for Quintilian language is in the service of the lawyer's specific purpose, and so the speaker must select only the methods which will get his

The Functions of Rhetorical Figures 51

argument accepted: 'What pleasure can an orator hope to produce, or what impression even of the most moderate learning, unless he knows how to fix one point in the minds of the audience by repetition, and another by dwelling on it, how to digress from and return to his theme. . . .' (9.2.4) and so on. In all such essential manœuvres the figures are vital, and can be varied to suit differing tones of emphasis. In this section Quintilian's literary sensitivity is seen in his intelligent choice of examples from Cicero, Virgil, Seneca and Terence, as again to illustrate his point that. 'The figures best adapted for intensifying emotion consist chiefly in simulation' (9.2.26–8). Not all the figures are treated with detailed reference to their poetic and emotional effect. For many, having established the functional principle, Quintilian is content to describe the figure and give examples of it; for others, he gives a brief account. Of the familiar figure *anaphora* he writes: 'a number of clauses may begin with the same word for the sake of force and emphasis' (9.3.30); on *asyndeton* and its relations: 'The origin of these figures is one and the same, namely that they make out utterances more vigorous and emphatic and produce outbursts of emotion' (9.3.50, 54). Here we see a wider awareness of the emotional states of the orator and his audience, and of the connection between the two. In developing this point later he brings out a constant assumption, that the orator must convince his audience of the genuineness of his feeling by suiting his style to subject and to the appropriate emotions, for anger cannot be credibly expressed in neat antitheses (9.3.102). It is a passage which provides an illuminating gloss on the failure of Brutus's rhetoric in *Julius Caesar* (Vickers [2], 241–5).

The lucid common sense shown here characterizes other valuable points, such as the important insistence on the need for an organic relation between form and content. Our pleasure should be derived 'both from the figurative form and the excellence of the sense' (9.3.71), for 'it is as ridiculous to hunt for figures without reference to the matter as it is to discuss dress and gesture without reference to the body' (9.3.100). Again we have the stress on the need to avoid display: '*Gradatio,* which the Greeks call *climax,* necessitates a more obvious and less natural application of art and should therefore be more sparingly employed' (9.3.54). This injunction is of a piece with his frequent stress on the need for selection, judgement and 'decorum' in its original sense of fitting outer to inner, of choosing the apt figure for the emotional or intellectual position. Still more illuminating is his automatic association of the figures with the emotions, even though he objects to creating new figures non-stop:

> I must repudiate the view of those who hold that there are as many types of figures as there are kinds of emotion, on the ground, not that emotions are not qualities of the mind, but that a figure, in its strict, not its general sense, is not simply the expression of anything you choose to select.

The mere expression of emotion does not create a figure, even though – a very enlightening point this – 'superficial observers are deceived by the feet that they find figures in all passages dealing with such themes', that is, expressions of 'anger, grief, pity, fear, confidence or contempt'. So the figures *are* the automatic repositories of emotion, and will be used in all states of excitement, but only some figures may legitimately be used for specific emotional effects (9.1.23–6). The relationship 'figures: emotions' is genuine, and a two-way process, but art is a selection from nature. From Quintilian alone the Elizabethan reader would have drawn a dear sense of the necessity for using rhetorical figures, and of their power as poetic channels of expression. And from the modesty and control of the exposition and the examples given, he would have seen that these were not 'dry formulae' or 'husks' of style, but the essential steps to eloquence and conviction.

Unfortunately Quintilian was not as widely used by later rhetoricians as he deserved to be, and a similar irony is that the most remarkable union of rhetoric and literary criticism in classical times (or since) disappeared altogether until 1554: the work *On the Sublime*, ascribed to one 'Longinus'. The loss to rhetoric here was great, for Longinus gives the best account of the organic nature of the figures, which form for him 'the third source of literary excellence' (chapters 16–29). Longinus's account is brief (but amounts to over half of the work preserved), and he selects only 'a few of those that contribute to a strong effect' (chapter 16, para. 43). His general thesis is that 'Figures naturally work in harmony with excellence of style and in turn receive marvellous reinforcement from it' (17.45). He at once meets the objection that the 'clever use of figures' draws attention to its own artificiality, by urging that such expertise should be accompanied by 'literary excellence and strong feeling', for 'When the craft with which it has been elaborated is concealed by its beauty and grandeur, the figure is no longer obvious and escapes all suspicion' (17.47). This injunction may be derived from Aristotle, Quintilian, or from Horace's famous *ars est celare artem*, but it is an intrinsic part of rhetoric's relation to natural speech.

Longinus's excellence as a rhetorician consists first in his power to analyse particular effects in extant literary works, as we see in his discussion of Demosthenes' use of an apostrophe to produce both 'pathos' and 'all the reasons for belief' (16.44), and the same orator's use of question and answer (*anthypophora*) to create an impression of 'spontaneous emotion' (18.48). His second excellence (seen always together with the first) is that of perceiving the connection between particular figures of rhetoric and particular emotional states, either in the *persona* presented in the literary work, or in the audience's reaction to it. He is in effect giving a psychological explanation of the power of rhetorical figures. So he writes of *asyndeton*:

> In the figure of *asyndeton*, the phrase fall unconnected as though in a torrent, almost getting ahead of the speaker himself – Xenophon writes: 'With their shields striking together, they pushed, they fought, they killed, they were killed' [*Hellenica*, IV.3.19].... Since the phrases are disconnected and yet rapid, they make emphatic the excitement which both hampers the man's speech and makes it more rapid. This the poet achieves by leaving out the connectives.
>
> (19.49)

From this analysis too we are given the suggestion of the genesis of a rhetorical figure. In real life, when men are excited, their words 'fall unconnected as though in a torrent'; the rhetorician observed this phenomenon, saw its syntactical root, and gave it a name; so the writer by using the figure can re-create the emotional state.

Longinus always brings out the emotional effect of the figures, especially those which break up an expected order in language or in life, for as in Demetrius or Puttenham there is seen to be a direct connection between a man's mind and his language: 'emotion, since it is a violent disturbance of the soul, is expressed by disorder' (20.50). He notes well how the orator, by combining various figures in the speech against Meidias, 'smites the mind of the jury with blow upon blow', and how this disorder produces 'the effect of breathless haste and roughness' (20.50; 21.51), Again like Demetrius he rewrites the passage, removes the figure, and demonstrates how the emotional power dwindles. The most impressive example of his perception of the emotional state underneath a figure is his account of *hyperbaton*.

> This consists in a violent disruption of the natural order of words and ideas, and seems to show the most unmistakable signs of violent feeling, because those who really are angry or afraid or violently irritated or in the grip of jealousy or some other passion (for there are so many emotions that no one can hope to number them) come forward with one idea and then rush off to some other, after having thrown in something quite irrational; then they circle back to the first, and in their excitement, as though driven by an uncertain wind, shift their words and ideas now in one direction, then to the very opposite, and change their arrangement from the natural into a thousand shifting forms. The best prose writers, using *hyperbaton* to imitate nature, get the same effect. For art is perfect when it seems to be nature, and nature succeeds when it has art concealed within.
>
> (22.52)

By further analysis of examples in Herodotus, Demosthenes, and Thucydides, Longinus brings out the sort of effect that this representation can have on the audience. To consider the accuracy of his account by appealing to life is hardly necessary, but from literature we might recall how well Shakespeare understood this state and the stylistic representation of it – as in Shylock's anguish at the double loss of Jessica and his ducats; or Richard III on the eve of Bosworth; or the jealousies of Othello and Leontes.

Although Longinus's discussion of the figures is brief, his insistence on their organic function is very stimulating. He writes as if it were quite obvious: 'Then there are the figures included under *polyptotes* – accumulations, startling turns, and climaxes – which, as you know, are very powerful aids in securing beauty and every kind of excellence and emotional effect' (23.54). He is presumably referring to such figures as *polyptoton, paronomasia, syllepsis,* and *gradatio* – several of which Elizabethan and other rhetoricians associate with specific effects. In his summing up Longinus states the functional nature of the figures most cogently. 'They all enable speeches to be more passionate and expressive of feeling, and emotion plays the same part in the most excellent compositions as character does in those that are merely pleasing' (29.62). If limited in width of discussion, the author of *On the Sublime* gives more than compensation by the intensity of his perception that the rhetorical figures are *channels* of emotional expression. As well as giving many excellent practical analyses, Longinus makes afresh the discovery that the schemes and tropes are basically stylizations or records of man's natural emotional behaviour as expressed in language, which when properly applied form the best stylistic means of re-creating the details of human emotion in literature. In those words of E. H. Gombrich that form an epigraph to this book, 'In classical writings on rhetoric we have perhaps the most careful analysis of any expressive medium ever undertaken' (374).

It is a minor tragedy that Longinus was lost to the Middle Ages and early Renaissance. Some of the functions of the figures would be evident from the *Ad Herennium,* but (accepting my limited knowledge of medieval rhetorical theory) the writers of the arts of poetry do not seem to have laid any stress on this point. One assumes that it must have been self-evident to them, or else they would hardly have expended so much energy on the figures, and certainly there is much evidence that the poets themselves understood the figures' emotional possibilities. A small proof of the figures' creative potential is given (as if by accident) by Manly in his lecture on 'Chaucer and the rhetoricians': 'But that some of Chaucer's freest and most delightful work should contain twice as much rhetoric as some of his least inspired compositions is a puzzle that demands investigation' (108). It is not 'a puzzle', for in my view of the functional nature of rhetoric it is self-evident that the greatest literature may often have been based on the greatest use of rhetoric, but it is a question that as regards the Middle Ages has not had nearly enough investigation, especially on the theoretical side, and I must leave this matter to more qualified (and, I hope, active) hands. (See R. O. Payne's brief survey.)

For the English Renaissance we are on more fruitful ground, and although we may not normally expect to find anything original in the literary theories expounded by our writers in this period, they seem to have absorbed the classical rhetoricians' advocacy of the imaginative power of rhetoric, and even to have improved on it. Of course there are still vague descriptions of the 'comeliness' or 'adornment' of rhetorical figures (as in the *Ad Herennium* or Quintilian), but there is ample evidence of English recognition of their functional possibilities. The most complete handbook of the figures is *The Garden of Eloquence* by Henry Peacham (1577, 1593). Its main source is the popular *Epitome troporum* of Susenbrotus, and of the classical rhetorics it comes closest to the *Ad Herennium* in its interest in the detailed techniques of rhetoric rather than its philosophical contexts. But it surpasses that work in its insistence on the functional nature of the figures, as can be seen in many places, and also by the fact that for the second edition of 1593 Peacham (perhaps noticing similar but only occasional caveats in the classical rhetoricians) systematically added a section on each figure giving 'The Use' and 'The Caution', stressing the need for the rhetorical device to be related to the sense and not to be used excessively – nature must conceal art. So in 1577 he had described the effect of *anaphora* in the same vague terms used in the *Ad Herennium*: 'when with much comelynesse one word is repeated in diuers clauses . . .' (Sig. Hiiii). But in 1593 he brings out its function: 'The use hereof is chiefly to repeate a word of importance, and effectual signification', and he adds the cautions that it must not be used too often, or tautologically, and that 'heede ought to be taken, that the word which is least worthie or most weake, be not taken to make the repetition, for that were very absurd' (41–2). An example of the correct use of *anaphora* is quoted by him from Psalm 29: 'The Lord sitteth above the water floods. The Lord remaineth a King for ever. The Lord shall give strength unto his people. The Lord shall give his people the blessing of peace.'

In many of these figures of repetition Peacham insists that the writer fit sound and structure to sense, laying great stress on the need for the figure to be founded on 'a word of importance' in the text. For the figure *epistrophe*, 'which endeth diuerse members or clauses still with one and the same word', he adds an awareness of the audience and the persuasive intent of rhetoric reminiscent of Quintilian: '*The use of this figure* ... it serueth to leave a word of importance in the ende of a sentence, that it may the longer hold the sound in the mind of the hearer' (43). Perhaps the most forceful example of this echoing figure is Leontes' savage *epistrophe* on 'nothing' (*Winter's Tale*, 1.2.284–96). Again for *diaphora* or *ploce*, the repetition of a word, Peacham urges that it should serve 'both to the pleasure of the eare and sense of the mind', and that here as in other figures the word repeated must be at the centre of meaning (45). *Epanalepsis*, he maintains, should place 'a word of importance in the beginning of a sentence to be considered, and in the end to be remembered' (46). *Paragmenon* – his name for *polyptoton* – ('a figure which of the word going before deriveth the word following') is used 'to delight the eare by the derived sound, and to move the mind with a consideration of the nigh affinitie and concord of the matter', for example, on the relationship between Adam and Christ (1 Cor. 15.45): 'The first man was of the earth earthly, the second man was the Lord from Heaven heavenly' (55). He recalls the classical rhetoricians in stressing the avoidance of artifice. The figure *paronomasia* 'ought to be sparingly used, and especially in graue and weightie cases, both in respect of the light and illuding forme, and also forasmuch as it seemeth not to be found without meditation and affected labour' (56). More specifically he recalls Longinus in describing the effect of *articulus* (or *asyndeton* – the image he uses looks like a Renaissance updating of Quintilian's sword-fighting metaphor). This figure is 'very convenient to express any vehement affections: in peacable and quiet causes it may be compared to a sembreefe in Musicke, but in causes of perturbation and haste it may be likened to thicke and violent strokes in fight, or to a thick and thundring peale of ordinance' (57).

Peacham is so convinced of the potential of the figures to express feeling that he actually groups them according to their degree of emotional power. Figures of 'the second order' ('Figures of sentences') are such as do make the oration not onely pleasant and plausible but also verie sharpe and vehement, by which the sundrie affections and passions of the minde are properly and elegantly uttered (by a forme of outcrie) and that either by the figures of Exclamation, Moderation, Consultation, or Permission' (61–2). Later he says that these figures 'do attend upon affections, as ready handmaids at commaundement to express most aptly whatsoever the heart doth affect or suffer' (120). And within this group he distinguishes between the more violent forms of exclamation and the 'lesse vehement than those', which 'pertaine to more milde affections, and do require a more moderate form of pronunciation' (84). The criteria for classification of the figures are emotional and psychological. (At about the same time in France the author of a rhetoric-book for dramatists, which we know Racine owned, was writing that 'the tragic poet's business being to express and excite passions he will make copious use of' such 'figures of sentence'; France, 33, 39). Although there are less perceptive references to 'the profit and pleasure' or the 'comeliness' of figures, Peacham shows himself to be intelligently aware of their emotional function – and indeed of their intellectual or argumentative force. Thus he says of the figure *apodixis* (*evidens probatio*) that 'Of all the formes of speech there is not one more apt, or more mighty to confirme or confute then this, which is grounded upon the strong foundation of experience confirmed by all times . . .' (87). A similar power is given to *antimetabole*, quoting the example used in the *Ad Herennium*, but giving a more intelligent account of it than that work's mere epithet 'neat': '*Antimetabole*, is a forme of speech which inverteth a sentence by the contrary, thus: "It behoueth-thee to eate that thou maist liue, and not to liue that thou maist eate". . . . The use hereof serveth properlie to praise, dispraise, to distinguish, but most commonly to confute by the inversion of the sentence' (164). No reader of Peacham could come away without seeing that the figures of rhetoric have a great persuasive power, appealing both to the emotions and to the intellect.

Of the many other Elizabethan rhetoricians, the least interested in stressing the imaginative potential of rhetoric are the Ramists, surprisingly so in view of their 'literary' illustrations of the tropes and figures. One looks in vain for any advance on the common-place concept of rhetoric as being ornament or 'garnishing' in Dudley Fenner's *Artes of Logike and Rhetorik* (1584) or Charles Butler's *Rhetorical Libri Duo* (1597), and in a more adventurous Ramist work, Abraham Fraunce's *Arcadian Rhetoric* (1588), there are only a few signs of a more intelligent awareness. In one of these places, discussing the power of 'figures in Sentences, which in the whole sentence express some motion of the minde', he seems to be merely echoing Peacham: 'These are more forcible & apt to perswade, than those of words, which be rather pleasant and fit to delight' (63). But in discussing figures such as *epanorthosis* or *aposiopesis* he seems to make a more original psychological point: 'The calling backe of a mans selfe followeth, when any thing is revoked, and it is as it were, a cooling of that heate of exclamation. . . .' (78). This stress on 'cooling', however, is opposed to the traditional interpretations of the figure's pathetic or passionate effect, such as Peacham's: '*Aposiopesis:* by which the Orator through some affection, as either of feare, anger, sorrow, bashfulness or such like, breaketh off his speech before it be all ended. *Virgil:* "How doth the childe Ascanius, whom tymely *Troy* to thee –" breaking off by the interruption of sorrow.'

Weak though the Ramists are on this point, further evidence of the literary-psychological relations of rhetoric is found in, a writer often (if on dubious grounds) associated with the Ramists, Sir Philip Sidney. In the *Apology for Poetry* he attacks the misuse of imitation: although Cicero and Demosthenes are 'most worthie to be imitated' it should not be done mechanically and without regard to context. Sidney illustrates his point by reference to the famous opening of the first *In Catilinam*, which both Quintilian and the young King Edward VI had analysed:

> *Tully* when he was to drive out *Catiline,* as it were with a thunderbolt of eloquence, often useth the figure of reptation, as *Vivit & vincit, imo in senatum, venit imo, in senatum venit, &c.* Indeede enflamed, with a well grounded rage, hee would have his words (as it were) double out of his mouth, and so do that artificially, which we see men in choller doo naturally. And we, having noted the grace of those words, hale them in sometimes in a familiar Epistle, when it were too much choller to be chollericke.
>
> (*Works*, III.42)

The Functions of Rhetorical Figures

By his scornful concluding *polyptoton* ('choller... chollericke') as by his allusion to the figure *conduplicatio* in 'double out of his mouth' (*ploce* is called by Puttenham 'the doubler') Sidney shows his familiarity with rhetoric. More interesting is his explicit connection of rhetoric to its natural sources in human emotion: 'So do that artificially, which we see men in choller doo naturally.' And in an earlier passage in the *Apology*, arguing that all the liberal arts derive their subject-matter from nature, Sidney concisely indicated the relationship here between nature and art; 'the *Rhetoritian* and *Logitian*, considering what in nature wil soonest proove, and perswade thereon, give artificiall rules' (III.7), that is – in no pejorative sense – rules made by art.

If the Ramists are on the whole disappointing, by contrast psychological penetration is the key point of the *Directions for Speech and Style* by John Hoskins (*c.* 1599), who in this might be called the English Longinus. Here too is evidence of a considerable literary intelligence, a rare sensitivity to the style of individual writers, and here too the work is tantalizingly brief. Hoskins fellows Peacham, but adds several explanations of his own. So in discussing figures of repetition he moves from the unexceptionable position that 'The ears of men are not only delighted with store and exchange of divers words but feel great delight in repetition of the same' to the remarkably perceptive pre-Freudian position that 'as no man is sick in thought upon one thing but for some vehemency or distress, so in speech there is no repetition without importance' (12), This is both a psychological and an artistic justification for a figure, and the insights of Demetrius and Longinus into the significance of linguistic obsession are here validated. Elsewhere he combines artistic and more utilitarian ends, as did Quintilian and Peacham (105) before him: the figure *anaphora* 'beats upon one thing to cause the quicker feeling in the audience, and to awake a sleepy or dull person' (13).

Already we see Hoskins's ability to take a familiar figure and give to some fresh interpretation, in a natural and human way. Of all the accounts of *antimetabole* (e.g. from Sidney: 'they misliked what themselves did, and yet did still what themselves misliked'), none is as acute as his: 'this is a sharp and witty figure and shows out of the same words a pithy distinction of meaning...' (15). Intelligent, too, is his association of it with logical techniques (the schoolmen) and his comment on the frequency with which Sidney used it. Hoskins, like Peacham, stresses the need to tie figure to sense and structure: 'let discretion [i.e. decorum] be the greatest and general figure of figures' (15), and again, the use of a figure should 'come from some choice and not from barrenness' (17). He is clearly aware of the organic needs of the artistic moment: 'In these two sorts of amplifying you may insert all figures *as the passion of the matter shall serve*' (21; my italics), and has a good sense of the varying effects possible from any one channel – so *polyptoton* 'is a good figure, and may be used *with or without passion*' (17). Some figures, such as exclamation, are so emotionally intense that they are 'not lawful but in extremity of motion, as Piracies, seeing the mild Philoelea innocently beheaded, cried out: "O tyrant heaven, traitor earth, blind providence, no justice! How is this done! How is this suffered? Hath this world a government?"' (33). His sympathy with one of Sidney's favourite figures, *synoeciosis* (or *oxymoron*, 'a composition of contraries' – such as 'witty ignorance') again takes a psychological turn: 'This is a fine course to stir admiration in the hearer and make them think it a strange harmony which must be expressed in such discords' (36). (For another example of this psychological state we think of Claudius's insincere welcome to Hamlet: 'With mirth in funeral, and with dirge in marriage' – I.ii. 10–14.) One other virtue of Hoskins is his remarkable sensitivity to changes in style in his lifetime (as he shrewdly said of *synoeciosis* or *oxymoron:* 'This is an easy figure now in fashion, not like ever to be so usual', 37). In connection with the current vogue for *sententia* he made a prophecy of the decline of rhetoric which came uncannily true:

> For now there are such schisms of eloquence that it is enough for any ten year that all the bravest wits do imitate some one figure which a critic hath taught some great personage. [He is perhaps referring to the figure *contentio,* which, he records, Ascham taught Queen Elizabeth – 37.] So it may be within this two hundred years we shall go through the whole body of rhetoric.
>
> (39)

He was right almost to the day: 1799; 1800 saw the Preface to the *Lyrical Ballads.* In trying to re-create the 'body of rhetoric' as the Renaissance knew it, John Hoskins is one of the most intelligent and helpful guides, and his perception of the connections between the figures and the psychology of emotion is extremely important.

If Hoskins is the Longinus of Elizabethan rhetoric, then Puttenham is its Quintilian, for the author of *The Arte of English Poesie* moves with equal ease from philosophical and historical aspects down to both technicalities and *jeux d'esprit.* Here are given the strongest arguments in favour of rhetoric, for it is indeed the highest reach of art, as he explains in the first chapter of the third book, 'Of Ornament': 'the chief prayse and cunning of our Poet is in the discreet using of his figures . . . with a delectable varietie, by all measure and iust proportion, and in places most aptly to be bestowed' (138). In the next chapter he argues that just as it is wrong 'to use figurative speeches foolishly', so is it wrong not to use them at all, by which we make our writing or speeches, 'but as our ordinary talk, then which nothing can be more vnsavourie and farre from all ciuilitie'. If the highest persons in the land were to speak, they 'ought to doe it cunningly and eloquently, which can not be without the use of figures' (138–9). Here is the basis of Renaissance literary language: figures are the *sine qua non* of excellence, and 'plain Speeche' is simply crude. Puttenham also provides the best statement of the organic relation between the figures and the sense, in commenting on such a clumsy repetition as

> 'To loue him and loue him, as sinners should doo.' These repentions be not figuratiue but phantastical, *for a figure is euer used to a purpose, either of beautie or of efficacie:* and these last recited be to no purpose, for neither can ye say that it vrges affection, nor that it bcautifieth or enforceth the sence, not hath any other subtilitie in it, and therefore is a very foolish impertinency of speech, and not a figure.
>
> (202; my italics)

The harshness of tone there, from this generally urbane writer, is an additional sign of the seriousness with which the Renaissance took its rhetoric.

The writer must use the figures, then, and he must use them in an organic relationship to his subject-matter, either for emotional or intellectual conviction, or just for beauty. So he urges the poet to use the sententious figures, which are not only pregnant with meaning but also have a melodious, 'auricular' effect, 'because the eare is no lesse rauished with their currant tune, than the mind is with their sententiousness. For the eare is properly but an instrument of conveyance for the minde, to apprehend the sence by the sound' (196). This is surely for its date a remarkable insistence on the organic relationship between sound and sense, and a further imaginative expansion of the power of rhetoric. In his comments on particular figures Puttenham is just as perceptive. Of *aposiopesis* (166–7), which he describes as 'the figure of silence, or of interruption', he gives several possible psychological motives, 'If we doo interrupt our speech for feare' it is suitable, or 'for shame', or 'for anger or by way of menace' – as for example, we might add, with Lear to Goneril and Regan:

No, yon unnatural hags,
I will have revenges on you both,
That all the world shall – I will do such things;
What they are, yet I know not, but they shall be
The terrors of the earth.

(II.iv.281)

The figure is equally apt 'to show a moderation of wrath as the graue and discreeter sort of men do', or just 'upon some sodaine occasion', and he adds a further hint as to the sort of character who might be shown using it: 'This figure is fit for phantasticall heads and such as be sodaine or lacke memorie' – and one thinks of Shakespeare's Polonius, or Shallow. Here are five possible states of mind which the figure *aposiopesis* can correctly record, demonstrating a sharp awareness by Puttenham of the emotional-psychological flexibility of the figures. Again, like contemporary and classical rhetoricians, he sees the peculiar power of *asyndeton:* 'we vtter it in that fashion, when either we be earnest, or would seeme to make hast' (213). Like Hoskins, he has a good sense of the particular figures which characterize a writer's style, noting Raleigh's frequent use of figures of repetition (*anaphora,* 198; *epizeuxis and ploce,* 201), Sidney's involuted wit (202), and making a shrewd comment on writers using *antithesis:* '*Isocrates* the Greek Oratour was a little too full of this figure, & so was the Spaniard [Guevara] that wrote the life of *Marcus Aurelius,* & many of our moderne writers in vulgar, vse it in excesse & incurre the vice of fond affection: otherwise the figure is very comendable' (211). It is a fair comment on *Euphues.*

In addition to his insights into the organic nature of rhetorical figures' their auricular and emotional effect, Puttenham provides the most intelligent statement known to me of the relationship between rhetoric and life. Longinus had argued that rhetorical figures were created by observation of human speech in certain emotional states, and the idea that in our normal speech we use rhetorical figures without knowing it was conceived again by Abraham Fraunce, as we have seen (p. 87). Puttenham also makes this point, but extends it into a fully thought-out concept of the function of rhetoric in recording and representing human emotions.

> And with these examples I thinke sufficient to leaue, geuing you information of this one point, that all your figures Poeticall or Rhetoricall, are but observations of strange speeches [i.e. outside the norm of human communication: Aristotle's 'foreign'], and such as without any arte at all we should use, and commonly do, euen by very nature without discipline [instruction]. But more or less aptly and decently, or scarcely, or abouundantly, or of this kind or that kind of figure, and one of us more than another, according to the disposition of our nature, constitution of the heart, and facilitie of each mans vtterance: so as we may conclude, that nature her selfe suggesteth the figure in this or that forme: but arte aydeth the iudgement of his vse and application. . . .
>
> (290)

This remarkably coherent presentation of rhetoric as the image of human thought and emotion makes a useful movement towards the psychology of style (what is it that makes different writers choose different figures?). It also raises the crucial dispute between nature and art, which Puttenham resolves into a philosophical view of the artistic process which suggests at once Plato and Coleridge. Of the three liberal arts which make up the traditional trivium

> I call those artes of Grammer, *Logicks*, and *Rhetorick* not bare imitations, as the painters or keruers craft and worke in a forraine subject viz a liuely purtraite in his table or wood, but by long and studious observation rather a repetition or reminiscens naturall, reduced into perfection, and made prompt by use and exercise.
>
> (306)

The ancient triad 'Art, Imitation, Exercise' is thus given a philosophical extension. It follows then that the poet having mastered the art of expressing himself in the most effective 'maner of language and stile . . . whereof the many moodes and strange phrases are called figures' must transcend this art and return to nature, where he began. His work, 'even as nature herselfe working by her owne peculiar vertue and proper instinct and not by example or meditation or exercise as all other artificers do, is then most admired when he is most naturall and least artificial' (301). The excellence of Puttenham's book should be as evident today as it was then, and we should take for granted the organic connection between rhetoric and poetry in the way that Sir John Harington did in 1591, appending 'A Brief Apology for Poetry' to his translation of *Orlando furioso*, and earnestly recommending his readers to read the *Arte of English Poesie* 'where, as it were, a whole receit of Poetrie is described, with so manie new named figures as would put me in great hope in this age to come would breed manie excellent Poets' (Smith, 2.196). The living proof that in this period theory was put into practice can be found in the supremely fluid 'reminiscens naturall' of rhetoric in the works of Sidney, Shakespeare, Donne, George Herbert, Milton. Art and nature were one.

The Renaissance idea of the functional, organic nature of rhetoric is formulated most clearly by Puttenham, but is fully operative in Peacham and Hoskins. Given that both classical rhetoricians and the leading contemporary theorists affirmed the imaginative power of rhetoric, it is hardly likely that an educated Elizabethan would have regarded the figures as 'dry formulae'. It must be agreed that the English Renaissance developed a remarkably perceptive and organic theory of style and of the emotional-psychological function of the figures, one which in my view improves even on that of Longinus and Quintilian. If theirs was 'the most *careful* analysis of any expressive medium ever undertaken', this was even more sensitive to its literary value, and to its importance for the practising poet. The flourishing of rhetoric attended the emergence of Greek literature, as it did that of the great age of Latin literature: evidently rhetoric played a key role in the rise of a language as well as of its greatest literature. Certainly its development in England coincided with the 'triumph of the English language', and the period from 1570 to 1640, say, deserves to be known as the third great age of rhetoric, with London rivalling Athens and Rome.

But as rhetoric did not disappear in the seventeenth century, despite the odium heaped upon it, we can find continuing evidence of the functional nature of the rhetorical figures. So in his *Apology for Heroic Poetry and Poetic Licence* (1677) Dryden develops the hint of Longinus that rhetoric originally drew from life. The first poets, he writes, showed how to raise the passions by drawing directly from life before the conventions were formalized: 'From hence have sprung the tropes and figures for which they wanted a name who first practised them, and succeeded in them.' Therefore it follows 'that those things which delight all ages must have been an imitation of nature', and 'Therefore is rhetoric made an art; therefore the names of so many tropes and figures were invented; because it was observed they had such, and such effect upon the audience' (*Essays*, 1.200–1). Drawing nearer Longinus, Dryden outlines the occasions on which the 'bolder' or more forceful figures may be used, but not flaunted, so that they can

> work their effect upon the mind without discovering the art which caused it. And therefore they are principally to be used in passion; when we speak more warmly, and with more precipitation, than at other times: for then, *si vis me flere, dolendum est primum ipsi tibi;* the poet must put on the passion he endeavours to represent: a man in such an occasion is not cool enough, either to reason rightly, or to talk calmly. Aggravations are then in their proper places; interrogations, exclamations, hyperbata, or a disordered connection of disemine, are graceful there because they are natural.
>
> (203)

Dryden here joins the tradition extending from Puttenham back to Demetrius two thousand years before him: language reveals the inner man. In the words of Ben Jonson, translating Vives, '*Language* most shewes a man: speake that I may see thee. It springs out of the most retired, and inmost parts of us, and is the Image of the Parent of it, the mind. No glasse renders a mans forme, or likenesse, so true as his speech' (*Timber; Works,* VIII.625). In *Volpone* we are still in the world of Cicero and Quintilian when Mosca's praise of the brilliant advocate Voltore compasses the whole sequence of rhetorical composition:

> had you heard him first
> Draw it to certain heads, then aggravate,
> Then use his vehement figures. . . .
> (v.i)

Just as we find in the Augustan period the traditional ideas of rhetoric as being first a stylized record of human speech and secondly a means of representing human emotional and psychological extremes, we likewise see that in this Neoclassic world the figures still have a persuasive function. Thus Pope in the *Essay on Criticism* praises the *Institutes of Oratory;*

> In grave Quintilian's copious Work we find
> The justest Rules, and clearest *Method* join'd;
> Thus *useful Arms* in Magazines we place,
> All rang'd with *Order,* and dispos'd with *Grace,*
> But less to please the *Eye,* than arm the Hand,
> Still fit for Use, and ready at Command.
> (669–74)

That is, the figures are not ornaments but weapons, and Pope is here at one with Peacham or Martianus Capella or the *Ad Herennium*. We also find that the Augustans are aware of the specific nature of the various figures (they were still learning them at school), and rather amusing evidence of this is provided by the only parody of a rhetoric-book which I know of. As Longinus's treatise was called *Peri Hupsous* (the word does not mean 'sublime', but rather 'concerning height' or 'elevation' in style), so in 1727 Pope and his friends produced a *Peri Bathous,* by one Martin Scriblerus. The *Art of Sinking in Poetry* is a detailed burlesque of the manuals of rhetoric, for example, *Aposiopesis:* 'An excellent Figure for the Ignorant, as *What shall I say?* when one has nothing to say; or *I can no more,* when one really can no more' (46). One chapter parodies the *loci* ('places, storehouses') by offering to outline 'a *Rhetorical Chest of Drawers*', and the writer suggests that the figures should be re-allocated to various occupations in life, so reversing the process by which rhetoric imitated nature. The parody shows incidentally how specific still was the consciousness of each figure and its particular effects:

> Nothing is more evident than that divers Persons, no other war remarkable, have each a strong Disposition to the Formation of some particular Trope or Figure. *Aristotle* saith [*Rhetoric,* 3.11] that the *Hyperbole* is an Ornament of Speech fit *for young Men of Quality* [he in fact says that it is a sign of juvenility]; accordingly we find in those Gentlemen a wonderful Propensity toward it, which is marvellously improv'd by *travelling. Soldiers* also and *Seamen* are very happy in the same Figure, The *Periphrasis* or *Circumlocution* is the peculiar Talent of Country Farmers, the Proverb and Apologue of *old Men* at their Clubs, the *Ellipsis* or Speech by half-words of *Ministers* and *Politicians,* the *Aposiopesis* of *Courtiers,* the *Litote* or Diminution of *Ladies, Whisperers* and *Backbiters;* and the *Anadyplosis* of Common *Cryers* and *Hawkers,* who by redoubling the same Words, persuade People to buy their Oysters, green Hastings, or new Ballads.
> (72–3)

The figures of rhetoric are thus restored to their original sources in real life, if at a rather unflattering level. I am tempted to continue the quotation further, for it is a brilliant piece of satire which almost needs glossing, but my point is that the Scriblerians were writing within the framework of traditional rhetoric, with a keen sense of the particularity of each rhetorical figure. It is not an 'in-group' joke, but rather one which any educated man would have understood and enjoyed, Fielding or Quintilian.

As we saw earlier that rhetoric persisted as the central influence on literary theory till the very end of the eighteenth century, it is to be expected that the figures continued to have an emotional and psychological function. On this point too P. W. K. Stone's analysis is illuminating: 'Neo-classic tenets about the expression of feeling are so closely bound up with opinions about figurative language and its function that the two questions cannot easily be separated' (58). Tropes are still distinguished from figures, and 'a special function was reserved for figures alone: that of expressing and arousing feeling' (61). The tradition from Longinus to Sidney, Puttenham and Dryden that rhetoric springs directly from human emotion continues. 'It is very widely held that figurative language occurs spontaneously to the mind in a state of emotion' (62), and the extension of it to the person of the orator (stated by Dryden in the tag from Horace's *Art of Poetry*: 'If you wish me to grieve you must first grieve yourself') and so to the audience is still accepted. 'Figures are obviously useful only as they *demonstrate* feeling: they are signs of a state of mind in the speaker which his audience will readily interpret, and instinctively react to' (64 – here as often Mr Stone's clear analysis brings out the fundamental suppositions behind rhetorical method). So Joseph Priestley writes in 1777 that 'Figurative speech ... is indicative of a person's real feelings and state of mind, not by means of the words it consists of, considered as *signs of separate ideas* ... but as circumstances naturally attending those feelings which compose any state of mind' (66). It follows that particular figures will have special associations, and Mr Stone wisely picks out (69) the figure *asyndeton* for its continuing connection with emotional disturbance. Thus an anonymous writer in 1762 says that 'Joy, grief, and anger are most naturally expressed by exclamations, sudden starts and broken sentences'; James Beattie in 1783 states that 'The Language of enthusiasm, and of all those passions that strongly agitate the soul, is naturally incoherent'; Robert Lowth lecturing *On The Sacred Poetry of the Hebrews* in 1753 observes that the more violent affections of the heart 'break and interrupt the enunciation by their impetuosity; they burst forth in sentences pointed, earnest, rapid, and tremulous', while in 1774 Alexander Gerard provides an elaborate psychological explanation of the phenomenon. The reader may well feel here that this is where he came in, for clearly these writers are rediscovering the truth of those observations on dislocated style first made by Demetrius (no doubt they partly derive them from the vogue for Longinus). To the very end of the eighteenth century the concept of the figures as being channels for emotional and psychological expression remains active. But the last word had better be given to Croce, who in the early 1900s was able to pronounce the death of the traditional view of the figures as weapons, which goes from the *Essay* on *Criticism* back to the *Marriage of Mercury and Philology* and to the *Ad Herennium*, by simply inverting the metaphor; 'Language is not an arsenal of arms already made' (Wimsatt and Brooks, 513).

From the evidence presented here (and I am sure that more could be found) we can see that throughout its two thousand years of active life rhetoric taught that the figures had definite potential for expressing emotional and psychological states. This seemed such a self-evident point to La Rochefoucauld that he made a penetrating maxim by simply inverting the connection between rhetoric and the emotions: 'Les passions sont les seuls orateurs qui persuadent toujours' (France, 164). It is true that sometimes, as Mr Stone has observed (67), these functions only apply to extreme states of mind, as with *asyndeton* or *hyperbaton,* but these by their very nature describe extreme states, and most of the other figures can be used for delicate and subtle effects as well as more vigorous ones. Hoskins noted that *polyptoton* 'may be used with or without passion' and one could follow through any great writer's varying and complex uses of a figure (see, for example, the index to Rubel, Tuve, Vickers [1], Vickers [2]). To offer one brief example, the figure *antimetabole* (only later known as *chiasmus,* not until 1871 according to the *Oxford English Dictionary*) can be used for a great range of effects: at the level of witty interchange, as in the *bon-mot* about the success of *The Beggar's Opera:* it 'made Gay rich, and Rich gay', or in Pope's sly dig at the nobleman's motive for making the Grand Tour: 'Europe he saw, and Europe saw him too.' But it can have a much sharper sting, recalling Hoskins's description – 'a sharp and witty figure and shows out of the same words a pithy distinction of meaning.' So in the Overbury collection of *Characters,* of the Ordinary Widow' (the professional widow, always marrying afresh, rather like the Wife of Bath) we read that 'The end of her husband begins in tears, and the end of her tears begins in a husband'. No more concise or witty form of words could be devised for this suggested reflex action. But the same figure has a quite serious function (Peacham: 'to confute by the inversion of the sentence'), as in Montaigne's melancholy reflection on human life (here the suffixes interchange): 'La vie est un songe ... nous veillons dormants et veillants dormons', or in Balzac's claim that his *Cantes drôles* were 'designed rather to impart the morality of pleasure than to preach the pleasure of morality' (Booth, 179), or in Brecht's dialectical use of it in *The Messingkauf Dialogues* (Brecht, 34, 47, 57, 92). The time-scale of those three examples shows that the special effects obtainable from *antimetabole* continue to be needed long after the decline of the rhetorical tradition proper. Its range continues to be great, as we can see in two contrasted examples from novelists. First, serious and sardonic, one of the many ways in which Conrad deflates Mr Verloc in *The Secret Agent* is through this figure, with its ability to sustain paradoxes, even absurd ones: 'His idleness was not hygienic, but it suited him very well. He was in a manner devoted to it with a sort of inert fanaticism, or perhaps rather with a fanatical inertness.' Secondly, part-comic, part-serious, Sterne's curiously divided emotional reactions to his own writing: 'I laugh till I cry, and in the same tender moment cry till I laugh.' As a last example in a list which could he vastly extended, it provided a form for some of President Kennedy's key statements in his 1961 Inaugural: 'Let us never negotiate out of fear, but let us never fear to negotiate', and more famous, 'ask not what your country can do for you; ask what you can do for your country' (Corbett, 504–18). *Antimetabole* has served these and many other ends.

The figures are not fixed, then: they are flexible, and can be effective channels for quite varied states of mind or levels of argument. For a very important point, which I have reserved till now, is that the rhetoricians discuss the figures in terms of the physical shape of the word-patterns alone, and hardly ever with reference to their meaning. Given the multiple levels of sense in addition, then each figure has within its own proper field a great variety of applications, an endless range of reference for literature. But at the same time the figures are not automatic guarantees of literary excellence. Isocrates as early as the fourth century B.C. had criticized those handbooks which treated rhetoric 'over-confidently as a perfect machine that was bound to function without fail, no matter what the mental ability of the person applying it' (Marrou, 84). This is indeed Outrageous optimism', for as I said earlier, rhetoric is a tool which depends on its user. In incompetent hands the figures can be stiff and banal, and like every other artistic convention they need a great artist to fully extend them – in the hands of Virgil, Shakespeare, Racine they become an organic part of literature. But in many lesser hands they were still of great potential, because they were in themselves representations of human emotional and psychological states. No-one who has read this chapter sympathetically will want to call them 'husks' or 'dry formulae', but even the less pejorative metaphor of 'tools' makes them too static. We should perhaps think of them as pockets of energy, for as I hope I have adequately shown, they did have their own resources. 'A figure has always a function.'

Bibliography

(A) Primary Texts

Ad Herennium: *Rhetorica ad Herennium*, tr. and ed. H. Caplan (Loeb Library: 1954).
Aristotle: *The Works of Aristotle translated into English*, ed. W. D. Ross, II vols (Oxford, 1924).
Brecht: Bertold Brecht, *The Messingkauf Dialogues*, tr. John Willett (1965).
Cicero: *De Oratore*, tr. E. W. Sutton and H. Rackham (Loeb Library: 1942).
Demetrius: G. M. Grube, *A Greek Critic: Demetrius on Style* (Toronto, 1961): translation and commentary.
Dryden: J. Dryden, *Of Dramatic Poesy and other Critical Essays*, ed. G. Watson, 2 vols (1962).
Hoskins: John Hoskins, *Directions for Speech and Style*, ed. H. Hudson (Princeton, 1935).
Jonson: Ben Jonson, *Works*, ed. C. H. Herford, P. and E. Simpson, II vols (Oxford, 1925–52).
Longinus: *On the Sublime*, tr. and ed. A. H. Gilbert, above.
Peacham: Henry Peacham, *The Garden of Eloquence* (1935), ed. W. G. Crane (Florida, 1954).
Plato: *The Collected Dialogues*, ed. E. Hamilton and H. Cairns (New York, 1963): various translators.
Pope: *The Poems of Alexander Pope. A one-volume edition of the Twickenham Text*, ed. J. Butt (1963).
Puttenham: George Puttenham, *The Arte of English Poesie*, ed. G. Willcock and A. Walker (Cambridge, 1936).
Quintilian: *Institutio Oratoria*, tr. H. E. Butler, 4 vols (Loeb Library: 1922).
Sidney: *Prose Works*, ed. A. Feuillerat, 4 vols (Cambridge, 1962).
Smith: G. G. Smith, *Elizabethan Critical Essays*, 2 vols (Oxford, 1904).
Vives: *Vives: On Education. A Translation of the 'De Tradendis Disciplinis'*, by F. Watson (Cambridge, 1913).

(B) Secondary Texts

C. S. Baldwin, *Medieval Rhetoric and Poetic (to 1400)* (New York, 1928).
W. C. Booth, *The Rhetoric of Fiction* (Chicago, 1961).

D. L. Clark [I], *Rhetoric and Poetry in the Renaissance. A Study of Rhetorical Terms in English Renaissance Literary Criticism* (New York, 1922).
M. L. Clarke, *Rhetoric at Rome. A Historical Survey* (1953).
E. P. Corbett, *Classical Rhetoric for the Modern Student* (New York, 1965).
H. Craig, *The Enchanted Glass. The Elizabethan Mind in Literature* (Oxford, 1959).
W. G. Crane, *Wit and Rhetoric in the Renaissance. The Formal Basis of Elizabethan Prose Style* (New York, 1937).
J. F. D'Alton, *Roman Literary Theory and Criticism* (1931).
M. Doran, *Endeavours of Art: A Study of Form in Elizabethan Drama* (Wisconsin, 1954).
G. F. Else, *Aristotle's Poetics: The Argument* (Harvard U.P., 1957, 1963).
E. Faral, *Les Arts poétiques du XIIe et du XIIIe siècle* (Paris, 1924).
P. France, *Racine's Rhetoric* (Oxford, 1965).
W. S. Howell, *Logic and Rhetoric in England 1500–1700* (Princeton, 1956).
B. L. Joseph, *Elizabethan Acting* (1951).
Sister M. Joseph, *Shakespeare's Use of the Arts of Language* (New York, 1947).
G. A. Kennedy, *The Art of Persuasion in Greece* (1963).
M. Mahood, *Shakespeare's Wordplay* (1957).
H. I. Marrou, *A History of Education in Antiquity*, tr. G. Lamb (1956).
V. L. Rubel, *Poetic Diction in the English Renaissance. From Skelton through Spenser* (New York, 1941).
E. Salter, *'Piers Plowman': An Introduction* (Oxford, 1962).
L. A. Sonnino, *A Handbook to Sixteenth-Century Rhetoric* (1968).
P. W. K. Stone, *The Art of Poetry 1750–1820. Theories of poetic composition and style in the late Neo-Classic and early Romantic periods* (1967).
E. Sweeting, *Early Tudor Criticism, Linguistic & Literary* (Oxford, 1940).
R. Tuve, *Elizabethan and Metaphysical Imagery. Renaissance Poetic and Twentieth-Century Critics* (Chicago, 1947).
B. W. Vickers [1], *Francis Bacon and Renaissance Prose* (Cambridge, 1968).
B. W. Vickers [2], *The Artistry of Shakespeare's Prose* (1968).
W. K. Wimsatt and C. Brooks, *Literary Criticism. A Short History* (New York, 1957).

3.
ELOCUTION OR STYLE
Sister Miriam Joseph

The rhetoricians of the sixteenth century agreed in conceiving elocution or style as concerned mainly with the figures of speech, but they differed as to the scope of the figures and their number. The figures have a long history. Plato and Aristotle reprehended the excessive ornateness of Gorgias. Isocrates, the pupil of Gorgias, reduced this extravagance of ornament and used figures with more art. In the third book of his *Rhetoric* Aristotle took up the discussion of style, for, as he remarked,

> The arts of language cannot help having a small but real importance, whatever it is we have to expound to others: the way in which a thing is said does affect its intelligibility.
>
> (1404 ^{a}8)

With regard to style Aristotle was concerned principally with lucidity, vividness, appropriateness, structure, and prose rhythm, but he devoted some attention to figures. He did not name many of those which he described, but he favored metaphor, simile, synecdoche, prosopopoeia, antonomasia, periphrasis, all of which tend to promote vividness; likewise antithesis, isocolon, homoioteleuton, anaphora, epistrophe, polysyndeton, and asyndeton, figures which emphasize balance in periodic structure and affect prose rhythm. He counseled the avoidance of zeugma, parenthesis, and in general whatever tends to ambiguity and obscurity, although he liked antanaclasis and paronomasia, which are figures of deliberate ambiguity. Nearly half of the *Rhetorica ad C. Herennium,* contemporary with Cicero and influential as a school text throughout the Middle Ages and the Renaissance, was devoted to style, chiefly the figures. Cicero treated the same elements of style as did Aristotle, but he was more hospitable to the figures, enumerating them in *De oratore* and again, reducing their number, in *Orator.* He used them extensively in his orations, especially those which rise to the lofty style. Quintilian reviewed Cicero's presentation of the figures before giving his own more detailed treatment, and he told why he excluded some which Cicero had included. He stated clearly his own concept of figures.

> Consider what we are to understand by the word figure; for it is used in two senses; signifying, in the one, any form of words, whatever it may be, as bodies, of whatever they be composed, have some certain shape; in the other, in which it is *properly* termed a figure, any

---

Joseph, Sister Miriam. "Elocution or Style." *Shakespeare's Use of the Arts of Language.* New York: Columbia University Press, 1947: 31–40.

deviation, either in thought or expression, from the ordinary and simple method of speaking, as our bodies assume different postures when we sit, lie, or look back.... If we adopt the first and general sense, then, there will be no part of language that is not *figured*.... But if particular habits, and, as it were, gestures of language, are to receive this designation, that only must here be regarded as a figure, which deviates, by poetical or oratorical phraseology, from the simple and ordinary modes of speaking. Thus we shall be right in saying that one sort of style is . . . destitute of figures, (and this is no small fault) and another . . . diversified with figures. . . . Let the definition of a figure, then, be *a form of speech artfully varied from common usage.*[1]

This definition was accepted by the Tudor rhetoricians of all three groups. For example, Puttenham analyzes the purpose and scope of figurative language.

> Figurative speech is a noveltie of language evidently (and yet not absurdly) estranged from the ordinarie habite and manner of our dayly talke and writing and figure it selfe is a certaine lively or good grace set upon wordes, speaches and sentences to some purpose and not in vaine, giving them ornament or efficacie by many maner of alterations in shape, in sounde, and also in sence, sometime by way of surplusage, sometime by defect, sometime by disorder, or mutation, & also by putting into our speaches more pithe and substance, subtiltie, quicknesse, efficacie or moderation, in this or that sort tuning and tempring them, by amplification, abridgement, opening, closing, enforcing, meekening or otherwise disposing them to the best purpose.
>
> (p. 159)

With the exception of Hoskyns, the rhetoricians of the three Renaissance groups employed the traditional division of figures into tropes and schemes, and the further division of schemes into those that are grammatical and those that are rhetorical. A trope, such as a metaphor, turns the significance of a word or sentence from its proper meaning to another not proper, but yet near it in order to increase its force. Grammatical schemes were subdivided into orthographical and syntactical schemes; rhetorical schemes, into figures of words and figures of sentence or thought. The rhetorical figures of words were figures of repetition. Some authors gave the name figures of amplification to a certain group of the figures of thought. In *The Arcadian Rhetorike* Fraunce remarked that tropes confer on language a certain grace, figures of words a kind of delicacy fit to delight, and figures of thought a majesty and force apt to persuade. (Sig. E 4^r)

The table on page 70 shows how the figures in the Renaissance works[2] compare in number with those in the *Rhetorica ad C. Herennium*,[3] in Cicero's *De orators,* and in Quintilian's *Institutio oratoria.*

According to the number of figures dealt with, the Ramists represent one extreme and the figurists the other. Yet they are not so far apart as the difference in number might suggest, for the figurists incorporated in their figures much of what the Ramists treated in their logic texts, since, as the former often remarked, many of the figures are derived from the topics of invention. The figurists, like the traditionalists and the Ramists, had a high regard for invention. Sherry included a brief but pointed section on invention and proofs in his *Treatise of Schemes and Trope* (1550). Angel Day speaks of

Elocution or Style

invention first, wherein plentifully is searched and considered, what kinde of matter, how much variety of sentences, what sorts of figures, how many similitudes, what approbations, diminutions, insinuations, and circumstances are presently needfull, or furthering to the matter in handling.

(p. 14)

It would be a mistake to regard the treatises of the figurists as limited to a discussion of style in the narrow sense.[4] Puttenham, eager to bestow upon the poet the right to use the rhetorical figures of thought, which he considered pre-eminent, declared the poet to be the most ancient orator (p. 196). Peacham emphasized the value of the figures as means of persuasion, considering

the knowledge of them so necessary, that no man can reade profytably, or understand perfectlye eyther Poets, Oratours, or the holy Scriptures, without them: nor any Oratoure able by the waight of his wordes, to perswade his hearers, having no helpe of them.
(Epistle dedicatory, A. iii^r, 1577 edition)

In terms of the three-fold means of persuasion basic in Aristotle's *Rhetoric*, namely, *logos, pathos*, and *ethos*, and of the aesthetic aspects of grammar such as are touched on in his discussion of style, the fundamental likeness among the three groups of sixteenth-century works becomes clear. When the approximately two hundred figures which the Tudor theorists distinguished are arranged under these four headings, it becomes evident that the work of the figurists covered practically the same ground as the combined works on logic and rhetoric, whether traditionalist or Ramist. The figures under *logos*, constituting by far the most numerous and the most important group, best illustrate the parallel between the works of the logicians and the figurists, for many of the examples cited by the logicians to illustrate the topics and forms of logic are exactly parallel to those cited by the figurists as figures. Some of the figures are identical with logical forms, for example, the dilemma, which was regarded as both a figure and a form of reasoning. That the figures of thought were understood to function under *logos* is clear from the fact that the Ramists treated the substance of them in their logic texts and the figurists frequently mentioned the topics and forms of logic on which they are based. The tropes likewise function under *logos*, as the Ramists recognized, for although they treated them in their rhetoric texts, they related them strictly to the logical topics from which they are derived.[5] The figures may accordingly be reorganized as follows:

Grammar: schemes of words; of construction
the vices of language
figures of repetition
Logos: the figures related to
(*a*) logical topics: testimony, definition, division, genus, species, adjunct, contrary, contradictory, similarity, dissimilarity, comparison, cause, effect, antecedent, consequent, notation, conjugates
(*b*) logical forms, as the syllogism, enthymeme, sorites, dilemma
(*c*) the devices of disputation

Table 3.1 Figures of Speech[a]

	I. Tropes		II. Schemes Grammatical			III. Schemes Rhetorical			
	Of Words	Of Sentences	Ortho-graphical	Syntactical	Of Words	Of Thought and Amplification	Total	Vices
1. Rhet. ad. Her.	10				35	20	65	
2. Cic. De or.	4				41	46	91	
3. Quintilian	14			8	29	38	89	14
4. Wilson	8	1(5)	6		24	41	80	
5. Talacus	4				9	10	23	
6. Fenner	4(8)				9	10	23(27)	2
7. Fraunce	4(8)				9	10(11)	23(28)	
8. Butler	4(11)		13		8(10)	10(31)	22(65)	21
9. Hoskyns	6			3	13	28	50	
10. Susenbrotus	9	10	15	32	14	60	132	
11. Sherry 1550	7	8	11	12	41	25	104	16
12. Sherry 1555	7	8	12	12	20	60	119	22
13. Peacham 1577	9	10	14	42	24	85	184	
14. Peacham 1593	8	10			24	123	165	10
15. Puttenham	10	12	6	18	9	52	107	15
16. Day	7	9		21	12	44	93	

[a] Because some authors list separately figures which others treat as subdivisions, a comparison of mere numbers is misleading. The same figure is sometimes treated in more than one section of a work and counted each time. For example, Wilson names five tropes of sentences but prefers to treat four of them under other classifications. In his table of figures Butler agrees with the other Ramists, but in his text he introduces additional figures which bring the number up to the totals indicated in parentheses. Similar additions of other writers are similarly indicated. Because Hoskyns uses a different and original classification, his figures have been reclassified here in the traditional groupings for purposes of comparison. The classification by Puttenham is novel in words rather than in meaning. He himself says (pp. 160, 163) that his auricular figures are orthographical and syntactical; his sensable figures are tropes, and his sententious figures, with some exceptions, are figures of thought. (For a more precise comment on Puttenham's classification in relation to the traditional one, especially Quintilian's, and for parallels with Quintilian see La Rue Van Hook, "Greek Rhetorical Terminology in Puttenham's 'The Arte of English Poesie,'" in *Transactions of the American Philological Association*, XLIV [1914], 113, note 9). The vices of speech are listed above only where they are distinguished from the figures, not where they themselves are called figures, as in the work of Susenbrotus, of Day, and of Peacham in 1577.

Pathos: the figures of affection and vehemence

Ethos: the figures revealing courtesy, gratitude, commendation, forgiveness of injury

This reorganization makes the numerous figures more significant by ordering them in groups fulfilling four fundamental functions, somewhat as the periodic table makes the chemical elements more significant by ordering them in families having similar properties. By thus correlating the figures with the whole body of theory in logic and in the parts of rhetoric other than elocution this reorganization emphasizes the completeness of the pattern and the interdependence of its parts, for every part gains meaning from its relation to the other parts and to the whole.

The essential general theory of composition and of reading current in Shakespeare's England, as expressed in the definitions, illustrations, and comments of the Tudor logicians and rhetoricians, is presented at the end of this volume in an eclectic handbook constructed by selecting each item from the author who seems to have treated it best and by arranging the whole in the pattern outlined above. The entire theory, with a few negligible exceptions, is illustrated from Shakespeare's plays and poems in the following chapters.[6]

The Renaissance figures seem to us remarkable for their inclusiveness. They deal with words, in the figures of orthography; with grammar, in such matters as interrogation, exclamation, the unfinished sentence, the periodic sentence, ellipsis, rhythm, and the means of varying through them; with coherence, through figures of conjunction and transition; with emphasis, through word order and the figures of repetition; with clarity and obscurity; with amplification and condensation; with beauty, through exergasia and all the figures of exornation; with force, through vehemence (*pathos*); with proof, through *logos;* with *ethos;* even with gesture (mimesis and mycterismus), and voice (pathopopoeia and tasis). The Tudor rhetoricians were tireless in their distinctions, unflagging in their faith in art and artifice, eager to assist in transplanting to the vernacular the adornments of Latin, Greek, and Hebrew literatures assiduously noted in the grammar schools and the universities. They anatomized composition and reading in an age that, delighted in anatomies, as of wit, of flattery, of absurdity, and they showed composition interpenetrated with logic.

The Tudor rhetoricians classified the figures in the traditional manner indicated by the table on page 70, not under grammar, *logos, pathos,* and *ethos*. There is warrant for the present reclassification, however, in Aristotle, who furnished the pattern, and in the Renaissance rhetoricians, who implicitly adapted it. Aristotle, discussing style in his *Rhetoric,* gave some attention to the figures of grammar and, in relation to them, to figures of repetition. In discussing the substance of rhetorical discourse he emphasized its function to effect an interrelated threefold persuasion: by *logos,* the speaker convinces his hearers of the truth of his argument by appealing to their reason; by *pathos* he puts them into a favorable, not a hostile, frame of mind by appealing to the emotions which color their judgment; by *ethos* he inspires their confidence in his own character and trustworthiness by convincing them of his honesty and goodness, his competence and judgment, and above all his good will toward them. The importance which

Aristotle attached to *ethos, logos,* and *pathos* is indicated by the fact that his final words on the art of rhetoric emphasize the necessity of including this threefold persuasion in the epilogue of an oration:

> The Epilogue has four parts. You must (1) make the audience well-disposed towards, yourself and ill-disposed towards your opponent, (2) magnify or minimize the leading facts, (3) excite the required sute of emotion in your hearers, and (4) refresh their memories.
> (*Rhetoric*, 19, 1419 ^{b}10)

Renaissance rhetoricians, although accepting the traditional classification of figures under schemes of grammar, tropes, rhetorical figures of words, and rhetorical figures of thought, nevertheless did take account of these three modes of persuasion. For example, in his revised and improved work of 1593 Peacham subdivided his figures into those whose function is: repetition, omission, conjunction, and separation (grammatical); distribution, description, comparison, collection (*logos*); the stirring of affection and vehemence (*pathos*); nor is the hearer's impression of the speaker (*ethos*) left out of account, for some figures are directly designed to win good will and a favorable hearing. In other words, Peacham divides his figures of thought according to their functions into those of amplification (*logos*) and those of affection (*pathos*). Some promote *ethos*. In his *Elementa rhetorices* (1531) Melanchthon classified approximately forty of the figures of thought under selected topics of logic (definition, division, cause, contraries, similitudes, genus, circumstances and signs). The studious reader, he says, will observe that these especially take their origin from the places of dialectic, for the same places, when they are applied to proving or disproving a matter are called sinews of argument; when they are applied to illuminating it, they are called ornaments and many times add weight to the argument.[7] We should not, however, be too exact and superstitious in comparing the places of dialectic and the figures of elocution. It is enough to employ a moderate prudence and to see some relation between them.[8]

Peacham's subdivisions and Melanchthon's classification furnish contemporary evidence indicating that the Renaissance rhetoricians would regard the reorganization of the figures under grammar, *logos, pathos,* and *ethos* as a clarification of what is partly explicit and partly implicit in their work. The present study undertakes to reclassify not merely the figures of thought, which have long been recognized as related to dialectic, but all of the two hundred Tudor figures, in terms of these four functions, and that without resorting to a miscellaneous catch-all such as Melanchthon's circumstances and signs. This reclassification of the figures makes no claim to apodictic exactitude. Their classification, by whatever method, has always proved baffling, for one figure may fit into any one of a number of classes, and some figures may not fit precisely into any one. For instance, a figure of collection or summary does not precisely fit in with figures of division; yet it may reasonably be placed with them because it is understood in relation to division as a reverse process. In addition to making the figures more intelligible and significant, the reorganization here presented accentuates the basic agreement of the Renaissance rhetoricians and logicians among themselves and with the ancient tradition.

It is difficult for a modern to keep in mind the ancient and the Renaissance conception of ornament as something more integral than we conceive it to be. According to Aristotle,

> Ornament is attained by induction and distinction of things closely akin . . . , an instance of the kind of thing meant is . . . the distinction of sciences into speculative, practical, and productive. For everything of this kind lends additional ornament to the argument, though there is no necessity to say them, so far as the conclusion goes.
>
> (*Topics*, 8.1.157 ᵃ7)

Hermogenes constantly spoke of the enthymeme and the epicheirema as embellishments. Cicero also delighted in them and recognized that ever to discuss style and ornament apart from thought involves an unnatural separation.

> It is impossible to achieve an ornate style without first procuring ideas and putting them into shape, and . . . no idea can possess distinction without lucidity of style.[9]

> This is the reason why that genuine and perfect eloquence we are speaking of, has been yet attained by no one; because the art of *reasoning* has been supposed to be one thing, and that of *speaking* another; and we have had recourse to different instructors for the knowledge of things and words.[10]

The figures of thought evoked great enthusiasm in the Renaissance, an age that delighted in logical exercise. As Sherry remarked at the close of his *Treatise of the Figures of Grammer and Rhetorike* (1555), they were called

> ornamentes of maner, because by them, not only the oration and wordes, but the body of the matter groweth and is increased.
>
> (fol. lviiʳ)

Since the figures of thought bulk largest in both number and importance, logic emerges as the dominant factor in composition not only for the Ramists and the traditionalists but for the figurists as well. Elizabethan literature was produced by a technique which, while giving attention to patterns of sound and movement and heaping up a rich profusion of imagery, was deeply rooted in thought and emotion.

Notes

1 Quare primum intuendum est, quid accipere debeamus figuram. Nam duobus modis dicitur: uno qualiscunque forma sententiae, sicut in corporibus, quibus, quoquo modo sunt composita, utique habitus est aliquis; altero, quo proprie schema dicitur, in sensu vel sermone aliqua a vulgari et simplici specie cum ratione mutatio, sicut nos sedemus, incumbimus, respicimus. . . . In quo ita loquimur, tanquam omnis sermo habeat figuram. . . . Sed si habitus quidam et quasi gestus sic appellandi sunt, id demum hoc loco accipi schema oportebit, quod sit a simplici atque in promptu posito dicendi modo poetice vel oratorie mutatum. Sic enim verum erit, aliam esse orationem . . . carentem figuris, quod vitium non inter minima est, aliam . . . est figuratam. . . . Ergo figura sit arte aliqua novata forma dicendi. (*Institutio oratoria*, 9.1.10–14 [Loeb Classical Library]. Translation by J. S. Watson [Bohn's Classical Library], II, 146.)

2. Rainolde gives almost no attention to figures; Cox, none at all.
3. Faral, *op. cit.*, pp. 52–54, presents a table showing the degree of correspondence of the figures in nine leading rhetorical works of the twelfth and thirteenth centuries to those in the *Rhetorica ad C. Herennium*.
4. All the Renaissance groups valued the figures as means to enhance style. In the words of Puttenham's recent editors: "The figures are the sum of all the resources (others than metrical) by which poetry conveys its special overplus of excitement or stimulation; they are the sum, expressed in Elizabethan terms, of the types of ambiguity, the obliquities, the transferences, the echoes and controlled associations, which lift poetry above mere statement and by which the poet lets odd and unexpected lights into his subject, 'drawing it,' says Puttenham, 'from plainnesse and simplicitie to a certaine doublenesse.'" (p. lxxx)
5. The Ramists admitted four tropes. They distinguished metonymy of cause, of effect, of subject, of adjunct; synecdoche of genus, of species, of the whole, of the parts. They explained that irony is based on the contrary; metaphor, on similitude.
6. The reader may study the theory in Part Three (Chapters VI–IX) either a section at a time or a chapter at a time before he reads the illustration of it from Shakespeare in Part Two (Chapters II–V). He may even want to read all of Part Three before beginning Chapter II. The headings of sections and the order of topics within sections in Parts Two and Three are identical to facilitate reference. The reader who is not interested in the theory either for proof or for flavor may disregard Part III entirely, since the chapters on Shakespeare are intelligible without it.
7. Melanchthon, *Opera*, XIII, 479–80: "Observet autem studiosus lector figuras omnes, praesertim has, quae augent orationem ex locis dialecticis oriri, ad quos si quis prudenter sciet eas referre, pleraque in causis subtiliter et acute iudicare, et definitas negotii regiones melius videre poterit. Nam iidem loci cum confirmandi aut confutandi causa adhibentur argumenta sunt ac nervi, ut vocant. Cum adhibentur illuminandi causa, dicuntur ornamenta. Ac pleraque non tantum ad pugnae speciem comparata sunt, sed argumentis pondus addunt."
8. *Ibid.*, p. 4.83: "Utimur autem in hac comparatione locarum dialecticorum et figurarum elocutionis non nimis subtili ac superstitiosa ratione. Satis est enim ad eam rem adhibere mediocrem quandam prudentiam, et aliqua ex parte cognationem videre, ut fontes ornamentorum et negociorum regiones animadverti queant."
9. "... tantum significabo brevi, neque verborum ornatum inveniri posse non partis expressisque sententiis, neque esse ullam sententiam illustrem sine luce verborum." (Cicero *De oratore* 3.6.24), tr. by E. W. Sutton and H. Rackham (Loeb Classical Library).
10. "... quo fit ut veram illam et absolutam eloquentiam nemo consequatur, quod alia intelligendi alia dicendi disciplina est et ab aliis rerum ab aliis verborum doctrina quaeritur." (Cicero *Orator* 5.17); tr. by E. Jones, whose translation of this passage is preferable to that in the Loeb edition.

4.
MANUALS OF TROPES AND FIGURES
Peter Mack

Special uses of language which impress and move an audience were considered to be a central part of rhetorical teaching from the Hellenistic period onwards. Brian Vickers has effectively shown how great an impact the tropes and figures had on renaissance writing and on English poetry more generally.[1] When E. H. Gombrich called rhetoric 'perhaps the most careful analysis of an expressive medium ever undertaken',[2] he had in mind primarily the tropes and figures. All the evidence we have suggests that when properly used these forms and strategies are astonishingly effective.[3]

The tropes and figures were very widely available in the renaissance in different ways. Many renaissance grammars, some of which were printed in enormous numbers of editions, included a selection of the figures. The tropes and figures were fully described in two of the most printed classical manuals of rhetoric, *Rhetorica ad Herennium* and Quintilian's *Institutio oratoria*, with a combined total of 278 editions. Almost all the general manuals of rhetoric described in earlier chapters included comprehensive treatments of the tropes and figures. Finally the tropes and figures were described in a group of specialized manuals, with a combined total publication of around 180 editions, which are the subject of this chapter. Together all these works ensured a very wide availability of the tropes and figures, which probably conditioned the way educated people read books and set about constructing sentences of their own. Teachers were instructed to point out the use of tropes and figures when reading classical texts with their pupils. Pupils were expected to use particular figures in their school compositions, whether imitated or original.

Manuals of tropes and figures mainly copy from each other, but individual manuals innovate in three main ways. Some manuals aim to be more comprehensive than others, including additional figures, sometimes at the cost of inadvertent repetition. By contrast other manuals aim to simplify the list, so as to make it easier for a pupil to memorize, as a preparation for its practical use in reading and in composition. Many of the manuals respond to the length of the list and the differences in kind between the figures by trying to devise new ways of grouping the figures. The manuals generally name each figure, sometimes giving both Greek and Latin names, then define it, and then give examples from classical literature. Some manuals add subdivisions of particular tropes and figures, and advice on their use.

Mack, Peter. "Manuals of Tropes and Figures," *A History of Renaissance Rhetoric 1380–1620.* Oxford: Oxford University Press., 2011: 208–227.

The verbal patterns and linguistic techniques described through the tropes and figures are much more varied than might at first appear. Figures like anaphora and antistrophe describe patterning of words; homoeoptoton and homoeoteleuton provide for similar case-endings or final sounds in a group of individual words; paronomasia suggests changes in the spelling and sound of a word in order to effect wordplay. Colon, clause, and period analyse the way in which a sentence is built up; asyntedon and polysyntedon discuss the absence or addition of conjunctions within the sentence; hysteron proteron and parenthesis show how normal order within a sentence can effectively be altered. Apostrophe and rhetorical question have clear grammatical markers but describe ways of presenting material to achieve a certain effect. Figures like hypophora (also called subiectio), dubitatio, and permissio suggest attitudes the speaker might take to an audience. Correctio and aposiopesis describe ways of emphasizing something while seeming to retract or to be overcome with emotion. Description, expolitio, character portrayal, and comparison label sections of writing which one might include in a speech. Metaphor and metonymy, while suggesting striking forms of expression, invite questions about the operation of language itself. Renaissance rhetorics set themselves the task of categorizing and ordering these and other figures.[4]

In renaissance schools it seems that the tropes and figures were taught to students after they had learnt the basic Latin grammar and alongside their reading of middle-school texts, such as Cicero's letters, Terence, and Virgil. There is some overlap between grammar and rhetoric textbooks here, with some grammars including only figures which describe ways of organizing sentences and others including many figures which rhetoric also discusses.[5] In their reading of classical texts with their classes, teachers were instructed to point out the way in which writers used particular tropes.[6] This assumes that the names and descriptions of a range of figures had already been given to students. Reading texts and their own writing exercises would then have been ways of reinforcing this teaching. Knowing the names of the figures enables students to notice how a particular writer uses a particular technique. The names, which can sometimes seem to us excessively technical, actually make possible observation and the drawing of lessons. Renaissance grammar books often list some figures of speech, as part of the ancillary material, alongside the rules of prosody.[7] Pedagogically, the figures and tropes belong almost as much to the teaching of grammar as to rhetoric.

Our earliest thorough descriptions of the tropes and figures form part of comprehensive Latin rhetorics, *Rhetorica ad Herennium* 4 and Quintilian's *Institutio oratoria* 8 and 9. Book 4 of *Rhetorica ad Herennium* remained the best known classical account of the tropes and figures. It generally provides a Latin name for the figure with description, explanation, and examples, sometimes quite lengthy. Quite a number of the figures are treated at greater length, with subdivisions, instructions for composing, and/or advice on how a particular figure should be used. The work treats sixty-four figures, divided into thirty-five figures of words, ten tropes, and nineteen figures of thought.[8] Quintilian discusses fourteen tropes, some of them at considerable length at 8.6, twenty-nine figures of thought at 9.2.7–71, and fifty-three figures of speech at 9.3.6–87, within a very comprehensive account of style.[9]

We also have short Latin treatises focused entirely on the figures and tropes by Rutilius Lupus (first century AD), Aquila Romanus (third century), and Julius Rufinianus (fourth century). These were rediscovered in the renaissance and first printed in 1519 and 1521.[10] They use Greek names for the figures. Rutilius Lupus, who is a source for the others, seems to base his work on the lost first-century BC Greek work of Gorgias.[11] The relatively short lists of Rutilius (forty-one figures, undivided) and Aquila (thirty-eight figures, divided into figures of words and figures of thought) describe some figures not listed in *Rhetorica ad Herennium* and Quintilian. Renaissance rhetoricians also used short treatises on the tropes and figures by the classical Latin grammarians Diomedes and Donatus.[12] They probably also made use of the Venerable Bede's *Liber de schematibus et tropis*, which gives biblical examples for each figure.[13]

Rhetorica ad Herennium 4 remained the most important treatment of the figures and tropes in the middle ages. A highly influential medieval treatise by Marbod of Rennes (c.1035–1123) was *De ornamentis verborum*, which paraphrases *Ad Herennium*'s definitions of thirty figures of speech, adding verse illustrations of each figure. This work survives in fifty-one manuscripts and it was printed once (Rennes, 1524).[14] Geoffrey de Vinsauf's *Poetria nova* (c.1200), which survives in 204 manuscripts,[15] devotes around a quarter of its 2116 lines to descriptions and (especially) examples of ten tropes, thirty-five figures of speech (examples only), and nineteen figures of thought (as in *Rhetorica ad Herennium*). Later medieval treatments of the figures include those in Eberhard the German's *Laborintus* (after 1213, before 1280), Joannes Balbus of Genoa's *Catholicon* (1280), and the anonymous fourteenth-century *Tria sunt*.[16]

Perotti

The earliest renaissance treatment of the tropes and figures and one which was very widely circulated in the late fifteenth century was the relatively brief section *De figuris* in Perotti's *Rudimenta grammatices*, composed in 1468, first printed in 1473, and printed a total of 133 times (115 times before 1500).[17] The division of this section of the work into barbarism, solecism, metaplasm, figures of words, tropes, and figures of construction, suggests that it is based on a Latin grammatical source. Perotti gives Greek names, defines each figure in response to a question, and adds an example of each figure and each subtype.[18]

Antonio Mancinelli (1452–1505)

Some renaissance teachers took the view that their audiences required brief verse texts which could more easily be learned by heart. Antonio Mancinelli was a Latin teacher in Perugia, Rome, and other Italian cities who composed a number of textbooks on grammar and composition. His *Carmen de figuris* (Rome, 1489) was printed forty times up to 1590, latterly together with Mosellanus's *Epitome* which superseded it. Mancinelli's poem of 268 lines describes some ninety-eight figures, divided into faults (twenty-seven), schemes (eighteen), and a rather broad group of tropes (fifty-three). After the three- to four-line segment of the poem devoted to each figure, which generally gives a definition and an example, Mancinelli provides a prose commentary, including definition of the figure, an explanation of how the Greek term denotes the figure, some comments from other authorities (most often Diomedes, Donatus, or Quintilian), and examples of the figure. Mancinelli's main sources are Quintilian, *Rhetorica ad Herennium* (which he refers to as Cicero), and the grammarians Diomedes and Donatus.

> When various words are set out without conjunctions, certainly we achieve dialyton or asyntedon. You may take this example: the thing, the soldier, the people deny that. Dialyton may be called 'set free', for it is derived from the word Dialyo which is 'I untie'. Dialytos means 'dissolved'; Dialysis is 'dissolving'. Dialyton or asyntedon is a phrase without conjunctions. 'Bear arms in haste; hand out weapons; climb up on the walls' (*Aeneid* 9.37). The same in 'I came; I saw; I conquered' ... This is also called brachylogia by Diomedes; also in Quintilian book 9 (9.3.50). Asyndetos is called disjoined; Asynthetos uncomposed.[19]

> Anaphora is called repetitio or relatio ... Anaphora is, as Diomedes says the placing of the same word or a similar one at the beginning of several verses.[20]

Johannes Despauterius (Jean Despautère, c. 1460–1520)

Johannes Despauterius was a Flemish grammarian who studied and taught at Louvain. His *De figuris* (1512) was printed fourteen times before 1620. Despauterius's work consists of a 100-line poem (heavily dependent on Mancinelli) defining ninety-two figures. He begins by defining a figure as 'a form of speech altered by a certain art', and dividing into metaplasm (the changes which poets make in order to observe the rules of metre), schemes, and tropes.[21] Later he distinguishes between schemes of words and schemes of thought but he only describes the former, perhaps because he regards the latter as part of rhetoric and therefore outside his remit.[22] This may be the reason why frequently used figures like conversio, permissio, dubitatio, correctio, and licentia do not appear in either Mancinelli or Despauterius.

The line of poetry devoted to each figure is followed by a short commentary in which Despauterius defines the figure in prose and adds an example (usually from Virgil). Sometimes he adds a comment on similarities between this figure and others. His list of figures is more thoroughly organized than Mancinelli's, though for the most part he gives the same figures in the same order (with three or four changes of terminology). He begins with fifteen vices of style (subdivided into *barbarum, obscurum, and inordinatum*, a division Diomedes also made). Then there are fourteen figures of metaplasm, eighteen schemes of words, twenty-seven tropes, and eighteen other figures. Most of his omissions in comparison to Mancinelli are in this last category (which Mancinelli included under tropes). Within the tropes proper Despauterius distinguishes thirteen main types of trope, with the others treated as species of hyperbaton, allegory, and homoeosis.[23]

> I call metonymy, I drink Bacchus, Vines crown. Metonymy is a change of names, which occurs when we understand the invention instead of the inventor, the contents instead of the container, the effect instead of the efficient cause, the possessor instead of the thing possessed and vice versa. Metonymy is translated as 'change of name' from meta, that is 'trans' and onoma, that is name.[24]

Despauterius's division of metonymy into these types recalls *Rhetorica ad Herennium* 4.32.43.

Peter Schade (1493–1524)

Peter Schade, known as Mosellanus because of his birth in Bruttig on the Mosel, studied with Caesarius and learnt Greek at Cologne (1512–14). He taught Greek in Freiburg and Leipzig where he studied theology and was rector in 1520 and 1523. He was a correspondent and supporter of Erasmus. His *Tabulae de schematibus et tropis* (Frankfurt, 1516) was the most successful of the sixteenth-century handbooks of tropes and figures, with eighty-six printings up to 1590. The main part of the book lists and defines the figures and tropes. In later editions this is supplemented with Georg Major's tabular summary of the whole of rhetoric, based on Melanchthon's *Institutiones rhetoricae*, and his (slightly longer) analysis and summary of Erasmus's De copia.[25]

Schade's introduction emphasizes the importance of the figures in capturing the attention of an audience and delighting them. Because there are so many figures and because it is as important to remember them all as it is difficult, Schade thought that it would be useful to collect information about all of them briefly so that students could easily have them all before their eyes. He even suggests that the lists and definitions should be put up on the wall of the school, somewhere where pupils would often see them, in order to refresh their memories. He will start with figures of speech, and then move on to vices and virtues of expression. For each entry he will give the Greek name, a Latin equivalent taken from Cicero (by which he means *Rhetorica ad Herennium*), Quintilian, or Diomedes. Then he will give explanations, definitions, and examples. Finally he claims to have included a few figures which others have omitted.[26]

Very clear organization is a strength of Schade's work. Figures are divided into figures of diction, locution, and construction. Schade also recognizes the class of figures of thought, but omits them because they lie outside his present grammatical purpose.[27] He gives fourteen figures of diction, corresponding to Despauterius's category of metaplasm, twenty-four of locution (and three subtypes), most of which are taken from Despauterius's schemes of words,[28] and five types of figures of construction, taken from the grammarians and showing some overlap with the figures of locution. As in Despauterius vices of style are divided into three categories: *obscurum* (eight types), *inordinatum* (six types), *barbarum* (three types). Most of the figures listed are the same as we find in Despauterius and Mancinelli, who took them from Diomedes. Virtues of style are divided into propriety (three qualities) and *ornatus*, whose main element is the tropes. Schade recognizes fourteen main types of trope, with eight subtypes of allegory, five subtypes of hyperbaton, and three subtypes of homoeosis. Like Despauterius he explains why genres like topography and chronography should not be regarded as tropes. In all Schade discusses ninety-three figures, a comparable total to Despauterius and Mancinelli. Like them he includes no figures of thought.

In general Schade's descriptions of figures are very short, offering the Greek name, a transcription into the Roman alphabet (or occasionally a Latin equivalent), a short explanation, and an example. Sometimes he adds a short comment on the use of a topic.

Προσωποποιΐα Prosopopoeia, a feigning of persons, certainly when speech is given to many things. The poets allowed themselves much in this and the Orators took it over from them, as when Cicero in the speeches against Catilina fits speech to the country.

Ἀποσιώπησις Aposiopesis, which Cicero calls reticence, when because of anger or indignation we stop speaking for part of the speech. 'Which I—but better to still the raging waves.'

(*Aeneid* 1. 135).

He stops before saying 'will punish'.[29]

There are exceptions to this brevity, notably the discussions of metaphor and synecdoche. Some of the entries show a very clear verbal dependence on Despauterius (and behind him on Mancinelli and Diomedes), though Schade almost always alters the phrasing slightly. In many cases he chooses his own words or relies on a different source. He refers to Erasmus, Diomedes, Cicero, and Quintilian as sources. His uncharacteristically lengthy accounts of metaphor and synecdoche use Quintilian, Erasmus, and *Rhetorica ad Herennium*.[30] But the main features of Schade's account are the clear organization, the short entries for each figure, the reliance on Despauterius's lists, and the absence of figures of thought.

Melanchthon

Melanchthon introduced important changes to the presentation of the tropes and figures in his *Institutiones rhetoricae* (1521) and again later in the even more successful *Elementa rhetorices* (1529). As we saw in Chapter 6, these two manuals were published a total of 101 times up to 1610. The 1521 changes appear to have had the greater influence on later manuals of the tropes and figures. In 1521 Melanchthon begins with the tropes, which he has reduced to seven (metaphor, synecdoche, metonymy, antonomasia, onomatopoeia, catachresis, and metalepsis), adding a separate treatment of allegory (with eight subtypes including enigma, irony, sarcasm, proverb, and fable).[31] The figures are divided into grammatical (seven figures) and rhetorical in three orders: figures concerned with individual words (twelve figures: including repetition, polysyntedon, hypallage, and paronomasia), figures of thought (ten figures including question, exclamation, dubitatio, communicatio, prosopopeia, and parrhesia), and figures associated with amplification (thirty-three figures including climax, synonyms, distribution, aitiology, antithesis, antimetabole, prosopopeia again, and sententia.)[32] In 1529 grammatical figures are omitted and figures of amplification are subdivided according to the topics of invention from which they are derived.[33] In comparison with Schade, Melanchthon has considerably reduced the total number of figures (now seventy-nine) at the same time as including the figures of thought, which authors working primarily from the grammatical tradition had omitted. He has also introduced a new and relatively straightforward division of the figures.

> SYNECDOCHE, the use of the part instead of the whole, as when I use the name of 'edge' instead of 'sword', or the name of 'sword' instead of the noun 'war'. The same thing: 'If someone strikes you on the right cheek, you should offer him also the left one'.

Correctio, in Greek ἐπανόρθωσκ, he takes away what he has said replacing it with another more suitable word, as 'Theologian, or rather nitpicker' or 'Cruel man, really not a man at all'. What Rutilius calls μετάνοΙαν is obviously correctio.[34]

Johannes Reusch

The Leipzig schoolmaster Johannes Reusch composed a brief *De tropis orationis et dictionis* (1521), which supplements Rufinianus's description of the figures of speech (which Reusch regards as the best explanation of the figures[35]) with an account of the tropes, based on *Rhetorica ad Herennium* and Quintilian. Reusch gives examples from the Bible and Cicero and quotes Erasmus's De copia on metaphor. The tropes of diction are metaphor, synecdoche, metonymy, antonomasia, onomatopoeia, catachresis, and metalepsis; the tropes of oration are allegory, irony, and their subtypes, such as enigma. Reusch adds a very brief account of comparisons and examples. The work was printed eleven times, mostly before 1542.[36]

Susenbrotus (c.1485–1543)

Melanchthon's 1521 division of the material and inclusion of the figures of thought was taken up by the Ravensburg schoolmaster Susenbrotus in his *Epitome troporum ac schematum* (Zurich, 1540), which was printed twenty-six times up to 1620. Susenbrotus, however, hugely expanded the number of figures, reinstating many and finding further figures through an exhaustive comparison of sources, to reach a total of 132.[37] He divides the figures into tropes and schemes. Tropes are subdivided into tropes of words (nine kinds: Melanchthon's 1521 list, plus acrylogia and antiphrasis) and tropes of discourse (ten kinds: a slightly expanded list of the species of allegory, plus hyperbole). Schemes can be grammatical, subdivided into orthography (fifteen types), syntactical (thirty-two types, including aposiopesis and figures which involve changes in word-order, such as hysteron proteron and parenthesis; the list also includes some figures which could go in many places[38]) or rhetorical. Among rhetorical schemes, schemes of words include fourteen figures, schemes of thought nineteen figures, and schemes of amplification forty-one figures. A few figures appear in more than one category.[39]

In the address to his students which serves as a preface Susenbrotus insists that teachers need to identify the tropes and figures in texts they are reading just as much as they need to explain unusual words and difficult constructions. Ignorance of the tropes and figures will hinder or even prevent pupils from understanding classical texts. In his own teaching he has always tried to point out the figures both in order to help students interpret the texts correctly and to provide them with materials for their own speaking and writing. Since the students have previously had nothing to help them beyond Mosellanus's *Tabulae* he has now attempted to collect together from ancient and modern authors whatever can help in reading classical literature. In setting out the figures and tropes he has followed the order established by Melanchthon.[40]

Brennan has shown with admirable exactness how Susenbrotus constructed the individual entries through constant references to, and comparisons between: *Rhetorica ad Herennium*, Quintilian, Erasmus's De copia (including weltkirchius's commentary and an epitome) and Ecclesiastes, Diomedes, the minor Latin orators Rutilius Lupus, Aquila Romanus, and Rufinianus, Mancinelli, Despauterius, Schade, Linacre's *Grammar,* and Melanchthon.[41]

Susenbrotus defines a figure as 'a certain method, by which the direct and simple kind of speaking is altered with a certain strength in the expression'.[42] He explains that figures are supported by the best authorities and are useful in varying our expression and making it more delightful to listeners, in words taken over from Quintilian.[43] His definition of trope ('a variation of a phrase or a word from its proper meaning to a related one for the sake of charm') is close to Quintilian, while the definition of scheme ('a form of speaking and writing altered in some way') is slightly altered from Despauterius.[44] Susenbrotus gives a relatively short account of metaphor, with a definition related to one given by Erasmus, a commendation, various examples, and an explanation that metaphors may be used for necessity (when no appropriate word exists), for emphasis, or for ornament, with examples of each type, taken from Quintilian.[45] In the longer entries on synecdoche and metonymy he follows Schade, who is here drawing on Erasmus.[46]

The general pattern of Susenbrotus's entries on figures of speech is to give a Latin term (often but not always a transliteration of the Greek); the associated Greek term; another Latin equivalent, if appropriate; an explanation; and several examples. Occasionally he adds a division of the figure (with examples of each type); more often he adds at the end a comment on the use of the figure or on alternative names or related figures. He quite often quotes Mancinelli's verse definitions and sometimes invents examples related to religious topics, as Melanchthon had. From time to time he adds a separate note (*Observatiuncula*) on the use of a particular figure or group of figures.

> Subjectio occurs when we reply to our own question. This is effected in three ways. First when we object to ourselves what might be objected by our auditors, and we reply just as if the objection had really been made; secondly when we compel our adversaries to respond and we refute them just as though they had responded; third when we propose various replies, as though deliberating, but then confute them one by one. The first method, according to Erasmus is fitting to argument. The second is appropriate for the conclusion and both for the introduction. The third is apt for deliberating. [He gives lengthy examples of each type.] There is another species of subjectio in which we ourselves propose a question and then answer it, and thereby render the hearer attentive. [Another example.] There is yet another form of subjectio by which we concede something as though it were an objection posed by our adversary, and thereupon add a further qualification by which we turn his objection to our own advantage … This scheme is somewhat related to *erotemata, dialogismus, occupatio*, and *dubitatio*. It is not useful for any one occasion in discourse; it makes for perspicuity, for vehemence or gravity, for docility.[47]

While Susenbrotus normally only quotes his examples, sometimes he adds comments on the way a particular author has used a figure or on the interpretation of a particular passage. He gives more advice than other post-classical writers on the uses of particular figures. By allocating a number of figures primarily to amplification and by the way he uses material from *De copia* and the commentary on it by weltkirchius in describing these figures, Susenbrotus in a way absorbs the teaching of *De copia* into the manual of tropes and figures.[48] The thorough accounts of comparison, types of description, and *sententiae* (also taken from Erasmus) have the effect of incorporating also sections from the *progymnasmata*, so that the book prepares for several different aspects of the grammar-school rhetoric course.[49]

Susenbrotus is very impressive in his scholarship, clarity of expression, and thoughtfulness. The entries are much too long to be learnt by heart but the student who read this book frequently and used it as a reference while reading would have access to an immense amount of information about the figures and many examples of each figure.

Lawrence Green has shown that T. W. Baldwin's comments on the ubiquity of Susenbrotus's *Epitome* are overstated in view of the comparatively small number of editions.[50] While we do not know exactly how many editions any of these works went through, it is now safe to assume that there were far fewer editions of any of these handbooks of tropes and figures than there were of standard grammar texts, such as the Lily-Colet grammar in England. Green points out that a few of the figures were taught in the grammar texts, and they may have been supplemented by notes dictated by individual teachers, such as those which survive in Conybeare's *Notebook*.[51]

Talon's *Rhetorica*

After Susenbrotus, the next major contribution to the study of the tropes and figures was the publication of Omer Talon's *Rhetorica* (Paris, 1548), which went through more than 100 editions before 1620. Since three-quarters of this work (in the later and most printed editions) was given over to the tropes and figures, it must often have been used largely as a guide to them. As we saw in Chapter 7, Talon (and Ramus) reduced the tropes to four (metonymy, irony, metaphor, and synecdoche), treating allegory and hyperbole as types of metaphor.[52] This change proved to be very influential. Later writers who would not contemplate considering themselves as Ramists were nevertheless happy to focus their attention on these four essential tropes (usually in a different order). Equally influential was Talon's decision to place poetic metre and prose-rhythm alongside the tropes at the centre of rhetoric. From now on most handbooks would do the same. This move also helped Talon to reduce the number of figures by including the requirements of rhythm and metre without the need for the numerous figures specified by the grammarians.

More controversial (and less influential on later writers) was Talon's decision to reduce the figures of rhetoric to nineteen. Talon's subdivisions make the whole system much easier to recall, and retain the most frequently used figures. He divides figures of words into those which involve the same sound (seven, including anadiplosis, climax, anaphora, and epanados) and those which use similar sounds (two: paronomasia and polyptoton). Figures of thought are divided into monologic (exclamatio, correctio, aposiopesis, apostrophe, and prosopopeia) and dialogic (addubitatio, communicatio, occupatio, permissio, and concessio). Short though the list is, most of the most frequently used and most effective figures are included. Often Talon's accounts of particular figures are preceded by definition and division of the genus to which they belong. Generally he gives a definition followed by several examples, mainly from Cicero, Virgil, and Terence.[53] Because the list is so short Talon can give more examples of each figure and because the system is easier to understand and remember pupils will more quickly move on to the real point of what they are learning, observing how the best classical authors use the tropes and figures in their works. Talon's treatment of the tropes, in particular, is more subdivided and nuanced (and makes more of the logical bases of metonymy and synecdoche) than Susenbrotus or Mosellanus.[54]

> Apostrophe, turning aside, is when the speech is turned to another person than the oration we have undertaken dictates. This figure comes not far short of Exclamatio in its emotional force and is often joined with it. But Apostrophe can be differentiated according to the different condition of the persons. Sometimes the turning is towards a human person. [Examples from Cicero and Virgil.] Sometimes the turning is from men to Gods. [Examples.] In the poets the invocation is a conspicuous example of Apostrophe. [Examples.] At other times the speech is transferred to an inarticulate and inanimate object, as if it were a person. [Examples.] This figure is rare but it is found from time to time, especially in exordia. [Example.][55]

Julius Caesar Scaliger (1484–1558)

Julius Caesar Scaliger was a Paduan physician, philosopher, grammarian, and naturalist who lived for most of his adult life in Agen in France. His posthumously published *Poetices libri septem* (1561), which was printed ten times up to 1617, contains two treatments of the figures of speech, in books 3 and 4. He defines a figure as 'an acceptable delineation of notions which are in the mind, different from ordinary usage' and refuses to distinguish between figures and tropes.[56] Whereas grammar and dialectic have their own kinds of figures (for dialectic Scaliger is thinking of the figures of the syllogism), oratory, history, and poetics share the common figures.[57] Book 3, supposedly concerned with figures of meaning, and using mainly Latin terms, divides ninety-seven figures into five classes. Since figures are a way of representing notions in the mind they must be either equal to (sixty-six figures), greater than (seven), less than (ten), different from (one), or contrary to (thirteen) the idea expressed. Book 4, supposedly devoted to figures of words, and using mainly Greek terms, divides thirty-eight figures into nine classes: from omission (two), from inclusion of the same word (eleven: anaphora, climax, etc.), from inclusion of the meaning (two), from inclusion of similar things (three: allusion, paronomasia, etc.), from different things (nine: pleonasmus, periphrasis, metonymy, etc.), from inclusion of contrary things (six), change of position within the sentence (six: hyperbaton, parenthesis, etc.), from quantity (three: parison, synthesis, tmesis), and from quality (two: homeoptoton and homeoteleuton). This division of the figures is certainly logical and original but not particularly helpful, especially in book 3 where most of the figures lie within the same class. Scaliger's treatment of individual figures is very brief, usually giving only a definition of the figure and an example from Virgil. Rather surprisingly in a work of poetics, metaphor is treated only once and very briefly.[58]

Luc Deitz has shown that in book 3 Scaliger based his account of the figures mainly on Latin sources, especially on Aquila Romanus, Julius Rufinianus, *Ad Herennium*, Quintilian, and George Trapezuntius, while in book 4, as Francis Cairns showed, he worked directly from the Greek *De figuris* by Alexander, son of Numenius, printed in the *Rhetores Graeci* of 1508. Deitz documents the overlaps between the two lists, explaining that Scaliger followed his Greek source very closely, apparently without noticing the repetition, which is explained by a lost common source for Aquila and Alexander.[59]

Simon Verepaeus (c.1522–1598)

Simon Verepaeus was a Catholic Dutch grammar-school teacher who wrote textbooks on grammar and letter-writing, and prayers. His *Praeceptiones de figuris seu de tropis et schematibus* (Cologne, 1582), which stretches to 160 octavo pages written in the question-and-answer form of the catechism, was printed six times before 1620, sometimes alongside his *Praeceptiones de verborum et rerum copia*. Verepaeus divides his textbook into faults, tropes, and figures. As in Diomedes, Despauterius, and Schade, the faults are divided into *barbarum, obscurum,* and *inordinatum*, though with fewer figures in each class. He discusses eight tropes of words and four of discourse, including seven types of allegory, which is close to Melanchthon (who as a Protestant is not named). He follows Susenbrotus in dividing figures between grammatical and rhetorical. As in Melanchthon and Susenbrotus, the rhetorical figures are divided into figures of words (fifteen figures, including anaphora and its associates), figures of thought (nine), and figures of amplification (thirty), but with some omissions and usually fewer figures assigned to each class. Verepaeus is extremely thorough in his treatment of the tropes, making many subdivisions, particularly in metaphor, metonymy, and synecdoche.[60] He makes considerable use of Schade and Susenbrotus in his treatment of individual figures.

> Gradatio, climax, is what it is called when the sentence rises as if by steps so that the word ending the preceding clause begins the following one.[61]

Keckermann, Vossius, Caussin

The large encyclopedic textbooks of rhetoric of the early seventeenth century, which we discussed in the previous chapter, make some use of the specialized textbooks of tropes and figures. Keckermann focuses on Talon's four main tropes (metonymy, synecdoche, metaphor, and irony).[62] He divides figures of thought into six classes according to their uses: explanation, proof, amplification, emotions in general, relation to others (like Talon's category of dialogue), and figures connected with specific emotions.[63] Figures of speech are divided into four classes on the basis of form: figures of omission, figures of addition or excess, changes in order, and figures of repetition.[64] Vossius concentrates mainly on four tropes (metaphor, metonymy, synecdoche, and irony), some types of allegory, and three lesser tropes. He tells us that he takes his division of the figures from Scaliger's third book, but it would be better to say that there are some similarities between Vossius's classification and particular sections of Scaliger's two versions of a division. While Vossius's first and second classes resemble the first two groups from Scaliger's fourth book, both in the terms of the description and the content, his third and fourth classes resemble Scaliger's 4.38–41 in description but not in content and his sixth and eleventh groups have some connections with sections 2, 3 and 5 of Scaliger's book 3 division. Caussin's main treatment of the figures combines an inclusive approach with the abandonment of classification, giving brief accounts of 207 figures in alphabetical order, including several repetitions.[65] Later he adds a section on the use of figures, suggesting seven classes for a selection from his longer list: those which express a picture of something in a few words, figures for longer descriptions, repetition, improving the sweetness of the sentence, for weightiness, for argument, and for emotions.[66] He includes tropes and figures of thought but does not separate them from figures of words.

Other new textbooks which were intended for grammar school use were the letter-writing manuals (to be discussed in the next chapter), new versions of the *progymasmata*, particularly from Spanish authors,[67] and adaptations of Erasmus's De copia. The latter included Georg Major's summary printed with later editions of Schade's *Tabulae* and Verepaeus's *Praeceptiones de verborum et rerum copia* (Cologne, 1582).[68]

The existence of separate manuals of tropes and figures, of which around 180 editions are known to have been printed between 1489 and 1620, confirms the importance of the tropes and figures within rhetorical education. These doctrines were also available to readers in *Rhetorica ad Herennium* and Quintilian's *Institutio oratoria*, which together went through more than 280 editions, as well as in all the major renaissance manuals of the whole of rhetoric, totalling more than 550 editions. The large numbers of editions of these manuals confirm the implications of school statutes and instructions for reading, that pupils should be introduced to the figures and tropes once they had passed beyond the elementary stage of Latin reading. Teachers were supposed to point out the ways in which classical authors used the tropes and figures. To do this they needed handbooks of tropes and figures to be studied in advance of the full course in rhetoric. The brevity of the earlier manuals can be explained by the way in which they were to be used. The focus was on learning the names and definitions by heart so that figures could be recognized in reading. Recognizing and naming the figures made it possible to observe the ways in which classical authors used the tools of their trade and made this aspect of their reading available to pupils for imitation in their own writing.

In the course of the sixteenth century textbook writers made various attempts to develop categorizations of the tropes and figures which would help pupils understand and remember them better. None of these attempts was entirely successful, because even those that were followed widely tended to produce some categories (such as Melanchthon's category of figures associated with amplification) which included very numerous and diverse figures. The result was that one of the most important *summae* of rhetoric of the early seventeenth century abandoned classification in favour of a huge and repetitive alphabetical list. Probably the most effective of the new systems of organization was devised by Omer Talon, but at the cost of a radical reduction in the number of figures. His identification of four principal tropes was largely adopted by later writers.

Within the developing tradition of descriptions of the tropes and figures we notice a tension between an expansive impulse, caused by the scholarly desire to incorporate the teaching of a widening range of classical texts, and an impulse to shorten and simplify derived from a pedagogic preference for teaching which can be learnt more quickly and remembered more easily. So while Susenbrotus and Caussin, for example, enlarge the scope of the book, Melanchthon and Talon look for ways to shorten it.

Another characteristic of these manuals is their conservatism. We have seen how Schade copies from Despauterius, who copies Mancinelli, who relies very heavily on the Latin grammarian Diomedes. This tradition also makes a strong impression on all the later writers. One striking effect of this is that the figures of thought only enter the sixteenth-century manuals of tropes and figures at a rather late stage. Thus of the roughly 180 editions of manuals of the tropes and figures, about 140 lack the figures of thought. In later editions of Schade, Major's table of the whole of rhetoric names several figures which Schade's *Tabulae de schematibus* has not described or exemplified.[69]

In contrast we can also see how a little later the manual of tropes and figures begins to incorporate the approach of Erasmus's De copia, first in the attachment of Major's summary of De copia to later editions of Schade's manual, then in the adoption of the category of figures assisting amplification, and eventually in the reuse of sections from Erasmus in Susenbrotus and Verepaeus.

The overall pattern of publication suggests two conclusions. It very much looks as if independent publication of Mancinelli is superseded by the appearance of Schade's *Tabulae* in 1516. Twenty-four editions of Mancinelli appear before 1518. There are no editions between 1520 and 1540. All the editions after 1540 are part of a collection of texts based on Schade. Considering the group of texts as a whole it seems that there was strong regular production of such manuals between 1500 and 1580, with at least ten editions per decade. There was a peak of around twenty-five editions per decade between 1530 and 1550 and a middle plateau of sixteen editions per decade 1550–1570. Production peaks in the heyday of northern humanism, and tails off at about the same time as Ciceronian rhetoric declines more generally.

Notes

1 B. Vickers, *Classical Rhetoric in English Poetry* (London, 1970); *In Defence of Rhetoric* (Oxford, 1988), 294–339, 491–8.
2 E. H. Gombrich, *Art and Illusion* (Princeton, 1960), 374–5.
3 On the figures more generally, see R. Lanham, *A Handlist of Rhetorical Terms* (Berkeley, 1991); H. Lausberg, *Handbuch der literarischen rhetorik*, 3rd edn. (Stuttgart, 1990), 282–455, tr. as *Handbook of Literary Rhetoric* (Leiden, 1998), 248–411; J. Knape, 'Elocutio', in G. Ueding (ed.), *Historisches Wörterbuch der Rhetorik*, ii (Tübingen, 1994), 1022–83; and Gideon Burton's website 'Silva rhetoricae' at http://rhetoric.byu.edu. On the development of the doctrine see G. Calboli, 'From Aristotelian λέξις to elocutio', *Rhetorica*, 16 (1998), 47–80, and 'The Metaphor after Aristotle', in D. C. Mirhady (ed.), *Influences on Peripatetic Rhetoric* (Leiden, 2007), 123–50.
4 On the tropes and figures in the renaissance see L. Sonnino, *A Handbook to Sixteenth Century Rhetoric* (London, 1968); S. Adamson et al. (eds.), *Renaissance Figures of Speech* (Cambridge, 2007).
5 L. Green, 'Grammatica movet', in P. Osterreich and T. Sloane (eds.), *Rhetorica Movet: Studies in Honour of H. F. Plett* (Leiden, 1999), 81–104.
6 P. Mack, *Elizabethan Rhetoric* (Cambridge, 2002), 14–16, 22–4, 45–6. J. Susenbrotus, *Epitome troporum et schematum* (Zurich, n.d.), sig. A2[r-v]. Repr. in J. Brennan's dissertation: see n. 12 below.
7 Green, 'Grammatica movet', 79–83.
8 On the doctrine of the figures see Cornifici, *Rhetorica ad C. Herennium*, ed. G. Calboli, 2nd edn. (Bologna, 1993), 50–4.

9 Quintilian, *Institution oratoire*, ed. J. Cousin, v. *Livres VIII et IX* (Paris, 1978), 129–51. On the tropes and figures in classical rhetoric see R. E. Volkmann, *Die Rhetorik der Griechen und Römer* (Leipzig, 1885), 415–505.
10 C. Halm, *Rhetores Latini Minores* (Leipzig, 1863), pp. v–vii, 1–62.
11 D. A. Russell, *Criticism in Antiquity* (London, 1981), 145–6. G. Kennedy, *The Art of Rhetoric in the Roman World* (Princeton, 1972), 337–8. P. Rutilius Lupus, *Schemata dianoeas et lexeos*, with study by G. Barabino (Genoa, 1967); *De figuris sententiarum et elocutionis*, ed. E. Brooks (Leiden, 1970).
12 J. Brennan, 'The Epitome Troporum ac Schematum of Joannes Susenbrotus: Text, Translation and Commentary', Ph.D. dissertation, University of Illinois, 1953, pp. iii–vii. H. Keil (ed.), *Grammatici Latini*, i (Leipzig, 1867), iv (Leipzig, 1864).
13 Halm, *Rhetores Latini Minores*, 606–18. Brennan, 'Epitome', p. xviii.
14 Marbodo di Rennes, '*De ornamentis verborum*', ed. R. Leotta (Florence, 1998), pp. xxxiii–xlii, 2–25.
15 M. C. Woods, *Classroom Commentaries* (Columbus, Ohio, 2010), 289–307.
16 M. Camargo, 'Latin Composition Textbooks and *Ad Herennium* Glossing: The Missing Link?', in Cox and Ward (eds.), *The Rhetoric of Cicero* (Leiden, 2006), 267–88. I am indebted to Martin Camargo for the information in this paragraph.
17 This work is discussed in more detail in the next chapter because of its influential section on letter-writing.
18 N. Perotti, *Rudimenta grammatices* (Milan, 1480), sigs. I4[v]–K1[v].
19 'Cum sine iunctura voces variae locitantur / Dialyton certe vel asyndeton efficimus: / Exemplum capies: res miles plebs negat illud. / Dialyton dici potest absolutum: nam descendit a verbo Dialyo quod est dissolvo. Dialytos vero dissolutus. Dialysis dissolutio. Dialyton vel asyndeton est oratio sine coniunctionibus: ut . . . Ferte citi ferrum; date tela [ascendite muros] . . . Item in veni vidi vici . . . Haec etiam Bracchilochia nominatur, ut Diomedes ait; et Fabius libro ix. Asyndetos disiunctus dicitur Asynthetos incompositus.' Sulpitius Verulanus, *Gremmatice Quinta recognitio atque additio* (London, 1514), STC 23427a.7, sigs. H2[v]–3[r].
20 'Anaphora dicitur repetitio vel relatio . . . Anaphora est, ut Diomedes ait, relatio verbi eiusdem aut similis per principia versuum plurimorum.' Ibid., sig. H3[v].
21 'Arte novata aliqua dicendi forma figura est.' J. de Spauter, *Artis versificatoriae compendium . . . Item de Figuris liber* (Edinburgh, 1631), sig. C1[v].
22 Despauter, *De Figuris*, sigs. C3[v]–4[r].
23 Ibid., sigs. C5[r], C6[r–v].
24 'Dico Metonymiam, Bacchum bibo, Vina coronant. / Metonymia est nominum transmutatio, quoties pro inventore inventum, pro continente contentum, pro efficiente effectum, pro possesso possessorem aut contra capimus. Metonymia transfertur nominis transmutatio, a meta, id est trans, et onoma id est nomen.' Ibid., sig. C5[v]. Compare: 'Pone tenens lector pro contento: aut vice versa / Nunc pateras libate iovi vel vina coronant / Pone inventorem pro inventis: sive deum quem / Pro re cui praesit: seu pro coitu Venerem dic / Nempe Metonymiam concedimus esse figuram.' Mancinelli, *Carmen de figuris* (as in n. 19 above), H5[r].
25 Mosellanus, *Tabulae de schematibus et tropis* (Antwerp, 1529), sigs. B7[v], D7[r].
26 P. Mosellanus, Tabulae de schematibus et tropis in rhetorica (London, 1573), sigs. A1[v]–2[r].
27 Ibid., sig. A2[v].
28 Eighteen are from Despauterius's figures of words, five are from the miscellaneous figures at the end of Despauterius's work; antimetabole is added from one of the classical lists.
29 'Π ροσωποποιία Prosopopoeia, Personarum fictio, nimirum cum multis sermo tribuitur. In qua quanquam Poëtae multum sibi permittunt, tamen et Oratores usurpant, ut Cicero in Catilinam patriae sermonem accommodat . . . 'Αποσιώπησίς Aposiopesis, quam Cicero reticentiam appellat, cum per iram vel indignationem, orationis partem reticemus. Quos ego, sed motos praestat componere fluctus. Tacet enim, puniam.' Mosellanus, *Tabulae*, sig. A6[r–v].
30 Ibid., sigs. B3[r]–4[v].
31 Melanchthon, *Institutiones*, C3[v]–D1[v.] *Elementa*, 463–6, 472–3. *Elementa* slightly shortens both these lists.
32 Melanchthon, *Institutiones*, D2[r]–E3[v].

33 Melanchthon, *Elementa*, 475–92.
34 'SYNECDOCHE, partis est pro toto usurpatio, ut cum pro gladii voce, utor mucro-nis adpellatione, pro belli nomine gladii. Tale est, si quis percusserit te in dextram maxillam tuam, porrige ei et sinistram. Correctio, graece ἐπανόρθωσίς, tollit quod dictum est, supponens aliud magis idoneum, ut, Theologus, immo nugator; crudelis homo, immo ne homo quidem. Quam vocat Rutilius μετάνοιαν ea plane est correctio.' Melanchthon, *Institutiones rhetoricae* (Hagenau, 1521), sigs. C3^v, E2^r. Matthew 5: 39.
35 J. Rufinianus, *De figuris lexeos*, with Reuschius, *De tropis orationis et dictionis* (Leipzig, 1521), sig. A2^r.
36 Rufinianus, ibid., sigs. B4^v–C5^v.
37 Susenbrotus, *Epitome*, repr. in Brennan, 'Epitome', sigs. A2^v–3^v
38 Susenbrotus, *Epitome*, repr. in Brennan, 'Epitome', sig. B5^v.
39 e.g. Susenbrotus, *Epitome*, sigs A7^v, B1^v (antiphrasis), E2^v, F3^{r-v} (prosopopeia).
40 Ibid., sigs. A2^{r-v}, D1^r.
41 Brennan, 'Epitome', pp. xvi–xxii, xxv, 107–41. Occasionally Brennan under-reports the changes Susenbrotus made to his sources. This valuable thesis should be made more widely available.
42 'Figura est ratio quaedam, qua de recto ac simplici loquendi genere cum aliquo dicendi virtute deflectitur.' Susenbrotus, *Epitome*, sig. A4^v.
43 Ibid., sig. A4^v. Brennan, 'Epitome', 110. Quintilian 9.3.3–4.
44 'Tropus est dictionis sive orationis a propria significatione in cognatam ornandi gratia variatio ... Schema, vel figura proprie, est aliqua novata et scribendi et dicendi forma.' Susenbrotus, *Epitome*, sig. A4^v. Brennan, 'Epitome', 110. Quintilian 8.6.1. Despauterius, *De Figuris*, sig. C1^v.
45 Susenbrotus, *Epitome*, sig. A5^r. Brennan, 'Epitome', 110. Erasmus, *De copia, Opecoronnia*, i/6, 62–4. Quintilian 8.6.4.
46 Susenbrotus, *Epitome*, sig. A5^r–6^r. Brennan, 'Epitome', 110–11. Mosellanus, *Tabulae*, sig. B4^{r-v}. Erasmus, *De copia*, 68–72.
47 'Subjectio est cum ipsi nostrae interrogatione respondemus. Id fit tribus modis. Primo cum nobisipsis obiicimus quod ab adversaribus obiici poterat, et quasi obiectum sit respondemus. Secundo, cum adversarios compellamus ut respondeant, et quasi responderint, refellimus. Tertio, cum quasi deliberantes varia proponemus, ac singula confutamus. Primus modus auctore Erasmo convenit argumentatione; Secundus epilogo, uterque convenit introductione. Tertius aptus est ad deliberandum ... Est praeterea subjectionis species, qua, dum ipsi questionem proponimus ac mox ad eam respondemus, reddimus auditorem attentum ac docilem ... Est et alia subjectionis forma qua quiddam veluti ab adversario nobis obiectum concedimus, sed subiicimus aliud, quo illius obiectionem ad nos detorquemus ... Habet autem hoc schema nonnihil affinitatis cum erotemate, dialogismo, occupatione, et cum dubitatione. Nec ad unam orationis commoditatem utilis est. Facit ad perspicuitatem, et ad vehementiam sive gravitatem, et ad docilitatem.' Susenbrotus, *Epitome*, sigs. D6^r–7^r, tr. Brennan.
48 e.g. Susenbrotus, *Epitome*, sig. E3^r–4^r.
49 Ibid., sigs. E4^v–5^v, F3^r–4^v, F6^v–7^r.
50 Green, 'Grammatica movet', 77, 105–10.
51 Ibid. 84–104, 110–15. Mack, *Elizabethan Rhetoric*, 45–6.
52 O. Talon, *Rhetorica* (Cambridge, 1631), sigs. A8^v–B1^r.
53 e.g. ibid., sigs. C4^{r-v}, C7^r–8^r.
54 Ibid., sigs. A4^r–7^r, B1^r–3^r.
55 'Apostrophe, aversio, est quando oratio ad alienam personam convertitur, quam instituta oratio requirit. Figura non multum cedens elationis genere Exclamationi, et persaepe cum ea conjugitur. Sed Apostrophe ex conditione personarum varie distingui potest. Alias enim ad humanam personam sit aversion ... Alias ab hominibus ad deos sit aversion ... In Apostrophe Invocatio insignis est apud poetas ... Alias ad rem mutam et inanimatam, velut ad personam, transfertur oratio ... Haec figura raro quidem, sed tamen aliquando protinus in proemio adhibatur.' Ibid., sigs. C8^r–D1^r.
56 'Figura est notionum quae in mente sunt, tolerabilis delineatio, alia ab usu commune.' J. C. Scaliger, *Poetices libri septem* (Lyon, 1561; repr. Stuttgart, 1964), 120. He acknowledges but does not observe the distinction between figures of words and figures of things, p. 121.

57 Ibid. 121.
58 Ibid. 127.
59 J. C. Scaliger, *Poetices libri septem*, ii, ed. L. Deitz (Stuttgart, 1994), 30–59 (esp. pp. 35–6). F. Cairns, 'The Poetices libri septem: An Unexplored Source', *Res Publica Litterarum*, 9 (1986), 49–57.
60 Verepaeus, *Praeceptiones de figuris seu de tropis et schematibus* (Cologne, 1590), sigs. B8^v–C6^v.
61 'Gradatio, climax, dicitur, cum ita quasi per gradus ascendit oratio, ut dictio finiens clausulam precedentem, inchoat sequentem.' Ibid., sig. h6^r.
62 Keckermann, *Systema Rhetoricae*, M5^v–O7^v.
63 Ibid., R2^r–V3^r.
64 Ibid., V3^r–Y2^r.
65 Caussin, Parallela, 256–80.
66 Ibid. 281–93.
67 Anon, Progymnasmata in artem oratoriam (Paris, 1520), which was printed nine times up to 1620 and see L. López Grigera, *La rétorica en la España del siglo de oro* (Salamanca, 1994), 55, 59, 69–83, 185, mentioning Juan Pérez, *Progymnasmata artis rhetoricae* (Alcala, 1539), Antonio Lulio's *Progymnasmata rhetorica* (Basel, 1548), Lorenzo Palmireno, *Aphthonii progymnasmata* (Valencia, 1553), Juan Mal Lara, *Aphthonii progymnasmata scholia* (Hispali, 1567), Alfonso Torres, *Exercitationes rhetoricae* (Alcala, 1569), and Pedro Juan Nuñez, *Progymnasmata* (Zaragoza, 1596).
68 Johann Possel, *Calligraphia oratoria linguae Grecae, ad proprietatem, elegantiam et* copiam graeci sermonis parandam (Frankfurt 1585), which went through eight edns., is a Latin–Greek phrasebook organized alphabetically by subject.
69 Mosellanus, *Tabulae*, sigs. C3^v–4^v.

5.
FOUR MASTER TROPES
Kenneth Burke

I REFER to metaphor, metonymy, synecdoche, and irony. And my primary concern with them here will be not with their purely figurative usage, but with their rôle in the discovery and description of "the truth." It is an evanescent moment that we shall deal with—for not only does the dividing line between the figurative and literal usages shift, but also the four tropes shade into one another. Give a man but one of them, tell him to exploit its possibilities, and if he is thorough in doing so, he will come upon the other three.

The "literal" or "realistic" applications of the four tropes usually go by a different set of names. Thus:

For *metaphor* we could substitute *perspective;*
For *metonymy* we could substitute *reduction;*
For *synecdoche* we could substitute *representation;*
For *irony* we could substitute *dialectic.*

We must subsequently try to make it clear in what respects we think these substitutions are justifiable. It should, however, be apparent at a glance that, regardless of whether our proposed substitutions are justifiable, considered in themselves they do shade into another, as we have said that the four tropes do. A dialectic, for instance, aims to give us a representation by the use of mutually related or interacting perspectives—and this resultant perspective of perspectives will necessarily be a reduction in the sense that a chart drawn to scale is a reduction of the area charted.

Metaphor is a device for seeing something *in terms of* something else. It brings out the thisness of a that, or the thatness of a this. If we employ the word "character" as a general term for whatever can be thought of as distinct (any thing, pattern, situation, structure, nature, person, object, act, rôle, process, event, etc.,) then we could say that metaphor tells us something about one character as considered from the point of view of another character. And to consider A from the point of view of B is, of course, to use B as a *perspective* upon A.

It is customary to think that objective reality is dissolved by such relativity of terms as we get through the shifting of perspectives (the perception of one character in terms of many diverse characters). But on the contrary, it is by the approach through a variety of perspectives that we establish a character's reality. If we are in doubt as to what an object is, for instance, we deliberately try to consider it in as many different

---

Burke, Kenneth. "Four Master Tropes." *The Kenyon Review*, 3.4 (1941): 421–438.

terms as its nature permits: lifting, smelling, tasting, tapping, holding in different lights, subjecting to different pressures, dividing, matching, contrasting, etc.

Indeed, in keeping with the older theory of realism (what we might call "poetic realism," in contrast with modern "scientific realism") we could say that characters possess *degrees of being* in proportion to the variety of perspectives from which they can with justice be perceived. Thus we could say that plants have "more being" than minerals, animals have more being than plants, and men have more being than animals, because each higher order admits and requires a new dimension of terms not literally relevant to the lower orders.

By deliberate coaching and criticism of the perspective process, characters can be considered tentatively, in terms of other characters, for experimental or heuristic purposes. Examples may be offered at random: for instance, human motivation may, with varying degrees of relevance and reward, be considered in terms of conditioned reflexes, or chemicals, or the class struggles, or the love of God, or neurosis, or pilgrimage, or power, or movements of the planets, or geography, or sun spots, etc. Various kinds of scientific specialists now carry out the implications of one or another of such perspectives with much more perseverance than that with which a 17th Century poet might in one poem pursue the exploitation of a "conceit."

In *Permanence and Change* I have developed at some length the relationship between metaphor and perspective. I there dealt with such perspectives as an "incongruity," because the seeing of something in terms of something else involves the "carrying-over" of a term from one realm into another, a process that necessarily involves varying degrees of incongruity in that the two realms are never identical. But besides the mere desire not to restate this earlier material, there is another reason why we can hurry on to our next pair (metonymy and reduction). For since the four pairs overlap upon one another, we shall be carrying the first pair with us as we proceed.

2.

Science, concerned with processes and "processing," is not properly concerned with substance (that is, it is not concerned with "being," as "poetic realism" is). Hence, it need not be concerned with motivation. All it need know is correlation. The limits of science, *qua* science, do not go beyond the statement that, when certain conditions are met, certain new conditions may be expected to follow. It is true that, in the history of the actual development of science, the discovery of such correlations has been regularly guided by philosophies of causation ("substantial" philosophies that were subsequently "discredited" or were so radically redefined as to become in effect totally different philosophies). And it is equally true that the discovery of correlations has been guided by ideational forms developed through theology and governmental law. Such "impurities" will always be detectible *behind* science as the act of given scientists; but science *qua* science is abstracted from them.

Be the world "mind," or "matter," or "both," or "several," you will follow the same procedure in striking a match. It is in this sense that science, *qua* science, is concerned with operations rather than with substances, even though the many inventions to do with the chemistry of a match can be traced back to a source in very explicit beliefs about substances and motivations of nature—and even of the supernatural.

However, as soon as you move into the social realm, involving the relation of man to man, mere *correlation* is not enough. Human relationships must be *substantial*, related by the copulative, the "is" of "being." In contrast with "scientific realism," "poetic realism" is centered in this emphasis. It seeks (except insofar as it is affected by the norms of "scientific realism") to place the motives of action, as with the relation between the seminal (potential) and the growing (actualized). Again and again, there have been attempts to give us a "science of human relations" after the analogy of the natural sciences. But there is a strategic or crucial respect in which this is impossible; namely: there can be no "science" of substance, except insofar as one is willing to call philosophy, metaphysics, or theology "sciences" (and they are not sciences in the sense of the positive scientific departments).

Hence, any attempt to deal with human relationships after the analogy of naturalistic correlations becomes necessarily the *reduction* of some higher or more complex realm of being to the terms of a lower or less complex realm of being. And, recalling that we propose to treat *metonymy* and *reduction* as substitutes for each other, one may realize why we thought it necessary thus to introduce the subject of metonymy.

The basic "strategy" in metonymy is this: to convey some incorporeal or intangible state in terms of the corporeal or tangible. E.g., to speak of "the heart" rather than "the emotions." If you trail language back far enough, of course, you will find that all our terms for "spiritual" states were metonymic in origin. We think of "the emotions," for instance, as applying solely to the realm of consciousness, yet obviously the word is rooted in the most "materialistic" term of all, "motion" (a key strategy in Western materialism has been the reduction of "consciousness" to "motion"). In his *Principles of Literary Criticism*, Richards is being quite "metonymic" in proposing that we speak not of the "emotions" aroused in the reader by the work of art, but the "commotions."

Language develops by metaphorical extension, in borrowing words from the realm of the corporeal, visible, tangible and applying them by analogy to the realm of the incorporeal, invisible, intangible; then in the course of time, the original corporeal reference is forgotten, and only the incorporeal, metaphorical extension survives (often because the very conditions of living that reminded one of the corporeal reference have so altered that the cross reference no longer exists with near the same degree of apparentness in the "objective situation" itself); and finally, poets regain the original relation, in reverse, by a "metaphorical extension" back from the intangible into a tangible equivalent (the first "carrying-over" from the material to the spiritual being compensated by a second "carrying-over" from the spiritual back into the material); and this "archaicizing" device we call "metonymy."

"Metonymy" is a device of "poetic realism"—but its partner, "reduction," is a device of "scientific realism." Here "poetry" and "behaviorism" meet. For the poet spontaneously knows that "beauty *is as* beauty *does*" (that the "state" must be "embodied" in an actualization). He knows that human relations require actions, which are *dramatizations*, and that the essential medium of drama is the posturing, tonalizing body placed in a material scene. He knows that "shame," for instance, is not merely a "state," but a movement of the eye, a color of the cheek, a certain quality of voice and set of the muscles; he knows this as "behavioristically" as the formal scientific behaviorist who would "reduce" the state itself to these corresponding bodily equivalents.

He also knows, however, that these bodily equivalents are but part of the *idiom of expression* involved in the act. They are "figures." They are hardly other than "symbolizations." Hence, for all his "archaicizing" usage here, he is not offering his metonymy as a *substantial* reduction. For in "poetic realism," states of mind as the motives of action are not reducible to materialistic terms. Thus, though there is a sense in which both the poetic behaviorist and the scientific behaviorist are exemplifying the strategy of metonymy (as the poet translates the spiritual into an idiom of material equivalents, and may even select for attention the same bodily responses that the scientist may later seek to measure), the first is using metonymy as a *terminological* reduction whereas the scientific behaviorist offers his reduction as a "real" reduction. (However, he does not do this *qua* scientist, but only by reason of the materialist metaphysics, with its assumptions about substance and motive, that is implicit in his system.)

3.

Now, note that a reduction is a *representation*. If I reduce the contours of the United States, for instance, to the terms of a relief map, I have within these limits "represented" the United States. As a mental state is the "representation" of certain material conditions, so we could—reversing the process—say that the material conditions are "representative" of the mental state. That is, if there is some kind of correspondence between what we call the act of perception and what we call the thing perceived, then either of these equivalents can be taken as "representative" of the other. Thus, as reduction (metonymy) overlaps upon metaphor (perspective) so likewise it overlaps upon synecdoche (representation).

For this purpose we consider synecdoche in the usual range of dictionary sense, with such meanings as: part for the whole, whole for the part, container for the contained, sign for the thing signified, material for the thing made (which brings us nearer to metonymy), cause for effect, effect for cause, genus for species, species for genus, etc. All such conversions imply an integral rerelationship, a relationship of convertibility, between the two terms.

The "noblest synecdoche," the perfect paradigm or prototype for all lesser usages, is found in metaphysical doctrines proclaiming the identity of "microcosm" and "macrocosm." In such doctrines, where the individual is treated as a replica of the universe, and vice versa, we have the ideal synecdoche, since microcosm is related to macrocosm as part to whole, and either the whole can represent the part or the part can represent the whole. (For "represent" here we could substitute "be identified with.") One could thus look through the remotest astronomical distances to the "truth within," or could look within to learn the "truth in all the universe without." Leibniz's monadology is a good instance of the synecdochic on this grand scale. (And "representation" is his word for this synecdochic relationship.)

A similar synecdochic form is present in all theories of political representation, where some part of the social body (either traditionally established, or elected, or coming into authority by revolution) is held to be "representative" of the society as a whole. The pattern is essential to Rousseau's theory of the *volonté générale,* for instance. And though there are many disagreements within a society as to what part should represent the whole and how this representation should be accomplished, in a complex civilization any act of representation automatically implies a synecdochic relationship (insofar as the act is, or is held to be, "truly representative").

Sensory representation is, of course, synecdochic in that the senses abstract certain qualities from some bundle of electro-chemical activities we call, say, a tree, and these qualities (such as size, shape, color, texture, weight, etc.) can be said "truly to represent" a tree. Similarly, artistic representation is synecdochic, in that certain relations within the medium "stand for" corresponding relations outside it. There is also a sense in which the well-formed work of art is internally synecdochic, as the beginning of a drama contains its close or the close sums up the beginning, the parts all thus being consubstantially related. Indeed, one may think what he will of microcosm-macrocosm relationships as they are applied to "society" or "the universe," the fact remains that, as regards such a "universe" as we get in a well-organized work of art, at every point the paradoxes of the synecdochic present themselves to the critic for analysis. Similarly, the realm of psychology (and particularly the psychology of art) requires the use of the synecdochic reversals. Indeed, I would want deliberately to "coach" the concept of the synecdochic by extending it to cover such relations (and their reversals) as: before for after, implicit for explicit, temporal sequence for logical sequence, name for narrative, disease for cure, hero for villain, active for passive. At the opening of *The Ancient Mariner,* for instance, the Albatross is a *gerundive:* its nature when introduced is that of something *to be* murdered, and it implicitly contains the future that is to become explicit. In *Moby Dick,* Ahab as pursuer is pursued; his action is a passion.

Metonymy may be treated as a special application of synecdoche. If, for instance, after the analogy of a correlation between "mind and body" or "consciousness and matter (or motion)" we selected quality and quantity as a "synecdochically related pair," then we might propose to treat as synecdoche the substitution of either quantity for quality or quality for quantity (since either side could be considered as the sign, or symptom, of the other). But only *one* of these, the substitution of quantity for quality, would be a metonymy. We might say that representation (synecdoche) stresses a *relationship* or *connectedness* between two sides of an equation, a connectedness that, like a road, extends in either direction, from quantity to quality or from quality to quantity; but reduction follows along this road in only *one* direction, from quality to quantity.[1]

Now "poetic realism," in contrast with "scientific realism," cannot confine itself to representation in this metonymic, one-direction sense. True, every art, in its nature as a medium, reduces a state of consciousness to a "corresponding" sensory body (so material that it can be reproduced, bought and sold). But the aim of such *embodiment* is to produce in the observer a corresponding state of *consciousness* (that is, the artist proceeds from "mind" to "body" that his representative reduction may induce the audience to proceed from "body" to "mind"). But there is an important difference between representing the quality of an experience thus and reducing the quality to a quantity. One might even "represent" the human body in the latter, reductive sense, by reducing it to ashes and offering a formula for the resultant chemicals. Otto Neurath's "isotypes" (see his *Modern Man in the Making,* or our review of it, "Quantity and Quality," in the appendix of *The Philosophy of Literary Form*) are representations in the latter, reductive sense, in contrast with the kind of representation we get in realistic portrait-painting.

Our point in going over this old ground is to use it as a way of revealing a tactical error in the attempt to treat of *social* motivations. We refer to the widespread belief that the mathematico-quantitative ideal of the physical sciences can and should serve as the ideal of the "social sciences," a belief that has led, for instance, to the almost fabulous amassing of statistical surveys in the name of "sociology." Or, if one insisted upon the right to build "sciences" after this model (since no one could deny that statistics are often revealing) our claim would be that science in this restricted sense (that explains higher orders by reduction to lower orders, organic complexities by reduction to atomistic simplicities, being by reduction to motion, or quality by reduction to number, etc.) could not *take the place* of metaphysics or religion, but would have to return to the role of "handmaiden."

Let us get at the point thus: *A terminology of conceptual analysis, if it is not to lead to misrepresentation, must be constructed in conformity with a representative anecdote—whereas anecdotes "scientifically" selected for reductive purposes are not representative.* E.g., think of the scientist who, in seeking an entrance into the analysis of human motivations, selects as his "informative anecdote" for this purpose some laboratory experiment having to do with the responses of animals. Obviously, such an anecdote has its peculiarly simplificatory ("reductive") character, or genius — and the scientist who develops his analytic terminology about this anecdote as his informative case must be expected to have, as a result, a terminology whose character or genius is restricted by the character or genius of the model for the description of which it is formed. He next proceeds to transfer (to "metaphor") this terminology to the interpretation of a different order of cases, turning for instance from animals to infants and from infants to the acts of fully developed adults. And when he has made these steps, applying his terminology to a kind of anecdote so different from the kind about which it was formed, this misapplication of his terminology would not give him a representative interpretation at all, but a mere "debunking." Only insofar as the analyst had not lived up to his claims, only insofar as his terminology for the analysis of a higher order of cases was *not* restricted to the limits proper to the analysis of a lower order of cases, could he hope to discuss the higher order of cases in an adequate set of terms. Otherwise, the genius of his restricted terminology must "drag the interpretation down to their level."

This observation goes for any terminological approach to the analysis of human acts or relationships that is shaped in conformity with an unrepresentative case (or that selects as the "way in" to one's subject an "informative anecdote" belonging in some other order than the case to be considered). For instance, insofar as Anton Korzybski really does form his terminology for the analysis of meaning in conformity with that contraption of string, plugs, and tin he calls the "Structural Differential," his analysis of meaning is "predestined" to misrepresentation, since the genius of the contraption itself is not a representative example of meaning. It is a "reduction" of meaning, a reduction in the restricted sense of the term, as Thurman Arnold's reduction of social relations into terms of the psychiatric metaphor is reductive.

What then, it may be asked, would be a "representative anecdote?" But that takes us into the fourth pair: irony and dialectic.

4.

A treatment of the irony-dialectic pair will be much easier to follow if we first delay long enough to consider the equatability of "dialectic" with "dramatic."

A human rôle (such as we get in drama) may be summed up in certain slogans, or formulae, or epigrams, or "ideas" that characterize the agent's situation or strategy. The rôle involves properties both intrinsic to the agent and developed with relation to the scene and to other agents. And the "summings-up" ("ideas") similarly possess properties derived both from the agent and from the various factors with which the agent is in relationship. Where the ideas are in action, we have drama; where the agents are in ideation, we have dialectic.

Obviously, there are elements of "dramatic personality" in dialectic ideation, and elements of dialectic in the mutual influence of dramatic agents in contributing to one another's ideational development. You might state all this another way by saying that you cannot have ideas without persons or persons without ideas. Thus, one might speak of "Socratic irony" as "dramatic," and of "dramatic irony" as "Socratic."

Relativism is got by the fragmentation of either drama or dialectic. That is, if you isolate any one agent in a drama, or any one advocate in a dialogue, and see the whole in terms of his position alone, you have the purely relativistic. And in relativism there is no irony. (Indeed, as Cleanth Brooks might say, it is the very absence of irony in relativism that makes it so susceptible to irony. For relativism sees everything in but one set of terms—and since there are endless other terms in which things could be seen, the irony of the monologue that makes everything in its image would be in this ratio: the greater the *absolutism* of the statements, the greater the *subjectivity* and *relativity* in the position of the agent making the statements.)

Irony arises when one tries, by the interaction of terms upon one another, to produce a *development* which uses all the terms. Hence, from the standpoint of this total form (this "perspective of perspectives"), none of the participating "sub-perspectives" can be treated as either precisely right or precisely wrong. They are all voices, or personalities, or positions, integrally affecting one another. When the dialectic is properly formed, they are the number of characters needed to produce the total development. Hence, reverting to our suggestion that we might extend the synecdochic pattern to include such reversible pairs as disease-cure, hero-villain, active-passive, we should "ironically" note the function of the disease in "perfecting" the cure, or the function of the cure in "perpetuating" the influences of the disease. Or we should note that only through an internal and external experiencing of folly could we possess (in our intelligence or imagination) sufficient "characters" for some measure of development beyond folly.

People usually confuse the dialectic with the relativistic. Noting that the dialectic (or dramatic) explicitly attempts to establish a distinct set of characters, all of which protest variously at odds or on the bias with one another, they think no further. It is certainly relativistic, for instance, to state that any term (as per metaphor-perspective) can be seen from the point of view of any other term. But insofar as terms are thus encouraged to participate in an orderly parliamentary development, the dialectic of this participation produces (in the observer who considers the whole from the standpoint of the participation of all the terms rather than from the standpoint of any one participant) a "resultant certainty" of a different quality, necessarily ironic, since it requires that all the sub-certainties be considered as neither true nor false, but *contributory* (as were we to think of the resultant certainty or "perspective of perspectives" as a noun, and to think of all the contributory voices as necessary modifiers of that noun).

To be sure, relativism is the constant *temptation* of either dialectic or drama (consider how often, for instance, Shakespeare is called a relativist). And historians for the most part *are relativistic*. But where one considers different historical characters from the standpoint of a total development, one could encourage each character to comment upon the others without thereby sacrificing a perspective upon the lot. This could be got particularly, I think, if historical characters themselves (i.e., periods or cultures treated as "individual persons") were considered never to begin or end, but rather to change in intensity or poignancy. History, in this sense, would be a dialectic of characters in which, for instance, we should never expect to see "feudalism" overthrown by "capitalism" and "capitalism" succeeded by some manner of national or international or non-national or neo-national or post-national socialism—but rather should note elements of all such positions (or "voices") existing always, but attaining greater clarity of expression or imperiousness of proportion at one period than another.

Irony is never Pharisaic, but there is a Pharisaic temptation in irony. To illustrate the point, I should like to cite a passage from a poet and critic who knows a good deal about irony, and who is discussing a poet who knows a good deal about irony—but in this particular instance, I submit, he is wrong. I refer to a passage in which Allen Tate characterizes the seduction scene in *The Waste Land* as "ironic" and the poet's attitude as that of "humility." (I agree that "humility" is the proper partner of irony—but I question whether the passage is ironic enough to embody humility.)

Mr. Tate characterizes irony as "that arrangement of experience, either premeditated by art or accidentally appearing in the affairs of men, which permits to the spectator an insight superior to that of the actor." And he continues:

> The seduction scene is the picture of modern and dominating man. The arrogance and pride of conquest of the "small house agent's clerk" are the badge of science, bumptious practicality, overweening secular faith. The very success of this conquest witnesses its aimless character; it succeeds as a wheel succeeds in turning; he can only conquer again.
>
> His own failure to understand his position is irony, and the poet's insight into it is humility. But for the grace of God, says the poet in effect, there go I. There is essentially the poetic attitude, an attitude that Eliot has been approaching with increasing purity.

We need not try to decide whether or not the poet was justified in feeling "superior" to the clerk. But we may ask how one could *possibly* exemplify an attitude of "humility" by feeling "superior"? There is, to be sure, a brand of irony, called "romantic irony," that might fit in with such a pattern—the kind of irony that did, as a matter of fact, arise as an aesthetic opposition to cultural philistinism, and in which the artist considered himself *outside of* and *superior to* the rôle he was rejecting. And though not "essentially *the* poetic attitude," it is essentially *a* poetic attitude, an attitude exemplified by much romantic art (a sort of pamphleteering, or external, attitude towards "the enemy").

True irony, however, irony that really does justify the attribute of "humility," is not "superior" to the enemy. (I might even here rephrase my discussion of Eliot in *Attitudes Toward History* by saying that Eliot's problem in religion has resided precisely in his attempt to convert romantic irony into classic irony, really to replace a state of "superiority" by a state of "humility"—and *Murder in the Cathedral* is a ritual aimed at precisely such purification of motives.) True irony, humble irony, is based upon a sense of fundamental kinship with the enemy, as one *needs* him, is *indebted* to him, is not merely outside him as an observer but contains him *within*, being consubstantial with him. This is the irony of Flaubert, when he recognizes that Madame Bovary is himself. One sees it in Thomas Mann—and in what he once called, when applying the term to another, "Judas psychology." And there was, if not the humility of strength, at least a humility of gentle surrender, in Anatole France.

In *The Waste Land*, the poet is not saying "there but for the grace of God go I." On the contrary, he is, if not thanking God, at least congratulating himself, that he is not like other men, such other men as this petty clerk. If this was "humility." then the Pharisee is Humble Citizen No. 1. With Newton, on the other hand, there was no "superiority" in his exclamation as he observed the criminal. He did not mean that that man was a criminal but he, Newton, thank God, was not; he meant that *he too was a criminal, but that the other man was going to prison for him.* Here was true irony-and-humility, since Newton was simultaneously both outside the criminal and within him.

"Superiority" in the dialectic can arise only in the sense that one may feel the need of *more characters* than the particular foolish characters under consideration. But in one sense he can *never* be superior, for he must realize that he also *needs this particular foolish character as one of the necessary modifiers*. Dialectic irony (or humility) here, we might even say, provides us with a kind of "technical equivalent for the doctrine of original sin." Folly and villainy are integral motives, necessary to wisdom or virtue. [2]

A third temptation of irony is its tendency towards the simplification of literalness. That is: although *all* the characters in a dramatic or dialectic development are necessary qualifiers of the definition, there is usually some one character that enjoys the rôle of *primus inter pares*. For whereas any of the characters may be viewed in terms of any other, this one character may be taken as the summarizing vessel, or synecdochic representative, of the development as a whole. This is the rôle of Socrates in the Platonic dialogue, for instance — and we could similarly call the proletariat the Socrates of the Marxist Symposium of History, as they are not merely equal participants along with the other characters, but also represent the *end* or *logic* of the development as a whole.

This "most representative" character thus has a dual function: one we might call "adjectival" and the other "substantial." The character is "adjectival," as embodying one of the qualifications necessary to the total definition, but is "substantial" as embodying the conclusions of the development as a whole. Irony is sacrificed to "the simplification of literalness" when this duality of rôle is neglected (as it may be neglected by either the reader, the writer, or both). In Marxism as a literally libertarian philosophy, for instance, slavery is "bad," and *is* so treated in the rhetoric of proletarian emancipation (e.g., "wage slavery"). Yet from the standpoint of the development as a whole, slavery must be treated ironically, as with Engel's formula: "Without the slavery of antiquity, no modern socialism." Utilization of the vanquished by enslavement, he notes, was a great cultural advance over the wasteful practice of slaying the vanquished.

5.

Irony, as approached through either drama or dialectic, moves us into the area of "law" and "justice" (the "necessity" or "inevitability" of the *lex talionis*) that involves matters of form in art (as form affects anticipation and fulfilment) and matters of prophecy and prediction in history. There is a level of generalization at which predictions about "inevitable" developments in history are quite justified. We may state with confidence, for instance, that what arose in time must fall in time (hence, that any given structure of society must "inevitably" perish). We may make such prophecy more precise, with the help of irony, in saying that the developments that led to the rise will, by the further course of their development, "inevitably" lead to the fall (true irony always, we hold, thus involving an "internal fatality," a principle operating from within, though its logic may also be grounded in the nature of the extrinsic scene, whose properties contribute to the same development.)

The point at which different casuistries appear (for fitting these "general laws of inevitability" to the unique cases of history) is the point where one tries to decide exactly what new characters, born of a given prior character, will be the "inevitable" vessels of the prior character's deposition. As an over-all ironic formula here, and one that has the quality of "inevitability," we could lay it down that "what goes forth as A returns as non-A." This is the basic pattern that places the essence of drama and dialectic in the irony of the "peripety," the strategic moment of reversal.

Notes

1 Unfortunately, we must modify this remark somewhat. Reduction, *as per scientific realism,* would be confined to but one direction. Reduction, that is, as the word is now generally used. But originally, "reduction" was used in ways that make it closer rather to the margin of its overlap upon "perspective," as anything considered in terms of anything else could be said to be "reduced"—or "brought back" ("referred")—to it, so that the consideration of art in terms of morality, politics, or religion could have been called "the reduction" or art to morality, or politics, or religion.
2 I would consider Falstaff a gloriously ironic conception because we are so at one with him in his vices, while he himself embodies his vices in a mode of identification or brotherhood that is all but religious. Falstaff would not simply rob a man, from without. He *identifies himself* with the victim of a theft; he *represents* the victim. He would not crudely steal a purse; rather, he *joins forces* with the owner of the purse—and it *is* only when the harsh realities of this imperfect world have imposed a brutally divisive clarity upon the situation, that Falstaff is left holding the purse. He produces a new quality, a state of synthesis or merger—and it so happens that, when this synthesis is finally dissociated again into its analytic components (the crudities of the realm of practical property relationships having reduced this state of qualitative merger to a state of quantitative division), the

issue as so simplified sums up to the fact that the purse has changed hands. *He* converts "thine" into "ours"—and it is "circumstances over which he has no control" that go to convert this "ours" into a "mine." A mere thief would have directly converted "thine" into "mine." It is the addition of these intermediate steps that makes the vital difference between a mere thief and Falstaff; for it is precisely these intermediate steps that mark him with a conviviality, a sociality, essentially religious—and in this *sympathetic* distortion of religious values resides the irony of his conception.

We might bring out the point sharply by contrasting Falstaff with Tartuffe. Tartuffe, like Falstaff, exploits the coöperative values for competitive ends. He too would convert "thine" into "mine" by putting it through the social alembic of "ours." But the conception of Tartuffe is not ironic, since he is pure hypocrite. He uses the religious values simply as a swindler. Tartuffe's piety, which he uses to gain the confidence of his victims, is a mere deception. Whereas Tartuffe is all competition and merely *simulates* the sentiments of coöperation, Falstaff is genuinely coöperative, sympathetic, a synecdochic part of his victim—but along with such rich gifts of identification, what is to prevent a purse from changing hands?

6.
RHETORIC RESTRAINED
Gérard Genette

> G.C.: *Three or four years ago, journals, reviews, and essays were full of the word "metaphor." The fashion has changed. "Metonymy" is now replacing "metaphor."*
> J.L.B.: *I don't think there is much to be gained from this difference.*
> G.C.: *Certainly not.*
> Georges Charbonnier,
> Entretiens avec Jorge Luis Borges

The academic year 1969–70 saw the almost simultaneous appearance of three texts, different in scope, but bearing titles so similar as to be symptomatic: I am referring to *Rhétorique générale*, published by the Liège group,[1] the original title of which was *Rhétorique généralisée;* an article by Michel Deguy, "Pour une théorie de la figure généralisée";[2] and another by Jacques Sojcher, "La métaphore généralisée.[3] Rhetoric-figure-metaphor: under the disavowing—or compensatory—cover of a pseudo-Einsteinian generalization, we have here, outlined in its principal stages, the (approximately) historical course of a discipline that has witnessed, over the centuries, the gradual contraction of its field of competence, or at least of action, Aristotle's *Rhetoric* made no claims to be "general" (still less "generalized"): yet in its range it was so, and so much so that a theory of figures did not yet merit any particular mention in it; just a few pages on comparison and metaphor, in one Book (out of three) devoted to style and composition, a tiny territory, an out-of-the-way region, lost in the immensity of an Empire. Nowadays we call general rhetoric what is in fact a treatise on figures.[4] And if we have so much to "generalize," it is obviously because we have restricted it too much: from Corax to our own day, the history of rhetoric has been that of a *generalized restriction*.

It was in the early Middle Ages, it seems, that the balance peculiar to ancient rhetoric, as represented in the works of Aristotle and, better still, of Quintilian, began to be lost: to begin with, the balance between the genres (deliberative, judicial, epidictic), because the death of the republican institutions, which Tacitus had already seen as one of the causes of the decline of eloquence,[5] brought with it the disappearance of the deliberative genre, and also, it seems, of the epidictic, so bound up with the major events of civic life; Martianus Capella and Isidore of Seville both noted these defections: "rhetorica est bene dicendi scientia in civilibus quaestionibus";[6] next the balance between the "parts" (*inventio, dispositio, elocutio*), because the rhetoric of the *trivium*,

---

Genette, Gérard. "Rhetoric Restrained," *Figures of Literary Discourse*, Translated by Alan Sheridan, Introduction by Marie-Rose Logan. New York: Columbia University Press, 1982: 103–126.

crushed between grammar and dialectic, soon came to be confined to the study of *elocutio*, the ornaments of discourse, *colores rhetorici*. The classical period, especially in France, and even more especially in the eighteenth century, inherited this situation and carried it still further by constantly giving pride of place in its examples to the literary (and particularly poetic) corpus of oratory; Homer and Vergil (and soon Racine) supplanted Demosthenes and Cicero, and rhetoric tended to become for the most part a study of the poetic *lexis*.

What is needed, to fill out and correct this more than cavalier account,[7] is an immense historical investigation, which is well beyond my competence, but of which Roland Barthes has provided a sketch in his seminar at the École pratique des Hautes Études.[8] I would like to do no more here than to draw attention to the later stages of this movement—those marking the passage from classical rhetoric to modern neo-rhetoric—and to consider what their significance might be.

The first of these stages was the publication, in 1730, of César Dumarsais' treatise *Des Tropes*. This work did not claim of course to cover the entire field of rhetoric, and the point of view adopted by the grammarian of the *Encyclopédie* is not even exactly that of a rhetorician, but rather that of a linguist and, to be more precise, of a semantician (in the sense that Michel Bréal was later to give this term), as is made quite clear by his subtitle: ". . . or concerning the different senses in which the same word may be taken in the same language." But by its very existence and the prestige it acquired, it did much to place at the center of rhetorical studies, not so much the theory of figures in general but, in an even more specific way, that of the figures of meaning, "by which one gives a word a signification that is not exactly the literal signification of that word," and therefore to place at the center of historical thought the opposition between the *literal* and *the figurative* (which is dealt with in chapters VI and VII of the first part), and therefore to turn rhetoric into a consideration of figuration, a turnstile of the figurative defined as the other of the literal, and of the literal defined as the other of the figurative—and to enclose it for a long time to come in this meticulous vertigo.

Nothing illustrates better the influence of this *tropological reduction* on the development of French rhetoric than the work of the man who prided himself, nearly a hundred years later, not only on taking over, but also on destroying the legacy of Dumarsais by an *Aufhebung* that he first called *Commentaire raisonné des tropes* (1818), then *Traité générale des figures du discours* (1821–27). Indeed the way Pierre Fontanier "took over" from Dumarsais is, from the viewpoint that concerns us here, remarkably ambiguous: on the one hand, Fontanier once again enlarged the field of study to cover all figures, tropes and non-tropes; but, on the other hand, returning with increased vigor (by the exclusion of catachresis, as a non-figurative trope, because it is not a substitution: *feuille de papier*, for example, in which *feuille* does not replace any literal word) to the criterion of substitution that governs the tropological activity, and extending it to the figurative field as a whole (hence the exclusion of a "so-called figure of thought," on the grounds that it expresses nothing more than what it says), he tends to make of the trope the model for all figures, and therefore to stress still further, by giving it *de jure* foundation, the *de facto* restriction begun by his predecessor. Dumarsais was doing no more than offering a treatise on tropes; Fontanier imposes (by the adoption of his manual in public education) a treatise on figures, tropes, and "other than tropes" (the lameness of this terminology is eloquent enough in itself), the *object* of which is indeed all figures, but the *principle* (the criterion of admission and exclusion) of which is fundamentally and purely tropological.[9]

So the trope is installed at the paradigmatic heart of what is no longer simply a theory of figures but, through the effect of a singular and apparently universal lexical scarcity, will nevertheless continue to be called rhetoric:[10] a good example of generalizing synecdoche. But this first move by Fontanier was followed by another, which confirms him in his role as founder of modern rhetoric,[11] or rather of the modern idea of rhetoric, which is based on the classification or, in the language of the time, the *division* of the tropes.

Dumarsais had drawn up a rather chaotic and sometimes redundant list of eighteen tropes, which was duly shortened without too much trouble by reducing the doubles (irony-antiphrasis) or subspecies (antonomasia, euphemism, hypallage) and by including in other classes such "supposed tropes" as metalepsis, periphrasis, or onomatopoeia. But he had also suggested, in a special chapter,[12] which, curiously enough, had had no effect on the arrangement of his own inventory, the possibility of a "subordination of the tropes," that is to say, an indication of the "rank that they must occupy in relation to one another." Vossius had already posed such a hierarchy, in which all the tropes would be related, "like species to genera," to four principles; metaphor, metonymy, synecdoche, and irony. Dumarsais sketches a new conflation of synecdoche and metonymy, which are seen as connected since they are both based on a *relation,* or *connection* (together with "dependence" in the case of synecdoche), which is neither the relation of *resemblance* of metaphor nor the relation of *contrast* of irony: it was implicitly to "subordinate" all tropes to the free associative principles of similarity, contiguity, and opposition. Fontanier restored to the metonymy/synecdoche distinction all its hierarchical function, but on the other hand he excluded irony, on the grounds that it was a figure "of expression" (a trope in several words and therefore a pseudo-trope), and above all he was not content to "relate" all tropes to the three fundamental genera that he allowed to survive: he recognized only those three, the rest being a confused mass made up of non-figurative tropes., non-trope figures, and even non-figures and non-tropes. The only tropes worthy of the name were therefore (in order) metonymy, synecdoche, and metaphor. As one may already have realized, all that was needed now was to add up these two subtractions—Dumarsais' connection between metonymy and synecdoche and Fontainier's elimination of irony—to obtain the exemplary figurative pair, the irreplaceable bookends of our own modern rhetoric: metaphor and metonymy.

This new reduction was acquired, if I am not mistaken, in the vulgate of Russian Formalism, with Boris Eichenbaum's work on Anna Akhmatova, which dates from 1923, including the metonymy = prose, metaphor = poetry equivalences. It turns up again with the same value in 1935 in Jakobson's article on Pasternak's prose, and above all in his text of 1956, "Two Aspects of Language and Two Types of Aphasia," in which the classical opposition analogy/contiguity (which, it should be remembered, concerns the *signifieds* in a relation of substitution in metaphor and metonymy; gold and corn, iron and sword) is confirmed by a perhaps overly bold assimilation to the strictly linguistic oppositions (which concern the signifiers) between paradigm and syntagma, equivalence and succession.

This episode is too close to us and too well known to be labored. Perhaps we should, on the other hand, ask ourselves why so drastic a reduction could have been effected within the figurative domain itself. I have already remarked on the gradual displacement of the rhetorical object of eloquence toward poetry,[13] already very marked in the classical writers, which leads one's meta-rhetorical attention to be concentrated preferably on figures with a stronger semantic tenor (figures of signification in a single word) and, among these, preferably on figures of a "sensory" semanticism[14] (the spatio-temporal relation, the relation of analogy), to the exclusion of tropes with a reputedly more intellectual semanticism like antiphrasis, litotes, or hyperbole, which have been more and more firmly excluded from the poetic field or more generally from the esthetic function of language. This shift of object, of an obviously historical nature, contributes therefore to giving pride of place to the two relations of contiguity (and/or of inclusion) and of resemblance. But one could easily detect other convergent movements, like the one to be found in Freud in his analysis of the "principles of association" in *Totem and Taboo*. In his *Esquisse d'une théorie de la magie* (1902) Marcel Mauss, in line with a tradition that goes back to E. B. Tylor, defined the laws of magical association in terms of three associationist principles of contiguity, similarity, and contrast. In *Totem and Taboo* (1912), Freud, repeating on another terrain Fontanier's gesture of excluding irony from the list of tropes, keeps as principles of association only the first two, which in any case are subsumed together under the "more comprehensive" concept of *contact*, similarity being defined, somewhat amusingly as it happens, as a "contact in the metaphorical sense."[15]

The bringing together of synecdoche and metonymy had already, as we have seen, been proposed by Dumarsais, but the concept of "connection" was for him rather too broad (or too slack) to contain both the connections without "dependence" (that is to say, without inclusion) that govern metonymy and also the relations of inclusion that define synecdoche. The notion of *contiguity*, on the other hand, reveals or effects a choice in favor of "connection without dependence," and therefore a unilateral reduction of synecdoche to metonymy, which Jakobson makes explicit when he writes for example: "Uspensky had a penchant for metonymy, especially for synecdoche."[16] The justification for this gesture is given among others by Mauss in the text already mentioned: "The simplest form [of association by contiguity]," he says, "is the identification of the part with the whole."[17]

Yet it is not at all certain that one can legitimately regard inclusion, even in its most crudely spatial forms, as a particular case of contiguity. This reduction no doubt has its origin in an almost inevitable confusion between the relation of the part to the whole and the relation of this same part to the *other parts* that make up the whole: a relation, it might be said, of the part to the *remainder*. The sail is not contiguous to the ship, but it is contiguous to the mast and to the yard and, by extension, to the rest of the ship, to everything that is part of the ship except the sail itself. Most of the "dubious" cases derive from this always-open choice between considering either the relation of the part to the whole or that of the part to the remainder: hence the symbolic relation in its ancient etymon, in which one may read both a relation of contiguity between the two complementary halves of the *sumbolon,* and a relation of inclusion between each of these two halves and the whole that they constitute and reconstitute. Each demi-symbol both suggests the other and evokes their common totality. Similarly, one might read *ad libitum,* in the figure by attribute ("crown" for "monarch," for example), a metonymy or a synecdoche, depending on whether one regards the crown as simply linked to the monarch, or as forming part of him, by virtue of the implicit axiom: no monarch without a crown. One then sees that every metonymy can be converted into a synecdoche by appeal to the higher totality, and every synecdoche into a metonymy by recourse to the relations between constituent parts. The fact that each figure-event can be analysed in two ways at will certainly does not imply that these two ways are in fact one, any more than Archimedes is *in the same way* both a Prince and a geometrician, but one can see very well how in fact this kind of double membership might cause confusion. It remains of course to explain why this confusion has operated in one way rather than in the other, to the benefit of metonymy and not of synecdoche. It may be that here the pseudo-spatial notion of contiguity has played the role of a catalyst by proposing a model of the relation that is both simpler and more material than any other. But it should be noted once again that although this notion operates in favor of metonymy, it also effects, within the field of this figure, a new reduction; for many relations covered by classical metonymy (the effect for the cause and vice versa, the sign for the tiling, the instrument for the action, the physical for the moral, etc.) do not allow themselves so easily, except perhaps through metaphor, to be reduced to an effect of contact or spatial proximity: what kind of "contiguity" could be maintained by the heart and courage, the brain and intelligence, the bowels and mercy? To reduce every metonymy (*a fortiori* every synecdoche) to a pure spatial relation is obviously to restrict the play of these figures to their physical or sensory aspect alone, and here again one can see the privilege gradually acquired by poetic discourse in the field of rhetorical objects, and the displacement effected by this discourse itself, in the modern period, toward the more material forms of figuration.

To this gradual reduction of the figures of "connection" to the single model of spatial metonymy corresponds a noticeably symmetrical reduction on the other side (that of the figures of "resemblance"), which operates here to the benefit of metaphor alone. We know that the term metaphor tends increasingly to cover the whole of the analogical field: whereas the classical ethos saw in metaphor an implicit comparison,[18] modern thinking would tend to treat comparison as an explicit or motivated metaphor. The most typical example of this use is obviously to be found in Proust, who always called metaphor what in his work was generally pure comparison. Here again, the motives for the reduction appear fairly clearly in the perspective of a figuratics centered on poetic discourse or at least (as in Proust) on a poetics of discourse: we no longer have much use for Homeric comparisons, and the semantic concentration of the trope ensures its almost obvious esthetic superiority over the developed form of the figure. Mallarmé congratulated himself on having banished the words "like" and "as" from his vocabulary. Yet although explicit comparison is tending to desert poetic language, the same cannot be said, it should be remarked in passing, in literary discourse as a whole, and still less in spoken language, especially as the comparison can make up for the lack of intensity that characterizes it by an effect of semantic anomaly that metaphor can hardly allow itself under pain of remaining, in the absence of the compared, totally unintelligible. This effect in particular is what Jean Cohen calls inappropriateness.[19] There are famous examples like Eluard's line "La terre est bleue comme une orange" (the earth is blue as an orange), or Lautréamont's series of "beau comme . . ." (beautiful as . . .); one may also be reminded of the prevalence in popular language of arbitrary comparisons, "comme la lune" (like the moon), or antiphrastic ones, "aimable comme une porte de prison" (as pleasant as prison gates), "bronzé comme un cachet d'aspirine" (tanned as an aspirin tablet), "frisé comme un oeuf dur" (curly as a hard-boiled egg), or those deliriously farfetched ones, such as those to be found in Peter Cheyney, San Antonio, or Pierre Perret: "thighs open like a pious woman's missal." A theory of the figures of analogy excessively centered on the metaphoric form is doomed to neglect such effects, and others.

Lastly, it should be said that the reduction to the "metaphoric pole" of all the figures of analogy is detrimental not only to comparison, but also to several forms of figure the diversity of which does not seem to have been entirely appreciated until now. Metaphor and comparison are usually opposed in the name of the absence in one and the presence in the other of the compared term. This opposition does not seem to me to be very well formulated in these terms, for a syntagma of the type "pâtre promontoire" (promontory pasture—Hugo), or "soleil cou coupé" (sun neck cut—Aimé Césaire), which contains both a comparing and a compared element, is not regarded as a comparison, nor for that matter as a metaphor, and in the end has to be counted out for lack of a more complete analysis of the constituents of the figure of analogy. One should really consider the presence or absence not only of the comparing and compared elements ("vehicle" and "tenor," in I. A. Richards' vocabulary), also of the comparative modalizer ("like," "as," "to resemble," etc.), and of "motive" (ground) of the comparison. One then sees that what we generally call "comparison" can assume two quite different forms: an unmotivated comparison ("my love is like a flame"), and a motivated comparison ("my love burns like a flame), which is necessarily more limited in its analogical scope, since a single common seme (heat) is retained as motive, among others (light, lightness, mobility), which the unmotivated comparison might, at the very least, not exclude; one sees therefore that the distinction between these two forms is not entirely useless. It appears that the canonical comparison, under its two species, must include not only a comparing and a compared element, but also the modalizer without which one will be dealing with an *identification*,[20] motivated or not, either of the type "my love (is) a burning flame," or "my burning love (is) a flame" ("You are my proud and generous lion"), or of the type "my love (is) a flame" ("Achilles is a lion," "promontory pasture," already mentioned). The ellipsis of the compared element will determine two more forms of identification, one motivated, of the type "my ardent flame," and the other unmotivated, which is the metaphor in the strict sense: "my flame." Table 6.1 brings together these different forms, plus four elliptical, less canonical, but fairly conceivable states,[21] motivated or unmotivated comparisons

Table 6.1

Figures of Analogy	Compared	Motive	Modalizer	Comparing	Examples
Motivated comparison	+	+	+	+	*My love burns like a flame*
Unmotivated comparison	+		+	+	*My love is like a flame*
Motivated comparison without comparing'	+	+	+		*My love burns like . . .*
Motivated comparison without compared*		+	+	+	*. . . burning like a flame*
Unmotivated comparison without comparing*	+		+		*My love is like . . .*
Unmotivated comparison without compared'			+	+	*. . . like a flame*
Motivated identification	+	+		+	*My love (is) a burning flame*
Unmotivated identification	+			+	*My love (is) a flame*
Motivated identification without compared		+		+	*My burning flame*
Unmotivated identification without compared (metaphor)				+	*My flame*

*Elliptical states

with an ellipsis of the comparing element ("my love is burning like, . ." or "my love is like . . .") or the compared element (". . . like a burning flame," or ". . . like a flame"): these apparently hypothetical forms are not to be ignored, as Cohen has realized: who for example remembers the compared element of Lautréamont's "beautiful as . . ." series in which the disparity between the motive and the comparing element is obviously more important than the attribution of the total predicate to the Grand Duke of Virginia, the vulture, the beetle, Mervyn, or Maldoror himself?

This rather rough-and-ready table has no other aim than to show the extent to which metaphor is merely one form among many others,[22] and that its promotion to the rank of figure of analogy *par excellence* is the result of a sort of takeover. But we still have to consider one last reductionist movement,[23] by which again, metaphor, absorbing its ultimate adversary, turns itself into the "trope of tropes" (Sojcher), "the figure of figures" (Deguy), the kernel, the heart, and ultimately the essence and almost the whole of rhetoric.

Notes

1. Groupe μ, *Rhétorique générale* (Paris: Larousse, 1970).
2. Michel Deguy, "Pour une théorie de la figure généralisée," *Critique* (October 1969).
3. Jacques Sojcher, "La métaphore généralisée," *Revue internationale de philosophie*, no. 87, p. 1.

4. This "we" is not a polite form, used in accordance with the figure called *communication,* The reproach, if such it be, is addressed here just as much to its author, who, in the present relative abuse of the notion of *figure,* would find it difficult to maintain his complete innocence. The criticism here will take the disguised (and convenient) form of self-criticism.
5. Tacitus, *Dialogue of the Orators,* xxxvi–xxxvii.
6. Ernst Robert Curtius, *European Literature and the Latin Middle Ages,* Willard R. Trask, tr. (Princeton: Princeton University Press, 1973), p. 75.
7. A. Kibédi Varga, *Rhétorique et littérature* (Paris: Didier, 1970), pp. 16–17, challenges the notion that classical French rhetoric is, as I have said elsewhere, "above all a rhetoric of *elocutio,*" and the whole of his book demonstrates in effect the interest shown by certain seventeenth- and eighteenth-century rhetoricians in the techniques of argument and composition. This is a question of relative emphasis and proportion, and also of one's choice of references: Varga relies heavily on Barry, Legras, Crevier, and me on Lamy, Dumarsais, Fontanier. One would have to examine systematically, for example, the hundred or so titles collected by P. Kuentz (*XVIIe Siècle,* no. 80–81). It also seems to me that the part devoted to *elocutio,* even when it was not the largest, was already at that time the most vivid, the most original in relation to the ancient models and therefore the most productive (despite the new material provided by the sermon). Perhaps this is an effect of projection, but Varga himself brings grist to this mill by noting that, as early as the sixteenth century, Ramus suggested bringing *inventio* and *dispositie* under dialectics, leaving to rhetoric only the art of *elocution.*
8. Roland Barthes, 'L'ancienne rhétorique,' *Communications* (December 1970), vol. 16.
9. I refer here to my Introduction to the new edition of Fontanier's *Figures du discours* (Paris: Flammarion, 1968).
10. We must overcome, as best we can, this scarcity: thus I will propose to call this part of rhetoric *figuratics,* which has the virtue at least of being unequivocal.
11. A symbolic role, it should be said, for if his handbook was widely used in schools throughout the nineteenth century, its later influence seems to have been almost nonexistent, until his recent resurrection.
12. César Dumarsais, *Traité des tropes* (1730), II, ch. 21.
13. Or toward written prose regarded from the point of view of its esthetic function as is the case with modern stylistics.
14. We should recall Lamy's words, "Metaphors make all things sensible."
15. "The two principles of association—similarity and contiguity—are both included in the more comprehensive concept of 'contact.' Association by contiguity is contact in the literal sense; association by similarity is contact in the metaphorical sense. The use of the same word for the two kinds of relation is no doubt accounted for by some identity in the psychical processes concerned which we have not yet grasped." Sigmund Freud, *Totem and Taboo* (1912) in *Standard Edition,* (London: Hogarth Press, 1953–56) 13:85. This dichotomy obviously revives the opposition set up by Frazer between *imitation* and *contagion.* However, from *The Interpretation of Dreams* of 1900 and *Jokes and Their Relation to the Unconscious* of 1905, we know how large a role Freud gave to "representation by the opposite" in the work of the dream and of the joke, and how the figure of antiphrasis returns later in the rhetoric of denial in the article "Negation" of 1925.
16. Roman Jakobson and Morris Halle, *Fundamentals of Language* (The Hague: Mouton, 1956), p. 80. The reduction is already apparent, incidentally, in Dumarsais, *Tropes,* II::4—"Synecdoche, then, is a species of metonymy by which ... I take the *more* for the less, or the *less* for the *more.*"
17. Marcel Mauss, *Sociologie et anthropologie,* (Paris: P.U.F., 1950), p. 57. See also Jakobson, "Remarques sur la prose de Pasternak," French translation in *Poétique* (1971), 7:317: "The passage from the part to the whole and from the whole to the part is only a particular case of the process [of association by contiguity]."
18. "... by virtue of a comparison that is in the mind" (Dumarsais, *Tropes,* II, 10).
19. Jean Cohen, "La comparaison poétique: essai de systématique," *Langages* (December 1968), vol. 12.

20. I borrowed this term from Danielle Bouverot, "Comparaison et Métaphore," Le *Français moderne* (1969). The author proposes a division of "images" (figures of analogy) into four types: *comparison* ("night thickened like a wall"), which corresponds to our motivated comparison; *attenuated identification* ("and that immense night like chaos of old"), which corresponds to our unmotivated comparison; *identification* ("night, surly hostess"), which I specify as an unmotivated identification; *metaphor* ("listen to the gentle steps of night"). The essential difference between the two classifications concerns the importance accorded to the presence or absence of the modalizer, which determines for me the distinction between comparison and identification.
21. Marked here with an asterisk.
22. In particular it neglects the role of the copula and its various forms. On this subject cf. Christine Brooke-Rose, *A Grammar of Metaphor* (London: Secker and Warburg, 1958).
23. The adjective [last] is obviously not to be taken here in a strictly chronological sense. In the movement that I am describing, certain stages overlap, and Proust for example, represents a more "advanced" stage of restriction than Jakobson.

7.
CONCEPTUAL METAPHOR IN EVERYDAY LANGUAGE
George Lakoff and Mark Johnson

UNTIL recently philosophers have tended to berate metaphor as irrational and dangerous, or to ignore it, reducing it to the status of a subsidiary problem in the philosophy of language. Literal language, assumed to be mutually exclusive with metaphor, has been taken to be the real stuff of philosophy, the domain where issues of meaning and truth arise and can be dealt with. At best, metaphor is treated as if it were always the result of some operation performed upon the literal meaning of the utterance. The phenomenon of "conventional metaphor," where much of our ordinary conceptual system and the bulk of our everyday conventional language are structured and understood primarily in metaphorical terms, has gone either unnoticed or undiscussed.

As we will show directly, conventional metaphors are pervasive in our ordinary everyday way of thinking, speaking, and acting. We feel that an understanding of conventional metaphor and the way that metaphor structures our ordinary conceptual system will ultimately provide a new "experientialist" perspective on classical philosophical problems, such as the nature of meaning, truth, rationality, logic, and knowledge. In this present paper we can only focus on the nature and role of metaphor in our conceptual system, with a few suggestions concerning the larger implications of our account.[1]

I. Concepts That We Live By

Metaphor is for most people a device of the poetic imagination and the rhetorical flourish—a matter of extraordinary rather than ordinary language. Moreover, metaphor is typically viewed as characteristic of language alone, a matter of words rather than thought or action. For this reason, most people think they can get along perfectly well without metaphor. We have found, on the contrary, that metaphor is pervasive in everyday life, not just in language, but in thought and action. Our ordinary conceptual system, in terms of which we both think and act, is fundamentally metaphorical in nature.

The concepts that govern our thought are not just matters of the intellect. They also govern our everyday functioning, down to the most mundane details. Our concepts structure what we perceive, how we get around in the world, and how we relate to other people. Our conceptual system thus plays a central role in defining our everyday

---

Lakoff, George and Mark Johnson. "Conceptual Metaphor in Everyday Language," *The Journal of Philosophy*, Vol. 77, Issue 8, 1980: 453–486.

realities. If we are right in suggesting that our conceptual system is largely metaphorical, then the way we think, what we experience, and what we do every day is very much a matter of metaphor.

But our conceptual system is not something that we are normally aware of. In most of the little things we do every day, we simply think and act more or less automatically along certain lines. Just what these lines are is by no means obvious. One way to find out is by looking at language. Since communication is based on the same conceptual system in terms of which we think and act, language is an important source of evidence for what that system is like.

Primarily on the basis of linguistic evidence, we have found that most of our ordinary conceptual system is metaphorical in nature. And we have found a way to begin to identify in detail just what the metaphors are that structure how we perceive, how we think, and what we do.

To give some idea of what it could mean for a concept to be metaphorical and for such a concept to structure an everyday activity, let us start with the concept of an ARGUMENT, and the conceptual metaphor ARGUMENT IS WAR. This metaphor is reflected in our everyday language by a wide variety of expressions:

> ARGUMENT IS WAR
> Your claims are *indefensible.*
> He *attacked every weak point* in my argument.
> His criticisms were *right on target.*
> I *demolished* his argument.
> I've never *won* an argument with him.
> You disagree? Okay, *shoot!*
> If you use that *strategy,* he'll *wipe you out.*
> He *shot down* all my arguments.

It is important to see that we don't just *talk* about arguments in terms of war. We can actually win or lose arguments. We see the person we are arguing with as an opponent. We attack his positions and we defend our own. We gain and lose ground. We plan and use strategies. If we find a position indefensible, we can abandon it and take a new line of attack. Many of the things we *do* in arguing are partially structured by the concept of war. Though there is no physical battle, there is a verbal battle, and the structure of an argument—attack, defense, counterattack, etc.—reflects this. It is in this sense that we live by the ARGUMENT IS WAR metaphor in this culture; it structures the actions we perform in arguing.

Try to imagine a culture where arguments were not viewed in terms of war, where no one won or lost, where there was no sense of attacking or defending, gaining or losing ground. Imagine a culture where an argument is viewed as a dance, with the participants as performers, and the goal being to perform in a balanced and aesthetic way. In such a culture, people would view arguments differently, experience them differently, carry them out differently, and talk about them differently. But *we* would probably not view them as arguing at all. It would be strange even to call what they were doing "arguing." Perhaps the most neutral way of describing this difference between their culture and ours would be to say that we have a discourse form structured in terms of battle and they have one structured in terms of dance.

This is an example of what it means for a metaphorical concept, namely, ARGUMENT IS WAR, partially to structure what we do and how we understand what we do when we argue. *The essence of metaphor is understanding and experiencing one kind of thing or experience in terms of another.* It is not that arguments are a subspecies of wars. Arguments and wars are different kinds of things—verbal discourse and armed conflict—and the actions performed are different kinds of actions. But ARGUMENT is partially structured, understood, performed, and talked about in terms of WAR. The concept is metaphorically structured, the activity is metaphorically structured, and consequently, the language is metaphorically structured.

Moreover, this is the *ordinary* way of having an argument and talking about one. The normal way *for us* to talk about attacking a position is to use the words 'attack a position'. Our conventional ways of talking about arguments presuppose a metaphor we are hardly ever conscious of. The metaphor is not merely in the words we use—it is in our very concept of an argument. The language of argument is not poetic, fanciful, or rhetorical, but rather literal. We talk about arguments that way because we conceive of them that way—and we act according to the way we conceive of things.

II. The Systematicity of Metaphorical Concepts

Arguments usually follow patterns; that is, there are certain things we typically do and do not do in arguing. The fact that we in part conceptualize arguments in terms of battle systematically influences the shape arguments take and the way we talk about what we do in arguing. Because the metaphorical concept is systematic, the language we use to talk about that aspect of the concept is systematic.

We saw in the ARGUMENT IS WAR metaphor that expressions from the vocabulary of war, e.g., 'attack a position', 'indefensible', 'strategy', 'new line of attack', 'win', 'gain ground', etc. form a systematic way of talking about the battling aspects of arguing. It is no accident that these expressions mean what they mean when we use them to talk about arguments. A portion of the conceptual network of battle partially characterizes the concept of an argument, and the language follows suit. Since metaphorical expressions in our language are tied to metaphorical concepts in a systematic way, we can use metaphorical linguistic expressions to study the nature of metaphorical concepts and to gain an understanding of the metaphorical nature of our activities.

To get an idea of how metaphorical expressions in everyday language can give us insight into the metaphorical nature of the concepts that structure our everyday activities, let us consider the metaphorical concept TIME IS MONEY as it is reflected in contemporary English:

> TIME IS MONEY
> You're *wasting* my time.
> This gadget will *save* you hours.
> I don't *have* the time to *give* you.
> How do you *spend* your time these days?

That flat tire *cost* me an hour.
I've *invested* a lot of time in her.
I don't *have enough* time to *spare* for that.
You're *running out* of time.
You need to *budget* your time.
Put aside some time for ping pong.
Is that *worth your while*?
Do you *have* much time *left*?
You don't *use* your time *profitably*.
I *lost* a lot of time when I got sick.
Thank you for your time.

Time in our culture is a valuable commodity. It is a limited resource that we use to accomplish our goals. Because of the way that the concept of work has developed in modern Western culture, where work is typically associated with the time it takes and time is precisely quantified, it has become customary to pay people by the hour, week, or year. In our culture TIME IS MONEY in many ways: telephone message units, hourly wages, hotel room rates, yearly budgets, interest on loans, and paying your debt to society by serving time. These practices are relatively new in the history of the human race and by no means exist in all cultures. They have arisen in modern industrialized societies and structure our basic everyday activities in a very profound way. Corresponding to the fact that we *act* as if time were a valuable commodity, a limited resource, even money, so we *conceive* of time that way. Thus we understand and experience time as the kind of thing that can be spent, wasted, budgeted, invested wisely or poorly, saved or squandered.

TIME IS MONEY, TIME IS A LIMITED RESOURCE, and TIME IS A VALUABLE COMMODITY are all metaphorical concepts. They are metaphorical since we are using our everyday experience with money, limited resources, and valuable commodities to conceptualize time. This isn't a necessary way for human beings to conceptualize time; it is tied to our culture. There are cultures where time is none of these things.

The metaphorical concepts TIME IS MONEY, TIME IS A RESOURCE, and TIME IS A VALUABLE COMMODITY form a single system based on subcategorization, since in our society money is a limited resource and limited resources are valuable commodities. These subcategorization relationships characterize what we will call "entailment relationships" between the metaphors, TIME IS MONEY entails that TIME IS A LIMITED RESOURCE, which entails that TIME IS A VALUABLE COMMODITY. We can see the relationship in the following diagram:

MONEY	TIME IS MONEY
is	entails
A LIMITED RESOURCE	TIME IS A LIMITED RESOURCE
is	entails
A VALUABLE COMMODITY	TIME IS A VALUABLE COMMODITY

We are adopting the practice of using the most specific metaphorical concept, in this case TIME IS MONEY, to characterize the entire system, since TIME IS MONEY entails TIME IS A LIMITED RESOURCE and TIME IS A VALUABLE COMMODITY. Of the expressions

Conceptual Metaphor in Everyday Language

listed under the TIME IS MONEY metaphor, some refer specifically to money ('spend', 'invest', 'budget', 'profitably', 'cost'), others to limited resources ('use', 'use up', 'have enough of', 'run out of'), and still others to valuable commodities ('have', 'give', 'lose', 'thank you for'). This is an example of the way in which metaphorical entailments can characterize a coherent system of metaphorical concepts and a corresponding coherent system of metaphorical expressions for those concepts.[2]

III. Metaphorical Systematicity: Highlighting and Hiding

The very systematicity that allows us to comprehend one aspect of a concept in terms of another (e.g., comprehending an aspect of arguing in terms of battle) will necessarily hide other aspects of the concept. In allowing us to focus on one aspect of a concept (e.g., the battling aspects of arguing), a metaphorical concept can keep us from focusing on other aspects of the concept which are not coherent with that metaphor. For example, in the midst of a heated argument, where we are intent on attacking our opponent's position and defending our own, we can lose sight of the more cooperative aspects involved in an argument. Someone who is arguing with you can be viewed as giving you his time, a valuable commodity, in an effort at mutual understanding. But when we are preoccupied with the battle aspects, we will most often lose sight of the cooperative aspects.

A far more subtle case of how a metaphorical concept can hide an aspect of our experience can be seen in what Michael Reddy [3] has called the "conduit metaphor." Reddy observes that our language about language is structured roughly by the following complex metaphor: (i) ideas (or meanings) are objects; (ii) linguistic expressions are containers; (iii) communication is sending—the speaker puts ideas (objects) into words (containers) and sends them (along a conduit) to a hearer who takes the idea-objects out of the word-containers. Reddy documents this with over one hundred *types* of expressions in English, which he estimates account for at least seventy per cent of the expressions we use to talk about language. Here are some examples:

> THE CONDUIT METAPHOR
> It's hard to *get* that *idea* across to him.
> I *gave* you that idea.
> Your reasons *came through* to us.
> It's difficult to *put* my ideas *into* words.
> When you *have* a good idea, try to *capture* it immediately *in* words.
> Try to *pack* more thought *into* fewer words.
> You can't simply *stuff* ideas *into* a sentence any old way.
> The meaning is right there *in* the words.
> Don't *force* your meanings *into* the wrong words.
> His words *carry* little meaning.
> The introduction *has* a great deal of thought-*content*.
> Your words seem *hollow*.
> The sentence is *without* meaning.
> The idea is *buried in* terribly dense paragraphs.

In examples like these it is far more difficult to see that there is anything hidden by the metaphor, or even to see that there is a metaphor here at all. This is so much the conventional way of thinking about language that it is sometimes hard to imagine that it might not fit reality. But if we look at what the conduit metaphor entails, we can see some of the ways in which it masks aspects of the communicative process.

First, the LINGUISTIC EXPRESSIONS ARE CONTAINERS FOR MEANINGS aspect of the metaphor entails that words and sentences have meanings in themselves, independent of any context or speaker. The MEANINGS ARE OBJECTS part of the metaphor, for example, entails that meanings have an existence independent of people and contexts. The part of the metaphor that says that LINGUISTIC EXPRESSIONS ARE CONTAINERS FOR MEANING entails that words (and sentences) have meanings, again independent of contexts and speakers. These metaphors are appropriate in many situations—those where context differences don't matter and where all the participants in the conversation understand the sentences in the same way. These two entailments are exemplified by sentences like "The meaning is *right there in* the words," which, according to the conduit metaphor, can correctly be said of any sentence. But there are many cases where context does matter. Here is a celebrated example recorded in actual conversation by Pamela Downing: "Please sit in the apple-juice seat." In isolation this sentence has no meaning at all, since the compound 'apple-juice seat' is not a conventional way of referring to any kind of object. But the sentence made perfect sense in the context in which it was uttered: An overnight guest came down to breakfast. There were four place settings, three with orange juice and one with apple juice. It was clear what the apple-juice seat was. And even the next morning, when there was no apple juice, it was still clear which seat was the apple-juice seat.

In addition to sentences that have no meaning without context, there are cases where a single sentence will mean different things to different people. Consider: "We need new alternative sources of energy." This means something very different to the president of Mobil Oil than it does to the president of Friends of the Earth. The meaning is not right there in the sentence—it matters a lot who is saying or listening to the sentence and what his social and political attitudes are. The conduit metaphor does not fit cases where context is required to determine whether the sentence has any meaning at all, and, if so, what meaning it has.

These examples show that the metaphorical concepts we have looked at provide us with a partial understanding of what communication, argument, and time are, and that in so doing they hide other aspects of these concepts. It is important to see that the metaphorical structuring involved here is partial, not total. If it were total, one concept would *be* the other, would not merely be understood in terms of it. For example, time isn't actually money. If you *spend your time* trying to do something and it doesn't work, you can't *get your time back*. There are no *time banks*. I can *give* you *a lot of time*, but you can't *give me back the same time*, though you can *give me back the same amount of time*. And so on. Thus, part of a metaphorical concept does not and cannot fit.

On the other hand, metaphorical concepts can be extended beyond the range of ordinary literal ways of thinking and talking into the range of what is called figurative, poetic, colorful, or fanciful thought and language. Thus, if ideas are objects, we can *dress them up in fancy clothes, juggle them, line them up nice and neat,* etc. So when we say that a concept is structured by a metaphor, we mean that it is partially structured, and that it can be extended in some ways but not others.

IV. Types of Metaphor: Structural, Orientational, Physical

In order to see in more detail what is involved in the metaphorical structuring of a concept or system of concepts, it is useful to identify three basic domains of conceptual structure and to trace some of the systematic connections among and within them. These three domains—physical, cultural, and intellectual—are only roughly divided, because they cannot be sharply delineated and usually interact in significant ways.

So far we have examined what we might call "structural" metaphors, cases where one concept is metaphorically structured in terms of another (e.g., ARGUMENT is structured in terms of WAR). Structural metaphors often involve using a concept from one domain (WAR as a physical or cultural phenomenon) to structure a concept from another domain (ARGUMENT as primarily an intellectual concept, but with cultural content). But before we can look more closely at the various domains of conceptual structure, it is important to see that there are what might be called "physical" and "orientational" metaphors, in addition to structural metaphors of the conventional type. Briefly, "physical" metaphors involve the projection of entity or substance status upon something that does not have that status inherently. Such conventional metaphors allow us to view events, activities, emotions, ideas, etc., as entities for various purposes (e.g., in order to refer to them, categorize them, group them, or quantify them). For example, we find physical metaphors such as:

> My *fear of insects* is driving my wife crazy. (referring)
> You've got *too much hostility* in you. (quantifying)
> The *brutality of war* dehumanizes us all. (identifying aspects)
> The *pressures of his responsibilities* caused his breakdown. (identifying causes)
> Here's what to do to ensure *fame and fortune.* (setting goals and motivating actions)

Physical metaphors such as these are hardly ever noticed, because they are so basic to our everyday conceptualizing and functioning. But they are, nevertheless, conventional metaphors by means of which we understand either nonphysical or not clearly bounded things as entities. In most cases such metaphors involve the use of a concept from the physical domain to structure a concept from the cultural or intellectual domains.

A third kind of conventional metaphor is the "orientational" metaphor, which does not structure one concept in terms of another, but instead organizes a whole system of concepts with respect to one another. We call them "orientational" metaphors because most of them have to do with spatial orientation: UP-DOWN, FRONT-BACK, IN-OUT, ON-OFF, DEEP-SHALLOW, CENTRAL-PERIPHERAL. These spatial orientations arise from the facts that we have bodies of the sort we have and that they function as they do in our physical environment. Orientational metaphors give a concept a spatial orientation, for example, HAPPY IS UP. The fact that the concept HAPPY is oriented UP leads to English expressions like "I'm feeling up today."

In order to examine the way in which metaphors provide structure across the different domains of concepts (physical, cultural, intellectual) we shall focus briefly on orientational metaphors, as representative examples. Such metaphorical orientations are not arbitrary. They have a basis in our physical and cultural experience. Though the polar oppositions UP-DOWN, IN-OUT, etc. are physical in nature, the orientational metaphors can vary from culture to culture. For example, some cultures orient the future in front of us; others orient it in back. We will be looking at UP-DOWN spatialization metaphors, which have been studied intensively by William Nagy,[4] as an illustration. In each case, we will give a brief hint of how each metaphorical concept might have arisen from our physical and cultural experience. These accounts are meant to be suggestive and plausible, rather than definitive.

(1) Happy Is Up; Sad Is Down

I'm feeling up. That boosted my spirits. My spirits rose. You're in high spirits. Thinking about her always gives me a lift. I'm feeling down. I'm depressed. He's really low these days. I fell into a depression. My spirits sank.

Physical basis: Drooping posture typically goes along with sadness and depression, erect posture with a positive emotional state.

(2) Conscious Is Up; Unconscious Is Down

Get up. Wake up. I'm up already. He rises early in the morning. He fell asleep. He dropped off to sleep. He's under hypnosis. He sank down into a coma.

Physical basis: Humans and most animals sleep lying down and stand erect when they wake up.

(3) Health and Life Are Up; Sickness and Death Are Down

He's at the peak of health. Lazarus rose from the dead. He's in top shape. As to his health, he's way up there. He fell ill. He's sinking fast. He came down with the flu. His health is declining. He dropped dead.

Physical basis: Serious illness forces us physically to lie down. When you're dead you are physically down.

(4) Having Control or Force Is Up; Being Subject to Control or Force Is Down

I have control over her. I am on top of the situation. He's in a superior position. He's at the height of his power. He's in the high command. His power rose. He's in a dominating position. He ranks above me in strength. He is under my control. He fell from power. His power is on the decline. He's in an inferior position.

Physical basis: Physical size typically correlates with physical strength, and the victor in a fight is typically on top.

(5) More Is Up; Less Is Down

The number of books printed each year keeps going up. You made a high number of mistakes. My income rose last year. There is an overabundance of food in this country. My knowledge keeps increasing. The amount of artistic activity in this state has gone down in the past year. His number of errors is incredibly low. His income fell last year. He is underage. If you're too hot, turn the heat down.

Physical basis: If you add more of a substance or of physical objects to a container or pile, the level goes up.

(6) Foreseeable Future Events Are Up (and Ahead)

The up-and-coming events are listed in the paper. What's coming up this week? I'm afraid of what's up ahead of us. What's up?

Physical basis: Normally our eyes are in the direction in which we typically move (ahead, forward). As an object approaches a person (or the person approaches the object), the object appears larger. Since the ground is perceived as being fixed, the top of the object appears to be moving *upward* in the person's field of vision.

(7) High Status Is Up; Low Status Is Down

He has a high position. She'll rise to the top. He's at the peak of his career. He's climbing the ladder. He has little upward mobility. He has a low position. She fell in status.

Social and physical basis: Status is correlated with power (social) and power is UP (physical).

(8) Good Is Up; Bad Is Down

Things are looking up. We hit a peak last year, but it's been going downhill ever since. Things are at an all-time low. The quality of life is high these days.

Physical basis for personal well-being: HAPPINESS, HEALTH, LIFE, and CONTROL—the things that principally characterize what is GOOD for a person—are all UP.

(9) Virtue Is Up; Depravity Is Down

He is high-minded. She has high standards. She is upright. She is an upstanding citizen. That was a low trick. Don't be underhanded. I wouldn't stoop to that. That would be beneath me. He fell into the abyss of depravity. That was a low-down thing to do.

Physical and social basis: GOOD IS UP for a person (physical basis), together with the SOCIETY IS A PERSON metaphor (in the version where you are *not* identifying with your society). To be virtuous is to act in accordance with the standards set by the society-person to maintain its well-being. VIRTUE IS UP because virtuous actions correlate with social well-being from the society-person's point of view. Since socially based metaphors are part of the culture, it's the society-person's point of view that counts.

(10) Rational Is Up; Emotional Is Down

The discussion fell to the emotional level, but I raised it back up to the rational plane. We put our feelings aside and had a high-level intellectual discussion of the matter. He couldn't rise above his emotions.

Physical and cultural basis: In this culture people view themselves as being in control over animals, plants, and their physical environment, and it is their unique ability to reason that places human beings above other animals and gives them this control. CONTROL IS UP, which has a physical basis, thus provides a basis for MAN IS UP, and therefore for RATIONAL IS UP.

On the basis of these examples, we suggest the following conclusions about the experiential grounding, the coherence, and the systematicity of metaphorical concepts:

(i) Most of our fundamental concepts are organized in terms of one or more spatialization metaphors.

(ii) There is an internal systematicity to each spatialization metaphor. For example, HAPPY IS UP defines a coherent system, rather than a number of isolated and random cases. (An example of an incoherent system would be one where, say, "I'm feeling up" meant "I'm feeling happy," but "My spirits rose" meant "I became sadder").

(iii) There is an over-all external systematicity among the various spatialization metaphors, which defines coherence among them. Thus, GOOD IS UP gives an UP orientation to general well-being, which is coherent with special cases like HAPPY IS UP, HEALTHY IS UP, ALIVE IS UP, CONTROL IS UP. STATUS IS UP is coherent with CONTROL IS UP.

(iv) Spatialization metaphors are rooted in physical and cultural experience. They are not randomly assigned.

(v) There are many possible physical and social bases for metaphors. Coherence within the over-all system seems to be part of the reason why one is chosen and not another. For example, happiness also tends to correlate physically with a smile and a general feeling of expansiveness. This could in principle form the basis for a metaphor HAPPY IS WIDE; SAD IS NARROW. And in fact there are minor metaphorical expressions like "I'm feeling expansive" which pick out a different aspect of happiness than does "I'm feeling up." But the major metaphor *in our culture* is HAPPY IS UP; there is a reason why we speak of the height of ecstasy rather than the breadth of ecstasy. HAPPY IS UP is maximally coherent with GOOD IS UP, HEALTHY IS UP, etc.

(vi) In some cases spatialization is so essential a part of a concept that it is difficult for us to imagine any alternative metaphor that might structure the concept. In our society "high status" is such a concept. Other cases, like happiness, are less clear. Is the concept of happiness independent of the HAPPY IS UP metaphor, or is the up-down spatialization of happiness a part of the concept? We believe that it is a part of the concept within a given conceptual system. The HAPPY IS UP metaphor places happiness within a coherent metaphorical system, and part of its meaning comes from its role in that system.

(vii) So-called "purely intellectual" concepts, e.g., the concepts in a scientific theory, are often—and maybe even always—based on metaphors that have a physical or cultural basis. The 'high' in 'high-energy particles' is based on MORE IS UP. The 'high' in 'high-level functions', as in physiological psychology, is based on RATIONAL IS UP. The 'low' in 'low-level phonology' (which refers to detailed phonetic aspects of the sound systems of languages) is based on MUNDANE REALITY IS DOWN (as in 'down to earth'). The intuitive appeal of a scientific theory has to do with how well its metaphors fit one's experience.

(viii) Our physical and cultural experience provides many possible bases for spatialization metaphors. Which ones are chosen, and which ones are major, may vary from culture to culture.

(ix) It is hard to distinguish the physical from the cultural basis of a metaphor, since the choice of one from among many possible physical bases has to do with cultural coherence. It is to this connection between metaphor and cultural coherence that we now turn.

V. Metaphor and Cultural Coherence

The most fundamental values in a culture will be coherent with the metaphorical structure of the most fundamental concepts in the culture. As an example, let us consider some cultural values in our society which are coherent with our UP-DOWN spatialization metaphors and whose opposites would not be.

1. MORE IS BETTER is coherent with MORE IS UP and GOOD IS UP. LESS IS BETTER is not coherent with them.
2. BIGGER IS BETTER is coherent with MORE IS UP and GOOD IS UP; SMALLER IS BETTER is not coherent with them.
3. THE FUTURE WILL BE BETTER is coherent with THE FUTURE IS UP and GOOD IS UP; THE FUTURE WILL BE WORSE is not.
4. THERE WILL BE MORE IN THE FUTURE is coherent with MORE IS UP and THE FUTURE IS UP.
5. YOUR STATUS SHOULD BE HIGHER IN THE FUTURE is coherent with HIGH STATUS IS UP and THE FUTURE IS UP.

These are values deeply embedded in our culture. THE FUTURE WILL BE BETTER is a statement of the concept of progress. THERE WILL BE MORE IN THE FUTURE has as special cases the accumulation of goods and wage inflation. YOUR STATUS SHOULD BE HIGHER IN THE FUTURE is a statement of careerism. These are coherent with our present spatialization metaphors; their opposites would not be. So it seems that our values are not independent, but must form a coherent system with the metaphorical concepts we live by. We are not claiming that all cultural values coherent with a metaphorical system will exist, but only that those which do exist and are deeply entrenched will be consistent with the metaphorical system.

The values listed above hold in our culture in general—all things being equal. But because things are usually not equal, there are often conflicts among these values. To resolve such conflicts, one has to give different priorities to these values. There are certain constants. For instance, MORE IS UP seems always to have the highest priority since it has the clearest physical basis. The priority of MORE IS UP over GOOD IS UP can be seen in examples like "Inflation is rising" and "The crime rate is going up." Assuming that inflation and the crime rate are BAD, these sentences mean what they do because MORE IS UP always has top priority.

In general, which values are given priority is partly a matter of the subculture you live in and partly a matter of personal values. The various subcultures of a mainstream culture share basic values, but give them different priorities. For example, the value BIGGER IS BETTER may be in conflict with THERE WILL BE MORE IN THE FUTURE when it comes to the question of whether to buy a big car now with large time payments that will eat up future salary or whether to buy a smaller cheaper car. There are American subcultures where you buy the big car and don't worry about the future, and there are others where the future comes first and you buy the small car. There was a time (before inflation and the energy crisis) when owning a small car had a high status within the subculture where VIRTUE IS UP and SAVING RESOURCES IS VIRTUOUS took priority over BIGGER IS BETTER. Nowadays the number of small car owners has gone up drastically because there is a large subculture where SAVING MORE MONEY IS BETTER has priority over BIGGER IS BETTER.

In addition to subcultures, there are groups whose defining characteristic is that they have certain important values that conflict with those of the mainstream culture. But in less obvious ways they preserve other mainstream values. Take monastic orders like the Trappists. There LESS IS BETTER and SMALLER IS BETTER with respect to material possessions, which are viewed as hindering what is important, namely, spiritual growth. The Trappists share the mainstream value VIRTUE IS UP, though they give it the highest priority and a very different definition, MORE is still BETTER, though it applies to VIRTUE; and STATUS is still UP, though it is not of this world but of a HIGHER one, the Kingdom of God. Moreover, THE FUTURE WILL BE BETTER in terms of spiritual growth (UP) and ultimately salvation (REALLY UP). This is typical of groups that are out of mainstream culture, VIRTUE, GOODNESS, and STATUS may be radically redefined, but they are still UP. It is still BETTER to have MORE of what is important, the FUTURE WILL BE BETTER with respect to what is important, and so on. Relative to what is important for such a monastic group, the value system is both internally coherent and, with respect to what is important for the group, coherent with the major orientational metaphors of the mainstream culture.

Individuals, like groups, will vary in their priorities and in the way they define what is GOOD or VIRTUOUS to them. In this sense, they are like subgroups of one. Relative to what is important for them, their individual value systems are coherent with the major orientational metaphors of their mainstream culture.

Not all cultures give the priorities we do to UP-DOWN orientation. There are cultures where BALANCE or CENTRALITY plays a much more important role than it does in our culture. Or consider the nonspatial orientation ACTIVE-PASSIVE. For us ACTIVE IS UP and PASSIVE IS DOWN in most matters. But there are cultures where passivity is valued more than activity. In general the major orientations UP-DOWN, IN-OUT, CENTRAL-PERIPHERAL, ACTIVE-PASSIVE, etc., seem to cut across all cultures, but which concepts will be oriented which way, and which orientations will be most important, will vary from culture to culture.

Conceptual Metaphor in Everyday Language

VI. An Apparent Metaphorical Contradiction

Charles Fillmore has observed (in conversation) that English appears to have two contradictory organizations of time. In the first the future is in front and the past behind.

> In the weeks ahead of us... (future)
> That's all behind us now... (past)

In the second, the future is behind and the past is in front.

> In the following weeks... (future)
> In the preceding weeks... (past)

This appears to be a contradiction in the metaphorical organization of time. Moreover, the apparently contradictory metaphors can mix with no ill effect, as in "We're looking *ahead* to the *following* weeks." Here it appears that *ahead* organizes the future in front, while *following* organizes it behind.

To see that there is, in fact, a coherence here, we first have to consider some facts about back and front organization. Some things have inherent fronts and backs, for example, people and cars, but not trees. A rock may receive a front-back organization under certain circumstances. Suppose you are looking at a medium-sized rock and there is a ball between you and the rock, say, a foot from the rock. Then it is appropriate for you to say "The ball is in front of the rock." The rock has received a front-back orientation, as if it had a front that faced you. This is not universal. There are languages, for instance Hausa, where the rock would receive the reverse orientation and you would say that the ball was behind the rock, if it was between you and the rock.

Moving objects generally receive a front-back orientation so that the front is in the direction of motion (or in the canonical direction of motion, so that a car backing up retains its front). A spherical satellite, for example, that has no front while standing still, gets a front while in orbit by virtue of the direction in which it is moving.

Now time in English is structured in terms of the TIME IS A MOVING OBJECT metaphor, with the future moving toward us.

> The time will come when...
> The time has long since gone when...
> The time for action has arrived.

The proverb "Time flies" is an instance of the TIME IS A MOVING OBJECT metaphor. Since we are facing toward the future, we get:

> In the weeks ahead of us...
> I look forward to doing that.
> Before us is a great opportunity.

By virtue of the TIME IS A MOVING OBJECT metaphor, time receives a front-back orientation facing in the direction of motion, just as any moving object would. Thus the future is facing toward us as it moves toward us, and we find expressions like:

> I can't face the future.
> The face of things to come...
> Let's meet the future head-on.

Now, although expressions like 'ahead of us', 'I look forward', and 'before us' orient times with respect to people, expressions like 'precede' and 'follow' orient times with respect to times. Thus we get:

> Next week and the week following it...

but not:

> The week following me...

Since future times are facing toward us, the times following them are further in the future, and all future times follow the present. That is why the *weeks to follow* are the same as *the weeks ahead of us*.

The point of this example is not merely to show that there is no contradiction, but also to show all the subtle details that are involved in the coherence: the TIME IS A MOVING OBJECT metaphor, the front-back orientation given to time by virtue of its being a moving object, and the consistent application of words like 'follow', 'precede', and 'face' when applied to time on the basis of the metaphor. All of this coherent detailed metaphorical structure is part of our everyday literal language about time, so familiar that we would normally not notice it.

VII. Some Further Examples

We have been claiming that metaphors partially structure our everyday concepts, and that this structure is reflected in our literal language. Before we can get an over-all picture of the philosophical implications of these claims, we need a few more examples. In each of the following cases we give a metaphor and a list of ordinary expressions that are special cases of the metaphor. The English expressions are of two sorts—simple literal expressions and idioms that fit the metaphor and are part of the normal everyday way of talking about the subject.

Theories (and Arguments) Are Buildings

Is that the *foundation* for your theory? The theory needs more *support*. The argument is *shaky*. We need some more facts or the arguments will *fall apart*. We need to *construct* a *strong* argument for that. I haven't figured out yet what the *form* of the argument will be. We need some more facts to *shore up* the theory. We need to *buttress* the theory with *solid* arguments. The theory will *stand* or *fall* on the *strength* of that argument. The argument *collapsed*. They *exploded* his latest theory. We will show that theory is *without foundation*. So far we have only put together the *framework* of the theory.

Ideas Are Food

What he said *left a bad taste in my mouth*. All this paper has in it are *raw facts, half-baked ideas,* and *warmed-over theories*. There were too many facts in the paper for me to *digest* them all. I just can't *swallow* that claim. That argument *smells fishy*. Let me *stew over* that for a while. Now there's a theory you can really *sink your teeth into*. We need to let that idea *percolate* for a while. That's *food for thought*. He's a *voracious* reader. We don't need to *spoon-feed* our students. He *devoured* the book. Let's let that idea *simmer on the back burner* for a while. This is the *meaty* part of the paper.

Love Is a Journey

Look *how far we've come*. We're *at a crossroads*. We can't *turn back* now. I don't think this relationship is *going anywhere*. This relationship is *a dead-end street*. Our marriage is *on the rocks*. We've gotten *off the track*. *Where* are we? We're *stuck*. It's been a *long, bumpy road*.

Seeing Is Understanding; Ideas Are Light Sources; Discourse Is a Light Medium

I *see* what you're saying. It *looks* different from my *point of view*. What is your *outlook* on that? I *view* it differently. Now I've got the *whole picture*. Let me *point something out* to you. That's an *insightful* idea. That was a *brilliant* remark. It really *shed light* on the subject. It was an *illuminating* remark. The argument is *clear*. It was a *murky* discussion. Could you *elucidate* your remarks? It's a *transparent* argument. The discussion was *opaque*.

Life Is a Game of Chance

I'll *take my chances*. *The odds are against us*. I've *got an ace up my sleeve*. He's *holding all the aces*. It's a *toss-up*. If you *play your cards right*, you can do it. He *won big*. He's *a real loser*. Where is he when *the chips are down*? That's my *ace in the hole*.

In the last example we have a collection of what are called "speech formulas," or "fixed-form expressions," or "phrasal lexical items." These function in many ways like single words, and the language has thousands of them. In the example given, a set of such phrasal lexical items are coherently structured by a single metaphor. Although each of them is an instance of the LIFE IS A GAME OF CHANCE metaphor, they are typically used to speak of life, not of gambling situations. They are normal ways of talking about life situations, just as using the word 'construct' is a normal way to talk about theories. It is in this sense that we include them as what we have called "literal" or "conventional" metaphors. If you say "the odds are against us," or "we'll have to take our chances," you will not be viewed as speaking metaphorically, but rather as using the normal everyday language appropriate to the situation.

VIII. The Partial Nature of Metaphorical Structuring

So far we have described the systematic character of metaphorically defined concepts. Such concepts are understood in terms of a number of different metaphors (e.g., TIME IS MONEY, TIME IS A MOVING OBJECT, etc.). The metaphorical structuring of concepts is necessarily partial, and is reflected in the lexicon of the language—including the phrasal lexicon, which contains fixed-form expressions such as 'be without foundation'. Because concepts are metaphorically structured in a systematic way, e.g., THEORIES ARE BUILDINGS, it is possible for us to use expressions (*construct, foundation*) from one domain (BUILDINGS) to talk about corresponding concepts in the metaphorically defined domain (THEORIES). What *foundation,* for example, means in the metaphorically defined domain (THEORY) will depend on the details of how the metaphorical concept THEORIES ARE BUILDINGS are used to structure the concept of a THEORY.

The parts of the concept of a building which are used to structure the concept of a theory are the foundation and outer shell. The roof, internal rooms, staircases, and hallways are parts of a building not used as part of the concept of a theory. Thus the metaphorical concept THEORIES ARE BUILDINGS has a "used" part (foundation and outer shell) and an "unused" part (rooms, staircases, etc.). Expressions such as *construct* and *foundation* are instances of the used part of such a metaphorical concept and are part of our ordinary literal language about theories.

But what of the linguistic expressions that reflect the "unused" part of a metaphor like THEORIES ARE BUILDINGS? Here are four examples:

> His theory has thousands of little rooms and long, winding corridors.
> His theories are always baroque.
> He prefers massive Gothic theories covered with gargoyles.
> Complex theories usually have problems with the plumbing.

These sentences fall outside the domain of normal literal language and are part of what is usually called "figurative" or "imaginative" language. Thus literal expressions ("He has constructed a theory") and imaginative expressions ("His theory is covered with gargoyles") can be instances of the same general metaphor (THEORIES ARE BUILDINGS).

Here we can distinguish three different subspecies of imaginative (or nonliteral) metaphor:

(1) Extensions of the used part of the metaphor, e.g., "These facts are the bricks and mortar of my theory." Here the outer shell of the building is referred to, but the metaphor stops short of mentioning the materials used.

(2) Instances of the unused part of the literal metaphor, e.g., "His theory has thousands of little rooms and long, winding corridors."

(3) Instances of novel metaphor, that is, a metaphor not used to structure part of our normal conceptual system, but a new way of thinking about something, e.g., "Classical theories are patriarchs who father many children, most of whom fight incessantly." Each of these subspecies lies outside of the *used* part of a metaphorical concept that structures our normal conceptual system.

We note in passing that all the linguistic expressions that we have given to characterize general, metaphorical concepts are figurative. Examples are TIME IS MONEY, TIME IS A MOVING OBJECT, CONTROL IS UP, IDEAS ARE FOOD, THEORIES ARE BUILDINGS, etc. None of these is literal. This is a consequence of the fact that they are only *partly* used to structure our normal concepts. Since they necessarily contain parts that are not used in our normal concepts, they go beyond the realm of the literal.

Each of the metaphorical expressions we have talked about so far (e.g., the *time* will *come*, *construct* a theory, *attack* a *position*) is used within a whole system of metaphorical concepts—concepts that we live and think in terms of. These expressions, like all other words and phrasal lexical items in the language, are fixed by convention. In addition to these cases, which are part of whole metaphorical systems, there are idiosyncratic metaphorical expressions that stand alone and are not systematically used in our language or thought. These are well-known expressions like the *foot* of the mountain, a *head* of cabbage, the *leg* of a table, etc. These expressions are isolated instances of metaphorical concepts, where there is only one instance of a used part (or maybe two or three). Thus the *foot* of the mountain is the only used part of the metaphorical concept A MOUNTAIN IS A PERSON. In normal discourse we do not speak of the *head, shoulders,* or *trunk* of a mountain, though in special contexts it is possible to construct novel metaphors about mountains based on these unused parts. In fact, there is an aspect of the metaphorical concept A MOUNTAIN IS A PERSON in which mountain climbers will speak of the *shoulder* of a mountain (namely, a ridge near the top) and of *conquering, fighting,* and even *being killed* by a mountain. And there are cartoon conventions where mountains become animate and their peaks become heads. The point here is that there are metaphorical concepts like A MOUNTAIN IS A PERSON which are marginal in our culture and our language, whose used part may consist of only one conventionally fixed expression of the language, and which do not systematically interact with other metaphorical concepts, because so little of them is used. This makes them relatively uninteresting for our purposes, but not completely uninteresting, since they can be extended to their unused part in framing novel metaphors, making jokes, etc. And our ability to extend them to unused parts indicates that, however marginal they are, they do exist.

Examples like the *foot* of the mountain are idiosyncratic, unsystematic, and isolated. They do not interact with other metaphors, play no particularly interesting role in our conceptual system, and hence are not metaphors that we live by. The only signs of life that they have is that they can be extended in subcultures, and that their unused portions can be the basis for (relatively uninteresting) novel metaphors. If any metaphorical expressions deserve to be called "dead," it is these, though they do have a bare spark of life, in that they are understood partly in terms of marginal metaphorical concepts like A MOUNTAIN IS A PERSON.

It is important to distinguish these isolated and unsystematic cases from the systematic metaphorical expressions we have been discussing. Expressions like 'wasting time', 'attacking positions', 'going our separate ways', etc., are reflections of systematic metaphorical concepts that structure our actions and thoughts. They are "alive" in the most fundamental sense—they are metaphors we live by. The fact that they are conventionally fixed within the lexicon of English makes them no less alive.

IX. Inadequacies of a Theory of Abstraction

On the basis of our previous analysis of the nature of literal metaphor we may now begin to draw out what we consider to be the more important implications for recent linguistic and philosophical treatments of language. We shall begin with the theory of abstraction, one strategy which linguists have occasionally tried for dealing with isolated cases of literal metaphor.[5] For example, consider 'construct' in "We constructed a theory" and "We constructed a building." According to the abstraction proposal, 'construct' has a very general, abstract meaning which is neutral between buildings and theories and can apply to both. Another example would be the 'in' of 'in the kitchen', 'in the ruling class', and 'in love'. The abstraction solution is that 'in' has an abstract meaning which is neutral among space, social groups, and love, and which can apply to all. This proposal has typically been suggested only for isolated lexical items rather than whole domains of literal metaphor, so it is not clear that there is any proposal for abstraction that is relevant. Still, the idea keeps popping up that it ought to be a viable program; so we shall indicate several shortcomings of this view relative to our account of literal metaphor.

(1) Under the abstraction view, there would be no conventional metaphors and, therefore, no partial metaphorical structuring such as we have proposed. But then how can one explain the apparent systematic grouping of expressions under single metaphors and the fact that different metaphors based on a single concept may have different partial structurings? Consider the metaphors LOVE IS WAR, RATIONAL DISCOURSE IS WAR, STOPPING INFLATION IS WAR, and CANCER IS WAR. ATTACK is in CANCER, INFLATION, and DISCOURSE. STRATEGY is in LOVE, DISCOURSE, and INFLATION. CONQUERING is in LOVE, INFLATION, and CANCER, VICTORIES and SETBACKS are in all of them. There is a FIRST LINE OF DEFENSE in INFLATION and CANCER. On our hypothesis, WAR is the basis for all four metaphors, each of which has a different partial structuring. On the abstraction hypothesis, there is no unity at all, but only a hodgepodge of different abstract concepts of different sorts.

(2) Since the abstraction proposal has no partial metaphorical structuring, it cannot account for metaphorical extensions into the unused part of the metaphor, as in "Your theory is constructed out of cheap stucco" and many others that fall within the unused portion of the THEORIES ARE BUILDINGS metaphor.

(3) The abstraction proposal does not seem to make any sense at all for UP-DOWN spatialization metaphors, such as HAPPY IS UP, CONTROL IS UP, MORE IS UP, VIRTUE IS UP, THE FUTURE IS UP, REASON IS UP, NORTH IS UP, etc. It seems impossible to imagine a single general concept with any content at all that would be an abstraction of HEIGHT, HAPPINESS,

CONTROL, MORE, VIRTUE, THE FUTURE, REASON, and NORTH and which would precisely fit them all. Moreover, it would seem that UP and DOWN could not be at the same level of abstraction, since UP applies to the FUTURE, while DOWN does not apply to the PAST. We account for this by partial metaphorical structuring, but under the abstraction proposal UP would have to be more abstract in some sense than DOWN, and that does not seem to make sense.

(4) The abstraction theory would not distinguish between metaphors of the form "A is B" and those of the form "B is A," since it would claim that there are neutral terms covering both domains. For example, English has the LOVE IS A JOURNEY metaphor, but no JOURNEYS ARE LOVE metaphor. The abstraction view would deny that love is understood in terms of journeys, and would be left with the counterintuitive claim that love and journeys are understood in terms of some abstract concept neutral between them.

(5) Different conventional metaphors can structure different aspects of a single concept. For example, LOVE IS A JOURNEY; LOVE IS WAR; LOVE IS AN ELECTROMAGNETIC PHENOMENON; LOVE IS MADNESS; LOVE IS A GAME. Each of these provides one perspective on the concept of love and structures one of many aspects of the concept. The abstraction hypothesis would seek a single general concept of love which is abstract enough to fit all of these. This would miss the point that these metaphors are not jointly characterizing a core concept of love, but are separately characterizing different aspects of the concept of love.

(6) Finally, the abstraction hypothesis assumes, in the case of LOVE IS A JOURNEY, for example, that there is a set of abstract concepts, neutral with respect to love and journeys, which can "fit" or "apply to" both of them. But in order for such abstract concepts to "fit" or "apply to" love, the concept of love must be independently structured, so that there can be such a "fit." As we will show, love is, on its own terms, not a concept that has a clearly delineated structure; it gets such structure only via conventional metaphors. But the abstraction view, which has no conventional metaphors to do the structuring, must assume that a structure as clearly delineated as the relevant aspects of journeys exists independently for the concept of love. It's hard to imagine how.

X. How Is Our Conceptual System Grounded?

We claim that most of our normal conceptual system is metaphorically structured; that is, most concepts are partially understood in terms of other concepts. This raises an important question about the grounding of our conceptual system. Are there any concepts at all that are understood directly without metaphor? If not, how can we understand anything at all?

The prime candidates for concepts that are understood directly are the simple spatial concepts, such as UP. Our spatial concept UP arises out of our spatial experience. We have bodies and stand erect. Virtually every motor movement that we make involves a motor program that either changes our UP-DOWN orientation, maintains it, presupposes it, or takes it into account in some way. Our constant physical activity in the world, even when we sleep, makes UP-DOWN orientation not merely relevant to our physical activity, but centrally relevant. The centrality of UP-DOWN orientation in our motor programs and everyday functioning might make one think that there could be no alternative to such an orientational concept. Objectively speaking, however, there are many possible frameworks for spatial orientation, including Cartesian coordinates, which don't in themselves have UP-DOWN orientation. Human spatial concepts, however, include UP-DOWN, FRONT-BACK, IN-OUT, NEAR-FAR, etc. It is these that are relevant to our continual everyday bodily functioning, which gives them a relative priority over other possible structurings of space *for us*. In other words, the structure of our spatial concepts emerges from our constant spatial experience, that is, our interaction with our physical environment. Concepts that emerge in this way are concepts that we live by in the most fundamental way.

Thus, UP is *not* understood purely in its own terms, but emerges from the collection of constantly performed motor functions that have to do with our erect position relative to the gravitational field we live in. Imagine a spherical being living outside of any gravitational field, with no knowledge or imagination of any other kind of experience. What could UP possibly mean to such a being?

Some of the central concepts in terms of which our bodies function—UP-DOWN, IN-OUT, FRONT-BACK, LIGHT-DARK, WARM-COLD, MALE-FEMALE, etc.—are more sharply delineated than others. Our emotional experience is as basic as our spatial and perceptual experience, but our emotional experiences are much less sharply delineated in terms of what we do with our bodies. Although a sharply delineated conceptual structure for space emerges from our perceptual-motor functioning, no sharply defined conceptual structure for the emotions emerges from our emotional functioning alone. Since there are *systematic correlates* between our emotions (like happiness) and our sensory-motor experiences (like erect posture), these form the basis of orientational metaphorical concepts (such as HAPPY IS UP). Such metaphors allow us to conceptualize our emotions in more sharply defined terms and also to relate them to other concepts having to do with general well-being (e.g., HEALTH, LIFE, CONTROL, etc.). In this sense, we can speak of *emergent metaphors* as well as emergent concepts.

The concepts of OBJECT, SUBSTANCE, and CONTAINER also emerge directly. We experience ourselves as entities, separate from the rest of the world—CONTAINERS with an inside and an outside. We also experience things external to us as entities—often also CONTAINERS with insides and outsides. We experience ourselves as being made up of SUBSTANCES, e.g., flesh and bone, and external objects as being made up of various *kinds* of SUBSTANCES—wood, stone, metal, etc. We experience many things, through sight and touch, as having distinct boundaries. And when things have no distinct boundaries, we often project boundaries upon them—conceptualizing them as entities and often as containers (for example, forests, clearings, clouds, etc.).

Like orientational metaphors, basic physical metaphors are grounded by virtue of *systematic correlates within our experience*. For example, the metaphor THE VISUAL FIELD IS A CONTAINER is grounded in the correlation of what we see with a bounded physical space. The TIME IS A MOVING OBJECT metaphor is based on the correlation between an object moving toward us and the time it takes to get to us. The same correlation is a basis for the TIME IS A CONTAINER metaphor (as in "He did it *in* ten minutes"), with the *bounded* space traversed by the object correlated with the time the object takes to traverse it. EVENTS and ACTIONS are correlated with bounded time spans, which makes them CONTAINER-OBJECTS.

Perhaps the most important thing to stress about grounding is the distinction between an experience and the way we conceptualize it. We are *not* claiming that physical experience is in any way more basic than other kinds of experience, whether emotional, mental, cultural, or whatever. All these experiences may be just as basic as physical experiences. Rather, what we *are* claiming about grounding is that we typically *conceptualize* the nonphysical in terms of the physical—or the less clearly delineated in terms of the more clearly delineated. To see this more clearly, consider the following examples:

(1) Harry is *in* the kitchen.
(2) Harry is *in* the Elks Club.
(3) Harry is *in* love.

The sentences refer to three different domains of experience: spatial, social, and emotional. None of these has experiential priority over the others; they are all equally basic kinds of experience.

But with respect to conceptual structuring there is a difference. The concept IN expressed in (1) emerges *directly* from spatial experience in a clearly delineated fashion. It is not an instance of a metaphorical concept. The other two sentences *are* instances of metaphorical concepts. (2) is an instance of the SOCIAL GROUPS ARE CONTAINERS metaphor, in terms of which the concept of a social group is structured. This metaphor allows us to "get a handle on" the concept of a social group by means of a spatialization. Both the word 'in' and the concept IN are the *same* in all three examples; we do not have three different concepts of IN or three homophonous words 'in'. We have one emergent concept IN, one word for it, and two metaphorical concepts which partially define social groups and emotional states. What these cases show is that it is possible to have equally basic kinds of experiences while having conceptualizations of them that are not equally basic.

Thus, (1) happens to be, according to our account, a nonmetaphoric literal sentence, containing a directly spatial nonmetaphoric instance of the spatial concept IN. But for most linguistic purposes this doesn't give it any particularly special status over (2) and (3). However, sentences like (1) do seem to have special status in philosophical papers dealing with literal meaning. Sentences like (1) are much more likely to be used as clear examples of literal meaning than are sentences like (2) and (3), since philosophers seem instinctively to shy away from using sentences containing conventional metaphors as examples of literal meaning. That is the reason for the predominance of examples such as "The cat is on the mat," "Snow is white," "Brutus killed Caesar," etc.

XI. An Example of an Emergent Category

Our discussion in the two previous sections of the grounding of our conceptual system and the nature of nonmetaphoric literal meaning may seem to provide a framework for a "building-block" theory, in which all meaningful utterances either are or are constructed from certain unanalyzable semantic units. But we reject the notion of unanalyzable simples which might serve as the atoms for a linguistic or epistemological foundationalism. Instead, we wish to identify emergent categories and concepts that are best understood as experiential gestalts, which, though decomposable into other elements, are yet basic and irreducible in terms of grounding our conceptual system.

To explain this important notion, let us now move beyond our use of spatial examples of concepts that emerge from our successful functioning in our environment (e.g., UP-DOWN, IN-OUT, etc.) to a consideration of the concept of causation. Piaget has hypothesized that infants first learn about causation through the realization of their ability to manipulate directly objects around them—pulling off their blankets, throwing their bottles, dropping toys. There is, in fact, a stage in which infants seem to "practice" these manipulations, e.g., repeatedly dropping their spoons. As the child masters these more primitive manipulations of external objects, it moves on to other tasks which are to become part of its constant everyday functioning in its environment, for example, flipping lightswitches, opening doors, buttoning shirts, adjusting glasses. Though each of these actions is different, the overwhelming proportion of them share common features of what we may call a "prototypical" or "paradigmatic" case of direct causation. Among these shared features are included:

1. The agent has as a goal some change of state in the patient.
2. The change of state is physical.
3. The agent has a "plan" for carrying out this goal.
4. The plan requires the agent's use of a motor program.
5. The agent is in control of that motor program.
6. The agent is primarily responsible for carrying out the plan.
7. The agent is the energy source (i.e., the agent is directing his energies toward the patient) and the patient is the energy goal (i.e., the change in the patient is due to an external source of energy).
8. The agent touches the patient either with his body or with an instrument (i.e., the change in the patient is due to an external source of energy).
9. The agent successfully carries out the plan.
10. The change in the patient is perceptible.
11. The agent monitors the change in the patient through sensory perception.
12. There is a single specific agent and a single specific patient.

This set of properties characterizes "prototypical" direct manipulations, and these are cases of causation par excellence. We are using the word 'prototypical' in the sense used by Eleanor Rosch in her theory of human categorization.[6] Her experiments indicate that people categorize objects, not in set-theoretical terms, but in terms of prototypes and family resemblances. For example, small flying singing birds like sparrows, robins, etc., are prototypical birds. Chickens, ostriches, and penguins are birds, but not central members of the category—they are nonprototypical birds. But they are birds, nonetheless, because they bear sufficient family resemblances to the prototype; that is, they share enough of the relevant properties of the prototype to be classified by people as birds.

The twelve properties given above characterize a prototype of causation in the following sense. They recur together over and over in action after action as we go through our daily lives. We experience them as a gestalt, in which the complex of properties occurring together is more basic to our experience than their separate occurrences. Through their constant recurrence in our everyday functioning, the category of causation emerges with this complex of properties characterizing prototypical causations. Other kinds of causation, which are less prototypical, are actions or events that bear sufficient family resemblances to the prototype. These would include action at a distance, nonhuman agency, the use of an intermediate agent, the occurrence of two or more agents, involuntary or uncontrolled use of the motor program, etc. In physical causation the agent and patient are events, a physical law takes the place of plan, goal, and motor activity, and all the peculiarly human aspects are factored out. When there is not sufficient family resemblance to the prototype, we cease to characterize what happens as causation; for example, if there were multiple agents, if what the agents did was remote in space and time from the patient's change, and if there were neither desire nor plan nor control, then we probably wouldn't say that this was an instance of causation, or at least we would have questions about it.

Although the category of causation has fuzzy boundaries, it is clearly delineated in an enormous range of instances. Our successful functioning in the world involves the application of the concept of causation to ever new domains of activity—through intention, planning, drawing inferences, etc. The concept is stable, because we continue to function successfully in terms of it. Given a concept of causation that emerges from our experience, that concept can be applied to metaphorical concepts. In "Harry raised our morale by telling jokes," for example, we have an instance of causation where what Harry did made our morale go UP, as in the HAPPY IS UP metaphor.

Though the concept of causation as we have characterized it is basic to human activity, it is not a "primitive" in the usual building-block sense; that is, it is not unanalyzable and undecomposable. Since it is defined in terms of a prototype that is characterized by a recurrent complex of properties, our concept of causation is both analyzable into those properties and capable of a wide range of variation. The terms into which the causation prototype is analyzed (e.g., control, motor program, volition, etc.) are probably also characterized by prototype and capable of further analysis. This permits us to have concepts that are at once experientially basic and indefinitely analyzable.

XII. Novel Metaphor

We have already discussed some cases of novel metaphor as instances of the extensions of a conventional metaphor drawn from ordinary language. We gave examples of extensions of both the "used" and "unused" portion of the THEORIES ARE BUILDINGS metaphor and also of a truly novel metaphor not normally used to structure our conceptual system (for example, the CLASSICAL THEORIES ARE PATRIARCHS metaphor). We now want to explore more fully the workings of novel metaphor by focusing on two problems of special philosophical importance. First, what makes one metaphor more appropriate or fitting than another, and second, in what sense, if any, may we speak of the truth of a metaphor?

A. What Makes a Novel Metaphor Appropriate?

Consider the new metaphor: LOVE IS A COLLABORATIVE WORK OF ART. This is a metaphor that we personally find particularly forceful, insightful, and appropriate, given our experiences as members of our generation and our culture. The reason is that it makes our experiences coherent—it makes sense of them. But how can a mere metaphor make coherent a large and diverse range of experiences? The answer, we believe, comes out of the fact that metaphors have entailments. A novel metaphor may entail both other novel metaphors and literal statements. For example, the entailments of LOVE IS A COLLABORATIVE WORK OF ART arise from our knowledge and experience of what it means for something to be a collaborative work of art. Here are some of the entailments of this metaphor, based on our own experiences of what a collaborative work of art entails.

LOVE IS WORK.	LOVE IS AN AESTHETIC EXPERIENCE.
LOVE IS ACTIVE.	LOVE IS VALUABLE IN ITSELF.
LOVE REQUIRES HELPING.	LOVE IS AN EXPRESSION OF DEEPEST EMOTION.
LOVE REQUIRES COMPROMISE.	LOVE IS CREATIVE.
LOVE REQUIRES PATIENCE.	LOVE INVOLVES BEAUTY.
LOVE REQUIRES SHARED VALUES AND GOALS.	LOVE REQUIRES HARMONY.
LOVE DEMANDS SACRIFICE.	LOVE CANNOT BE ACHIEVED BY FORMULA.
LOVE INVOLVES FRUSTRATION.	LOVE IS UNIQUE IN EACH INSTANCE.
LOVE REQUIRES DISCIPLINE.	LOVE IS UNPREDICTABLE IN ITS OUTCOME.
LOVE BRINGS JOY AND PAIN.	LOVE IS AN ACT OF COMMUNICATION.

Some of these entailments are literal (e.g., LOVE REQUIRES PATIENCE); others are themselves novel metaphors (e.g., LOVE IS AN AESTHETIC EXPERIENCE). Each of these entailments may itself have further entailments. The result is a large and coherent network of entailments which may, on the whole, either fit or not fit our experiences of love. When such a coherent network of entailments fits our experiences, those experiences form a coherent whole as instances of the metaphor. What we experience with such a metaphor is a kind of reverberation down through the network of entailments which awakens and connects our memories of our past love experiences and serves as a possible guide for future ones.

Let's get more specific about what we mean by "reverberations" in the metaphor LOVE IS A COLLABORATIVE WORK OF ART.

(1) The metaphor highlights certain features while suppressing others. For example, the ACTIVE side of love is brought into the foreground through the notion of WORK both in COLLABORATIVE WORK and in WORK OF ART. This requires the masking of certain aspects of love which are viewed passively. In fact, the emotional

aspects of love are almost never viewed as being under active control in our literal language. Even in the LOVE IS A JOURNEY metaphor, the relationship is viewed as a vehicle that is not in the couple's active control, one that can be OFF THE TRACKS, or ON THE ROCKS, or NOT GOING ANYWHERE. In the LOVE IS MADNESS metaphor ("I'm crazy about her," "She's driving me wild"), there is the ultimate lack of control. In the LOVE IS HEALTH metaphor, where the relationship is a patient ("It's a healthy relationship," "It's a sick relationship," "Their relationship is reviving"), the passivity of health in this culture is transferred to love. Thus, in focusing on various aspects of activity (e.g., WORK, CREATION, PURSUING GOALS, BUILDING, HELPING, etc.), the metaphor provides an organization of important love experiences that the literal language does not make available.

(2) The metaphor does not merely entail other concepts, like WORK or PURSUING SHARED GOALS, but it entails very specific *aspects* of these concepts. It is not just any work, like working on an automobile assembly line, for instance. It is work that requires special balance of power and letting go which is appropriate to artistic creation. It is not just any kind of goal that is pursued, but a joint aesthetic goal. And though the metaphor may suppress the out-of-control aspects of the LOVE IS MADNESS metaphor, it highlights another aspect, namely, the sense of almost demonic possession which lies behind our culture's connection between artistic genius and madness.

(3) Because the metaphor highlights important love experiences and makes them coherent, while it masks other love experiences, the metaphor gives love a new meaning. If those things entailed by the metaphor are for us the most important aspects of our love experiences, then the metaphor can acquire the status of a truth—for many people, love *is* a collaborative work of art. And because it is, the metaphor can have a feedback effect, guiding our future actions in accordance with the metaphor.

(4) Thus, metaphors can be appropriate because they sanction actions, justify inferences, and help us set goals. For example, certain actions, inferences, and goals are dictated by the LOVE IS A COLLABORATIVE WORK OF ART metaphor but not by the LOVE IS MADNESS metaphor. If love is MADNESS, I do not concentrate on what I have to do to maintain it. But if it is WORK, then it requires activity, and if it is a WORK OF ART, it requires a very special *kind* of activity, and if it is COLLABORATIVE, then it is even further restricted and specified.

(5) The meaning a metaphor will have for me will be partly culturally determined and partly tied to my past experiences. The cultural differences can be enormous because each of the concepts in the metaphor under discussion can vary widely from culture to culture—ART, WORK, COLLABORATION, and LOVE. Thus LOVE IS A COLLABORATIVE WORK OF ART would mean very different things to a nineteenth-century European romantic than to a Greenland Eskimo of the same time period. There will also be differences within a culture based on the structure and significance of one's past experiences. LOVE IS A COLLABORATIVE WORK OF ART will mean something very different to two fourteen-year-olds on their first date than to a mature artist-couple. Only when the entailments of a metaphor fit our cultural and personal experience closely enough and when it seems reasonable to ignore what it hides, can we speak of it as being appropriate, and perhaps even true.

Typically this involves understanding less concrete experiences in terms of more concrete and more highly structured experiences.

Many concepts are defined metaphorically, in terms of concrete experiences that we can comprehend, rather than in terms of necessary and sufficient conditions.

This permits cross-cultural differences in conceptual systems: different cultures have different ways of comprehending experience via conceptual metaphor. Such differences will typically be reflected in linguistic differences.

We are thus led to a theory of truth that is dependent on understanding: a sentence is true in a situation when our understanding of the sentence fits our understanding of the situation.

An account of understanding is worked out in terms of a theory of experiential gestalts, that is, structurings of experience along certain natural dimensions: perceptual, functional, etc.

For the present, we hope to have shown only that metaphor is conceptual in nature, that it is pervasive in our everyday conventional language, and that no account of meaning and truth can pretend to be complete, or basically correct, or even on the right track if it cannot account for the kind of phenomena discussed above.

Notes

1 For a more comprehensive and thorough working out of the implications for several areas, especially philosophy and linguistics, see our *Metaphors We Live By* (Chicago: University of Chicago Press, 1980).
2 The account of systematicity and coherence we are developing may seem similar to Nelson Goodman's claim that metaphor involves a transfer in which "(a) label along with others constituting a scheme is in effect detached from the home realm of that scheme and applied for the sorting and organizing of an alien realm. Partly by thus carrying with it a reorientation of a whole network of labels does a metaphor give clues for its development and elaboration" [*Languages of Art* (Indianapolis: Bobbs-Merrill, 1968), p. 72]. Here Goodman comes down squarely on the side of those who view metaphor as a matter of language (that is, "labels") rather than as a matter of thought. We are at odds with Goodman on this, as well as other matters. For example, Goodman does not seem to regard most everyday conventional language as metaphorical. Nor, presumably, would he go along with our experientialist account of truth, in which truth is secondary to understanding (cf. our *Metaphors We Live By, op. cit.*).
3 "The Conduit Metaphor," in A. Ortony, ed., *Metaphor and Thought* (New York: Cambridge, 1979).
4 *Figurative Patterns and Redundancy in the Lexicon,* unpublished dissertation, University of California at San Diego, 1974.
5 A philosophical example of the abstractionist position is contained in L. Jonathan Cohen and Avishai Margalit, "The Role of Inductive Reasoning in the Interpretation of Metaphor," in D. Davidson and G. Harman, eds., *Semantics of Natural Language* (Boston: Reidel, 1972), pp. 722–740. "The metaphorical meanings of a word or phrase in a natural language are all contained, as it were, within its literal meaning or meanings. They are reached by removing any restrictions in relation to certain variables from the appropriate section or sections of its semantical hypothesis" (735). The result of merely removing restrictions would always result in a very general meaning in common between the metaphorical and literal meanings.
6 "Human Categorization," in N. Warren, ed., *Advances in Cross-cultural Psychology* (New York: Academic Press, 1977), vol. I.

Part 2:
Applications

Literary Criticism

8.
THE LITERARY CRITICISM OF ORATORY
Herbert A. Wichelns

I

SAMUEL JOHNSON once projected a history of criticism "as it relates to judging of authors." Had the great eighteenth-century critic ever carried out his intention, he would have included some interesting comments on the orators and their judges. Histories of criticism, in whole or in part, we now have, and histories of orators. But that section of the history of criticism which deals with judging of orators is still unwritten. Yet the problem is an interesting one, and one which involves some important conceptions. Oratory—the waning influence of which is often discussed in current periodicals—has definitely lost the established place in literature that it once had. Demosthenes and Cicero, Bossuet and Burke, all hold their places in literary histories. But Webster inspires more than one modern critic to ponder the question whether oratory is literature; and if we may judge by the emphasis of literary historians generally, both in England and in America, oratory is either an outcast or a poor relation. What are the reasons for this change? It is a question not easily answered. Involved in it is some shift in the conception of oratory or of literature, or of both; nor can these conceptions have changed except in response to the life of which oratory, as well as literature, is part.

This essay, it should be said, is merely an attempt to spy out the land, to see what some critics have said of some orators, to discover what their mode of criticism has been. The discussion is limited in the main to Burke and a few nineteenth-century figures—Webster, Lincoln, Gladstone; Bright, Cobden—and to the verdicts on these found in the surveys of literary history, in critical essays, in histories of oratory, and in biographies.

Of course, we are not here concerned with the disparagement of oratory. With that, John Morley once dealt in a phrase: "Yet, after all, to disparage eloquence is to depreciate mankind."[1] Nor is the praise of eloquence of moment here. What interests us is the method of the critic: his standards, his categories of judgment, what he regards as important. These will show, not so much what he thinks of a great and ancient literary type, as how he thinks in dealing with that type. The chief aim is to know how critics have spoken of orators.

We have not much serious criticism of oratory. The reasons are patent. Oratory is intimately associated with statecraft; it is bound up with the things of the moment; its

---

Wichelns, Herbert A. "The Literary Criticism of Oratory". In: Alexander M. Drummond (ed.), *Studies in Rhetoric and Public Speaking in Honor of James Albert Winans.* New York: The Century Company, 1925: 181–216.

occasion, its terms, its background, can often be understood only by the careful student of history. Again, the publication of orations as pamphlets leaves us free to regard any speech merely as an essay, as a literary effort deposited at the shrine of the muses in hope of being blessed with immortality. This view is encouraged by the difficulty of reconstructing the conditions under which the speech was delivered; by the doubt, often, whether the printed text of the speech represents what was actually said, or what the orator elaborated afterwards. Burke's corrections are said to have been the despair of his printers.[2] Some of Chatham's speeches, by a paradox of fate, have been reported to us by Samuel Johnson, whose style is as remote as possible from that of the Great Commoner, and who wrote without even having heard the speeches pronounced.[3] Only in comparatively recent times has parliamentary reporting pretended to give full records of what was actually said; and even now speeches are published for literary or political purposes which justify the corrector's pencil in changes both great and small. Under such conditions the historical study of speech making is far from easy.

Yet the conditions of democracy necessitate both the making of speeches and the study of the art. It is true that other ways of influencing opinion have long been practised, that oratory is no longer the chief means of communicating ideas to the masses. And the change is emphasized by the fact that the newer methods are now beginning to be investigated, sometimes from the point of view of the political student, sometimes from that of the "publicity expert." But, human nature being what it is, there is no likelihood that face to face persuasion will cease to be a principal mode of exerting influence, whether in courts, in senate-houses, or on the platform. It follows that the critical study of oratorical method is the study, not of a mode outworn, but of a permanent and important human activity.

Upon the great figures of the past who have used the art of public address, countless judgments have been given. These judgments have varied with the bias and preoccupation of the critics, who have been historians, biographers, or literary men, and have written accordingly. The context in which we find criticism of speeches, we must, for the purposes of this essay at least, both note and set aside. For though the aim of the critic conditions his approach to our more limited problem—the method of dealing with oratory—still we find that an historian may view an orator in the same light as does a biographer or an essayist. The literary form in which criticism of oratory is set does not afford a classification of the critics.

"There are," says a critic of literary critics, "three definite points, on one of which, or all of which, criticism must base itself. There is the date, and the author, and the work."[4] The points on which writers base their judgments of orators do afford a classification. The man, his work, his times, are the necessary common topics of criticism; no one of them can be wholly disregarded by any critic. But mere difference in emphasis on one or another of them is important enough to suggest a rough grouping. The writers with whom this essay deals give but a subordinate position to the date; they are interested chiefly in the man or in his works. Accordingly, we have as the first type of criticism that which is predominantly personal or biographical, is occupied with the character and the mind of the orator, goes behind the work to the man. The second type attempts to hold the scales even between the biographical and the literary interest. The third is occupied with the work and tends to ignore the man. These three classes, then, seem to represent the practice of modern writers in dealing with orators. Each merits a more detailed examination.

II

We may begin with that type of critic whose interest is in personality, who seeks the man behind the work. Critics of this type furnish forth the appreciative essays and the occasional addresses on the orators. They are as the sands of the sea. Lord Rosebery's two speeches on Burke, Whitelaw Reid's on Lincoln and on Burke, may stand as examples of the character sketch.[5] The second part of Birrell's essay on Burke will serve for the mental character sketch (the first half of the essay is biographical); other examples are Sir Walter Raleigh's essay on Burke and that by Robert Lynd.[6] All these emphasize the concrete nature of Burke's thought, the realism of his imagination, his peculiar combination of breadth of vision with intensity; they pass to the guiding principles of his thought: his hatred of abstraction, his love of order and of settled ways. But they do not occupy themselves with Burke as a speaker, nor even with him as a writer; their first and their last concern is with the man rather than with his works; and their method is to fuse into a single impression whatever of knowledge or opinion they may have of the orator's life and works. These critics, in dealing with the public speaker, think of him as something other than a speaker. Since this type of writing makes but an indirect contribution to our judgment of the orator, there is no need of a more extended account of the method, except as we find it combined with a discussion of the orator's works.

III

Embedded in biographies and histories of literature, we find another type of criticism, that which combines the sketch of mind and character with some discussion of style. Of the general interest of such essays there can be no doubt. Nine-tenths of so-called literary criticism deals with the lives and personalities of authors, and for the obvious reason, that every one is interested in them, whereas few will follow a technical study, however broadly based. At its best, the type of study that starts with the orator's mind and character is justified by the fact that nothing can better illuminate his work as a persuader of men. But when not at its best, the description of a man's general cast of mind stands utterly unrelated to his art: the critic fails to fuse his comment on the individual with his comment on the artist; and as a result we get some statements about the man, and some statements about the orator, but neither casts light on the other. Almost any of the literary histories will supply examples of the gulf that may yawn between a stylistic study and a study of personality.

The best example of the successful combination of the two strains is Grierson's essay on Burke in the *Cambridge History of English Literature*. In this, Burke's style, though in largest outline only, is seen to emerge from the essential nature of the man. Yet of this essay, too, it must be said that the analysis of the orator is incomplete, being overshadowed by the treatment of Burke as a writer, though, as we shall see, the passages on style have the rare virtue of keeping to the high road of criticism. The majority of critics who use the mixed method, however, do not make their study of personality fruitful for a study of style, do not separate literary style from oratorical style even to the extent that Grierson does, and do conceive of literary style as a matter of details. In fact, most of the critics of this group tend to supply a discussion of style by jotting down what has occurred to them about the author's management of words; and in the main, they notice the lesser strokes of literary art, but not its broader aspects. They have an eye for tactics, but not for strategy. This is the more strange, as these same writers habitually take large views of the orator himself, considered as a personality, and because they often remark the speaker's great themes and his leading ideas. The management of ideas—what the Romans called invention and disposition—the critics do not observe; their practice is the *salto mortale* from the largest to the smallest considerations. And it needs no mention that a critic who does not observe the management of ideas even from the point of view of structure and arrangement can have nothing to say of the adaptation of ideas to the orator's audience.

It is thus with Professor McLaughlin in his chapter in the *Cambridge History of American Literature* on Clay and Calhoun and some lesser lights. The pages are covered with such expressions as diffuse, florid, diction restrained and strong, neatly phrased, power of attack, invective, gracious persuasiveness. Of the structure of the speeches by which Clay and Calhoun exercised their influence—nothing. The drive of ideas is not represented. The background of habitual feeling which the orators at times appealed to and at times modified, is hinted at in a passage about Clay's awakening the spirit of nationalism, and in another passage contrasting the full-blooded oratory of Benton with the more polished speech of Quincy and Everett; but these are the merest hints. In the main, style for McLaughlin is neither the expression of personality nor the order and movement given to thought, but a thing of shreds and patches. It is thus, too, with Morley's pages on Burke's style in his life of the orator, and with Lodge's treatment of Webster in his life of the great American. A rather better analysis, though on the same plane of detail, may be used as an example. Oliver Elton says of Burke :

> He embodies, more powerfully than any one, the mental tendencies and changes that are seen gathering force through the eighteenth century. A volume of positive knowledge, critically sifted and ascertained; a constructive vision of the past and its institutions; the imagination, under this guidance, everywhere at play; all these elements unite in Burke. His main field is political philosophy.... His favorite form is oratory, uttered or written. His medium is prose, and the work of his later years, alone, outweighs all contemporary prose in power.... His whole body of production has the unity of some large cathedral, whose successive accretions reveal the natural growth of a single mind, without any change or essential break....
>
> Already [in the *Thoughts* and in the *Observations*] the characteristics of Burke's thought and style appear, as well as his profound conversance with constitutional history, finance, and affairs. There is a constant reference to general principles, as in the famous defence of Party. The maxims that come into play go far beyond the occasion. There is a perpetual groundswell of passion, embanked and held in check, but ever breaking out into sombre irony and sometimes into figure; but metaphors and other tropes are not yet very frequent....
>
> In the art of unfolding and amplifying, Burke is the rival of the ancients....

The Literary Criticism of Oratory

> In the speech on Conciliation the [oft-repeated] key-word is peace.... This iteration makes us see the stubborn faces on the opposite benches. There is contempt in it; their ears must be dinned, they must remember the word peace through the long intricate survey that is to follow....
>
> Often he has a turn that would have aroused the fervor of the great appreciator known to us by the name of Longinus. In his speech on Economical Reform (1780) Burke risks an appeal, in the face of the Commons, to the example of the enemy. He has described ... the reforms of the French revenue. He says: "The French have imitated us; let us, through them, imitate ourselves, ourselves in our better and happier days." A speaker who was willing to offend for the sake of startling, and to defeat his purpose, would simply have said, "The French have imitated us; let us imitate them." Burke comes to the verge of this imprudence, but he sees the outcry on the lips of the adversary, and silences them by the word *ourselves;* and then, seizing the moment of bewilderment, repeats it and explains it by the noble past; he does not say when those days were; the days of Elizabeth or of Cromwell? Let the House choose! This is true oratory, honest diplomacy.[7]

Here, in some twenty pages, we have but two hints that Burke had to put his ideas in a form adapted to his audience; only the reiterated *peace* in all Burke's writings reminds the critic of Burke's hearers; only one stroke of tact draws his attention. Most of his account is devoted to Burke's style in the limited use of the term: to his power of amplification—his conduct of the paragraph, his use of clauses now long, now short—to his figures, comparisons, and metaphors, to his management of the sentence pattern, and to his rhythms. For Professor Elton, evidently, Burke was a man, and a mind, and an artist in prose; but he was not an orator. Interest in the minutiæ of style has kept Elton from bringing his view of Burke the man to bear on his view of Burke's writings. The fusing point evidently is in the strategic purpose of the works, in their function as speeches. By holding steadily to the conception of Burke as a public man, one could make the analysis of mind and the analysis of art more illuminating for each other than Elton does.

It cannot be said that in all respects Stephenson's chapter on Lincoln in the *Cambridge History of American Literature* is more successful than Elton's treatment of Burke; but it is a better interweaving of the biographical and the literary strands of interest. Stephenson's study of the personality of Lincoln is directly and persistently used in the study of Lincoln's style.

> Is it fanciful to find a connection between the way in which his mysticism develops—its atmospheric, non-dogmatic pervasiveness—and the way in which his style develops? Certainly the literary part of him works into all the portions of his utterance with the gradualness of daylight through a shadowy wood.... And it is to be noted that the literary quality ... is of the whole, not of the detail. It does not appear as a gift of phrases. Rather it is the slow unfolding of those two original characteristics, taste and rhythm. What is growing is the degree of both things. The man is becoming deeper, and as he does so he imposes himself, in this atmospheric way, more steadily on his language.[8]

The psychology of mystical experience may appear a poor support for the study of style. It is but one factor of many, and Stephenson may justly be reproached for leaning too heavily upon it. Compared to Grierson's subtler analysis of Burke's mind and art, the essay of Stephenson seems forced and one-sided. Yet he illuminates his subject more than many of the writers so far mentioned, because he begins with a vigorous effort to bring his knowledge of the man to bear upon his interpretation of the work. But though we find in Stephenson's pages a suggestive study of Lincoln as literary man, we find no special regard for Lincoln as orator. The qualities of style that Stephenson mentions are the qualities of prose generally :

> At last he has his second manner, a manner quite his own. It is not his final manner, the one that was to give him his assured place in literature. However, in a wonderful blend of simplicity, directness, candor, joined with a clearness beyond praise, and a delightful cadence, it has outstripped every other politician of the hour. And back of its words, subtly affecting its phrases, . . . is that brooding sadness which was to be with him to the end.[9]

The final manner, it appears, is a sublimation of the qualities of the earlier, which was "keen, powerful, full of character, melodious, impressive";[10] and it is a sublimation which has the power to awaken the imagination by its flexibility, directness, pregnancy, wealth.

In this we have nothing new, unless it be the choice of stylistic categories that emphasize the larger pattern of ideas rather than the minute pattern of grammatical units, such as we have found in Elton and to some extent shall find in Saintsbury; it must be granted, too, that Stephenson has dispensed with detail and gained his larger view at the cost of no little vagueness. "Two things," says Stephenson of the Lincoln of 1849–1858, "grew upon him. The first was his understanding of men, the generality of men. . . . The other thing that grew upon him was his power to reach and influence them through words."[11] We have here the text for any study of Lincoln as orator; but the study itself this critic does not give us.

Elton's characterization of Burke's style stands out from the usual run of superficial comment by the closeness of its analysis and its regard for the architectonic element. Stephenson's characterization of Lincoln's style is distinguished by a vigorous if forced effort to unite the study of the man and of the work. With both we may contrast a better essay, by a critic of greater insight. Grierson says of Burke:

> What Burke has of the deeper spirit of that movement [the romantic revival] is seen not so much in the poetic imagery of his finest prose as in the philosophical imagination which informs his conception of the state, in virtue of which he transcends the rationalism of the century. . . . This temper of Burke's mind is reflected in his prose. . . . To the direct, conversational prose of Dryden and Swift, changed social circumstances and the influence of Johnson had given a more oratorical cast, more dignity and weight, but, also, more of heaviness and conventional elegance. From the latter faults, Burke is saved by his passionate temperament, his ardent imagination, and the fact that he was a speaker conscious always of his audience. . . . [Burke] could delight, astound, and convince an audience. He did not easily conciliate and win them over. He lacked the first essential and index of the conciliatory speaker, *lenitas vocis;* his voice was harsh and unmusical, his gesture ungainly. . . . And, even in the text of his speeches there is a strain of irony and scorn which is not well fitted to conciliate. . . . We have evidence that he could do both things on which Cicero lays

stress—move his audience to tears and delight them by his wit.... Yet, neither pathos nor humor is Burke's *forte*.... Burke's unique power as an orator lies in the peculiar interpenetration of thought and passion. Like the poet and the prophet, he thinks most profoundly when he thinks most passionately. When he is not deeply moved, his oratory verges toward the turgid; when he indulges feeling for his own sake, as in parts of *Letters on a Regicide Peace,* it becomes hysterical. But, in his greatest speeches and pamphlets, the passion of Burke's mind shows itself in the luminous thoughts which it emits, in the imagery which at once moves *and* teaches, throwing a flood of light not only on the point in question, but on the whole neighboring sphere of man's moral and political nature.[12]

The most notable feature of these passages is not their recognition that Burke was a speaker, but their recognition that his being a speaker conditioned his style, and that he is to be judged in part at least as one who attempted to influence men by the spoken word. Grierson, like Elton, attends to the element of structure and has something to say of the nature of Burke's prose; but, unlike Elton, he distinguishes this from the description of Burke's oratory—although without maintaining the distinction: he illustrates Burke's peculiar oratorical power from a pamphlet as readily as from a speech. His categories seem less mechanical than those of Elton, who is more concerned with the development of the paragraph than with the general cast of Burke's style; nor is his judgment warped, as is Stephenson's, by having a theory to market. Each has suffered from the necessity of compression. Yet, all told, Grierson realizes better than the others that Burke's task was not merely to express his thoughts and his feelings in distinguished prose, but to communicate his thoughts and his feelings effectively. It is hardly true, however, that Grierson has in mind the actual audience of Burke; the audience of Grierson's vision seems to be universalized, to consist of the judicious listeners or readers of any age. Those judicious listeners have no practical interest in the situation; they have only a philosophical and aesthetic interest.

Of Taine in his description of Burke it cannot be said that he descends to the minutiæ of style. He deals with his author's character and ideas, as do all the critics of this group, but his comments on style are simply a single impression, vivid and picturesque :

Burke had one of those fertile and precise imaginations which believe that finished knowledge is an inner view, which never quits a subject without having clothed it in its colors and forms.... To all these powers of mind, which constitute a man of system, he added all those energies of heart which constitute an enthusiast.... He brought to politics a horror of crime, a vivacity and sincerity of conscience, a sensibility, which seem suitable only to a young man.

... The vast amount of his works rolls impetuously in a current of eloquence. Sometimes a spoken or written discourse needs a whole volume to unfold the train of his multiplied proofs and courageous anger. It is either the exposé of a ministry, or the whole history of British India, or the complete theory of revolutions ... which comes down like a vast overflowing stream.... Doubtless there is foam on its eddies, mud in its bed; thousands of strange creatures sport wildly on its surface: he does not select, he lavishes.... Nothing strikes him as in excess.... He continues half a barbarian, battening in exaggeration and violence; but his fire is so sustained, his conviction so strong, his emotion so warm and abundant, that we suffer him to go on, forget our repugnance, see in his irregularities and his trespasses only the outpourings of a great heart and a deep mind, too open and too full.[13]

This is brilliant writing, unencumbered by the subaltern's interest in tactics, but it is strategy as described by a war-correspondent, not by a general. We get from it little light on how Burke solved the problem that confronts every orator: so to present ideas as to bring them into the consciousness of his hearers.

Where the critic divides his interest between the man and the work, without allowing either interest to predominate, he is often compelled to consider the work *in toto*, and we get only observations so generalized as not to include consideration of the form of the work. The speech is not thought of as essentially a means of influence; it is regarded as a specimen of prose, or as an example of philosophic thought. The date, the historical interest, the orator's own intention, are often lost from view; and criticism suffers in consequence.

IV

We have seen that the critic who is occupied chiefly with the orator as a man can contribute, although indirectly, to the study of the orator as such, and that the critic who divides his attention between the man and the work must effect a fusion of the two interests if he is to help materially in the understanding of the orator. We come now to critics more distinctly literary in aim. Within this group several classes may be discriminated: the first comprises the judicial critics; the second includes the interpretative critics who take the point of view of literary style generally, regarding the speech as an essay, or as a specimen of prose; the third and last group is composed of the writers who tend to regard the speech as a special literary form.

The type of criticism that attempts a judicial evaluation of the literary merits of the work—of the orator's "literary remains"—tends to center the inquiry on the question: Is this literature? The futility of the question appears equally in the affirmative and in the negative replies to it. The fault is less with the query, however, than with the hastiness of the answers generally given. For the most part, the critics who raise this problem are not disposed really to consider it: they formulate no conception either of literature or of oratory; they will not consider their own literary standards critically and comprehensively. In short, the question is employed as a way to dispose briefly of the subject of a lecture or of a short essay in a survey of a national literature.

Thus Phelps, in his treatment of Webster and Lincoln in *Some Makers of American Literature*,[14] tells us that they have a place in literature by virtue of their style, gives us some excerpts from Lincoln and some comments on Webster's politics, but offers no reasoned criticism. St. Peter swings wide the gates of the literary heaven, but does not explain his action. We may suspect that the solemn award of a "place in literature" sometimes conceals the absence of any real principle of judgment.

Professor Trent is less easily satisfied that Webster deserves a "place in literature." He grants Webster's power to stimulate patriotism, his sonorous dignity and massiveness, his clearness and strength of style, his powers of dramatic description. But he finds only occasional splendor of imagination, discovers no soaring quality of intelligence, and is not dazzled by his philosophy or his grasp of history. Mr. Trent would like more vivacity and humor and color in Webster's style.[15] This mode of deciding Webster's place in or out of literature is important to us only as it reveals the critic's method of judging. Trent looks for clearness and strength, imagination, philosophic grasp, vivacity, humor, color in style. This is excellent so far as it goes, but goes no further than to suggest some qualities which are to be sought in any and all works of literary art: in dramas, in essays, in lyric poems, as well as in speeches.

Let us take a third judge. Gosse will not allow Burke to be a complete master of English prose: "Notwithstanding all its magnificence, it appears to me that the prose of Burke lacks the variety, the delicacy, the modulated music of the very finest writers."[16] Gosse adds that Burke lacks flexibility, humor, and pathos. As critical method, this is one with that of Trent.

Gosse, with his question about mastery of prose, does not directly ask, "Is this literature?" Henry Cabot Lodge does, and his treatment of Webster (in the *Cambridge History of American Literature*) is curious. Lodge is concerned to show that Webster belongs to literature, and to explain the quality in his work that gives him a place among the best makers of literature. The test applied is permanence: Is Webster still read? The answer is, yes, for he is part of every schoolboy's education, and is the most quoted author in Congress. The sight of a literary critic resigning the judicial bench to the schoolmaster and the Congressman is an enjoyable one; as enjoyable as Mr. H. L. Mencken's reaction to it would be; but one could wish for grounds more relative than this. Mr. Lodge goes on to account for Webster's permanence: it lies in his power to impart to rhetoric the literary touch. The distinction between rhetoric and literature is not explained, but apparently the matter lies thus: rhetorical verse may be poetry; Byron is an example. Rhetorical prose is not literature until there is added the literary touch. We get a clue as to how the literary touch may be added: put in something imaginative, something that strikes the hearer at once. The example chosen by Lodge is a passage from Webster in which the imaginative or literary touch is given by the single word "mildew."[17] This method of criticism, too, we may reduce to that of Trent, with the exception that only one quality—imagination—is requisite for admission to the literary Valhalla.

Whether the critic's standard be imagination, or this together with other qualities such as intelligence, vivacity, humor, or whether it be merely "style," undefined and unexplained, the point of view is always that of the printed page. The oration is lost from view, and becomes an exercise in prose, musical, colorful, varied, and delicate, but, so far as the critic is concerned, formless and purposeless. Distinctions of literary type or kind are erased; the architectonic element is neglected; and the speech is regarded as a musical meditation might be regarded: as a kind of harmonious musing that drifts pleasantly along, with little of inner form and nothing of objective purpose. This, it should be recognized, is not the result of judicial criticism so much as the result of the attempt to decide too hastily whether a given work is to be admitted into the canon of literature.

V

It is, perhaps, natural for the historian of literature to reduce all literary production to one standard, and thus to discuss only the common elements in all prose. One can understand also that the biographer, when in the course of his task he must turn literary critic, finds himself often inadequately equipped and his judgment of little value, except on the scale of literature generally rather than of oratory or of any given type. More is to be expected, however, of those who set up as literary critics in the first instance: those who deal directly with Webster's style, or with Lincoln as man of letters. We shall find such critics as Whipple, Hazlitt, and Saintsbury devoting themselves to the description of literary style in the orators whom they discuss. Like the summary judicial critics we have mentioned, their center of interest is the work; but they are less hurried than Gosse and Lodge and Phelps and Trent; and their aim is not judgment so much as understanding. Yet their interpretations, in the main, take the point of view of the printed page, of the prose essay. Only to a slight degree is there a shift to another point of view, that of the orator in relation to the audience on whom he exerts his influence; the immediate public begins to loom a little larger; the essential nature of the oration as a type begins to be suggested.

Saintsbury has a procedure which much resembles that of Elton, though we must note the fact that the former omits consideration of Burke as a personality and centers attention on his work. We saw that Elton, in his passages on Burke's style, attends both to the larger elements of structure and to such relatively minute points as the management of the sentence and the clause. In Saintsbury the range of considerations is the same. At times, indeed, the juxtaposition of large and small ideas is ludicrous, as when one sentence ends by awarding to Burke literary immortality, and the next describes the sentences of an early work as "short and crisp, arranged with succinct antithetic parallels, which seldom exceed a single pair of clauses."[18] The award of immortality is not, it should be said, based entirely on the shortness of Burke's sentences in his earliest works. Indeed much of Saintsbury's comment is of decided interest:

> The style of Burke is necessarily to be considered throughout as conditioned by oratory.... In other words, he was first of all a rhetorician, and probably the greatest that modern times have ever produced. But his rhetoric always inclined much more to the written than to the spoken form, with results annoying perhaps to him at the time, but even to him satisfactory afterwards, and an inestimable gain to the world....
>
> The most important of these properties of Burke's style, in so far as it is possible to enumerate them here, are as follows. First of all, and most distinctive, so much so as to have escaped no competent critic, is a very curious and, until his example made it imitable, nearly unique faculty of building up an argument or a picture by a succession of complementary strokes, not added at haphazard but growing out of and onto one another. No one has ever been such a master of the best and grandest kind of the figure called ... Amplification, and this ... is the direct implement by which he achieves his greatest effects.
>
> ... The piece [*Present Discontents*] may be said to consist of a certain number of specially labored paragraphs in which the arguments or pictures just spoken of are put as forcibly as the author can put them, and as a rule in a succession of shortish sentences, built up and glued together with the strength and flexibility of a newly fashioned fishing-rod. In the intervals the texts thus given are turned about, commented on, justified, or discussed in detail, in a rhetoric for the most part, though not always, rather less serried, less evidently burnished, and in less full dress. And this general arrangement proceeds through the rest of his works.[19]

After a number of comments on Burke's skill in handling various kinds of ornament, such as humor, epigram, simile, Saintsbury returns to the idea that Burke's special and definite weapon was "imaginative argument, and the marshalling of vast masses of complicated detail into properly rhetorical battalions or (to alter the image) mosaic pictures of enduring beauty."[20] Saintsbury's attitude toward the communicative, impulsive nature of the orator's task is indicated in a passage on the well-known description of Windsor Castle. This description the critic terms "at once ... a perfect harmonic chord, a complete visual picture, and a forcible argument."[21] It is significant that he adds, "The minor rhetoric, the suasive purpose [presumably the argumentative intent] must be kept in view; if it be left out the thing loses"; and holds Burke "far below Browne, who had no need of purpose."[22] It is less important that a critic think well of the suasive purpose than that he reckon with it, and of Saintsbury at least it must be said that he recognizes it, although grudgingly; but it cannot be said that Saintsbury has a clear conception of rhetoric as the art of communication: sometimes it means the art of prose, sometimes that of suasion.

Hazlitt's method of dealing with Burke resembles Taine's as Saintsbury's resembles that of Elton. In Hazlitt we have a critic who deals with style in the large; details of rhythm, of sentence pattern, of imagery, are ignored. His principal criticism of Burke as orator is contained in the well-known contrast with Chatham, really a contrast of mind and temperament in relation to oratorical style. He follows this with some excellent comment on Burke's prose style; nothing more is said of his oratory; only in a few passages do we get a flash of light on the relation of Burke to his audience, as in the remark about his eagerness to impress his reader, and in the description of his conversational quality. It is notable too that Hazlitt finds those works which never had the form of speeches the most significant and most typical of Burke's style.

> Burke was so far from being a gaudy or flowery writer, that he was one of the severest writers we have. His words are the most like things; his style is the most strictly limited to the subject. He unites every extreme and every variety of composition; the lowest and the meanest words and descriptions with the highest.... He had no other object but to produce the strongest impression on his reader, by giving the truest, the most characteristic, the fullest, and most forcible description of things, trusting to the power of his own mind to mold them into grace and beauty.... Burke most frequently produced an effect by the remoteness and novelty of his combinations, by the force of contrast, by the striking manner in which the most opposite and unpromising materials were harmoniously blended together; not by laying his hands on all the fine things he could think of, but by bringing together those things which he knew would blaze out into glorious light by their collision.[23]

Twelve years after writing the essay from which we have quoted, Hazlitt had occasion to revise his estimate of Burke as a statesman; but his sketch of Burke's style is essentially unaltered.[24] In Hazlitt we find a sense of style as an instrument of communication; that sense is no stronger in dealing with Burke's speeches than in dealing with his pamphlets, but it gives to Hazlitt's criticisms a reality not often found. What is lacking is a clear sense of Burke's communicative impulse, of his persuasive purpose, as operating in a concrete situation. Hazlitt does not suggest the background of Burke's speeches, ignores the events that called them forth. He views his subject, in a sense, as Grierson does: as speaking to the judicious but disinterested hearer of any age other than Burke's own. But the problem of the speaker, as well as of the pamphleteer, is to interest men here and now; the understanding of that problem requires, on the part of the critic, a strong historical sense for the ideas and attitudes of the people (not merely of their leaders), and a full knowledge of the public opinion of the times in which the orator spoke. This we do not find in Hazlitt.

Two recent writers on Lincoln commit the opposite error: they devote themselves so completely to description of the situation in which Lincoln wrote as to leave no room for criticism. L. E. Robinson's *Lincoln as Man of Letters*[25] is a biography rewritten around Lincoln's writings. It is nothing more. Instead of giving us a criticism, Professor Robinson has furnished us with some of the materials of the critic; his own judgments are too largely laudatory to cast much light. The book, therefore, is not all that its title implies. A single chapter of accurate summary and evaluation would do much to increase our understanding of Lincoln as man of letters, even though it said nothing of Lincoln as speaker. A chapter or two on Lincoln's work in various kinds—letters, state papers, speeches—would help us to a finer discrimination than Professor Robinson's book offers. Again, the proper estimate of style in any satisfactory sense requires us to do more than to weigh the soundness of an author's thought and to notice the isolated beauties of his expression. Something should be said of structure, something of adaptation to the immediate audience, whose convictions and habits of thought, whose literary usages, and whose general cultural background all condition the work both of writer and speaker. Mr. Robinson has given us the political situation as a problem in controlling political forces, with little regard to the force even of public opinion, and with almost none to the cultural background. Lincoln's works, therefore, emerge as items in a political sequence, but not as resultants of the life of his time.

Some of the deficiencies of Robinson's volume are supplied by Dodge's essay, *Lincoln as Master of Words*.[26] Dodge considers, more definitely than Robinson, the types in which Lincoln worked: he separates messages from campaign speeches, letters from occasional addresses. He has an eye on Lincoln's relation to his audience, but this manifests itself chiefly in an account of the immediate reception of a work. Reports of newspaper comments on the speeches may be a notable addition to Lincolniana; supported by more political information and more insight than Mr. Dodge's short book reveals, they might become an aid to the critical evaluation of the speeches. But in themselves they are neither a criticism nor an interpretation of Lincoln's mastery of words.

Robinson and Dodge, then, stand at opposite poles to Saintsbury and Hazlitt. The date is put in opposition to the work as a center of critical interest. If the two writers on Lincoln lack a full perception of their author's background, they do not lack a sense of its importance. If the critics of Burke do not produce a complete and rounded criticism, neither do they lose themselves in preparatory studies. Each method is incomplete; each should supplement the other.

We turn now to a critic who neglects the contribution of history to the study of oratory, but who has two compensating merits: the merit of recognizing the types in which his subject worked, and the merit of remembering that an orator has as his audience, not posterity, but certain classes of his own contemporaries. Whipple's essay on Webster is open to attack from various directions: it is padded, it "dates," it is overlaudatory, it is overpatriotic, it lacks distinction of style. But there is wheat in the chaff. Scattered through the customary discussion of Webster's choice of words, his power of epithet, his compactness of statement, his images, the development of his style, are definite suggestions of a new point of view. It is the point of view of the actual audience. To Whipple, at times at least, Webster was not a writer, but a speaker; the critic tries to imagine the man, and also his hearers; he thinks of the speech as a communication to a certain body of auditors. A phrase often betrays a mental attitude; Whipple alone of the critics we have mentioned would have written of "the eloquence, the moral power, he infused into his reasoning, so as to make the dullest citation of legal authority *tell* on the minds he addressed."[27] Nor would any other writer of this group have attempted to distinguish the types of audience Webster met. That Whipple's effort is a rambling and incoherent one, is not here. in point. Nor is it pertinent that the critic goes completely astray in explaining why Webster's speeches have the nature of "organic formations, or at least of skilful engineering or architectural constructions"; though to say that the art of giving objective reality to a speech consists only of "a happy collocation and combination of words"[28] is certainly as far as possible from explaining Webster's sense of structure. What is significant in Whipple's essay is the occasional indication of a point of view that includes the audience. Such an indication is the passage in which the critic explains the source of Webster's influence:

> What gave Webster his immense influence over the opinions of the people of New England, was first, his power of so "putting things" that everybody could understand his statements; secondly, his power of so framing his arguments that all the steps, from one point to another, in a logical series, could be clearly apprehended by every intelligent farmer or mechanic who had a thoughtful interest in the affairs of the country; and thirdly, his power of inflaming the sentiment of patriotism in all honest and well-intentioned men by overwhelming appeals to that sentiment, so that after convincing their understandings, he clinched the matter by sweeping away their wills.
>
> Perhaps to these sources of influence may be added . . . a genuine respect for the intellect, as well as for the manhood, of average men.[29]

In various ways the descriptive critics recognize the orator's function. In some, that recognition takes the form of a regard to the background of the speeches; in others, it takes the form of a regard to the effectiveness of the work, though that effectiveness is often construed as for the reader rather than for the listener. The "minor rhetoric, the suasive purpose" is beginning to be felt, though not always recognized and never fully taken into account.

VI

The distinction involved in the presence of a persuasive purpose is clearly recognized by some of those who have written on oratory, and by some biographers and historians.

The writers now to be mentioned are aware, more keenly than any of those we have so far met, of the speech as a literary form—or if not as a literary form, then as a form of power; they tend accordingly to deal with the orator's work as limited by the conditions of the platform and the occasion, and to summon history to the aid of criticism.

The method of approach of the critics of oratory as oratory is well put by Lord Curzon at the beginning of his essay, *Modern Parliamentary Eloquence:*

> In dealing with the Parliamentary speakers of our time I shall, accordingly, confine myself to those whom I have myself heard, or for whom I can quote the testimony of others who heard them; and I shall not regard them as prose writers or literary men, still less as purveyors of instruction to their own or to future generations, but as men who produced, by the exercise of certain talents of speech, a definite impression upon contemporary audiences, and whose reputation for eloquence must be judged by that test, and that test alone.[30]

The last phrase, "that test alone," would be scanned; the judgment of orators is not solely to be determined by the impression of contemporary audiences. For the present it will be enough to note the topics touched in Curzon's anecdotes and reminiscences—his lecture is far from a systematic or searching inquiry into the subject, and is of interest rather for its method of approach than for any considered study of an orator or of a period. We value him for his promises rather than for his performance. Curzon deals with the relative rank of speakers, with the comparative value of various speeches by a single man, with the orator's appearance and demeanor, with his mode of preparation and of delivery, with his mastery of epigram or image. Skill in seizing upon the dominant characteristics of each of his subjects saves the author from the worst triviality of reminiscence. Throughout, the point of view is that of the man experienced in public life discussing the eloquence of other public men, most of whom he had known and actually heard. That this is not the point of view of criticism in any strict sense, is of course true; but the *naiveté* and directness of this observer correct forcibly some of the extravagances we have been examining.

The lecture on Chatham as an orator by H. M. Butler exemplifies a very different method arising from a different subject and purpose. The lecturer is thinking, he tells us, "of Oratory partly as an art, partly as a branch of literature, partly as a power of making history."[31] His method is first to touch lightly upon Chatham's early training and upon his mode of preparing and delivering his speeches; next, to present some of the general judgments upon the Great Commoner, whether of contemporaries or of later historians; then to re-create a few of the most important speeches, partly by picturing the historical setting, partly by quotation, partly by the comments of contemporary writers. The purpose of the essay is "to reawaken, however faintly, some echoes of the kingly voice of a genuine Patriot, of whom his country is still justly proud."[32] The patriotic purpose we may ignore, but the wish to reconstruct the *mise en scène* of Chatham's speeches, to put the modern Oxford audience at the point of view of those who listened to the voice of Pitt, saw the flash of his eye and felt the force of his noble bearing, this is a purpose different from that of the critics whom we have examined. It may be objected that Butler's lecture has the defects of its method: the amenities observed by a Cambridge don delivering a formal lecture at Oxford keep us from getting on with the subject; the brevity of the discourse prevents anything like a full treatment; the aim, revivification of the past, must be very broadly interpreted if it is to be really critical. Let us admit these things; it still is true that in a few pages the essential features of Pitt's eloquence are brought vividly before us, and that this is accomplished by thinking of the speech as originally delivered to its first audience rather than as read by the modern reader.

The same sense of the speaker in his relation to his audience appears in Lecky's account of Burke. This account, too, is marked by the use of contemporary witnesses, and of comparisons with Burke's great rivals. But let Lecky's method speak in part for itself:

> He spoke too often, too vehemently, and much too long; and his eloquence, though in the highest degree intellectual, powerful, various, and original, was not well adapted to a popular audience. He had little or nothing of that fire and majesty of declamation with which Chatham thrilled his hearers, and often almost overawed opposition; and as a parliamentary debater he was far inferior to Charles Fox. . . . Burke was not inferior to Fox in readiness, and in the power of clear and cogent reasoning. His wit, though not of the highest order, was only equalled by that of Townshend, Sheridan, and perhaps North, and it rarely failed in its effect upon the House. He far surpassed every other speaker in the copiousness and correctness of his diction, in the range of knowledge he brought to bear on every subject of debate, in the richness and variety of his imagination, in the gorgeous beauty of his descriptive passages, in the depth of the philosophical reflections and the felicity of the personal sketches which he delighted in scattering over his speeches. But these gifts were frequently marred by a strange want of judgment, measure, and self-control. His speeches were full of episodes and digressions, of excessive ornamentation and illustration, of dissertations on general principles of politics, which were invaluable in themselves, but very unpalatable to a tired or excited House waiting eagerly for a division.[33]

These sentences suggest, and the pages from which they are excerpted show, that historical imagination has led Lecky to regard Burke as primarily a speaker, both limited and formed by the conditions of his platform; and they exemplify, too, a happier use of stylistic categories than do the essays of Curzon and Butler. The requirements of the historian's art have fused the character sketch and the literary criticism; the fusing agent has been the conception of Burke as a public man, and of his work as public address. Both Lecky's biographical interpretation and his literary criticism are less subtle than that of Grierson; but Lecky is more definitely guided in his treatment of Burke by the conception of oratory as a special form of the literature of power and as a form molded always by the pressure of the time.

The merits of Lecky are contained, in ampler form, in Morley's biography of Gladstone. The long and varied career of the great parliamentarian makes a general summary and final judgment difficult and perhaps inadvisable; Morley does not attempt them. But his running account of Gladstone as orator, if assembled from his thousand pages, is an admirable example of what can be done by one who has the point of view of the public man, sympathy with his subject, and understanding of the speaker's art. Morley gives us much contemporary reporting: the descriptions and judgments of journalists at various stages in Gladstone's career, the impression made by the speeches upon delivery, comparison with other speakers of the time. Here history is contemporary: the biographer was himself the witness of much that he describes, and has the experienced parliamentarian's flair for the scene and the situation. Gladstone's temperament and physical equipment for the platform, his training in the art of speaking, the nature of his chief appeals, the factor of character and personality, these are some of the topics repeatedly touched. There is added a sense for the permanent results of Gladstone's speaking: not the votes in the House merely, but the changed state of public opinion brought about by the speeches.

> Mr. Gladstone conquered the House, because he was saturated with a subject and its arguments; because he could state and enforce his case; because he plainly believed every word he said, and earnestly wished to press the same belief into the minds of his hearers; finally because he was from the first an eager and a powerful athlete.... Yet with this inborn readiness for combat, nobody was less addicted to aggression or provocation....
>
> In finance, the most important of all the many fields of his activity, Mr. Gladstone had the signal distinction of creating the public opinion by which he worked, and warming the climate in which his projects throve.... Nobody denies that he was often declamatory and discursive, that he often overargued and overrefined; [but] he nowhere exerted greater influence than in that department of affairs where words out of relation to fact are most surely exposed. If he often carried the proper rhetorical arts of amplification and development to excess, yet the basis of fact was both sound and clear.... Just as Macaulay made thousands read history, who before had turned from it as dry and repulsive, so Mr. Gladstone made thousands eager to follow the public balance-sheet, and the whole nation became his audience....
>
> [In the Midlothian campaign] it was the orator of concrete detail, of inductive instances, of energetic and immediate object; the orator confidently and by sure touch startling into watchfulness the whole spirit of civil duty in man; elastic and supple, pressing fact and figure with a fervid insistence that was known from his career and character to be neither forced nor feigned, but to be himself. In a word, it was a man—a man impressing himself upon the kindled throngs by the breadth of his survey of great affairs of life and nations, by the depth of his vision, by the power of his stroke.[34]

Objections may be made to Morley's method, chiefly on the ground of omissions. Though much is done to re-create the scene, though ample use is made of the date and the man, there is little formal analysis of the work. It is as if one had come from the House of Commons after hearing the speeches, stirred to enthusiasm but a little confused by the wealth of argument; not as if one came from a calm study of the speeches; not even as if one had corrected personal impressions by such a study. Of the structure of the speeches, little is said; but a few perorations are quoted; the details of style, one feels, although noticed at too great length by some critics, might well receive a modicum of attention here.

Although these deficiencies of Morley's treatment are not supplied by Bryce in his short and popular sketch of Gladstone, there is a summary which well supplements the running account offered by Morley. It has the merit of dealing explicitly with the orator as orator, and it offers more analysis and an adequate judgment by a qualified critic.

> Twenty years hence Mr. Gladstone's [speeches] will not be read, except of course by historians. They are too long, too diffuse, too minute in their handling of details, too elaborately qualified in their enunciation of general principles. They contain few epigrams and few ... weighty thoughts put into telling phrases.... The style, in short, is not sufficiently rich or finished to give a perpetual interest to matters whose practical importance has vanished....
>
> If, on the other hand, Mr. Gladstone be judged by the impression he made on his own time, his place will be high in the front rank.... His oratory had many conspicuous merits. There was a lively imagination, which enabled him to relieve even dull matter by pleasing figures, together with a large command of quotations and illustrations.... There was admirable lucidity and accuracy in exposition. There was great skill in the disposition and marshalling of his arguments, and finally ... there was a wonderful variety and grace of appropriate gesture. But above and beyond everything else which enthralled the listener, there were four qualities, two specially conspicuous in the substance of his eloquence—inventiveness and elevation; two not less remarkable in his manner—force in the delivery, expressive modulation in the voice.[35]

One is tempted to say that Morley has provided the historical setting, Bryce the critical verdict. The statement would be only partially true, for Morley does much more than set the scene. He enacts the drama; and thus he conveys his judgment—not, it is true, in the form of a critical estimate, but in the course of his narrative. The difference between these two excellent accounts is a difference in emphasis. The one lays stress on the setting; the other takes it for granted. The one tries to suggest his judgment by description; the other employs the formal categories of criticism.

Less full and rounded than either of these descriptions of an orator's style is Trevelyan's estimate of Bright. Yet in a few pages the biographer has indicated clearly the two distinguishing features of Bright's eloquence—the moral weight he carried with his audience, the persuasiveness of his visible earnestness and of his reputation for integrity, and his "sense for the value of words and for the rhythm of words and sentences";[36] has drawn a contrast between Bright and Gladstone; and has added a description of Bright's mode of work, together with some comments on the permanence of the speeches and various examples of details of his style. Only the mass and weight of that style are not represented.

If we leave the biographers and return to those who, like Curzon and Butler, have written directly upon eloquence, we find little of importance. Of the two general histories of oratory that we have in English, Hardwicke's[37] is so ill organized and so ill written as to be negligible; that by Sears[38] may deserve mention. It is uneven and inaccurate. It is rather a popular handbook which strings together the great names than a history: the author does not seriously consider the evolution of oratory. His sketches are of unequal merit; some give way to the interest in mere anecdote; some yield too large a place to biographical detail; others are given over to moralizing. Sears touches most of the topics of rhetorical criticism without making the point of view of public address dominant; his work is too episodic for that. And any given criticism shows marked defects in execution. It would not be fair to compare Sears's show-piece, his chapter on Webster, with Morley or Bryce on Gladstone; but compare it with Trevelyan's few pages on Bright. With far greater economy, Trevelyan tells us more of Bright as a speaker than Sears can of Webster. The *History of Oratory* gives us little more than hints and suggestions of a good method.

With a single exception, the collections of eloquence have no critical significance. The exception is *Select British Eloquence*,[39] edited by Chauncey A. Goodrich, who prefaced the works of each of his orators with a sketch partly biographical and partly critical. The criticisms of Goodrich, like those of Sears, are of unequal value; some are slight, yet none descends to mere anecdote, and at his best, as in the characterizations of the eloquence of Chatham, Fox, and Burke, Goodrich reveals a more powerful grasp and a more comprehensive view of his problem than does Sears, as well as a more consistent view of his subject as a speaker. Sears at times takes the point of view of the printed page; Goodrich consistently thinks of the speeches he discusses as intended for oral delivery.

Goodrich's topics of criticism are: the orator's training, mode of work, personal (physical) qualifications, character as known to his audience, range of powers, dominant traits as a speaker. He deals too, of course, with those topics to which certain of the critics we have noticed confine themselves: illustration, ornament, gift of phrase, diction, wit, imagination, arrangement. But these he does not overemphasize, nor view as independent of their effect upon an audience. Thus he can say of Chatham's sentence structure: "The sentences are not rounded or balanced periods, but are made up of short clauses, which flash themselves upon the mind with all the vividness of distinct ideas, and yet are closely connected together as tending to the same point, and uniting to form larger masses of thought."[40] Perhaps the best brief indication of Goodrich's quality is his statement of Fox's "leading peculiarities."[41] According to Goodrich, Fox had a luminous simplicity, which combined unity of impression with irregular arrangement; he took everything in the concrete; he struck instantly at the heart of his subject, going to the issue at once; he did not amplify, he repeated; he rarely employed a preconceived order of argument; reasoning was his *forte*, but it was the reasoning of the debater; he abounded in *hits*—abrupt and startling turns of thought—and in sideblows delivered in passing; he was often dramatic; he had astonishing skill in turning the course of debate to his own advantage. Here is the point of view of public address, expressed as clearly as in Morley or in Curzon, though in a different idiom, and without the biographer's fulness of treatment.

But probably the best single specimen of the kind of criticism now under discussion is Morley's chapter on Cobden as an agitator. This is as admirable a summary sketch as the same writer's account of Gladstone is a detailed historical picture. Bryce's brief essay on Gladstone is inferior to it both in the range of its technical criticisms and in the extent to which the critic realizes the situation in which his subject was an actor. In a few pages Morley has drawn the physical characteristics of his subject, his bent of mind, temperament, idiosyncrasies; has compared and contrasted Cobden with his great associate, Bright; has given us contemporary judgments; has sketched out the dominant quality of his style, its variety and range; has noted Cobden's attitude to his hearers, his view of human nature; and has dealt with the impression given by Cobden's printed speeches and the total impression of his personality on the platform. The method, the angle of approach, the categories of description or of criticism, are the same as those employed in the great life of Gladstone; but we find them here condensed into twenty pages. It will be worth while to present the most interesing parts of Morley's criticism, if only for comparison with some of the passages already given:

> I have asked many scores of those who knew him, Conservatives as well as Liberals, what this secret [of his oratorical success] was, and in no single case did my interlocutor fail to begin, and in nearly every case he ended as he had begun, with the word *persuasiveness*. Cobden made his way to men's hearts by the union which they saw in him of simplicity, earnestness, and conviction, with a singular facility of exposition. This facility consisted in a remarkable power of apt and homely illustration, and a curious ingenuity in framing the argument that happened to be wanted. Besides his skill in thus hitting on the right argument, Cobden had the oratorical art of presenting it in the way that made its admission to the understanding of a listener easy and undenied. He always seemed to have made exactly the right degree of allowance for the difficulty with which men follow a speech, as compared with the ease of following the same argument on a printed page. . . .
>
> Though he abounded in matter, Cobden can hardly be described as copious. He is neat and pointed, nor is his argument ever left unclinched; but he permits himself no large excursions. What he was thinking of was the matter immediately in hand, the audience before his eyes, the point that would tell best then and there, and would be most likely to remain in men's recollections. . . . What is remarkable is, that while he kept close to the matter and substance of his case, and resorted comparatively little to sarcasm, humor, invective, pathos, or the other elements that are catalogued in manuals of rhetoric, yet no speaker was ever further removed from prosiness, or came into more real and sympathetic contact with his audience. . . .
>
> After all, it is not tropes and perorations that make the popular speaker; it is the whole impression of his personality. We who only read them can discern certain admirable qualities in Cobden's speeches; aptness in choosing topics, lucidity in presenting them, buoyant confidence in pressing them home. But those who listened to them felt much more than all this. They were delighted by mingled vivacity and ease, by directness, by spontaneousness and reality, by the charm . . . of personal friendliness and undisguised cordiality.[42]

These passages are written in the spirit of the critic of public speaking. They have the point of view that is but faintly suggested in Elton and Grierson, that Saintsbury recognizes but does not use, and Hazlitt uses but does not recognize, and that Whipple, however irregularly, both understands and employs. But such critics as Curzon and Butler, Sears and Goodrich, Trevelyan and Bryce, think differently of their problem; they take the point of view of public address consistently and without question. Morley's superiority is not m conception, but in execution. In all the writers of this group, whether historians, biographers, or professed students of oratory, there is a consciousness that oratory is partly an art, partly a power of making history, and occasionally a branch of literature. Style is less considered for its own sake than for its effect in a given situation. The question of literary immortality is regarded as beside the mark, or else, as in Bryce, as a separate question requiring separate consideration. There are, of course, differences of emphasis. Some of the biographers may be thought to deal too lightly with style. Sears perhaps thinks too little of the time, of the drama of the situation, and too much of style. But we have arrived at a different attitude towards the orator; his function is recognized for what it is: the art of influencing men in some concrete situation. Neither the personal nor the literary evaluation is the primary object. The critic speaks of the orator as a public man whose function it is to exert his influence by speech.

VII

Any attempt to sum up the results of this casual survey of what some writers have said of some public speakers must deal with the differences between literary criticism as represented by Gosse and Trent, by Elton and Grierson, and rhetorical criticism as represented by Curzon, Morley, Bryce, and Trevelyan. The literary critics seem at first to have no common point of view and no agreement as to the categories of judgment or description. But by reading between their lines and searching for the main endeavor of these critics, one can discover at least a unity of purpose. Different in method as are Gosse, Elton, Saintsbury, Whipple, Hazlitt, the ends they have in view are not different.

Coupled with almost every description of the excellences of prose and with every attempt to describe the man in connection with his work, is the same effort as we find clearly and even arbitrarily expressed by those whom we have termed judicial critics. All the literary critics unite in the attempt to interpret the permanent value that they find in the work under consideration. That permanent value is not precisely indicated by the term beauty, but the two strands of æsthetic excellence and permanence are clearly found, not only in the avowed judicial criticism but in those writers who emphasize description rather than judgment. Thus Grierson says of Burke:

> His preoccupation at every juncture with the fundamental issues of wise government, and the splendor of the eloquence in which he set forth these principles, an eloquence in which the wisdom of his thought and the felicity of his language and imagery seem inseparable from one another ... have made his speeches and pamphlets a source of perennial freshness and interest.[43]

Perhaps a critic of temper different from Grierson's—Saintsbury, for example—would turn from the wisdom of Burke's thought to the felicity of his language and imagery. But always there is implicit in the critic's mind the absolute standard of a timeless world: the wisdom of Burke's thought (found in the principles to which his mind always gravitates rather than in his decisions on points of policy) and the felicity of his language are not considered as of an age, but for all time. Whether the critic considers the technical excellence merely, or both technique and substance, his preoccupation is with that which age cannot wither nor custom stale. (From this point of view, the distinction between the speech and the pamphlet is of no moment, and Elton wisely speaks of Burke's favorite form as "oratory, uttered or written";[44] for a speech cannot be the subject of a permanent evaluation unless it is preserved in print.)

This is the implied attitude of all the literary critics. On this common ground their differences disappear or become merely differences of method or of competence. They are all, in various ways, interpreters of the permanent and universal values they find in the works of which they treat. Nor can there be any quarrel with this attitude—unless all standards be swept away. The impressionist and the historian of the evolution of literature as a self-contained activity may deny the utility or the possibility of a truly judicial criticism. But the human mind insists upon judgment *sub specie æternitatis*. The motive often appears as a merely practical one: the reader wishes to be apprised of the best that has been said and thought in all ages; he is less concerned with the descent of literary species or with the critic's adventures among masterpieces than with the perennial freshness and interest those masterpieces may hold for him. There is, of course, much more than a practical motive to justify the interest in permanent values; but this is not the place to raise a moot question of general critical theory. We wished only to note the common ground of literary criticism in its preoccupation with the thought and the eloquence which is permanent.

If now we turn to rhetorical criticism as we found it exemplified in the preceding section, we find that its point of view is patently single. It is not concerned with permanence, nor yet with beauty. It is concerned with effect. It regards a speech as a communication to a specific audience, and holds its business to be the analysis and appreciation of the orator's method of imparting his ideas to his hearers.

Rhetoric, however, is a word that requires explanation; its use in connection with criticism is neither general nor consistent. The merely depreciatory sense in which it is often applied to bombast or false ornament need not delay us. The limited meaning which confines the term to the devices of a correct and even of an elegant prose style—in the sense of manner of writing and speaking—may also be eliminated, as likewise the broad interpretation which makes rhetoric inclusive of all style whether in prose or in poetry. There remain some definitions which have greater promise. We may mention first that of Aristotle: "the faculty of observing in any given case the available means of persuasion";[45] this readily turns into the art of persuasion, as the editors of the *New English Dictionary* recognize when they define rhetoric as "the art of using language so as to persuade or influence others." The gloss on "persuade" afforded by the additional term "influence" is worthy of note. Jebb achieves the same result by defining rhetoric as "the art of using language in such a way as to produce a desired impression upon the hearer or reader."[46] There is yet a fourth definition, one which serves to illuminate the others as well as to emphasize their essential agreement: "taken broadly [rhetoric is] the science and art of communication in language";[47] the framers of this definition add that to throw the emphasis on communication is to emphasize prose, poetry being regarded as more distinctly expressive than communicative. A German writer has made a similar distinction between poetic as the art of poetry and rhetoric as the art of prose, but rather on the basis that prose is of the intellect, poetry of the imagination.[48] Wackernagel's basis for the distinction will hardly stand in face of the attitude of modern psychology to the "faculties"; yet the distinction itself is suggestive, and it does not contravene the more significant opposition of expression and communication. That opposition has been well stated, though with some exaggeration, by Professor Hudson:

> The writer in pure literature has his eye on his subject; his subject has filled his mind and engaged his interest, and he must tell about it; his task is expression; his form and style are organic with his subject. The writer of rhetorical discourse has his eye upon the audience and occasion; his task is persuasion; his form and style are organic with the occasion.[49]

The element of the author's personality should not be lost from sight in the case of the writer of pure literature; nor may the critic think of the audience and the occasion as alone conditioning the work of the composer of rhetorical discourse, unless indeed he include in the occasion both the personality of the speaker and the subject. The distinction is better put by Professor Baldwin:

> Rhetoric meant to the ancient world the art of instructing and moving men in their affairs; poetic the art of sharpening and expanding their vision.... The one is composition of ideas; the other, composition of images. In the one field life is discussed; in the other it is presented. The type of the one is a public address, moving us to assent and action; the type of the other is a play, showing us [an] action moving to an end of character. The one argues and urges; the other represents. Though both appeal to imagination, the method of rhetoric is logical; the method of poetic, as well as its detail, is imaginative.[50]

It is noteworthy that in this passage there is nothing to oppose poetry, in its common acceptation of verse, to prose. Indeed, in discussing the four forms of discourse usually treated in textbooks, Baldwin explicitly classes exposition and argument under rhetoric, leaving narrative and description to the other field. But rhetoric has been applied to the art of prose by some who include under the term even nonmetrical works of fiction. This is the attitude of Wackernagel, already mentioned, and of Saintsbury, who observes that Aristotle's *Rhetoric* holds, "if not intentionally, yet actually, something of the same position towards Prose as that which the *Poetics* holds towards verse."[51] In Saintsbury's view, the *Rhetoric* achieves this position in virtue of its third book, that on style and arrangement: the first two books contain "a great deal of matter which has either the faintest connection with literary criticism or else no connection with it at all."[52] Saintsbury finds it objectionable in Aristotle that to him, "prose as prose is merely and avowedly a secondary consideration: it is always in the main, and sometimes wholly, a mere necessary instrument of divers practical purposes,"[53] and that "he does not *wish* to consider a piece of prose as a work of art destined, first of all, if not finally, to fulfil its own laws on the one hand, and to give pleasure on the other."[54] The distinction between verse and prose has often troubled the waters of criticism. The explanation is probably that the outer form of a work is more easily understood and more constantly present to the mind than is the real form. Yet it is strange that those who find the distinction between verse and prose important should parallel this with a distinction between imagination and intellect, as if a novel had more affinities with a speech than with an epic. It is strange, too, that Saintsbury's own phrase about the right way to consider a "piece of prose"—as a work of art destined "to fulfil its own laws"—did not suggest to him the fundamental importance of a distinction between what he terms the minor or suasive rhetoric on the one hand, and on the other poetic, whether or not in verse. For poetry always is free to fulfil its own law, but the writer of rhetorical discourse is, in a sense, perpetually in bondage to the occasion and the audience; and in that fact we find the line of cleavage between rhetoric and poetic.

The distinction between rhetoric as theory of public address and poetic as theory of pure literature, says Professor Baldwin, "seems not to have controlled any consecutive movement of modern criticism."[55] That it has not controlled the procedure of critics in dealing with orators is indicated in the foregoing pages; yet we have found, too, many suggestions of a better method, and some few critical performances against which the only charge is overcondensation.

Rhetorical criticism is necessarily analytical. The scheme of a rhetorical study includes the element of the speaker's personality as a conditioning factor; it includes also the public character of the man—not what he was, but what he was thought to be. It requires a description of the speaker's audience, and of the leading ideas with which he plied his hearers—his topics, the motives to which he appealed, the nature of the proofs he offered. These will reveal his own judgment of human nature in his audiences, and also his judgment on the questions which he discussed. Attention must be paid, too, to the relation of the surviving texts to what was actually uttered: in case the nature of the changes is known, there may be occasion to consider adaptation to two audiences—that which heard and that which read. Nor can rhetorical criticism omit the speaker's mode of arrangement and his mode of expression, nor his habit of preparation and his manner of delivery from the platform; though the last two are perhaps less significant. "Style"— in the sense which corresponds to diction and sentence movement—must receive attention, but only as one among various means that secure for the speaker ready access to the minds of his auditors. Finally, the effect of the discourse on its immediate hearers is not to be ignored, either in the testimony of witnesses, nor in the record of events. And throughout such a study one must conceive of the public man as influencing the men of his own times by the power of his discourse.

VIII

What is the relation of rhetorical criticism, so understood, to literary criticism? The latter is at once broader and more limited than rhetorical criticism. It is broader because of its concern with permanent values: because it takes no account of special purpose nor of immediate effect; because it views a literary work as the voice of a human spirit addressing itself to men of all ages and times; because the critic speaks as the spectator of all time and all existence. But this universalizing of attitude brings its own limits with it: the influence of the period is necessarily relegated to the background; interpretation in the light of the writer's intention and of his situation may be ignored or slighted; and the speaker who directed his words to a definite and limited group of hearers may be made to address a universal audience. The result can only be confusion. In short, the point of view of literary criticism is proper only to its own objects, the permanent works. Upon such as are found to lie without the pale, the verdict of literary criticism is of negative value merely, and its interpretation is false and misleading because it proceeds upon a wrong assumption. If Henry Clay and Charles Fox are to be dealt with at all, it must not be on the assumption that their works, in respect of wisdom and eloquence, are or ought to be sources of perennial freshness and interest. Morley has put the matter well :

> The statesman who makes or dominates a crisis, who has to rouse and mold the mind of senate or nation, has something else to think about than the production of literary masterpieces. The great political speech, which for that matter is a sort of drama, is not made by passages for elegant extract or anthologies, but by personality, movement, climax, spectacle, and the action of the time.[56]

But we cannot always divorce rhetorical criticism from literary. In the case of Fox or Clay or Cobden, as opposed to Fielding or Addison or De Quincey, it is proper to do so; the fact that language is a common medium to the writer of rhetorical discourse and to the writer in pure literature will give to the critics of each a common vocabulary of stylistic terms, but not a common standard. In the case of Burke the relation of the two points of view is more complex. Burke belongs to literature; but in all his important works he was a practitioner of public address written or uttered. Since his approach to *belles-lettres* was through rhetoric, it follows that rhetorical criticism is at least a preliminary to literary criticism, for it will erect the factual basis for the understanding of the works: will not merely explain allusions and establish dates, but recall the setting, reconstruct the author's own intention, and analyze his method. But the rhetorical inquiry is more than a mere preliminary; it permeates and governs all subsequent interpretation and criticism. For the statesman in letters is a statesman still: compare Burke to Charles Lamb, or even to Montaigne, and it is clear that the public man is in a sense inseparable from his audience. A statesman's wisdom and eloquence are not to be read without some share of his own sense of the body politic, and of the body politic not merely as a construct of thought, but as a living human society. A speech, like a satire, like a comedy of manners, grows directly out of a social situation; it is a man's response to a condition in human affairs. However broadly typical the situation may be when its essential elements are laid bare, it never appears without its coverings. On no plane of thought—philosophical, literary, political—is Burke to be understood without reference to the great events in America, India, France, which evoked his eloquence; nor is he to be understood without reference to the state of English society. (It is this last that is lacking in Grierson's essay: the page of comment on Burke's qualities in actual debate wants its supplement in some account of the House of Commons and the national life it represented. Perhaps the latter is the more needful to a full understanding of the abiding excellence in Burke's pages.) Something of the spirit of Morley's chapter on Cobden, and more of the spirit of the social historian (which Morley has in other parts of the biography) is necessary to the literary critic in dealing with the statesman who is also a man of letters.

In the case of Burke, then, one of the functions of rhetorical criticism is as a preliminary, but an essential and governing preliminary, to the literary criticism which occupies itself with the permanent values of wisdom and of eloquence, of thought and of beauty, that are found in the works of the orator.

Rhetorical criticism may also be regarded as an end in itself. Even Burke may be studied from that point of view alone. Fox and Cobden and the majority of public speakers are not to be regarded from any other. No one will offer Cobden's works a place in pure literature. Yet the method of the great agitator has a place in the history of his times. That place is not in the history of *belles-lettres;* nor is it in the literary history which is a "survey of the life of a people as expressed in their writings." The idea of "writings" is a merely mechanical one; it does not really provide a point of view or a method; it is a book-maker's cloak for many and diverse points of view. Such a compilation as the *Cambridge History of American Literature,* for example, in spite of the excellence of single essays, may not unjustly be characterized as an uneven commentary on the literary life of the country and as a still more uneven commentary on its social and political life. It may be questioned whether the scant treatment of public men in such a compilation throws light either on the creators of pure literature, or on the makers of rhetorical discourse, or on the life of the times.

Rhetorical criticism lies at the boundary of politics (in the broadest sense) and literature; its atmosphere is that of the public life,[57] its tools are those of literature, its concern is with the ideas of the people as influenced by their leaders. The effective wielder of public discourse, like the military man, belongs to social and political history because he is one of its makers. Like the soldier, he has an art of his own which is the source of his power; but the soldier's art is distinct from the life which his conquests affect. The rhetorician's art represents a natural and normal process within that life. It includes the work of the speaker, of the pamphleteer, of the writer of editorials, and of the sermon maker. It is to be thought of as the art of popularization. Its practitioners are the Huxleys, not the Darwins, of science; the Jeffersons, not the Lockes and the Rousseaus, of politics.

Of late years the art of popularization has received a degree of attention: propaganda and publicity have been words much used; the influence of the press has been discussed; there have been some studies of public opinion. Professor Robinson's *Humanizing of Knowledge*[58] is a cogent statement of the need for popularization by the instructed element in the state, and of the need for a technique in doing so. But the book indicates, too, how little is known of the methods its author so earnestly desires to see put to use. Yet ever since Homer's day men have woven the web of words and counsel in the face of all. And ever since Aristotle's day there has been a mode of analysis of public address. Perhaps the preoccupation of literary criticism with "style" rather than with composition in the large has diverted interest from the more significant problem. Perhaps the conventional categories of historical thought have helped to obscure the problem: the history of thought, for example, is generally interpreted as the history of invention and discovery, both physical and intellectual. Yet the history of the thought of the people is at least as potent a factor in the progress of the race. True, the popular thought may often represent a resisting force, and we need not marvel that the many movements of a poet's mind more readily capture the critic's attention than the few and uncertain movements of that Leviathan, the public mind. Nor is it surprising that the historians tend to be occupied with the acts and the motives of leaders. But those historians who find the spirit of an age in the total mass of its literary productions, as well as all who would tame Leviathan to the end that he shall not threaten civilization, must examine more thoroughly than they as yet have done the interactions of the inventive genius, the popularizing talent, and the public mind.

Notes

1 *Life of William Ewart Gladstone,* New York, 1903, II, 593.
2 *Select Works,* ed. E. J. Payne Oxford, 1892, I, xxxviii.
3 Basil Williams, *Life of William Pitt,* New York, 1913, II, 335–337.
4 D. Nichol Smith, *Functions of Criticism,* Oxford, 1909, p. 15.
5 See Rosebery, *Appreciations and Addresses,* London, 1899, and Whitelaw Reid, *American and English Studies,* New York, 1913, II.
6 See Augustine Birrell, *Obiter Dicta,* New York, 1887, II; Walter Raleigh, *Some Authors,* Oxford, 1923; Robert Lynd, *Books and Authors.* London, 1922.
7 Oliver Elton, *Survey of English Literature, 1780–1830,* I, 234–53.
8 *Cambridge History of American Literature,* New York, 1921, III, 374–5.
9 *Cambridge History of American Literature,* III, 378.
10 *Ibid.,* pp. 381–2.
11 *Ibid.,* p. 377.
12 *Cambridge History of English Literature,* New York, 1914, XI, 30–5.
13 H. A. Taine, *History of English Literature,* tr. H. Van Laun, London, 1878, II, 81–3.
14 Boston, 1923.
15 W. P. Trent, *History of American Literature, 1607–1865,* New York, 1917, pp. 576–7.
16 Edmund Gosse, *History of Eighteenth Century English Literature, 1660–1780,* London, 1889, pp. 365–6.
17 *Cambridge History of American Literature,* New York, 1918, II, 101.
18 G. E. B. Saintsbury, *Short History of English Literature,* New York, 1915, p. 630.
19 *Ibid.,* pp. 629–30.
20 *Ibid.,* p. 631.
21 *Ibid.*
22 *Ibid.*
23 *Sketches and Essays,* ed. W. C Hazlitt, London, 1872, II, 420–1.
24 *Political Essays with Sketches of Public Characters,* London, 1819, pp. 264–79.
25 New York, 1923.
26 New York, 1924.
27 E. P. Whipple, "Daniel Webster as a Master of English Style," in *American Literature,* Boston, 1887, p. 157.
28 *Ibid.,* p. 208.
29 *Ibid.,* p. 144.
30 London, 1914, p. 7.
31 *Lord Chatham as an Orator,* Oxford, 1912, p. 5.
32 *Ibid.,* pp. 39–40.
33 'W. E. H. Lecky, *History of England in the Eighteenth Century,* New York, 1888, III, 203–4.
34 *Life of William Ewart Gladstone,* I, 193–4; II. 54–5, 593.
35 *Gladstone, his Characteristics as Man and Statesman,* New York, 1898, pp. 41–4.
36 G. M. Trevelyan, *Life of John Bright,* Boston, 1913, p. 384.
37 Henry Hardwicke, *History of Oratory and Orators,* New York, 1896.
38 Lorenzo Sears, *History of Oratory,* Chicago, 1896.

39 New York, 1852.
40 P. 75.
41 P. 461.
42 *Life of Richard Cobden,* Boston, 1881, pp. 130–2.
43 *Cambridge History of English Literature,* New York, 1914, XI, 8.
44 Oliver Elton, *Survey of English Literature, 1780–1830,* London, 1912, I, 234.
45 *Rhetoric,* ii, 2, tr. W. Rhys Roberts in *The Works of Aristotle,* XI, Oxford, 1924.
46 Article "Rhetoric" in the *Encyclopædia Britannica,* 9th and nth editions.
47 J. L. Gerig and F. N. Scott, article "Rhetoric" in the *New International Encyclopædia.*
48 K. H. W. Wackernagel, *Poetik, Rhetorik und Stilistik,* ed. L. Sieber, Halle, 1873, p. 11.
49 'H. H. Hudson, "The Field of Rhetoric," *Quarterly Journal of Speech Education,* IX (1923), 177. See also the same writer's "Rhetoric and Poetry," *ibid.,* X (1924), 143 ff.
50 C. S. Baldwin, *Ancient Rhetoric and Poetic,* New York, 1924, p. 134.
51 G. E. B. Saintsbury, *History of Criticism and Literary Taste in Europe,* New York, 1900, I, 39.
52 *Ibid.,* p. 42.
53 *History of Criticism and Literary Taste in Europe,* p. 48.
54 *Ibid.,* p. 52.
55 *Op. cit.,* p. 4.
56 *Life of William Ewart Gladstone,* II, 589–90.
57 For a popular but suggestive presentation of the background of rhetorical discourse, see J. A. Spender, *The Public Life,* New York, 1925.
58 New York, 1923.

9.
THE FIGURES OF RHETORIC IN SPENSER'S *COLIN CLOUT*
Sam Meyer

MODERN CRITICISM has given increasing recognition to the functional, as distinguished from the decorative, aspect of rhetorical figures in the poetry of the English Renaissance.[1] The continuance of this emphasis is particularly appropriate to Spenser's pastoral, *Colin Clouts Come Home Againe* (1595), where the relevance of the figures to the larger considerations of style—indeed, to the total discourse—is so cardinal. The importance of the figures is enhanced by the natural use of rhetorical arts by characters, set in a kind of *mise en scène,* whose suasory speeches largely comprise the poem. Stress of the functional side of the rhetorical elements in the poem need not deny or denigrate the role of the figures in conferring upon the verse an aura of conspicuous beauty. The office of the figures in this respect is simply another manifestation of the same taste for elegance which reflected itself in Renaissance dress, manners, ceremonial processions, and décor. The beautifying characteristics of the numerous word orders, comprised of tropes and schemes, were recognized and frankly accepted by literati of the Tudor period. In their eyes, figures possessed value as ornament by reason of their constituting departures from everyday speech patterns. The idea is conventionally phrased by Abraham Fraunce, whom many believe to be the Corydon praised in lines 383–384: of the poem:[2] "A figure is a certeine decking of speach, whereby the vsual and simple fashion thereof is altered and changed to that which is more elegant and conceipted."[3]

To belletrists of the Renaissance most assuredly—and it requires some effort for us to accept this—there was no discrepancy between the functional and embellishing aspects of figures. In that favored pamphlet of the era, the *Ars Poetica* of Horace, the aims of poetry are enunciated as being to teach (*prodesse*) or to delight (*delectare*), or to do both at once. To this dictum, which is rhetorical in its conception of the poetic art, the Renaissance conjoined Cicero's third aim of oratory—to persuade or sway—and applied it to the poet. To this humanistic formulation of moving as an object of eloquence in all forms, it required, in a Christian era, little extension on the part of critics and poets to make the direction of movement specifically ethical and moral.[4] Applied to poetry, the threefold aim of oratory meant that poetry teaches through its appeal to the intellect of the reader or listener by means of its content or *doctrina;* pleases through its appeal to the aesthetic sense by means of its style, elaborated largely through figures of speech; and

---

Meyer, Sam. 1964. "The Figures of Rhetoric in Spenser's *Colin Clout.*" PMLA, Vol. 79, No. 3 (1964): 206–218.

moves to virtuous action by means of its appeal to emotion, acting through message and mode together. Thus, delight in poetry, whether achieved by means of pleasing fables or of patterned language, was not considered by discerning men of the period to exist for its own sake; and we may be reasonably certain that to mature critics like Sidney and George Puttenham, who were also practicing poets, and to poetic craftsmen like Spenser, who was also a critic,[5] rhetorical figures would hardly be thought of as elements super-added to poetry even though they were often referred to as ornament.[6]

Of course, where taste is deficient and conception weak, abuses are inevitable. Renewed awareness of this gloomy truism doubtless prompted Henry Peacham to add a section entitled "Caution" to the discussion of each of his figures when he issued his revised edition of *The Garden of Eloquence* in 1593. Indeed, dutiful injunctions against abuse of the figures accompanied treatment of them in both ancient and Renaissance treatises. Classical authors of textbooks still used in the educational system of the sixteenth century warned, for instance, against inflated speech ("sufflata oratio"), outlandish metaphors ("verbis ... duriter aliunde translatis")[7] and excessive reliance upon the colors of rhetoric ("magis infucata vitia").[8] That those vices of overabundant and tasteless rhetoric which the anonymous author of the *Ad Herennium* and Cicero had inveighed against were by no means absent from the Elizabethan literary scene is made evident by Sidney himself in the famous passage about Matron Eloquence being at times "with figures and flowers, extreamelie winter-starued."[9]

Sidney's strictures here allude, one must not forget, to the *improper* employment of "figures and flowers." In their proper employment, formal patterns of words, phrases, and larger elements of discourse, together with locutions accorded special meanings, could hardly exist as appliquéd ornament. On the contrary, the conception and deployment of these rhetorical devices are linked on a general plane through content and through emotional appeal with the exacting disciplines of logic and rhetoric respectively—the heart and core of formal education during the period in which Spenser lived.[10] Inasmuch as many of the figures, particularly those which lend themselves to amplification of matter, derive from, or are identical to, the places of rhetorical or dialectical investigation, their connection with the basic compositional arts becomes integral rather than incidental.[11] The precise way in which figures of rhetoric, especially those of comparison, are elaborated from the dialectical places is more than a matter of historical interest. This methodology and its relevance to meaning in *Colin Clout* is special and significant, but adequate treatment of this aspect would carry us considerably beyond the bounds of the present inquiry.

The specific aim of this investigation is to exhibit and discuss the figures of rhetoric found in a single Renaissance poem. But figurative elements in an age which deferred so much to tradition can hardly be studied profitably, or even intelligibly, without reference to literary positions which supply a context for their employment. In touching on relevant aspects of these positions, I strive, for the sake of brevity, to stick to the critical high roads. What I have said thus far has been intended to provide, in highly synoptic form, a frame of reference compatible with the canons of the age in which to examine figures in *Colin Clout*. These canons suggest that the contribution of the figures to the whole poem can be approached from two separate but related points of view: that of rhetoric, the open hand, which views figures in their overt aspect as patterns of a given variety, with specific textbook names; and that of logic, the closed fist, which views figures, more limited in number and type, as elaboration of ways to discover places and follow a method of inquiry. I shall confine myself here to the first and more inclusive of these approaches, with the reservation, in Howell's words, that to Englishmen of the sixteenth and seventeenth centuries "poetry was considered to be the third great form of communication, open and popular but not fully explained by rhetoric, concise and lean but not fully explained by logic."[12]

The Figures Illustrated for the Last One Hundred Lines of *Colin Clout*[13]

Lines	Quotation	Rhetorical Figure(s)
851–854	So being former foes, they wexed friends, And gan by litle learne to loue each other: So being knit, they brought forth other kynds Out of the fruitfull wombe of their great mother.	compar antithesis
855–860	Then first gan heauen out of darknesse dread For to appeare, and brought forth chearfull day: Next gan the earth to shew her naked head, Out of deep waters which her drownd alway. And shortly after euerie liuing wight, Crept forth like wormes out of her slimie nature.	distributio auxesis prosopopoeia
863–864	Thenceforth they gan each one his like to loue, And like himselfe desire for to beget.	ploce
865–866	The Lyon chose his mate, the Turtle Doue Her deare, the Dolphin his own Dolphinet.	zeugma synonymia
871–874	For beautie is the bayt which with delightD oth man allure, for to enlarge his kynd, Beautie the burning lamp of heauens light, Darting her beames into each feeble mynd.	sententiaploce metaphora
883–886	So loue is Lord of all the world by right, And rules the creatures by his powrfull saw: All being made the vassalls of his might, Through secret sence which therto doth them draw.	sententia acclamatio
891–894	For their desire is base, and doth not merit, The name of loue, but of disloyall lust: Ne mongst true louers they shall place inherit, But as Exuls out of his court be thrust.	aetiologia synonymia antithesis comparatio
896–898	*Colin*, thou now full deeply hast divynd: Of loue and beautie and with wondrous skill, Hast *Cupid* selfe depainted in his kynd.	transitio
911–914	But who can tell what cause had that faire Mayd To vse him so that vsed her so well: Or who with blame can iustly her vpbrayd, For louing not? for who can loue compell?	pysma antanaclasis sententia

Lines	Quotation	Rhetorical Figure(s)
919–924	And well I wote, that oft I heard it spoken, / How one that fairest *Helene* did reuile, / Through iudgement of the Gods to been ywroken / Lost both his eyes and so remaynd long while, / Till he recanted had his wicked rimes, / And made amends to her with treble praise.	periphrasis [Rix, p. 71] prothesis
925–926	Beware therefore, ye roomes, I read betimes, / How rashly blame of *Rosalind* ye raise.	apostrophe
935–938	Not then to her that scorned thing so base, / But to my selfe the blame that lookt so hie: / So hie her thoughts as she her selfe haue place, / And loath each lowly thing with loftie eie.	anadiplosis antithesis
939–946	Yet so much grace let her vouchsafe to grant / To simple swaine, sith her I may not loue: / Yet that I may her honour paravant, / And praise her worth, though far my wit aboue. / Such grace shall be some guerdon for the griefe, / And long affliction which I haue endured: / Such grace sometimes shall giue me some reliefe, / And ease of paine which cannot be recured.	ploce compar anaphora meiosis paroemion
947–950	And ye my fellow shepheardes which do see / And heare the languours of my too long dying, / Vnto the world for euer witnesse bee, / That hers I die, nought to the world denying.	apostrophe polyptoton
952–955	So hauing ended, he from ground did rise, / And after him vprose eke all the rest: / All loth to part, but that the glooming skies / Warnd them to draw their bleating flocke to rest.	hyperbaton chronographia

    The real ubiquity of tropes and schemes in *Colin Clout* may be unsuspected by the reader who has merely noted Rix's incidental reference to the "profusion of tropes and schemes"[14] or Miss Rubel's statement that, "as far as the rhetoric of *Colin Clout* is concerned, it is not so lavishly ornamental as that of the poetry which was intended to be more polite."[15] The Table shown above, identifying the figures for the last hundred lines, will give a more adequate idea of their almost unbelievable multiplicity. Selection of the closing lines for the purpose of exhibiting the figures is a purely arbitrary choice; almost any section would show about the same relative frequency of figures. Counting only once alliteration (*paroemion*), which is well-nigh omnipresent, and reversals of normal syntactical order (*hyperbaton*), which occurs on the average of once in every six lines, I have found thirty-five figures in the last one hundred lines. On the same basis, I have counted thirty-one figures in the first one hundred lines. The average throughout the poem is approximately one figure for every three lines. Besides indicating the number and variety of figures, the Table, by presenting a consecutive listing of the figures in context, permits the reader to observe the complexity of rhetorical patterning—that is, the way in which the figures are interwoven within a passage. This interlacing is a conventional as well as integral part of the lore.

Among the numerous tropes, schemes of words, and schemes of thought and amplification,[16] Spenser employs, under Greek and Latin appellations, many standard compositional devices found in current writing, but his use of the figures differs most significantly from that in vogue today because, following typical Renaissance practice, he employs them to a degree heightened beyond that of the moderns to accomplish one or more of three distinct functions: (1) to constitute the framework and the substance of blocks of verse; (2) to control the stylistic level; and (3) to provide emotional fervor. The first of these ends has to do mainly with development or amplification, which is subsumed within the two standard rhetorical divisions of *inventio* and *dispositio*, which are processes of discovering matter and arranging it. The latter two ends are aspects of tone and emotion.

With reference to the first end to which use of the figures is directed, the two famous passages evaluating contemporary poets and praising the ladies at court (ll. 377–449, 488–575) may serve to exemplify the efficacy of figures in providing both the form of the material and the material itself. These passages both employ *divisio* or *distributio*, by which figure, according to Peacham's rendering of Susenbrotus' Latin, "we dilate and spread abroade the generall kinde, by numbering and reckning vp the speciall kindes."[17] That is, the sections set forth concrete details to support a generality. They possess the character of a formal design, achieved to some extent in the section on the poets by the repetition of the transitional phrase "There is," and in the section on the ladies by the phrase "ne lesse praise worthie." That the second formula for transition was part of a common lore for the use of *distributio* or *merismus* is suggested by Puttenham's treatment and illustration in *The Arte of English Poesie* (1589), where he cites a passage in praise of the maiden Queen with the "*merismus* in the negatiue for the better grace."[18] *Distributio*, then, operates to create an orderly channel through which the poet can apply individualizing comments to persons in the two groups. The raw material, as it were, of the verse is constructed in the two passages largely out of another figure—*epitheton* or *appositum*, defined by Peacham as "when we ioyne adiectiues to those Substantiues, to whome they doe properly belong, and that eyther to prayse, disprayse, to amplify or extenuate."[19] With respect to *epitheton* or epithet, one might assume from the two illustrative lines cited by Rix out of *The Faerie Queene* that the figures might be limited, as in the modern conception, to adherent adjectives. The first of these illustrations, taken from the second edition of the elder Alexander Gill's *Logonomia Anglia* (1619), revised in 1621, is "But wise *Speranza* gave him comfort sweet." The second is "So false *Duessa*, but vile *Ate* thus." However, as King James VI of Scotland's *Ane Schort Treatise* (1584) and Puttenham's *Arte* clearly show,[20] the interchangeable terms *epitheton* or *appositum* could properly embrace not only prepositional adjectives but postpositional adjectives and substantive phrases as well. Thus, in the passage on the poets one finds "good *Harpalus* now woxen aged, / In faithfull seruice of faire *Cynthia*" (ll. 380–381); "*Corydon* though meanly waged, / Yet hablest wit of most I know this day" (ll. 382–383); "sad *Alcyon* bent to mourne" (l. 384), etc.; and in the passage on the ladies one finds "*Vrania* sister vnto *Astrofell* (l. 487);

"faire *Marian*, the *Muses* onely darling" (l. 505); "*Mansilia*, / Best knowne by bearing vp great *Cynthiaes* traine" (ll. 508–509), etc. In short, two important sections of the poem are organized by one figure—*distributio*, and their content is derived largely from another—*epitheton*.

This use of figures to supply *copia* is so pervasive in *Colin Clout* that it will be profitable to observe the principle at work in more detail. For this purpose, we may select almost at random four additional examples. The first three show the process for separate figures. The fourth demonstrates the more complex technique of interweaving. The first example is the speech (ll. 22–31) of Hobbinol, in which all nature is represented as lamenting Colin's absence. Though this passage is in the main line of classical pastoral tradition by way of Ronsard's *Adonis*,[21] it is nevertheless built upon *prosopopoeia*, the personification of Nature in this case, which is the *raison d'être* of the unit. The second example is the *allegoria* of the ocean as Cynthia's pasture (ll. 240–251)—the "marine pastoral"[22] motif. The description is given a mythological coloring, but the chief element is the extended metaphor likening the sea to a meadow. Spenser's dispraise of the courtiers who pervert the sacred concept of love is the third example showing how he uses the figures to furnish the main substance of his units. The figure (ll. 786–792) through which Spenser has Colin ring the changes on the key words *serve* and *use* in their contrasting shades of meaning is *antanaclasis*, a play on words in their varying senses.

The final example of Spenser's use of figures to supply *copia* is Colin's blazon (ll. 464–479) in which he praises his mistress and protests devoted service and undying love. The passage is typical of the many in *Colin Clout* that employ an elaborate blending of figures to make up the block of verse, in this case, a lyric cry. It is one of two extended tributes by Colin to his mistress, Rosalind. The complaint opens with a mild *exclamatio*, followed by *aetiologia*, the reason that the speaker does not deserve ill of "gentle Mayds" (l. 465). The heart of the next six lines is *expolitio*, termed by Puttenham "the Gorgious," and said by him to be used to "polish our speech & as it were attire it with copious & pleasant amplifications and much varietie of sentences all running vpon one point & to one intēt" (p. 247). The entire speech is then rounded off with two lines of *acclamatio*, the summing up, and two lines of complicated word play, combining with epigrammatic neatness *antimetabole* and *antistrophe*.

While figures in *Colin Clout* perform the basic function of filling out details of a passage, they are also instrumental, along with diction generally, in achieving the second major objective of rhetorical patterning—that of adjusting the style to suit Renaissance notions of decorum respecting genre, subject, and persons, with genre being the most impelling determinant. The general relationship between the figures and the styles, as conceived by men of the period, is clear. Abundant use of figures is a distinguishing characteristic of the high style. The middle and low styles are marked by decreasing employment of the figures. The bald application of the principle governing decorum of the kinds would have resulted in *Colin Clout's* being written throughout in "the lawe kinde, when we vse no *Metaphores* nor translated words, nor yet vse any amplifications but goe plainly to worke, and speake altogether in common wordes."[23] No poet of consequence, however, applies the theory undiscriminatingly. To do sso would be to forgo the rich possibilities for registering fine discriminations in value—and consequent aesthetic effects—when changing from one subject or one person to another subject or another person.

In the Dedicatory Letter to Sir Walter Raleigh, when Spenser refers to *Colin Clout* as a "simple pastorall" and apologizes for the "meanesse of the style," which is "vnworthie of your higher conceipt," he is using in the first two quoted phrases terms familiar to the critical discussions of the time. The conventional designation of pastoral was "simple" and, as Puttenham makes quite clear, the "low and base stile" was understood to be reserved for "all *Eglogues* and pastorall poemes" (p. 153). In view of the multiplicity of figures in *Colin Clout*, hardly compatible with conventions governing the low style, one may feel that Spenser's statement in the Dedication is inconsistent with his practice, or that he is simply throwing the standard theory overboard. Actually, neither alternative reflects the true situation. His statement, when taken in a larger context, does not identify the poem unreservedly as written in unadorned style, nor would Sir Walter, in all likelihood, have construed the deprecatory phrases so to identify it. Perhaps the reasons for discounting Spenser's statement as an indication of his intention to eschew elevation should be specified. First, one has to make ample allowances for the convention of humility and disparagement in dedications to one's patron in the 1590's. Part of this engaging air of self-disparagement reflects also the courtly fashion of *sprezzatura*, the word Castiglione first uses in his influential *Il Libro del Cortegiano* (1528) to characterize the temper by which a gentleman conceals a purpose of high seriousness with a show of studied negligence.[24] Had not Spenser in his Dedicatory Sonnets disparaged even the high style of *The Faerie Queene* itself in such lines as the following to "The Right Honourable the Earle of Ormund and Ossory":

> Receiue most noble Lord a simple taste
> Of the wilde fruit, which saluage soyle hath bred,
> Which being through long wars left almost waste,
> With Brutish barbarisme is ouerspredd;
>   (*Works*, III, 193)

or in such lines as the following to "The Most renowned and valiant Lord, the Lord Grey of Wilton, knight of the Noble order of the Garter, & Cn"?—

> Rude rymes, the which a rustick Muse did weaue
> In sauadge soyle, far from Parnasso mount.
>   (*Works*, III, 194)

In alluding to the poem as "simple," Spenser was in little danger of creating for his immediate readers a misleading supposition as to its actual quality.

Second, Spenser may well have been using the word "meanesse" to accord with the conventional classification of style into three levels, "mean" being the term commonly employed to designate the intermediate level. Finally, even if, as is conceivable, Spenser meant "meanesse" to suggest a degree of baseness, the convention implied that *all* poetry was raised above common discourse (Puttenham, pp. 8–9) and that the lower flight merely restricted the kinds of figures and modes of using them, not the figures themselves. The copiousness of figures in an out-and-out pastoral like Spenser's *The Shepheardes Calender* indicates convincingly that the low style, at least in poetry, did not outlaw the figures. *Colin Clout,* moreover, being far from "pure pastoral" in genre, by reason of its containing matters "that concerne the Gods and diuine things" and the "noble gests and great fortunes of Princes" (Puttenham, p. 152), would be pushed upward under the principle of decorum toward conventions of middle and high style.

Though all the figures inasmuch as they "passe the ordinary limits of common vtterance" (Puttenham, p. 154) serve to raise the style, certain figures are more efficacious to this end than others. I shall confine myself to those figures in the poem which best exemplify this function: *comparatio* and *allegoria; antonomasia* and *epitheton; periphrasis, sententia;* and *acclamatio*. The first of these is quite common. The main way in which *comparatio,* defined as "a comparing of thinges, persons, deedes, examples, contrairies, lyke, or vnlyke" (Rix, p. 55), imparts elevation of style is in the drawing of its subject matter from Biblical or mythological sources, with their rich store of associations for Christian humanists of the time. Cases involving the use of *comparatio* to call up Biblical associations for the reader are the praise of Urania

> In whose braue mynd as in a golden cofer,
> All heauenly gifts and riches locked are:
> More rich than pearles of *Ynde* or gold of *Opher;*
>
> (ll. 488–490)

and the figurative deification of Cynthia, whose

> thoughts are like the fume of Franckincence,
> Which from a golden Censer forth doth rise
> . . . .
> Emongst the seats of Angels heauenly wrought,
> Much like an Angell in all forme and fashion.
>
> (ll. 608–609; 614–615)

An example of a comparison depending upon mythological lore for its effectiveness is the injunction by Colin to Daniel bidding that poet to "rouze thy feathers quickly" (l. 424) and "to what course thou please thy selfe aduance" (l. 425).[25] Thus the author of the sonnet-sequence *Delia* (which Spenser probably saw in manuscript)[26] is equated with, or considered to be under the inspiration of, the Muse of Poetry by way of Pegasus, the winged horse on which the Muses sometimes traveled. Similarly, the one clear example of *allegoria*—in Peacham's phrase, "a contynued Metaphor" (Rix, p. 24)—derives its tone from the classical tradition. This is the ocean-meadow fancy (ll. 240–251) contained in "the shepheards" description of Cynthia's "Regiment" at sea. The marine divinities Triton and Proteus figure prominently in this description.

From one point of view, of course, *Colin Clout* is in its entirety an extended metaphor—an *allegoria,* in which a thin veil is thrown over all by the poet's casting the poem in the pastoral mode. Colin's life is placed in an atmosphere of shepherds and shepherdesses, bearing names appearing in prestigious classical works—the idylls of Theocritus and the eclogues of Virgil, for the most part. All locutions which arise from the pastoral mode were well understood by the convention to designate an order of things and beings different from such empirical things and beings as Ireland, Kilcolman, England, the English Court, Queen Elizabeth, Raleigh, Spenser, Harvey, Bryskett.

With reference to *epitheton* and *antonomasia*, the two succeeding figures in the above list of those serving to raise the style, both represent adaptations of utterances to reflect real or attributed differences in rank or dignity between the speaker, the shepherd Colin, and the person spoken about. *Epitheton* and *antonomasia*, distinguished by Puttenham as "the Qualifier" and "the figure of attribution" (pp. 176–177), serve to register the speaker's awareness of special difference owing to the subject persons. They create a kind of aesthetic distance between him and them. As pointed out in the discussion of the passages on poets and ladies as set pieces of conventional formalism, these two long passages (ll. 377–449, 485–575) are interpenetrated with epithets, each person, in fact, being honored by one or more appropriate "qualifiers." Among the poets, for instance, there is "*Alabaster* throughly taught, / In all this skill, though knowen yet to few" (ll. 400–401); among the maids of honor, there are "Faire *Galathea* with bright shining beames" (l. 518), and Neaera, "the blosome of grace and curtesie" (l. 528). Interestingly enough, of the ten ladies lauded, only Stella has no epithet bestowed upon her. The reason for this, given by Colin himself, is that Sidney has already "prais'd [her] and rais'd [her] aboue each other starre" (l.535).

There can be little question as to the efficacy of these qualifiers to enhance the dignity of the person to whom a description or qualifying word or phrase is attached and at the same time to indicate the speaker's awareness of his comparative unworthiness. The value of *antonomasia* in creating a sense of aesthetic distance between speaker and subject is even greater than that of the epithet. Puttenham terms *antonomasia* "the surnamer" and defines it as "the manner of naming of persons or things . . . by a conuenient difference, and such as is true or esteemed and likely to be true." His illustrations of the figure include reference to "the Westerne king" (King Phillip II of Spain) and to "*The maiden Queene,* for that is her hiest peculiar among all the Queenes of the World" (p. 181). In *Colin Clout,* too, *antonomasia* is used to register the speaker's humble position in relation to persons of high estate: the speaker's refusal to mention Queen Elizabeth's name outright, referring to her instead as "*Cynthia* the Ladie of the sea" (l. 166), "that Goddesse grace" (l. 359), "dreaded Dread" (l. 406) ; and Colin's reference to Sir Walter Raleigh as "a straunge shepheard" (l. 60) and "the shepheard of the Ocean" (l. 358).

Of other figures calculated to raise the style, *periphrasis,* or circumlocution, is exceedingly rare in *Colin Clout,* being employed in only two instances. The first is the phraseology chosen by the speaker, Colin, to indicate that he had actually been in Elizabeth's presence: "since I saw that Angels blessed eie" (l. 40). In this case, the circumlocution permits Colin to avoid direct reference to a person greatly above him in rank and dignity. Thus, *periphrasis,* like *antonomasia,* is used to create aesthetic distance. The second instance is the *periphrasis* for Stesichorus:

> And well I wote, that oft I heard it spoken,
> How one that fairest *Helene* did reuile,
> Through iudgement of the Gods to been ywroken
> Lost both his eyes and so remaynd long while.
> (ll. 919–922)

Here *periphrasis* acts to ennoble the language by bringing in an implied comparison between the shepherd Colin and Stesichorus, a character connected with epic matter *par excellence*—that of Helen and of Troy.

Sententia, or the apothegmatic statement, is somewhat more common than *periphrasis,* though it must be conceded that the modern reader can easily overlook some aphorisms that Elizabethan readers recognized at once.[27] The gnomic figure is also more adaptable than *periphrasis* for varying the stylistic level because it may be either learned or folkish in origin. Whatever the origin, however, *sententia* may be regarded as operating to elevate the tone. Something of this idea is contained in Erasmus' Preface to his *Apophthegmata* (1531), where he says that "all these uniuersalle sorte of writyinges, as doe comprehende prouerbes, sage sentencies, and notable saiynges or actes, is moste fitte for Princes and noble menne."[28] The vogue of the commonplace books, which many compiled for themselves or had convenient access to in printed works like Erasmus' *Apophthegmata* or his earlier *Adagia,* testify to the value placed by men of Spenser's era on sententious materials as aids to wit.[29] Moreover, the tragedies of Seneca the Younger, abounding in quotable declarations, gave impressive classical sanction to the use of *sententiae* as an elevating device. In the *Apologie,* Sidney indirectly specifies the peculiar value Seneca possessed in the eyes of literary Londoners when he praises the English blood-and-thunder play *Gorboduc* for its "stately speeches and well sounding Phrases, clyming to the height of *Seneca* his stile, and as full of notable moralitie."[30] William Cornwallis' *Discourse upon Seneca the Tragedian* (1601) also reflects the strong interest of Elizabethan writers in the Stoic playwright's sententious line, which often took precedence over their interest in the tragedies themselves.[31]

In *Colin Clout,* gnomes with a vaguely bookish cast sometimes appear in the dialogue, as when Colin defends his reason for leaving the court to return "back to my sheep to tourne" (l. 672) rather than, "hauing learned repentance late, to mourne / Emongst those wretches which I there descryde" (ll. 674–675). The repentance reference is a slight turn of the proverb cited as "Repentance never comes too late" by Morris Palmer Tilley in *A Dictionary of the Proverbs in the Sixteenth and Seventeenth Centuries* (p. 569, R80). Another example of proverbs appearing in the dialogue is the question by which Lucida seeks to excuse Rosalind's lack of reciprocity in love: "for who can loue compell?" (l. 914). This truism receives more formal expression in the river myth passage earlier in the poem when Colin explains why Mulla refused to follow her father Mole's wish for her union with Allo: "For loue will not be drawne, but must be ledde" (l. 129). Tilley's entry for a series of quotations current in Spenser's time expressing the same idea is "Love cannot be compelled (forced)" (p. 395, l. 499).

The foregoing examples of *sententiae* in the poem illustrate their customary office of raising the style. Because of their currency in untutored language, proverbs were also available for the purpose of lowering the level of utterance. King James VI of Scotland, writing in *Ane Schort Treatise,* obviously has in mind the adaptability of proverbs for varying the style when, in a short section on "thrie speciall ornamentis to verse," he warns: "As for the *Prouerbis,* they man be proper for the subiect." They must, he adds, be chosen on the same basis as comparisons. Of the latter, he had just specified that they ought to be "sa proper for the subiect that nather they beouer bas, gif your subiect be heich, for then sould your subiect disgrace your *Cornparisoun,* nather your *Comparisoun* be heich quhen your subiect is basse, for then sail your *Comparisoun* disgrace your subiect."[32] An outstanding example of the use of a proverb to deliberately debase the style occurs in the satirical passage in *Colin Clout* containing the most bitter denunciation of bad courtiers to be found in Spenser's poetry outside of *Mother Hubberds Tale* (1591):

> For each mans worth is measured by his weed,
> As harts by hornes, or asses by their eares.
>
> (ll. 711–712)

The proverbial nature of the "tailor-made man" concept is established by Tilley's numerous citations under the entry, "Apparel makes (Clothes make) the man" (p. 16, A283). While Tilley gives no proverb referring directly to horns as a distinguishing mark of the hart, he does cite the comparable byword of the Devil's being known by his horns (p. 152, D252). There is no dearth of variations by sixteenth- and seventeenth-century writers on the theme that "An Ass is known by his ears" (p. 20, A355).

It remains true, nevertheless, that the customary effect of the *sententia* in *Colin Clout* is to confer dignity upon the places where it is used. Its contribution to this end is nowhere more clearly marked than in the miniature "Hymne in Honour of Love" near the end of the poem. Here the two lofty utterances of general truth combine *sententia* and another figure, *acclamatio,* the pithy restatement or summing up of preceding matter, to give added grandeur to the whole discourse:

> For beautie is the bayt which with delight
> Doth man allure,[33] for to enlarge his kynd.
> . . . .
> So loue is Lord of all the world by right
> And rules the creatures by his powrfull saw.[34]
>
> (ll. 871–872, 883–884)

Acclamatio, without *sententia* but in combination with other figures, appears at intervals and elevates the style because of the stately and considered calm which it engenders. Note, for example, the following epitomizing declaration which Spenser has Colin make—a declaration of importance, moreover, since it helps clear away the apparent paradox in Colin's position: Why does a vicious element continue to exist in English court and society which otherwise are of such surpassing virtue and refinement? The answer is contained in the *acclamatio:*

> For end, all good, all grace there freely growes,
> Had people grace it gratefully to vse:
> For God his gifts there plenteously bestowes,
> But gracelesse men them greatly do abuse.
> (ll. 324–327)

The fact that Spenser's use of rhetorical figures in *Colin Clout* reflects a conscious and deliberate control for clearly envisaged ends now seems evident. His use of the figures to build up blocks of verse is not thereby necessarily mechanical or "unpoetic." Indeed, to let one example stand for many, one of the most admired passages of the entire poem, the charming river myth concerning the love of Mulla and Bregog (ll. 103–153) is a set piece embodying in the figure *topographia* the poet's imaginative conception. Spenser could have found numerous models in Boccaccio and in later Renaissance poets of Florence and Naples for the myth of locality.[35] Yet on this conventional pattern he has superimposed a story in which the actual physical environs of his Kilcolman estate, with meticulous accuracy of detail, are interwoven. This employment of the figures to fill out the matter of the poem is the first main use to which Spenser put rhetoric in *Colin Clout*. The second main use—to vary the style—has just been discussed. In general, Spenser applies the elevating power of rhetoric to maintain that studied level of tone and style which would not ascend too high for pastoral nor yet fall too low for the praise of noble persons and causes with which the poem is chiefly concerned.

I should like now to consider the most powerful of Spenser's three main overt uses of the figures—that of moving the affections or passions. The standard doctrine of the three styles is particularly relevant to a consideration of Spenser's reliance upon figures to "inueigle and appassionate the mind."[36] It is true that the doctrine of the styles was originally a concept applicable to oratory, but in an age like the Renaissance, when men like Richard Stanyhurst could praise Virgil indifferently as a poet, an orator, or a philosopher,[37] the influence of rhetorical precept on poetic practice was bound to be immense. In the *Orator*, Cicero has a section describing the perfect orator and the highest eloquence. In it he comments that a poet deserves credit for seeking the virtues of the orator and that, despite the differences between the two arts of poetry and oratory, they are identical in the fact that both require discrimination in selection of subject matter and in choice of words. A large part of that discrimination, Cicero's subsequent discussion makes clear, lies in the ability of the man of eloquence to choose, control, and combine the three different styles, each of which has its particular forte. For each of the three aims—to prove, to please, and to sway—one style is most effective. The plain style is for proof, the middle style for pleasure, and the high style for persuasion. And of the three purposes, the last is the most important since, in the final analysis, the judge or deliberative body must be moved before it will accede to the pleasure of the speaker.[38] Elsewhere in the same work Cicero relates the figures to stylistic levels by telling us that figures are used sparingly in the plain style, moderately in the middle style, and lavishly in the grand style.[39] Quintilian stresses, in the *Institutio Oratoria*, the efficacy of the intermediate and high styles for emotional persuasion. He distinguishes these styles from the low by their comparatively high proportion of ornamental devices. The pleader who uses the high style will, according to him, be able to call the dead to life, inspire anger or pity, and cause the listening judges to be swept impetuously from one emotion to another, as they weep and call upon the gods.[40]

The relevance of this kind of rhetorical teaching to which the Tudor scholar was almost continuously exposed in its application to poetry need hardly be labored. In connection with the three aims of eloquence, one should note in passing that they are considered complementary, not mutually exclusive. The Renaissance followed the classical writers in making no hard and fast distinction between feeling and intellect. Puttenham, for instance, emphasizes the inseparable nature of emotion and thought, in contradistinction to our modern dichotomy, in these words: "For to say truely, what els is man but his minde? ... He therefore that hath vanquished the minde of man, hath made the greatest and most glorious conquest. But the minde is not assailable vnlesse it be by sensible approches."[41] "Sensible," it need hardly be added, is employed in its usual sixteenth-century denotation of affecting the senses or passions.

As one might anticipate, the figures of principal import in helping achieve the aim of moving the passions are in the category of schemes of thought and amplification rather than of tropes—turns of a single word—or schemes of words only. Unlike similes, definitions, metaphors, and the like, these figures tend not to be definable by reference to common places or standard positions of argument. In Ramist manuals, therefore, most of them appear in the rhetorics rather than in the logics. This class of figures, which includes exclamations, moderations, or revocations of exclamations (*epanorthosis*), apostrophe, and other fashionings largely in imitation of the spoken word, is called "figures of sentences" in *The Arcadian Rhetorike* of Abraham Fraunce. Fraunce recognizes the emotional force of this group in the paragraph introducing them: "now folow the figures in Sentences, which in the whole sentēce expres some motion of the minde. These are more forcible & apt to perswade, than those of words, which be rather pleasant and fit to delight. Generallie, as in tropes there is a certaine grace, in figures of words a kind of delicacie, so in these of sentences appeareth force and maiestie" (p. 63). The schemes of thought and amplification that contribute so much to the emotive and dramatic effect of the poem are *exclamatio* or exclamation; *interrogatio* or rhetorical question; *pysma*, the extended form of *interrogatio; apostrophe* or direct address; and *synathroismus* or a "heaping up of many different things" (Rix, p. 42 n.). In stressing the emotive force of such figures as these, the Ramist rhetoricians were simply confirming what the older ones, following Cicero and Quintilian, had been saying all along. It is significant, for example, that the definitions of these figures from Susenbrotus, translated by Peacham, reflect the critics' awareness of the exclamatory quality of the particular figures, e.g., "Apostrophe, when we sodeinly forsake the former frame of our speach and goe to another" (Rix, p. 41); "Pysma, when we aske often times together, and vse many questions in one place, wherby we do make the oration sharp and vehement" (p. 39). Collectively, these figures account in no small measure for the generally spirited tone of the entire poem, and, as a result of their very frequent occurrence, constitute the leading means by which the emotions of friendship, love, and indignation are strongly imitated.

Though it is necessary to isolate the figures for the purpose of detailing their special office, it is not necessarily helpful to do so when one is attempting to show their cumulative force. Indeed, as the Table presented earlier shows, the figures seldom occur alone in Spenser; rather they frequently reinforce one another; and for key passages are often massed to make a triple assault, as it were, upon the reader or listener. This triple assault combines the possible effects envisaged by Puttenham in grouping all the figures into the three categories of auricular, "sensible," and sententious, that is, affecting the ear, mind, and all faculties respectively (pp. 159–160). This massing is sometimes used to heighten the emotional quality even in passages of lesser importance. In the lines giving recognition to Alabaster, for instance, Spenser employs a combination of *exclamatio, interrogatio,* and *apostrophe:*

> Yet were he knowne to *Cynthia* as he ought,
> His Eliseïs would be redde anew.
> Who liues that can match that heroick song,
> Which he hath of that mightie Princesse made?
> O dreaded Dread, do not thy selfe that wrong,
> To let thy fame lie so in hidden shade:
> But call it forth, O call him forth to thee,
> To end thy glorie which he hath begun.
> (ll. 402–409)

There are three other cases of *apostrophe* in the same section on the poets. The figure, by reason of its purposeful abruptness, injects life into a passage which might otherwise lull the reader to sleep. Two of these invocations—those to Alcyon (ll. 388–391) and to Daniel (ll. 424–425)—are of lesser intensity. The third to Amyntas gains strength through being reinforced by *anaphora*, initial repetition, sometimes used, according to John Hoskins, to beat "upon one thing to cause the quicker feeling in the audience."[42]

> Helpe, O ye shepheards helpe ye all in this.
> Help *Amaryllis* this her losse to mourne.
> (ll. 436–437)

The poem closes, except for the completion of the narrative frame in the form of *chronographia* or description of the time of day, on the forceful and eloquent plea by Colin to his fellow-shepherds to witness his undying devotion to Rosalind:

> And ye my fellow shepheardes which do see
> And heare the languours of my too long dying,
> Vnto the world for euer witnesse bee,
> That hers I die, nought to the world denying,
> This simple trophe of her great conquest.
> (ll. 947–951)

Interrogatio in the form of the rhetorical question is relatively abundant. At the conclusion of the first panegyric to Queen Elizabeth, Spenser has Colin exclaim:

> Why then do I base shepheard bold and blind,
> Presume the things so sacred to prophane?
> (ll. 348–349)

This figure has particularly incisive force in Colin's encomium to Love, where he poses the great crux: What is the secret force that attracts unlike elements to each other, causing them to unite and eventually to culminate in the creation of man?

> For how should else things so far from attone
> And so great enemies as of them bee,
> Be euer drawne together into one,
> And taught in such accordance to agree?
> (ll. 843–846)

With reference to the expanded form of *interrogatio*, there is only one passage employing *pysma*, a series of rhetorical questions. It is the comment by Lucida, one of the interlocutors, in response to Hobbinol's snide remark about how poorly women have requited Colin for stating the cause of love so well:

> But who can tell what cause had that faire Mayd
> To vse him so that vsed her so well:
> Or who with blame can iustly her vpbrayd,
> For louing not? for who can loue compell?
> (ll. 911–914)

The employment by Spenser of *synathroismus*, or congeries, aptly called the "heaping figure" by Puttenham (p. 236), to stimulate emotion can be well illustrated by the passage in which Colin characterizes England by contrasting it with Ireland. In England

> No wayling there nor wretchednesse is heard,
> No bloodie issues nor no leprosies,
> No griesly famine, nor no raging sweard,
> No nightly bodrags, nor no hue and cries;
> The shepheards there abroad may safely lie,
> On hills and downes, withouten dread or daunger:
> No rauenous wolues the good mans hope destroy,
> No outlawes fell affray the forest raunger.
> (ll. 312–319)

While some of the sense of excitement in this passage derives from the verbs, particularly the active participles, the repetitive insistence that in England no factors exist which are disruptive of peace and harmony compels attention and conviction. *Anaphora*, iteration of the same sound at the beginning of successive lines, and *paroemion*, consonantal alliteration, help reinforce the sense. *Synathroismus* is also one important element of the rhetorically-rich passage in which Colin ecstatically expresses his chivalric devotion to his mistress:

> To her my thoughts I daily dedicate,
> To her my heart I nightly martyrize;
> To her my loue I lowly do prostrate,
> To her my life I wholly sacrifice:
> My thought, my heart, my loue, my life is shee.
> (ll. 472–476)

Here again, the insistent repetition, underscored by *anaphora* and alliteration and climaxed by *acclamatio*, takes on extraordinary passional force.

The foregoing account of the figures considers them as comprising all the linguistic patterns to which names are assigned in rhetorical manuals of the Renaissance. At the same time it takes cognizance of the fact that these patterns are by no means formulations distinctive to that period. The discussion attempts to set forth the main ways in which the figures are consciously used in one important poem of the high Renaissance in England for what we can be almost certain were ends predetermined by the poet. To recapitulate, the three main groupings of figures, conceived in terms of their special functions in *Colin Clout*, are: to furnish details of the matter, to give variety and elevation to the style, and to generate affective power at important junctures. To particularize the functional efficacy of the figures of rhetoric is not, again, to denigrate their aesthetic contribution. Poets of the Renaissance found it exhilarating to experiment with fashioning in the vernacular figurative formations which they had been taught to admire in Isocrates, Cicero, Virgil, Ovid, and Seneca. Readers of the time took frank delight in the figures as leading resources in providing the formal beauty of design which they deemed essential to a good poem. That delight was enhanced for those readers when the poet displayed logical aptness in turning up places and figures which in many cases amounted to the same thing. This study reveals something of the part that internal pressure played in shaping outward expression—in producing a style nicely toned and modulated to changes in subject, person, and circumstances by the studied application of figures. It conveys how important the figures are to the texture and the architecture of *Colin Clout*. In this sense, they tend to exemplify the aesthetic principle enunciated elsewhere by Spenser in these lines:

> That Beautie is not, as fond men misdeeme,
> An outward she we of things, that onely seeme;
>
> For of the soule the bodie forme doth take.[43]

J. Sterling Morton Junior College
Cicero, Ill.

Notes

1 Rosemond Tuve, *Elizabethan and Metaphysical Imagery: Renaissance Poetic and Twentieth-Century Critics* (Chicago, 1947), maintains that all elements in figures of comparison assist in conveying meaning; and that classification of figures of any time would be clearer if similarities in logical nature (e.g., images of "quality" or "manner of doing") were observed. Herbert David Rix, *Rhetoric in Spenser's Poetry,* Penn. State Coll. Studies, No. 7 (State College, 1940), applies the ideological concept of the figures and other rhetorical formulae to the poetry of Spenser.

2 *Daphnaïda and Other Poems,* ed. W. L. Renwick, An Elizabethan Gallery, No. 4 (London, 1929), p. 186; Kathrine Koller, "Abraham Fraunce and Edmund Spenser," *ELH,* VII (1940), 108.

3 *The Arcadian Rhetorike,* ed. Ethel Seaton, Luttrell Society Reprints, No. 9 (Oxford, 1950), p. 26.

4 See Bernard Weinberg, *A History of Literary Criticism in the Italian Renaissance* (Chicago, 1961), II, 721–724, for Daniello's view of the similarity between oratory and poetry in having for their object pleasurable teaching of exemplary morality; also pp. 737, 748, for emphasis on the same point by Minturno and Scalinger, whose *De Poeta* (1559) and *Poetices Libri Septem* (1561) respectively were prime sources for Sir Philip Sidney's *Apologie for Poetrie* (c. 1583, printed in 1595). G. Gregory Smith's notes to the *Apologie* in *Elizabethan Critical Essays* (Oxford, 1904), I, 382–403, reveal how closely Sidney, in numerous passages, echoes his Italian models.

5 The writer of the Argument to the *October* eclogue of *The Shepheardes Calender* refers to a book of the author's called the *English Poete,* which had just recently come into his hands. In *A Discourse of English Poetrie* (1586), William Webbe expresses the wish that he might see the *English Poet,* which E. K., the author's friend, had promised to publish (*Eliz. Critical Essays,* I, 232).

6 Father Ong's reminder that the first meaning of *ornamentum* in Latin rhetorical terminology is "equipment or accoutrements, which the 'naked causes' of dialectic, like naked persons, would need rather more than pretty clothing to get along in this world," is pertinent here. He recalls that Miss Tuve (in Ch. iv of *Elizabethan and Metaphysical Imagery*) and others have shown that the Renaissance notion of ornament "does not necessarily mean appliqué work in the way the English term ornament suggests today" (Rev. Walter J. Ong, S. J., *Ramus: Method, and the Decay of Dialogue,* Cambridge, Mass., 1958, p. 277).

7 *Rhetorica ad Herennium* iv.10.15, Loeb Classical Library, trans. Harry Caplan (Cambridge, Mass., 1944), p. 264.

8 Cicero, *De Oratore* iii.25.100, Loeb Classical Library, trans. H. Rackham (Cambridge, Mass., 1942), p. 80.

9 *Apologie for Poetrie,* in *Eliz. Critical Essays,* I, 201–202. Another less familiar but equally zestful contemporary diatribe against rhetorical affectation (which borrows its imagery directly from Cicero) is contained in a commencement oration delivered at Oxford University in 1572 by John Rainolds, a candidate for the M. A. (*Oratio in Laudem Artis Poeticae,* ed. William Ringler; trans. Walter Allen, Jr., Princeton Univ. Studies in English, No. 20, Princeton, 1940, p. 48).

10 For a selective list of references detailing the teaching of composition through the media of the trivium in English educational institutions of the Renaissance, see Wilbur Samuel Howell, *Logic and Rhetoric in England, 1500–1700* (Princeton, 1956), n. 1, p. 64. To this list should be added Donald Lemen Clark, *John Milton at St. Paul's School: A Study of Ancient Rhetoric in English Renaissance Education* (New York, 1948).

11 See William G. Crane, *Wit and Rhetoric in the Renaissance: The Formal Basis of Elizabethan Prose Style* (New York, 1937), p. 5, for a summary of the vital connection between the figures and the places. Also see p. 55 for a brief statement on the effects of the Ramist reorganization of logic and rhetoric in relation to figures. For an expanded account of the whole movement for the reform of the Aristotelian and Ciceronian system of logic and rhetoric, see Howell, *Logic and Rhetoric in England,* Ch. iv. According to Howell, by the fifteen-seventies the struggle to keep Aristotle and Cicero supreme in logic and rhetoric respectively was beginning to be lost (p. 178). The supremacy of Cicero was challenged at Cambridge University as early as 1574, the year Spenser received his B.A. degree from Pembroke College. In this year Spenser's best friend, Gabriel Harvey (Hobbinol in the poem), as praelector in rhetoric at Cambridge, began preparation of the lectures delivered in 1575–76 and published in 1577 (pp. 247–248).

Whether Spenser came to adopt the Ramist reorganization is not known, although his acquaintance with the Cambridge and Sidney circles which advocated it would make his familiarity with the reformed disciplines virtually certain. Some details concerning Spenser's place in these circles is given in Miss Roller's article on "Edmund Spenser and Abraham Fraunce." *The Lawiers Logicke* and *The Arcadian Rhetoricke,* which Fraunce, a confirmed Ramist, published at London in 1588, are liberally interspersed with illustrative passages of poetry, including some one hundred from Spenser in the former and three in the latter work. These works of Fraunce serve to demonstrate not only the extent to which Ramist books in England point up places and figures with quotations from poetry but also to show how closely proponents of the reformed program of liberal arts continue to associate rhetoric and poetry. (See also Father Ong, *Ramus,* pp. 282–283, on Ramist conceptions of the relationship between poetry and rhetoric.) If Spenser can be counted among those who embraced the new approaches, his adoption in whole or in part of the revised system would not have required any basic readjustment of ingrained habit patterns as regards composition through logical and rhetorical modes. In Ch. xii of *Elizabethan and Metaphysical Imagery,* Miss Tuve treats, under the title "Ramist Logic: Certain General Conceptions Affecting Imagery," the possible effects of the redirection of peripatetic logic on the creation of poetic images during the latter part of the sixteenth and early part of the seventeenth centuries in England. She holds the influence of Ramus to have been inescapable on the part of writers of this era (p. 339). (This conclusion is strongly fortified by Father Ong in his recent book on Ramus.) However, Miss Tuve believes this influence, whether direct or indirect, resulted, not in images with new qualities, but in images with old qualities highlighted (p. 351). The change of emphasis fostered by the Ramists would, in her view, operate to produce images more notable for logical toughness and intellectual fineness (p. 353).

12 Howell, p. 4.
13 Rix, *Rhetoric in Spenser's Poetry,* p. 62.
14 Veré L. Rubel, *Poetic Diction in the English Renaissance from Skelton through Spenser* (New York, 1941), p. 258.
15 All citations from Spenser follow the text of *The Works of Edmund Spenser: A Variorum Edition,* eds. Edwin Greenlaw et al., 10 vols. in 11 (Baltimore, 1932–57). Line citations only will be given for *Colin Clout,* which appears in *Minor Poems,* Vol. I (*Works,* VII), edited by C. G. Osgood and H. G. Lotspeich, assisted by D. E. Malone. Except that the editors have corrected misprints and made a few relatively minor emendations, the *Variorum* version reproduces the text of the poem as contained in the revised issue of the 1595 Quarto, a collection titled from the pastoral under consideration. For a detailed study of the genesis and transmission of the text, see my "*Colin Clout*: The Poem and the Book," *PBSA,* LVI (fourth quarter, 1962), 397–413.
16 I assume as standard for the Elizabethan period the meanings ascribed to the figures by Rix, pp. 22–61. These meanings are made clear by definitions and specimens. The definitions quoted by Rix in this section are nearly all from Joannes Susenbrotus, *Epitome Troporum ac Schematum* (1563). The English translations of the Latin definitions are mostly from Henry Peacham, *The Garden of Eloquence* (1577). A great many of the specimens are from Alexander Gill, *Logonomia Anglica* (1619, rev. 1621). Gill devotes four chapters of his work to the various figures and illustrates many of them by quotations from *The Faerie Queene, The Ruines of Time,* and *The Shepheardes Calender.* On pp. 19–20 of *Rhetoric in Spenser's Poetry,* Rix explains his division of the figures into tropes (words employed in other than their literal meanings, as in metaphor and metonymy) and schemes (words or longer units arranged or repeated according to a definite pattern, as in alliteration and simile). Rix refines the category of schemes by subdividing them into schemes of words and schemes of thought and amplification. His system of classification is an adaptation of one of the commonly accepted groupings in Spenser's period, although no two Renaissance sources agree *in toto* on precise classifications of different figures. In the ensuing discussion of the wide variety of stylistic devices which appear in *Colin Clout* and which are encompassed by the term figures in its Renaissance acceptation, I have found no need to maintain these distinctions in categories. I have profited much from the way in which Rix treats Spenser's use of rhetorical figures. For *Colin Clout,* however, Rix's coverage is negligible, since he includes only ten illustrative figures from the poem in his Table of Figures (pp. 21–61) and mentions in passing another figure (p. 71).

17 Rix, p. 48.
18 George Puttenham, *The Arte of English Poesie*, eds. Gladys Doidge Willcock and Alice Walker (Cambridge, Eng., 1938), p. 223.
19 Rix, p. 31.
20 King James VI of Scotland, in *Eliz. Critical Essays*, I, 219; Puttenham, pp. 176–177.
21 Merritt Y. Hughes, "Spenser and the Greek Pastoral Triad," *SP*, xx (1929), 208–209, cited in *Works*, VII, 410.
22 Elkin Calhoun Wilson, *England's Eliza*, Harvard Studies in English, xx (Cambridge, Mass., 1939), 302.
23 Thomas Wilson, *Wilson's Arte of Rhetorique, 1560*, ed. George Herbert Mair (Oxford, 1909), p. 169.
24 *Il Libro del Cortegiano de Conte Baldesar Castiglione* (Venice, 1528), sig. biiiir.
25 The comparison would now be called a metaphor, but Renaissance criticism normally has *metaphora* denote a single word "translated from the proper and natural signification, to another not proper, yet nie and/likely" (Peacham, in Rix, p. 22).
26 *Daphnaïda and Other Poems*, ed. Renwick, p. 187.
27 See Morris Palmer Tilley, *A Dictionary of the Proverbs in England in the Sixteenth and Seventeenth Centuries* (Ann Arbor, Mich., 1940), p. v.
28 *The Apophtegmes of Erasmus*, trans. Nicolas Udall, from the edition of 1564, ed. Robert Roberts (Boston, 1877), p. xxii.
29 See Crane, *Wit and Rhetoric in the Renaissance*, Chs. ii and iii, for a discussion of commonplace books and the way in which they were utilized by men of the Renaissance as helps to composition.
30 In *Eliz. Critical Essays*, I, 196–197.
31 *Discourses upon Seneca the Tragedian*, ed. Robert Hood Bowers (Gainesville, Fla., 1952), pp. iv–ix. For a full account of Seneca's influence on English letters, which, in opposition to Ciceronianism, was on the rise during the latter part of the sixteenth century, see George Williamson, *The Senecan Amble* (Chicago, 1951).
32 Quotations from *Ane Schort Treatise* in *Eliz. Critical Essays*, I, 219.
33 Cf. Tilley, p. 28, B50, citations from Pettie, *A Petite Pallace of Pettie His Pleasure* (1576): "he bit so greedily at the bait of her beauty, that he swallowed down the hook of hateful hurt"; also from Lyly, *Euphues, The Anatomy of Wit* (1578): "Beautie . . . was a deceiptfull bayte with a deadly hooke."
34 Cf. ibid., p. 398, L527, citations from Wilmot et al., *Gismond* (1566–68): "Loue rules the world, Loue onely is the Lorde"; and from Wilmot, *Tancred and Gismond* (1591–92): "I . . . am that great God of loue, who with high might Ruleth the wast wide world, and liuing things."
35 Rudolph B. Gottfried, "Spenser and the Italian Myth of Locality," *SP*, xxxiv (1937), 111–114, 117–124.
36 Puttenham, p. 154. See Tuve, Ch. ix, for a valuable discussion concerning the way in which Renaissance notions of decorum and the styles affected the fashioning of figurative devices in poetic writing.
37 Dedication to *Thee First Foure Bookes of Virgil his Aeneis*, in *Eliz. Critical Essays*, I, 137.
38 Cicero, *Orator*, 67–70, Loeb Classical Library, trans. H. M. Hubbell, (Cambridge, Mass., 1939), pp. 354, 356.
39 Ibid., 20–22, pp. 318, 320; 79–82, pp. 364, 366.
40 *Institutio Oratoria* xii.10.58–65, rv. 482, 484, 486.
41 P. 197. See Tuve, pp. 166–175, 396–402, for a succinct discussion of Renaissance psychological theories, with particular reference to tropical language in poetry. Her note on p. 396 lists a few selected references on the mental operations as conceived by learned Elizabethans and Jacobeans.
42 *Directions for Speech and Style*, ed. Hoyt H. Hudson, Princeton Studies in English, No. 12 (Princeton, 1935), p. 13.
43 *An Hymne in Honour of Beautie*, ll. 90–91, *Works*, VII, 206, and l. 132, p. 207.

10.
RHETORIC OF TROPES (NIETZSCHE)
Paul de Man

IT MAY SEEM FAR-FETCHED TO CENTER A CONSIDERATION of Nietzsche's relationship to literature on his theory of rhetoric. Why should one choose to consider what, by all evidence, appears to be an eccentric and minor part of Nietzsche's enterprise as a way of access to the complex question of his reflection on literature and on the specifically literary aspects of his own philosophical discourse? An abundance of other, less oblique approaches to the question may appear preferable. The configuration of the earlier literary examples explicitly mentioned by Nietzsche, a constellation that includes a wide variety of writers ranging from Goethe, Schiller, and Hölderlin to Emerson, Montaigne, and Sterne could certainly yield interpretative insights. Or one could consider Nietzsche's literary ofispring, which is certainly even more extensive and informative than one suspects. The repertory of the revealed or hidden presence of Nietzsche in the main literary works of the twentieth century still has to be completed. It would reveal many surprises of value to an understanding of our period and literature in general.[1] For Nietzsche is obviously one of those figures like Plato, Augustine, Montaigne, or Rousseau whose work straddles the two activities of the human intellect that are both the closest and the most impenetrable to each other—literature and philosophy.

Nevertheless, the apparently crooked byways of the neglected and inconspicuous corner of the Nietzsche canon dealing with rhetoric will take us quicker to our destination than the usual itinerary that starts out from studies of individual cases and progresses from there to synthetic generalizations. That this area has been neglected or discarded as a possible mainroad to central problems in the interinterpretation of Nietzsche is clear from bibliographical evidence: one of the few books dealing with the subject, a recent German work by Joachim Goth entitled *Nietzsche und die Rhetorik* (Tübingen, 1970), starting out from a suggestion that goes back to Ernst Robert Curtius, remains strictly confined to stylistic description and never pretends to engage wider questions of interpretation. That, on the other hand, the consideration of Nietzsche's theory of rhetoric, however marginal it may be, offers at least some promise, is clear from the work of some recent French commentators such as Philippe Lacoue-Labarthe, Bernard Pautrat, Sarah Kofinan, and others.[2] Writing under the influence of a renewed interest, in France, in the theory of language, their work is oriented towards the philosophical implications of Nietzsche's concerns with rhetoric rather than towards the techniques of oratory and persuasion that are obviously present in his

---

de Man, Paul. "Rhetoric of Tropes (Nietzsche)." *Allegories of Reading: Figural Language in Rousseau, Nietzsche, Rilke, and Proust.* New Haven, CN: Yale University Press, 1979: 103–118.

style. I do not plan to deal with these particular contributions which are still preparatory and tentative at best, but will try instead to indicate, in too broad and too hasty an outline, how the question of rhetoric can be brought to bear on some of Nietzsche's texts, early us well as late.

It is well known that Nietzsche's explicit concern with rhetoric is confined to the notes for a semester course taught at the University of Basel during the winter semester of 1872–73, with no more than two students present. Parts of these notes have been published in Volume V of the Kröner-Musarion edition. Only with their complete publication, presumably in the new Colli-Montinari edition, will we be able to judge if the former editors were justified in their claim that, after the seventh paragraph, the interest of the notes no longer warranted their publication. It is also well known that Nietzsche's course on rhetoric was not original and drew abundantly on the textbooks that were current at the time in the academic study of classical rhetoric, especially Richard Volkmann, *Die Rhetorik der Griechen und Römer in systematischer Übersicht* (1872), Gustav Gerber's *Die Sprache als Kunst* (1872) and, on the question of eloquence, the works of Blass (1868).[3] There is sufficient manipulation of these sources and sufficient new emphases in Nietzsche's notes to justify their consideration despite their mixed origins. To claim, however, that they are of more than local significance takes some more elaboration. At first sight there is little in these notes to single them out for special attention.

Two main points that can be deduced from the notes deserve to be stressed. Nietzsche moves the study of rhetoric away from techniques of eloquence and persuasion [*Beredsamkeit*] by making these dependent on a previous theory of figures of speech or tropes. The notes contain explicit discussion of at least three tropes: metaphor, metonymy, and synecdoche, and announce Nietzsche's intention to follow this up with a taxonomy of tropes that would include catachresis, allegory, irony, metalepsis, etc. Eloquence and style are an applied form derived from the theory of figures. Nietzsche writes: "There is no difference between the correct rules of eloquence [*Rede*] and the so-called rhetorical figures. Actually, all that is generally called eloquence is figural language."[4]

The dependence of eloquence on figure is only a further consequence of a more fundamental observation: tropes are not understood aesthetically, as ornament, nor are they understood semantically as a figurative meaning that derives from literal, proper denomination. Rather, the reverse is the case. The trope is not a derived, marginal, or aberrant form of language but the linguistic paradigm par excellence. The figurative structure is not one linguistic mode among others but it characterizes language as such. A series of successive elaborations show Nietzsche characteristically radicalizing his remarks until they reach this conclusion:

> It is not difficult to demonstrate that what is called "rhetorical," as the devices of a conscious art, is present as a device of unconscious art in language and its development. We can go so far as to say that rhetoric is an extension [*Fortbildung*] of the devices embedded in language: at the clear light of reason. No such thing as an unrhetorical, "natural" language exists that could be used as a point of reference: language is itself the result of purely rhetorical tricks

and devices. . . . Language is rhetoric, for it only intends to convey a *doxa* (opinion), not an *episteme* (truth). . . . Tropes are not something that can be added or subtracted from language at will; they are its truest nature. There is no such thing as a proper meaning than can be communicated only in certain particular cases.[5]

Although it may seem daringly paradoxical, the statement has affinities with similarly oriented formulations in Gerber's *Die Sprache als Kunst*. This is not so surprising if one bears in mind Gerber's antecedents in German Romanticism, especially in Friedrich Schlegel and Jean Paul Richter; the relationship of Nietzsche to his so-called Romantic predecessors is still largely obscured by our lack of understanding of Romantic linguistic theory. Yet, the straightforward affirmation that the paradigmatic structure of language is rhetorical rather than representational or expressive of a referential, proper meaning is more categorical, in this relatively early Nietzsche text, than in the predecessors from which it stems. It marks a full reversal of the established priorities which traditionally root the authority of the language in its adequation to an extralinguistic referent or meaning, rather than in the intralinguistic resources of figures.

A passage such as this one could still be understood as a belated echo of earlier speculations, long since overcome in the post-Kantian and post-Hegelian syntheses that have put rhetoric back in its proper place, or dismissed it as a form of the aesthetic decadence that Nietzsche will be one of the first to denounce in later, anti-Wagnerian and anti-Schopenhauerian writings. The question remains however whether some of the implications of the early speculations on rhetoric are carried out in later works. At first sight, this hardly seems to be the case. The rhetorical vocabulary, still much in evidence in the *Philosphenbuch* (which dates from the fall of 1872 and thus immediately precedes the course on rhetoric) disappears almost entirely from *Human all too Human* on. It seems as if Nietzsche had turned away from the problems of language to questions of the self and to the assertion of a philosophy rooted in the unmediated sense of existential pathos which has been so prevalent in the interpretation of his work.

The validity of this scheme can be put in question by examining one single but typical passage from a later text. It dates from 1888 and is part of the posthumous fragments known as *The Will to Power*. The passage is characteristic of many later Nietzsche texts and is not to be considered as an anomaly. I am not primarily interested in its specific "thesis" but rather in the manner in which the argument is conducted.

The passage has to do with what Nietzsche calls the phenomenalism of consciousness, the tendency to describe mental events such as recollection or emotion in terms derived from the experience of the phenomenal world: sense perception, the interpretation of spatial structures, etc. Under the heading "phenomenalism of the inner world," Nietzsche writes as follows:

> The *chronological reversal* which makes the cause reach consciousness later than the effect.—We have seen how pain is projected in a part of the body without having its origin there; we have seen that the perceptions which one naïvely considers as determined by the outside world are much rather determined from the inside; that the actual impact of the

outside world is never a *conscious* one . . . The fragment of outside world of which we are conscious is a correlative of the effect that has reached us from outside and that is then projected, *a posteriori*, as its "cause" . . .[6]

The argument starts out from a binary polarity of classical banality in the history of metaphysics: the opposition of subject to object based on the spatial model of an "inside" to an "outside" world. As such, there is nothing unusual about the stress on the unreliability, the subjectivity of sense impressions. But the working hypothesis of polarity becomes soon itself the target of the analysis. This occurs, first of all, by showing that the priority status of the two poles can be reversed. The outer, objective event in the world was supposed to determine the inner, conscious event as cause determines effect. It turns out however that will was assumed to be the objective, external cause is itself the result of an internal effect. What had been considered to be a cause, is, in fact, the effect of an effect, and what had been considered to be an effect can in its turn seem to function as the cause of its own cause.

The two sets of polarities, inside/outside and cause/effect, which seemed to make up a closed and coherent system (outside causes producing inside effects) has now been scrambled into an arbitrary, open system in which the attributes of causality and of location can be deceptively exchanged, substituted for each other at will. As a consequence, our confidence in the original, binary model that was used as a starting point is bound to be shaken. The main impact of this deconstruction of the classical cause/effect, subject/object scheme becomes clear in the second part of the passage. It is based, as we saw, on an inversion or reversal of attributes which, in this particular case, is said to be temporal in nature. Logical priority is uncritically deduced from a contingent temporal priority: we pair the polarities outside/inside with cause/effect on the basis of a temporal polarity before/after (or early/late) that remains un-reflected. The result is cumulative error, "the consequence of all previous causal fictions," which as far as the "objective" world is concerned, are forever tied to "the old error of original Cause."[7] This entire process of substitution and reversal is conceived by Nietzsche—and this is the main point for us in this context—as a linguistic event. The passage concludes as follows:

The whole notion of an "inner experience" enters our consciousness only after it has found a language that the individual *understands*—i.e., a translation of a situation into a *familiar situation*—: 'to understand,' naïvely put merely means: to be able to express something old and familiar.[8]

What is here called "language" is the medium within which the play of reversals and substitutions that the passage describes takes place. This medium, or property of language, is therefore the possibility of substituting binary polarities such as before for after, early for late, outside for inside, cause for effect, without regard for the truth-value of these structures. But this is precisely how Nietzsche also defines the rhetorical figure, the paradigm of all language. In the Course on Rhetoric, metonymy is characterized as what rhetoricians also call metalepsis, "the exchange or substitution of cause and effect" and one of the examples given is, revealingly enough, the substitution of "tongue" for language. Later in the same notes metonymy is also defined as hypallagus and characterized as follows:

> The abstract nouns are properties within and outside ourselves that are being torn away from their supports and considered to be autonomous entities. . . . Such concepts, which owe their existence only to our feelings, are posited as if they were the inner essence of things: we attribute to events a cause which in truth is only on effect. The abstractions create the illusion as if *they* were the entity that causes the properties, whereas they receive their objective, iconic existence [*bildliches Dasein*] only from us as a consequence of these very properties.[9]

Practically the same text that, in 1872, explicitly defines metonymy as the prototype of all figural language, describes, in 1888, a metaphysical construct (the phenomenalism of consciousness) as susceptible of being deconstructed as soon as one is made aware of its linguistic, rhetorical structure. We are not here concerned with the consequences of this critique of phenomenalism which is also, in many respects, a prefigurative critique of what will later become known a phenomenology. Readers of *The Will to Power* know that this critique by no means pretends to discard phenomenalism, but puts us on our guard against the tendency to hypostatize consciousness into an authoritative ontological category. And they will also recognize that the pattern of argument here directed against the concept of consciousness is the same pattern that underlies the critique of the main categories that make up traditional metaphysics: the concepts of identity, of causality, of the object and the subject, of truth, etc. We can legitimately assert therefore that the key to Nietzsche's critique of metaphysics—which has, perhaps misleadingly, been described as a mere *reversal* of metaphysics or of Plato—lies in the rhetorical model of the trope or, if one prefers to call it that way, in literature as the language most explicitly grounded in rhetoric.

The idea of a reversal or an exchange of properties (in the previous example, it is the exchange of the attributes of place and causality) is constitutively paired by Nietzsche to the idea of error: the critical deconstruction shows that philosophical models such as the phenomenalism of consciousness are indeed aberrations whose systematic recurrence extends throughout the entirety of classical metaphysics. Would it not follow that, since the aberration turns out to be based on a rhetorical substitution, it would suffice to become aware of this in order to undo the pattern and restore the properties to their "proper" place? If attributes of time and attributes of cause have been improperly associated with each other, one might be able to uncross, so to speak, the polarities that have been exchanged in order to recover a measure of truth. In the example at hand, we could conceivably eliminate the misleading temporal scheme that led to the confusion, and substitute for the derived cause, mistakenly assumed to have an objective existence in the outside world, an authentic cause that could be inferred from the critical deconstruction of the aberrant one. Granted that the misinterpretation of reality that Nietzsche finds systematically repeated throughout the tradition is indeed rooted in the rhetorical structure of language, can we then not hope to escape from it by an equally systematic cleansing of this language from its dangerously seductive figural properties? Is it not possible to progress from the rhetorical language of literature to a language that, like the language of science or mathematics, would be epistemologically more reliable? The ambivalence of Nietzsche's attitude towards science and literature, as it appears, for example, in the use of the term science in the title of "la gaya scienza" or in the later fragments that look back upon *The Birth of Tragedy,* indicates the complexity of his position. One can read these texts as a glorification as well as a denunciation of literature. The general drift of Nietzsche's thought, on this point, can be better understood by taking into account texts that precede the 1873 Course on Rhetoric, especially the never completed *Philosophenbuch.*

For the very question we are considering, the possibility of escaping from the pitfalls of rhetoric by becoming aware of the rhetoricity of language, is central to the entire *Philosophenbuch* and its only completed unit, the essay. *On Truth and Lie in an Extra-Moral Sense* [*Über Wahrheit und Lüge im aussermoralischen Sinn*]. This essay flatly states the necessary subversion of truth by rhetoric us the distinctive feature of all language. "What is truth?" asks Nietzsche, and he answers:

> A moving army of metaphors, metonymies and anthropomorphisms, in short a summa of human relationships that are being poetically and rhetorically sublimated, transposed, and beautified until, alter long and repeated use, a people considers them as solid, canonical, and unavoidable. Truths are illusions whose illusionary nature has been forgotten, metaphores that have been used up and have lost their imprint and that now operate as mere metal, no longer as coins.[10]

What is being forgotten in this false literalism is precisely the rhetorical, symbolic quality of all language. The degradation of metaphor into literal meaning is not condemned because it is the forgetting of a truth but much rather because it forgets the un-truth, the lie that the metaphor was in the first place. It is a naïve belief in the proper meaning of the metaphor without awareness of the problematic nature of its factual, referential foundation.

The first step of the Nietzschean deconstruction therefore reminds us, as in the above quotation, of the figurality of all language. In this text, contrary to what happens in *The Birth of Tragedy,* this insight is openly stated as the main theme of the essay. Does it follow that the text therefore escapes from the kind of error it denounces? And since we can make the possibility of this error distinctive of literature in general, does it then follow that the essay *On Lie and Truth* is no longer literature but something closer to science—as *Wittgenstein's Tractatus* could claim to be scientific rather than literary? Or, if we call a hybrid text like this one "philosophical," can we then define philosophy as the systematic demystification of literary rhetoric?

The text proceeds in its deconstructive enterprise by putting into question some of the concepts that will also be targets of the later critique of metaphysics in *The Will to Power.* It shows, for example, that the idea of individuation, of the human subject as a privileged viewpoint, is a mere metaphor by means of which man protects himself from his insignificance by forcing his own interpretation of the world upon the entire universe, substituting a human-centered set of meanings that is reassuring to his vanity for a set of meanings that reduces him to being a mere transitory accident in the cosmic order. The metaphorical substitution is aberrant but no human self could come into being without this error. Faced with the truth of its nonexistence, the self would be consumed as an insect is consumed by the flame that attracts it. But the text that asserts this annihilation of the self is not consumed, because it still sees itself as the center that produces the affirmation. The attributes of centrality and of selfhood are being exchanged in the medium of the language. Making the language that denies the self into a center rescues the self linguistically at the same time that it asserts its insignificance, its emptiness as a mere figure of speech. It can only persist as self if it is displaced into the text that denies it. The self which was at first the center of the language as its empirical referent now becomes the language of the center as fiction, as metaphor of the self. What was originally a simply referential text now becomes the text of a text, the figure of a figure. The deconstruction of the self as a metaphor does not end in the rigorous separation of the two categories (self and figure) from each other but ends instead in an exchange of properties that allows for their mutual persistence at the expense of literal truth. This process is exactly the same as what Nietzsche describes as the exemplary "lie" of language: "The liar uses the valid designations, words, to make the unreal appear real.... He misuses the established linguistic conventions by *arbitrary substitutions or even reversals* of the names."[11] By calling the subject a text, the text calls itself, to some extent, a subject. The lie is raised to a new figural power, but it is nonetheless a lie. By asserting in the mode of truth that the self is a lie, we have not escaped from deception. We have merely reversed the usual scheme which derives truth from the convergence of self and other by showing that the fiction of such a convergence is used to allow for the illusion of selfhood to originate.

The pattern is perhaps clearest in the reversal of the categories of good and evil as they combine with those of truth and lie. The usual scheme derives good from truth and evil from falsehood. But Nietzsche tells the tale of the reversed pattern: in order to survive in society, man began by lying.

> [Then] man forgets that this is the case: his lying then is no longer conscious and is founded on age-old habit—and it is *by this nonawareness,* by this forgetting that he develops a sense of truth. Because he feels obliged to designate a certain thing as "red," another as "cold," a third as "mute," a moral impulse oriented towards truth is awakened: in opposition to the liar, who is trusted by no one and excluded from the group, man discovers the respectability, the reliability and the use of truth.[12]

Thus moral virtue is shown to originate out of lies. But the text cannot go to rest in this deconstruction that would justify, to some extent, the morality of deceit (as we find it, for example, within a political context, in Machiavelli or in Rousseau). For we believe in the morality of deceit, we also have to believe in the evil or truth, and to the extent that the society is held together by means of deceit, the open assertion of this fact will also destroy the moral order. It could hardly be said, without further qualification, that a text like this one is socially or morally uplifting. Once again, the reversal of polarities has not led to a restoration of literal truth—in this case, it would be the assertion that moral education should increase one's skill at lying—but has driven us further into the complications of rhetorical delusion. We may have changed the rhetorical mode but we certainly have not escaped from rhetoric. This could hardly have been expected. The original pairing of rhetoric with error, as we encounter it from the Course on Rhetoric to *The Will to Power* was based on the cross-shaped reversal of properties that rhetoricians call chiasmus. And it turns out that the very process of deconstruction, as it functions in this text, is one more such reversal that repeats the selfsame rhetorical structure. All rhetorical structures, whether we call them metaphor, metonymy, chiasmus, metalepsis, hypallagus, or whatever, are based on substitutive reversals, and it seems unlikely that one more such reversal over and above the ones that have already taken place would suffice to restore things to their proper order. One more "turn" or trope added to a series of earlier reversals will not stop the turn towards error. A text like *On Truth and lie*, although it presents itself legitimately as a demystification of literary rhetoric remains entirely literary, rhetorical, and deceptive itself. Does this mean that it will end up in a glorification of literature over science or, as is sometimes claimed of Nietzsche, in a purely literary conception of philosophy?

Two quotations from the *Philosophenbuch*, closely contemporary to *On Truth and Lie*, fully reveal the ambiguity inherent in the question. On the one hand, the truth-value of literature, albeit a negative one, is recognized and asserted. Art is no longer associated with the Dionysian immediacy of music but is now openly Socratic in its deconstructive function. It is therefore, of all human activities, the only one that can lay claim to truth: "Art treats appearance as appearance; its aim is precisely *not* to deceive, it is therefore *true*."[13] But the truth of appearance, unlike the truth of being, is not a threat or a passion that could be described in terms similar to those used in *The Birth of Tragedy* to evoke the Dionysian pathos of truth. It can therefore be said that it stands above pleasure and pain, in the ordinary sense of these terms. The artist, who is truthful in his recognition of illusion and of lie for what they are, thus gains a special kind of affective freedom, a euphoria which is that of *joyful* wisdom or of the Homeric *Heiterkeit* and that differs entirely from the pleasure principle tied to libido and desire. "As long as man looks for truth *in the world*, he stands under the dominance of desire [*unter der Herrschaft des Triebes*]: he wants pleasure, not truth; he wants the belief in truth and the pleasurable effects of this belief."[14] Only the artist who can conceive of the entire world as appearance is able to consider it without desire: this leads to the feeling of liberation and weightlessness that characterizes the man freed from the constraints of referential truth, what Barthes, in more recent times, has referred to as "la libération du signifiant." *On Truth and Lie* describes the euphoria of this type of "truth":

> The intellect, this master of deceit, feels itself freed from its habitual servitude when it is allowed to deceive without direct harm. Then it celebrates its own saturnalia. It is never so rich, so seductive, proud, clever and outrageous: with inventive satisfaction, it juggles metaphores and tears out [*verrückt*] the bordermarks of abstractions. For example, he considers the river as if it were the moving roadway that carries man to where he would otherwise have to walk. . . . It imitates human existence as if it were a fine thing and declares itself entirely pleased with it.[15]

This attractive pairing of Heraclites with Stendhal is however not devoid of warning signals. It has its own pseudo-teleology, the flow of time delighting in the self-sufficient, innocent spectacle of its own motion. But if this movement is reduced to the mere appearance that it is, it also loses its foundation and becomes one among the various other metaphors of self-destruction disseminated throughout this brief text: the insect and the fluttering light, the conceptual pyramid that turns out to be a tomb, the painter deprived of his hands, man asleep on the back of a tiger.[16] The implicit threat in all these images is very similar to the threat implied in mistaking a river for a road. The critical deconstruction that leads to the discovery of the literary, rhetorical nature of the philosophical claim to truth is genuine enough and cannot be refuted: literature turns out to be the main topic of philosophy and the model for the kind of truth to which it aspires. But when literature seduces us with the freedom of its figural combinations, so much airier and lighter than the labored constructs of concepts, it is not the less deceitful because it asserts its own deceitful properties. The conclusion of the essay shows the artist in a not particularly enviable situation: he is indeed freer but "he suffers more [than the conceptual philosopher] *when* he suffers; and he suffers more often, because he does not learn from experience and always again falls in the same trap in which he fell in the first place. In his suffering, he is then just as foolish [*unvernünftig*] as in his happiness: he complains loudly and can find no consolation."[17] An aphorism that dates from exactly the same period puts it more bluntly and from a less personal point of view: it may be true that art sets the right norm for truth, but "Truth kills, indeed kills itself (insofar that it realizes its own foundation in error)."[18] Philosophy turns out to be an endless reflection on its own destruction at the hands of literature.

This endless reflection is itself a rhetorical mode, since it la unable ever to escape from the rhetorical deceit it denounces. The definition of this mode lies beyond our present scope, though we get some indication from the just-quoted description of the artist's plight in *On Truth and Lie* as well as from the general tonality and structure of this text. First of all, the description is certainly not a tragic one: the suffering described in the passage, as well as the happiness that precedes it, cannot be taken seriously, since both are so clearly the result of foolishness. The same foolishness extends to the text itself, for the artist-author of the text, as artist, is just as vulnerable to it as the artist-figure described in the text. The wisdom of the text is self-destructive (art is true but truth kills itself), but this self-destruction is infinitely displaced in a series of successive rhetorical reversals which, by the endless repetition of the same figure, keep it suspended between truth and the death of this truth. A threat of immediate destruction, stating itself as a figure of speech, thus becomes the permanent repetition of this threat. Since this repetition is a temporal event, it can be narrated sequentially, but what it narrates, the subject matter of the story, is itself a mere figure. A nonreferential, repetitive text narrates the story of a literally destructive but nontragic linguistic event. We could call this rhetorical mode, which is that of the "conte philosophique" *On Truth and Lie* and, by extension, of all philosophical discourse, an ironic allegory—but only if we understand "irony" more in the sense of Friedrich Schlegel than of Thomas Mann. The place where we might recover some of this sense is in Nietzsche's own work, not in that of his assumed continuators.

This conclusion as to the fundamentally ironic and allegorical nature of Nietzsche's discourse projects its effect on the works that follow and on those that precede the *Philosophenbuch* as well as on the relationship between the two segments that are thus being more or less arbitrarily isolated. How an ironic reading of an allegorical text such as *Zarathustra* or *The Genealogy of Morals,* or the allegorical reading of ironic aphoristic sequences from *The Gay Science* or *The Will to Power* would have to proceed cannot be outlined here, however sketchily. It may be more productive, in conclusion, to observe how an early text such as *The Birth of Tragedy* fits into this pattern. For one of the most persistent ways in which the illusion that rhetorical blindness can be overcome manifests itself is by the transference of what Nietzsche calls "the old error of original cause" from the *statement* to the *history* of the text. While granting the ambivalence of the later Nietzsche on the subject of truth, one may contrast this wariness with the relative naïveté of the earlier works. Particular texts from, say, *On Truth and Lie* on, can be considered to be epistemologically destructive, but by presenting them as a development moving beyond the assumed mystification of the earlier writings, the "history" of Nietzsche's work as a whole remains that of a narrative moving from false to true, from blindness to insight. But the question remains whether the pattern of this narrative is "historical," i.e., revelatory of a teleological meaning, or "allegorical," i.e., repetitive of a potential confusion between figural and referential statement. Is Nietzsche's work structured as a process, a movement of "becoming"—and Nietzsche's late reference to "the innocence of becoming" is well known—or as a repetition? The importance of the question is apparent from the near-obsessive way in which Nietzsche himself, as well as his interpreters, have been returning to the enigmas of the early *Birth of Tragedy.*

The obvious pathos and exaltation of *The Birth of Tragedy* seems entirely incompatible with irony. It is difficult not to read it as a plea for the unmediated presence of the will, for a truly tragic over an ironic art. If this were indeed the case, then one would have to assume a genuine development, even a conversion within Nietzsche's thought during the years immediately following the writing of *The Birth of Tragedy.* The conversion could have been brought about by his reflections on rhetoric as they appear in the *Philosophenbuch* and in the 1873 course notes, and it would also be apparent in the reaction against Wagner and Schopenhauer in the *Unzeitgemässe Betrachtungen.* The structure of the work as a whole would then be essentially different from that described and acted out in *On Truth and Lie.*

A more rhetorically aware reading of *The Birth of Tragedy* shows that all the authoritative claims that it seems to make can be undermined by means of statements provided by the text itself. And if one also takes into account notes written for *The Birth of Tragedy* but not incorporated in the published text, the ironization implicitly present in the final version becomes quite explicit. Moreover, the forthcoming publication, in the new critical edition of Nietzsche's works, of further lateral material for *The Birth of Tragedy,* shows that the exclusion of these notes was dictated by considerations that disrupt the system of epistemological authority even more deeply. We are told, in these fragments, that the valorization of Dionysos as the primary source of truth is a tactical necessity rather than a substantial affirmation. Nietzsche's auditors have to be spoken to in Dionysian terms because, unlike the Greeks, they are unable to understand the Apollonian language of figure and appearance. In pseudo-historical arguments, reminiscent of Hölderlin's considerations on the dialectical relationship between the Hellenic and the Western world, Nietzsche writes: "The epic fable of the Ancients represented the Dionysian in images. For us, it is the Dionysian that represents (symbolizes) the image. In Antiquity, the Dionysian was explained by the image. Now it is the image that is explained by Dionysos. We have therefore an exactly reversed relationship.... For them, the world of representation was clear; for us, it is the Dionysian world that we understand."[19] It follows that the entire system of valorization at work in *The Birth of Tragedy* can be reversed at will. The Dionysian vocabulary is used only to make the Apollonian mode that deconstructs it more intelligible to a mystified audience. This exchange of attributes involving the categories of truth and appearance deprives the two poles of their authority. The binary polarity that structures the narrative of the text turns out to be the same figure we have encountered in all previous examples, the same "reversal of names" that was mentioned in *On Truth and Lie*. If we read Nietzsche with the rhetorical awareness provided by his own theory of rhetoric we find that the general structure of his work resembles the endlessly repeated gesture of the artist "who does not learn from experience and always again falls in the same trap." What seems to be most difficult to admit is that this allegory of errors is the very model of philosophical rigor.

Notes

1. As one example among many, I was struck to find many more traces of Nietzsche in Proust than assumed, often in connection with Wagner and with the theme of music in general.
2. Sec Bernard Pautrat, *Versions du soleil; Figures et système de Nietzsche* (Paris, 1971); Sarah Kofman, "Nietzsche et la métaphore," *Poétique* 5 (1971): 77–98; Philippe Lacoue-Labarthe, "Le détour," *Poétique* 5 (1971): 53–76.
3. See Friedrich Nietzsche, "Rhétorique et langage," texts translated, presented, and annotated by Philippe Lacoue-Labarthe and Jean-Lac Nancy in *Poétique* 5 (1971): 100.
4. Friedrich Nietzsche, *Gesammelte Werke* (Munich: Musarion Verlag, 1922), 5:300.
5. Ibid.
6. Friedrich Nietzsche, *Werke in drei Bänden,* ed. Karl Schlechta (Munich: Hanser Verlag, 1956), 3:804–05.
7. Ibid, 3:805.
8. Ibid.
9. Musarion, 5:319.
10. Schlechin, 3:314
11. Ibid., 3.311 (my italics).
12. Ibid., 3:314.
13. Musarion, 6:98.
14. Ibid.
15. Schlechta, 3:320.
16. Ibid., 3:310, 315, 317, 311, respectively.
17. Ibid., 3:322.
18. Musarioo, 6.93.
19. Quoted from galley proofs of the forthcoming Colli and Montinari edition of *The Birth of Tragedy;* no reference available.

Politics

11.
JOHN F. KENNEDY: INAUGURAL ADDRESS
(January 20, 1961)
Edward P. J. Corbett and Robert J. Connors

1 We observe today not a victory of party but a celebration of freedom, symbolizing an end as well as a beginning, signifying renewal as well as change. For I have sworn before you and Almighty God the same solemn oath our forebears prescribed nearly a century and three-quarters ago.

2 The world is very different now. For man holds in his mortal hands the power to abolish all forms of human poverty and all forms of human life. And yet the same revolutionary belief for which our forebears fought is still at issue around the globe, the belief that the rights of man come not from the generosity of the state but from the hand of God.

3 We dare not forget today that we are the heirs of that first revolution. Let the word go forth from this time and place, to friend and foe alike, that the torch has been passed to a new generation of Americans, born in this century, tempered by war, disciplined by a hard and bitter peace, proud of our ancient heritage, and unwilling to witness or permit the slow undoing of those human rights to which this nation has always been committed, and to which we are committed today at home and around the world.

4 Let every nation know, whether it wishes us well or ill, that we shall pay any price, bear any burden, meet any hardship, support any friend, oppose any foe to assure the survival and the success of liberty.

5 This much we pledge—and more.

6 To those old allies whose cultural and spiritual origins we share, we pledge the loyalty of faithful friends. United, there is little we cannot do in a host of co-operative ventures. Divided, there is little we can do, for we dare not meet a powerful challenge at odds and split assunder.

7 To those new states whom we welcome to the ranks of the free, we pledge our word that one form of colonial control shall not have passed away merely to be replaced by a far more iron tyranny. We shall not always expect to find them supporting our view. But we shall always hope to find them strongly supporting their own freedom, and to remember that, in the past, those who foolishly sought power by riding the back of the tiger ended up inside.

Corbett, Edward P. J. and Robert J. Connors. "John F. Kennedy: Inaugural Address," *Classical Rhetoric for the Modern Student*. Oxford: Oxford University Press, 1999: 459–472.

8 To those people in the huts and villages of half the globe struggling to break the bonds of mass misery, we pledge our best efforts to help them help themselves, for whatever period is required, not because the Communists may be doing it, not because we seek their votes, but because it is right. If a free society cannot help the many who are poor, it cannot save the few who are rich.

9 To our sister republics south of our border, we offer a special pledge: to convert our good words into good deeds, in a new alliance for progress, to assist free men and free governments in casting off the chains of poverty. But this peaceful revolution of hope cannot become the prey of hostile powers. Let all our neighbors know that we shall join with them to oppose aggression or subversion anywhere in the Americas. And let every other power know that this hemisphere intends to remain the master of its own house.

10 To that world assembly of sovereign stales, the United Nations, our last best hope in an age where the instruments of war have far outpaced the instruments of peace, we renew our pledge of support: to prevent it from becoming merely a forum for invective, to strengthen its shield of the new and the weak, and to enlarge the area in which its writ may run.

11 Finally, to those nations who would make themselves our adversary, we offer not a pledge but a request: that both sides begin anew the quest for peace, before the dark powers of destruction unleashed by science engulf all humanity in planned or accidental self-destruction.

12 We dare not tempt them with weakness. For only when our arms are sufficient beyond doubt can we be certain beyond doubt that they will never be employed.

13 But neither can two great and powerful groups of nations take comfort from our present course—both sides over-burdened by the cost of modern weapons, both rightly alarmed by the steady spread of the deadly atom, yet both racing to alter that uncertain balance of terror that stays the hand of mankind's final war.

14 So let us begin anew, remembering on both sides that civility is not a sign of weakness, and sincerity is always subject to proof. Let us never negotiate out of fear, but let us never fear to negotiate.

15 Let both sides explore what problems unite us instead of belaboring those problems which divide us.

16 Let both sides, for the first time, formulate serious and precise proposals for the inspection and control of arms, and bring the absolute power to destroy other nations under the absolute control of all nations.

17 Let both sides seek to invoke the wonders of science instead of its terrors. Together let us explore the stars, conquer the deserts, eradicate disease, tap the ocean depths and encourage the arts and commerce.

18 Let both sides unite to heed in all corners of the earth the command of Isaiah to "undo the heavy burdens . . . [and] let the oppressed go free."

19 And if a beachhead of co-operation may push back the jungle of suspicion, let both sides join in creating a new endeavor, not a new balance of power, but a new world of law, where the strong are just and the weak secure and the peace preserved.

20 All this will not be finished in the first one hundred days. Nor will it be finished in the first one thousand days, nor in the life of this Administration, nor even perhaps in our lifetime on this planet. But let us begin.

21 In your hand, my fellow citizens, more than mine, will rest the final success or failure of our course. Since this country was founded, each generation of Americans has been summoned to give testimony to its national loyalty. The graves of young Americans who answered the call to service surround the globe.

22 Now the trumpet summons us again—not as a call to bear arms, though arms we need; not as a call to battle, though embattled we are; but a call to bear the burden of a long twilight struggle, year in and year out, "rejoicing in hope, patient in tribulation," a struggle against the common enemies of man: tyranny, poverty, disease and war itself.

23 Can we forge against these enemies a grand and global alliance, North and South, East and West, that can assure a more fruitful life for all mankind? Will you join in that historic effort?

24 In the long history of the world, only a few generations have been granted the role of defending freedom in its hour of maximum danger. I do not shrink from this responsibility; I welcome it. I do not believe that any of us would exchange places with any other people or any other generation. The energy, the faith, the devotion which we bring to this endeavor will light our country and all who serve it, and the glow from that fire can truly light the world.

25 And so, my fellow Americans, ask not what your country can do for you; ask what you can do for your country.

26 My fellow citizens of the world, ask not what America will do for you, but what together we can do for the freedom of man.

27 Finally, whether you are citizens of America or citizens of the world, ask of us here the same high standards of strength and sacrifice which we ask of you. With a good conscience our only sure reward, with history the final judge of our deeds, let us go forth to lead the land we love, asking His blessing and His help, but knowing that here on earth God's work must truly be our own.

The Editors of *The New Yorker*: John F. Kennedy's Inaugural Address

As rhetoric has become an increasingly dispensable member of the liberal arts, people have abandoned the idea, held so firmly by the ancient Greeks and Romans, that eloquence is indispensable to politics. Perhaps President Kennedy's achievements in both spheres will revive a taste for good oratory—a taste that has been alternately frustrated by inarticulateness and dulled by bombast. There have been a few notable orators in our day—most recently Adlai Stevenson—but they have been the exceptions, and it has taken Mr. Kennedy's success as a politician to suggest that the power to "enchant souls through words" (Socrates) may soon be at a premium once more. Whatever the impact of the Inaugural Address on contemporary New Frontiersmen, we find it hard to believe that an Athenian or Roman citizen could have listened to it unmoved, or that Cicero, however jealous of his own reputation, would have found reason to object to it.

We are all familiar by now with the generally high praise the President received for his first speech, but before the responsibility for a final judgment is yielded to Time it would be a shame not to seek the opinion of a couple of true professionals. Both Aristotle and Cicero, the one a theorist and the other a theorizing orator, believed that rhetoric could be an art to the extent that the orator was, first, a logician and, second, a psychologist with an appreciation and understanding of words. Cicero felt further, that the ideal orator was the thoroughly educated man. (He would be pleased by Mr. Kennedy's background, with its strong emphasis on affairs of state: the philosopher-orator-statesman.) Of the three types of oratory defined by the ancients—political, forensic, and display (in which audience participation was limited to a judgment of style)—the political was esteemed most highly, because it dealt with the loftiest of issues; namely, the fate of peoples, rather than of individuals. ("Now the trumpet summons us again . . . against the common enemies of man. . . .") The ideal speech was thought to be one in which three kinds of persuasion were used by the speaker: logical, to present the facts of the case and construct an argument based on them; emotional, to reach the audience psychologically; and "ethical," to appeal to the audience by establishing one's own integrity and sincerity. The Inaugural Address, being a variation on the single theme of man's rights and obligations, is not primarily logical, although it contains no illogic; it is an appeal to men's souls rather than to their minds. During the Presidential campaign, Mr. Kennedy tested and patented an exercise in American psychology that proved to be all the emotional appeal he required for the inaugural speech: "And so, my fellow-Americans, ask not what your country can do for you, ask what you can do for your country." His ethical persuasion, or indication of this personal probity, consisted of an extension of that appeal: ". . . ask of us here the same high standards of strength and sacrifice which we ask of you."

Aristotle recognized only one (good) style, while Cicero thought that there were three styles—the plain, the middle, and the grand. To Aristotle, who considered it sufficient for a style to be clear and appropriate, avoiding undue elevation (whence bombast) and excessive lowliness, it would have seemed that Mr. Kennedy had achieved the Golden Mean. The formality of the Inaugural Address ("To that world assembly of sovereign stales, the United Nations . . .") is appropriate to the subject; the language ("In your hands, my fellow-citizens, more than mine, will rest the final success or failure of our course") is clear and direct. Cicero's ideal orator was able to speak in all three styles, in accordance with the demands of his subject, and in that respect Mr. Kennedy filled the role by speaking plainly on the practical ("All this will not be finished in the first one hundred days"), by speaking formally but directly on the purpose of national defense ("For only when our arms are sufficient beyond doubt can we be certain beyond doubt that they will never be employed"), and by speaking grandly on the potential accomplishments of the movement toward the New Frontier ("The energy, the faith, the devotion which we bring to this endeavour will light our country and all who serve it—and the glow from that fire can truly light the world").

The address, however, is largely in the grand style, which is characterized by Cicero as the ultimate source of emotional persuasion, through figures of speech and a certain degree of dignified periodic rhythm, not iambic ("The world is very different now. For man holds in his mortal hands the power to abolish all forms of human poverty, and all forms of human life"). The oration is so rich in figures of speech—the many metaphors include a torch, a beachhead, jungles, a trumpet, a tiger—that we can imagine students of the future studying it for examples of antithesis ("If a free society cannot help the many who are poor, it cannot save the few who are rich"), personification ("... the hand of mankind's final war"), and anaphora ("Not as a call to bear arms, though arms we need; not as a call to battle, though embattled we are ..."). "Battle" and "embattled"—an excellent example of paronomasia.

And so we leave the speech to the students of rhetoric, having invoked for Mr. Kennedy the blessings of Aristotle and Cicero, and for ourself the hope that he has re-established the tradition of political eloquence.

Analysis of the Style of John F. Kennedy's Inaugural Address

> "If, in the effective use of language, style is the man, style is the nation too; men, countries, and entire civilizations have been tested and judged by their literary tone."
>
> —John F. Kennedy

General Situation for the Speech

If we are to relate the style of the Inaugural Address to its content, we must take into account the subject matter, the occasion, the audience, and the ethos of the speaker. An inauguration is a solemn, ceremonial event, attended by certain traditions and rituals. A speech delivered on such an occasion is usually of the ceremonial variety, although there may be deliberative elements in it. What the people have come to expect is not so much a speech that lays down a specific program as a speech that sets a mood. In striking the keynote of the coming administration, the speaker will try to heal the wounds that may have been inflicted during the campaign, to remind the audience of a common heritage and a common purpose, to set forth, in a general way, the policies and objectives of the new administration, and to reassure the international community of the continuity and determination of the nation.

Since a ceremonial speech like this deals in generalities rather than in particulars, it can very easily slip off into platitude and pious cant. In seeking to please everyone with a "safe" speech, the speaker runs the risk of pleasing no one. In striving for that happy mean between the general and the specific, between the trite and the bizarre, and between the offensive and the fulsome, the speaker will have to draw on all his or her ingenuity to come up with a content and a form that will impress the audience without boring them.

Having characterized the kind of speech that is usually delivered at an inauguration, we might consider now the special situation that faced President Kennedy on that January morning in 1961. John Fitzgerald Kennedy was the youngest man and the first

Catholic to be elected to the highest office in America, and he had been elected by a narrow margin of votes. His youth, his religious affiliation, and his narrow victory at the polls—all these combined to establish some doubts about him in the minds of his own people and the people of other countries. Having created an image, during the campaign, of enormous vitality and considerable political shrewdness, this leader of the New Frontier had to fulfill his promise to push the country forward. Clearly, this was an occasion when a powerful ethical appeal would have to be exerted if the confidence and initiative of the people were to be aroused.

What about the audience for this address? There would be the immediate audience—the high dignitaries on the platform and the thousands of people gathered in the plaza in front of the Capitol building. Then there were the millions of people who would see and hear the speaker through the medium of television. And finally there would be the millions of people in foreign lands who would read accounts of the speech in their newspapers the next day. Taken together, this was a vast, heterogeneous audience, posing special problems for the speaker. As we have remarked before, the larger and more heterogeneous the audience is, the more difficult it is to adjust the discourse to fit the audience. In his content and his style, the President must strike some common denominator—but a common denominator that does not fall below the dignity that the occasion demands.

Having looked at the general situation that prevailed for the speech, let us now see how the President accommodated his means to his end. In this analysis, of course, we are going to investigate only the way in which the President accommodated his *style* to the subject matter, occasion, audience, and his own personality.

The Speech as a Whole

One of the first things that strikes the reader is the relative brevity of the speech—1343 words, which at the normal rate for public address would take between nine and ten minutes to deliver. When the President wrote this speech he could not have known that the "live" audience for the speech would be standing in the biting cold that followed a heavy snowstorm in the Washington area on the day before the inauguration. So the President had not made his speech brief out of consideration for his wind-chilled audience. In preparing the speech, however, he might have taken into consideration that it would be delivered at the end of some lengthy preliminary speech-making. But perhaps the consideration that mainly determined the brevity of the speech was the traditional nature of inaugural addresses. As we have observed, inaugural addresses usually deal in broad, undeveloped generalizaties. Principles, policies, and promises are enunciated without elaboration.

Paragraphs

The relative brevity of the speech is reflected in the paragraph and sentence structure. A glance at the printed text of the speech reveals a succession of short paragraphs. Of the twenty-seven paragraphs in the speech, ten have only one sentence; seven paragraphs are two sentences long; and another seven are three sentences long. The longest paragraphs (9 and 24) contain only four sentences. In terms of averages, there are 49.3 words per paragraph and 1.92 sentences per paragraph.

The President is trying to cover a lot of ground in this short speech. In order to do this, he enunciates his principles, promises, and policies in a litany of capsule paragraphs. The effect of these unelaborated paragraphs would have been slight if the President had not rendered many of those paragraphs memorable by the brilliance of his style.

Sentences: Length

Descending to the next smallest unit of discourse, the sentence, we note some interesting facts about the length and kinds of sentences. The two extremes of sentence length are represented by the sentence of eighty words (second sentence of paragraph 3) and the sentence of four words (third sentence of paragraph 20). The average length of the President's sentences is 25.8 words. But what is more revealing about the President's style is the variation above and below this average. Fourteen of the fifty-two sentences (27 percent) in the speech are ten words or more *above* the average; but twenty-three sentences (44 percent) are five words or more *below* the average. Although the President has a number of unusually long sentences—66 words (paragraph 10), 64 words (paragraph 22), 54 words (paragraphs 8 and 13)—an unusually high proportion of his sentences are composed of twenty words or less. Even by modern journalistic standards, a twenty-word sentence is short. This high proportion of short sentences matches the over-all brevity of the speech and the short paragraphs. Although the President displays an admirable variety in sentence-length, his heavy use of the short sentence docs suggest that he had his *listening* audience in mind when he composed his speech. Another consideration that may have influenced the President in the use of short sentences is that short sentences help to create the effect of sententiousness that is appropriate for a ceremonial speech.

Sentences: Grammatical Types

Having noted a high proportion of relatively short sentences, we might expect that a majority of the sentences would be of the simple or compound type. But a close investigation of the grammatical types reveals that this is not so. Twenty (38.4 percent) of the sentences are simple, only six (11.6 percent) sentences are compound. But twenty-six sentences (exactly 50 percent) are complex. Taken together, the simple and compound sentences constitute 50 percent of the whole, but the predominant grammatical type is the complex sentence. What this reveals is that the President manages the expansion of his sentences mainly through the sophisticated powers of subordination. A study of the sequence of sentences, however, shows how well the President has mixed the grammatical types in order to avoid monotony of structure. Only in a half dozen or so places in the speech does he string together two or more sentences of the same grammatical type.

Sentences: Rhetorical Types

When we study the rhetorical patterns of the speech, we note another interesting feature of President Kennedy's style. The predominant rhetorical structure is antithesis. This recurring structure was perhaps dictated by the fact that the speech deals mainly with comparisons of opposite (end–beginning, old–new, rich–poor, friend–enemy). He strikes the theme of the speech and the antithetical keynote in the first sentence: "We observe today *not a victory of party / but a celebration of freedom*—symbolizing *an end / as well as a beginning*—signifying *renewal / as well as change.*" Additional examples of antithesis are not hard to find:

> to friend and foe alike (paragraph 3)
> United . . . Divided (paragraph 6)
> To those old allies . . . To those new states (paragraphs 6, 7)
> If a free society cannot help the many who are poor, it cannot save the few who are rich. (paragraph 8)
> What problems unit us . . . those problems which divide us (paragraph 15)

And the most memorable line of the speech is cast in the form of an antithesis:

> . . . Ask not what your country can do for you—ask what you can do for your country.

Most of these antitheses of thought are laid out in parallel grammatical structure. The recurring parallelism is appropriate here because although the President is pointing up opposites by his antitheses he wants to suggest that these opposites can be reconciled. Opposites can be reconciled only if they are co-ordinate, and one way to emphasize the co-ordinate value of opposites is to juxtapose them in a parallel grammatical structure.

The other use that the President makes of parallelism is for the purpose of specification or enumeration, as in these three examples:

> born in this century, tempered by war, disciplined by a hard and bitter peace, proud of our ancient heritage (paragraph 3)

> pay any price, bear any burden, meet any hardship, support any friend, oppose any foe (paragraph 4)

> Together let us explore the stars, conquer the deserts, eradicate disease, and encourage the arts and commerce (paragraph 17)

As we shall see when we come to study the figures of speech, there are additional schemes intertwined in many of these parallel and antithetical patterns.

Before concluding this section on rhetorical patterns, we shall point out some other features of style. If students needed any evidence to justify their use of a co-ordinating conjunction at the beginning of the sentence, they could cite this speech. The President begins fourteen of his sentences (over 25 percent) with a co-ordinating conjunction. There is, of course, ample precedent for this usage in modern prose and the prose of earlier centuries. But it is interesting to note how effective rhetorically this means of articulating sentences is in the President's speech. Let us look at just one example of this usage:

> We dare not tempt them with weakness. For only when our arms are sufficient beyond doubt can we be certain beyond doubt that they will never be employed. (paragraph 12)

Contrast the effect of this with the following:

> We dare not tempt them with weakness, for only when our arms ate sufficient beyond doubt can we be certain beyond doubt that they will never be employed.

The content and rhetorical scheme of both sentences is exactly the same, and perhaps if one were *reading* the second sentence aloud, one could produce the same effect as the first sentence has. But on the printed page, a special emphasis is achieved by setting off the second clause in a sentence by itself and by signaling the syllogistic relationship .of the two clauses by the capitalized initial *For*. If you analyze the other uses of initial co-ordinating conjunctions, you will usually find some rhetorical purpose being served.

Sentences: Functional Types

The overwhelming majority of the sentences are declarative. This proportion is appropriate in a speech that is designed to inform and reassure the world about the objectives of the new administration. Occasionally, however, the President uses some other functional types of sentence. In paragraph 23, he uses two rhetorical questions ("Can we forge against these enemies a grand and global alliance, North and South, East and West, that can assure a more fruitful life for all mankind? Will you join in that historic effort?"). These questions occur at the point in the speech when the President is about to launch into his peroration. Up to this point the President has been declaring what he will do, what the American people will do. Now he wants to suggest what the international community can do to support his program of peace and prosperity. But he can only suggest—he cannot dictate or predict—what other countries will do. The rhetorical questions are phrased in such a way, however, that the natural answer to them is a resounding *Yes*.

The President groups together two other types of functional sentences—imperatives and hortatives. In paragraphs 25, 26, 27 (the concluding paragraphs of the speech), we see three sharp imperatives, using the verb *to ask,* which leave the citizens with a call to action. Up to this point, the audience have been mere listeners to this ceremonial discourse. Now the audience must be engaged actively. The imperatives point to the general line of action that they must take.

The series of fourteen hortative sentences ("Let us ... Let both sides ...") in paragraphs 14 through 20 also lays down a program of action, but the directives are softened by being cast in a hortatory form. (The Latin and Greek languages would have used the subjunctive mood of the verb to create this effect.) The President here is seeking to induce action, not command it. In other words, he wants to persuade rather than coerce.

Diction

The diction of the speech unobtrusively but unmistakably exerts an influence on the effect of the speech. The simplicity of the diction is perhaps not immediately noticeable, but when one studies it, one notes that there is almost no word that a moderate intelligent high-school graduate would have to look up in a dictionary. A closer study of the diction reveals a high proportion of monosyllabic words: some 951 words in the speech (71 percent) are monosyllabic. In paragraphs 19 and 20, the proportion of monosyllabic words is as high as 80 percent. Even in the peroration of the speech, where one might expect the orator to make use of the sonorous cadence that can be achieved with polysyllabic diction, one finds a high proportion of one-syllable words. This monosyllabism helps to account not only for the impression of simplicity but also for the note of strength in the speech—a note that people had come to associate with the vigor of this youthful public figure. In working over the drafts of the speech, the President must consciously have sought out simple, Anglo-Saxon words.

Having noted the high proportion of monosyllabic words, one might expect to find also a high proportion of concrete words. But this is not the case. Investigation of the nouns in the speech turns up many abstract words—words like *freedom, poverty, tyranny, loyalty, devotion, responsibility, aggression, subversion*. And most of this abstract diction is Latinate and polysyllabic. Aside from the figures of speech—which we will investigate later—there are surprisingly few concrete words—*huts, villages, stars, deserts, graves*. Whatever air of concreteness the speech has is created by the figures of speech. Perhaps the high proportion of abstract words is the natural consequence of the brief, unelaborated character of the speech. Once the President had decided to enunciate only the broad, general policy of his administration, it was almost inevitable that most of his substantive words would be abstract. What we have in this short speech really is a series of undeveloped topic sentences.

Another thing that accounts for the formal quality of this ceremonial speech is the occasional use of slightly archaic diction. We find the President using such words as *forebears* (twice), *host, anew, asunder, foe, adversary, writ*. Besides echoing the tone of Lincoln's *Gettysburg Address* ("Fourscore and seven years ago," "our fathers," "final resting-place," "hallow"), this quaint diction has Biblical overtones and a certain appropriateness to the old-new motif. The President reinforced the effect of this kind of diction by two quotations from the Old Testament and the folksy adage about riding the back of the tiger. The repetition of certain honorific key terms, like *pledge, citizens, peace* also helps to reinforce the reverential tone of the speech.

Figures of Speech: Schemes

First of all, let us look at some of the schemes—those patternings of words which represent departures from the ordinary way of speaking. Since we have already remarked about the pervasive parallelism and antithesis in the speech, we will concentrate here on some of the other schemes.

There are a number of schemes of repetition. The most notable of these is anaphora—repetition of the same words at the beginning of successive clauses. Anaphora is conspicuous in two key passages in the speech: the section (paragraphs 6–11) in which the President is making a series of pledges ("To those . . ."); and the section (paragraphs 15–18) in which the President is suggesting a course of action ("Let both sides . . ."). We have previously observed that these two sections make use of parallelism. The addition of *anaphora* to these passages performs two functions: it combines with the parallelism to mark off and emphasize the co-ordinateness of the series, and it helps to establish the rhythm of the passages. The speech has no example of the opposite scheme, epistrophe (repetition of the same word at the end of successive clauses), but it does have two examples of repetition of similar words in a medial position: "bear *any* burden, meet *any* hardship, support *any* friend, oppose *any* foe" (paragraph 4); "sufficient *beyond doubt* . . . certain *beyond doubt*" (paragraph 12).

The most remembered sentence in the speech—"ask not what your country can do for you—ask what you can do for your country"—contains a figure of repetition known as antimetabole (repetition of words in converse order). Another memorable utterance—"Let us never negotiate out of fear. But never fear to negotiate"—appears to be another example of antimetabole, but it is more accurately classified as polyptoton (repetition of words derived from the same root). Here we have different conjugates of the word *fear*—serving as a noun in the first clause and as an infinitive in the second clause. There is another example of polyptoton in paragraph 23 ("Not as a call to *battle*, though *embattled* we are")—although, as the editors of *The New Yorker* observed, there is a suggestion here too of the trope called paronomasia (play on words).

President Kennedy made sparing use of the scheme of repetition known as alliteration. There are only two instances of noticeable alliteration in the speech—"the area in which its *w*rit may *r*un" (paragraph 10); "to *l*ead the *l*and we *l*ove" (paragraph 27). Perhaps in accord with his personality, the President avoided frequent use of alliteration because of the soft, effeminate sound-effect often produced by this figure; the President was striving for a note of strength and vigor. One wonders, though, whether the President did not intend some sound-effect of appropriate harshness in the succession of *s* and *d* sounds in "before the dark powers of destruction unleashed by science engulf all humanity in planned or accidental self-destruction" (paragraph 11).

Let us look briefly at a few more schemes. In most of his parallel series, the President shows a preference for the hurried rhythms that can be achieved with asyndeton (omission of conjunctions)—e.g., "born in this century, tempered by war, disciplined by a hard and bitter peace, proud of our ancient heritage" (paragraph 3). The President makes little use of the scheme called anastrophe (unusual word order). In the entire speech, there is only one structure that is inverted: "*United*, there is little we cannot do in a host of co-operative ventures. *Divided*, there is little we can do" (paragraph 6). It is easy to see the special emphasis the President achieves here by placing the past participles in the initial position, even though these participles do not modify, as they normally do in this position, the subject of the main clause. One could regard this structure, however, as ellipsis rather than anastrophe. The closest the President comes to the figure known as climax is in graphs 25, 26, 27; but even here we have to strain a bit to find any element of rising importance in the series.

Figures of Speech: Tropes

Although the President makes rather skillful use of the schemes, he is less satisfactory in his use of tropes. There are a number of metaphors in the speech, and those metaphors represent, as we remarked earlier, the chief way in which the President introduces concreteness into the speech. But many of these metaphors—"the torch," "bonds of mass misery," "the chains of poverty," "corners of the earth," "the trumpet," "the glow from that fire"—are rather hackneyed. He achieves a little more freshness in some of his more subtle metaphors, like "iron tyranny," "destruction unleashed," "twilight struggle," "forge." Perhaps his most successful metaphor is the one in paragraph 19—"And if a beachhead of co-operation may push back the jungle of suspicion." By themselves, *beachhead* and *jungle* are rather shopworn metaphors, but they acquire a certain freshness by being combined in a complex metaphor.

The several uses of "hands" (part of the whole) and "arms" (genus for the species) can be looked upon as examples of synecdoche, but those tropes too are fairly trite. The use of "hand" in paragraph 13—"that uncertain balance of terror that stays the hand of mankind's final war"—should be classified as in instance of personification rather than of synecdoche. Perhaps the only other expression in the speech which might be read as an instance of personification is found in the last paragraph—"with history the final judge of our deeds."

Style of Delivery

Undoubtedly, a good deal of the effect of this speech was produced by the "style" of delivery. Those who watched the inauguration ceremonies on television may recall the President's clear, crisp voice, the distinctive Bostonian accent, the mannerisms of the jabbing finger, the pauses, the inflections, the stresses. All of these features of voice and gesture helped to put the speech across; combined with the carefully worked-out style, they helped to communicate the President's message to the electorate and to the world. And perhaps it would be well for the student who has read this close analysis of the style to put the speech together again by listening to it on one of the many memorial records that were issued shortly after the President's assassination. Listening to a recording of the speech will make the student aware that this was a discourse designed for oral delivery, and it might prove interesting to note how much of the highly refined style of the speech comes through to the student once he or she has had the devices of style pointed out.

Concluding Remark

The various stylistic devices we have been observing may be looked upon by some people as the ornamentation of the speech. These devices do "dress up" the speech, but if they are regarded as no more than ornamentation, they have failed to perform the functions that rhetoricians traditionally assigned to them. These formal devices should be one of the carriers of meaning. If the diction, the composition of words, and the figures of speech are not functioning to clarify, enliven, and emphasize the thought, if they are not exerting an ethical, emotional, or logical appeal, then indeed the style of a piece is so much sounding brass and tinkling cymbals, so much sound and fury signifying nothing.

It is not so important that the style of the speech be recognizable as the "Kennedy style" as it is that the style be seen as appropriate to the subject matter, the occasion, the purpose, and the audience. Just as Lincoln's *Gettysburg Address* was not particularly impressive to the audience who heard it in the National Cemetery on November 19, 1863, so Kennedy's Inaugural Address was not—if we may judge from the restrained applause that greeted it while it was being delivered—notably impressive to the audience who heard it in the snow-packed Capitol Plaza on January 20, 1961. It is only when we get a chance to read and reread Lincoln's and Kennedy's speeches that we realize what splendid performances they were. Only a close analysis such as we have engaged in can make us aware of the great care and deliberation President Kennedy devoted to the "expression" of his speech. So much eloquence did not come by chance. It had to come from calculated choices from among a number of possibilities.

We should now be in a better position to judge whether the President's choices were judicious. And we should be in a better position to predict whether future generations will judge this Inaugural Address to be one of the noblest utterances to issue from the lips of an American statesman.

Note

"Notes and Comment," from *The New Yorker,* 36 (Feb. 4, 1961), 23–24; Copyright © 1961, 1989. The New Yorker Magazine, Inc. Reprinted by permission of the publisher.

12.
LINCOLN AT COOPER UNION: A RHETORICAL ANALYSIS OF THE TEXT
Michael C. Leff and Gerald P. Mohrmann

WHEN Abraham Lincoln spoke at the Cooper Union on the evening of February 27, 1860, his audience responded enthusiastically, and the speech has continued to elicit praise throughout the intervening years. Biographers, historians, and literary scholars agree that it was "one of his most significant speeches,"[1] one that illustrated "his abilities as a reasoner,"[2] and one to which posterity has ascribed his "subsequent nomination and election to the presidency."[3] Ironically, however, this model of "logical analysis and construction"[4] has failed to generate a critical response in kind. Most of what has been written treats of the background, and, too often, the man as myth has intruded; caught up in the drama of the performance, writers find no bit of information too trivial to report, whether it be the price of tickets or the fit of Lincoln's new shoes.[5] Such details can deepen our appreciation of the event, but they do not illuminate the speech as a speech.

Unhappily, little light is shed by those who do comment on the speech text. Nicolay and Hay assert, for example, that Lincoln's conclusions "were irresistibly convincing,"[6] but their sole piece of supporting evidence is a four-hundred word excerpt. And if they happen to be "firmly in the hero-worshipping tradition,"[7] those of sterner stuff fare no better. Basler makes the curious claim that the rhetorical "high-water mark" occurs toward the end of the first section;[8] Nevins mistakenly argues that the speech "fell into two halves",[9] reputable scholars equate summary and quotation with explication;[10] and it is generally accepted that Lincoln demonstrated a conciliatory attitude toward the South."[11]

Certainly all is not dross in previous studies, but wherever one turns in the literature, no satisfying account of the speech is to be found.[12] We are convinced that a systematic rhetorical analysis can help rectify the situation, and what follows is our attempt to accomplish such an analysis. In that attempt, we center on the text of the speech, but our purpose demands some preliminary remarks about the rhetorical context.

Although it was not until after the speech that Lincoln frankly admitted his presidential aspirations, saying, "The taste *is* in my mouth a little,"[13] he had been savoring the possibility for months. The preceding November, he had written that the next canvas would find him laboring "faithfully in the ranks" unless "the judgment of

---

Leff, Michael C. and Gerald P. Mohrmann. 1974. "Lincoln at Cooper Union: A Rhetorical Analysis of the Text," *Quarterly Journal of Speech*, Vol. 60, No. 3 (1974): 346–358.

the party shall assign me a different position,"[14] but even as he wrote, Lincoln was grasping for a different assignment, "busy using the knife on his rivals . . . and doing all he could to enhance his reputation as an outstanding Republican leader."[15] Small wonder that he decided early to "make a political speech of it" in New York.[16] Here was the opportunity to make himself more available to Republicans in the East. The appearance alone would make for greater recognition, but political availability required more; Lincoln had to be an acceptable Republican, and he had to be an attractive alternative to the Democratic candidate.

William A. Seward and Stephen A. Douglas were the presumptive nominees, and they, patently, were Lincoln's antagonists. Moreover, their views on slavery created an intertwining threat that menaced his conception of the party and his personal ambitions. When Seward spoke about a "higher law" and an "irrepressible conflict," he strained Lincoln's sense of moral and political conservatism; these pronouncements smacked too much of radicalism.[17] Douglas, meanwhile, exacerbated the situation with his doctrine of popular sovereignty. Lincoln feared that this siren song would cause wholesale apostasy in Republican ranks, an eventuality all the more likely if the party nominee was tinctured with radicalism. He knew, however, that a middle ground existed, and he long had occupied it with his insistence that slavery should be protected but not extended. Consequently, when Lincoln addressed the Eastern Republicans, both principle and expediency permitted, even dictated, that he speak for party and for self and that he maintain party and self in a position between those taken by Seward and Douglas.

That he took such a course is revealed by an examination of the speech text, but all the external evidence shows a man running hard, if humbly, for political office, and while Lincoln spoke for his party, he spoke first for his own nomination. In fact, the Cooper Union Address is best characterized as a campaign oration, a speech designed to win nomination for the speaker. This identification of genre is basic to our analysis, and the nature of the genre is suggested by Rosenthal's distinction between non-personal and personal persuasion;[18] in the former, the speaker attempts to influence audience attitudes about a particular issue, and ethos is important insofar as it lends credence to the substance of the argument. In the latter the process is reversed. The focal point is the speaker, and the message becomes a vehicle for enhancing ethos. Campaign orations, on this basis, tend to be examples of personal persuasion, for while "the ostensible purpose of a given speech may be to gain acceptance of a particular policy, . . . the actual purpose is to gain votes for the candidate."[19] In other words, the ultimate goal of the campaign orator is to promote himself as a candidate. Both policies and character are in question, but the treatment of issues is subsidiary to the purpose of creating a general identification between the speaker and the audience. The objective, then, in a campaign oration is ingratiation.

With genre and purpose in mind, we can approach the speech through familiar topics. Addressing himself first to the people of New York, then to the South and finally to the Republican Party, Lincoln divides his speech into three sections, and this pattern of organization invites seriatim analysis of the major dispositional units. Furthermore argument and style immediately loom as important elements, since they disclose essential characteristics in and significant interrelationships among the main units of the discourse. Consequently, our critique will follow Lincoln's pattern of organization and will have special reference to matters of argument and style. This approach, however, is not without its hazards. The convenience of tracing the natural sequence of the argument may foster fragmentary analysis and obscure the dominant rhetorical motive. Yet to be mindful of the genre is to find a corrective. The central concern is ingratiation, and recognition of this purpose unifies the elements of analysis by giving them a more precise focus; awareness of the ultimate goal becomes shuttle to the threads of structure, argument, and style.

In the address, Lincoln deals exclusively with slavery, and although this inflamatory issue might seem a shaky bridge to ingratiation, the choice is a fitting response to the rhetorical problem. What better point of departure than the paramount issue of the day, the issue with which he was most closely identified, and the issue that had spawned the Republican Party?[20] And Lincoln starts with the very motivation that had driven men to Ripon only a few years before, the question of slavery in the territories. Capitalizing on these initial associations, he counters the emotionalism inherent in the topic by assuming a severely rational posture and enunciating a moderate but firm set of principles. The approach distinguishes him from his chief rivals and solicits an intensified association from Eastern Republicans. These objectives govern the matter and manner of the opening argument, and this argument lays a foundation for subsequent developments in the speech. In the opening section and throughout, Lincoln associates himself and Republicans with the founding fathers and Constitutional principle, and he dissociates rival candidates and factions from those fathers and that principle.

Acknowledging his "fellow citizens of New York," Lincoln begins by adopting a "text for this discourse."[21] The text is a statement in which Stephen A. Douglas had asserted, "Our fathers, when they framed the government under which we live, understood this question just as well and even better than we do now." Defining terms in catechistic sequence, Lincoln maintains that "the frame of government under which we live" consists of the Constitution and the "twelve subsequently framed amendments" and that "our fathers" are "the 'thirty-nine' who signed the original instrument." He then asks, what is the question "those fathers understood 'just as well and even better, than we do now'?" The answer "is this: Does the proper division of local from Federal authority or anything else in the Constitution, forbid our Federal Government to control as to slavery in our Federal Territories?" The question joins the issue because it is a matter upon which "Senator Douglas holds the affirmative, and the Republicans the negative."

That Douglas should play the foil is most fitting. National newspaper coverage of the 1858 senatorial campaign had linked the two men together, and the debates were to be published in March.[22] Moreover, Lincoln had continued the argument during 1859, worrying whether the Republican Party would "maintain it's [sic] identity, or be broken up to form the tail of Douglas' new kite."[23] Nevertheless, Lincoln knew that Douglas was vulnerable. The Freeport Doctrine had convinced many in the North that the man was only too "willing to subordinate moral considerations to political expediency."[24] Douglas, then, was an established rival, one whom Lincoln perceived as a threat to party unity, and one whose strategic position was open to attack from principle.

On a tactical level, the "text" quoted from Douglas affords Lincoln an ideal starting point. The allusion to the fathers is a symbolic reference with the potential for universal respect, and Douglas' implicit attack upon the principles that had generated the Republican Party creates an antithesis binding speaker and audience together in opposition to a common enemy. This antithesis is a channel for ingratiation; Lincoln makes Republicanism the voice of rational analysis, and the precise terms of Douglas' assertion form the premises of logical inquiry. Moving into the inquiry, Lincoln pursues a vigorous *ad hominem* attack.[25] He accepts Douglas' logic and then turns it against him.

The argument of the first section develops out of a single hypothetical proposition: if the better understanding evinced by our fathers shows that they believed nothing forbade federal control of slavery in the territories, then such regulatory power is inherent in the governmental frame. Lincoln affirms the antecedent with an elaborate chain of inductive evidence. Instances in the induction consist of actions by the fathers before and after they signed the Constitution because the question "seems not to have been directly before the convention."[26] From the Northwest Ordinance of 1784 to the Missouri Compromise of 1820, Lincoln enumerates seven statutes regulating slavery in the territories, and he accounts for votes by twenty-three of the fathers.[27] Twenty-one voted in favor of such regulation. Since these men were bound by "official responsibility and their corporal oaths" to uphold the Constitution, the implication of their affirmative votes is beyond question. To conclude that the twenty-one would have condoned federal regulation if they thought it unconstitutional would be to accuse these fathers of "gross political impropriety and willful perjury," and "as actions speak louder than words, so actions under such responsibility speak still louder."

Emphasizing deeds and "adhering rigidly to the text," Lincoln cannot offer in evidence "whatever understanding may have been manifested by any person" other than the thirty-nine, nor can he cite the sixteen who left no voting records. But the latter include the likes of Franklin, Hamilton, and Morris, and he believes that this group "would probably have acted just as the twenty-three did." In any event, "a clear majority of the whole" understood that nothing "forbade the Federal Government to control slavery in the Federal Territories," and with the remaining lathers probably agreeing, there can be little doubt about "the understanding of our fathers who framed the original Constitution; and the text affirms that they understood the question 'better than we.'"

Lincoln now uses this understanding to discredit arguments based on the fifth and tenth amendments; he says it is "a little presumptuous" to suggest that the fathers embraced one principle when writing the Constitution and another when writing the amendments. And does not this suggestion "become impudently absurd when coupled with the other affirmation, from the same mouth, that those who did the two things alleged to be inconsistent, understood whether they really were inconsistent better than we—better than he who affirms that they are inconsistent?" The touch of sarcasm reveals a more aggressive attitude, but it is justified by the inductive process; Douglas' own criterion forces the conclusion that he does not comprehend the understanding of the fathers. Lincoln will become even more combative before he brings the first section to a close, but some comments on style are merited, and they will lead us into his conclusion.

The style of this section is entirely consistent with Lincoln's severely rational approach. The audience probably did not expect the "rhetorical fireworks of a Western stump-speaker,"[28] but Lincoln is most circumspect. There are none of the "many excuses" that made him a Uriah Heep to some of his opponents,[29] and he avoids all display, indulging neither in anecdotes nor figurative language. The syntax is complex at times, but the complexity is that of legal rather than literary prose, as is evidenced in the following sentence: "It, therefore, would be unsafe to set down even the two who voted against the prohibition as having done so because, in their understanding, any proper division of local from Federal authority, or anything in the Constitution, forbade the Federal Government to control as to slavery in Federal territory."

The preceding quotation, with its echo of the text, points to a noteworthy stylistic element: repetition. Lincoln includes fifteen extended citations of the issue and an equal number from the "text," repetitions that accentuate the single line of argument. He adds to the emphasis by stressing certain key words and phrases. For example, there are over thirty uses of the root "understand," usually in the participial "understanding," and Lincoln alludes to the "fathers" more than thirty-five times. None of these repetitions is blatant or forced because he weaves them into the fabric of the inductive process. Furthermore, the repetitions concomitantly reinforce and control the emotional association with the fathers and their understanding of the Constitution. This point is crucial to an appreciation of Lincoln's rhetorical method. Both the direction of the argument and the symbols expressing it are fiercely emotional; yet, all is enmeshed in an incisive logical and linguistic structure, and while the tone remains rationalistic and legalistic, it also creates a subtle emotive nexus between the Republican audience and the founding fathers.

As noted above, style and argument shift in the concluding paragraphs, after Lincoln already has established his logical credentials. The argument becomes bolder, and the style alters appropriately. When developing the induction, Lincoln refers to the framers of the Constitution as the "thirty-nine," but they become "our fathers" again in the conclusion of the long first section of the speech. And there periods become more polished and sophisticated:

> If any man at this day sincerely believes that a proper division of local from Federal authority, or any part of the Constitution, forbids the Federal Government to control as to slavery in the Federal Territories, he is right to say so, and to enforce his position by all truthful evidence and fair argument which he can. But he has no right to mislead others, who have less access to history, and less leisure to study it, into the false belief that 'our fathers who framed the government under which we live' were of the same opinion—thus substituting falsehood and deception for truthful evidence and fair argument.

This passage completes the negative phase of Lincoln's argumentation. Both matter and manner drive a rational wedge between the speaker and his rivals. Clearly, Lincoln suggests that Douglas may be guilty of deliberate "falsehood and deception," and just as clearly, his own position represents "truthful evidence and fair argument." Lincoln, one of those with "access to history" and some "leisure to study it," attempts to set the record straight. Another direct slash at Douglas, the very source of the text and issue. At the same time, Lincoln indirectly differentiates himself from Seward and his radical posture. Lincoln's position is more to the right, closer to the demands of objective inquiry, closer also to the demands of political availability, and it is important to remark that he achieves this dissociation without recourse to divisive rhetoric. The foray against the man and his position is patent, but it is completely inferential.

Although less obtrusive than the refutation, an equally important constructive movement exists within this part of the oration. Not only does Lincoln distinguish himself from his opponents, he nurtures Republican unity because he makes himself and party the vessels for transmitting the faith of the fathers. Avoiding self-references, he presents himself as the voice of Republicanism, and he caps this appeal with words both to and from the party:

> But enough! Let all who believe that 'our fathers who framed the government under which we live understood this question just as well, and even better, than we do now,' speak as they spoke, and act as they acted upon it. This is all Republicans ask—all Republicans desire—in relation to slavery. As those fathers marked it, so let it be again marked, as an evil not to be extended, but to be tolerated and protected only because of and so far as its actual presence among us makes that toleration and protection a necessity. Let all the guarantees those fathers gave it be not grudgingly, but fully and fairly, maintained. For this Republicans contend, and with this, so far as I know or believe, they will be content.

At this point in the speech, Lincoln has associated himself and his audience with the spirit, the principles and the actions of the founding fathers, and in doing so, he has taken the first steps toward ingratiation.

Comprising nearly half the speech, this initial section is so clearly logical that it regularly is cited as a demonstration of Lincoln's powers as a reasoner, but to say no more is to grossly underestimate his achievement. The next section, too, is remarkable for its logical development, and all that follows in the speech is anticipated and controlled by the attack upon Douglas. Failure to appreciate this unity has confounded commentators, and their confusion is strikingly illustrated in the generally accepted conclusion that Lincoln follows his attack with remarks "conciliatory toward the South."[30]

The second section does begin with an ostensible change in audience: "And now, if they would listen,—as I suppose they will not,—I would address a few words to the Southern people." But we learn more about the beholders than the object when we are told that the next twenty-six paragraphs are filled with "words of kindly admonition and protest,"[31] words of "sweet reasonableness to allay Southern fears."[32] Presuming that he will not be heard, Lincoln notes that "our party gets no votes" in the South, and he flatly asserts later that "the Southern people will not so much as listen to us." These are not idle reservations. They represent the realistic assessment of an astute politician who knows that the coming election will be won or lost in the North; it is hardly plausible that this man would detract from his ultimate purpose by directing nearly forty per cent of his speech to an unavailable audience.

In truth, the audience does not change. Lincoln merely casts the second section of the speech in the form of a *prosopopoeia*, a figure he had rehearsed five months earlier in Cincinnati.[33] The device suits his purposes admirably. It enables him to create a mock debate between Republicans and the South, a debate in which he becomes spokesman for the party. In this role, Lincoln can strengthen the identification between himself and the available Republican audience. He is careful to extend the refutation of Douglas into the second section and thus carry over the lines of association and disassociation begun earlier in the discourse. If Lincoln leaves Douglas with little ground on which to stand, he performs the same argumentative service for the South, and the debate he manufactures is far from being conciliatory.

The *prosopopoeia* develops into another *ad hominem* argument. This time, however, the presentation is complicated by the need to deal with the collective contentions of a collective opposition. To provide control, Lincoln again begins by stressing reason, saying to the South, "I consider that in the general qualities of reason and justice you are not inferior to any other people." Yet, in the specific case, rational discourse is stymied because the Southerners never refer to Republicans except "to denounce us as reptiles, or, at the best, as no better than outlaws." Such responses are unjust to both sides. The proper course would be to "bring forward your charges and specifications, and then be patient long enough to hear us deny or justify." Obviously, the South is unwilling and unable to follow this procedure, and becoming persona for both Republicanism and reason, Lincoln reconstructs the charges and specifications; these include sectionalism, radicalism, agitation of the slavery question, and slave insurrections.

The putative debate begins: "You say we are sectional. We deny it. That makes an issue; and the burden of proof is upon you." The crux of the matter is whether Republicans repel the South with "some wrong principle." Republican principle, however, is based in the beliefs and actions of the fathers, and Lincoln challenges the South to respond to this fact. "Do you accept the challenge? No! Then you really believe that the principle which 'our fathers who framed the government under which we live' thought so clearly right as to adopt it, and indorse it again and again, upon their official oaths, is in fact so clearly wrong as to demand your condemnation without a moment's consideration." Closing and reinforcing this line of reasoning Lincoln refers to the pre-eminent father: "Some of you delight to flaunt in our faces the warning ... given by Washington in his Farewell Address," but if he were to speak for himself "would he cast the blame of that sectionalism upon us, who sustain his policy, or upon you, who repudiate it? We respect that warning of Washington, and we commend it to you, together with his example pointing to the right application of it."[34] Thus, the South claims to be the injured party, but analysis of the charge proves that the wounds are self-inflicted.

Lincoln uses the same refutational method for each of the other issues; first defining the charge with a series of rhetorical questions, he then turns the argument against the adversary. The South proclaims itself the bastion of conservatism and denounces Republican radicalism, but "what is conservatism? Is it not adherence to the old and tried, against the new and untried? We stick to, contend for, the identical old policy ... which was adopted by 'our fathers who framed the government under which we live'; while you with one accord reject, and scout, and spit upon that old policy, and insist upon substituting something new." The South alleges that Republicans have made the slavery issue more prominent. True, the issue is more prominent, but this situation arose because the South "discarded the old policy of the fathers." Finally, Southerners complain that Republicans foment insurrection among the slaves, but they can adduce no evidence to support this allegation, cannot "implicate a single Republican" and ignore that "Republican doctrines and declarations are accompanied with a continual protest against any interference whatever" with the institution in the slave states. Indeed, were it not for the loud and misleading protestations of Southern politicians, the slaves would hardly know that the Republican Party existed. Worse yet, the South refuses to acknowledge a simple truth contained in Republican doctrine, a truth articulated "many years ago" when Jefferson indicated that the cause of slave insurrections was slavery itself. Like Jefferson, Republicans would not interfere with slavery where it exists, but Republicans do insist, as the fathers did, that the federal government "has the power of restraining the extension of the institution—the power to insure that a slave insurrection shall never occur on any American soil which is now free."

Finishing his treatment of specific charges, Lincoln builds to a more forceful and aggressive tone, just as he did at the end of the first section. His arrangement of responses to Southern allegations is itself climatic, the issue of insurrections being both last and most critical. Always volatile, this issue had become extremely explosive in the wake of the Harper's Ferry raid and the trial of John Brown, and Lincoln understandably chooses this matter as the instrument for his most extensive defense of party and principle. He is not content, however, to assume a merely defensive posture; the entire pattern of his argumentation reveals a movement from reply to attack that gathers momentum as the discourse proceeds. Thus, having disposed of the insurrection controversy, Lincoln assails the very character of the Southern position, and he concludes this section with an examination of threats emanating from the South.

The South hopes to "break up the Republican organization." That failing, "you will break up the Union rather than submit to a denial of your constitutional rights." This is a course of "rule or ruin"; the union will be destroyed unless people are permitted to take slaves into the federal territories. But no such right exists in the Constitution, and Southern threats are fruitless. Neither the Constitution nor the Republican Party are so malleable as to bend at the touch of Southern fancy. Not even the Dred Scott decision offers a refuge. That verdict was made "in a divided court, by a bare majority of the judges, and they not quite agreeing with one another in the reasons for making it." The decision rests upon "the opinion that 'the right of property in a slave is distinctly and expressly affirmed in the Constitution,'" but careful analysis shows that this right is not even implied. Surely it is reasonable to expect the Court to retract "the mistaken statement" when apprised of its error. Furthermore, the verdict runs contrary to the judgment of the fathers, those who decided the same question long ago "without division among themselves when making the decision," without division "about the meaning of it after it was made," and without "basing it upon any mistaken statement of facts." Having thus contrasted the babel of the Court with the unity of the fathers and their lineal descendants, Lincoln builds to a striking analogy:

Under these circumstances, do you really feel yourselves justified to break up this government unless such a court decision as yours is shall be at once submitted to as a conclusive and final rule of political action? But you will not abide the election of a Republican president! In that supposed event, you say, you will destroy the Union; and then, you say, the crime of having destroyed it will be upon us! That is cool. A highwayman holds a pistol to my ear, and mutters through his teeth, 'Stand and deliver, or I shall kill you, and then you will be a murderer!'

Adding that the highwayman's threat can "scarcely be distinguished in principle" from "the threat of destruction to the Union," Lincoln completes his *ad hominem* assault against the Southern position, and the *prosopopoeia* ends.

The parallels and interrelationships between the first and the second sections of the speech are evident. Some shifts in invention and style between the two sections are occasioned by the change of antagonist, but it is more significant that Lincoln elects to argue against adversaries in both and that he uses the same fundamental argument to dispatch them all. In both sections, he strives to become spokesman for the party by demonstrating that he is a man of reason and that this characteristic melds himself and party with the principles of the founding fathers. In addition, the same characteristic distinguishes him from other candidates. Finally, each section is based on a severely rational framework and builds to a terminal climax that unifies and heightens logical and emotional dimensions.

Merging style and argument within and between parts of the discourse, Lincoln unquestionably remains in touch with his immediate audience, and he unquestionably has his eye on ingratiation. In the first movement, he separates himself and party from Douglas and Seward; in the second, he favorably contrasts the position of the party with that of its most vociferous opponent.[35] But one further step remains. To this juncture, the identification of speaker, party, and principle has been closely tied to a series of negative definitions. A positive gesture seems necessary, and in the final section of the speech, Lincoln fuses his audience together through more directly constructive appeals.

He begins by saying he will address "a few words now to Republicans," and though he puts aside both text and issue, his remarks evolve naturally from what has proceeded. Once more reason is the point of departure. Having, in the highwayman metaphor, implied a contrast between cool reason and hot passion, Lincoln urges Republicans to "do nothing through passion and ill-temper" that might cause discord within the nation, and, as he draws out the ultimate implications of the Southern position, antithesis becomes the dominant mode of argument and style. The section centers on a contrast between the Republicans and the South (between "we" and "they"); it extends and amplifies the distinction between word and deed that is present throughout the speech; and the argument is couched in and reinforced by antithetical syntax.

Recognizing Southern intransigence, Lincoln still wants his party to "calmly consider their demands" and reach conclusions based on all "they say and do." Pursuing the inquiry, he asks, "Will they be satisfied if the Territories be unconditionally surrendered to them? We know they will not." And "will it satisfy them if, in the future, we have nothing to do with invasions and insurrections? We know it will not." It will not because past abstention has not exempted "us from the charge and the denunciation." To satisfy them, "we must not only leave them alone, but we must somehow convince them that we do let them alone." Experience shows that this is no easy task because Republican policy and actions have been misconstrued consistently. The only recourse seems to be "this and only this: cease to call slavery wrong, and join them in calling it right. And this must be done thoroughly—done in acts as well as words. Silence will not be tolerated—we must place ourselves avowedly with them." Republicans must suppress all "declarations that slavery is wrong," must return "fugitive slaves with greedy pleasure," and must pull down all free state constitutions "before they will cease to believe that all their troubles proceed from us."

Most Southerners, Lincoln admits, would not put the argument in this extreme form. Most would simply claim that they want to be left alone, but "we do let them alone." Consequently, it is apparent that "they will continue to accuse us of doing, until we cease saying." Given the nature of their arguments and the character of their actions, the Southerners cannot stop short of the demand that all Republicans desist from speaking and acting out of conviction. Those who hold that "slavery is morally right and socially elevating" must necessarily call for its recognition "as a legal right and a social blessing." Stripped of its veneer and examined in the cold light of reason, the Southern position reveals the disagreement governing the entire conflict; it also underscores the principle from which Republicans cannot retreat. Lincoln expresses both points in a final antithesis that reduces the issue of slavery to a matter of right and wrong, to a matter of moral conviction:

> Their thinking it right and our thinking it wrong is the precise fact upon which depends the whole controversy. Thinking it right, as they do, they are not to blame for desiring its full recognition as being right; but thinking it wrong, as we do, can we yield to them? Can we cast our votes with their view, and against our own? In view of our moral, social, and political responsibilities, can we do this?

Providing no answers because they are only too obvious, Lincoln moves on to merge self and party with the fathers, and Washington is the exemplar.

Style changes appropriately as Lincoln makes his final call for unity. Antithetical elements appear in the penultimate paragraph, but the opposed clauses are subordinated within the long, periodic flow of the final sentence, a flow that builds emotionally to a union with Washington's words and deeds. Lincoln repeats that slavery can be left alone where it exists, but he insists that there can be no temporizing when it comes to the extension of slavery:

> If our sense of duty forbids this, then let us stand by our duty fearlessly and effectively. Let us be diverted by none of those sophistical contrivances wherewith we are so industriously plied, and belabored—contrivances such as groping for some middle ground between the right and the wrong: vain as the search for a man who should be neither a living man nor a dead man: such as a policy of 'don't care' on a question about which all true men do care; such as Union

appeals beseeching true Union men to yield to Disunionists, reversing the divine rule, and calling, not the sinners, but the righteous to repentance: such as invocations to Washington, imploring men to unsay what Washington said and undo what Washington did.

Neither let us be slandered from our duty by false accusations against us, nor frightened from it by menaces of destruction to the government, nor of dungeons to ourselves. Let us have faith that right makes might, and in that faith let us to the end dare to do our duty as we understand it.

This short third section, constituting less than fifteen per cent of the text, is a fitting climax to Lincoln's efforts. Rational principle develops into moral conviction, and the resulting emotional intensity emerges from and synthesizes all that has gone before. Yet the intensity is controlled. Speaker and audience are resolute and principled, but at the same time, they are poised and logical. Others may indulge in "false accusations" and "menaces of destruction," but Lincoln and Republicans will have faith in right and in their understanding.

With this closing suggestion of antithetical behavior, Lincoln harks back to all he has said, and with it, he completes his exercise in ingratiation. Douglas is a pitiful example of one who argues misguided principle in maladroit fashion, and Seward's notion of an irrepressible conflict is at odds with the true spirit of the Republican Party, a party whose words and deeds follow from what the framers of the government said and did. Neither opponent measures up to the new and higher self-conception that the speaker has created for his audience. Furthermore, Lincoln has, by this very performance, demonstrated that he is the one who will best represent party and principle. Starting with reason and principle, he has shunted aside opposition, differentiated between Republicans and the South, and pushed on to unite the party in the faith that will "let us to the end dare to do our duty as we understand it."

The very wording of the concluding paragraphs reflects the organic quality of Lincoln's quest for unity. "Understand" echoes the "text"; Washington is a synecdochic reminder of the fathers; and the antithetical language recalls dissociations that are fundamental. In examining the discourse, we have attempted to explicate this internal coherence by tracing the sequence of arguments and images as they appear in the text, by dealing with the speech on its own terms. We are satisfied that the analysis has produced a reading that is more accurate than those previously available, a reading that goes farther toward explaining why the Cooper Union Address was one of Lincoln's most significant speeches.

Our interpretation is at odds, of course, with the conventional wisdom concerning his attitude toward the South. Where others have found him conciliatory, we argue that his position on slavery was calculated to win the nomination, not to propitiate an unavailable audience. That he had made "many similar declarations, and had never recanted any of them"[36] unquestionably contributed to the triumph of availability that was to be his, but his position ultimately pointed to an ideological conflict between North and South. Some Southerners took solace from Lincoln's assurances that slavery would be left alone where it existed, but extremists perceived him as the personification of Black Republicanism, even as the source of the irrepressible conflict doctrine.[37]

The latter perceptions were distorted. So are ours, if we blink the realities of political rhetoric, and whatever else the speech might have been, it was certainly an oration designed to meet the immediate problems of a political campaign.

This perspective emphasizes that alternatives sometimes really do exclude and that rhetoric may nurture exclusion. Such a perspective may be uncomfortable for those who want to cast Lincoln as the Great Conciliator, but we are convinced that an accurate reading of the Cooper Union Address demands a frank recognition of the immediate rhetorical motives. Despite the mythology, the man was human, perhaps gloriously so, and it does him no disservice to accept this speech as evidence of his political skill, as evidence that "he was an astute and dextrous operator of the political machine."[38] Nor does this acceptance detract from the speech as literature and as logical exposition. The political artistry and the rhetorical artistry are functions of each other, and an appreciation of this coalescence can only enhance our understanding of the Cooper Union Address. And viewing the speech as a whole, we are quite content to close with a slightly altered evaluation from another context: "The speech is—to put it as crudely as possible—an immortal masterpiece."[39]

Notes

1 J. G. Randall, *Lincoln the President* (New York: Dodd, Mead, 1945), I, 135.
2 Howard Mumford Jones and Ernest E. Leisy, eds., *Major American Writers* (New York: Harcourt, Brace, 1945), p. 681.
3 Benjamin Barondess, *Three Lincoln Masterpieces* (Charleston: Education Foundation of West Virginia, 1954), p. 3.
4 R. Franklin Smith, "A Night at Cooper Union," *Central States Speech Journal* 13 (Autumn 1962), 272.
5 The most influential account of this sort is Carl Sandburg, *The Prairie Years* (New York: Harcourt, Brace, 1927), II, 200–216, but the most complete is Andrew A. Freeman, *Abraham Lincoln Goes to New York* (New York: Coward-McCann, 1960).
6 John G. Nicolay and John Hay, *Abraham Lincoln: A History* (New York: Century, 1917), II, 219–220.
7 Richard Hofstadter, *The American Political Tradition* (New York: Alfred A. Knopf, 1948), p. 364.
8 *Abraham Lincoln: His Speeches and Writings* ed. Roy P. Basler (Cleveland: World, 1946), p. 32.
9 Allan Nevins, *The Emergence of Lincoln* (New York: Charles Scribner's Sons, 1950), II. 186.
10 Randall, pp. 136–137; Basler, pp. 32–33; Nevins, pp. 186–187; Reinhard H. Luthin, *The Real Abraham Lincoln* (Englewood Cliffs, New Jersey: Prentice-Hall, 1960), p. 210.
11 Randall, p. 136; Barondess, p. 18; Nicholay and Hay, p. 220, Nevins, p. 186; Luthin, pp. 243–244.
12 Freeman treats of the text briefly, pp. 84–88, and although Barondess ranges from preparation to audience reaction, pp. 3–30, Hofstadter's observation applies, n. 7 above. Earl W. Wiley discusses the address in *Four Speeches by Lincoln* (Columbus: Ohio State Univ. Press, 1927), pp. 15–27, but he limits analysis to the first section of the speech, a limitation also applied in his "Abraham Lincoln: His Emergence as the Voice of the People," in *A History and Criticism of American Public Address*, ed. William N. Brigance (New York: McGraw-Hill, 1943), II, 859–877. In the same volume, the speech is the basis for comments on delivery in Mildred Freburg Berry, "Abraham Lincoln: His Development in the Skills of the Platform," pp. 828–858.
13 Letter to Lyman Trumbull, April 29, 1860, *The Collected Works of Abraham Lincoln*, ed. Roy P. Basler (New Brunswick, New Jersey: Rutgers Univ. Press, 1955), IV, 45.
14 Letter to William E. Frazer, November 1, 1859, *Collected Works*, III, 491.

15 Richard N. Current, *The Lincoln Nobody Knows* (New, York: McGraw-Hill, 1958), p. 199. For an indication of Lincoln's activities see *Collected Works*, III, 384–521.
16 Letter to James A. Briggs, *Collected Works*, III, 494.
17 See Letter to Salmon P. Chase, June 9, 1859, *Collected Works*, III, 384; Letter to Nathan Sargent, June 23, 1859, *Collected Works*, III, 387–388; Letter to Richard M. Corwine, April 6, 1860, *Collected Works*, IV, 36.
18 Paul I. Rosenthal, "The Concept of Ethos and the Structure of Persuasion," *Speech Monographs* 33 (June 1966), 114–126.
19 Rosenthal, p. 120.
20 In 1854, "northern whigs persuaded that their old party was moribund, Democrats weary of planting dominance, and free-soilers eager to exclude slavery from the territories began to draw together to resist the advance of the planting power"; Charles A. Beard and Mary R. Beard, *The Rise of American Civilization* (New York: Macmillan, 1937), II, 22. Cf. Don E. Fehrenbacher, "Lincoln and the Formation of the Republican Party," in *Prelude to Greatness* (Stanford: Stanford Univ. Press, 1962), pp. 19–47.
21 We follow the text in *Complete Works*, ed. John G. Nicolay and John Hay (New York: Francis D. Tandy, 1905), V, 293–328; we include no footnotes because aside from unimportant exceptions, citations are sequential. This text is more conservative in typography than that edited and published as a campaign document by Charles C. Nott and Cephas Brainerd. The latter appears in *Collected Works*, III, 522–550; 1860, p. 1. Substantive variations in extant see also the *New York Times*, February 28, texts are minuscule, and this consistency deserves comment. Lincoln ignored suggested alterations in the original (Sandburg, II, 210 and 215–216); he proofread the newspaper copy (Freeman, pp. 92–93); pamphlet copies were available by the first of April *(Collected Works*, IV, 38–39); and Lincoln adamantly resisted editorial changes by Nott *(Collected Works*, IV, 58–59). This evidence emphasizes the care with which he constructed the speech, but it also suggests that he anticipated a wider audience from the outset. Publication practices and his own experience told Lincoln that he would teach many who would not hear him speak.
22 General interest in the debates is underlined by the favorable editorial notice appearing in the Brooklyn *Daily Times*, August 26, 1858, an editorial written by one Walt Whitman; Walt Whitman, *I Sit and Look Out*, ed. Emory Holloway and Vernolian Schwartz (New York: Columbia Univ. Press, 1932), p. 96. For letters referring to publication of the debates, see *Collected Works*, III. 341, 343, 372–374, 515. and 516.
23 Letter to Lyman Trumbull, Dec. 11, 1858, *Collected Works*, III, 345..
24 Harry J. Carman and Harold C Syrett, *A History of the American People* (New York: Alfred A. Knopf, 1952), I, 588. Cf. Fehrenbacher, "The Famous 'Freeport Question,'" in *Prelude to Greatness*, pp. 121–142.
25 Logicians often define *ad hominem* as a fallacy resulting from an attack upon the character of a man rather than the quality of argument. In this essay, however, we use the term as Schopenhauer does in distinguishing between *ad hominem* and *ad rem* as the two basic modes of refutation. He differentiates in this manner: "We may show either that the proposition is not in accordance with the nature of things, *i.e.*, with absolute, objective truth [ad *rem*]; or that it is inconsistent with other statements or admissions of our opponent, *i.e.*, with truth as it appears to him [*ad hominem*]"; Arthur Schopenhauer, "The Art of Controversy," in *The Will to Live: Selected Writings of Arthur Schopenhauer*, ed. Richard Taylor (New York: Anchor Books, 1962), p. 341. See Henry W. Johnstone, Jr., "Philosophy and *Argumentum ad Hominem*," *Journal of Philosophy* 49 (July 1952), 489–498.
26 Lincoln undoubtedly knew that James Wilson, Patrick Henry and Edmund Randolph had discussed the topic (See *Collected Works*, III, 526–527, n. 9.), but he is accurate in asserting that the subject did not come "directly" before the convention.
27 Washington's vote was his signature, as President, on the Act of 1789 which enforced the Ordinance of 1787.
28 Nicolay and Hay, *Abraham Lincoln*, II, 220.
29 See Hofstadter, p. 94; *Collected Works*, III. 396.

30 Randall, I, 136.
31 Nicolay and Hay, *Abraham Lincoln*, II, 220.
32 Nevins, II, 186.
33 *Collected Works*, III, 438–454. Speaking at Cincinnati, September 17, 1859, Lincoln directs so much of his speech across the river "to the Kentuckians" (p. 440.) that one listener complained aloud, "Speak to Ohio men, and not to Kentuckians!' (p. 445.) Interestingly, Nevins appreciates the *prosopopoeia* in this speech, noting that Lincoln was "ostensibly speaking to Kentuckians," II, 56.
34 The varied interpretations of Washington's warning and their longevity are illustrated in debates, early in 1850, over the purchase of the Farewell Address manuscript for the Library of Congress. Much of the debate is reproduced in William Dawson Johnston, *History of the Library of Congress* (Washington: Government Printing Office, 1904), I, 326–340.
35 The second movement continues the implicit attack upon Seward, and all texts indicate a mimicking of Douglas' "gur-reat pur-rinciple" Buchanan also is a victim here, for he had championed popular sovereignty in his "Third Annual Message," December 19, 1859; *The Works of James Buchanan*, ed. John Bassett More (1908–1911; rpt. New York: Antiquarian Press Ltd., 1960), X. 342. Lincoln's efforts were not lost on a New York *Evening Post* reporter who wrote that "the speaker places the Republican party on the very ground occupied by the framers of our constitution and the fathers oᶜ our Republic" and that "in this great controversy the Republicans are the real conservative party." His report is reprinted in the *Chicago Tribune*, 1 Mar. 1860, p. 1.
36 Abraham Lincoln, "First Inaugural Address" in Collected Works, IV, 263.
37 Michael Davis, *The Image of Lincoln in the South* (Knoxville: Univ. of Tennessee, 1971), pp. 7–40; traces Southern views from nomination through inauguration. See *Southern Editorials on Secession*, ed. Dwight L. Dumond (1931; rpt. Gloucester, Mass.: Peter-Smith, 1964), pp. 103–105, 112–115, 159–162, *et passim*.
38 David Donald, *Lincoln Reconsidered* (New York: Alfred A. Knopf, 1956), p. 65.
39 The original is Randall Jarrell's comment on a poem, Robert Frost's "Provide Provide," in *Poetry and the Age* (New York: Vintage-Knopf, 1953), p. 41.

13.
LINCOLN AND GORGIAS
Charles N. Smiley

Seven years ago I carried with me to Berlin as an antidote against Prussian bureaucracy and despotism the Everyman selection of Lincoln's speeches and letters. I had bought it in Paternoster Row behind St. Paul's in London (may Heaven defend that sacred place against Zeppelin and his bombs!). The little book was also to serve as an antidote against certain other noxious influences to which I was about to subject myself. I am not referring now to the Lessing Theater, the Royal Opera, or to any of the stimulating lecturers whom it was my good fortune to hear (may Heaven defend them also!). But a small portion of my winter had been dedicated to a journey across that high and arid tableland, Spengel's *Rhetores Graeci*. It was to be a sort of botanical expedition—an investigation of the flora, so to speak, a more careful study of the flowers of speech in the ancient world. After a long *Gänsemarsch* through fields of artificial flowers, what could be more refreshing than a look into some old-fashioned garden—into some book unbedizened with any form of meretricious embellishment? Lincoln's speeches seemed the very book. In fact, Ambassador Bryce, who had made the Everyman selection, gave assurance (at least by implication) in his excellent introduction that Lincoln and Gorgias represented the two antipodes of the stylistic world. But before the winter was over my mind became so infected with the Gorgian figures that I could see them everywhere without effort, and even in Lincoln's speeches. It was a pleasant discovery to find some affinity between the great Sicilian and the still greater American; it seemed to give an added glory to them both. The fact that Lincoln, without any training in formal rhetoric, by a certain divine intuition had rediscovered for himself some of the Gorgian figures and had used them to give power to the expression of his thought seemed to add some fraction of a cubit to his intellectual stature; but still more it seemed to make amends for the harsh criticism which Gorgias had suffered through the centuries since Aristotle. The rhetorical forms that had been so severely censured as the marks of superficial sham and insincerity had somehow proved themselves capable of sincerity. We all hate mere rhetoric, i.e., form without content; we hate the art that cannot conceal itself. It is a rather difficult matter to conceal a Gorgian figure, and the thought must be indeed profound and fundamental that can make the reader forget balanced clauses, antitheses, alliterations, and other assonances. But the thought which Lincoln had to present could stand the strain. Put the matter to the test; cut the nightingale to pieces and try to discover the song. Read over the Gettysburg speech.

A careful examination will reveal in twenty-seven lines two antitheses, five cases of anaphora, eight instances of balanced phrases and clauses, thirteen alliterations. Yet the thought is so compelling that ordinarily we do not notice the subtle means that are used to intensify the emotional content of the speech. But take another instance in which the Gorgian element makes no attempt to conceal itself, the letter addressed to Horace Greeley, August 22, 1862. In forty-four lines we have six completely balanced sentences, eight cases of anaphora, six instances of similar clause endings, six antitheses, Even the encomium of Helen attributed to Gorgias is not so completely Gorgian in its embellishment. And yet no one today would attempt to revise this letter in the hope that he could set forth the same thought with greater power and impressiveness, or with such perspicuity, appropriateness, and brevity. The historical importance of the letter is sufficient to justify reprinting it entire, even if it did not illustrate the matter under discussion.

> I have just read yours of the 19th instant, addressed to myself through the *New York Tribune*.
>
> If there be in it any statements or assumptions of fact which I may know to be erroneous, I do not now and here controvert them.
>
> If there be in it any inferences which I believe to be falsely drawn, I do not now and here argue against them.
>
> If there be perceptible in it an impatient and dictatorial tone, I waive it, in deference to an old friend whose heart I have always supposed to be right.
>
> As to the policy I "seem to be pursuing," as you say, I have not meant to leave anyone in doubt. I would save the Union. I would save it the shortest way under the Constitution.
>
> The sooner the national authority can be restored, the nearer the Union will be—the Union as it was.
>
> If there be those who would not save the Union unless they could at the same time save slavery, I do not agree with them.
>
> If there be those who would not save the Union unless they could at the same time destroy slavery, I do not agree with them.
>
> My paramount object in this struggle is to save the Union, and not either to save or destroy slavery.
>
> If I could save the Union without freeing any slave, I would do it; if I could save it by freeing all the slaves, I would do it; and if I could save it by freeing some and leaving others alone, I would also do that.
>
> What I do about slavery and the coloured race, I do because I believe it helps to save the Union; and what I forbear, I forbear because I do not believe it would help to save the Union.
>
> I shall do less whenever I shall believe that what I am doing hurts the cause; and I shall do more whenever I shall believe doing more will help the cause.
>
> I shall try to correct errors where shown to be errors, and I shall adopt new views as fast as they shall appear to be true views.
>
> I have here stated my purpose according to my views of official duty, and I intend no modification of my oft-expressed personal wish that all men everywhere could be free.

A study of Lincoln's speech of June 17, 1858, reveals similar tendencies. The following passage of eleven lines offers six antitheses, six instances of balanced sentence structure, two cases of anaphora, and four alliterations:

I believe the government cannot endure permanently, half slave and half free. I do not expect the Union to be dissolved—I do not expect the house to fall; but I do expect it to cease to be divided. It will become all one thing, or all the other. Either the opponents of slavery will arrest the further spread of it and place it where the public mind shall rest in the belief that it is in the course of ultimate extinction; or its advocates will push it forward till it shall become alike lawful in all the states, old as well as new, North as well as South.

The rest of the speech, which is nine pages in length, presents sixteen additional cases of anaphora, forty-five instances of marked alliteration, seventeen rhetorical questions, fourteen instances of balanced sentence structure.

Lincoln's reply to Douglas, July 10, 1858, is a speech of seventeen and a half pages; in it we find forty pronounced alliterations, forty-eight examples of anaphora, thirty instances of balanced sentence structure, thirty-four rhetorical questions.

A careful examination of the following sentences will throw some light on the question under investigation:

The former unprofaned by the foot of the invader, the latter undecayed by the lapse of time [page 4].

Let it be preached from the pulpit, proclaimed in legislative halls, and enforced in courts of justice [page 5].

That we improved to the last, that we remained free to the last, that we revered his name to the last [page 6].

They were a fortress of strength, they were a forest of great oaks. . . . . Despoiled of its verdure, shorn of its foliage, unshaded and unshading [page 8].

Our fathers, our brothers, our sons, our friends. . . . . To command his action, to dictate to his judgment, to mark him at once to be shunned and despised [page 15].

Repeal the Missouri Compromise, repeal all compromise, repeal the Declaration of Independence, repeal all past history, still you cannot repeal human nature [page 34].

The South flushed with triumph and tempted to excess, the North, betrayed, as they believed, brooding on wrong and burning for revenge. One side will provoke, the other will resent; the one will taunt, the other defy; one aggresses, the other retaliates. Already a few in the North defy all constitutional restraint, resist the execution of the Fugitive Slave Law, and even menace the institution of slavery in the states where it exists. Already a few in the South claim the constitutional right to take and hold slaves in the free states, demand the revival of the slave trade, and demand a treaty with Great Britain by which fugitive slaves may be reclaimed from Canada [page 32].

Stand with anybody who stands right. Stand with him while he is right and part with him when he goes wrong. Stand with the Abolitionist in restoring the Missouri Compromise, and stand against him when he attempts to repeal the Fugitive Slave Law [page 33].

. . . . it was conceived in violence, is maintained in violence and is being executed in violence [page 37].

. . . . blood of the blood and flesh of the flesh of the men who wrote the Declaration; and so they are.

That is the electric cord in that Declaration that links the hearts of patriotic and liberty-loving men together; that will link those patriotic hearts as long as the love of freedom exists in the minds of men throughout the world [page 93].

It is the first of its kind, it is the astonisher of legal history, it is a new wonder of the world.

He tells you he is for the Cincinnati platform; he tells you he is for the Dred Scott decision; he tells you he cares not if slavery is voted up or down; he tells you the struggle on Lecompton is past [page 88].

I am not a master of language, I have not a fine education, I am not capable of entering upon a disquisition in dialectics [page 83].

From the mouth of a king, an excuse for enslaving the people of a country; from the mouth of one race as a reason for enslaving the men of another race [page 93].

If I had made any mistake, I was ready to be corrected; if I had drawn any false inference with regard to Judge Douglas, I was fully prepared to modify it [page 96].

All the anxious politicians of our party, or who have been of the party for years past, have been looking upon him, as certainly at no distant day, to be President of the United States. They have seen in his round, jolly, fruitful face, post-offices, land-offices, marshalships and cabinet appointments, charge-ships and foreign missions, bursting and sprouting out in wonderful exuberance, ready to be laid hold of by their greedy hands [page 95].

In a rather hasty scrutiny of one hundred and seven pages I found eighty-four antitheses, one hundred and ninety-five cases of anaphora, four hundred and one cases of pronounced alliteration, and one hundred and seventy-six instances of balanced sentence structure—an average of eight Gorgian figures to the page. The number of figures found is not large enough to justify us in calling Lincoln a Gorgian in matters of style, but it is too large for us to overlook. It is plain that he was not innocent of the subtle arts of the public speaker. He cared more for his thought than for his style; but he cared so much for his thought that he studied with care the means of making it incisive and effective. He would drive it home with the trip-hammer blows of the anaphora; he would set it in high relief by an antithetic presentation of that which might serve as its foil; and he did not forget that the mind easily remembers alliterative phrases.

14.
THE PUBLIC LETTER AS A RHETORICAL FORM: STRUCTURE, LOGIC, AND STYLE IN KING'S "LETTER FROM BIRMINGHAM JAIL"
Richard P. Fulkerson

IN Birmingham, Alabama, on 12 April 1963, the Reverend Martin Luther King, Jr., in order to have himself arrested on a symbolic day (Good Friday), disobeyed an Alabama Supreme Court injunction against demonstrations.[1] That same day, in the *Birmingham News,* King saw a public letter signed by eight leading (white) Birmingham clergymen calling on the protesters to cease their activities and to work through the courts for the redress of their grievances.

On the morning following his arrest, while being held in solitary confinement, King began to write in response to the clergymen the now famous "Letter from Birmingham Jail." As he wrote later, "Begun on the margins of the newspaper in which the statement appeared while I was in jail, the letter was continued on scraps of writing paper supplied by a friendly Negro trusty, and concluded on a pad my attorneys were eventually permitted to leave me."[2] The "Letter" was completed on Tuesday, and the American Friends Service Committee had 50,000 copies printed for distribution.[3] Later, after polishing, it became a central chapter in King's *Why We Can't Wait* (1964).[4]

Judged by the frequency with which it has been reprinted, the "Letter" has already become an American classic.[5] It has been characterized as a "compelling argument,"[6] "a virtuoso performance,"[7] "a model of effective persuasive writing,"[8] and "one of the strongest pieces of persuasive writing to come out of twentieth-century America."[9] Despite these comments, the "Letter" has been the subject of only one rather cursory study.[10] Most of the published commentary on it constitutes praise rather than criticism.

The "Letter" deserves more extensive study, for it is an instance of superb rhetoric in action. Designed apparently as a refutative response to the clergymen, King's essay actually addresses two audiences simultaneously: the limited and precisely defined group of eight clergymen and a broader and less exactly defined group of intelligent and religious moderates. The purposes of this study are, first, to consider the nature and relationship of King's two audiences and the rhetorical benefits King gained from using one audience to provide a focus through which the other could be addressed, and,

---

Fulkerson, Richard P. "The Public Letter as a Rhetorical Form: Structure, Logic, and Style in King's 'Letter from Birmingham Jail'," *The Quarterly Journal of Speech*, Vol. 65, No. 2 (1979): 121–36.

second, to demonstrate how carefully and effectively King adapted his presentation to suit both audiences on three levels: structural, logical, and stylistic.

The Clergymen's Letter

In their letter, the eight clergymen, representing both Christian and Jewish faiths, address not the issue of racism, but the propriety of civil disobedience and the timing of the protest. A restrained document of seven paragraphs and slightly more than 400 words, the clergymen's letter supports the theses that "these demonstrations are unwise and untimely," and that, "When rights are consistently denied, a cause should be pressed in the courts."[11] It is a clear statement of the moderate position: Injustice may exist, but the methods of remediation must lie in compromise and in the appropriate legal channels. Typically moderate also is the tone of optimism; the clergymen refer to a "new constructive and realistic approach" and "increased forbearance" which make these "days of new hope." Such positive signs, along with the patience and restraint now being shown by the police, make this an especially inappropriate time for protest.

Specifically the clergymen accuse King and his followers of (1) being led "in part by outsiders," (2) failing to negotiate, (3) inciting hatred and violence, (4) choosing an inappropriate time to act, (5) using extreme measures, (6) ignoring the courts as the correct avenue of redress, and (7) not observing the principles of "law and order."

Two "Fictionalized" Audiences

Since King's response to these charges is a "Letter" to "My dear Fellow Clergymen," one might assume the eight clergymen to be the audience. On the other hand, it is a public letter in the tradition of Emile Zola's Dreyfus letter. Thus, because the letter has an apparent audience (the clergymen) and a larger, more diverse one (King's public reader), the question of audience is complex.

Ong has recently argued that "the writer's audience is always a fiction," since no writer addresses the audience at the moment of writing but must imaginatively project both the audience and its potential response.[12] This becomes more true and thus presents a more difficult rhetorical problem as the distance between writer and reader widens. While seeming to address the clergymen and to respond to their charges, King had also to address his broader readership; thus as he wrote he had to fictionalize two audiences, one sharing his clerical perspective, the other more diverse. Such a perspective obviously creates some difficulties. The writer, for example, must not assume (i.e., fictionalize) anything about the ostensible audience that would not also apply to the broader real audience. Structure, logic, and style, all have to be appropriate not just for a single defined audience but for the larger one as well.

Yet King turned the rhetorically complex situation into an advantage. Had he chosen to defend his actions directly to a public audience, he would have had to fictionalize his audience with virtually no guidelines. Instead, he wrote as if he were addressing the clergymen, about whom he could reasonably make certain assumptions;

he took them—or rather his fictionalized image of them—as a metaphor for his broader readership.

By using the clergymen as his ostensible audience, King found the guidelines for fictionalizing the broader audience, much the more important one to address under the circumstances. The clergymen, of course, were religious, white, moderate, educated leaders of public opinion. Thus they were representative of only a segment of the broader public, but it was a segment which King had both a need to and a possibility of persuading. Little, if anything, was to be gained in addressing white segregationists, black revolutionists, or people indifferent to civil rights. The situation called instead for an address to as wide a range of moderate-to-liberal, involved readers as possible; so much the better if a substantial number of them were also leaders of public opinion.

All social movements face the potential problem of splintering; and the civil rights movement, then in its infancy, was in danger of falling apart because of disagreement over the propriety of King's tactics. In addition to persuading a broad public, King thus needed also to unify civil rights proponents by persuading the more moderate among them that his course of action was the right one. By answering the clergymen, he in effect answered the mental reservations held by those whose dedication to equality fell short of support of public demonstrations.

The rhetorical advantages of addressing the broader audience in terms of the clerical audience are clearer if King and the clergymen are perceived as opponents in a written debate. Debaters seem to address each other, and they do respond to each other, but the response is determined by its intended effect on a third party, the judge or audience.

Despite the complexity resulting from the dual audience, this debater's stance gave King five argumentative advantages. First, the already existing document defined the key issues. Instead of having to fictionalize all potential arguments that an audience might hold against protest, King had only to respond to assertions in the clergymen's letter. Fortunately for his purposes, their letter was a synthesis of almost every likely criticism. This allowed King the fullest range of issues to discuss and thus allowed the greatest opportunity for persuasion; had the clergy disagreed with King on only one matter, such as timing, he could have answered that charge, but his response could not have become a refutative manifesto for a broader audience, a defense of his movement and the theory of peaceful civil disobedience on which it was based.

Second, refutation of an existent paper allowed a clear, easy to follow, point by point organization. Purely by enumeration, if King wished, he could handle each argument as it had been brought up by the opponents. The only necessary scaffolding was the transition, "You also argued . . ."

Third, refutation worked particularly well since the clergymen were in a weak position to begin with. They could not deny the charge that Birmingham was a thoroughly segregated city; at best they could argue that the means being used to remedy segregation were improper and/or that they were pursued at the wrong time.

Fourth, it is simpler to disprove someone else's moral argument than to build a case for one's own. Demonstrating that an opponent's position is unsoundly argued does not logically validate one's own argument, but rhetorically it often seems to a reader to do so.

A reader-judge does not engage in argument but, rather, compares the two cases presented. Instead of listening to King to decide whether he is right, a public reader is more likely to judge which of two presentations is the more persuasive. And, although a reader might be unconvinced by the "Letter" as an independent entity, when it is compared with the clergymen's argument, King's case is clearly superior on all counts.[13]

Finally, adapting his presentation to his ostensible audience, instead of having to launch it into the dark, allowed King to create a warm, personal tone. His essay is stylistically and tonally a real letter with a real personality behind it.

The "Letter's" Structure

King's essay is primarily a series of refutations of the arguments made by the clergymen, a point made by several commentators.[14] But saying this tends to obscure its more subtle features. In constructing his essay King, by design or accident, adapted the pattern of the classical oration to suit the situation in Birmingham, the clergymen's letter, and the wider audience as well. He reduced the classical *confirmatio* to utmost brevity and expanded the *refutatio* to carry the burden of argument.

The letter opens without an impassioned *exordium*, and this seems entirely appropriate to the already heated circumstances. Instead, the salutation, "My dear Fellow Clergymen," establishes immediately the warm, tactful tone prevalent in the essay. How different would have been the more formal "Dear Sirs," or "Dear Clergymen," or even "My Fellow Clergymen." The body of the letter begins with the classical *narratio*, "the exposition of the state of affairs at the moment,"[15] the facts that have motivated the writing. Subtly emphasizing the irony of a minister's being in prison, King notes, "While confined here in the Birmingham City Jail, I came across your recent statement calling our present activities 'unwise and untimely.' . . . I would like to answer your statement in what I hope will be patient and reasonable terms." Both the "patient and reasonable" tone and the intimacy of direct address continue throughout the essay.

King quickly deviates (pars. 2 and 3) from the pattern of the classical oration, however, by addressing one point in the clergy's letter: "I think I should give the reason for my being in Birmingham, since you have been influenced by the argument of 'outsiders coming in.'" The reason for refuting this argument before presenting the constructive case seems clear; if the argument about "outsiders" has any validity in the minds of either audience, then King has no right to discuss circumstances in Birmingham. He must earn the right to talk.

After his response to the "outsiders" argument, King states (par. 4) his *propositio*, that the Negro in Birmingham has had no choice but protest. Then, using the classical *partitio*, King notes (par. 5) that four steps are necessary in a protest campaign: "(1) collection of the facts to determine whether injustices are alive; (2) negotiation; (3) self-purification; and (4) direct action." King now takes up successively (pars. 5–7) the first three steps to show that in fact the Birmingham protesters had gone through them before determining to use direct action (par. 8).

These few paragraphs constitute King's unusually brief *confirmatio*, his constructive case for civil disobedience in Birmingham at this time, an argument built on what

Bosmajian has called the "Method of Residues."[16] Altogether, proposition, partition, and confirmation comprise only five of the essay's forty-eight paragraphs.

King now turns (par. 9) to the first of six major issues: "You may well ask, 'Why direct action? Why sit-ins, marches, etc.? Isn't negotiation a better path?'" This was not the first point raised by the clergymen, but King wisely adapts the order of his main arguments to move from the obvious to the more complex, presumably for the benefit of the wider audience. By agreeing, King logically and gracefully turns the argument back on the clergymen: Certainly negotiation is desirable; the *goal* of the protest is precisely to make the other side willing to negotiate. In the succeeding paragraphs (10–20), King handles the second and third major issues, the charges that the protests were ill-timed and violations of "law and order."

At this point King interrupts his refutative pattern with one of the personal sections that Larson calls digressions.[17] If the section is digressive, it is progressive at the same time; and such asides, merged into the rigid refutative structure, enhance the feeling that this is a personal letter in which personal feeling and digression (of sorts) are acceptable. In this "digression," King moves by association from the clergy's "law and order" argument to the first of "two honest confessions." He feels compelled to "confess" (par. 21) that he has been profoundly disappointed in the Southern white liberal for making arguments such as the "law and order" one instead of joining the Negro cause. Suddenly the clergy are on the defensive; not just their argument but their inaction is criticized. King does not attack angrily; he is merely forced (against his own good will) to admit that he has been saddened by such behavior and "almost" made to conclude that the people who make up his audiences are more dangerous to the Negro than outright segregationists. This tone of sadness and compulsion is effective precisely because it allows King to attack without seeming aggressive.

After two paragraphs (21–22) on his first disappointment, King returns (par. 23) to his refutative strategy and disposes of the argument that his nonviolent actions are evil because they precipitate violence from others. Then he refutes (pars. 24–25) what he calls "the myth of time," an argument that Negroes should wait for the natural course of social evolution to solve their problems. The clergymen had not made this argument, although it might have been suggested in their assertion that the protest in Birmingham was untimely. So to provide this view explicitly, and consequently maintain his refutative pattern, King quotes another letter, one from "a white brother in Texas" who had argued, "All Christians know that the colored people will receive equal rights eventually, but is it possible that you are in too great of a religious hurry? It has taken Christianity almost 2000 years to accomplish what it has." The "white brother," and perhaps the clergymen, is answered quickly. Then King devotes three paragraphs (26–28) in response to the argument that his actions are "extreme."

His second "disappointment," this one sadder and more pointed, follows; it is not only disappointment with the white liberal Southerner, but also disappointment with the Southern white church, which King sees as having sacrificed the "extremism" of moral commitment historically typical of the Christian faith. In the characteristic sad tone, King devotes twelve paragraphs (30–41) to the irony of the Southern churches' professing equality in the eyes of God, and the spirit of Christian fellowship, while allowing the ungodly and immoral practice of segregation to continue unopposed. By implication this is a direct attack on precisely the behavior of the eight clergymen to whom he is responding, for they profess a religiously rooted equality and fellowship but are arguing to allow the continuation of an ungodly segregation. King cannot understand such an "other-worldly religion which made a strange distinction between body and soul, the sacred and the secular."[18] Whereas the major *confirmatio* received only five paragraphs, the *refutatio* with its two attendant confessions extends for thirty-three paragraphs.[19]

King then begins (par. 42) his moving *peroratio,* stopping once (pars. 43–44) to refute the clergymen's praise of the restraint shown by the Birmingham police. The peroration, in its apology for having written at such length, recalls both the calm tone and the prison reference of the opening: "what else is there to do when you are alone for days in the dull monotony of a narrow jail cell other than write long letters, think strange thoughts, and pray long prayers?" The closing paragraph reasserts the identity of his viewpoint with that of his ostensible audience and speaks confidently of the future, when they may all meet and the "deep fog of misunderstanding will be lifted from our fear-drenched communities."

Schematically, then, the essay's structure looks like this:

A. *Narratio* (pars. 1–4)
   1. Clergy's letter
   2. King's reasons for being in Birmingham
B. *Propositio*— "the white power structure of this city left the Negro community with no other alternative" (par. 4)
C. *Confirmatio*—the four steps to protest (pars. 5–8)
D. *Refutatio* (pars. 9–41)
   1. Negotiation
   2. Timing
   3. Breaking laws
      (First "Confession": Disappointment in white liberals for not breaking laws)
   4. Precipitating violence
   5. The myth of time
   6. Extremism
      (Second "Confession": Disappointment in white Southern church for not being extreme)
E. *Peroratio* (pars. 42–48)
   1. Confidence in the future
   2. Clergy's praise for police (refuted)
   3. Hope to meet in a better future

The interjection of the two "disappointments" into the six main refutations, as well as the length of some of the refutations, may create the impression of looseness.[20] So may the informal, epistolary style. But the essay is actually tightly and elaborately structured. It combines the clarity, efficiency, and persuasive force of the classical oration with the personal warmth and associative structure of a letter to a friend.

The "Letter's" Refutative Logic

Even more impressive than the overall arrangement of the "Letter" is its internal logic in each refutative segment. King characteristically refutes the charges brought against him with a dual pattern. Never satisfied with one response, he answers each argument on at least two levels, usually a practical, immediate level, perhaps most appealing to a public audience, and an abstract, philosophical level involving unstated moral premises, an argument appealing more to the ostensible audience and others with some concern for philosophical abstractions. Multiple refutation is especially effective for the onlooking audience because it creates the impression that the other side's reasoning is not just weak but so unsound as to be unacceptable.

For example, in response to the charge that he is an outsider who has no business in Birmingham, King has four answers. First, he explains that the black leaders of Birmingham had invited him to come assist in the protest (rather than being a cause of it); second, that as president of the Southern Christian Leadership Conference of which the Alabama Christian Movement for Human Rights is an affiliate, "I am here because I have basic organizational ties here." These are the practical answers. They establish (if accepted) that he is not in fact an outsider, or at least not a complete outsider. But beyond these, King moves to attack the concept of the "outsider." Thus his third response is that, in the tradition of Paul and other Christian prophets and missionaries, he has gone wherever there was need. Such a view is the direct consequence of a historical, religious precedent that neither of his audiences could reject. Fourth, since all communities and states in the modern world are interrelated, King argues, no man can be an outsider in his own nation. With that he has turned to the attack: "Whatever affects one directly affects all indirectly. Never again can we afford to live with the narrow, provincial 'outside agitator' idea."

For refutative purposes King, here and throughout, expands the clergymen's enthymemes into syllogisms, without using the dry and formidable phrasing of formal logic. In formal terms their reasoning had to be as follows:

> Outsiders have no right to protest.
> King is an outsider.
> Therefore, King has no right to protest.

In response, King first attacks the minor premise by showing the ties that make him other than an outsider in Birmingham. But if this is not convincing, he also attacks the major premise by citing the tradition of Christian missionary work and by arguing that in our interdependent nation, no citizen is an outsider anywhere.

Perhaps the clearest example of King's strategy of dual refutation is his answer to the label "extreme measures." The phrase masks a full syllogism:

> Extremism is wrong.
> King and his followers' actions are
>   extreme.
> Therefore, their actions are wrong.

At first King attacks the minor premise by pointing out that in fact among the Negro community his is precisely the moderate position, midway between the passive complacency of some older Negroes and the violent militance of the young. Then, upon rethinking the matter, King attacks the unstated major premise by citing historical precedents of great extremists whom his opponents and the observing audience cannot help but revere: Christ, Paul, Martin Luther, John Bunyan, Lincoln, Thomas Jefferson. To deny first that one is an extremist, and then to argue that in fact extremism in moral matters is desirable, not wrong, seems self-contradictory. Actually King works on two definitions of extremism: The first is holding a position far from the norm (which King says he does not); the second is holding a view, no matter what, without compromise. Since the clergymen's brief letter did not define the term, King takes the two possible definitions and shows his own position superior in either case. His position is not an *extreme* one, but he holds to it with extreme commitment.

Throughout the essay similarly, precise meanings of key terms are used as the bases for arguments. In answering the most important charge, that it is improper to break a law, in this instance a court-ordered injunction, King graciously acknowledges the apparent inconsistency: "Since we so diligently urge people to obey the Supreme Court's decision of 1954 outlawing segregation in the public schools, it is rather strange and paradoxical to find us consciously breaking laws." Because this is in fact the central issue and the one probably most likely to evoke disagreement, King devotes the longest refutation to it, eight paragraphs, and gives the greatest number of different answers. This time King cannot attack the minor premise; he had in fact broken a law. Instead he answers the implied major premise (that it is always wrong to break the law) on several levels, each carefully calculated to persuade both his ostensible and his observing audiences, both of whom were likely to be hostile to such a claim.

King's fundamental answer is drawn from the premise that laws are not *ends* in themselves but *means* of achieving justice. If so, justice, and not the law per se, must be served. In fact, he asserts, initiating another key distinction, there are just laws and unjust laws, and it is one's moral duty to disobey unjust laws because they subvert the purpose of law—justice. By subtle implication then, if he is right, his audiences have not lived up to their moral duties.

King offers three definitions of the difference between just and unjust laws, presumably in the event that one of the distinctions proves less than persuasive. First, "A just law is a man-made code that squares with the moral law or the law of God. An unjust law is a code that is out of harmony with the moral law." Second, an unjust law is any law forced on a minority not followed also by the majority. And third, an unjust law is any law that a minority had no voice in making.

On all three counts, King argues, segregation laws (and presumably laws against or used against public protests) are unjust. His audience might not agree with his definitions, but few could deny that some laws are unjust. However one defines injustice, the opponents of protest are in the untenable position of defending at least temporary obedience to unjust law.

King then turns again to historical tradition for key instances of disobedience to patently unjust laws. Several examples from the Judeo-Christian tradition can scarcely be rejected by the ostensible audience, and probably not by most members of the wider one. As a more current instance King alludes to Hitler, who in persecuting the Jews was following the law. Anyone who does not accept, at this point, the notion that it is sometimes moral to break the law must also accept the implication of defending on similar grounds obedience to the antisemitic decrees of the Nazi regime.[21]

In this instance King's argument rests on premises similar to those underlying the "Higher Law" argument of the nineteenth century abolitionists and the "Natural Law" argument of the eighteenth century revolutionists. Thus, in outline, the argument is one with which his audience was likely to be familiar and sympathetic. King's position, consequently, is well adapted to both of his audiences and increases his chances of being persuasive. Moreover, King's use of the historical tradition here (as throughout) has the rhetorical virtue of presenting him as a traditionalist, an image likely to be valued by his moderate audience, who tend to regard him as a radical bent on "extreme measures."

Reading the "Letter" a first or second time, one is not yet fully aware of the shape of King's refutation, but, as in many affective situations, awareness is not requisite. King's combination of definition, precedent, and multipremise refutation is rhetorically effective, both directly and indirectly. Because the refutation seems at once precise, clear, and elegant without ostentation, the reader-judge is encouraged to assume not only "this is a sound position," but also "this is a master at work. He knows his subject, he knows his audience, he knows his art." And, I believe, a reader comes unconsciously to feel that "a man who can perform these tasks is able and honest and worthy of belief." In short, as he argues, King not only adapts to a fictionalized audience, but creates for that audience an image of himself through his adaptation. In classical terms, he creates his *ethos*. To extend Ong's argument, in any instance of *written* communication, the rhetor—whether the image be true or false—is always a fiction created for the audience and based on the writer's fictionalizing of them.

Any rhetorical choice thus has two dimensions. A choice effective in its own right becomes doubly effective because it fictionalizes a writer as the sort of person who makes such choices—a wise, shrewd rhetor worth listening to. Likewise, a choice that fails presents an image of a rhetor who had no better judgment than to make that choice. Persuasion results not only from the *logos* of content but also from the *ethos* created through the performance, and King's "Letter" is outstanding on both grounds.

Style as Persuasion in the "Letter"

The positive ethical image does not result only from the chosen audience conceptualization and refutative strategies discussed above, however. It also results from the essay's style. Although this is not the place for a complete descriptive analysis of King's stylistic versatility in "Letter from Birmingham Jail," I would like to highlight some of its more striking stylistic features and to speculate on the ways they reinforce the total persuasive effort. The essay's style is supple and sophisticated yet readable. An audience is likely to be favorably impressed, without being overwhelmed. The stylistic manipulations both create an image of competence and sincerity and operate on the reader's emotions.

Like all rhetorical choices, stylistic decisions have multiple effects. But to clarify the relation between stylistic choice and persuasion, it may be useful to assert that an effective stylistic choice will work in one or more of the following three ways. It may adapt the style in order to carry meaning more effectively to the audience as fictionalized by the rhetor, such as a decision to use a simpler synonym in place of a more elaborate equivalent. This is the *adaptive* dimension of style. Or the choice may operate on the reader's emotions in a less than obvious way, such as in a decision to use words that alliterate. This is the *affective* dimension of style, as I hope to clarify below. Finally the stylistic choice may be effective primarily because it helps enhance the rhetor's image and thus the rhetor's credibility. This is the *ethical* dimension of style. These three varieties of stylistic impact correspond closely to the three classical modes of persuasion; the adaptive choice is a rational technique (logos), the affective choice works on the emotions (pathos), and the ethical choice is a technique for enhancing ethos.

To illustrate these three persuasive dimensions of King's style, it may be well to start with an obvious and relatively simple feature of the essay. A reader can scarcely help noticing how often King refers to other famous men whom he expects his reader to recognize. These allusions are directly effective in their adaptive and affective appeals to both the limited and broader audiences and indirectly effective in the image of him they help create.

King unabashedly puts himself into a great tradition of protest beginning with Socrates, referred to three times, and extending down through primarily Christian history, from the early prophets to Christ himself, to Paul, to Aquinas, Augustine, Martin Luther, and Bunyan. In addition to such historical allusions, King also buttresses his argument by quoting or paraphrasing Reinhold Niebuhr, Martin Buber, and Paul Tillich, leading modern spokesmen from both Christian and Jewish faiths and thus presumably adaptive references for all of the eight clergymen at one time or another as well as to virtually all of King's broader audience. He even manages to quote an unidentified justice of the United States Supreme Court and T. S. Eliot. This man, who is potentially suspect as an outsider, a rabble-rouser, even a criminal, reveals himself to be educated, wise, and widely read. At least that is the impression such allusions make in discourse. They have multiplicative ethical impact, since an auditor assumes they are a carefully chosen sample drawn from a much larger store of information.

King's style in the essay is also marked by the extensive use of metaphors, generally of two types: either enduring archetypal metaphors or metaphors drawn from contemporary technology. Two archetypal patterns are dominant, that of depth versus height and dark versus light. The present system and segregation are repeatedly characterized as being *down* and *dark,* while the hope for the future involves rising and coming into the *light.* The Negroes live in a "dark shadow" and must "rise from the dark depths." They are "plunged into an abyss of injustice where they experience the bleakness of corroding despair." Policy must be lifted from "quicksand" to "rock," and "we have fallen below our environment"; Negroes are in a "dark dungeon"; in the emphatic and optimistic final paragraph (quoted below) America now suffers under the "dark clouds of racial prejudice" in a "deep fog of misunderstanding," but "tomorrow the radiant stars of love and brotherhood will shine."

As Osborn has argued, "Because of their strong positive and negative associations with survival and developmental motives, such metaphors express intense value judgments and may thus be expected to elicit significant value responses." Such "argument by archetype" also appeals to an audience's desire for simplification through its built-in, two-valued orientation.[22]

Other metaphors come from modern technology. The nations of Africa are moving forward with "jet-like speed" while we go at "a horse and buggy pace"; and the church stands "as a tail light behind other community agencies rather than a headlight leading men to higher levels of justice." The church is now merely a "thermometer" recording popular opinion instead of what it once was, "a thermostat that transformed the mores of society."

Specifically medical metaphors unite the technological imagery with the archetypal metaphor of disease and health. Segregation is a disease and later a boil that must be exposed to the healing sun. The liberal argument to wait has "been a tranquilizing thalidomide, relieving the emotional stress for a moment, only to give birth to an ill-formed infant of frustration."[23] Some whites have sensed the need for "antidotes" to segregation, but others have remained silent "behind the anesthetizing security of stained glass windows." All told, I count seventy-two metaphors, including both explicit and suppressed forms. Almost none are presented through cliches (common verbal formulas). They share several stylistic functions. On the adaptive level they are memorable for their ingenuity, and they help make an abstract philosophical argument vividly concrete. On the affective level, the archetypal metaphors speak to fundamental urges in us all and thus enhance the message indirectly. Finally, like all rhetorical choices, the stylistic decision to use metaphors also affects King's image. The archetypal references create the image of a sincere man of deep feeling who is fundamentally like the reader and who has confidence both in his own moral judgment and in the inevitability of a better tomorrow. The technological images help build an identification between King and his readers; both speaker and listener inhabit the same world of jet planes, thermometers, and wonder drugs, a world of rapid change in which only one element—the status of blacks—has not kept up.

This same identity of rhetor and reader is also enhanced by a series of stylistic choices which, taken together, constitute the conciliatory tone that characterizes the essay and serves to unite a variety of other tones. From the salutation onward, King is not out to criticize or belittle, but merely to explain patiently and sadly to those who do not (yet) see the light of the truth. Throughout the essay King may be righteous, hurt, disappointed, ironic, sorry that he must say some unavoidably critical things, but neither angry nor despairing. He has "almost reached the regrettable conclusion that the Negroes' great stumbling block in the stride toward freedom is not the White Citizens' 'Counciler' or the Ku Klux Klanner, but the white moderate": almost but not quite. And he has paid his clerical audience the compliment of having listened carefully to their views. His essay thus fulfills Carl Rogers' demand that one must first hear a position and be able to repeat it with understanding and clarity before real communication can occur.[24] Throughout the essay King shows his respect for his reader. He knows that his clerical audience is composed of sincere and devout men, men who share his basic religious values and whom he can call "My dear Fellow Clergymen" and "My Christian brothers." King even praises some by name for their own (limited) efforts to move toward integration. He can criticize such men only with regret. Echoing through the essay are phrases such as "I must say" and "I feel impelled to mention." Such a stylistic stance flatters him as well as his addressees. It serves the positive image he wants; this writer is not a shouting, belligerent, troublemaker, but a sincere and understanding human being whose views are forced out of him by his concern for their misguided positions.

The identification with the audience and the conciliatory tone are further created by one of the most subtle stylistic elements in the "Letter," the use of personal pronouns. Since the "Letter" is a deeply personal apologia, it is not surprising that *I* occurs regularly—139 times to be exact, 100 times as the subject of a main clause. Similarly King often addresses his ostensible audience directly: in rephrasing their arguments ("you stated"), in asking for understanding ("I hope that you can see"), in direct address ("Each of you has taken some significant stands"), and in personal appeal ("I beg you to forgive me." "I hope this letter finds you strong in the faith."). There are forty uses of *you* to refer to the clergymen, not to mention other generic uses of the word, which also carry personal overtones. The net effect is an impression of informality as well as personal commitment on the part of the *I*.

More subtle still is King's manipulation of ambiguous first-person-plural pronouns. Often *we* and *our* and *us* in the essay refer clearly to some or all of the Birmingham protesters: "Several months ago our local affiliate here . . . invited us to be on call . . . We readily consented." In other places, the *we* is more general, as in "Never again can we afford to live with the narrow, provincial 'outside agitator' idea." Yet frequently a *we, our,* or *us* seems to refer to the protesters but may also include the audience, in effect reinforcing the frequent direct addresses by gathering King and his opponents into a unit sharing a single outlook. Consider this sentence: "I have tried to stand between these two forces saying that we need not follow the 'do-nothingism' of the complacent or the hatred and despair of the black nationalist." *We* here at first seems to mean "we the moderate protesters," but it may equally well mean "we who recognize the problem and want to see it solved." We, all of us, you clergymen as well as my followers, may take this middle road. The union is subtle, but is at least subconsciously forced on the reader by King's choice of pronouns.

A similar movement from "I-you" to *we* operates in the closing paragraph of the essay in conjunction with extended archetypal imagery:

> *I* hope this letter finds *you* strong in the faith.
>
> *I* also hope that circumstances will soon make it possible for *me* to meet each of *you*, not as an integrationist or a civil rights leader, but as a fellow clergymen and a Christian brother. Let *us* all hope that the dark clouds of racial prejudice will soon pass away and the deep fog of misunderstanding will be lifted from *our* fear-drenched communities and in some not too distant tomorrow the radiant stars of love and brotherhood will shine over *our* great nation with all their scintillating beauty (italics added).

In the first two sentences, the current separation between *I* and *you* is both stated and reinforced by the pronouns, but after the conciliatory "fellow clergymen," in the third sentence, both groups merge in a vision of future unity in "our communities" and "our great nation" under the scintillating beauty of the high, bright stars.

King's style in the "Letter," as Larson has pointed out,[25] is primarily characterized by variety. It shows in the allusions and metaphors already discussed and in the range of tones united by the dominant conciliatory stance, but it is nowhere more obvious than in the essay's syntactic structures.

The original published text of King's "Letter" consisted of 48 paragraphs, 325 sentences, and 7,110 words, with a moderate average sentence of 22 words and an average paragraph of almost 7 sentences or 149 words. The average sentence, not so long as that of normal American intellectual prose, is consequently appropriate for King's extensive audience. But such statistics mask the variety of King's syntax. Of the 325 sentences, many are short; 62 have 10 or fewer words. Some are aphoristic, such as "We are caught in an inescapable network of mutuality tied in a single garment of destiny. Whatever affects one directly affects all indirectly." Thus parts of the essay are quite easy to read and eminently quotable. On the other hand, 18 sentences are more than 50 words long and 2 exceed 100 words. I know of no other modern public prose including sentences of such length. Although some readers are likely to stumble over such sentences, my impression is that, overall, the style is clear and vivid and relatively easy to read but with no hint of condescension. The extreme variations in sentence length as well as similar variety in clausal construction and levels of formality seem primarily to work on the ethical level. That is, they dramatize for the readers a rhetor who is a master manipulator of language.

The one syntactic feature that emerges as common within the variation is elaborate parallelism. In it, as in the metaphors, it is easy to hear the cadences of the evangelist, another dimension of King's self-dramatization through style. Sometimes King's parallelism is tight and aphoristic as in "Shallow understanding from people of good will is more frustrating than absolute misunderstanding from people of ill will," or "Whatever affects one directly affects all indirectly." More often, however, it is spread out and rhythmic: "I say it as a minister of the gospel, who loves the Church; who was nurtured in its bosom; who has been sustained by its spiritual blessings and who will remain true to it as long as the cord of life shall lengthen." Or,

> I have almost reached the regrettable conclusion that the Negroes' great stumbling block in the stride toward freedom is not the White Citizens' "Counciler" or the Ku Klux Klanner, but the white moderate who is more devoted to "order" than to justice; who prefers a negative peace which is the absence of tension to a positive peace which is the presence of justice; who constantly says "I agree with you in the goal you seek, but I can't agree with your methods of direct action"; who paternalistically feels that he can set the time-table for another man's freedom; who lives by the myth of time and who constantly advises the Negro to wait until a "more convenient season."

Frequently this extended parallelism continues through several sentences:

> They have left their secure congregations and walked the streets of Albany, Georgia, with us. They have gone through the highways of the South on torturous rides for freedom. Yes,

they have gone to jail with us. Some have been kicked out of their churches and lost the support of their bishops and fellow ministers. But they have gone with the faith that right defeated is stronger than evil triumphant.

In all, I count 15 instances of sustained parallelism, some involving as many as 6 sentences and one (discussed below) a single sentence of more than 300 words.

The effects of such parallelism must be largely conjectural, but it is difficult to imagine that they can lie in the adaptive domain. That is, there seems to be no reason to think that parallel syntax is any more clear or easy to follow than are other syntactic structures. On the other hand, the rhythms and balance created by parallelism, especially when a series of parallel constructions is used to build to a climax, probably have an affective impact, much as they would in oral discourse but to a lesser degree. The major effect is ethical, portraying the rhetor as a man who can balance various views and who has his ideas under complete control.

The "Letter's" most impressive stylistic feat is its longest sentence. Unique form serves to emphasize unique content since it is the one place in the essay where the evil of segregation, rather than the necessity of protest, is delineated. Because it contains in miniature so much that is syntactically and metaphorically characteristic of the essay, I quote it in full. It occurs (par. 12) within the refutation of the argument that now is not the proper time for protest. It opens, as do many of the sentences, with a conjunctive turn:

> But when you have seen vicious mobs lynch your mothers and fathers at will and drown your sisters and brothers at whim; when you have seen hate filled policemen curse, kick, brutalize, and even kill your black brothers and sisters with impunity; when you see the vast majority of your twenty million Negro brothers smothering in an air-tight cage of poverty in the midst of an affluent society; when you suddenly find your tongue twisted and your speech stammering as you seek to explain to your six-year-old daughter why she can't go to the public amusement park that has just been advertised on television, and see tears welling up in her little eyes when she is told that Funtown is closed to colored children, and see the depressing clouds of inferiority begin to form in her little mental sky, and see her begin to distort her little personality by unconsciously developing a bitterness toward white people; when you have to concoct an answer for a five-year-old son asking in agonizing pathos: "Daddy, why do white people treat colored people so mean?"; when you take a cross country drive and find it necessary to sleep night after night in the uncomfortable corners of your automobile because no motel will accept you; when you are humiliated day in and day out by nagging signs reading "white" men and "colored"; when your first name becomes "nigger" and your middle name becomes "boy" (however old you are) and your last name becomes "John," and when your wife and mother are never given the respected title "Mrs."; when you are harried by day and haunted by night by the fact that you are a Negro, living constantly at tip-toe stance never quite knowing what to expect next, and plagued with inner fears and outer resentments; when you are forever fighting a degenerating sense of "nobodiness";—then you will understand why we find it difficult to wait.

This most impressive periodic sentence of 331 words is highlighted through contrast with the preceding sentence of 19 words and succeeding sentences of 33, 11, 13, and 6 words. Its nine major subordinate clauses are each addressed directly to the audience with "when you," and they comprise an elaborate catalogue, frequently with metaphor, of the injustices suffered daily by the Negro in America. The sentence builds to a climax after detail is piled on detail, only to end with the one main clause of magnificently understated direct address: "then you will understand why we find it difficult to wait." Here the pronouns create no union: *you* are distinctly not *we*. It is appropriate that this single indictment of American racism, the only point in the essay at which pathos is used as a major suasive mode, should be the longest sentence. But it is also appropriate that it not be dominant. For the subject of the essay is not racial injustice. That is, except here, a given.

Conclusion

Presumably a public letter, to be credible, must suit the ostensible audience; one of the virtues of the form is that it provides a relatively well-defined (ostensible) audience on which rhetorical and stylistic choices may be based. But this fact in turn both defines and controls the onlooking audience. We can never know who King's readers were (or will be), but we can deduce who his fictionalized audience must have been. The refutative logic, discussed above, is careful and complex. Precise definitions are used involving careful distinctions. Uncommon (primarily Christian) allusions, some impressive vocabulary, complex syntax, and elaborate metaphor mark this, not as a piece of popular propaganda, but as a moral argument carefully designed for an audience of some sophistication.

The "Letter" lacks the elaborate pathos that might be persuasive to a purely popular audience, the emotional fireworks it could easily have employed about the evils of segregation. It uses instead a combination of logical and ethical persuasion, effective for a broad but generally well-educated audience, "sincere" readers "of genuine good will." Further, it is written for a concerned religious audience, an essentially conservative and traditional audience who would generally oppose civil disobedience but who would take the time to listen and not be alienated by extensive citing of other thinkers.

To lose the moral and social content of King's argument in critical analysis of nuances would, of course, be a mistake. Central to this examination is the attempt to bring about a more refined appreciation of King's text as an instance of rhetoric in the classical sense, a conspicuously compelling effort to persuade. It cannot be fully understood in isolation. As a public letter it stands in the context of its time and place, and it has a precise dialectical relationship to the document which provoked it. It is thus a very real effort to use language as a medium of social-problem solving, as a medium of change. Nevertheless, it also exists, especially for readers today, as a permanent articulation of human perception of an issue, which justifies examining it in all of its eloquent, rhetorical complexities. As an exercise in clarity and logic, King's essay well deserves the fame it has gained. Its structure makes it both readable and thorough. Its refutative stance makes it alive with the fire of heated but courteous controversy, and the dual nature of the refutation makes it simultaneously persuasive and logically compelling. Its stylistic variety and nuance portray a personality in print, manipulate a reader's emotions, and create a union of reader and rhetor.

Notes

1 David L. Lewis, *King: A Critical Biography* (New York: Praeger, 1970), p. 182.
2 Martin Luther King, Jr., *Why We Can't Wait* (New York: Harper & Row, 1963), p. 78.
3 Alan F. Westin and Barry Mahoney, *The Trial of Martin Luther King* (New York: Crowell, 1974), p. 140.
4 My analysis is based on the first published version. In all major respects the two versions are almost identical. King's editing was restricted to minor alterations of diction and syntax in more than 200 sentences. Six other sentences were deleted, and one was added. In fourteen instances two sentences were combined in revision; and four original sentences were divided. The changes seem to have been made in the interests of economy and a move toward slightly more formality. Anyone reading the two versions, however, must search carefully to find the changes. The overall difference in impact is negligible.
5 The "Letter" is included in a number of college anthologies: Charles Muscatine and Marlene Griffith, eds., *The Borzoi College Reader*, 3rd ed. (New York: Knopf, 1976); Arthur M. Eastman et al., eds., *The Norton Reader*, 4th ed. (New York: Norton, 1977); Caroline Shrodes, Harry Finestone, and Michael Shugrue, eds., *The Conscious Reader*, 2nd ed. (New York: Macmillan, 1978); Richard E. Young, Alton L. Becker, and Kenneth L. Pike, *Rhetoric: Discovery and Change* (New York: Harcourt, Brace & World, 1970); Halsey P. Taylor and Victor N. Okada, eds., *The Craft of the Essay* (New York: Harcourt Brace Jovanovich, 1977); and Forrest D. Burt and E. Cleve Want, eds., *Invention & Design: A Rhetorical Reader* (New York: Random House, 1978). It also appears in Edward P. J. Corbett, *Classical Rhetoric for the Modern Student*, 2nd ed. (New York: Oxford, 1971); Staughton Lynd, ed., *Nonviolence in America: A Documentary History* (Indianapolis: Bobbs-Merrill, 1966); George Ducas and Charles Van Doren, eds., *Great Documents in Black American History* (New York: Praeger, 1970); and Herbert J. Storing, ed., *What Country Have I? Political Writings by Black Americans* (New York: St. Martin's, 1970).
6 Craig Bradford Snow, *A Guide to The Norton Reader, Fourth Edition* (New York: Norton, 1977), p. 173.
7 Richard L. Larson, *Rhetorical Guide to The Borzoi College Reader* (New York: Knopf, 1967), p. 87.
8 Burt and Want, p. 354.
9 Taylor and Okada, p. 310.
10 Haig A. Bosmajian, "Rhetoric of Martin Luther King's Letter From Birmingham Jail," *Midwest Quarterly*, 8 (Jan. 1967), 127–43.
11 The clergymen's letter along with the earlier version of King's response is reprinted in Muscatine and Griffith, pp. 233–34.
12 Walter J. Ong, "The Writer's Audience Is Always a Fiction," *PMLA*, 90 (1975), 9–21.
13 I do not mean to imply that a reader of King's essay must be familiar with the clergy's letter. It is quite enough to "know" their letter through King's restatements of its main points. He "responds" to the clergy's arguments but does not allow them to structure his essay; they only seem to do so. If one knows the clergy's letter well, it is even clear that King slightly restates some arguments to make them more refutable.
14 The refutative structure has been pointed out by Larson and Bosmajian.
15 Corbett, p. 27.
16 Bosmajian, p. 130.
17 Larson, p. 84.
18 It may not be too farfetched to argue that these two digressions actually constitute the real constructive case of the essay. They do not directly support the proposition as I have described it, but they do make a case for concerted action against, rather than endurance of, segregation. And motivating such action may be the real implicit purpose.
19 Actually one of the clergy's corollary claims, that King and his followers had ignored the courts, is never answered. Since King, in fact, had chosen protest in the streets rather than action in the courts, he can scarcely answer such a charge directly. The whole letter is, however, a justification of ignoring the courts.

20 Larson, in his valuable set of notes on the essay, has characterized it as "randomly interconnected" (p. 84); obviously, I disagree.
21 In his revision, King added a further historical example, the Boston Tea Party.
22 Michael Osborn, "Archetypal Metaphor in Rhetoric: The Light-Dark Family," *Quarterly Journal of Speech,* 53 (1967), 117.
23 In the revised version, King cut out three of his metaphors, apparently because they were too harsh. Both the "thalidomide" and the "tail light" images were omitted, as was a reference to the few whites who had joined the black protest as "the leaven in the lump of race."
24 Carl R. Rogers, "Communication: Its Blocking and Its Facilitation," in Young, Becker, and Pike, pp. 284–89.
25 Larson says, "It is, indeed, unfair to speak of the 'tone' of the 'Letter,' for in its varied tones the 'Letter' is more like a musical performance than a piece of argument" (p. 86). True, but, as in a piece of music, the varied tones are all brought into harmony by the tonic note, in this instance the generous, conciliatory stance with which King states his uncompromising case.

15.
INTRODUCTION TO RHETORICAL STYLE: THE USES OF LANGUAGE IN PERSUASION
Jeanne Fahnestock

IN 1984, AN archivist for the U.S. Congress discovered a text that had been missing for forty-three years: the "podium" copy of the speech President Franklin D. Roosevelt delivered on December 8, 1941, asking Congress to declare war on Japan. Roosevelt had evidently left this copy behind in the House of Representatives, and it had been duly filed away. This typed version of the President's address contains four corrections in his handwriting, and during the actual delivery, Roosevelt made several more changes. These continuing adjustments to the exact wording of his text represent the last stages of a process of revision that began the preceding day, shortly after news of the attack on Pearl Harbor, when Roosevelt dictated the first version to his typist Grace Tully, complete with punctuation marks, and then began to work over the language. Below are the opening sentences of that dictated first draft with the changes that Roosevelt made by hand.[1]

>   infamy –
> Yesterday, December 7, 1941, ̭ a date which will live in ~~world history~~, ̭
>   suddenly
> the United States of America was ~~simultaneously~~ and deliberately attacked by
>   ~~without warning~~
> naval and air forces of the Empire of Japan. ̭
>   at the solicitation of Japan
> The United States was at the moment at peace with that nation and ̭ was
>   still in
> ~~continuing the~~ conversations with its Government and its Emperor looking toward the maintenance of peace in the Pacific. Indeed, one hour after Japanese air
>   Oahu
> squadrons had commenced bombing in ~~Hawaii and the Philippine~~s, the Japanese Ambassador to the United States and his colleague delivered to the Secretary of
>   recent American   While
> State a formal reply to a ~~former~~ message, ~~from the secretary~~. ̭ This reply

---

Fahnestock, Jeanne. "Introduction." *Rhetorical Style: The Uses of Language in Persuasion*. Oxford: Oxford University Press, 2011: 3–6.

>   stated   it seemed useless to continue the existing
> ~~contained a statement~~ that ˄ diplomatic negotiations ~~must be considered at an end~~
>   it   or   war or
> ~~but~~ ˄ contained no threat ~~and no~~ hint of ˄ ~~an~~ armed attack.
>   It will be recorded that the distance~~s of Manila, and especially~~ of Hawaii,
>   s   was
> from Japan make ˄ it obvious that these attack~~s=were~~ ˄ deliberately planned many
>   or even weeks
> days ˄ ago.

How can the language of both FDR's original phrasing and his changes be described? And what further principles of analysis can account for his stylistic decisions and his second thoughts? Any description of his language will depend on what the describer is prepared to notice, and any explanation of the features noticed will depend on the analyst's preferences for what counts as a satisfactory explanatory rationale. One obvious rationale would consider Roosevelt's language based on his purpose. Roosevelt wants Congress to pass a declaration of war (or actually acknowledge a state of war), and he has to give them reasons for doing so. At the same time, in a speech broadcast live on radio, he is addressing the entire nation, and he must also secure their support for war and for the coming sacrifices. His text is a means to accomplish these goals. It is, in the ancient and enduring sense of the word, *rhetorical,* constructed to have an impact on the attitudes, beliefs, and actions of its audiences. And while justifying a declaration of war after an attack may seem an easy goal given the circumstances, nevertheless an argument had to be made explicitly and war had to be declared formally.

Roosevelt's opening strategy for accomplishing his purpose is, first, to amplify the treachery of the enemy, a common move in deliberative speeches calling for war. His language choices in the passage above can be assessed against that particular strategy. It is therefore not surprising that he opens by citing what is on everyone's mind, the attack of the day before, and his choice of passive voice in his first sentence correctly makes the United States, while filling the role of grammatical subject, nevertheless the recipient and victim, while Japan is the agent: *the United States . . . was . . . attacked . . . by . . . the forces of* collectively and formally—*the United States of America*—since, collectively and formally, a unified nation had to respond.

The opening words of Roosevelt's first sentence locate the attack in time in a series of renamings ordered by their expanding perspective (Stelzner 1993, 111). The first word, *Yesterday,* places the crucial event in terms of the present moment for Roosevelt and his listeners; it happened on their *yesterday.* The second identifying phrase gives the precise date of the attack, *December 7, 1941,* widening the temporal location to a calendar address that will not change when it is no longer yesterday. The third appositive identifies this *date* in a new and still wider frame of reference. Here Roosevelt's first and most stunning revision occurs in naming this final location: his replacing *world history* with *infamy.* A word that came into English from Norman French, *infamie* (originally meaning "dishonor" or "ill repute") carries the military and even chivalric associations of many such French-sourced terms, and it arguably has greater force than a more familiar alternative like Old English *shame* or a less familiar one like the Latin *perfidy*.[2] The term also fits well in its grammatical place in the sentence as the third and final in the series of locations. In the first version, the attack is lodged in the storehouse of *world history*. As a destination, *world history* does serve Roosevelt's argument as a standard of evaluation: this attack ranks with other similar acts of treachery significant enough to be recorded in world history, and this ranking justifies a declaration of war in response. The revision to *infamy* replaces this standard with a vaguer but much more powerful one, a qualitative measure of heinousness transposed into a place, like a reserved spot in Dante's hell where acts of evil live forever. To highlight this new standard, Roosevelt, ever mindful of prosodic effects, also changed the punctuation around this third appositive, replacing the commas with dashes to remind himself to set this third phrase off from the rest of the sentence. In speaking, these slightly longer pauses before and after emphasize an internal sentence element that might not otherwise receive emphasis from its mid-sentence position. Altogether, in his opening phrases, Roosevelt amplifies the attack with a series whose items increase in length and significance, precisely the method of heightening recommended by Quintilian two thousand years ago (see chapter 18).

Many of Roosevelt's other changes in this opening follow from his second thoughts about citing the attack on the Philippines along with the attack on Hawaii. The air assault on the Philippines occurred several hours after the attack on Pearl Harbor (causing a subsequent controversy about lack of preparation), and Roosevelt first paired them as attacks on U.S. territories and forces. But he later made a significant decision, perhaps as more military intelligence came in, to argue by partitioning events differently, isolating the attack on *Qahu* from all the others that occurred that day; in a subsequent draft, these are all mentioned in a dramatic listing of Japans multiple targets (see below, p. 227). In his actual delivery, Roosevelt added the identifying epithet *the American Island of* before *Oahu*, an identification that is both geographical and patriotic. Roosevelt's strategy of heightening this one much more devastating attack—the one earlier, first reported, and closer to home—fixes his audiences on the single event they were already aware of and neither divides their attention nor complicates their outrage. Amplification through quantity will come later in the speech. Having made the decision to focus, Roosevelt crosses out a *simultaneously* that no longer applies, though he still wants the cadence of the multisyllabic double adverbs and wisely chooses *suddenly* instead. He also needs to change the two calculations of distance, from Manila and Hawaii, to one, and the multiple attacks become *the attack* planned not only days but *even weeks* ago.

Much more could be said about Roosevelt's language in relation to his argument. His many constitutive choices deserve mention, such as his use of static linking verb constructions in the second sentence or the agentless *it seemed* in the fourth. But to focus only on changes, his crossing out of *without warning* removes the redundancy with *suddenly*, and it also preserves the end-of-sentence emphasis on the first mention of the enemy, notably named more formally with the longer and more significant sounding epithetical name, *the Empire of Japan* (changed again in delivery). Also, because the first paragraph grounds treachery in hypocrisy, Roosevelt must tell a complicated story of peace negotiations initiated by an enemy intent on war and of diplomatic memos exchanged while an attack was underway. To simplify, he removes the confusing and too alliterative *formal reply to a former message from*, dropping in *American* in the process. And he wisely changes the entire architecture of the last sentence of the first paragraph, from a single independent clause with parallel verbs (*this reply contained a statement. . . but contained no threat*) to a sentence with an opening adverbial clause delivering the qualifications, followed by the main clause carrying the main point about what the message did not contain, *no threat or hint of war or armed attack,* a phrasing that balances symmetrical doubles around the preposition *of*. This prosodically satisfying final phrase also delivers an *a fortiori* argument, defined in rhetorical manuals as a comparison argument from the lesser or the greater. Since the second item in each pair is the lesser of the two, the construction is understood as furthering the case for the enemy's duplicity by pointing out that they did not indicate their true intent or even some lesser version of it: they did not threaten "or even" *hint* at war "or even" at *armed attack.* Without a glimpse of this underlying argument, there is otherwise no explanation for the downstep in each pair.

16.
WINSTON CHURCHILL: METAPHOR AND HEROIC MYTH
Jonathan Charteris-Black

16.1 Background

Churchill was the past master of twentieth-century political oratory and has set the standards that subsequent politicians have often sought to emulate – especially in crisis situations for which his rhetorical style is the benchmark. Soon after his election George W. Bush declared that he had placed a bust of Churchill in the White House Oval Office. His post September 11 speeches adopted Churchill's rhetorical style and in early 2004 Bush claimed that Churchill was not just 'the rallying voice of the Second World War' but also 'a prophet of the Cold War'.[1] It is significant that a politician who attached great personal importance to oratory in the classical sense was also the one who had the greatest opportunity to employ it for that most vital of political objectives: national survival. Churchill has been able to set the benchmark for political speaking in the modern period precisely because he believed in the power of the spoken word to motivate by winning over hearts and minds and demonstrated this belief through command of wartime rhetoric; as he said in 1954 'To jaw-jaw is better than to war-war'.

Churchill had unknowingly spent much of his earlier life preparing for his role as a wartime orator. He published the first volume of his speeches before he was 30 and eventually went on to publish 18 volumes. In 1897 he published an essay 'The Scaffolding of Rhetoric' arguing for the importance of oratory, and yet it was not until 43 years later that his mastery of persuasion directly led to his appointment as Prime Minister. His command of delivery was such that he memorised by heart the complete preprepared scripts for his speeches. Although his radio broadcasts provided leadership during a time of national crisis, his greatest political performances were in the House of Commons. For Churchill oratory was both the artist's brush and the bully's cudgel that could goad opponents into submission – he also knew when to use the brush and when the cudgel.

His most successful oratory was certainly during the Second World War when the impression of strength and inflexibility conveyed through his gravelly tone made him the symbol of a national resolve to withstand invasion. As Cassirer (1946: 278) argues:

Charteris-Black, Jonathan. "Winston Churchill: Metaphor and Heroic Myth." *Politicians and Rhetoric: The Persuasive Power of Metaphor*. Second edition. Basingstoke, UK: Palgrave Macmillan, 2011[2005]: pp. 52–78.

> Even in primitive societies where myth pervades and governs the whole of man's social feeling and social life it is not always operative in the same way nor does it always appear with the same strength. It reaches its full force when man has to face an unusual and dangerous situation ... In desperate situations man will always have recourse to desperate means – and our present-day political myths have been such desperate means.

In 1939 after the collapse of the Munich agreement and faced with the threat of an aggressive force expanding over Central Europe, Britain was in precisely such a position of danger. Churchill's appointment to the Admiralty on 3 September 1939 was against an unpromising background:

> He was politically déconsidéré, largely ignored even by those who agreed with his attitudes on foreign affairs. His career since 1915 had been, in the main, a story of failure. Now in his sixty-fifth year, after some forty years in active political life, he was given his opportunity.
> (James 1973: 108)

However, the loss of confidence in the government created a situation in which there were opportunities for myth creation. Indeed, his subsequent elevation to Prime Minister on 10 May 1940 can be attributed to the impact that his speeches were having in the early part of that year. The social function of his radio broadcasts was to raise morale by communicating the impression of specific actions being planned and implemented. The creation of a sense of strategy – even though often illusory – was essential if the public were to retain confidence in their leader's capacity to attain the stated objective of military victory. This use of the media was a completely novel, and effective, leadership strategy. As James argues – 'What will always be remembered as the "blood, sweat and tears" speech was a real turning point' (ibid.: 108). He goes on to claim:

> Here was the authentic voice of leadership and defiance. It was Churchill's outstanding quality as a war leader that he made the struggle seem not merely essential for national survival, but worthwhile and noble.
> (Ibid.: 109)

16.2 The Rhetoric of Winston Churchill

In the following analysis I will argue that Churchill's primary rhetorical objective was telling a story in which the actions of Hitler and Germany are represented as forces of evil in contrast to those of Britain and its Allies that are represented as forces of good. I describe this narrative as a heroic myth and argue that metaphor was the prime rhetorical method for expressing this myth. This is evident in the metaphors – in particular personifications – as in the following excerpt:

> Side by side, unaided except by their kith and kin in the great Dominions and by the wide empires which rest beneath their shield – side by side, the British and French peoples have advanced to rescue not only Europe but mankind from the foulest and most soul-destroying tyranny which has ever darkened and stained the pages of history. Behind them – behind us

– behind the Armies and Fleets of Britain and France – gather a group of shattered States and bludgeoned races: the Czechs, the Poles, the Norwegians, the Danes, the Dutch, the Belgians – upon all of whom the long night of barbarism will descend, unbroken even by a star of hope, unless we conquer, as conquer we must; as conquer we shall.

(19 May 1940)

Central to Churchill's heroic myth is the claim that Britain was not fighting purely for national self-interest but was the embodiment of forces of good that would rescue all mankind from tyranny and barbarism.

A hallmark of Churchill's use of metaphor is that nation states are conceptualised as human heroes, villains or victims. In his rhetoric nations are attributed with mental and affective states that lead them to have thoughts, beliefs and feelings and this contributes to his sounding right. It was, of course, the people who inhabited these nations who may have undergone such experiences, but Churchill's heroic myth described international political and military affairs *as if they were* personal hopes and anxieties. Metaphor created the possibility for representation of Britain and its allies as motivated by altruism and as having the right intentions and for Germany and its allies as motivated by self- interest. This use of personification can be represented by an underlying metaphor – THE NATION IS A PERSON.[2]

For Churchill metaphor had a dual rhetorical role of sounding right and establishing himself as having the right intentions; this was crucial to creating confidence and confirming his identity as a successful leader. At other times, metaphor could be seen as a distraction from the primary goal of deliberating on political decisions. Metaphor was a resource for projecting a set of beliefs, and for creating social cohesion by telling the right story; this contrasts with the way that Hitler used metaphor for the conceptualisation and formation of actual political policy. It is for this reason that I describe Churchill's use of metaphor as heroic myth – a myth in which Churchill serves as a metonym for a righteous and heroic Britain.

Metaphor was only one amongst several rhetorical strategies. Quite large sections of Churchill's wartime speeches are characterised by a complete absence of metaphor; this is especially when he is describing the current military situation and summarising military strategy. There are very few occurrences of metaphor in a number of the most famous quotations for which Churchill is remembered. If we consider his first speech as Prime Minister – the 'blood, sweat and tears' speech – images of physical and mental suffering combine hyperbole with metonymy because the *effects* of blood, sweat and tears refer to the suffering and hard work that *cause* them, so the effects are used to refer to their cause. The speech also contains extensive use of repetition, matching clauses (parisons) and rhetorical questions. In the following excerpt from this speech repeated matched items are underlined and questions are shown in italics:

> We have before us an ordeal of the most grievous kind. <u>We have before us</u> many, many long months of struggle and of suffering. You ask, *what is our policy*? I can say: It is to wage war, by sea, land and air, with all our might and <u>with all</u> the strength that God can give us; <u>to wage war</u> against a monstrous tyranny, never surpassed in the dark, lamentable catalogue of human crime. That is <u>our policy</u>. <u>You ask,</u> *what is our aim*? I can answer in one word: It is victory,

> <u>victory</u> at all costs, <u>victory</u> in spite of all terror, <u>victory</u>, however long and hard the road may be; for without <u>victory</u>, there is no survival. Let that be realised; <u>no survival</u> for the British Empire, <u>no survival</u> for all that <u>the British Empire</u> has stood for, <u>no survival</u> for the urge and impulse of the ages, that mankind will move forward towards its goal.
>
> (13 May 1940)

While the speech also contains metaphors, the essence of its rhetorical force is in repeated elements and rhetorical questions rather than metaphors. The effect of repetition and reiteration is to convey persistence and obduracy that sounds right because it is based on conviction. The structure of this part of the speech is organised around repetition in response to rhetorical questions; in answer to the first question about policy 'wage war' is repeated, in answer to the second regarding aims, 'victory' is repeated. Reiteration also assists in generalisation from *British* war 'policy' and 'aims' to the 'goals' of *mankind in general*. Here the underlying intention is to equate specific British objectives with general human aspirations and so to raise the status of military action from the personal to the heroic, from the prosaic to the sublime.

Often lexical repetition is combined with parallelism to produce an even more marked use of repetition at the levels of both vocabulary and grammar, as perhaps is most well known in:

> We shall go on to the end, <u>we shall fight</u> in France, <u>we shall fight</u> on the seas and oceans, <u>we shall fight</u> with growing confidence and growing strength in the air, <u>we shall defend</u> our Island, whatever the cost may be, <u>we shall fight</u> on the beaches, <u>we shall fight</u> on the landing grounds, <u>we shall fight</u> in the fields and in the streets, <u>we shall fight</u> in the hills; <u>we shall never surrender.</u>
>
> (4 June 1940)

Repetition of 'we' implies unity of purpose and 'shall' clearly predicts the future; particular locations, landing grounds, etc. are then slotted into a syntactical frame:

WE + SHALL + 'MILITARY' VERB + LOCATION.

Repetition implies physical and mental obduracy since, like the staccato effect of a machine gun, opposition will continue – even when the bullets run out: it sounds right! Reiteration of the syntactical structure communicates strength and conviction and Churchill also sometimes uses it with poetic effect:

> The empires of the future are the empires of the mind.
>
> (6 September 1943)

Hyperbole is such a favoured rhetorical strategy that it becomes a mode of discourse for Churchill, as in his tribute and eulogy to the airmen who fought in the Battle of Britain:

> The gratitude of every home in our Island, in our Empire, and indeed throughout the world, except in the abodes of the guilty, goes out to the British airmen who, undaunted by odds, unwearied in their constant challenge and mortal danger, are turning the tide of the

World War by their prowess and by their devotion. Never in the field of human conflict was so much owed by so many to so few.

(20 August 1940)

Rhetorical force is achieved by the strategy of combining reiteration with contrast ('so much', 'so many': 'so few'). Metaphor also plays a marginal role for example in conceptualising the war as a sea with a changing tide. In other cases hyperbole is created by the use of superlative forms:

Let us therefore brace ourselves to our duties, and so bear ourselves that, if the British Empire and its Commonwealth last for a thousand years, men will still say, 'This was their finest hour.'

(18 June 1940)

In yet other cases contrast (or antithesis) is employed for an effect that can be both memorable and witty as in the following:

There is nothing wrong with change, if it is in the right direction.

The problems of victory are more agreeable than those of defeat, but they are no less difficult.

In some instances this is combined with chiasmus (clause inversion):

An optimist sees an opportunity in every calamity; a pessimist sees a calamity in every opportunity.

Chiasmus could be used for morale raising in memorable fashion when describing the various stages of the war:

Now this is not the end. It is not even the beginning of the end. But it is, perhaps, the end of the beginning.

(10 November 1942)

This reminds us that in addition to strategies such as repetition, clause matching, inversion, antithesis and hyperbole, another hallmark of Churchill's oratory is his ability to replicate the structural patterns and discourse function of English phraseology. Consider, for example, his use of proverb-like utterances such as: 'We make a living by what we get, we make a life by what we give'; or 'If you mean to profit, learn to please' and 'It is better to do the wrong thing than to do nothing.' These clearly have a discourse function of warning similar to that of many English proverbs but they are also characterised by their formal linguistic pattern. They are comprised of two phrases in a relation of symmetry in which the second phrase reiterates structural elements from the first.

In other cases – again those that are often quoted because structural reiteration encourages memorisation – there are the characteristics of maxims or adages. Examples would include: 'The price of greatness is responsibility'; 'I never worry about action, but only inaction'; 'Censure is often useful, praise often deceitful' and 'Success is going from failure to failure without losing your enthusiasm'. All these phrases replicate ideas and linguistic patterns with which his audience would be familiar because they characterise the phraseology of the English language. This enhances the likelihood for subsequent quotation and these are therefore key linguistic techniques for myth creation. It is the ability to coin phrases that share the structural patterns of familiar maxims and express widely held cultural outlooks that enhanced Churchill's persuasiveness. It is no coincidence, then, that the phrase 'blood, sweat and tears' has entered into English phraseology and provides evidence of how sounding right contributes to linguistic innovation.

16.3 Metaphor Analysis

For the analysis I selected a corpus of 25 of the major wartime speeches (see Appendix 1). There is a bias towards those speeches given in the earlier part of the war because this was a period when persuasive communication was most necessary to sustain public morale after the fall of France, the evacuation from Dunkirk and during the Battle of Britain. This was a crucial period in determining the outcome of the war. As A.J.P. Taylor (1969: 31) has put it:

> His confidence that victory, though perhaps not easy, was certain, in time inspired others, and appeasement seemed to be unnecessary as well as dishonourable. Churchill's arguments mattered less than the tone in which he said them and his voice ultimately made him, in British eyes, the architect of victory.

The corpus contains approximately 50,000 words and at least 385 metaphors; therefore, one expression that is classifiable as a metaphor (using the definition given in Chapter 1) occurs on average every 130 words. For comparative purposes I also examined a 50,000-word corpus of Hitler's speeches; this revealed over double the frequency of metaphors found in the Churchill corpus.

Initially, I classified metaphors according to their source domains; this is because in establishing how metaphor can be used to create myth we need to identify the typical social values that are attached to the domains on which metaphor draws (see Appendix 2). These values arise from our bodily experience and knowledge of the value attached to these domains in particular cultural practices; for example, we know that light is a prerequisite for growth as well as sight while darkness is associated with inability to see and the resulting possibility of dangerous experiences. We know that families are normally associated with close human relationships and therefore associated with a positive evaluation. Our experience of journeys is that they are normally purposeful and goal orientated and that different types of experiences, difficulties, etc. may be encountered. Analysis of how metaphors are used to create the myths that underlie an ideology begins with identification of their source domains.

The approach summarised in Appendix 2 allows us to identify the preferred metaphor types of a particular politician; this facilitates comparison of different speakers and is valuable in identifying the metaphors that characterise their oratorical style. I should first comment briefly on the above figures: they are not necessarily comprehensive and I do not claim that other metaphor analysts would come up with slightly different numerical classifications. A particular difficulty, as we will see later, is when a number of different source domains occur in close proximity in what I will describe as 'nested metaphors' (see section 3.7); consider, for example, the following italicised metaphors:

> Very few wars have been won by mere numbers alone. Quality, will power, geographical advantages, natural and financial resources, the command of the sea, and, above all, a cause which rouses the spontaneous *surgings* (1) of the human spirit in millions of hearts – these have proved to be the decisive factors in *the human story* (2). If it were otherwise, how would the race of men have risen above the apes; how otherwise would they have conquered and extirpated dragons and monsters; how would they have ever evolved the moral theme; how would they have *marched forward* (3) across the centuries to broad conceptions of compassion, of freedom, and of right? How would they ever have discerned those *beacon lights* (4) which summon and guide us across the *rough dark waters* (5) and presently will guide us across *the flaming lines of battle* (6) towards better days which lie beyond?
> (20 January 1940)

I suggest that the numbered metaphors draw on the following conceptualisations:

1. The spirit is an ocean
2. Evolution is a narrative
3. Human progress is a journey
4. Safety/hope is light
5. Danger/fear is darkness
6. War is fire

According to my analysis, there is a water metaphor (1), a narrative or 'story' metaphor (2), a journey metaphor (3), two light and darkness metaphors (4 and 5) and a fire metaphor (6). However, the journey metaphor is extended over several phrases (e.g. from 'marched forward' to a double repetition of 'guide'); similarly, the light metaphor occurs in 'beacon light' and 'dark waters' and the fire metaphor is in both 'beacon' and in 'flaming'. So in such cases is there one metaphor or two? ('Beacon' is particularly problematic since it is potentially both a light metaphor and a fire metaphor.)

Where metaphors from the same source domain occur in the same phrase my method was to count them as *single* metaphors. Where there is evidence of different source domains in the same phrase, I would identify which source domain was *primary* and only count this – especially where the secondary use was also part of *another* metaphor. For example, 'beacon' – though potentially part of a fire metaphor – is primarily a light metaphor (because the function of a beacon is to create light rather than heat) so I did not *also* count it as a fire metaphor. A similar practice was followed when the same source domain occurs in different phrases, so although 'guide' is potentially a journey metaphor, since 'march' had already led me to identify a journey metaphor and 'guide' is *also* part of a light metaphor it is not counted again. This procedure aims to avoid counting the same word or phrase as more than one metaphor and gives a rather conservative count of the number of metaphors used. The purpose of counting metaphors was to direct our interest towards underlying conceptualisations that were important in influencing core value judgements in Churchill's creation of political myth. Quantitative data are helpful in determining the relative importance to be attached to each of the different source domains for metaphor that he employed.

Appendix 2 shows that a relatively small number of domains provide the linguistic and cognitive basis for Churchill's metaphors. They include those for which the potential audience may be assumed to have had some experience – journeys, animals, buildings, family, etc. – and some that would be naturally resonant for British people because of their cultural and historical experience – such as the sea and the weather. Comparison with the Hitler corpus showed that Churchill draws on a much wider range of source domains. This may reflect a different discourse role for metaphor as Churchill is more concerned with sounding right and having the right intentions, while Hitler employs metaphor in actual policy formulation – that is thinking about what in his view was right. The stylistic preference for use of personification by Churchill reflects a preference for a grandiloquent and classical rhetorical style that is motivated by a desire to sound right as a national leader. This literary and aesthetic role for metaphor as a source of embellishment can be related to his earlier experience of historical writing. I used the findings shown in Appendix 2 to identify those domains worthy of a detailed analysis; these were personification, journeys, light and darkness and slavery.

16.4 Personification

Personification was easily the most common figure in Churchill's oratory, accounting for around 37 per cent of all his metaphors. It is a linguistic figure in which an abstract and inanimate entity is described or referred to using a word or phrase that in other contexts would be used to describe a person. We may therefore think of 'person' as the source domain. Personification is persuasive because it evokes our attitudes, feelings and beliefs about people and applies them to our attitudes, feelings and beliefs about abstract political entities and is therefore a way of heightening the emotional appeal. Typically, the ideological basis for using personification is either to arouse empathy for a social group, ideology or belief evaluated as heroic, or to arouse opposition towards a social group, ideology or belief that is evaluated as villainous, This is done by associating social groups, ideologies and beliefs that are positively evaluated with heroic human attributes – such as courage and determination – and by associating negatively evaluated social groups, ideas, etc. with villainous attributes – such as cowardice and treachery. A typical example of positive evaluation is when 'Britain' or 'us' is described as if it is a plucky hero who is prepared to fight to the death:

> And now it has come to us to stand alone in the breach, and face the worst that the tyrant's might and enmity can do . . . here, girt about by the seas and oceans where the Navy reigns; shielded from above by the prowess and devotion of our airmen – we await undismayed the impending assault.
>
> (14 July 1940)

Britain, other nations thought, had drawn a sponge across her slate. But instead our country stood in the gap. There was no flinching and no thought of giving in, never give in, never, never, never.

(29 October 1941)

... to look ahead to those days which will surely come when we shall have finally beaten down Satan under our feet and find ourselves with other great allies at once the masters and the servants of the future.

(3 September 1943)

In these metaphors there is evidence of the concepts: BRITAIN IS A HERO and GERMANY IS A VILLAIN. In the corpus there are 11 occurrences where Churchill uses personifications to refer to 'we', 'us' or 'ourselves' – this forms a metonymic chain in which he stands for the people and the people stand for nation. The chain implies that the qualities that are attributed to the nation are also to be attributed to himself and the people. In this way, Churchill's rhetoric was successful in representing himself and his country as a champion prize fighter and identifying the people and himself with the acts of bravery and physical courage undertaken by servicemen. The effect of sounding right was to satisfy the political objective of harnessing the efforts of the civilian population to the military effort. This use of personification combined with first-person reference was a highly effective linguistic instrument for creating a myth in which he is a symbol of a heroic nation. The heroic myth of BRITAIN IS A HERO is quite evident in his speech to the VE day crowds:

This is not victory of a party or of any class. It's a victory of the great British nation as a whole. We were the first, in this ancient island, to draw the sword against tyranny. After a while we were left all alone against the most tremendous military power that has been seen. We were all alone for a whole year.

(8 May 1945)

Hawkins (2001) describes an iconographic frame of reference comprised of three images: the hero, the villain and the victim; and he refers to this as the 'Warrior Iconography'. Though, of course, these roles are also implied by Edelman's Valiant Leader and Conspiratorial Enemy myths. Churchill's warrior iconography is one in which Churchill and Britain are the hero, Hitler and Germany are the villain and France and other conquered nations of Europe are the victims. The villain and victim roles are evident in the following:

... and against that other enemy who, without the slightest provocation, coldly and deliberately, for greed and gain, stabbed France in the back in the moment of her agony, and is now marching against us in Africa.

(20 August 1940)

This activates a mental representation for treacherous and cowardly behaviour that is associated with the type of unprovoked assault one would expect of a villain – someone who has the wrong intentions. Everything that is associated with life is positively valued while everything that is associated with death carries an extreme negative value. It seems that what is important here in communicating value judgements is the creation of a polar contrast between forces of good and evil as well as those of life and death. In some instances personification creates an emotive link between Nazism and death as in the following:

> So we came back after long months from the jaws of death, out of the mouth of hell, while all the world wondered.
>
> (8 May 1945)

In other places the mythic role of 'monster' replaces that of 'villain':

> ... so many States and kingdoms torn to pieces in a few weeks or even days by the *monstrous force* of the Nazi war machine.
>
> (14 July 1940)

> It is to wage war, by sea, land and air, with all our might and with all the strength that God can give us; to wage war against a *monstrous tyranny*, never surpassed in the dark, lamentable catalogue of human crime.
>
> (13 May 1940)

> ... because, while France had been bled white and England was supine and bewildered, a *monstrous growth* of aggression sprang up in Germany, in Italy and Japan.
>
> (3 September 1943)

In this iconographic frame if Germany is the villain, then Nazism is the monster created by it; this provides evidence of an underlying concept NAZISM IS A MONSTER. I would like to suggest that motivating this concept is a combination of a conceptual metaphor and a conceptual metonym. The conceptual metaphor is A NATION IS A PERSON; it is this which permits the actions of nations to be represented as if they were either the actions of heroes or villains and other passive nations to be cast in the role of victim. The conceptual metonym is POLITICAL LEADER FOR NATION; the leader of the government of a nation is taken to represent that nation because he has an ultimate decision-making capacity. We see this in conventional expressions such as 'Mussolini has reeled back in Albania' or 'the smear of Hitler has been wiped from the human path'. The metonym and the metaphor work in conjunction with each other – since the metonym encourages us to think of the political actions of countries as if they were the actions of a particular person in those countries. The conventional use of metonym creates the conceptual basis for personifications motivated by the conceptual metaphor A NATION IS A PERSON.

Against this cognitive background, battles between nation states are conceived in heroic terms appropriate to a struggle between medieval warriors:

> *Shielded by* overwhelming sea power, possessed of invaluable strategic bases and of ample funds, France might have remained one of the *great combatants* in the struggle. By so doing,

Table 16.1 Summary of metaphor targets in Churchill's personifications

	Positive evaluation	Total	Negative evaluation	Total	Total
Country/ political grouping	France (9) Nations (5) Countries (4) British nation (4)	41	Japan Germany	3	44
Abstract concept	Destiny(4) Freedom (4) Justice (2) Progress (2) History (2)	21	Death (4) War (3) Disaster (2) Woe (2)	17	38
Social grouping	We/us (11) Mankind (4) Motherland (2)	22	Foe (3) Enemy Evil doers	5	27
Military grouping	British army French army Navy	9	Gestapo German aircraft	2	11
Ideology	Western democracies	1	Nazi regime Communism Tyranny (5)	8	9
Other		11		4	15
Total		105		39	144

> France would have preserved the continuity of her life, and the French Empire might have advanced with the British Empire to the rescue of the independence and integrity of the French Motherland . . . The Czechs, the Poles, the Norwegians, the Dutch, the Belgians are still *in the field, sword in hand,* recognized by Great Britain and the United States as the sole representative authorities and lawful Governments of their respective States.
>
> (20 August 1940)

Churchill's use of personifications based around the conceptual metaphor THE NATION IS A PERSON implies an evaluation based on a historical schema for medieval warfare in which allies are heroes and enemies are villains.

Because of the importance of personification in conveying value judgements and ideology through an emotional appeal I decided to quantify the types of metaphorical targets for which evaluation is given by a personification (see Table 16.1).

Not surprisingly, the most preferred target for a personification is a country/a political grouping or an abstract concept – these accounted for around two-thirds of the total uses of this figure. The metaphors in the following speech to the VE-day crowd refer to historical processes:

> London can take it. So we came back after long months from *the jaws of death,* out of *the mouth of hell,* while all the world wondered. When shall the reputation and faith of this generation of English men and women fail? I say that in the long years to come not only will

the people of this island but of the world, wherever *the bird of freedom chirps* in human hearts, look back to what we've done and they will say 'do not despair, *do not yield to violence and tyranny,* march straightforward and die – if need be – unconquered'.

(8 May 1945)

Churchill shifts from personifications of abstract entities that have a negative evaluation (e.g. death and tyranny) and are linked to negatively evaluated targets (e.g. Germany and Japan) to those that have a positive evaluation (e.g. freedom) and are linked with positively evaluated targets (e.g. the British Empire and its Allies). This gives a mythical dimension to the struggle between good and evil and creates a polar relation between them: the use of personification is effective when combined with antithesis as it creates an evaluation based on a metaphysical domain. Personification was therefore a major rhetorical means for persuasion in Churchill's efforts to unify and to raise morale during a period of military conflict because it allowed him both to sound right and to express the right intentions,

16.5 Journey Metaphors

Journey metaphors were originally introduced into cognitive linguistics by Lakoff and Johnson (1980) who proposed a metaphor LOVE IS A JOURNEY to account for expressions such as 'our relationship is at a crossroads', though this was later developed into the more general LIFE IS A JOURNEY (Lakoff and Turner 1989). They trace the literary and biblical origins of this metaphor in terms of how choices can be made between good and evil paths and how God can be conceived as 'a guide' and death as 'a departure' (ibid.: 10). This was later reformulated into PURPOSEFUL ACTIVITY IS TRAVELLING ALONG A PATH TOWARD A DESTINATION (Lakoff 1993). Charteris-Black (2004: 74) suggests that *social* purposes can be viewed as destinations just as much as individual ones. Evidence for this idea can be found in metaphoric uses of 'step', 'burden', 'forward', etc. I also propose that Conservative discourse typically employs journey metaphors to refer to movements forward in time while in Labour discourse movement is typically spatial rather than temporal. Chilton (2004) highlights the importance of spatial concepts in political discourse and argues that what is *close* to the speaker is evaluated as morally and legally *good,* while what is *distant* from the speaker is evaluated as morally and legally *bad.*

Journeys are a potent source domain for metaphor because of the availability of a clear schema that includes *required* elements – such as start and end points connected by a path and entities that move along the path; this is usually represented in cognitive linguistics as a SOURCE–PATH–GOAL. However, *optional* elements are equally important in political speeches; these include mode of travel, guides, companions, etc. It is the flexibility of these optional elements that serves as a richer basis for inferential reasoning and evaluation than the required elements that are so much part of our experience that we are barely conscious of them. For example, we know that on journeys there is the potential for both positive experiences – such as making friends and seeing new places – and for negative ones – such as meeting a dead end or getting lost. However, unlike personifications that create relations of contrast between the poles of good and evil, the rhetorical purpose of journey metaphors is to create solidarity in order that positively evaluated purposes may be successfully attained. In this respect journey metaphors encourage followers to accept short-term suffering for worthwhile long-term objectives.[3]

'Journeys' was the second most common source domain for metaphor in the corpus with a total of 48 linguistic forms. Typical linguistic forms were: *road, path, journey, toiling up a hill, milestone, feet, forward* and *march*. Over 75 per cent of the journey metaphors had one of four metaphor targets; these were: the British war effort ($n = 15$), human progress in general ($n = 10$), military victory ($n = 7$) and the American war effort ($n = 5$). All the metaphors convey a strong positive evaluation of these targets as we can see from the following examples which are chosen to illustrate the first three of these metaphor targets:

> ... And the whole preparation of our munitions industries under the spell of war has *rolled forward* with gathering momentum.
> (27 January 1940)

> The course of world history is the noblest prize of victory. *We are still toiling up the hill; we have not yet reached the crest-line of it;* we cannot survey the landscape or even imagine what its condition will be when that longed-for morning comes.
> (10 August 1940)

> Duty inescapable remains. So long as our *pathway to victory* is not impeded, we are ready to discharge such offices of good will toward the French Government as may be possible ...
> (14 July 1940)

While all Churchill's journey metaphors carry a positive evaluation of the overriding war aim of defeating Germany, different aspects of the source domain are highlighted according to the rhetorical intention within the context of the speech. For example, when the metaphor target is some aspect of the British war effort – whether in terms of military or civilian activity – it is usually the knowledge that journeys involve expenditure of effort that is highlighted by the metaphor, So typically, movement towards a desirable social goal is difficult and involves some form of short-term suffering or struggle to overcome resistance. This was clearly effective in giving a sense of purpose to the suffering and difficulty that people encountered in their everyday lives during war. However, there are also other related ideas that realised Churchill's rhetorical intention of persuading by telling the right story. He sought to emphasise that journeys once started have to be completed (whatever the cost in human suffering) and that there was no 'going back' because of the desirability of the 'destination':

> ... the Prime Minister *led us forward* in one great body into a struggle against aggression and oppression, against a wrong-doing, faithlessness and cruelty, from which there can be *no going back*.
> (27 January 1940)[4]

Some optional elements from the journey source domain are explicitly rejected – for example, the knowledge that rests are sometimes taken during a journey:

> But from them also we may draw the force and inspiration to *carry us forward upon our journey* and *not to pause or rest* till liberation is achieved and justice done.
>
> (27 January 1940)

However, since the purpose of journey metaphors was to raise morale and create a feeling of optimism, they are also frequently goal-focused and refer explicitly to the end point, or destination, of the journey – and here the metaphor target is military victory:

> The *road to victory* may not be so long as we expect. But we have no right to count upon this. Be it long or short, rough or smooth, we mean *to reach our journey's end*.
>
> (10 August 1940)

Churchill frequently used the phrase 'the road to victory' as it emphasises the fact that there is always a predetermined destination – unlike say a path which could either meander around in circles or take us to an unknown destination. Churchill's use of journey metaphors shifts from emphasising personal suffering to highlighting the irreversibility of the war effort according to the rhetorical objective of the stage in the speech.

The most important example of the power of language to influence political outcomes through the journey schema was when Churchill persuaded the USA to join the Allied cause – in this respect they contributed also to right thinking by providing a political argument. The choice of journey metaphors to describe both the British and the American war effort was a heuristic for forging a political link between the two countries – this was a vital objective in 1940 and journey metaphors encouraged the Anglo-American alliance. For example, the knowledge that journeys are generally social rather than solitary endeavours was exploited in the speech 'The Price of Greatness is Responsibility' which was designed to encourage American involvement in the war. Journey metaphors are shown in italics in the following excerpts:

> We may be quite sure that this process will be intensified with every *forward step the United States make* in wealth and power.

> Not only do we *march and strive shoulder to shoulder*[5] at this moment under the fire of the enemy on the fields of war or in the air, but also in those realms of thought which are consecrated to the rights and the dignity of man.

> I like to think of British and Americans *moving about freely* over each other's wide estates with hardly a sense of being foreigners to one another.
>
> (3 September 1943)

These metaphors show evidence of an underlying concept BRITAIN AND THE USA ARE TRAVELLING COMPANIONS. Here each use of the metaphor profiles a different aspect of the journey domain. First is the idea of journeys being purposeful, next is the idea of going on a journey together with someone else, and finally, the idea of travelling with someone implies unrestricted rights of access to each other's territory. This heuristic probably encouraged the government of the USA to enter the war and to commit itself to the rescue of its 'travelling companion'. Churchill's use of metaphor is systematically linked with underlying rhetorical and political intentions. These are achieved by highlighting different component elements of the schema that people have for journeys in the construction of an ideological perspective. Systematic extension and elaboration of a particular metaphor schema are a very effective way of using metaphor both to develop a political argument and to give stylistic coherence to a speech.

Another good example of how metaphor forms coherent mental representations or frames occurs in the speech 'The First Five Months' of 27 January 1940. There are a total of five metaphors from the source domain of journeys that are distributed at near equal distances throughout the speech as follows:

1. ... the Prime Minister *led us forward* in one great body into a struggle against aggression and oppression, against a wrong-doing, faithlessness and cruelty, from *which there can be no going back.*
2. ... the whole preparation of our munitions industries under the spell of war *has rolled forward* with gathering momentum ...
3. The men at the top may be very fierce and powerful, but their ears are deaf, their fingers are numb; they cannot feel their feet as *they move forward in the fog and darkness of the immeasurable and the unknown.*
4. ... wickedness has cast its shadow upon mankind and seeks *to bar its forward march ...*
5. But from them also we may draw the force and inspiration *to carry us forward upon our journey* and not to pause or rest till liberation is achieved and justice done.

The first two metaphors highlight the directionality and force of the war effort. In the first Churchill is a heroic leader inspired by a sense of moral self-righteousness. In the second we know that – like a journey – the war effort cannot be reversed; the third one then describes the Nazi command as being lost on a journey because they are ignorant of the route (perhaps because they have no guide or no adequate maps). The last two then describe the general notion of inevitability of human progress in terms of a successful and purposeful journey – but one which may encounter impediments that need to be overcome. This illustrates the flexibility of the journey metaphor in developing arguments. It is used to examine different aspects of the military and political conflict in such a way as to imply that the British efforts are successful because they have direction while those of their enemy are not because they are without direction.

Analysis of metaphors can add to our understanding of how specific rhetorical goals are achieved through the use of metaphors that match the speaker's intentions with the audience's mental schemata and scripts for journeys. Evidently the creation of such metaphorical coherence is an important skill in speech making and is likely to add to the attainment of its persuasive objectives. These were primarily the creation of social and political unity by telling the right story and reflects in the use of 'space' metaphors of the left rather than the 'time' journey metaphors of traditional Conservatives (cf. Charteris-Black 2004: 74–6).

16.6 Metaphors of Light and Darkness

Originally, Lakoff and Johnson (1980: 48) cited evidence for UNDERSTANDING IS SEEING in conventional expressions such as 'I see what you are saying' and 'can you elucidate your remarks'. In these expressions there is the implication that light is an experiential prerequisite for sight which is, in turn, a necessary precondition for knowledge. Lakoff and Turner (1989: 190) reformulated the metaphor as KNOWING IS SEEING and on Lakoff's home page there are other metaphors such as HOPE IS LIGHT, IDEAS ARE LIGHT SOURCES and INTELLIGENCE IS A LIGHT SOURCE. Since knowledge is equated with light in this schema, darkness is by implication equated with ignorance. Cognitive linguistic treatment of light metaphors has been traced to the association between light and life (plants rely on a light source) and between darkness and death (it is dark underground where we are buried). However, their origin in universal knowledge overlooks the importance of cultural and social knowledge in influencing the mythical quality of metaphors.

I would suggest that *cultural* knowledge is more important in determining the type of evaluation conveyed by light in Churchill's use of light metaphors. Light and dark metaphors are very common in Christian religious discourse and link light, faith, goodness and Jesus; for example, these notions are central to the creation of coherence in John's Gospel. Light metaphors contrast with dark metaphors in which there is an equivalence between darkness, spiritual ignorance, evil and Satan, leading to such familiar expressions in the domain of the supernatural as 'the forces of darkness' and 'the dark powers' (cf. Charteris-Black 2004: 185ff.). In this respect, within Christian discourse, 'light' carries a positive evaluation as being prototypically good while 'dark' carries the negative one of being prototypically bad. This is not necessarily mediated by any knowledge that we may have of the conditions necessary for plant survival – indeed some plants prefer dark and shady locations to light ones. This cultural knowledge contributes to Churchill's narrative of Britain as a force of light – and therefore heroic – and Germany as a force of darkness and therefore villainous.

In political speeches metaphors drawing on the source domain of light and darkness are frequently used as a way of offering evaluation through exploiting their potential for antithesis. This is typically how Churchill employs light and dark metaphors; in fact he uses more dark metaphors than light metaphors and the majority of his dark metaphors use a morphological variant of 'dark' such as 'darkness' – his most common metaphor is the phrase 'The Dark Ages'. By contrast, there is a wider diversity of light metaphors and these include 'beacon', 'shining', 'flickering' and 'gleam'. Table 16.2 shows how light and dark metaphors invariably convey a strong evaluation.

Typically, Churchill's light metaphors are based on the conceptual metaphor HOPE IS LIGHT which complies with the rhetorical purpose of raising morale. The only exceptions to this are when he uses light in relation to science as in 'the light of perverted science' ('The Few') which is motivated by the concept KNOWING IS SEEING. For added persuasive effect, Churchill frequently heightens the contrast between the forces of good and the forces of evil by juxtaposing light and dark metaphors, as in the following passage referring to Finland's struggle to prevent a Nazi invasion:

> ... *If the light of freedom which still burns so brightly* in the frozen North should be finally *quenched*, it might well herald a return *to the Dark Ages*, when every vestige of human progress during two thousand years would be *engulfed*.
> (20 January 1940)

In addition to a contrast between light and dark, there is evidence of fire metaphors nesting within a metaphor frame for light – hence the selection of 'burns', 'quenched' and 'engulfed' (since we know from experience that fires can be extinguished if they are absorbed by a liquid).[6] Fire and light when combined as metaphor source domains have the rhetorical effect of hyperbole.

As a stylistic feature, this type of intensification of meaning is important at particular stages in a speech and Churchill frequently uses light metaphors at the end position of speeches; for example, these are the final lines of the speech 'The Air Raids on London':

> Our qualities and deeds must burn and glow through the gloom of Europe until they become the veritable beacon of its salvation.
> (8 October 1940)

And the speech 'War of the Unknown Warriors' ends:

> ... but let all strive without failing in faith or in duty, and the dark curse of Hitler will be lifted from our age.
> (14 July 1940)

As well as the creation of contrast and the use of light and dark metaphors in speech endings he also uses them to create relations of cohesion between paragraphs. One important instance of this is the important post-war speech 'The Sinews of Peace' in which he outlines his vision for Anglo-American relations after the occupation of part of Germany by the Russian forces. Early on in the speech he describes 'opportunity'

Table 16.2 Evaluation in Light and Dark Metaphors

Light: positive evaluation	Dark: negative evaluation
Not so easily shall the *lights of freedom* die	Many hundreds of naval homes in our dockyard cities *have been darkened* by irreparable loss
The veritable *beacon of salvation*	Wickedness has *cast its shadow* upon mankind
The qualities of Allied troops *have shone*	*Long dark months* of trial and tribulation lie before us
British qualities *shine the brightest*	*The dark curse* of Hitler will be lifted from our age

as '*clear and shining* for both our countries'; subsequently he warns 'The *dark* ages may return, the Stone Age may return on the *gleaming* wings of science.' In the next paragraph he claims that: 'A *shadow* has fallen upon the scenes so lately *lighted* by the Allied victory ...'. Then the following paragraph commences: 'In front of the *iron curtain* which lies across Europe are other causes for anxiety.' Later in the speech he refers again to: 'In front of the *iron curtain* that lies across Europe ...' and in the next paragraph but one:

> I have felt bound to portray the *shadow* which, alike in the west or the east, falls upon the world.
>
> (5 March 1946)

Here it seems that the genesis of the politically potent image of the iron curtain can be analysed as an extension of the light-dark source domain. Our knowledge of the function of a curtain is that it is designed both to exclude light and to prevent someone outside from looking in; one made of iron would be all the more impenetrable to light and all the more secretive. This iconic metaphor implies that Russia was allied with forces of darkness and also did not wish to be seen – since it had drawn the curtain. This negative evaluation is reinforced by our knowledge that iron is visually unattractive and has the properties of being hard and inflexible (a heavy curtain would be much more difficult to draw). These attributes were later taken up and exploited by the Russians in the phrase 'the Iron Lady' to refer to Margaret Thatcher (a metaphor for which skilfully reversed the rhetorical effect by re-representing inflexibility as strength). So the iron curtain metaphor fits with the view of Russia as secretive, potentially dangerous and an obstacle to open communication.[7] Here we can see how influential and persuasive Churchill's choice of metaphor became since the metaphor in the original image weakened over time as 'the iron curtain' came to refer to a literal geopolitical reality. However, it is not clear that it ever lost the important connotative and evaluative meaning that underlay its original choice.

16.7 Nested Metaphors

'Nested metaphor' is the term that I have used to describe the rhetorical practice of placing a metaphor from one source domain within a metaphor from another source domain (cf. Charteris-Black 2004). In the last section I showed how fire and light metaphors could be nested within one another. There is no limit to the number of metaphors that can be connected in this way – and knowledge of both source domains as well of the relations between them is necessary to fully interpret the metaphor. 'Nested metaphor' is not to be confused with the term 'mixed metaphor'; this implies that there is a degree of inappropriateness or over-elaboration in metaphor choice.[8] We are not always aware of nested metaphors in the same way that we may be of 'mixed metaphors' because of the congruence of source domains and they can be highly persuasive ways of creating a subtle and sophisticated use of language.

Churchill often nests journey metaphors within other source domains in order to heighten their persuasive effect by creating interactions between a range of source domains. This use of metaphor is not conventional and can be described as poetic because of the novelty of the images that are created. Churchill's passion for English literature reflects in his desire to employ such poetic uses of metaphor. In the following a personification ('History is a person'), light and fire metaphors (in bold) and combat metaphors (underlined) are nested within a journey metaphor frame (in italics):

> History with its **flickering lamp** *stumbles along the trail* of the past, trying to reconstruct its scenes, to revive its echoes, and kindle with **pale gleams** the passion of former days. What is the worth of all this? The only *guide* to a man is his conscience; the only <u>shield</u> to his memory is the rectitude and sincerity of his actions. It is very imprudent *to walk through life* without <u>this shield</u>, because we are so often mocked by the failure of our hopes and the upsetting of our calculations; but <u>with this shield</u>, however the fates may play, *we march always* in the ranks of honour.
>
> (12 November 1940)

The past is represented as if it were the life of a man; a light metaphor based on UNDERSTANDING IS SEEING is blended with a fire metaphor based on INTENSE FEELING IS HEAT (ANGER IS HEAT; cf. Lakoff and Kövecses 1987). These domains are connected by the underlying metaphor LIFE IS A JOURNEY that is implied by 'stumbles', 'guide', 'walk' and 'march'. Then a combat metaphor is introduced; this we can represent as RIGHT ACTION IS A SHIELD. So – given that the 'destination' is death – and all that remains is our memory of a person, the combination of light, combat and journey metaphors provides a poetic account of the metaphor target of the whole text: 'the right way to live'. The genre of a eulogy permits an elaborate use of metaphor in which a range of different source domains interact with each other creating a diversity of images in order to evoke sentiments appropriate for this occasion. This would not of course always be an option in other speech-making contexts.

Nested metaphors are also in evidence when Churchill was at the height of his speech-making powers in terms of sounding right and telling the right story. Consider, for example, the last section of his crucial morale-raising speech paying tribute to the airmen who defended the country in the Battle of Britain:

> What General Weygand called the Battle of France is over. I expect that the Battle of Britain is about to begin. Upon this battle depends the <u>survival of Christian civilization</u>. Upon it depends <u>our own British life</u>, and the long continuity of our institutions and our Empire. The whole fury and might of the enemy must very soon be turned on us. Hitler knows that he will have to break us in this Island or lose the war. If we can stand up to him, all Europe may be free and <u>the life of the world</u> may *move forward into broad, sunlit uplands*. But if we fail, then the whole world, including the United States, including all that we have known and cared for, will sink into the abyss of *a new Dark Age* made more sinister, and perhaps more protracted, by *the lights of perverted science*. Let us therefore brace ourselves to our duties, and so bear ourselves that, if the British Empire and its Commonwealth last for a thousand years, men will still say, 'This was their finest hour'.
>
> (18 June 1940)

Here I have underlined three personifications and italicised the other metaphors; by using the *same* figure – personification – for three *different* metaphor targets ('Christian civilization', 'the British way of life' and 'the world') Churchill creates a relationship of equivalence between them. This is rhetorically persuasive as it implies that the interests of Britain are identical with – and representative of – those of Christian civilisation and the world in general. Britain has the right intentions because it is fighting for these global altruistic objectives. It also tells a story that contradicts the reality that Britain was at this time militarily isolated by implying that morally it is Germany that is alone. A journey metaphor is then conflated with a light metaphor in the image of 'the world' moving 'forward into broad, sunlit uplands' – here HOPE IS LIGHT, This is contrasted with 'Dark Age' where darkness implies absence of hope and – because it is 'sinister' – absence of morality too. This creates an antithesis to the underlying metaphor UNDERSTANDING IS SEEING by implying that knowledge can become 'perverted'. In this way Churchill employs metaphor effectively to construct ethos: a tone of morally inspired authority. This prepares the way for the famous use of hyperbole in the coda position of the speech in which his own evaluation of a social group (airmen) is attributed to mankind in general.

By identifying himself with all mankind and by appointing himself as an arbiter of morality, Churchill communicates the central idea that the British were a heroic people fighting for the cause of Christian civilisation; metaphor is therefore essential for expressing the legitimacy of their cause.

16.8 Summary

In this chapter I have argued that metaphor was vital in Churchill's speeches for the creation of a narrative I have described as a heroic myth in which Britain and her Allies are constructed as forces of goodness while Germany was constructed as a force of evil.

Although used along with other linguistic characteristics that contributed to sounding right such as repetition, reiteration, hyperbole and the coming of patterns based on English phraseology, metaphor was crucial to the formation of this heroic myth. Personification based on the conceptual metaphor THE NATION IS A PERSON was used to create a narrative in which Britain was a warrior, Germany a villain or a monster and France an innocent victim.

As I have illustrated, Churchill's systematic use of journey metaphors aimed to raise morale by giving a sense of purpose to the war effort but also had the political argument of engaging the Americans as fellow travelling companions. Light and dark metaphors were employed to offer evaluations of the combatants and sounded right by invoking cultural knowledge such as the metaphoric associations of light and dark in the Bible. I have also described his most contrived use of metaphor as nested metaphors where a number of different source domains interact to create myth. As Cassirer (1946: 280) summarises:

> In all critical moments of man's social life, the rational forces that resist the rise of old mythical conceptions are no longer sure of themselves. In these moments the time for myth has come again. For myth has not been really vanquished and subjugated. It is always there,

lurking in the dark and waiting for its hour and opportunity. This hour comes as soon as the other binding forces of man's social life, for one reason or another, lose their strength and are no longer able to combat the demonic mythical powers.

Churchill's mythic use of metaphor was precisely devised to combat the mythical powers that Hitler's oratory had revived in Germany and came at a time when the social forces binding the political structures of Europe were disintegrating. While Hitler's metaphors were directed to specific political arguments, as well as sounding right, Churchill's were chosen on the basis primarily of sounding right and on having the right intentions – he represented his struggle as being on behalf of civilization and mankind in general rather than part of it. The ideological struggle was therefore fundamentally also one of political communication in which metaphor was a weapon in the drawing of battle-lines, as competing narratives drew on competing metaphor systems for unifying and motivating participants. Churchill's creative use of metaphor extended the rhetorical methods developed in classical times, and which he knew about as a historian, to the purpose of persuasive wartime leadership.

Notes

1 Speech opening Churchill exhibition at the Library of Congress.
2 See Lakoff (1991) and Rohrer (1995) for a discussion of this metaphor in relation to the 1990 Gulf crisis.
3 Journey metaphors are also discussed in detail in sections 4.42 and 12.3.4.
4 Tony Blair used a similar journey metaphor to reject the idea of retreating from his chosen path when he claimed 'I can only go one way. I have not got a reverse gear' in his Labour Party conference speech of September 2003.
5 The same metaphor was subsequently used by Tony Blair in a speech intended to demonstrate British support for the USA following the September 11 attacks on the World Trade Center and the Pentagon.
6 The idea of one metaphor nesting within another is developed in section 3.7.
7 The 'Iron Curtain' metaphor is also discussed in relation to conventional metaphor in section 2.1.3.
8 For example, Brewer's defines a mixed metaphor as 'a figure of speech in which two or more inconsistent metaphors are combined' (Kirkpatrick 1992).

Bibliography

Cassirer, E. (1946) *The Myth of the State* (New Haven and London: Yale University Press).
Charteris-Black, J. (2004) *Corpus Approaches to Critical Metaphor Analysis* (Basingstoke: Palgrave Macmillan).
Chilton, P. (2004) *Analysing Political Discourse* (London and New York: Routledge).
James, R.R. (1973) *Churchill: a Study in Failure 1900–1939* (Harmondsworth: Penguin).
Kirkpatrick, B. (ed.) (1992) *Brewer's Concise Dictionary of Phrase and Fable* (London: Cassell).
Lakoff, G. (1991) 'The Metaphor System Used to Justify War in the Gulf', *Journal of Urban and Cultural Studies*, 2(1), 59–72.
Lakoff, G. (1993) 'The Contemporary Theory of Metaphor', in A. Ortony (ed.) *Metaphor and Thought*, 2nd edn (Cambridge: CUP), pp. 202–51.

Lakoff, G. and Johnson, M. (1980) *Metaphors We Live By* (Chicago: University of Chicago Press).
Lakoff, G. and Turner, M. (1989) *More than Cool Reason: a Field Guide to Poetic Metaphor* Chicago (London: University of Chicago Press).
Rohrer, T. (1995) 'The Metaphorical Logic of (Political) Rape: the New Wor(l)d Order', *Metaphor and Symbolic Activity,* 10(2), 115–37.
Taylor, A.J.P. (1969) *Churchill: Four Faces and the Man* (London: Allen Lane).

17.
PARADIASTOLE: REDESCRIBING THE VICES AS VIRTUES
Quentin Skinner

The earliest English rhetorical handbooks in which the figure of paradiastole is named and defined are Henry Peacham's *Garden of Eloquence* (1577) and George Puttenham's *Arte of English Poesie* (1589).[1] Peacham places paradiastole in the third order of the rhetorical schemates,[2] and thus among the figures of amplification used to 'garnish matters and causes'.[3] He turns to consider it immediately after discussing meiosis, to which it is said to be 'nye kin', and defines it as follows: '*Paradiastole* . . . is when by a mannerly interpretation, we doe excuse our own vices, or other mens whom we doe defend, by calling them vermes.' 'This figure is used', he summarises, 'when vices are excused.'[4]

Puttenham pursues the comparison between meiosis and paradiastole at greater length. If, he argues, 'you diminish and abbase a thing by way of spight or mallice, as it were to deprave it', this is an instance of meiosis. The contrast with paradiastole is said to be as follows: 'But if such moderation of words tend to flattery, or soothing, or excusing, it is by the figure *Paradiastole*, which therfore nothing improperly we call the *Curry-favell,* as when we make the best of a bad thing, or turne a signification to the more plausible sence . . . moderating and abating the force of the matter by craft, and for a pleasing purpose.'[5] Puttenham later reiterates that, whereas the figure of meiosis – which he labels 'the Disabler'[6] – has the effect of denigrating what is described, the figure of paradiastole or Curry-favell is used to exculpate.[7]

Both Peacham and Puttenham are self-conscious about the need to rework the conventions of classical rhetoric for a Tudor audience, an aspiration most clearly reflected in Puttenham's efforts to domesticate the outlandish names for the figures and tropes inherited by the Roman rhetoricians from their Greek authorities. But at the same time they remain heavily dependent on the body of ancient treatises in which the full range of the figures and tropes had already been anatomised and discussed. Within this ancient literature, the earliest work in which the figure of paradiastole had been defined and illustrated under that name was the *De figuris sententiarum et elocutionis* attributed to P. Rutilius Lupus and dated to *c.* 20 AD. Rutilius's handbook was printed in Venice as early as 1519, and subsequently republished in the Aldine collection of

---

Skinner, Quentin. "Paradiastole: Redescribing the Vices as Virtues," In: Sylvia Adamson, Gavin Alexander, and Katrin Ettenhuber (eds.), *Renaissance Figures of Speech*. Cambridge: Cambridge University Press, 2007: 149–166.

rhetorical texts edited by George of Trebizond in 1523, as well as in several editions later in the century.[8] The full entry on paradiastole reads as follows:

> This *schema* distinguishes between two or more things that seem to have the same force, and teaches us how far they are distinct from each other by assigning the right meaning to each of them. Hyperides: For when you attempt to deceive the opinion of others, you frustrate yourself. You are not able to show that you should be understood as wise rather than crafty, or courageous rather than reckless, or careful in family matters rather than niggardly, or severe rather than ill-willed. There is no vice in which you are able to glory by praising it as a virtue. The same *schema* can readily be used yet more impressively when a reason is added to the judgment. This can be done in the following way: Hence do not so often call yourself frugal when you are avaricious. For someone who is frugal makes use of what is sufficient; you on the contrary because of your avarice, want more than you have. So what will follow will not be the fruits of thrift but rather the miseries of destitution.[9]

Although this is the earliest discussion of paradiastole to have survived, the quotation from Hyperides (an Attic orator of the fourth century BC) indicates that, as we shall later see, the figure was already well-known at a much earlier date.

Rutilius may also have been indebted to the popular handbook generally known as the *Rhetorica ad Herennium*. This had been produced by a contemporary of Cicero's, and until the ascription was disproved by Raphael Regius in the 1490s it was frequently attributed to Cicero himself.[10] The *Ad Herennium* never uses the term paradiastole, but in the course of Book III we are treated to some hyperbolical advice about how to employ the technique in a court of law. Sometimes, we are told, it may even be possible to redescribe the cardinal virtues as instances of vice: 'What the person speaking against us calls justice we shall demonstrate to be cowardice, and a lazy and corrupt form of liberality; what he names prudence we shall say is inept, indiscreet and offensive cleverness; what he speaks of as temperance we shall speak of as lazy and dissolute negligence; what he names courage we shall call the heedless temerity of a gladiator.'[11] Like Rutilius, the author of the *Ad Herennium* is interested in rhetorical redescription as a means of challenging and undermining those who claim to be acting virtuously.

Rutilius's analysis was subsequently taken up, in an abbreviated form, in the most influential of all the surveys of the figures and tropes, that of Quintilian in his *Institutio oratoria* of c. 90 AD. At the same time, however, Quintilian modifies Rutilius's account in one fundamental respect. Rutilius had treated paradiastole as the name of the figure we employ when we seek to unmask someone for deceitfully laying claim to a virtue, and attempt to show that they deserve to be condemned. The ultimate aim is to denigrate our rivals and adversaries. Quintilian, by contrast, thinks of paradiastole as the figure in play when we seek to defend someone against an accusation of vice, and attempt to show that they deserve to be praised. The ultimate aim is to excuse, and normally to excuse ourselves.

Quintilian's revision, or perhaps misunderstanding, of Rutilius's argument becomes clear as soon as he turns to his examples. For Rutilius, it is an instance of paradiastole when we criticise someone for trying to claim that he is wise when he is merely crafty, or courageous when he is merely reckless, and so on. But for Quintilian, the figure is in use 'whenever you call *yourself* wise rather than crafty, or courageous rather than reckless, or careful rather than niggardly' ['Cum te pro astuto sapientem appelles, pro confidente fortem, pro illiberali diligentem'].[12] Although Quintilian takes over Rutilius's illustrations, he reverses their direction in every case.

When the *ars rhetorica* was revived in the Renaissance, it was Quintilian's view of paradiastole that largely prevailed. The earliest Renaissance text in which the figure is defined and illustrated is Antonio Mancinelli's *Carmen de Figuris,* which was printed in Venice as early as 1493 and frequently republished.[13] As he admits, Mancinelli is wholly reliant on Quintilian,[14] and simply quotes him to the effect that 'it is an instance of *paradiastole* when you call yourself wise rather than crafty, or courageous rather than reckless'.[15] His analysis served in turn as a major source for Johann Susenbrotus in his *Epitome Troporum ac Schematum,* perhaps the most widely used treatise on *elocutio* of the later sixteenth century. First printed in Germany, it was republished in London as early as 1562 and went through at least four editions in the next generation.[16] Susenbrotus summarises by noting that 'according to Mancinelli, it is said to be *paradiastole* when, instead of crafty, we say wise'.[17] His own list of examples begins by repeating Quintilian word-for-word: 'when you call yourself wise rather than crafty, or courageous rather than reckless, or careful rather than niggardly'.[18] It was largely through the conduit of Mancinelli's and Susenbrotus's treatises that Quintilian's analysis passed into the writings of the English rhetoricians of the sixteenth century, to whom we next need to turn.

The distinction of being the first to comment on rhetorical redescription falls to Thomas Wilson, whose neo-Ciceronian *Arte of Rhetorique* was first published in 1554.[19] Wilson never uses the term paradiastole, but in anatomising 'the firste kinde of Amplification', which is said to occur 'when by changing a woorde, in augmentynge we use a greater, but in diminishynge we use a lesse', he notes that this is the device we use whenever 'we give vices, the names of vertue'.[20] As we have already seen, the earliest English handbooks in which this technique is named as paradiastole are those of Peacham and Puttenham, after which the term passed into general currency. When, for example, Peacham reissued his *Garden of Eloquence* in an extended version in 1593, he defined paradiastole as a fit instrument of excuse' by means of which the vices are disguised as virtues.[21] Angel Day writes in similar terms in his *Declaration* of 1592, listing paradiastole among the 'schemes syntaxical' and explaining that this is the figure we deploy whenever 'with a milde interpretation' we palliate our own or other people's faults.[22]

The principal way in which the Tudor rhetoricians reveal their dependence on the Roman tradition lies in their choice of examples. As we have seen, the first illustration used by Rutilius and Quintilian had been that of trying to characterise yourself not as crafty (*astutus*) but rather as wise (*sapiens*), Mancinelli and Susenbrotus repeat the example, and Peacham likewise declares it an instance of paradiastole 'when we call him that is craftye, wyse', or when we justify 'deepe dissimulation' as 'singuler wisdome'.[23] Day slightly varies the vocabulary, speaking of calling 'a subtill person, wise',[24] but Peacham in the revised version of his text reverts to the standard formula, referring to those who defend 'craft and deceit' by redescribing it as 'wisdome and pollicie'.[25]

By similar lines of descent other examples suggested by Rutilius reappear as standard paradiastolic pairings in Renaissance handbooks: careful/niggardly, frugal/

avaricious, stern/spiteful, just/cruel. Rutilius's final example is the most familiar of all, and subsequently resurfaces in almost every Renaissance rhetorical text: that of a man who praises himself as *fortis* or courageous when he is in fact *confidens* or *temerarius,* a man of recklessness. Quintilian appropriates it, as do Mancinelli and Susenbrotus, and here again the Tudor rhetoricians follow suit. Peacham even suggests that one might justify a murder by calling it a manly deed,[26] while Puttenham writes of excusing 'the foolish-hardy' as 'valiant or couragious', and Day similarly notes that one can call 'a bold fellow, couragious' and 'a man furious or rash, valiant'.[27]

This last case is of particular significance. By contrast with the others I have examined, all of which appear for the first time in Roman sources, this example can already be found in a number of ancient Greek texts. Among these, undoubtedly the most influential was Aristotle's *Art of Rhetoric.* Aristotle's treatise became widely known after it was translated into Latin in the latter part of the fifteenth century, and by the end of the sixteenth century there were four separate Latin versions in print: those of George of Trebizond (1523), Ermolao Barbaro (1544), Carolo Sigonio (1565), and Antonio Maioragio (1591).[28] George of Trebizond introduces Aristotle's discussion by making him say that, if we aspire to speak persuasively, we must ensure that, 'when it comes to praise and blame, those things which are close to being morally worthy are accepted as having the quality itself' ['Ea quoque accipienda sunt, quae honestis propinqua sunt, tanquam ad laudem, vel vituperationem conferentia'].[29] One of his illustrations is that of trying to claim that someone who is merely *ferox* or savage is actually *fortis* or brave. This choice of terminology was closely followed by other sixteenth-century translators of Aristotle's text, which no doubt helps to explain why the example came to be one of the most frequently cited instances of paradiastole.[30]

Behind Aristotle's discussion, however, lies the celebrated analysis in Book III of Thucydides' *History* of how evaluative terms begin to be misapplied when communities fall into civil war. Thomas Nicolls published an English translation of Thucydides as early as 1550, in which Thucydides is made to say that, as soon as sedition and conflict broke out in the cities of Greece, 'all the evylles whiche they committed, they disguised and named by newe and unaccustomed names'. His first illustration is that 'temeritie and rashnes, they named magnanymytie and noblenes of courage, so that the rashe were named vertuous defenders of theyr frendes'.[31] Soon after the appearance of Nicolls s version, Thucydides' discussion caught the attention of Justus Lipsius, writing his *Politicorum libri sex* in Leiden in the 1580s at the height of the Dutch religious wars. When William Jones translated Lipsius's text into English in 1594, he rendered the passage by saying that, in the predicament described by Thucydides, 'whatsoever is rash and headie, that is deemed by them to be couragiously and valiauntly enterprised'.[32]

The excusing of rashness as courage may thus be said to constitute an unambiguous case in which an ancient Greek example of rhetorical redescription was taken up into Roman rhetorical theory and eventually came to be classified as an instance of paradiastole. It is striking, however, that there is no other case in the extant sources of such a transmission taking place. The Greek discussion appears to have remained a largely distinct strand of thought, illustrated with a distinct range of examples. It was only in the course of the sixteenth century that a number of rhetoricians began to enrich the discussion of rhetorical redescription (now universally known as paradiastole) by drawing examples eclectically from ancient Greek sources as well as from the Roman handbooks on which I have so far concentrated.

As I have intimated, the main conduit through which these additional examples flowed was undoubtedly Aristotle's *Art of Rhetoric*. But we also need to consider the remarkable discussion of rhetorical redescription in Book VIII of Plato's *Republic*, a discussion to which Aristotle's observations owe an obvious debt. Plato's analysis does not appear to have been known to the rhetorical theorists of the early Renaissance, but this situation was transformed after the appearance of Marsilio Ficino's *Platonis Opera*, his Latin version of the principal dialogues. Ficino's translation was printed in Venice in 1517, and repeated republications throughout the sixteenth century finally brought Plato's *oeuvre* to the attention of a wider audience.[33]

Plato examines the phenomenon of rhetorical redescription in the course of reflecting on how the soul adjusts itself from an oligarchic to a democratic form of life. One sign of this psychological decline is that many forms of behaviour previously recognised as corrupt begin to be exonerated. For instance, pride and insolence are redescribed as nobility and greatness. As Ficino's translation phrases it, 'they speak of insolence as the behaviour of those who have been nobly brought up'.[34] Aristotle repeats the example in his *Art of Rhetoric*, in which he argues – in the vocabulary developed by his sixteenth-century translators – that an arrogant, proud, or contumacious person can always hope to represent himself as magnificent, honourable, splendid, and great. Among Renaissance rhetoricians, Susenbrotus is the first to pick up the example, which he duly classifies as an instance of paradiastole and describes by saying that a man who is haughty or *fastidiosus* can always hope to claim that he is really noble or *magnanimous*.[36] His way of formulating the distinction was thereafter widely adopted. Angel Day, for example, notes in his *Declaration* of 1592 that it is a standard case of paradiastole to say of 'him that is proud' that he is really a man of magnanimity.[37] According to Plato, other consequences of the corruption of the soul under democracy are that prodigality comes to be redescribed as magnificence and unbridled behaviour as an expression of liberty, and that brazen and shameless persons begin to be praised for their courage and strength.[38] Aristotle omits this last example, but several Tudor rhetoricians nevertheless treat it as a standard case of paradiastole.[39]

One further contrast between the Greek and Roman discussions of rhetorical redescription needs to be emphasised. According to the understanding that eventually came to predominate in Roman thought, the point of using the technique is always to exonerate and excuse. Among the Greek writers, however, it is always assumed that the same device can equally well be employed to question and denigrate the virtues. It is true that Rutilius had adopted something like this perspective in treating paradiastole as a means of unmasking hypocrisies. Like the author of the *Ad Herennium*, however, Rutilius is chiefly interested in the complex possibility of criticising rivals and adversaries by countering and undermining their efforts to commend themselves. By contrast, the Greek writers focus on the simpler strategy of casting doubt on forms of behaviour normally regarded as unquestionably worthy of praise. One instance offered by Thucydides is that of impugning 'prudent consultation and deliberating in causes' as an expression of 'sensed and cloked deceate'.[40] A second possibility mentioned by Thucydides – and repeated by Plato – is that of ridiculing modesty of demeanour as nothing more than 'covered pusillanimytie or cowardenes'.[41] To which Thucydides adds – and Aristotle repeats – that 'an honest fear' can similarly be dismissed as mere slackness and faintness.[42]

One might finally ask what the Tudor rhetoricians managed to add to these earlier accounts. The answer is that they contribute almost nothing of their own at all. Wilson proposes one new example, which Peacham repeats: that of excusing gluttony and drunkenness as good fellowship.[43] Peacham adds two more, both of which gesture at his puritan sympathies: one is excusing idolatry as 'pure religion', the other excusing pride as 'cleanlynesse'.[44] Apart from this, however, the Tudor rhetoricians are little more than mouthpieces – in the case of this figure at least – of their ancient authorities.

Although the writers I have been examining undoubtedly isolate a distinct rhetorical technique, it remains to show how it could ever be practised with success. The numerous treatises on the good life circulating in early Tudor England all point to the obvious difficulty: that the virtues and vices appear to be names of diametrically opposed qualities. As John Larke, for example, puts it in his *Boke of Wysdome* of 1532, moral conflict is always between 'contraries':[45] between prudence and folly, chastity and lechery, liberality and covetousness, and even more antithetically between temperance and intemperance, constancy and inconstancy, justice and injustice.[46] But if the virtues and vices are such clearly opposed principles, how can we ever hope to redescribe the one as the other without being instantly accused of playing an obvious rhetorical trick?

By way of answer, the rhetoricians of the next generation appealed to one of the governing assumptions of Aristotelian moral philosophy: that every virtue consists in a mean between two opposed vices. Among the moral treatises of the early Elizabethan period, Sir Thomas Hoby's translation of Castiglione's *Cortegiano* furnished perhaps the most influential discussion of the claim. As Lord Octavian explains in Book IV, virtue is always 'placed in the middle between two extreme vyces, the one for the overmuch, and the other for the overlitle'.[47] Soon afterwards Cornelius Valerius, whose treatise on the virtues appeared as *The Casket of Jewels* in 1571, went on to add an explicit reference to the source of the argument. Agreeing that 'vertue is a meane in middes degree', he informs us that this insight is owed to Aristotle, by whom virtue is defined as 'a custome of the minde enterprised through reason situated in mediocritie'.[48]

If virtue is a mean, it follows that many of the vices, far from being 'contraries' of the virtues, will be likely to appear disconcertingly close to them. Castiglione draws the inference by invoking an image of neighbourliness. For every vice, he argues, there will always be a 'nexte vertue' and for every virtue a 'nexte vice'.[49] To which Valerius adds, still more troublingly, that in some cases the virtues and vices may turn out to be members of the same family. A number of vices, as he expresses it, are 'cousin germain to Vertue'.[50]

Castiglione and Valerius both acknowledge that, once this implication is recognised, it is easy to see how the vices can often be redescribed as virtues. As Aristotle had originally noted in the *Art of Rhetoric,* it will only be necessary to claim that (in the words of Sigonio's translation) 'those qualities which are in the neighbourhood of those actually present have an identical force'.[51] Both Castiglione and Valerius explicitly refer to the figure of paradiastole by way of making the point. As the Count observes in Book I of the *Cortegiano*, the neighbourly relationship between virtue and vice is such that we can always call 'him that is saucye, bolde: hym that is sober, drie: hym that is seelye, good: hym that is unhappye, wittie: and lykewyse in the reste'.[52] Valerius draws the same conclusion in still more anxious tones. He accepts that the distinction between virtue and vice can sometimes be 'apertly perceived'; we can readily see the difference, for example, 'when ignorance is set against wisdom, wrong against Justice, cowardnesse agaynst Fortitude'.[53] But there are other cases in which the vice 'is not so easely espied, as when craftinesse or subtiltie is gaiged agaynst wisedome, cruelty against Justice, lewdhardinesse agaynst manlinesse'.[54]

The power of paradiastole to disorder the vices and virtues is encapsulated by the rhetoricians in two favourite metaphors. One speaks of clothing and disguising the vices to lend them an outward appearance of good qualities. The Count in the *Cortegiano* observes that we can always hope to 'cover' a vice 'with the name of the nexte vertue' and to 'cover' a virtue 'with the name of the nexte vice'.[55] Henry Peacham in *The Garden of Eloquence* turns the image into the very definition of paradiastole, which he describes as the figure we use 'to cover vices with the mantles of verities'.[56]

The other metaphor speaks of colouring the vices in such a way as to make them appear 'colourable' or excusable. Sometimes this image is more broadly applied to characterise the figures of speech as a whole. Angel Day, for example, says of the figures at the start of his *Declaration* that they comprise 'the ornament, light and colours of Rhetorical speech'.[57] But the same metaphor is also used to refer more specifically to the power of paradiastole to make the vices seem more acceptable. Day defines paradiastole as the figure we employ 'when with a milde interpretation or speech, wee color others or our owne faultes'.[58]

It remains to consider what attitude the rhetoricians adopt towards the figure of paradiastole and its power to colour the vices. Classical writers on the *ars rhetorica* had always taken pride in the ability of powerful orators to make us change our minds about the right way of 'seeing' particular actions and events. Cicero had even put into the mouth of Crassus in the *De oratore* the view that this may be the highest rhetorical skill of all. There will always be two sides to any question, and the aim of the orator should be to show that a plausible argument can always be constructed *in utramque partem*, on either side of the case. 'We ought', as Crassus expresses it, 'to have enough intelligence, power and art to speak *in utramque partem* on all the leading issues in the moral sciences: 'on virtue, on duty, on equity and goodness, on dignity, benefit, honour, ignominy, reward, punishment and all similar things.'[59]

If one of the aims of eloquence is to make us examine the same question from different perspectives, then a skilful use of paradiastole will obviously be a valuable art to cultivate. Once the *ars rhetorica* was incorporated into Christian culture, however, this possibility came to be viewed with much greater nervousness, even by the rhetoricians themselves. They are anxious to insist that the question as to whether any given action ought properly to be described as virtuous can always be settled with finality. As they are obliged to recognise, however, this is precisely the kind of certainty that the figure of paradiastole tends to undermine. Susenbrotus concludes that this is one of the moments at which the art of rhetoric may be said to overreach itself: '*Paradiastole* is used whenever, by means of an excessively polite interpretation, we speak ingratiatingly so as to express approval of our own vices or those of others, as the wrong-headed reprobates of our own time are accustomed to do, who scratch each other's backs in exactly this way, as the proverb has it.'[60] Thomas Wilson[61] and especially Henry Peacham strongly endorse Susenbrotus's doubts. Although Peacham offers a neutral analysis of paradiastole in the 1577 edition of his *Garden of Eloquence,* his expanded edition of 1593 violently denounces the figure as a 'vice of speech'.[62] We are left confronting an ironic spectacle: that of the rhetoricians condemning the art of rhetoric for possessing the very power they generally liked to celebrate.

To those, however, with a professional interest in demonstrating that it is always possible to argue *in utramque partem,* the lure of paradiastole proved irresistible. So it is hardly surprising to find that, in the years immediately following the publication of the rhetorical handbooks I have been examining, there was a growing awareness of its literary as well as its forensic possibilities. John Lyly employs the figure in several of his orations in *Euphues,* and even alludes to Nicolls's translation of Thucydides when lamenting that the modest and shamefast are nowadays likely to be reviled for cowardice.[63] Marlowe was aware of this example, which he puts to dramatic use in Part II of *Tamburlaine,* in which the tyrant kills his own son for excusing his refusal to fight as 'manly wise' when Tamburlaine regards it as cowardly.[64] Shakespeare likewise displays an interest in such redescriptions from an early stage, and it is especially striking to find him making use of both the metaphors favoured by the rhetoricians to explain how it is possible for vices to be excused.

As we have seen, one of these metaphors had spoken of 'colouring' the vices to make them look like virtues. These are precisely the terms in which the politic Cardinal Beaufort responds to Queen Margaret in *2 Henry VI* when she proposes that Gloucester be summarily killed:

> That he should die is worthy policy;
> But yet we want a colour for his death.
> 'Tis meet he be condemned by course of law.[65]

It is ironic that Richard Gloucester should later complain – as he does when Catesby presents him with the head of the murdered Hastings – that he himself has been deceived by this very rhetorical trick:

> I took him for the plainest harmless creature
> That breathed upon the earth, a Christian,
> Made him my book wherein my soul recorded
> The history of all her secret thoughts.
> So smooth he daubed his vice with show of virtue.
>   (*Richard III*, 3.5.24–8)

As the use of 'daubed' implies, the colouring may not even have to be very skilful to be rhetorically effective.

Shakespeare also likes to invoke the image of 'covering' the vices to make them more pleasing to the eye. There are several instances in the early plays,[66] but the most elaborate occurs in *The Merchant of Venice* at the moment when Bassanio is trying to choose between the three caskets. Turning to the golden one, he sets it aside with these words:

So may the outward shows be least themselves.
The world is still deceived with ornament.
In law, what plea so tainted and corrupt
But, being seasoned with a gracious voice,
Obscures the show of evil? In religion,
What damned error but some sober brow
Will bless it and approve it with a text,
Hiding the grossness with fair ornament?
There is no vice so simple but assumes
Some mark of virtue on his outward parts.
(3.2.73–81)

When speaking of the verbal ornaments that deceive, Bassanio is partly referring in a general way to the *ornamenta*, the figures and tropes of speech. But when he speaks of hiding grossness with fair ornament, he appears to be referring more specifically to the power of paradiastole to 'cover' the vices by giving them an outward appearance of goodness.

Of far greater importance is the fact that Shakespeare is deeply interested in the dramatic exploration of paradiastole as (in Peacham's phrase) an instrument of excuse.[67] As we have seen, an instance of the technique given by Castiglione had been that of calling 'him that is saucye, bolde'. With this in mind, it is worth reconsidering the scene from *The Second Part of Henry the Fourth* in which Mistress Quickly informs the Lord Chief Justice that Falstaff has broken his promise to marry her, The Chief Justice rounds on Falstaff in tones remarkably reminiscent of Castiglione's Count, reproving him for his 'confident brow' and 'impudent sauciness' (2.1.113–15). But Falstaff responds by quoting Castiglione back at him: what you call 'impudent sauciness', he retorts, is really 'honourable boldness'.[68] It is part of the comedy, however, that Falstaff avails himself with such effrontery of one of the stock examples of paradiastole, and the Chief Justice knows too much about *the* art of rhetoric to let him to get away with it. He even appears to know about the specific objection that Henry Peacham had raised against the use of paradiastole: that it 'opposeth the truth by false tearmes'.[69] As the Chief Justice likewise objects, Falstaff is simply 'wrenching the true cause the false way' (112–13). He is instantly exposed for trying to play a well-known rhetorical trick.

A further stock example of paradiastole had been that of seeking to commend oneself for 'good husbandry', for being careful and thrifty, when one is in fact avaricious and covetous. This being so, it is similarly worth reconsidering the scene at the beginning of *The Merchant of Venice* in which Antonio and Bassanio meet Shylock to seal their bargain. As soon as he enters, Shylock declares his hatred of Antonio for lending out money gratis, for attacking his own taking of interest, and for accusing him, he later adds, of cut-throat practices (1.3.42, 49, 110). Reacting to Antonio's rebukes, Shylock offers precisely the account of himself that the rhetoricians had recommended. First he redescribes his alleged avarice as thrift:

> He hates our sacred nation, and he rails,
> Even there where merchants most do congregate,
> On me, my bargains, and my well-won thrift
> Which he calls interest.
> (46–9)

Next he tells the story of Jacob's good husbandry in grazing his uncle Laban's sheep. Jacob was promised all the lambs that were born parti-coloured, and found a way to increase their number:

> The skilful shepherd peeled me certain wands,
> And in the doing of the deed of kind
> He stuck them up before the fulsome ewes
> Who, then conceiving, did in eaning time
> Fall parti-coloured lambs; and those were Jacob's.
> This was a way to thrive; and he was blest;
> And thrift is blessing, if men steal it not.
> (83–9)

Shylock not only excuses his conduct; he redescribes it as positively virtuous: he has found a way to thrive without stealing, a form of increase sanctified by the Bible itself.

Shylock's use of paradiastole may at first sight seem a world away from Falstaff's effronteries. He not only pleads his case in passionate verse, but his sincerity is much harder to doubt. As in the case of Falstaff, however, he is playing a familiar rhetorical trick, and as before the trick is immediately exposed. Susenbrotus had warned that 'we have an example of *paradiastole* when vices show themselves under the guise of virtue, and by these means even the Devil himself can be transfigured into an Angel of light'.[70] Antonio reacts to Shylock's story of Jacobs good husbandry in remarkably similar terms:

> Mark you this, Bassanio?
> The devil can cite Scripture for his purpose.
> An evil soul producing holy witness
> Is like a villain with a smiling cheek,
> A goodly apple rotten at the heart.
> O, what a goodly outside falsehood hath!
> (96–101)

Antonio not only echoes Susenbrotus's view of paradiastole as a devilish force; his remark about giving falsehood a goodly outside alludes to one of the metaphors most frequently invoked by the rhetoricians to describe this specific figure of speech.

Modern readers of this scene are perhaps more likely to sympathise with Shylock than with his attackers. This makes it all the more important to recognise how unsympathetically the use of such redesenptions would have been viewed even by the rhetoricians themselves at the end of the sixteenth century. Seven years before the publication of *The Comical History of the Merchant of Venice* in 1600, Henry Peacham in his *Garden of Eloquence* had offered, as a standard case of paradiastole, the attempt to defend 'insatiable avarice' by calling it 'good husbandrie'.[71] But Peacham had immediately gone on to denounce such redescriptions as an 'instrument of excuse serving to selfe-love, partiall favour, blinde affection, and a shamelesse person',[72] For all his nobility of utterance, Shylock's self-justification is precisely the sort of thing to be expected, according to Peacham, from someone who is not merely shameless but whose basic purpose is 'the better maintenance of wickednesse'.[73]

Shakespeare's interest in paradiastole as a means of exculpation is not confined to these comedies of the late 1590s. To the same period belongs *Julius Caesar,* in which the tragic possibilities inherent in rhetorical redescription are profoundly explored. This aspect of the tragedy begins to unfold at the start of Act 2, when Brutus meditates on his intention to assassinate Caesar and then shares with the other conspirators his sense of how this action might be justified. In his soliloquy he reflects that Caesar 'would be crowned' and thus that, if Rome is to avoid this possible 'abuse of greatness', 'It must be by his death' (2.1.10, 12, 18). As he is obliged to admit, however, Caesar has not so far done anything to make him deserving of such a violent end (28–9). This in turn means that, as Brutus warns the conspirators later in the scene, they are liable to appear envious if they kill Caesar, and will be open to an accusation of sheer butchery (164,166,178),

If there is no possibility of justifying Caesar's assassination by considering – as Brutus puts it – 'the thing he is', how can it ever be justified? Brutus recognises that his own behaviour and that of his fellow conspirators will have to be rhetorically redescribed:

> Since the quarrel
> Will bear no colour for the thing he is,
> Fashion it thus.
>
> (28–30)

As he acknowledges—drawing on the distinctive vocabulary of the rhetoricians—he will need to 'fashion' his act, to give it an appealing rhetorical shape; more specifically, he will need to 'colour' it, to disguise and brighten it to yield a more attractive appearance.

How can this be done? Henry Peacham had suggested that murder can perhaps be excused by calling it a manly deed. As Brutus begins to converse with the conspirators, he appears for a moment to gesture at this possibility. One way, he suggests, to prevent the killing of Caesar from looking merely envious will be to 'kill him boldly, but not wrathfully' (172). Brutus's main suggestion, however, comes from a much more elevated source, the justification of Caesar's assassination to be found in Book III of

Cicero's *De officiis*. Cicero had appealed to the familiar image of the body politic and the importance of maintaining its health. To cite the earliest English translation, that of Robert Whytinton of 1534, tyrants are said to be 'poysonfull' and in need of being expelled from the body if it is to survive.[74] William Baldwin subsequently elaborated the image in his *Treatice of Morall Philosophy*, by far the most widely printed work on moral theory in later sixteenth-century England.[75] A good ruler, Baldwin declares, 'is lyke a common fountaine or springe'; if he becomes impure and poisonous, the people will be left without remedy 'untill the fountaine be purged'.[76]

This image of purgation is exactly the one that Brutus adopts to justify his killing of Caesar. In his soliloquy he compares Caesar with a serpent's egg, a source of venom that needs to be crushed in the shell if the body of Rome is to avoid being poisoned (14, 16, 32–4). In his speech to the conspirators he places the same image at the heart of the rhetorical redescription on which he finally takes his stand:

> This shall make
> Our purpose necessary, and not envious;
> Which so appearing to the common eyes,
> We shall be called purgers, not murderers.
> (177–80)

Purgers, not murderers. So convinced is Brutus by his redescription that he not only commends it to his fellow conspirators but predicts that it will be accepted without question by the people at large.

By contrast with Falstaff and even Shylock, Brutus's use of paradiastole owes nothing to the rhetoricians and their stock examples. He takes his redescription from one of the most widely respected works of moral philosophy of his own as well as Shakespeare's age. Nor is Brutus instantly challenged, as happens to Falstaff and Shylock alike. The conspirators silently accept his justification, and after the assassination it is shown to have exactly the power that Brutus had promised of making their action seem acceptable. Addressing the plebeians, Brutus explains that Caesar was ambitious, and that this is why he slew him (3.2.26–7). He does not repeat his earlier reference to purging the body politic of poison, but this is precisely how the plebeians spontaneously construct his act. 'This Caesar was a tyrant' declares the First Plebeian; to which the Third Plebeian adds 'We are blessed that Rome is rid of him' (70–1). They agree that the conspirators have rid the city of something noxious: they are purgers, not murderers.

Brutus's victory, however, is a rhetorical one, open to the danger that an orator adept at arguing *in utramque partem* may be capable of questioning and undermining his version of events. This is what Cassius dreads (3.1.234–7), and this is what Antony achieves with his intensely rhetorical response to Brutus's prose address to the people. Antony persuades them that Caesar was *not* ambitious: that Ambition should be made of sterner stuff (3.2.93). He is consequently able to insist that the conspirators *were* merely envious: 'See', he shows the people, 'what a rent the envious Casca made' (173). By this stage they have already repudiated Brutus s justification for his act. As soon as Antony refers to 'the honourable men | Whose daggers have stabbed Caesar' (152–3), the Fourth Plebeian suddenly shouts: 'They were villains, murderers' (156). Murderers, not purgers. Brutus's redescription is fatally inverted, and the next we hear of him is that he and Cassius 'Are rid like madmen through the gates of Rome' (262). We are left with a final, ironic play on the idea of purgation: they have rid through the gates, and Rome is rid of them.

Unlike Falstaff, or even Shylock, Brutus cannot simply be dismissed for attempting, in Peacham's phrase, to oppose the truth by false terms. But nor is he able to provide an unassailable justification of his act. Was he a purger or merely a murderer? It is part of his tragedy, we are made to realise, that this is a question without an answer: it will always be possible to argue in *utramque partem,* on either side of the case. Such is the power of rhetoric; more specifically, such is the power of paradiastole.

Notes

1. There is also a definition (but an unilluminating one) in Richard Sherry, *A Treatise of the Figures of Grammer and Rhetorike* (1555), fol. 39V. For recent discussions of paradiastole see Frank Whigham, *Ambition and Privilege: The Social Tropes of Elizabethan Courtesy Theory* (Berkeley: University of California Press, 1984), pp. 40–2, 204–5; Virginia Cox, 'Rhetoric and politics in Tasso's *Nifo*', *Studi Secenteschi* 30 (1989), 3–98 (53–5); Quentin Skinner, 'Thomas Hobbes: Rhetoric and the Construction of Morality', *Proceedings of the British Academy 76* (1991), 1–61 (esp. 4–40) and 'Moral Ambiguity and the Renaissance Art of Eloquence', *Essays in Criticism* 44 (1994), 267–92; Conal Condren, *The Language of Politics in Seventeenth-Century England* (Basingstoke: Macmillan, 1994), pp. 78–84; Quentin Skinner, *Reason and Rhetoric in the Philosophy of Hobbes* (Cambridge: Cambridge University Press, 1996), pp. 142–80; Richard Tuck, 'Hobbes's Moral Philosophy', in Tom Sorell (ed.), *The Cambridge Companion to Hobbes* (Cambridge: Cambridge University Press, 1996), pp. 175–207 (pp. 195–9).
2. See Henry Peacham, *The Garden of Eloquence* (1577), sig. B1r for his classification of the figures, which are divided into Tropes and Schemates, with the latter subdivided into grammatical and rhetorical schemes.
3. *Ibid.,* sig. N2r.
4. *Ibid.,* sig. N4V.
5. George Puttenham, *The Arte of English Poesie,* ed. Gladys Doidge Willcock and Alice Walker (Cambridge: Cambridge University Press, 1970), pp. 184–5.
6. *Ibid.,* p. 185, marginal gloss.
7. *Ibid.,* p. 220. 'To curry favell' [lit. = 'to groom the chestnut horse'] is the original of the modern idiom 'to curry favour', which developed from it, by folk etymology, during the 16th century. Puttenham's readers would have been familiar with its use in the proverb linking flattery with success at Court: 'He that wylle in courte abyde Must cory favell back and syde.' (For this and other versions, see M. P. Tilley, *Dictionary of the Proverbs in England in the Sixteenth and Seventeenth Centuries* (Ann Arbor: University of Michigan Press, 1950), p. 724.)
8. The Bibliothèque Nationale records editions in 1530 (Paris), 1540 (Lyon), and 1541 (Paris).
9. Publius Rutilius Lupus, *De figuris sententiarum etelocutionis,* ed. Edward Brooks (Leiden: Brill, 1970), p. 8.
10. For the debate over the authorship see Skinner, *Reason and Rhetoric,* pp. 32–3.
11. *Rhetorica ad Herennium,* 3.3.6.
12. Quintilian, *Institutio oratoria,* 9.3.65 (italics added).
13. The British Library records four editions published between 1493 and 1503.
14. Mancinelli explicitly states that he is writing 'teste Fabio libro nono', that is, according to the authority of Quintilian in Book ix of his *Institutio oratoria:* Antonio Mancinelli, *Carmen de figuris* (Venice, 1493), sig. H1r.

15. *Paradiastole* 'sit... quum te pro astuto sapientem appelles, pro confidente fortem' (*ibid.*). But in the same passage Mancinelli also contrasts being *fortis* with being *temerarius*.
16. The British Library lists London printings (all in Latin) in 1562, 1570, 1572, 1608, and 1621.
17. Johann Susenbrotus, *Epitome troporum ac schematum* (1562), p. 46: 'Mancin, Pro astuto sapiens sit Paradiastola dictus.'
18. *Ibid.*: 'cum pro astuto sapientem appelles: pro confidente, fortem: pro illiberali, diligentem'. Following Mancinelli, however, Susenbrotus also contrasts *fortis* with *temerarius*.
19. The title-page states that the work was published in January 1553, i.e. 1554 our style. On Wilson as rhetorician see Cathy Shrank, *Writing the Nation in Reformation England, 1530–1580* (Oxford: Clarendon Press, 2004), pp. 182–219.
20. Thomas Wilson, *The Arte of Rhetorique* (1554), fols. 66v, 67r.
21. Henry Peacham, *The Garden of Eloquence* (1593), p. 168.
22. Angel Day, *A Declaration of... Tropes, Figures or Schemes* (1592), p. 90.
23. Peacham, *The Garden of Eloquence* (1577), sig. N4V.
24. Day, *A Declaration of... Tropes, Figures or Schemes*, p. 90.
25. Peacham, *The Garden of Eloquence* (1593), p. 168.
26. Peacham, *The Garden of Eloquence* (1577), sig. N4V.
27. Puttenham, *The Arte of English Poesie*, p. 185; Day, *A Declaration of... Tropes, Figures or Schemes*, pp. 62–3.
28. Subsequent references will be by name of translator and to the following editions: *In Tres Rhetoricorum Aristotelis Libros* in *Rhetoricorum libri quinque*, trans. George of Trebizond (Venice, 1523), fols. 109–35; *De Arte Dicendi Libri III*, trans. Ermolao Barbaro (Paris, 1559); *De Arte Rhetorica Libri Tres*, trans. Carolo Sigonio (Bologna, 1565); and *De Arte Rhetorica Libri Tres*, trans. Antonio Maioragio (Venice, 1591).
29. George of Trebizond, fol. 114V.
30. See George of Trebizond, fol. 114V on *ferox/fortis*; cf. Barbaro, p. 32 on *temeritas/fortitudo*; Sigonio, p. 49 on *audax/fortis*; and Maioragio, fol. 70r, col. 1 on *temerarius/fortis*.
31. Thucydides, *The Hystory*, trans. Thomas Nicolls (1555), fol. 200r.
32. Justus Lipsius, *Sixe Bookes of Politickes or Civil Doctrine*, trans. William Jones (1594), p. 69.
33. There were later sixteenth-century printings in Basel, Frankfurt and Lyon as well as Venice.
34. Plato, *De republica vel de iusto* in *Platonis Opera*, trans. Marsilio Ficino (Venice, 1517), fol. 259V.
35. See George of Trebizond, fol. 114V on *arrogans/magnificus atque honestus*; Barbaro, p. 32 on *superbus/magnificus & splendidus*; Sigonio, p. 49 on *contumax/magnificus ac grandis*; and Maioragio, fol. 70r, col. 1 on *contumax/magnificus & gravis*.
36. Susenbrotus, *Epitome troporum ac schematum*, p. 46.
37. Day, *A Declaration of... Tropes, Figures or Schemes*, p. 63.
38. See Plato, *De republica*, trans. Ficino, fol, 259V on *prodigalitas/magnificentia, licentia/libertas,* and *impudentia/fortitudo*.
39. See Peacham, *The Garden of Eloquence* (1577), sig. N4V and Puttenham, *The Arte of English Poesie*, p. 185.
40. Thucydides, *The Hystory*, fol. 200r.
41. Thucydides, *The Hystory,* fol. 200r; cf, Plato, *De republica*, trans. Ficino, fol. 259V on *pudor/fatuitas*.
42. Thucydides, *The Hystory*, fol. 200r (Nicoll, however, reverses the direction of the example); for Aristotle cf. George of Trebizond, fol. 114V on *moderatus/timidus & insidiator*, and Barbaro, p. 32, Sigonio, p. 49, and Maioragio, fol. 70r, col, I on *cautus/insidiosus*.
43. The example already occurs in Sir Thomas Wyatt, 'Myne own John Poyntz', line 64, in R. A. Rebholz (ed.), *The Complete Poems* (Harmondsworth: Penguin, 1978): 'As dronkenes good fellowesnippe to call'. It became popular: William Fulbecke deplores the fact that nowadays 'a confederate in venereous practises' will be 'accounted immediatly a good felow' (*A Booke of Christian Ethicks or Moral Philosophie* (1587), sig. E2r).
44. Peacham, *The Garden of Eloquence* (1577), sig. N4V.
45. John Larke, *The boke of wysdome folowynge the auctoryties of auncyent pkyhsophers* (1532), fols. 7V, 9V, 27V, 45r, 50r, 56r.

46. *Ibid.*, fols. 9V, 27V, 56r; fols, 7V, 46V, 50r.
47. Baldassare Castiglione, *The Courtyer . . . Done into Englyshe by Thomas Hoby* (Edinburgh, 1899), p. 330.
48. Cornelius Valerius, *The Casket of Jewels: contaynynge a playne description of morall philosophie* (1571), sig. D1r–v.
49. Castiglione, *The Courtyer*, p. 44.
50. Valerius, *The Casket of Jewels*, sig. F2V.
51. *De Arte Rhetorica Libri Tres*, trans. Sigonio, p, 49.
52. Castiglione, *The Courtyer*, p. 44.
53. Valerius, *The Casket of Jewels*, sig. F2V.
54. *Ibid.*
55. Castiglione, *The Courtyer*, p. 44.
56. Peacham, *The Garden of Eloquence* (1593), p. 169.
57. Day, *A Declaration of . . . Tropes, Figures or Schemes*, p. 77.
58. *Ibid.*, p. 90.
59. Cicero, *De oratore*, 3.27.107.
60. Susenbrotus, *Epitome troporum ac schematum*, p. 46.
61. Wilson, *The Arte of Rhetorique*, fol. 69r.
62. Peacham, *The Garden of Eloquence* (1593), pp. 168–9.
63. John Lyly, *Euphues. The Anatomy of Wit*, ed. Edward Arber (London, 1868), p. 115.
64. Christopher Marlowe, *Tamburlaine the Great* Parts I and 2, ed. David Fuller, The Complete Works of Christopher Marlowe, vol. 5 (Oxford: Clarendon Press, 1998), 4.1.17 and 4.1.91.
65. 3.1.2.35–7, in William Shakespeare, *The Complete Works*, ed. Stanley Wells and Gary Taylor (Oxford, 1988). All further references to Shakespeare are to the texts in this edition.
66. So too in Shakespeare's poetry of the 1590s. See, for example, *The Rape of Lucrece*, line 246: Tarquin is said to speak in such a way that 'what is vile shows like a virtuous deed'.
67. Peacham, *The Garden of Eloquence* (1593), p. 168.
68. 2.1.125–6; Castiglione, *The Courtyer*, p. 44. Editors of *2 Henry IV* do not seem to have spotted the source of the remark.
69. Peacham, *The Garden of Eloquence* (1593), p. 167.
70. Susenbrotus, *Epitome troporum ac schematum*, p. 46.
71. Peacham, *The Garden of Eloquence* (1593), p. 168.
72. *Ibid.*, p. 169.
73. *Ibid.*
74. Cicero, *The thre bookes of Tullyes offices both in latyne tonge and in englysshe lately translated by Roberte Whytinton* (London, 1534), sig, Q8r.
75. Baldwin's treatise, first published in 1547, was reprinted at least three times in the 1550s. The text was enlarged by Thomas Palfreyman in 1567, and in this version, further enlarged in 1579, it went through at least ten further printings by the end of the century. The edition here used is that of 1579.
76. William Baldwin, *A Treatice of Morall Philosophy* (1579), fol. 72V.

Science

18.
THE ROYAL SOCIETY AND ENGLISH PROSE STYLE: A REASSESSMENT
Brian Vickers

1

IN 1667 THOMAS SPRAT, then aged twenty-eight, published *The History of The Royal-Society of London, For the Improving of Natural Knowledge*. Sprat, a young clergyman who subsequently became Bishop of Rochester, was not a scientist, and had a limited understanding of the nature of scientific research. But he had sufficient knowledge of, and sympathy with, the program formulated by Francis Bacon for the reformation of science, which had indeed swept through virtually all social, political, or religious groups in the seventeenth century,[1] to be able to write a defense of, or—as he called it—an "Apology" for, the Royal Society. The structure of this work, like so many of its ideas, derives from Bacon, especially from *The Advancement of Learning* (1605), the first book of which defended learning from its enemies, while the second went on to outline a program for its revival. Sprat's *History* is in three books: The first is an account of the "*Antient,* and *Modern* Philosophy"[2] up to and including' the foundation of the Society—an essay in history which celebrates those who have contributed to the advancement and restoration of learning, above all Bacon. The second book is a "*Narrative*" of the Society's proceedings, taken from its "*Registers,* and *Journals*" (4), with a description of its statutes, membership, and activities. The work ends, as Bacon's had begun, with a defense of learning from its adversaries, especially those who held it to be dangerous to religion.

Sprat's *History* is an official, quasi-commissioned document, written in straightforward English prose, but with a free use of rhetoric, both of figures (various forms of parallelism) and tropes (especially metaphor).[3] As an approved history of a distinguished institution it deserves attention, and some respect; yet as a document it is not easy to interpret, especially not if taken as gospel writ. We need to remind ourselves that the Royal Society, although mostly admirable, was the establishment organization for science; that it did not represent all the valuable work taking place in England—it was especially weak on chemistry; and that its own achievements were, and were seen by its own members to be, variable, and in some areas disappointing.[4] It represents one view, not necessarily the right one.

Vickers, Brian. "The Royal Society and English Prose Style: A Reassessment." In: Brian Vickers and Nancy S. Struever (eds.), *Rhetoric and the Pursuit of Truth. Language Change in the Seventeenth and Eighteenth Centuries*. Los Angeles: The William Andrews Clark Memorial Library, University of California, 1985: 3–76.

One of the most remarkable features of Sprat's *History* is the section in part 2 describing the Royal Society's attitude to style. Since the publication of Joel Spingarn's excellent and pioneering collection *Critical Essays of the Seventeenth Century* (1908–9), and especially since the work of Richard Foster Jones in the 1930s, this account of the Society's attitude to style has become famous, and few students of the seventeenth century can have escaped being exposed to it. Yet, because so much weight has been attached to it, we might note that it was hardly quoted before the present century (except in formal histories of the Royal Society) and that contemporary references to it are negligible.[5] It is an unusual passage, in that Sprat's generally balanced manner changes into a reformer's fury. The Society, he tells us, "has been most sollicitous" about

> the manner of their *Discourse:* which, unless they had been very watchful to keep in due temper, the whole spirit and vigor of their *Design,* had been soon eaten out, by the luxury and redundance of *speech.* The ill effects of this superfluity of talking, have already overwhelm'd most other *Arts* and *Professions* . . .

so much so that Sprat, Plato-like, is tempted to banish "*eloquence* . . . out of all *civil Societies,* as a thing fatal to Peace and good Manners" (*History,* 111). He refrains from doing so, however, since without the defensive power of rhetoric "the *naked Innocence* of vertue, would be upon all occasions expos'd to the *armed Malice* of the wicked." Originally the "Ornaments of speaking" were an "Instrument in the hands of *Wise Men*" used for purposes remarkably similar to those of the scientific program of the Royal Society: "to describe *Goodness, Honesty, Obedience*" (we recall that Sprat is writing after the Restoration of law and order); "to represent *Truth,* cloth'd with Bodies; and to bring *Knowledg* back again to our very senses, from whence it was at first deriv'd to our understandings" (111–12). Here we see the Baconian injunctions, endlessly repeated by all adherents to the New Sciences in the seventeenth century, that knowledge of reality must initially be read off from the external world through the senses, to the understanding, and not invented by the imagination. Nature is God's book: we read it, but we do not make it up. "For God forbid," Bacon wrote, "that we should give out a dream of our own imagination for a pattern of the world."[6] But in recent times, Sprat maintains, the tools of rhetoric

> are generally chang'd to worse uses: They make the *Fancy* disgust the best things, if they come sound, and unadorn'd: they are in open defiance against *Reason;* professing, not to hold much correspondence with that; but with its Slaves, *the Passions:* they give the mind a motion too changeable, and bewitching, to consist with *right practice.* Who can behold, without indignation, how many mists and uncertainties, these specious *Tropes* and *Figures* have brought on our Knowledg?
>
> (112)

As he contemplates the ill effects of "the easie vanity of *fine speaking*" Sprat professes himself to be "warm'd with" a "just Anger" against this easily acquired "vicious abundance of *Phrase,* this trick of *Metaphors,* this volubility of *Tongue,* which makes so great a noise in the World" (112). He continues his denunciation, elevating the misuse of language to the level of "those *general mischiefs;* such as the *dissention* of Christian Princes, the *want of practice* in Religion, and the like" (113).

These are hard accusations for a man of twenty-eight to be making; he diagnoses a general perversion of language and a misapplication of rhetoric (which he describes and evaluates with most effective rhetoric), putting this linguistic anarchy on the level of atheism and political dissension. Giving up hope of changing the rest of the world, he offers as exemplary "what has been done by the *Royal Society,* towards the correction of its excesses in *Natural Philosophy*" (113). Here follows his famous paragraph on stylistic reforms:

> They have therefore been most rigorous in putting in execution, the only Remedy, that can be found for this *extravagance:* and that has been, a constant Resolution, to reject all the amplifications, digressions, and swellings of style: to return back to the primitive purity, and shortness, when men deliver'd so many *things,* almost in an equal number of *words.* They have exacted from all their members, a close, naked, natural way of speaking; positive expressions; clear senses; a native easiness: bringing all things as near the Mathematical plainness, as they can: and preferring the language of Artizans, Countrymen, and Merchants, before that, of Wits, or Scholars.
>
> (113)

All in all, this is an impressive sequence: a diagnosis of a disease, or of what Bacon would have called "a distemper of learning," followed by a remedy, one that has apparently already been put into practice. It looks like a stylistic manifesto, but addressed rather to the immediate past than the future, since the cure has already been effected, disorder has been put down, ease and clarity reign once more in Charles II's London— or at least in his scientific society. Yet, convincing though the sequence seems on paper, it may be appropriate to ask the simple question, what is Sprat talking about? In what way had most of the other arts and professions been "overwhelm'd" by verbose language? How could the scientific program of the Royal Society have been "eaten out" by redundant speech? Sprat seems to be writing out of a situation of crisis, in panic—or is it paranoia? The feeling was certainly not restricted to him, for a few years later a central figure in the Royal Society, John Wilkins, introducing his *Essay Towards a Real Character and a Philosophical Language* (1668), spoke of words gobbling up things.[7] Obviously, then, to interpret this text properly we need to set it in its cultural and historical contexts. Before doing so, and before discussing the accepted interpretation, let us just deduce what we can from the plain meaning of the text:

(1) Sprat is not attacking language but the excesses of language: he speaks of a "luxury and redundance" of speech, a "superfluity" of talking, a "volubility" of tongue. He does not wish to abolish language but to bring it into some kind of economical relation to its subject matter. The Society has supposedly returned to "the primitive purity, and shortness, when men deliver'd so many *things,* almost in an equal number of *words.*" Here the demand for economy has become quantified, and the age-old rhetorical doctrine of the primacy of *res* over *verba* is being invoked almost on a one-to-one basis: one thing, one word. Here, evidently, the shift in some areas of seventeenth-century

thought (which A. C. Howell documented),[8] whereby *res* lost its meaning as "topic" or "subject matter" and became "thing," has taken place.

(2) Sprat is not attacking rhetoric but the abuse of rhetoric: it is the "specious" tropes and figures he protests against, those which produce "mists and uncertainties"; it is a "trick" of metaphors which prevents knowledge of reality directly, through the senses. Indeed, far from attacking rhetoric, he explicitly preserves it in its traditional role as the protector of good against evil. Elsewhere in his book he draws our attention to his use and reapplication of a metaphor (25); he praises Francis Bacon's style: "The Wit Bold, and Familiar: The comparisons fetch'd out of the way, and yet the most easie" (36); he assures students of grammar and rhetoric that the new "*Experimental Philosophy*" will have no "ill effects, on the usual *Arts*, whereby we are taught the Purity, and Elegance of *Languages*" (324); and he promises the "Wits" and "Gentlemen of our Nation" that the New Sciences, far from damaging wit, will actually offer, in place of the dying mythological sources of tropes, a whole new world of similitudes and comparisons, which will be "solid and lasting," "masculine and durable," since it will consist of "*Images* that are generally observ'd, and such visible things which are familiar to mens minds" (414–15). The comparisons so drawn "will be intelligible to all, becaus they proceed from things that enter into all mens Senses," and will thus make "the most vigorous impressions on mens *Fancies*, becaus they do even touch their *Eyes*, and are neerest to their *Nature*" (416). This last idea is a familiar concept in traditional rhetoric, that appeal to the imagination can be made most powerfully by visible effects—the concept of *enargeia*.[9] Again Sprat praises Bacon for his use of analogies drawn from science: he was "abundantly recompenc'd for his Noble Labors in that *Philosophy*, by a vast Treasure of admirable *Imaginations* which it afforded him, wherewith to express and adorn his thoughts about other matters" (416). But Sprat will not limit his praise to one author, "though he was one of the first and most artificial [meaning artistic, inventive] Managers of this way of *Wit*," but declares in general of the English tongue that "as it contains a greater stock of *Natural* and *Mechanical Discoveries*, so it is also more inrich'd with beautiful *Conceptions*, and inimitable *Similitudes*, gather'd from the *Arts* of mens hands, and the *Works of Nature*, than ever any other *Language* could produce" (417). Sprat's patriotism, touching, and in places ridiculous, was justified here, witness the freedom with which writers from Donne to Cowley, Swift to Thomson and beyond, applied and misapplied the findings of microscope and telescope, chemistry and physics, to the making of metaphor and simile.[10]

(3) Sprat is not attacking the imagination. That much is clear from his recommendation of similes drawn from experimental science as having "the most vigorous impressions on mens *Fancies*," or from his praise of Bacon's "Treasure of admirable *Imaginations*" (416), or his earlier description of Bacon as "a Man of strong, cleer, and powerful Imaginations" (36). What Sprat is attacking, as in the case of language and rhetoric, is not imagination itself, but its misuse, by which the "*Fancy*" is made to "disgust," or dislike, "the best things" if they are "unadorn'd." Here the tools of rhetoric, he claims, have been used "in open defiance against *Reason*; professing, not to hold much correspondence with that; but with its Slaves, *the Passions*." Sprat is expressing the well-known Renaissance and neoclassic distrust of imagination so conceived,[11] in

opposition to the reason and in service of the passions. When, in Swift's sublime formulation, "a Man's Fancy gets *astride* on his Reason, when Imagination is at Cuffs with the Senses,"[12] then anarchy reigns.

(4) Whatever the Royal Society is complaining of, it, too, has been guilty of the same thing: the remedies have been "towards the correcting of *its* excesses" (emphasis added) in natural philosophy, and the Society has "exacted from all [its] members" (113) adherence to the new style. We may expect to find the bad old style, then, perpetrated by the Royal Society's own members—perhaps Boyle, or Robert Hooke. . . .

(5) Finally, the new style is not to be that of "Wits" (although Sprat later spends so much time placating them) or of "Scholars." Whatever our conception of a scholar, we must remember that in the seventeenth century a scholar was, at the very least, one who could read Latin and who was familiar with the "Schools" of the universities, where, of course, throughout this period, instruction continued to be in Latin. One of the jokes in the Overbury character of "A Meere Scholer" is that "he speakes Latin better than his Mother-tongue."[13] What recommends "the language" of Sprat's "Artizans, Countrymen, and Merchants" is that it is English, with "a native easiness." Behind these words lies the whole seventeenth-century controversy about the proper language for science.

Those are a number of deductions that can be made from the passage on style by setting it in its own context within the *History*. The other questions which it raises cannot be settled without moving outside the text. Sprat seems to be referring to recent English history, to some "volubility of *Tongue*" that had disturbed our island. He is not simply talking about prose style: his words need to be put back into the context of political and religious history. (No seventeenth-century figure wrote in a vacuum, although some modern scholars do.) The passage in fact raises more questions than it answers. We should like to know, for instance, what was the "great . . . noise in the World" that Sprat complains of? what, exactly, did the members of the Society do to their prose style? who were they? who were the people or groups responsible for the misuse of language, rhetoric, and the imagination? and what effect, if any, did Sprat's account of an internal dispute have on writers outside the Society?

2

Richard Foster Jones, in a series of articles and books published between 1919 and 1963, provided a comprehensive answer to these questions, one that still governs the interpretation of the controversy over language.[14] Jones's main argument, about science, was accepted by Robert Adolph in his 1968 investigation of the rise of modern prose style, although William Youngren has disputed the resulting image of the "scientific," colorless, and neutral language of post-Restoration literature.[15] Jones's further argument, that the New Sciences influenced preaching style, was vigorously contested by W. Fraser Mitchell in 1932, and has been disputed by Jackson I. Cope and Adolph.[16]

Jones's main argument rests on the thesis of a profound change of mentality in England around 1660. He describes the writers of what he calls "the Puritan regime"— Taylor, Browne, and Milton (how odd that grouping looks today!)—as "rhetorical," and argues that "against this style there arose a movement which later became an organized revolt" (RFJ, 75–76). This is, to begin with, a rather melodramatic overstatement—we know of no "organized revolt"—and it has, from the outset, oversimplified the issue: if the "Puritans" are "rhetorical," the scientists must be antirhetorical. Bacon, he notes, was the pioneer of the Royal Society, and, Jones claims, Bacon had an "antagonism to rhetoric" (RFJ, 77). That judgment is surprising, since Jones came to know the range of Bacon's work better than most scholars do: suffice it to say that numerous studies have shown that Bacon expressed a lifelong interest in rhetoric, used it constantly, and made many intelligent proposals for its reform.[17] Jones may have been thinking of the famous attack on Ciceronianism in book I of the *Advancement of Learning,* but that is an attack on the excesses of fanatical *imitatio,* not on rhetoric itself. As for Bacon's attitude to the place of rhetoric in science, it resembles Aristotle's in the *Rhetoric.* Language, Aristotle wrote, is to be varied according to the situation: rhetoric for persuasion, logic for demonstration. Clarity is the ideal, so one should "avoid ambiguities; unless, indeed, you definitely desire to be ambiguous, as those do who have nothing to say but are pretending to mean something,"[18] Verbosity is also to be eschewed: ". . . for when the sense is plain, you only obscure and spoil its clearness by piling up words" (1406334–35). Otherwise, one should use the "arts of language" in their appropriate place: "All such arts are fanciful and meant to charm the hearer. Nobody uses fine language when teaching geometry" (1404311–13). It is a question of context, and appropriateness. Elsewhere Aristotle excludes metaphor from logic and reasoning, especially from philosophical definitions: he rejects Empedocles' description of the sea, "the sweat of the earth," as being "adequate, perhaps, for poetic purposes, but inadequate for the purposes of understanding the nature of the thing."[19]

Aristotle's distinction between the language of science or philosophy and the language of literature or history was preserved by Bacon, but with a further qualification. Bacon saw analogy as having a prime role in the invention as well as the transmission of knowledge: ". . . there is no proceeding in invention of knowledge but by similitude" (3:218). In transmitting knowledge analogy is also vital: ". . . if any one wish to let new light on any subject into men's minds . . . he must still . . . call in the aid of similitudes," which are "of prime use to the sciences, and sometimes indispensable" (6:698). This is all in accordance with his definition of the function of rhetoric as being "*to apply Reason to Imagination* for the better moving of the will" (3:409). As I have shown elsewhere, Bacon made constant, fluent, and imaginative use of metaphor in all his works, especially the scientific ones. He had no hostility to metaphor.[20] But there were two areas in which metaphor was not welcome: scientific method and scientific observation. The critique of previous scientific methods in book I of the *Novum Organum* includes an attack on the philological traditions of Aristotelian science, a science which consisted of a verbal commentary on a verbal text, with no recourse to physical reality. Part of Bacon's refutation of this circular, sterile method is to point out that the language which it used so confidently for text and discussion was not a stable, passive entity which could be manipulated at will. In his attack on the Idols of the Tribe—the phantasms, or false images, imposed on us by the nature of the human senses and human psychology—the deficiencies of language as a sole medium for science are exposed (4:54–55, 60–62, aphorisms 43, 59, 60).

This is not an attack on language in general—it is not true, as R. F. Jones claimed, that Bacon had an "antipathy" to language (RFJ, 143)—but on language in science when it merely reflects and reproduces age-old categories ("divisions of nature") which are not tested by reference to reality; when science is "sophistical and inactive," the discussions of learned men ending often "in disputes about words and names"; when science is preoccupied still with the fictions of scholastic science ("Fortune," "the Prime Mover," etc.), or with faultily defined abstract qualities such as "humid," or with the Aristotelian processes of generation and corruption and the qualitative concepts "*heavy, light, rare, dense*" (4:61–62). Bacon's argument is that science can only be properly established by going out and observing, experimenting: it cannot develop by purely verbal means. So he rejects as irrelevant here the practice of the mathematicians who begin with words "and so by means of definitions reduce them to order" (4:61), since that is a deductive process working within its own artificial, self-enclosed symbolism, a process having, for Bacon, the same negative value as the syllogism. The vital point, he insists, is that "even definitions cannot cure this evil in dealing with natural and material things; since the definitions themselves consist of words, and those words beget others: so that it is necessary to recur to individual instances, and those in due series and order," using the method of induction and the establishment of axioms (4:61–62). Science must be concerned with the natural world directly, not with language.

If a purely verbal solution is of no help at the level of scientific method, it is positively damaging to observation and experiment, the practice of science. In the "Parasceve, or Preparative towards a Natural and Experimental History," Bacon outlines the principles for the collection of observations and data on which axioms, or general laws of nature, can be established. His argument is that men must inspect nature, the physical universe, at first hand; therefore we should make away

> with antiquities, and citations or testimonies of authors; also with disputes and controversies and differing opinions; everything in short which is philological [merely textual disputes]. Never cite an author except in a matter of doubtful credit: never introduce a controversy unless in a matter of great moment. And for all that concerns ornaments of speech, similitudes, treasury of eloquence, and such like emptinesses, let it be utterly dismissed. Also let all those things which are admitted be themselves set down briefly and concisely, so that they may be nothing less than words.
>
> (4:254)

That final paradox implies that purely verbal science ends up with a status below that of language: it is meaningless. And in case his readers should think that this is a general attack on eloquence, Bacon adds a sentence to make absolutely clear that these injunctions apply *only* to the establishment of a storehouse of data:

> For no man who is collecting and storing up materials for shipbuilding or the like, thinks of arranging them elegantly, as in a shop, and displaying them so as to please the eye; all his

care is that they be sound and good, and that they be so arranged as to take up as little room as possible in the warehouse.

(4:254–55)

This careful qualification is completely omitted by George Williamson when he quotes the passage; ironically, in the accompanying footnote Williamson includes (but fails to connect) the comment of Peter Shaw, who edited Bacon in 1733 and drew attention to the crucial distinction being made here:

> The Business is not now to gain upon Men's Affections, or win them over to *Philosophy,* by Eloquence, Similitudes, or the Art of Writing; which the Author practised in the *De Augmentis;* but carefully to enquire into, and justly to copy, and describe, Nature, as she is in herself; and there the Style cannot well be too plain and simple.[21]

It is at this level—Bacon's concern about the language for science—that we must take his call for plainness of style, made, for example, in his remark in the *Advancement of Learning* that the "sophism of all sophisms" is equivocation or ambiguity "of words and phrase, specially of such words as are most general and intervene in every inquiry" (3:394), Evidently, Bacon made a clear distinction between the language of scientific method and the communication of experiment, and other language, in which an appeal to the imagination was legitimate.

The coherence of Bacon's program with that of Sprat's *History* must now be obvious. The statutes of the Royal Society, published in 1728, include this article:

> In all Reports of Experiments to be brought into the Society, the Matter of Fact shall be barely stated, without any Prefaces, Apologies, or Rhetorical Flourishes, and entered so into the Register-Book, by order of the Society.

(Quoted in RFJ, 84)

Everyone will agree that this is a proper rule for scientific papers, and the matter might perhaps have been left there. But Jones, neglecting Bacon's careful distinction between scientific prose and all other prose (a distinction understood and repeated by Sprat), and confusing conceptual and stylistic issues, went on to argue that seventeenth-century science, as a way of looking at the world characterized by objectivity, materiality (*Sachlichkeit*), and utilitarianism, changed the way English prose was written. He claimed that "in the concrete nature of the experimental philosophy is to be found the secret of the craving for a clear, accurate, plain style. . . . This obsession with the actual nature and appearance of things" profoundly altered the style for prose (RFJ, 107–8). Jones went on to argue that in his manifesto Sprat also had "poets, dramatists, and satirists in mind" (RFJ, 159). These claims seem to me mistaken, and neither proved by him nor likely to be proved. But I do not wish to engage myself in a mere refutation, overdue though it may be. I want to show that Jones used his material to refer to other things than in fact it did; that he neglected the cultural context; and that he in some way reversed the sequence of influence. It is essential to examine Jones's methodology, since the errors he made have continued to be made. The study of English seventeenth-century prose has yet to recover from the errors of. Jones, George Williamson, and Morris Croll,[22] all of whom imposed on prose style categories or labels which had no historical justification, and which neither defined the styles they purported to characterize nor succeeded in distinguishing styles one from another.

To begin, as every historian must, with the issue of chronology. Anyone arguing for the influence of A on B must be able to show that A is prior to B, was known or was likely to be known by B, and so on. As we work through Jones's essays, we are struck by the fact that many of. the books he quotes date from the 1640s, indeed some from the late 1630s. At one point, discussing the development of ideas about science, he himself writes that "every attitude of importance which later characterized the Royal Society and its defenders had been clearly expressed and defended before the Restoration."[23] But when it comes to discussing the question of style Jones cannot see that the same conclusion applies. To anticipate a little, my judgment would be that with respect to style as well as ideas, the Royal Society consolidated earlier positions, aligning itself with them, indeed sometimes appropriating them as if of its own invention. The Society's motto, "Nullius in verba," is an abridgment (dictated perhaps by the necessity of inserting it in the scroll which hangs at the top of the frontispiece to Sprat's *History*) of a phrase in Horace's first Epistle, "Nullius addictus iurare in verba magistri" (1.1.14), and students are sometimes taken in by the Society's presentation of itself as totally innovative.

Although Jones had read most of sixteenth- and seventeenth-century English literature, he did not always get things in the right order. Having noted Bacon's "advocacy of a naked style," he writes that the "plea for a plain style" is "heard again" in John Wilkins's *Ecclesiastes, or, a Discourse Concerning the Gift of Preaching* (1646). But it was surely heard in between, and afterwards, and before. Many such appeals were made in the sixteenth century; indeed in his later study *The Triumph of the English Language*[24] Jones quotes a number, especially from Puritan writers. The point to be settled in all attempts to write the history of style is whether an individual remark is specifically addressed to an immediate historical situation or is a generality always applicable. In "The Attack on Pulpit Eloquence in the Restoration" (RFJ, 111–42), Jones claims that "the scientific ideal of style—plainness, directness, clearness"— influenced preaching style, and that this "change was materially assisted by the determined efforts of numerous stylistic reformers, the first of which appeared, as we would expect, in scientific quarters," namely, again, Wilkins's *Ecclesiastes* of 1646 (RFJ, 113). Yet on the next page he asserts that "the real attack" began with a sermon by Robert South preached in Oxford on 30 April 1668 (RFJ, 114). We wonder how a "movement" can be constituted by two works appearing twenty-two years apart. Jones goes on to argue that there was a substantial attack on rhetoric in the Restoration period, and devotes several pages to its discussion (RFJ, 114–31). Then he turns to surveying the defense of figurative language, as in James Arderne's *Directions Concerning the Matter and Stile of Sermons,* and in Robert Ferguson's *The Interest of Reason in Religion: With the Import and Use of Scripture-Metaphors* (RFJ, 131–36): we note with surprise that these two books were published in 1671 and 1675 respectively, whereas South's sermon, preached in 1668, was apparently not published until 1717, in the fifth volume of his *Twelve Sermons . . . preached upon several . . . Occasions.* Rather than there having been a movement against pulpit rhetoric first, followed by one in defense of it, it appears that the two were carried on simultaneously. Jones has confused chronology in order to claim that the shape of his argument is the shape of history.[25]

Chronology is one vital tool for the historian; another is the interpretation of the documents. There are embarrassingly few documents for Jones's thesis, and those there are, or might be, he did not analyze. In 1930 he wrote of the Royal Society that "naturally its stylistic ideal was reflected in the scientific writings of its members" (RFJ, 88), but with the exception of works of Glanvill and Cowley (a marginal case), he did not analyze any of these writings—Hooke, Boyle, Power, and others were tacitly taken as supporting his thesis. In 1931 he claimed—again without giving any quotations or making any analyses—that Tillotson exemplifies "the new kind of preaching," and that the sermons of both Wilkins and Barrow illustrate "the new style" (RFJ, 113 n. 6). In order to show the figurative style of the Nonconformists he quoted one sentence only (RFJ, 131 n. 49). In a much later article, published in 1963, Jones argued that the style of the atomists Charleton and Digby "must have caused some misgivings" to the Royal Society,[26] but he cited no evidence for such misgivings, nor did he analyze the Society's "prose style"—if, indeed, it ever had a uniform style. Robert Adolph, a follower of Jones in part, accused both Sprat and Glanvill of blurring the "distinction between the 'natural' style of the artisans ... and the 'proper' style of the polite court."[27] But it should be evident that none of the scientists connected with the Society actually wrote like an artisan, a countryman, or a merchant. Is it not amazing that generations of scholars go on taking Sprat's "manifesto" literally, without ever reading Boyle, or Hooke, or the *Philosophical Transactions*? Critics of prose style seem to lack two essential qualities of the historian, skepticism about received hypotheses, and a sense of reality.

The documents cited by Jones in his 1930s articles were the writings of Glanvill and Cowley. To take the latter first: Jones noted, although with no extended analysis, the fact that Cowley's early style was stiff, his late style easy (RFJ, 98). Well, the same holds true for many writers, novelists, critics, or academics, and there would be various explanations, such as maturity, confidence, practice. The fact that the style of Cowley's *Vision Concerning Oliver Cromwell* is more "rhetorical" than that of his *Essays* is surely to be explained by the differing genres of the two works. Jones here lacked the true Baconian spirit, the appeal to negative instances to confirm or disprove a thesis.

In the case of Glanvill, though, he was able to show definite instances of stylistic revision by juxtaposing passages from three different editions of Glanvill's *Vanity of Dogmatizing*, a work first published in 1661 and originally written in what Jones fairly describes as "a highly rhetorical, exuberant, one might even say flamboyant, style" (RFJ, 89). Oldenburg, the secretary to the Royal Society, described Glanvill in 1667 as "a florid writer," an epithet usually applied to pre-Restoration prose, to Jeremy Taylor, or Sir Thomas Browne. In 1667 that judgment was accurate, for Glanvill republished the original version of the *Vanity* in 1665—by which time Sprat had probably finished writing the *History*—and gave it a new title, *Scepsis Scientifica*. Nonetheless, he added a dedication disclaiming its style in terms consonant with the "manifesto" of Sprat ("I must confess that *way of writing* to be less agreeable to my *present relish* and *Genius;* which is more gratified with *manly sense,* flowing in a *natural* and *unaffected Eloquence,* than in the *musick* and curiosity of *fine Metaphors* and *dancing periods*" [quoted in RFJ, 89]); he declared himself to be "grown too *cold*" toward the book to consider revising it. Yet when he reused the material a third time, as late as 1676, as the first essay in a volume called *Essays on Several Important Subjects in Philosophy and Religion*, he evidently felt that the old style could no longer pass, and he substantially revised it. His revisions were analyzed by Jones, who printed parallel passages, by Jackson I. Cope, and most recently by Stephen Medcalf, in an Oxford B. Litt. thesis and in the introduction to a useful facsimile reprint of the three versions.[28]

The first point to be made is that Glanvill was reducing a book to the length of an essay. Major cuts had to be made, but his motives for selecting one element of style as against another are not clear. Jones noted the cutting back of verbal redundance, the removal of a "touch of beauty," the achievement of a short, economical style by "merciless pruning" (RFJ, 90–97), Cope suggested that Glanvill's "apology for the style" was "made with an eye toward pacifying the radical element in the Society's plans for linguistic reform,"[29] while Medcalf studied the removal of metaphor and connected it with both Descartes and Locke.[30] But what none of these critics has noticed is that a passage in the 1661 *Vanity of Dogmatizing* is in fact a quotation from Boyle, for an identical passage appears in *The Sceptical Chymist*, also published in 1661. Glanvill says that "there are *experiments* that credit" this position; Boyle writes that "I did once, purposely, cause to be decocted in fair water . . ." and so on, adding the rider that "having made it but once I may possibly have been mistaken in it."[31] I cite this parallel not to accuse Glanvill of plagiarism: many writers connected with the Royal Society treated experiments as common property, and we know that Glanvill and Boyle were associated.[32] My point is that whatever Glanvill thought was wrong with his version must have been wrong with Boyle's also, according to the new taste. Therefore Sprat's comment that the Society was reforming its own excesses may have more point than we have so far realized.

3

The fact that Glanvill revised his style could, perhaps, be taken as one proof of Jones's thesis that science influenced prose style. It is a late piece of evidence, ten years after Sprat's *History*, and it can also be taken as evidence of self-criticism or maturity, since Glanvill, like other writers of the period, disclaimed his youthful excesses.[33] Yet if we do take it as evidence for the Jones thesis we must be careful not to assume a causal relationship between pronouncements on style and stylistic change, either in the form that one produced the other or in the form that the two exist on the same continuum. I offer the variant possibilities, first that a writer may change his style without reference to some formulated manifesto; and secondly that a writer's comments on style are not necessarily a program intended for his own reformation. I introduce this second point to account for a phenomenon which Jones noticed but could not explain, namely, the apparent contradiction between a writer's statements about style and his own practice. He quotes from a work by Samuel Parker of 1666 in which Parker attacks metaphor, and suggests that here is "another possible example of the influence of the Royal Society in sobering the style of its members" (RFJ, 101 n. 44). Yet Jones notes that "in spite of this expressed antipathy to rhetorical prose, the style of the *Censure* is far from being bare and unadorned." He quotes a passage, and comments, rather apologetically: "He had been for only a short time a member of the Royal Society, and perhaps its influence had not had time to bear fruit" (RFJ, 102 n. 44). Jones later quotes, in the name of plainness, Robert South's attack on "tropes" and "conceits," and comments that although South expressed a "distaste for all verbal embellishments ... [he] himself hardly lived up to his ideal" (RFJ, 115). Jones cites another attack on metaphor by Samuel Parker, this time directed against the Nonconformists, an attack on metaphor which—like all such attacks—has to rely on the figure it abuses. As in the famous rejections of metaphor by Hobbes and Locke, or in the rejections of rhetoric by Kant and Croce,[34] Parker uses metaphor as the indispensable figure for expressing and arousing feelings, advocating an act of Parliament "to abridge Preachers the-use of fulsom and lushious Metaphors," to cure "our present Distempers" by stripping the fanatics of "the Varnish of fine Metaphors and glittering Allusions" (quoted in RFJ, 118–19). Jones does not note the use of metaphor here; he did note that Simon Patrick's *Mensa Mystica* (1660) is replete with figures of speech and "enthusiastic" analogies; having quoted one, he comments: "This is as bad as anything he reprehends in the nonconformists" (RFJ, 117 n. 15). It is surely worse, since Patrick, like Parker, presents himself as a reformer.

The general point to be made is that it is extremely difficult, even today, to express a strong opinion or evaluation of anything without resorting to metaphor. (Try to praise or condemn any topic for one minute without using metaphors!) If we read only the excerpts quoted by Jones himself we will find the most exuberant use of metaphor in the prose of the 1640s, 1650s, and 1660s, especially by the Baconian scientists and propagandists, but also by Latitudinarians, Royalists, experimentalists.[35] The fact is that you cannot distinguish anyone from anyone in mid-seventeenth-century prose if the use or nonuse of metaphor is your criterion, since everyone used metaphor. In a late article Jones attempted to distinguish the style of the atomists from that of the experimentalists with half a syllogism—the atomists used metaphors: but, we must add, so did the experimentalists. Jones got tangled in his own categories when, having identified the atomists with a metaphorical style, he came to Hobbes and had to pronounce him "a glaring exception," since he "practiced verbal economy" and criticized metaphors.[36] But of course everything that Hobbes wrote is shot through with metaphor, to the verge of allegory—yet he is an atomist: not that that *makes* him an atomist, or that because he is an atomist he must be metaphorical. The two categories overlap here, but they are otherwise discrete, heterogeneous.

Later writers have also noted what they call contradictions. Robert Adolph accused Sprat and Glanvill of blurring distinctions, noted "the persistence of florid rhetoric" among the Fellows of the Royal Society,[37] and drew attention to the embarrassing case of Isaac Barrow. In an article originally published in 1930 Jones said of Barrow that as "a very early member" he "could hardly have escaped being influenced by the stylistic attitude of the Society" (RFJ, 102), but offered no analysis. Jones republished that article in his festschrift, *The Seventeenth Century,* in 1951, but neither he nor any of the other contributors to the festschrift referred to W. Fraser Mitchell's classic study, *English*

Pulpit Oratory from Andrewes to Tillotson, which was published in 1932. Mitchell showed that Barrow's pulpit style did not at all fit the stylistic ideals set out by Sprat. In fact, "Barrow's editor, Tillotson, felt compelled to simplify and 'improve' the original text."[38] Similar operations might have been performed on the prose of Sprat, or Boyle; *on* Seth Ward just as much as on his adversary John Webster, on Henry More as on his adversary Thomas Vaughan. The prose of this period is exuberant, inventive, imaginative, expressive, polemical, forceful, at times undisciplined, never "scientific." In his *Treatise of the Bulk and Selvedge of the World* (1674), Nathaniel Fairfax made a rather eccentric plea for purer English against the current of neologisms, and apologized resignedly for his "way of wording it," feeling that "'tis not trim enough for these Gay days of ours" in which the "borrowed words & gaynesses, that Englishmen have pickt and cull'd from other Tongues" have produced "those bewitcheries of speech that flow from Gloss and Chimingness" and to which his own style offers such a striking contrast.[39]

Fairfax is consistent in relating theory and practice, but many of the writers studied by R. F. Jones are, or appear to be, glaringly inconsistent. Jones never faced that issue squarely, but more recently, a computer stylist, Robert Cluett—although having enough literary sensitivity to analyze Sprat's style according to the genre he was using—diagnosed "a conflict between Sprat's rhetorical training, gifts, and tastes, and his distrust of the verbal imagination. This conflict produced a wide range of seemingly contradictory attitudes in his own statements about writing."[40] Unfortunately, in listing these so-called contradictions, Mr. Cluett does not consider in what part of the *History* they are found, or Sprat's explicit intentions at that point, but simply includes Sprat in a list of three "writers who have failed notoriously to follow their most renowned prescriptions."[41] Whatever the truth about Orwell or Swift may be, I cannot see that Sprat has contradicted himself, since he never disclaimed all use of rhetoric or of appeal to the imagination, but merely specified the situations in which the exercise of these faculties was permissible, indeed advisable. Sprat attacked the misuse of rhetoric and its tropes, in the writings of others. My simple point is that Jones and other scholars have taken seventeenth-century pronouncements on style at their face value. The writers of this period are not as schizoid as may seem from Jones or Cluett, since they are not enunciating, in a cool and balanced way, precepts of style which they intend that they themselves or others should follow. Samuel Parker's *A Discourse of Ecclesiastical Politie* is not a work of the same order as W. Strunk and E. B. White's *The Elements of Style.* Jones rightly calls Parker "that great champion of intolerance" (RFJ, 118), but he fails to see that Parker's violence and intolerance affect all that he writes, including his views on style, and most of all, on his enemies' style.

The crucial fact, which must never be lost sight of in discussing the seventeenth century, is that contemporary accounts of style are seldom neutral or accurately descriptive. They are the result of animus, or controversy, or party politics, or religious dispute. What so many of these writers give us is not a program or manifesto for how they themselves intend to write but an account of how their opponents write. And diagnosing their opponents' style is an action that does not exist on the same level as writing a prescriptive style manual. Nor, actually, is the dispute primarily one about style. You attack your enemies for their style, but that is part of your whole campaign;

or, equally, the style is a symptom of something else that you disapprove of. Either way the criticism does not work backwards, or reflexively, for you are right and they are wrong, so that you could never be guilty of the same faults as they are. It is your enemies who are at fault.

R. F. Jones did not see this. He tended to read all statements about language as, simply, statements about language, and not as elements in a wider dispute. Thus he takes Alexander Ross's violently destructive comments on Sir Thomas Browne's style as in some sense accurate or justified, and speculates that it was perhaps because of this assessment of his style that Browne did not join the Royal Society (RFJ, go n. 30). The fact is that most contemporary verdicts on style are polemical, as is seen most clearly in the attacks on the Nonconformists. Jones quotes a number of these attacks and seems indeed to side with the established church, concluding: "There is no doubt that there was some basis for the charges preferred against the style of the dissenters." Yet, characteristically, he adds a suggestion that "the object of attack was really wider than the nonconformists, that it was rhetoric in general" (RFJ, 131 n. 49). This is typical of his method, which tended to detach attacks from their actual target: instead of seeing the Established Church attacking Nonconformist Rhetoric he sees an attack on rhetoric. He believes that "the English . . . were imbued with a scientific spirit" which rejected rhetoric for "plainness," and states that "the scientists were so intent on the actual nature of things that they resented any form of expression that did not match exactly the thing described" (RFJ, 140). Jones elevates Sprat's comment to an unjustified level of generality, as he does again when he says that "the world has never witnessed such a thoroughgoing materialism . . . as characterized the mid-seventeenth century" (RFJ, 140)—and he writes this in the century of Lenin! Jones seems to me to unite history of ideas and literary criticism in an unfortunately linear or causal manner. It is one thing to claim that "the English were by nature more practical, more materialistic, more utilitarian," than others, although even here we would have to limit "the English" to a group of perhaps one hundred people around the Royal Society, and we would have to forget the nonpractical attitudes of King Charles's court, or of Restoration comedy, or foppery, or heroic drama, or the music of Purcell, or Traherne, Vaughan, Bunyan. But it is quite another thing to argue that these "attitudes" caused a transformation of prose style and of literature in general.

For Jones's model of an "organized revolt" in which Science somehow gained power over the English Mind in the late 1660s, with, Jones thought, disastrous effects on both literature and religion, I offer a model of a continuous series of disputes of a more or less partisan nature in which style or rhetoric or language is an element in a bigger quarrel. Jones had read very widely, but he read in order to find expressed views on style, which he then detached from their cultural context. In a later book he refers to "the bearing of experimental science upon the thought pattern in which we are interested."[42] but in practice such thought patterns become resolved into a generalized account of a "rationalistic spirit" that—a constant theme—"sees in language only an instrument for the expression of intellectual concepts" (RFJ, 118). Jones takes the interest in sign languages expressed by Descartes, Hartlib, Dalgarno, Petty, Wilkins, and others as a confirmation of his thesis of the materialistic nature of the New

Sciences. He claims that men, sick of religious controversies, "were beginning to discover in language the cause of the evil" (RFJ, 123), and it is true that Wilkins, for one, thought that his system of signs could eliminate ambiguity. (Actually, it would have led to much greater ambiguity.) It needs to be said that Wilkins did not speak for all of the scientists or reformers, and that no one else showed any sign of wishing to abolish written or spoken language.[43] When Jones refers to "that distrust of language and hatred of words, a unique characteristic of early modern science," we can see that he has again elevated a particular point to a false generalization.[44]

4

The occasion for Jones's remark about early modern scientists' supposed "distrust of language" is an attack by Sir William Petty on students' spending so much time learning foreign languages when there exist sufficient books in English.[45] Writing in 164.8, Petty was being rather disingenuous about the existence of ample, and adequate English texts for the sciences, but at least the context is clear, that he was protesting not against language but against the learning of foreign languages, by which he meant Latin and Greek. This complaint was heard on many occasions, and it led to various remedies being proposed, but never, I think, the abolition of language. Jones claims that "under the lead of Comenius, Dury, and others inspired by the Baconian philosophy, the study of the ancient languages was severely reprehended during the period in which Puritanism was triumphant" (RFJ, 146). Well, if that was the case, it had a singularly small effect, since the curricula of neither the schools nor the universities were altered, and instruction continued to be predominantly in Latin. The universities, in particular, were both conservative and complacent, and as Hugh Kearney's study has shown, had hardly changed over two hundred years. The same neo-Scholastic texts were used, and students' notebooks show a depressing persistence of traditional techniques.[46] The complaints of Webster and other Puritans against the universities were in some ways justified.

Yet the Puritans did not wish to abolish Latin. They objected to the time spent learning it, but Hartlib and others thought that they could reduce that time by using more efficient teaching methods—laying more stress on authors than on grammar, and employing the picture-book vocabularies of Comenius.[47] Nicholas Culpeper, the doctor, complained about the time spent learning languages and—because of a serious illness—was able to devote much of his life to translating medical books into English. Similar complaints about the time spent learning Greek and Latin were voiced by John Webster, George Snell, and others,[48] but this did not lead to an anti-Latin movement, let alone to an antilanguage one. William Petty was more extreme in rejecting "Latin and rhetoric, but Snell preserved both subjects.[40] Samuel Hartlib published *The True and Readie Way to Learne the Latine Tongue* in 1654,[50] while twenty years later Carew Reynell called for the arts and sciences to be "taught in the Mother Tongue" but did not wish study of the other languages to be abolished.[51] Jones is quite wrong to say that Latin "was in process of being depreciated and discarded" as a means of international communication (RFJ, 153). Charles Webster's admirable studies of Hartlib's circle have made it clear that the Puritan educationalist reformers were not out to abolish

Latin but to improve its teaching.[52] Rather than showing a distrust of language, these reformers were expressing an endless and almost childlike faith in their ability to change the world through language and through reorganization, as the many unpublished and unrealized schemes they have left behind in manuscript testify. Jones's later study *The Triumph of the English Language* records that many Englishmen of various schools of thought wished their mother tongue to be studied more: some of these were cranks, who boosted the Saxon elements in the language, or had an insane hatred for French; some were New Scientists or Puritans, and some were not.[53]

While there was a movement against Latin, there was also, in Jones's own words, "a far more important linguistic attitude" which "dominated the seventeenth century and extended far into the eighteenth": "the conviction of the instability of modern languages."[54] The best-known expression of this fear is perhaps Bacon's remark that "these modern languages will at one time or other play the bank-rowtes with books" (14:439): Jones collects five such references dating from the sixteenth century and twenty-five from the seventeenth. All agree that while Latin was immutable and eternal, an "unchanging and universal language," English was a mutable tongue with a life of three generations at the most. This attitude was shared by poets, historians, theorists of the language, compilers of dictionaries, and it had its effect on the language of science. Certainly scientific books had been written in English before 1640, but they were mostly practical manuals of navigation or mathematics. For William Gilbert, or Bacon, or William Harvey, as for Newton, Latin was the language for science. While the period from the 1640s onward saw an enormous boom in the writing of science in English, and in the translating of Continental Latin works into English, as a consequence other problems arose which have not been adequately noticed in the discussion of the Royal Society.

An early instance of the doubtful status of English as the language for science is provided by Sir Thomas Browne, in his *Pseudodoxia Epidemica, or Enquiries into Very many received tenents and commonly presumed truths* (1646). This is a catalogue of "vulgar errors," the drawing up of which Bacon had recommended (3:221, 4:169, 4:295). But although inspired by Bacon it takes a very different direction linguistically. Bacon's English style, like his attitude to scientific knowledge, stressed clarity and openness of communication. His major scientific works he either wrote in or had translated into Latin, but his English is clear and free of technical terms. In the preface Browne tells us:

> Our first intentions considering the common interest of Truth, resolved to propose it unto the Latine republique and equal Judges of *Europe,* but owing in the first place this service unto our Country, and therein especially unto its ingenuous Gentry, we have declared our self in a language best conceived. Although I confess the quality of the Subject will sometimes carry us into expressions beyond meer English apprehensions. And indeed, if elegancy still proceedeth, and English Pens maintain that stream, we have of late observed to flow from many; we shall within few years be fain to learn Latine to understand English, and a work will prove of equal facility in either.[55]

Browne's reference to the increased eloquence of English—by which he partly means its Latinity—seems to me consistent with several pieces of evidence from the 1640s, although this development did not fit into the scheme of R. F. Jones's pioneering study *The Triumph of the English Language*.[56] Yet, since Jones quotes so many writers from the first half of the seventeenth century who praised Latin over English, it should come as no surprise to find scientists stating that our language was simply not capable of expressing the scientific concepts or indeed processes which could be described by Latin. Browne had warned his readers that he would have to use expressions which "meer English apprehensions"—people who did not know Latin—would not be able to understand.

The absence of adequate scientific texts in English is attested by John Wilkins, in his *Mathematical Magick. Or, The Wonders That may be performed by Mechanicall Geometry . . . Not before treated of in this language* (1648). Discussing mechanics, Wilkins writes in his preface:

> Other discourses of this kind, are for the most part large and voluminous, of great price and hardly gotten; and besides, there are not any of them (that I know of) in our vulgar tongue, for which these Mechanicall arts of all others are most proper.[57]

Two years later Walter Charleton, in the preface to his first published work, a translation of Van Helmont, alludes to the limitations of the English language in such areas of science by appealing to those who truly know the subject and its literature

> *whether* the fine and mysterious nature of many things, treated of in that discourse, might not have suffered a grosse Eclipse, if drest in a meer-English veil? *Whether it be a Crime in me to trace the footsteps of those Worthies, who have infinitely both enriched and ennobled our Language, by admitting and naturalizing thousands of forraigne Words, providently brought home from the* Greek, Roman, Italian, *and* French *oratories; which, though in the untraveld ears of our* Fathers *they would have sounded . . . harsh . . . yet have a few years made so familiar unto us, that now even* Children *speak much of* Latine, *before they can well read a word of* English?[58]

Charleton protests that he has been accused of seeking a "*noveltie, or affected elegance of the* Phrase . . . *meerly because* I *rendered some* Physical Notions *in* terms *most amply and adequately exhibiting their* qualities; *and those no other, but such as are most frequent in the* Schools . . ."[59] He has had to use the language of the universities because there is no other. Similarly, in his *Two Treatises* (1644) Sir Kenelm Digby defended his use of "hard words," or the technical terms of the sciences, in Latinate English because

> the scarcity of our language is such, in subjects removed from ordinary Conversation (though in others, I think none is more copious) as affordeth us not apt words of our own to express significantly such notions as I must busy myself about in this discourse. Therefore I will presume to borrow them from the Latine Schoole, where there is much adoe about them.

R. F. Jones doubted Digby's seriousness, or sincerity, on this point, claiming that he could have found simpler English equivalents for some of the Latinate words he uses.[60] This may be true in some cases, but Digby was working within a unified scientific vocabulary, and it is not easy to make sporadic moves into the vernacular: one tends to think in the specific terms of a technical discussion.

It seems undeniable that many seventeenth-century scientists were conscious of using Latinate English but felt that there was really no alternative. Robert Boyle, in his *Sceptical Chymist* (1661), had his persona Carneades explain that in summarizing the arguments of the alchemist Sennertus he has

> thought fit to retain the language wherein the author proposes it, that I might also retaine the propriety of some Latine termes, to which I do not readily remember any that fully answer in English.
>
> (167)

Joseph Glanvill attacked the Enthusiasts, in his essay "Anti-fanatick Theologie, and Free Philosophy" of 1676, for their convoluted language, claiming that the established church preachers used no "*needless words of Art.*"[61] Yet in his *Essay Concerning Preaching* of 1678 Glanvill "reluctantly admits 'terms of art' from formal philosophy and divinity, as well as English words of Latin derivation. Some 'hard words' are now 'proper.'"[62] That the Latinism of scientific English continued to be unavoidable a generation after the Royal Society's foundation can be seen from Charleton's *Enquiries into Human Nature, in VI. Anatomic Prælections* (London, 1680). At the end of the preface Charleton writes:

> If my *Stile* shall sound somewhat harsh and ungrateful many times to Ears unaccustomed to any but their Mother tongue, as corning too near to the Latin; I intreat you to consider, this is either no indecency in this place, or such a one at worst, which I could not otherwise avoid, than by involving my sense in the obscurity of words less proper and significant; the nature and quality of Subjects treated of, being such, as cannot be fully expressed in our yet imperfect Language.
>
> (Sig. E3v; italics reversed)

From the 1640s to the 1680s, then, English scientists justified the Latinate quality of their writing in the vernacular on the grounds that English was not capable of inventing corresponding terms. Not everyone was happy with the situation, and anyone using these books today without a Latin dictionary at his elbow will be at a serious disadvantage. Indeed, in one of the most extraordinary examples of Latinate, aureate diction in our language, the translation by Richard Tomlinson of Renodaeus's *Dispensatory* (1657), the publisher felt obliged to issue for its purchasers *A Physical Dictionary. Or, An Interpretation of such crabbed Words and Terms of Art, as are derived from the Greek or Latin,* an aid whose usefulness is obvious to all, "especially such as are not Scholars," Tomlinson is an obvious eccentric, and one is grateful to have glosses for such words as "abstersive," "buccellation," "caliginous," "cardiogmos," "circumdated," "commaculate," "denigrate" ("that maketh black"), "deturpates," "erugates" ("takes away wrinckles"), "extruct," "frustaneous," "glumosity," "impetiginous," "mordacity," "suaveolent," "tenuifolious," "torcular," "vimineous," and so on.

It is a surprise to the modern reader to find words which we have accepted perhaps only recently—"anorexia," "contraindicant," "dentifrice"—how "modern" they sound!

Evidently neologizing occurs to fill a need. Yet Sprat and his colleagues can hardly have been happy.

The important point to make is that almost all scientists were guilty. The presence or absence of Latinisms is a criterion which distinguishes nothing. The "continuity of English prose," a famous theory of R. W. Chambers, was usually applied to specifically English elements. Yet for over forty years English science was written in a neo-Latin jargon. An early purist who expressed alarm at this development was John Evelyn, writing in 1665 to Sir Peter Wyche, chairman of the Royal Society's committee "for improving the English tongue," which had been set up on 7 December 1664. Unable to attend the meetings Evelyn sends an account of both the "additions to, and the corruption of, the English language" caused by war, travel, trade, and other factors, with some proposed remedies in grammar, spelling, and punctuation. As for vocabulary, he suggests the compilation of a lexicon "of all the pure English words by themselves; then those w^h are derivative from others, . . . so as no innovation might be us'd or favour'd, at least 'till there should arise some necessity." Secondly, there should be a lexicon of established "technical words." Lastly, he recommends that

> a full catalogue of exotic words, such as are daily minted by our *Logodædali*, were exhibited, and that it were resolved on what should be sufficient to render them current, *ut Civitate donentur*, since, without restraining that same *indomitam novandi verba licentiam*, it will in time quite disguisc the language: there are some elegant words introduce'd by physicians chiefly and philosophers, worthy to be retained; others, it may be, fitter to be abrogated; since there ought to be a law as well as a liberty in this particular.[63]

That Evelyn's alarm was justified can be seen from many scientific texts. Browne's *Pseudodoxia* is an appropriate starting place, for it would be hard to find any other piece of writing in English which included so much Latinate vocabulary or indeed so many neologisms, direct Latin coinages, many of which are noticeable because they failed to establish themselves. (By contrast Dr. Johnson gives us a pure stream of English.) To take some examples from books 1 and 2, without exerting ourselves greatly we can pick out single words like "indagation," "liquation," "numerosity," "induration," "verticity," "indubitate," "consectary," "cognation," "salinous," "circumjacent," "imbibition," "super-natation," "calefie," "vitrification," "lentous," "percolation," "coadjuvancy"; or longer sequences such as one relating how the Devil may sometimes "seem to be charmed with words of holy Scripture, and to flie from the letter and dead verbality, who must onely start at the life and animated interiors thereof: It may be feared they are but *Parthian* flights, *Ambuscado* retreats, and elusory tergiversations" (190); or how the Devil has "deluded many Nations in his Augurial and Extispicious inventions" (194).

One cannot simply dismiss these passages as harmless Browne mannerisms, for they are typical of a scientific discourse that has to resort to Latin in order to write English:

> I know that a decoction of wild gourd or Colocynthis (though somewhat qualified) will not from every hand be dulcified unto aliment by an addition of flower or meal . . . gall is very mundificative. . . .

(197)

> For if Crystal be a stone (as in the number thereof it is confessedly received,) it is not immediately concreted by the efficacy of cold, but rather by a Mineral spirit, and lapidifical principles of its own, and therefore while it lay *in solutis principiis,* and remained in a fluid Body, it was a subject very unapt for proper conglaciation....
>
> (203)

> Now such bodies as strike fire have sulphureous or ignitible parts within them, and those strike best, which abound most in them. For these scintillations are not the accension of the air, upon the collision of two hard bodies, but rather the inflamable effluencies or vitrified sparks discharged from the bodies collided.
>
> (208)

> But Ice receiveth its figure according unto the surface wherein it concreteth, or the circumambiency which conformeth it. So it is plain upon the surface of water, but round in Hayl (which is also a glaciation,) and figured in its guttnlous descent from the air, and so growing greater or lesser according unto the accretion or pluvious aggelation about the mother and fundamental Atomes thereof....
>
> (210–11)

The vocabulary is so abstruse, so artificial, as to be almost out of touch with the subject matter. It is as unsuitable for science as the language of the Ciceronianist fanatics was for religion or everyday reality. Browne writes what at its worst can only be called Latinate jargon, heavy and cumbrous, obscuring the meaning, dark and thick—or, as Dr. Johnson would say—inspissated:

> ... The difference of their concretion is collectible from their dissolution: which being many ways pertormable in Ice, is few ways effected in Crystal. Now the causes of liquation are contrary to those of concretion; and as the Atoms and indivisible parcels are united, so are they in an opposite way disjoyned. That which is concreted by exsiccation or expression of humidity, will be resolved by humectation, as Earth, Dirt, and Clay; that which is coagulated by a fiery siccity, will suffer colliquation from an aqueous humidity, as Salt and Sugar, which are easily dissoluble in water, but not without difficulty in oyl, and well rectified spirits of Wine.
>
> (205)

This Latinity defeats one of the main ideals of the New Sciences, communication and cooperation open to all classes of English readers, for such language is comprehensible only by an educated philologist, or esoteric scientist who works from books, not life. Of Browne can it be said (as Addison did, so unfairly, of Milton), "Our language sank under him"; only to him I suspect that it would have seemed an apotheosis.

Browne was excessive, perhaps, but the problem was widespread. John Webster's *Academiarum Examen,*[64] scornful though it is of the universities and all other examples of useless learning, nevertheless includes such Latinisms as "*Apodictically,*" "inscious," "innocont" (sig. A3V); "plumbeous," "putation" (sig. B2V); "*nocument*" (3); "*facundity*" (5); "the caliginous pit of meer putation, and doubtfull opinion" (16);

"consentaneous," "statuminated" (17); "Protoplast" (26); "fætiferous," "vive" (27); "Pamphoniacal" (28); "extrinsecally adventitious," "innate and inplantate" (29); "prolation" (30); "altercations and abjurgations" (33); "adæquation" (34); "concamerated" (46); "no appulsion, nor retrocession" nor "lation" (47); "reluctancy, and contranitency" (49); *"minutiloquious," "mortiferous"* (58); "caliginous" (60); "oscitancy," "lections" (62); "the true opifex, and dispositor of all the salutary, and morbifick lineaments" (74); "labefactation" (77); "luxuriously petulant" (as a verb, 84); "grandævity" (94); and "Auscultator" (95). Webster was a Nonconformist, at once a Baconian and a Paracelsian, refuted by two leading lights of the Oxford and London scientific societies: beyond the pale, one might think, and for that reason so desperately Latinate. Yet the same weakness for Latinism is to be seen in members of the Royal Society, who were religious conformists and Baconians. Boyle himself, although of a clear and inelegant style in general, claimed to have written *The Sceptical Chymist* "in a style more fashionable than that of mere scholars is wont to be," but by means of such a style he was only fulfilling "decorum," since "it was fit that in a book written by a gentleman, and wherein only gentlemen are introduced as speakers, the language should be more smooth and the expressions more civil than is usual in the more scholastic way of writing" (7).

Nevertheless Boyle affords the following list of Latinisms: "dissipable" (31); "comminution," "homogeneal," "factitious concrete," "oleagenous," "colliquated" (37); "candent," "calcination" (43); "dulcified colcothar" (56); "vitrification" (57); "glaciation," "congelation" (58); "compurgator" (68); "idoneous" (69); "graduations of coagulation, congelation, and fixation" (72); "ebullition," "affused" (74); "cohobations" (78); "mistion" (80); "vomitive" (124); "sapid" (133); "diaphoretick and very deopilative" (138); "effumability" (146); "porosity" (159); "mordicant" (172); "opacous," "adustion," "additaments" (173); "empyreumatical," "feculancy" (219). Of course we have retained some of these words but with a different prefix or suffix; the crucial point is that as science develops it makes claims upon a language which that language may not be prepared for. Ironically, perhaps, at this stage Latin was more "advanced" as a language for science than English.

Yet although we can explain the use of Latinisms, their presence in the writings of the New Scientists not only offended against the ideals of open communication of knowledge to men of all classes and trades, but could not help sounding ridiculous in itself. One of the targets in Shadwell's satire on the New Sciences in *The Virtuoso* (1676)[65] is this kind of language, recorded in the mouth of that untiring and indiscriminate advocate of experiment, Sir Nicholas Gimcrack, who abounds in such words and phrases as "detention of this filum or thread," "superficies or surface of this humid element" (44); "having sufficiently refrigerated my lungs by way of respiration" (45); "diffusive," "precelling in physico-mechanical investigations" (46); "fuliginous" (47); "follicular impulsion" (47–48); "emittent" (51); "cacochymious" (52); "testaceous," "stentrophonical" (55); "docible" (71); "coagulation of the aqueous juice," and "appulse" (111). The best passage is the following description of the process by which a plum turns blue: ". . . it comes first to fluidity, then to orbiculation, then fixation, so to angulization, then crystallization, from thence to germination or ebullition, then vegetation, then plant animation, perfect animation, sensation, local motion and the like" (102 [act 4, scene 3, lines 224–28]). If we feel tempted to dismiss this as a caricature by Shadwell we may be schocked to discover that the whole passage is taken from that seminal document of the New Sciences, Robert Hooke's *Micrographia* ([London, 1665], 127). It is a rather malicious quotation, since Hook's vocabulary is normally unexceptionably English. Yet all the same, we can see that when Sprat wished the Royal Society's members to avoid the language of "Wits and Scholar" he had good reasons.

Notes

1. On Bacon's influence in the seventeenth century see Richard Foster Jones, *Ancients and Modens: A Study of the Rise of the Scientific Movement in Seventeenth-Century England*, 2d ed. rev. (St. Louis: Washington University Press, 1961); Brian Vickers, *Francis Bacon and Renaissance Prose* (Cambridge: Cambridge University Press, 19ii8), 232–41, 264; and Charles Webster, *The Great Instauration: Science, Medicine, and Reform, 1620–1660* (London: Duckworth, 1975). On Sprat's Baconianism see H. Fisch and H. W. Jones, "Bacon's Influence on Sprat's *History of the Royal Society*," *Modem Language Quarterly* 12 (195t): 399–406. In "Bacon's So-called 'Utilitarianism': Sources and Influence" (*Francis Bacon: Terminología e fortuna nel XVII secolo*, ed. Marta Fattori [Rome; Ateneo, 1985], 281–313), I have objected to the anachronistic and misleading use of the term "utilitarianism" and have shown that Bacon derived from a much broader classical tradition of the *vita activa*.
2. *History of the Royal Society*, ed. Jackson I. Cope and Harold Whitmorc Jones (St. Louis: Washington University Press, 1958; London: Routledge and Kegan Paul, 1959), 4. All quotations are from this facsimile edition; page references are given subsequently in the text.
3. See Robert Cluett, "Style, Precept, Personality: A. Test Case (Thomas Sprat, 1655–1713)," *Computers and the Humanities* 5 (1970–71): 257–77. In this article Cluett presents material of interest to computer users, drawing on his as yet unpublished dissertation, "These Seeming Mysteries: The Mind and Style of Thomas Sprat" (Ph.D. diss., Columbia University, 1969 [*Dissertation Abstracts* 70: 6950])·
4. On the Society's nonrepresentative nature—violently asserted at the time by its archenemy, Henry Stubbe—see Michael Hunter, *Science and Society in Restoration England* (Cambridge: Cambridge University Press, 1981), 36ff., 46ff.; and on its variable achievement see Henry Oldenburg's letters, ibid., 40, 43, 45.
5. What contemporary references there were concern the Society's committee on the English language: see John Evelyn, *Publick Employment and an Active Life prefer'd to Solitude, and all its Appanages . . .* (London, 1667), a work written to oppose Sir George Mackenzie's anonymously published *A Moral Essay, preferring Solitude to Publick Employment* (Edinburgh, 1665). In his preface Evelyn identifies Mackenzie as an *"ingenious* Stranger" on the basis of his use of words and expressions, and comments that *"the felicity which we have of gracefully adopting so many* Languages *and* Idioms *into our own, frustrates all pretences of not infinitely improving it: This was once the* design *of the* Royal Society; *and as it was worthy their thoughts; so I hope they will resume it"* (sig. A8r). For Evelyn's more considered views on preserving the purity of the English language see his letter of 20 June 1665 to Sir Peter Wyche, reprinted in J. E, Spingarn, *Critical Essays of the Seventeenth Century*, 3 vols. (Oxford: Clarendon Press, 1908–9), 2:310–13.
6. *The Works of Francis Bacon*, ed. James Spedding, Robert Leslie Ellis, and Douglas Denon Heath, 14 vols. (London: Longman, 1857—74), 4:33–33. All quotations are from this edition; references, given subsequently in the text, are to volume and page.
7. Claiming that there has been an increase in ambiguity due to the sudden coming in of a great number of phrases which could bear several meanings, Wilkins warns that in "late times . . . this grand imposture of Phrases hath almost eaten out solid Knowledge in all professions" (John Wilkins, *An Essay Towards a Real Character and a Philosophical Language* [London, 1668], 18). On the universal language movement, see, for example, Paul Cornelius, *Languages in Seventeenth- and Early Eighteenth-Century Imaginary Voyages* (Geneva: Droz, 1965); James Knowlson,

Universal Language Schemes in England and France, 1600—1800 (Toronto and Buffalo: University of Toronto Press, 1975); Vivian Salmon, *The Works of Francis Lodwick: A Study of His Writings in the Intellectual Context of the Seventeenth Century* (London: Longman, 1972); and various essays in a collection of her work, *The Study of Language in Seventeenth-Century England* (Amsterdam: Benjamins, 1979).

8. A. C. Howell, "*Res et Verba*: Words and Things," *ELH* 13 (1946): 131–42. See also G. A. Padley, *Grammatical Theory in Western Europe, 1500–1700: The Latin Tradition* (Cambridge: Cambridge University Press, 1976), chap. 3, "The Seventeenth Century: Words versus Things," although I find this account oversimplified. It is not enough to say that "the seventeenth century"—as if so many diverse writers and attitudes could be lumped together under that label—suffered a "divorce between words and things" (Padley, 138–39), so that "the linguistic sign" was "no longer available to mediate between the mind and reality according to an arbitrary convention" (140). There were plenty of writers who held that words were *signs* of concepts, ideas, or objects: Bacon, Hobbes, and Locke, to start with. See Brian Vickers, "Analogy versus Identity: The Rejection of Occult Symbolism, 1580–1680," in Vickers, ed., *Occult and Scientific Mentalities in the Renaissance* (Cambridge and New York: Cambridge University Press, 1984), 102–5, 109–14.

9. On this trope see Quintilian, *Institutio oratoria*, 8.3.61–62. Related tropes include *evidentia, demonstratio* (hypotyposis), *effictio*: see Heinrich Lausberg, *Handbuch der literarischen Rhetorik: Eine Grundlegung der Literaturwissenschaft*, 2 vols. (Munich: M. Hueber, 1960); and Lee A. Sonnino, *A Handbook to Sixteenth-Century Rhetoric* (London: Routledge and Kegan Paul, 1968).

10. See, for example, Johnson's essay on Cowley and metaphysical poetry; Marjorie Nicolson, *Science and Imagination* (Ithaca, N.Y.: Cornell University Press, 1956), reprinting the essays "The Telescope and Imagination" and "The Microscope and English Imagination," both dating from 1935; and William Powell Jones, *The Rhetoric of Science: A Study of Scientific Ideas and Imagery in Eighteenth-Century English Poetry* (London: Routledge and Kegan Paul, 1966).

11. See also Pico della Mirandola, *On the Imagination*, ed. Harry Caplan (New Haven, Conn.: Yale University Press for Cornell University; London: H. Milford, Oxford University Press, 1930), chap, 7, for example: "On the numerous Evils which come from the Imagination"; Murray Wright Bundy, *The Theory of Imagination in Classical and Mediaeval Thought* (Urbana: University of Illinois Press, 1927); William Rossky, "Imagination in the English Renaissance: Psychology and Poetic," *Studies in the Renaissance* 5 (1958): 49–73; Donald F. Bond, "'Distrust' of Imagination in English Neo-Classicism," *Philological Quarterly* 14 (1935): 54–69; and idem, "The Neoclassical Psychology of the Imagination," *ELH* 4 (1937): 245–64.

12. From *A Tale of a Tub*, sec, 9, in *The Prose Works of Jonathan Swift*, ed. Herbert Davis, 14 vols. (Oxford: Basil Blackwell, 1939–68), 1:108.

13. *The Miscellaneous Works in Prose and Verse of Sir Thomas Overbury, Knt.*, ed. Edward F. Rimbault (London: J. R. Smith, 1856), 87.

14. See Richard Foster Jones, *The Seventeenth Century: Studies in the History of English Thought and Literature from Bacon to Pope* (Stanford, Calif.: Stanford University Press, 1951), cited subsequently in the text as RFJ. This volume collects the following essays: "Science and Criticism in the Neo-Classical Age of English Literature" (1940), 41–74; "Science and English Prose Style in the Third Quarter of the Seventeenth Century" (1930), 75–110; "The Attack on Pulpit Eloquence in the Restoration" (1931), 111–42; and "Science and Language in England of the Mid-Seventeenth Century" (1932), 143–60.

15. Robert Adolph, *The Rise of Modern Prose Style* (Cambridge, Mass.: M. I. T. Press, 1968). William Youngren ("Generality, Science, and Poetic Language in the Restoration," *ELH* 35 [1968]: 158–87) argues that post-Restoration literature does not reflect a mechanistic, colorless universe. It is difficult to imagine how anyone who had actually read, say, Dryden, Oldham, Rochester, Bunyan, Congreve, could get the idea that post-Restoration literature does portray such a universe. Historians of ideas can be dangerous guides to literary theory or practice.

16. W. Fraser Mitchell, *English Pulpit Oratory from Andrewes to Tillotson* (London: Society for Promoting Christian Knowledge, 1932); Jackson I. Cope, *Joseph Glanvill, Anglican Apologist* (St. Louis: Washington University Press, 1956); and Adolph, *The Rise of Modem, Prose Style.*

17. See, for example, Karl R. Wallace, *Francis Bacon on Communication and Rhetoric* (Chapel Hill: University of North Carolina Press, 1943); and John L. Harrison, "Bacon's View of Rhetoric, Poetry, and the Imagination," *Huntington Library Quarterly* 20 (1957): 91–126, reprinted in Brian Vickers, ed., *Essential Articles for the Study of Francis Bacon* (Hamden, Conn.: Archon, 1968; London: Sidgwick and Jackson, 1972), 253–71.
18. *Rheiorica,* trans. W. Rhys Roberts, in *The Works of Aristotle,* ed. W. D. Ross, 12 vols. (Oxford: Clarendon Press, 1908–52), vol. 11, 1407a33–35. References to Aristotle's *Rhetoric* are from this edition and volume; line numbers will be given subsequently.
19. See G. E. R. Lloyd, *Polarity and Analogy: Two Types of Argumentation in Early Greek Thought* (Cambridge: Cambridge University Press, 1966), 363–64, 403ff.; quotation (from Aristotle's *Meteorology*) on page 403.
20. Vickers, *Francis Bacon and Renaissance Prose,* 141–201, 211–31; and idem, "Bacon's Use of Theatrical Imagery," *Studies in the Literary Imagination,* 1971, no. 1: 189–226.
21. Quoted in George Williamson, *The Senecan Amble: A Study in Prose Form from Bacon to Collier* (London: Faber and Faber, 1951), 178n. 2.
22. See Morris Croll's essays, collected as *Style, Rhetoric, and Rhythm,* ed. J. Max Patrick et al. (Princeton, N.J.: Princeton University Press, 1966); and the critical evaluations of Croll's theories in Vickers, *Francis Bacon and Renaissance Prose,* 96–140, and in Adolph, *The Rise of Modern Prose. Style,* especially 10ff., 29ff., 62ff., 66, 89–90, 140ff., 161ff., 242.
23. Jones, *Ancients and Moderns,* 118.
24. Richard Foster Jones, *The Triumph of the English Language: A Survey of Opinions Concerning the Vernacular from the Introduction of Printing to the Restoration* (Stanford, Calif,: Stanford University Press, 1953).
25. This characteristic is shared by those who accept Jones's thesis; thus Robert Adolph discusses (inaccurately) the style of Boyle's *The Sceptical Chyrnist* (1661), and then introduces Wilkins's *Ecclesiastes* (1646) before going on to a work of 1669 (see Adolph, *The Rise of Modern Prose Style,* 192–95). He too claims that "toward the end of the century, understandably, a mild reaction against plainness in favor of 'Rhetorick' . . . set in" (206): yet the interest in rhetoric was constant throughout the seventeenth century. Every decade saw the publication of at least ten books in English on rhetoric, not to mention the countless Latin texts printed in England or imported from the Continent. In the middle of a later discussion of plain style Adolph suddenly introduces Puritan preachers arguing for plain style, in material dating from 1592, 1656, and 1659 (208–9), The great exemplar of confused chronology is of course George Williamson's *Senecan Amble,* a work which it is impossible to read without being plunged into muddle.
26. Richard Foster Jones, "The Rhetoric of Science in England of the Mid-Seventeenth Century," in *Restoration and Eighteenth-Century Literature,* ed. Carroll Camden (Chicago: University of Chicago Press, 1963), 21.
27. Adolph, *The Rise of Modern Prose Style,* 123.
28. *The Vanity of Dogrnatizing: The Three "Versions,"* ed. Stephen Medcalf (Hove, Sussex: Harvester Press, 1970), xxi–xxii, xxxiv–xxxix; Adolph, *The Rise of Modern Prose Style,* 78–128; and Cope, *Joseph Glanvill, Anglican Apologist,* 152–59.
29. Cope, *Joseph Glanvill, Anglican Apologist,* 149.
30. Medcalf, ed., *Vanity of Dogmatizing,* xxvi–xxxix.
31. See Boyle's *The Sceptical Chymist* (1661) in the Everyman Library reprint, ed. E. A. Moelwyn-Hughes (London: Dent, 1967), 1960–61; page references are given subsequently in the text. The passage in Boyle reads:
    . . . I may tell you, that I did once, purposely, cause to be decocted in fair water a plant abounding with sulphureous and spirituous parts, and having exposed the decoction to a keen north-wind in a very frosty night, 1 observed, that the more aqueous parts of it were turned by the next morning into ice, towards the innermost part of which, the more agile and spirituous parts, as I then conjectured, having retreated, to shun as much as might be their environing enemy, they had there preserved themselves unfrozen in the form of a high coloured liquor; the aqueous and spirituous parts having been so slightly (blended rather than) united in the

decoction, that they were easily separable by such a degree of cold, as would not have been able to have divorced the parts of urine or wine.... (60)

In Glanvill's *Vanity of Dogmatizing* we read:

> If after a decoction of *hearbs* in a Winter-night, we expose the liquor to the frigid air; we may observe in the morning under a crust of Ice, the perfect appearance both in *figure*, and *colour*, of the *Plants* that were taken from it. But if we break the *aqueous Crystal*, those pretty *images* dis-appear and are presently dissolved.

Now these *airy Vegetables* are presumed to have been made, by the reliques of these *plantal emissions* whose avolation was prevented by the *condensed inclosure*. And therefore playing up and down for a while within their liquid prison, they at last settle together in their natural order, and the *Atomes* of each part finding out their proper place, at length rest in their methodical Situation, till by breaking the *Ice* they are disturbed, and those counterfeit *compositions* are scatter'd into their first *Indivisibles*. (46–47)

> In the revision for the *Essays* of 1676 (Joseph Glanvill, *Essays on Several Important Subjects in Philosophy and Religion* [London, 1676]) we have:

And there is an experiment mentioned by approved Authors that looks the same way; It is, That after a decoction of Herbs in a frosty Night, the shape of the Plants will appear under the Ice in the Morning: which Images are supposed to be made by the congregated *Effluvia* of the Plants themselves, which loosely wandring up and down in the Water, at last settle in their natural place and order, and so make up an appearance of the Herbs from whence they were emitted. (11–12)

32. See Cope, *Joseph Glanvill, Anglican Apologist;* and the *Dictionary of National Biography*.
33. In a footnote Adolph criticizes the simplistic categories of Jones's 1963 paper "The Rhetoric of Science" (see n. 26 above) and argues that some Baconians can be rhetorical, as Sprat is, "or get caught up in jargon, as in the writings of Hooke" (*The Rise of Modern Prose Style*, 321). Mr. Adolph at least shows some signs of having read the New Scientists, but gives no commentary on them; he later refers to "Wren's florid manner" (338 n. 25).
34. See Brian Vickers, "Territorial Disputes: Philosophy versus Rhetoric," in Vickers, ed., *Rhetoric Revalued: Papers from the International Society for the History of Rhetoric* (Binghamton, N.Y.: Center for Medieval and Early Renaissance Studies, 1982), 247–66.
35. See, for instance, passages quoted in *Ancients and Moderns*, on the Baconians: 100, 132–33, 139, 140, 186, 329 n. 54, etc.; on the Latitudinarians: 186ff., 200; on the experimentalists: 192–93, 194–95, 197, etc.
36. Jones, "Rhetoric of Science," published in 1963 (see n. 26 above), 13, 13 n. 22. Adolph, in a 1968 work, also quotes Hobbes's attack on metaphor without noticing that it is entirely metaphorical (*The Rise of Modern Prose Style*, 215).
37. Adolph, *The Rise, of Modern Prose Style*, 122–23, 180, 181.
38. Ibid., 202.
39. Nathaniel Fairfax, *A Treatise of the Bulk and Selvedge of the World* (1674), in *Two Seventeenth-Century Prefaces*, ed. A. K. Groston (London: University Press of Liverpool, 1949), 36.
40. Cluett, "Style, Precept, Personality" (see n. 3 above), 258.
41. Ibid., 275.
42. Jones, *The Triumph of the English Language*, 310.
43. Despite the paucity of evidence critics have asserted that Wilkins had a great influence on the English language and prose style. See, for example, Francis Cliristensen, "John Wilkins and the Royal Society's Reform of Prose Style," *Modern Language Quarterly* 7 (1946): 179–87, 279–90; and B. C. Vickery, "The Significance of John Wilkins in the History of Bibliographical Classification," *Libri* 2 (1953): 326–43.
44. Jones, *Ancients and Moderns*, 91. Jones was followed, uncritically enough, by Cluett, who refers to Sprat and "the deep distrust of words that he shared with many of his co-Baconians, notably Wilkins," revealing "a pragmatic and anti-intellectual cast of mind" ("Style, Precept, Personality" [see n. 3 above], 258). G. A. Padley also follows Jones on Bacon's "antipathy to language," part of

the "utilitarianism of the new Puritan bourgeoisie" (*Grammatical Theory in Western Europe;* quotations on 138 and 135, respectively). Questions of style and questions of philosophy have become hopelessly confused here: there was no opposition to the intellect in Wilkins, nor to "words," *tout court,* in Bacon.
45. Jones, *Ancients and Moderns,* 91.
46. Hugh Kearney, *Scholars and Gentlemen: Universities and Society in Pre-Industrial Britain, 1500–1700* (London: Faber and Faber, 1970), 112–28.
47. Webster, *The Great Instauration,* passim.
48. Jones, *Ancients and Moderns,* 102, 139, 294 n. 27.
49. Jones, *The Triumph of the English Language,* 293–94, 293n.
50. Jones, *Ancients and Moderns,* 300 n. 66.
51. Jones, *The Triumph of the English Language,* 309n.
52. Charles Webster, ed., *Samuel Hartlib and the Advancement of Learning* (London: Cambridge University Press, 1970), 17–21, for example; and Webster, *The Great Instauration,* passim.
53. Jones, *The Triumph of the English Language,* 248, 249–50, 250–51, 258, 259–60, 307 n. 29, 309 n. 33, 317–18, 320 n. 63.
54. Ibid., 263ff.; quotation on 263.
55. *The Works of Sir Thomas Browne,* ed. Charles Sayle, 3 vols. (London: G. Richards, 1904–7), 1:117; italics reversed in this quotation. All further quotations are from volume 1 of this edition; page references are given subsequently in the text.
56. In *The Triumph of the English Language,* as in his later essays, Jones referred to the "strong neologizing movement, which ... reached its climax in the exuberant Elizabethan age" ("Rhetoric of Science" [see n. 26 above], 18). The fact is that the English language continued to import words from Latin, especially for scientific subjects, right through the seventeenth century. This can be easily checked by referring to Thomas Fihkenstaedt, Ernst Leisi, and Dieter Wolff, eds., *A Chronological English Dictionary* (Heidelberg: Carl Winter Universitätsverlag, 1970), where new words as recorded by the *Oxford English Dictionary* are listed alphabetically, year by year. See also Francis R. Johnson ("Latin versus English: The Sixteenth-Century Debate over Scientific Terminology," *Studies in Philology* 41 [1944]: 109–35), who shows that the problem of an inadequate English vocabulary for science was already an issue by the 1550s. Indeed, it was even felt necessary to add glossaries of new words: see Sanford V. Larkey, "Scientific Glossaries in Sixteenth-Century English Books," *Bulletin of the Institute of the History of Medicine* 5 (1937): 105–14.
57. John Wilkins, *Mathematical Magick. Or, The Wonders That may be performed by Mechanicall Geometry* ... (London, 1648), sig. A5r; quoted in Jones, *The Triumph of the English Language,* 310 n. 35·
58. Walter Charleton, *Deliramenta Catarrhi: Or, the Incongruities, Impossibilities, and Absurdities Couched under the Vulgar Opinion of Defluxions* (London, 1650), sig. A3r.
59. Ibid., sig. A3V.
60. See Jones, "Rhetoric of Science" (n, 26 above), 19 n. 25, for the quotation and comment.
61. Joseph Glanvill, "Antifanatick Theologie, and Free Philosophy," in *Essays on Several Important Subjects in Philosophy and Religion* (London, 1676), 42.
62. Adolph, *The Rise of Modern Prose Style,* 124; see also 123ff., and Joseph Glanyill. *Essay Concerning Preaching* (London, 1678), 13–17.
63. Spingarn, ed., *Critical Essays of the Seventeenth Century,* 2:310–64.
64. A facsimile edition of Webster's *Acaderniarum Examen, Or The Examination of Academies* is included in Allen G. Debus, ed., *Science and Education in the Seventeenth Century: The Webster-Ward Debate (London:* Macdonald, 1970); page references are given in the text.
65. Thomas Shadwell, *The Virtuoso,* ed. Marjorie Hope Nicolson and David Stuart Rodes (London: Arnold; Lincoln: University of Nebraska Press, 1966; all quotations are from this edition and page references are given in the text. See also Claude Lloyd, "Shadwell and the Virtuosi," *PMLA* 44 (1929): 472–94; and Joseph M. Gilde, "Shadwell and the Royal Society: Satire in *The Virtuoso,*" *Studies in English Literature, 1500–1900* 10 (1970): 469–90. For the wider background see the still essential study by Walter E. Houghton, Jr., "The English Virtuoso in the Seventeenth Century," *journal of the History of Ideas* 3 (1943): 51–73. 190–219.

# 19.
PLOCHE AND POLYPTOTON
Jeanne Fahnestock

In a 1992 issue of *Science*, two aeronautical engineers explained a new approach in the manufacturing of advanced materials for aircraft engines, an approach known as intelligent processing of materials (IPM), which they defined as "an integrated, comprehensive effort to apply mathematical modeling, sensor technologies, and control system methods to improve materials processes." IPM, they claimed, applied the scientific method "to deduce process behavior and establish extensible theories governing process performance" (Backman and Williams 1992, 1086). As part of their explanation of how IPM works, they wrote the following paragraph:

> Materials process understandings established early in the process development cycle by conducting statistically designed experiments and formulating physics-based models of the process. The derived knowledge is encoded in a process simulator. Process sensors are established to validate process models and to characterize the material product and process conditions for the designed experiments. The models and sensors serve as the foundation for subsequent process control development and act as the vehicle for technology transfer between the development and production environments. Process control can be applied at a variety of levels. Closed-loop control is used to counteract process disturbances that have short time constants, whereas supervisory and expert system control modules mimic the process corrections made by process operators and engineers.
>
> (1086–1087)

After taking this paragraph in, a reader should be convinced that there are some well formulated procedures in place for monitoring materials processing. The language of management and engineering combined in this sample is a well known if sometimes lamented linguistic register whose typical features include a high level of abstraction and a penchant for using noun clusters as prenoun modifiers (eg., "materials process understanding"). There certainty appear to be no figures of speech in this passage, particularly none of those discussed so far, antithesis, incrementum, or antimetabole. Yet this passage is as highly figured as any example from Henry Peacham's sixteenth-century *Garden of Eloquence*. Anyone reading it with some attention to the writers' choices is likely to notice the frequent repetition of the word "process." It appears twelve times, and its closest competitors are fairly distant, "control" occurring four times and "development" three. It is, in fact, the insistent repetition of the word

---

Fahnestock, Jeanne. "Ploche and Polyptoton," *Rhetorical Figures in Science*. Oxford: Oxford University Press, 1999: 156–177.

"process," primarily as an adjective and once as a noun, that epitomizes the arguers' point in this passage: That there is a specific kind of awareness and control being exercised throughout a manufacturing process by systems, equipment, and people especially dedicated to their task.

Figures of Repetition

Rhetoricians have always recognized the need for emphasizing key points and terms in an argument, and one device consistently praised in rhetorical manuals for achieving such emphasis b repetition. Quintilian recommended repetition as a hedge against wandering attention and idiosyncratic interpretation when he discussed the essentials of good style for the forensic orator before a judge who will

> have many other thoughts to distract him unless what we say is so clear that our words will thrust themselves into his mind even when he is not giving his attention, just as the sunlight forces itself upon the eyes. Therefore our aim must be not to put him in a position to understand our argument, but to force him to understand it. Consequently we shall frequently repeat anything which we think the judge has failed to take in as he should.
> (Quintilian 1921, III, 211)

The kind of repetition of key points that Quintilian talks of here can, of course, be accomplished by paraphrase, by saying the same thing again in different words. But another kind of repetition has an important place in the stylistic repertoire of classical rhetoric not just the repetition of ideas but the repetition of the same words and phrases.[1] Speakers who repeat the same words seem to stay on the same subject and make a place for that subject in the imperfect memories of their listeners; writers who repeat do the same and in addition provide visual chains across a text. Listeners and readers who absorb repetition, consciously or unconsciously, are also likely to infer that repeated terms have significance. Why else would they be repeated?

In the Classical and Renaissance lore of the figures, repetitions were categorized according to where they appeared in consecutive phrases or clauses. From the *Ad Herennium* on, the following schemes distinguished the strategic places for repetition:

> *Anaphora*:[2] Repetition of the openings of successive structures.
> (e.g., No one was there in the beginning; no one saw how it was put together.)
>
> *Epistrophe*: Repetition of the endings of successive structures.
> (e.g., When my hand works, my brain works.)
>
> *Epanalepsis*: Repetition of the opening of a structure at its ending.
> (e.g., Tune heals the sorrows inflicted by time.)
>
> *Anadiplosis*: Repetition of the ending of one structure in the opening of the next.
> (e.g., Cinderella loved the Prince. The Prince ignored her.)
>
> *Symploche*: Repetition of both the beginning and the ending in successive structures.
> (e.g., Time stays for no one. Time leaps for no one.)

Subjunctio: Immediate repetition of a word with nothing intervening.
(e.g., The camel came up short, short by Bedouin standards.)

Obviously more ingenious patterns of repetition can be identified, but these are the dominant ones marked in rhetorical texts over the centuries. There is nothing to prevent these patterns extending over three of four adjacent syntactic units or skipping sentence constituents and occurring in a first and third or second and fifth, etc., though the manuals stress repetition in immediately adjacent units.

Repetition in the openings and closings of phrases and douses, already positions of emphasis, creates patterns that can presumably be picked out or even registered only subliminally in the experience of a text. The importance of such patterns in aural texts is obvious; as a modern example, one thinks of the incantatory anaphora of Martin Luther King, Jr.'s "I have a dream" speech. Such structurally strategic repetition is a kind of aural glue. Listeners, and readers as crypto-listeners, are invited to detect the patterns superimposed by these repetitions, creating potential mini-schemes of organization across a text.

Perfect Repetition: Ploche

In addition to the basic schemes of strategic repetition cited above, Classical and Renaissance treatments of the figures also marked repetitions that do not occur in structurally significant slots. Perhaps in keeping with its protean character, versions of this formal feature of random repetition went by many names. The name preferred in this study is *ploche* (from the Greek πλοκή), referring to anything plaited or woven, a single word reappearing like a single strand in a braid or fabric. According to the first definition of this figure in the *Ad Herennium* (where its Latin name is *traductio*), the same word is "frequently reintroduced, not only without offense to good taste, but even so as to render the style more elegant, as follows: 'One who has nothing in life more desirable than life cannot cultivate a virtuous life'" ([Cicero] 1954, 279).[3]

Repetitions may occur in similar grammatical slots, the same word reappearing as an adjective within a sentence or across several. But these repetitions need not coincide with a syntactic pattern, like the opening and closing of a sentence. This lack of convergence with any other pattern makes ploche virtually disappear as a recognizable figure, and without a detectable pattern in the repetition, the signs of special authorial intention diminish. After all, it is normal practice for speakers and writers to repeat words occasionally. But me very invisibility of this figure makes it potentially more effective, and thus this least marked of the forms of repetition becomes, of all the figures discussed so far, an *experimentum crucis* in understanding the argumentative power of chosen forms of expression.

The figure of random repetition thrives in Renaissance manuals under a variety of aliases: *heratio, duplicatio, palilogia, diaphora* and *traductio*, as well as *ploche*. Some of these corollary figures concern repetition that is formal but not semantic; the same word is repeated orthographically, but the same exact meaning is not intended. In Susenbrotus, for example, ploche is a scheme "When the same word is repeated emphasizing by the repetition a particular aspect of its meaning" and Scaliger points out that "The meaning is inevitably altered on the second appearance of the word" (Sonnino 1968, 103). In Peacham, the device called *ploche* is very narrowly defined as one involving only proper names, but again with the stipulation that when repeated the name "signifieth another thing" (Peacham 1954, 44). As an example Peacham offers, "In that great victorie Caesar was Caesar, that is, a merecifull conquerer" (44), a use that also employs the trope *antonomasia,* in which a proper name becomes a term for a category or type of person (as in "Pol Pot was a Hitler"). These distinctions surely capture a valid insight about what sometimes happens when a term recurs. Readers may or may not understand the second appearance in the same way. From the perspective of logic and an insistence on univocal reference, a statement that repeats terms like "Caesar was Caesar," for example, is tautological nonsense? But no one would take this statement as meaningless when encountering it outside a logic text. To avoid the tautology, interpreters take the first instance of the term to mean one thing (the individual Caesar) and the second to mean another (in Peacham's version, the type, a "mercifull conquerer"). As *The New Rhetoric* puts it, "The formulation of an identity puts us on the track of an opposition" (Perelman and Olbrechts-Tyteca 1969, 217). Of course, the same strategy can be used even when the two terms are not proper names, as in "Boys will be boys," or in the alchemists naming of purified from impure sulphur as "the sulphur of sulphur" (Crosland 1962, 129). This repetition of ordinary terms in a way that exploits possible differences is identified by Quintilian as *antanaclasis,* "where the same word is used in two different meanings' (Quintilian 1921, III, 485) and by Peacham as *diaphora,* a figure that comes with the advice that "the word which is to be repeated, be a word of importance . . . and not every common word, for that were absurd: considering that many words may be repeated without change of signification" (Peacham 1954, 45).[4] In their careful distinctions among these figures, the rhetorical manuals are clearly marking intentional uses of the same word in different senses, but it is always possible for any repetition to be taken this way. Deconstructive readers obviously favor the unintended uses of antonomasia and antanaclasis in their pursuit of potential and presumably unconscious fissures in a text, and of course an interpreter need not wait for a word to be repeated but can find these potential double readings in a single occurrence.

But the argumentative intent of repetition may just as well be to keep the same signification from instance to instance as a common thread, maintaining consistency of concepts in consistency of terms, a notion inherent in the original Greek name for the figure, πλοκή, emphasizing braided interconnections, the tying together achieved by the repetition of something. When André Lwoff gave his exasperated definition, "A virus is a virus!" he did not mean the second instance of the term in a different sense; he intended a circular prediction to indicate an entity so unique it could not be defined (Eigen 1993, 43). Repetition of terms in the same sense is distinguished by Peacham, ever the most careful of catalogers, as *traduction* "a forme of speech which repeateth one word often times in one sentence, making the oration more pleasant to the care" (Peacham 1954, 49). Nowhere does Peacham mention changing meanings in his definition of this figure whose effect he compares to "pleasant repetitions and divisions in Musicke," and whose chief use is "either to garnish the sentence with oft repetition, or to note well the importance of the word repeated" (49). Furthermore, in all three of the examples Peacham offers of traductio [ploche], a word is repeated three times, a number of repetitions that certainly works against changing its meaning, while at the same time it suggests an author's deliberate choice. The fact that traductio marks repetition without change of meaning is also reinforced by Peacham's caution where the "disgrace' in this figure is lapsing into "Tautologia, which is a tedious and wearisome repetition of one word" (49). As an example of traductio [ploche] well used, Peacham offers no less than John 1:1, "In the beginning was the word, and the word was with God, and God was the word," a passage that is transformed significantly depending on whether it is read as traductio or diaphora, that is, on whether the repeated "word" is to be taken in different senses or in one.[5]

The Argumentative Effects of Ploche

The New Rhetoric emphasizes the rhetorical importance of presence, of foregrounding notions in an audience's consciousness, and it asserts that the "simplest way of creating this presence is repetition" (Perelman and Olbrechta-Tyteca 1969, 144). Here again is the general claim that the figures are like the fans in a stadium who are waving their hands, making them more visible then those sitting quietly. It is, however, possible to distinguish more specific argumentative effects from repetition than simply foregrounding.

Repetition can bring concepts together by giving them the same name or attributing the same property or action to them. It is, then, like gradatio, another device that can undo the work of antithesis, but only if the repeated term is taken to mean the same thing from use to use. If one predicates the same things of two terms, then these two things are joined, at least provisionally, in the act of listening or reading. If these two terms started out as antithetical in the minds of the audience, then this co-predication can have the effect of diminishing their opposition (see p 87).

The predication of the same qualities need not be drawn out or foregrounded in separate categorical propositions: X is A and Y is A. This work can occur more subtly anywhere in a sentence or across several sentences in repeated objects or verbs or adjectives positioned before nouns, and so on, although in each case the precise effect will depend on what function is repeated. Furthermore, in breaking with Peacham's examples, though not with his definition, repeating only twice in the same sense can still be argumentatively significant.

An illustration comes from the opening sentence of Roger Fowler and Gunther Kress's "Critical Linguistics," the concluding essay in *Language and Control*. "The language materials analyzed in this book suggest that there are strong and pervasive connections between linguistic structure and social structure" (Fowler and Kress 1979, 185). Here ploche carries the burden of the claim. The authors want to maintain that language and social organization map onto each other in significant ways; they could have said, "there are strong and pervasive connections between language and social organization," or "between language and society." Instead, they find pervasive connections between "linguistic structure and social structure," two entities that can be named by the same superordinate noun or genus term "structure." Since they are already the same thing by virtue of being named by the same noun—both are "structures"—it is less surprising that there should be "strong and pervasive" connections between them.

Making a claim less surprising and therefore more convincing is precisely the work of a figure of argument, illustrating once again that there are pervasive connections between linguistic structure and argumentative structure.

Stability in the phenomena under discussion can be an arguer's goal achieved by stability, that is, precise repetition of the nouns, the substance terms. The identity of the terms figures the identity of the reference, though of course these identities can be as vulnerable to refutation at any other attempted stability in an argument. Repetition of modifiers secures another kind of stability; it is a linguistic device used to produce connections among phenomena that are named differently.

Darwin's use of argumentative repetition is notable. Though in a corpus as large as Darwin's one can find examples of virtually any figure, Darwin generally avoids the more obvious devices of strategically positioned repetition such as anaphora, epanalepsis, and so forth. Instead he favors ploche, the subtler repetitions that declare identity in reference or the interconnections among phenomena. Darwin adeptly repeats strategic adjectives in the following critical passage that contains his defense of the concept of a struggle for existence.

> The dependency of one organic being on another, as of a parasite on his prey, lies generally between beings remote in the scale of the nature. This is likewise sometimes the case with those which may be strictly said to struggle with each other for existence, as in the case of locusts and grass-feeding quadrupeds. But the struggle will almost invariably be most severe between individuals of the same species, for they frequent the same districts, require the same food, and are exposed to me same dangers.
>
> (Darwin 1965, 60)

It would be no exaggeration to say that the repetition of "same" carries the argument in this passage. Darwin is, in his usual manner, establishing a quantitatively graded series, ordered degrees in the severity of the struggle for existence (see chapter 3). To reach the final item in this series, intraspecific competition, and to make this item a "most," requires amplification of the causes of competition among members of the same species, since the more they have in common, the more they struggle. The repetition of "same" accomplishes this intensification, linking districts, food sources, and dangers as common properties of the "same" species. The point could have been made without the repetition of "same," but the repetition epitomizes the argument.

The repetition of "different" proves critical in an article that appeared in *Science*, which in many ways typifies a generation of arguments in neurophysiology once functional magnetic resonance imaging technology became available. Brain researchers attempt to localize specific areas associated with cognitive tasks by MRIs indicating blood flow patterns. The goal of much of this research is to make robust distinctions in the tasks performed and then to associate those tasks with certain areas of the brain in ways more precise than have been possible before. The following passage summarizes the result of one such set of experiments on visual processing: "The main result was that different regions of extrastriate visual cortex were activated when [a subject was] attending to different attributes of a visual display" (Corbetta et al. 1990, 1556). This sentence delivers the primary claim of its authors: That there is a correlation between parts of the brain and parts of a specially constructed visual task. (There is no surprise in the localization of function, but some in the precisian of division of the visual task.) The argument for this claim is carried by the repetition of the key word "different," the verbal trace of the standard correlation argument Activation of *different* parts of the brain corresponds with *different* parts of the visual display. Two entities or concepts that can be modified by the same adjective are more likely to be taken as connected in some way. The logical appeal of adjective repetition, so simple and even simplistic when unpacked, nevertheless moves by quickly, without drawing the attention and potential refutation of explicit claims. Across a longer passage, the repetition of an unstressed adjective can work to associate a set of concepts that might otherwise remain dispersed. In a single sentence, the closer juxtaposition of repeated words is even more likely to take effect.[6] Ploche confounds the stylistic rule that repeating the same word in the same or in an adjacent sentence is inartistic, the result of an impoverished vocabulary. Yet what is sometimes seen as an aesthetic defect can be an argumentative virtue in a case like the following.

Koch's Postulates

One of the most celebrated events in the history of medicine, made famous by Paul De Kruif's hyperbolic account in *The Microbe Hunters,* was Robert Koch's discovery of the tuberculosis bacillus in 1882. A corollary of this discovery, as famous among microbiologists, were Koch's procedural innovations. In a popular book on viruses written in 1992, Arnold Levine of Princeton University, a distinguished researcher on tumor viruses and a former editor of the *Journal of Virology,* explains that a series of criteria first established by Koch is still in use as the standard for identifying a microbial disease agent. Levine phrases what are now widely known as "Koch's postulates" in the following way:

> (1) the organism must be regularly found in the lesions of the disease, (2) the organism must be isolated in pure culture (hence the need for sterile techniques) (3) inoculation of such a culture of pure organisms into the host should initiate the disease, and (4) the organism must be recovered once again from the lesions of this host (Levine 5; see the note for similar textbook versions of the postulates).[7]

What is stylistically noticeable about this version of Koch's postulates is the repetition of the word "organism" in each of the four elements. This use of ploche epitomizes perfectly the standard demanded by the postulates: that a consistent disease-causing agent persist through a precise experimental route, from an infected disease-ridden host to a pure culture to a new host that manifests the disease to another isolation and identification procedure. If an organism maintains its identity through each step of this process, the way the word itself is maintained in each sentence of the postulates, then there is "proof" that it is a disease-causing agent. Ploche, then, is the figurative epitome of Koch's postulates, stability of the term representing stability of the referent and, in this case, of the organism under scrutiny.

Koch's postulates figure in the recent controversy over whether the HIV virus is the true causal agent of AIDS and, indirectly, of its many end-stage pathologies. Peter

Duesberg, outspoken critic of the prevailing view, bases his main charge against the HIV paradigm on the fact that the virus has never been consistently identified through each of the required stages of Koch's postulates (Duesberg 1996, 35).[8] It is not always recoverable from the tissues of patients with full-blown AIDS nor has it proved possible to reproduce it for transmission to hosts of other species (174–186). In practice, however, the stage of isolation and in vitro culturing of the potential disease-causing organism is not a requirement. In experiments to identify the agent in the transmission of Bovine Spongiform Encephalopathy (BSE or "mad cow disease"), an agent not assumed to be self-replicating anyway, the brains of infected mice are ground up and injected directly into new mice (Lasmézas et al. 1997, 403–404; a method closer to that used by Pasteur to study rabies than that used by Koch to study tuberculosis). Nevertheless, if the presumed disease-causing agent is not detectable in animals down the chain when aspects of the disease are present, it is ruled out as a sufficient cause. Researchers in France have in fact been unable to complete Koch's ploche in the case of the malformed prion supposedly capable of causing spongiform encephalopathies across species and so have been forced to conclude that "a further unidentified agent may actually transmit BSE."(402)

Given the continuing importance of Koch's postulates and the consequent insistence on ploche in epitomes of research on microbial disease-causing agents, it is interesting to question how Koch himself phrased the frequently paraphrased postulates attributed to him. K. Codell Carter examined Koch's extensive writings and identified at least two variants of general criteria for identifying disease-causing agents (Carter 1985, 357, 361). Nowhere, according to Carter, does Koch produce a clear version of the multistep formula currently disseminated under his name. Perhaps the closest approximation to a general set of standards occurs in his most famous paper, his 1884 account of his tuberculosis research, "Die Aetiologie der Tuberkulose":

> First, it was necessary to determine whether the diseased organs contained elements that were not constituents of the body or composed of such constituents. If such allen *structures* [*Gebilde*] could be demonstrated, it was necessary to determine whether they were organised and showed any sign of independent life. Such signs include motility—which is often confused with molecular motion—growth, propagation, and fructification. Moreover, it was necessary to consider the relation of such *structures* (not in the original) to their surroundings, their relation to nearby tissues, their distribution in the body, their occurrence in various states of the disease, and other similar considerations. Such considerations enable one to conclude, with more or less probability, that there is a causal connection between these *structures and the disease* [*Gebilden und der Krankheit*] itself. Facts gained in these ways can provide so much evidence that only the most extreme skeptic would still object that the microorganism may not be the cause, but only a concomitant of the disease. Often this objection has a certain Justice, and, therefore, establishing the coincidence of the disease *and the parasite* [*der Krankheit und der Parasiten*] is not a complete proof. One requires, in addition, a direct proof that the *parasite* [*Parasiten*] is the actual cause. This can only be achieved by completely separating the parasites [*Parasiten*] from the diseased organism and from all products of the disease to which one could ascribe a causal significance. The isolated *parasites* [*Parasiten*], if introduced into healthy organisms, must then cause the disease with all its characteristics (see note for original passage in German).[9]
>
> (Koch 1987, 131)

This version of Koch's generalized procedures uses two repeating terms. The first stage of inquiry involves identification of "structures" that are not, to begin with, necessarily microorganisms. Though a master of the then best available techniques for mounting and staining tissue specimens and the inventor of many new techniques, Koch no doubt appreciated the potentially confusing artifacts observable under the microscopes of the late nineteenth century. Alien structures were not always easy to distinguish from the normal constituents of a cell. If they could be—and Koch includes illustrations with his 1884 article of tissues filled with a night-marish ploche of identical black rods—correlation at least could be established. The part of the passage dealing with "structures" concerns such correlation.[10] The passage then hands off causal agency to "parasites" (by overlapping with the term "disease") if they can be separated, isolated, and introduced into healthy animals, which then manifest the original disease. Koch's ploche with "parasites" in this passage is an adequate if not rigorous epitome of his method, but once formulated, the postulates themselves have undergone a ploche-like repetition from text to text for over one hundred years.

The pathway established by the postulates for a potential disease-causing entity in an experimental trial can be followed even in the absence of actually establishing that the entity exists. In other words, it is possible to move an agent verbally through the postulates without a physical referent. The discovery of viruses, in fact, followed that route. In the late 1880s, Adolf Mayr identified a disease of the tobacco plant that discolored its leaves. By grinding up the infected areas and soaking them in water, he produced a supernatant that easily caused the same effect when it was spread on healthy leaves. But Mayr could never identify a microorganism in his leaf cultures. Instead, "something" could be extracted from the infected tissue, "something" could sustain itself in a separate solution, and "something" could infect a new host. A consistent term was inferable from the protocol but its referent could not be isolated. Mayr was, of course, working with a virus (once a term for an infectious agent in general), a then submicroscopic form whose existence was eventually hypothesized because of the persistence of "something" when filtrations of preparations that would remove any known bacteria still yielded an infectious agent. Viruses were not identified visually until the 1930s, when Wendell Stanley succeeded in crystallizing the tobacco mosaic virus, and it was later observed in the newly available electron microscope (Levine 1992, 6–8). Until then, research with viruses could not visually identify them as demanded in Koch's postulates, yet viruses could be written about, and they were widely believed to be stable, disease-causing agents in animals, plants, and even bacteria long before their physical identification.

The current understanding of the interaction of a virus with its host cell stretches even further any application of Koch's postulates. Many viruses are now understood to follow two different pathways of infection. They can enter a cell, release their DNA or RNA, multiply exponentially, create their own structural proteins, reassemble, break out of the cell, usually killing it in the process, and go on to infect new cells, as though following Koch's postulates on their own. Or they can enter a cell and insert their DNA into the DNA of the host, where it can wait for year. In that latent form, the viral genome is difficult to distinguish from the host's genes, and the virus ceases to be recognizable as an independent entity until the viral genes are somehow turned on again, the viral constituents manufactured, and the reproduced virus released. Tracing out this pathway represented a significant conceptual achievement, but it is questionable whether the "organism" really maintains its identity through the middle step (prophage) of the second process (see the citation from Davis et al., note 7, which deletes an identifiable entity from step 3). Either pathway, however, can be epitomized not only verbally, by a custom version of Koch's postulates using the special strain name, but also visually, in diagrams that employ an icon for the infectious agent. The precise replication of the icon claims that the agent remains consistently identifiable when it enters and exits a cell In actual fact, given the high rate of mutation and recombination during replication, especially of RNA viruses, many of the progeny that exit a cell are likely to differ genetically from the virus that entered it. In some ways, the figure polyptoton, discussed below, would be a better verbal icon for the process than the exact replication implied by exact repetition, the ploche of words or images.

Partial Repetition: Agnominatio

In addition to perfect repetition, the figural tradition also marked the partial or near repetition that occurs when words look or sound alike.[11] Students of poetry are familiar with figures in this category (alliteration, the repetition of initial sounds or consonants, and assonance, the repetition of vowel sounds) as factors in the aural architecture of a text. But a more general device, identified in the figure manuals, encompasses these and extends their significance beyond aesthetic effects to argumentative ends.

Under the name *agnomination* or *agnominatio,* John Hoskins defines this figure as the repetition of "some syllables" in consecutive words and offers a simple example from Sidney's *Arcadia*: "Alas, what can saying make them believe whom seeing cannot persuade" (Hoskins 1935, 16). "Saying" and "seeing" here share initial consonants, the same final syllables, and an equal number of syllables and their resemblance enhances their role as parallel modes of persuasion, verbal and visual, although overall the phrase suggests an a fortiori argument: If "they" do not respond to the much stronger appeal of showing why should "they" respond to telling? When the resemblance of words it pushed, it can approach *paronomasia,* the pun, as in Hoskins' example from a sermon indulging in half-comic denunciations: "Our paradise is a pair of dice, our almes-deed are turned into all misdeeds, our praying into playing, our tasting into feasting" (Hoskins 1935, 16). The first two of the four transformations in this passage turn on puns, but the last two are "agnominations," the strong resemblance between "praying" and "playing" and between "fasting" and "feasting" enhancing the case with which frail humanity slides into sin.

Agnominatio has constructed many temporary and more enduring maxims: "Use it or lose it" (more aural than visual); "America. Love it or leave it"; "Praise the Lord and pass the ammunition." Citing Plato's use of sôma and sêma in "the body is a tomb," Olivier Reboul points out that the force of the repetition of phonemes in this pair disappears as soon as the phrase is translated. As Reboul explains, such verbal resemblance functions "as if—an 'as if' which quite exactly constitute the figure—the arbitrariness of the sign were abolished, as if the sequence of phonemes responded to a sequence of thoughts to which it brought an added measure of proof" (Reboul 1989, 170). Such a figure seems "to show that the resemblance between words attests to a relationship between things" (a claim that in translation uses agnominatio) (178).

An agnominatio that has had enduring force in psychology and genetics is Francis Gallon's powerful construction of two forces shaping bodies and behavior as "nature" and "nurture."[12] First introduced in 1874, this pair, sometimes in the agonistic formulation "nature versus nurture," has divided between them the complex factors that produce the observable organism and all its actions. In the 1860s and 1870s, Galton studied the consequences of his cousin Charles Darwin's theories of evolution as they might apply to human populations, eventually advocating policies that would encourage this "fit" to breed, for which he coined the name "eugenics." In 1869 he published his first treatise on the importance of lineage in creativity and talent. In response to Alphonse de Candolle's 1872 rebuttal of his work (with Candolle maintaining the influence of broad social factors in the promotion of scientific talent), Galton did his own survey-based research of over a hundred members of the Royal Society, concluding that their scientific inclinations were innate and hence due primarily to heredity. Galton's published version of his results appeared in 1874 as *English Men of Science: Their Nature and Nurture.* Galton was aware of the cleverness of the coinage in his subtitle and its powerful role in setting the conditions of his argument.

> The phrase "nature and nurture" is a convenient jingle of words, for it separates under two distinct beads the innumerable elements of which personality is composed. Nature is all that a man brings with himself into the world; nurture is every influence from without that affects him after his birth.
>
> (Galton 1970, 12)

Undoubtedly the agnominatio "nature and nurture" has had a great deal to do with constructing the following decades of debate, for the close resemblance of Galton's terms suggests the parity of these forces. Nurture, of course, has a more restricted connotation than Galton's stipulated definition allows. It meant then, and still does, an overseeing benevolence surrounding the developing organism, so Galton's pair also suggests an antithesis between what is beyond human control and what is not, an antithesis reinforced in the figure that concludes the passage quoted above. Since the two terms are so close in sound and appearance, differing only in one phoneme, it becomes more plausible to believe that they represent well-matched rivals. Parity is their theoretical condition in Galton's mind, though he believed as a result of his research that the more familiar and resonant of the two, "nature," was dominant: "When nature and nurture compete for supremacy on equal terms in the sense to be explained, the former proves the stronger" (12). Contemporary students of psychology and behavioral genetics hove replaced Galton's agnominatio with the unfigured pair "heredity and environment," but the terms of the debate between these two are still set by Galton's agnominatio in the sense that there is still a presumption of two forces in conflict in the creation of a fully realized organism and sometimes even a presumption that one should normally expect a fifty-fifty contribution from these two (see Gottesman 1997, 1522–1523). Though the pair "nature and nurture" may only appear now is self-consciously used synonyms, the relative contributions of genetic makeup and individual surroundings are still being prized apart according to the size of their respective shares of a "whole" in studies of intelligence, disease, violence, and addiction.

Notes

1. The classical rhetorical perspective on repetition has to be distinguished from repetition as characterized by twentieth-century text linguists who mention repetition as a device present in cohesive texts. Among the cohesive devices in English identified by Halliday and Hasan in *Cohesion in English* (1976), speakers and writers can maintain the same subject from sentence to sentence by repeating key words as well as by using synonyms or by using pronouns that clearly refer to previously introduced nouns. Repetition also has its place in the descriptions of information flow achieved in Functional Sentence Perspective. Writers and speakers can use essentially the same topic in the openings of consecutive sentences, the slot for "given" information, or they can pick up a new idea introduced toward the end of one sentence in the beginning of the next. These kinds of repetition can certainly have rhetorical importance, but the notions of cohesion or topic maintenance used by text linguists are not found in classical rhetoric.
2. Also known as *apanaphora*.
3. It could be argued that the recurrence of "life" three times in this sentence-inevitably divides it in three units so that by default "life" occurs at the end of each of these units.
4. Peacham also lists antanaclasis as "a figure which repeateth a word that hath two significations, and the one of them contrary, or at least, unlike to the other. An example:
   Care for those things which may discharge you of all care. Care in the first place signifieth to provide, in the last the solicitude and dread of the minde" (Peacham 1954, 56–57). Here is another interesting case where the same device can be described from the perspective of the double signification as a trope and from another, emphasizing the repetition, as a scheme.
5. For a similar lability according to the chosen figure of reading, see chapter 3 for the differences among the series figures.
6. The connection achieved by repeated adjectives can change from correlation to cause when the same word modifies what an arguer would like an audience to take as a cause-and-effect pair. In a letter to parents, a college president announced a donor's magnificent challenge grant in order to prepare for a funding campaign. He wanted the donor's generosity to spur the generosity of others and so he used repeated adjectives to make a causal connection: "I want you to know, however, that I have complete confidence in our ability to meet and even exceed the requirements of this challenge. Extraordinary events have a way of inspiring extraordinary response." The similarity in essence between a cause and its effect claimed by the repetition of "extraordinary" might be characterized as a fallacy, or a bit of shaman's word magic, but it is precisely the offered similarity that the president wants to establish in order to give the impression of inevitable future action.
7. A 1963 textbook, *The Microbial World*, second edition, credits Koch's teacher, Jacob Henle, with laying down the required causal criteria that Koch later instantiated. This text phrases "Koch's postulates" as follows: "(1) the microorganism must be present in every case of the disease; (2) the microorganism must be isolated from the diseased host and grown in pure culture; (3) the specific disease must be reproduced when a pure culture of the microorganism is inoculated into a healthy susceptible host; and (4) the microorganism must be recoverable once again from the experimentally infected host" (Stanier et al. 1963, 26).
   In a 1977 textbook, James H. Otto and Albert Towle's *Modern Biology*, the postulates are given in the imperative as a set of directions, "(i) Isolate the organism suspected of causing the disease. (ii) Grow the organism in laboratory cultures. (iii) Inoculate a healthy animal with the cultured organism. See if the animal contracts the disease, (iv) If the animal contracts the disease, examine the animal and re-isolate the organisms that caused the disease" (Carter 1985, 353, n. 2).

In the third edition of a textbook intended for medical students, *Microbiology: Including Immunology and Molecular Genetics* by Davis, Dulbecco, Eisen, and Ginsberg, the postulates are phrased without the rigor of ploche, and in fact the "organism" in a sense disappears after the first step and only re-emerges in the fourth: "(1) the organism is regularly found in the lesions of the disease, (2) it can be isolated in pure culture on artificial media, (3) inoculation of this culture produces a similar disease in experimental animals, and (4) the organism can be recovered from the lesions in these animals" (Davis et al. 1980, 7). In most situations, language users readily resort to pronoun substitution (see steps one to two in the previous example) rather than to exactly repeated terms. Thus it is an index to a different kind of rhetorical situation when language users "decide" that they must repeat terms precisely. In the informal register of a popular work, the British microbiologist John Postgate is comfortable with a pronoun but uses it with the consistency of ploche:

"One of the earliest bacteriologists, Dr. Robert Koch of Berlin, crystallized this dilemma [deciding if a particular microbe is really the cause of a disease] in a set of conditions known as Koch's postulates: a microbe may be accepted as the cause of a disease if (1) it is present in unusual numbers when and where the disease is active, (2) it can be isolated from the diseased patient, and (3) it causes disease when inoculated into a healthy subject" (Postgate 1992, 100).

8. Duesberg, like others, uses ploche in his presentation of the postulates: "First, the germ must be found abundantly growing in every patient and every diseased tissue. Second, the germ must be isolated and grown in the laboratory. Third, the purified germ must cause the disease again in another host" (Duesberg 1996, 35). A formulation later in the book uses the word "microbe" instead of "germ" (174–186).

9. "Zunächst war festzustellen, ob in den erkrankten Teilen Formelemente vorkommen, welche nicht zu den Bestandteilen des Körpers gehören oder aus solchen hervorgegangen sind. Wenn sich solche fremdartigen Gebilde nachweisen ließen, dann war weiter zu untersuchen, ob dieselben organisiert sind und ob sie irgendwelche Anzeichen von selbständigem Leben bieten, wohin besonders eigene Bewegung, mit welcher sehr oft noch die Molekularbewegung verwechselt wird, Wachstum, Vermehrung, Fruchtbildung zu rechnen sind. Ferner waren die Beziehungen zu ihrer Umgebung, das Verhalten der benachbarten Gewebsbestandteile, ihre Verteilung im Körper, ihr Auftreten in denverschiedenen Stadien der Krankheit und ähnliche Umstande zu eruieren, welche schon mit mehr oder weniger großer Wahrscheinlichkeit auf einen ursächlichen Zusammenhang zwischen diesen Gebilden und der Krankheit schliepen lassen [sic]. Die auf diesem Wege gewonnenen Tatsachen können möglicherweise schon soviel Beweismaterialliefern, daß nur noch der äußerste Skeptizismus den Einwand erheben kann, daß die gefundenen Mikroorganismen nicht Ursache, sondern nur eine Begleiterscheinung der Krankheit seien. Oft wird dieser Einwand allerdings eine gewisse Berechtigung haben, und es gehört deswegen zur vollsttindigen Beweisführung, daß man sich night allein damit begnügt, das Zusammentreffen der Krankheit und der Parasiten zu konstatieren, sondern daß außerdem direkt diese Parasiten als die eigentliche Ursache der Krankheit nachgewiesen werden. Dies kann nur in der Weise geschehen, daß die Parasiten von dem erkrankten Organismus vollständig abgetrennt und von allen Produkten der Krankheit, welchen etwa ein krankmachender Einfluß zugeschrieben werden könnte, befreit werden, und daß durch Einführung der isolierten Parasiten in den gesunden Organismus die Krankheit mit allen ihren eigentümlichen Eigenschaften von neuem hervorgerufen wird" (Koch 1912, 1:469–470).

10. According to K. Codell Carter, Koch formulated two different sets of general rules for establishing that a particular organism causes a disease. The first set appeared in his 1878 paper on wound infections, "Untersuchungen über die Aetiologie der Wundinfektionskrankheiten" and specified that an organism be found in every instance of the disease, that it correlate with and explain the disease, and that each disease be associated with a distinct micro-organism (357). The standard here is primarily one of association or correlation; it depends on the assumption that microorganisms are likely to cause disease. Koch's 1882–1884 work on tuberculosis adds the further criteria that the organism be isolated, cultured, and then inoculated into test animals, causing the disease. Both of these protocols combine in the passage from the 1884 paper cited in the text and together produce the current version of Koch's postulates.

11. Word play and specifically the creation of words that resemble each other was so well codified in Renaissance manuals that a set of figures was defined that marked the internal changes a word could be subjected to by certain additions, deletions, and transpositions of letters. *Prothesis* adds a letter or syllable to the beginning of a word and *aphaeresis* takes it away, *syncope* takes a letter or syllable away from the middle, and *epenthesis* puts one in; *apocope* removes an ending letter or syllable and *paragoge* adds one (Smith 1973, 170–171). Nothing in the word lore of rhetoric could seem further either from argumentative import or from the practices of scientists. Yet an *epenthesis* figures in the recent controversy over whether a meteorite from Mars shows signs of microbial life. The scientists making that claim used the notion first put forth by a geologist, Robert L. Folk, that there exists a hitherto unrecognized kind of extremely small microbial life, 0.05-.2µm, which are extremely abundant and which "run most of the earth's surface chemistry" (Folk 1997). Folk calls these forms *nannobacteria*, the term, and the proposed type of life, picked up by the NASA scientists in their sensational announcement. The prefix that would indicate the range of size here is nano meaning one billionth, used in combined forms like nanometer and nanogram. But Folk deliberately used a spelling with an added n, conforming to the practice of geologists who have coined the term *nannoplankton* for minute ocean life (Wade 1997, C1). This spelling then is an act of addressing a disciplinary community more hospitable to his claims. It may also be a way of hedging on ultimate claims about size. (For a similar use of variant spelling, and specifically adding letters see Fahnestock [1993, 178, 327].)
12. Galton, who quotes Shakespeare frequently in his writings, may have drawn his pair from a passage in *The Tempest* where Prospero says of Caliban, "A devil, a born devil, on whose nature nurture can never stick" (4.1.187–189; see Gottesman 1997, 1523).

References

Backman, Daniel G., and James C. Williams 1992. Advanced materials for aircraft engine applications. *Science* 255 (28 February): 1086–1087.

Carter, K. Codell, 1985. Koch's postulates in relation to the work of Jacob Henle and Edwin Klebs. *Medical History* 29:353–374.

Chipman, R. A. 1954. An unpublished letter of Stephen Gray on electrical experiments, 1707–1708. *Isis* 45:33–40.

[Cicero], 1954. *Rhetorica ad Herennium*. Translated by H. Caplan. Cambridge, MA: Harvard University Press.

Corbetta, Maurizio, Francis M. Miczin, Susan Dobmeyer, Gordon L. Shulman, Steven E. Peterson, 1990. Attentional modulation of neural processing of shape, color, and velocity in humans. *Science* 248: 1556–1559.

Crosland, Maurice P. 1962. *Historical Studies in the Language of Chemistry*. Cambridge, MA: Harvard University Press.

Darwin, Charles. 1965. *The Expression of the Emotions in Man and Animals* [1872]. Chicago: University of Chicago Press.

Davis, Bernard D., Renato Dulbecco, Herman N. Elsen and Harold S. Ginsberg. 1980. *Microbiology: Including Immunology and Molecular Genetics 3rd ed.* Philadelphia: Harper & Row.

Duesberg, Peter. 1996. *Inventing the AIDS Virus*. Washington, DC: Regnery.

Eigen, Manfred. 1993. Viral quasispecies. *Scientific American*. 269: 43–49.

Fahnestock, Jeanne. 1993. Tactics of evaluation in Gould and Lewontin's "The Spandrels of San Marco." *Understanding Scientific Prose*. Edited by Jack Selzer. Madison, WI: University of Wisconsin Press, pp. 158–179.

Folk, Robert L. 1997. Nannobacteria: Surely not figments but what under heaven are they natural SCIENCE. *A World Wide Web Journal* Vol I, Article 3, 1997. [http://naturalscience.com/ns/articles/01-03/ns_folk.html]

Fowler, Roger and Gunther Kress. 1979. *Language and Control* London: Routledge.

Galton, Francis, 1970. *English Men of Science: Their Nature and Nurture* [1874]. London: Cass

Gottesman, Irving I. 1997. Twins en route to QTLs for cognition. *Science* 276: 1522–1523.

Gray, Stephen. 1720. An account of some new electrical experiments. *Philosophical Transactions* 31:104–107.

Gray, Stephen. 1731. A letter to Cromwell Mortimer, M.D. Secr. R.S. containing several experiments concerning electricity. *Philosophical Transactions* 37:17–44.

Gray, Stephen. 1732. A letter concerning the electricity of water. *Philosophical Transactions.* 37:227–230.

Gray, Stephen. 1735. Experiments and observations upon the light that it produced by communicating electrical attraction to animal or inanimate bodies, together with some of its most surprising effects. *Philosophical Transactions* 39:16–24.

Halliday, M. A. K. and R. Hasan. 1976. *Cohesion in English.* London: Longmans.

Heilbron, J. L. 1979. *Electricity in the 17th and 18th Centuries: A Study of Early Modern Physics.* Berkeley: University of California Press.

Hoskins, John. 1935. *Directions for Speech and Style.* Edited by Hoyt H. Hudson. Princeton: Princeton University Press.

Janofsky, Michael. 1995. Demons and conspiracies haunt a "Patriot" World. *New York Times*, 31 May, A18.

Kennedy, George A., trans. 1991. *Aristotle On Rhetoric: A* Theory *of Civic Discourse.* New York: Oxford University Press.

Koch, Robert. 1987. *Essays of Robert Koch.* Translated by K. Codell Carter. New York: Greenwood.

Koch, Robert. 1912. *Gesammelts Werke* Leipzig: George Thieme.

Levine, Arnold. 1992. *Viruses.* New York Scientific American Library.

Needham, Turbervill. 1746. Extract of a letter from Mr. Turbervill Needham to Martin Folkes, esq; Pr. R.S. concerning some new electrical experiments lately made at Paris. *Philosophical Transactions* 44: 247–263.

Peacham, Henry. 1954. *The Garden of Eloquence* [1593]. Gainesville, FL: Scholars' Facsimiles & Reprints.

Perelman, Chalm and Lucie Otbrechts-Tyteca. 1969. *The New Rhetoric: A Treatise on Argumentation.* Translated by J. Wilkinson and P. Weaver. Notre Dame, IN: University of Notre Dame Press.

Postgate, John. 1992. *Microbes and Man.* 3d ed. Cambridge: Cambridge University Press.

Puttenham, George. 1970. *The Arte of English Poesie* [1589]. Kent. OH: Kent State University Press.

Quintilian. 1921. *Institutio Oratorio.* Translated by H. E. Butler. Cambridge, MA: Harvard University Press.

Reboul, Oliver. 1989. The figure and the argument. In *From Metaphysics to Rhetoric.* Edited by Michel Meyer. Dodrecht, Netherlands: Kluwer, pp. 169–181.

Smith, John. 1973. *The Mysterie of Rhetorique unvail'd* [1657]. New York: Hildesheim.

Sonnino, Lee A. 1968. *A Handbook to Sixteenth-Century Rhetoric.* New York: Barnes and Noble.

Stanier, Roger K., Michael Doudoroff and Edward A. Adelberg. 1963. *The Microbial World.* 2d ed. Eaglewood Cliffs, NJ: Prentice Hall.

Wade, Nicholas, 1997. Mars meteorite fuels debate on life on Earth. *New York Times,* 29 July, C1, C6.

Advertising

20.
FIGURES OF RHETORIC IN ADVERTISING LANGUAGE
Edward F. McQuarrie and David Glen Mick

A rhetorical figure can be defined as an artful deviation in the form taken by a statement. Since antiquity dozens of figures have been cataloged, ranging from the familiar (rhyme, pun) to the obscure (antimetabole). Despite the frequent appearance of rhetorical figures in print advertisements, their incorporation into advertising theory and research has been minimal. This article develops a framework for classifying rhetorical figures that distinguishes between figurative and nonfigurative text, between two types of figures (schemes and tropes), and among four rhetorical operations that underlie individual figures (repetition, reversal, substitution, and destabilization). These differentiations in the framework are supported by preliminary validation data and are linked to suggested consumer responses. The article also considers the theoretical import of the proposed framework for future research on rhetorical structure in advertising.

From Aristotle through the advent of modern social psychology, the discipline of rhetoric was the primary repository of Western thinking about persuasion (Barthes [1970] 1988). The central concern of rhetoric has always been method and manner: how to discover the most effective way to express a thought in a given situation, and how to alter its expression to suit different situations. Unfortunately, the many techniques cataloged by rhetoricians since antiquity (e.g., rhyme, antimetabole, pun, hyperbole) have remained largely unacknowledged, undifferentiated, and uninfluential in advertising theory. This article attempts to correct that neglect.

There exist three major reasons why consumer research needs to address the topic of rhetorical figures (also known as figures of speech). First, newly available content analyses have demonstrated the pervasiveness of figuration in the language of advertising (Leigh 1994). Moreover, the reliance on rhetoric is not exclusive to American or European culture (see Fernandez 1991). The second reason stems from the continued, inadvertent use of rhetorical figures in experimental protocols, without appreciation of their history and distinctiveness.[1] Third, the paradigmatic ferment associated with the advent of postmodern (Sherry 1991), semiotic (Mick 1986), and text-based perspectives (Hirschman and Holbrook 1992) is conducive to a focus on rhetorical phenomena in advertising (see also Deighton 1985; McQuarrie and Mick 1992; Scott 1990; Sherry 1987; Stern 1988; Wells 1988). Now that consumer researchers have at last permitted

---

McQuarrie, Edward F. and David Glen Mick. "Figures of Rhetoric in Advertising Language," *The Journal of Consumer Research*, Vol. 22, No. 4 (1996): 424–438.

themselves to talk about meaning as well as information, interpretation as well as stimulation, perhaps rhetorical phenomena can be grasped and integrated into consumer research (McCracken 1987; Scott 1994a).

The principal purpose of this article is to contribute a richer and more systematic conceptual understanding of rhetorical structure in advertising language. In contrast to previous analyses of rhetorical figures in consumer research that focused on isolated cases (e.g., rhetorical questions, Swasy and Munch [1985]; puns, McQuarrie and Mick [1992]), we provide a framework that integrates a wide range of figures appearing in advertisements.

Rhetorical Figures in Advertising

Rhetoricians maintain that any proposition can be expressed in a variety of ways and that in any given situation one of these ways will be the most effective in swaying an audience. Hence, when persuasion is the overriding goal, the rhetorical perspective suggests that the manner in which a statement is expressed may be more important than its propositional content. Moreover, rhetoric promises a system for identifying the most effective form of expression in any given case. Specifically, a rhetorical approach to advertising language rests on three premises: (1) that variations in the style of advertising language, in particular the presence of rhetorical figures, can be expected to have important consequences for how the ad is processed, (2) that these consequences can in turn be derived from the formal properties of the rhetorical figures themselves, and (3) that these formal properties are systematically interrelated.

Classification of Figures

Rhetorical figures were first identified and discussed over two thousand years ago in classical antiquity (Todorov 1982). Efforts to systematize the wealth of available figures are almost as old (Wenzel 1990). Modern efforts at systematization begin with Jakobson and Halle (1956) and Burke (1950) and culminate in the elaborate typologies of Dubois et al. (1970) and Durand (1987). Despite some attention to individual figures, no effort in the social sciences to date has incorporated a wide range of rhetorical figures (see Gibbs 1993; Kreuz and Roberts 1993). In fact, from the perspective of advertising theory, previous efforts to systematize the set of rhetorical figures have all been handicapped by one or more of the following shortcomings: the taxonomic categories are vague or too coarse grained, the categories are not linked to consumer responses, or the focus is on outcomes other than persuasion.

To overcome these limitations we proceeded on a dual front by (1) reading the literature on classical rhetoric, drawing on Corbett (1990), Leech (1969), and Vickers (1988) in particular, and (2) immersing ourselves in a large sample of contemporary magazine ads.[2] We sought a framework that would be both comprehensive and parsimonious, capable of reflecting the range of rhetorical figures present in advertisements but also restricted to include only those rhetorical figures that actually appear in ads. Because the framework is grounded in real ads, we present examples of both non-figurative and figurative headlines for purposes of illustration and clarification. To complete the framework we suggest how the underlying concepts that unite or distinguish different figures may be connected to standard ideas about consumer advertising response.

As shown in Figure 20.1 [see page 350], the framework takes the form of a tree diagram with three levels corresponding to figuration per se, to two different modes of figuration, and to four fundamental, generative rhetorical operations. These operations are arrayed on a gradient of deviation and also vary in complexity. The third level of the framework maps onto the individual figures found in our sample of ads. In building the framework we adopted the rule that a figure would only be included if a clear instance could be found in our sample. Future expansion of the framework can thus occur as more evidence accumulates.

Figuration

A rhetorical figure has traditionally been defined as an artful deviation (Corbett 1990). More formally, we submit that a rhetorical figure occurs when an expression deviates from expectation, the expression is not rejected as nonsensical or faulty, the deviation occurs at the level of form rather than content, and the deviation conforms to a template that is invariant across a variety of content and contexts. This definition supplies the standard against which deviation is to be measured (i.e., expectations), sets a limit on the amount and kind of deviation (i.e., short of a mistake), situates the deviation at the level of the formal structure of a text, and imposes a grouping requirement (i.e., there are a limited number of templates, each with distinct characteristics).

The exact nature of the deviation that constitutes a figure has been the subject of dispute (see Cohen 1982; Genette 1982). For classical authors, a figure was an artful deviation from the normal or ordinary manner of expression (Corbett 1990). However, it has been shown that metaphor and other figurative expressions are common in everyday speech (see Pollio, Smith, and Pollio 1990; Todorov 1982). Hence, we conceptualize the deviation relative to expectation in order to overcome the difficulties associated with defining figures as abnormalities. Our use of expectation is consistent with several aspects of the classical tradition, particularly the notion that a figure represents an unorthodox use or a violation of some norm or convention.

In terms of speech act theory, every communication encounter sets up expectations as it proceeds, and more general expectations that hold across encounters function as conventions or constraints (Grice 1989). Consider the case of metaphor. Listeners are aware of conventions with respect to the use of words, one of which might be formulated as follows: words are generally used to convey one of the lead meanings given in their dictionary entry. However, a metaphor violates that convention, as in this headline for Johnson & Johnson Band-Aids, "Say hello to your child's new bodyguards," accompanied by a picture of Band-Aids emblazoned with cartoon characters. In the dictionary, a bodyguard is a large, strong individual, often assigned to a celebrity or political figure for protection against violent assault, but in this context the ad is describing a Band-Aid decorated with imaginary beings. Sperber and Wilson (1986) contend that listeners know exactly what to do when a speaker violates a convention: they search for a context that will render the violation intelligible. If context permits an inference that the Band-Aid is particularly strong or that the world inhabited by children is particularly threatening, then the consumer will achieve an understanding of the advertiser's statement. If the ad had said, "Say hello to your child's new petunias," however, most consumers would have considerable difficulty. Nonsensical or anomalous statements represent a double violation or a deviation of the second degree. In other words, consumers have conventions available to deal with violations of convention. When a search for context successfully restores understanding, the consumer assumes a figurative use and responds accordingly (discussed further below). Else, the consumer assumes some failure of communication.

Because it is a deviation, any figure carries at least one additional meaning (Genette 1982). This overlaid meaning might be expressed as "Look, I chose to violate a convention here—take note." When told that the Band-Aid is a bodyguard, the consumer both finds a translation supported by context—this Band-Aid is particularly strong, provides a greater degree of protection, will treat your child like a celebrity, and so on—and understands that the advertiser was unwilling to simply say, "Band-Aids are strong," "Band-Aids provide extra protection," or "Your child is important." The implication is that none of these three paraphrases just given quite succeeds in capturing the advertiser's intent; in fact, no single, univocal predication applied to the Band-Aid appears adequate to capture the advertiser's thought. Thus, the resort to a figure prompts the consumer to consider a variety of predications concerning Band-Aids that will be consistent with the use of "bodyguard" and, therefore, render it comprehensible in context (see Sperber and Wilson 1986, pp. 231–237). In Genette's (1982) terms, every figure represents a "gap." The figure both points to a translation (it is the impossibility in this context of translating "Say hello to your child's new petunias" that is the key to its incomprehensibility) and denies the adequacy of that translation, thus encouraging further interpretation.

Deviation is used here in the neutral sense of a swerve or departure—a way of marking the text (Mukarovsky 1964; van Peer 1986). Like aesthetic objects generally (Berlyne 1971), a rhetorical figure provides a means for making the familiar strange. Deviation, then, is a matter of creating what consumer researchers might have called incongruity. A key contribution of rhetoric is to explain how certain kinds of text structure (i.e., rhetorical figures) can produce incongruity in advertising texts.

It is important to acknowledge that any particular figurative expression can deviate to a greater or lesser extent and, thus, be more or less incongruous (Leech 1969). This corollary applies to both individual instances of any figure (e.g., a particular occurrence of a pun) and to entire categories of figures (some types of figure, e.g., puns, may in general involve a greater degree of deviation than others, such as alliteration). All of our statements that compare rhetorical figures or situate them on the gradient of deviation (Fig. 20.1 [page 350]) refer to the hypothetical "average" instance of that category of figure. Moreover, if the deviation drops below some threshold, then it is no longer a figure. This occurs, for example, in the case of metaphors that have become frozen or conventional (e.g., the sports car that "hugs" the road). Because deviation may be temporally situated, what once was a figure need not always remain one. This example, together with the bodyguard metaphor, also serves as a reminder that rhetorical structure resides and operates in a complex web of sociocultural signs and meanings (Eco 1979; Mick 1986; Scott 1994a). The three limiting conditions in the definition of figuration presented earlier are intended to clarify the concept by explaining what it does not include. Bad grammar and faulty diction also deviate from expectations, but these constitute a failure of expression. Figures deviate but do not err. Deviations in message content are also not figures. For example, a claim that "cereal X is preferred by retired airplane mechanics" would deviate from our expectations but would not constitute a rhetorical figure because the deviation lies at the level of content: the reference to retired airplane mechanics rather than the more customary reference to champions or athletes. The final limiting condition distinguishes figures in the broader category of stylistic device. For a deviation to be a figure, it must be possible to define the deviation independent of any individual occurrence. Skillful deviations in form that have a onetime character, or where a rule applicable across content elements cannot be formulated, are only stylistic devices.

Figuration and Consumer Response

A rhetorician must assume that the widespread use of rhetorical figures is deliberate and designed to serve as an effective adaptation to the circumstances in which the advertisement is encountered. A fundamental feature of field exposure conditions is that the consumer has complete freedom to ignore an ad or to devote the barest minimum of processing effort to it (Greenwald and Leavitt 1984). Because consumers are under no compulsion to start reading a headline, finish reading it, or continue on to read the rest of the ad, an important function of rhetorical figures is to motivate the potential reader. In this regard, Berlyne (1971) found that incongruity (i.e., deviation) is among those factors that attract and arrest attention. Hence, when ad exposure is not forced, consumers should allocate a greater amount of attention to figurative ad language as compared to non-figurative ad language, ceteris paribus.[3] (For examples of nonfigurative ads, see Table 20.1.)

Figures also yield what the semiotician Barthes (1985) called a "pleasure of the text"—the reward that comes from processing a clever arrangement of signs. This in turn corresponds to Berlyne's (1971) argument, based on his research in experimental aesthetics, that incongruity (i.e., deviation) can produce a pleasurable degree of arousal. The rewarding character of artful deviation thus suggests that figurative ad language, as compared with literal ad language, should produce a more positive attitude toward the ad (A_{ad}).

Last, we expect figurative ad language to be more memorable. However, because the processes underlying memorability are quite different for schemes and for tropes, we will defer discussion of this consumer response until the next section.

Because positive effects on attention, ad liking, and recall derive from the artful deviation that constitutes a figure, all rhetorical figures can be expected to confer these advantages to some extent. This may explain why Leigh (1994) found rhetorical figures in three-fourths of the magazine ads studied. However, as we move down the taxonomy (see Fig. 20.1 [page 350]), we come to properties that differentiate specific types of figures. Here both qualitative and quantitative distinctions can be drawn. These distinctions indicate that consumer responses are not uniform across all kinds of rhetorical figures and suggest circumstances in which we can expect one kind of figure to be more effective than another in a particular respect.

Figurative Mode

These modes (Fig. 20.1 [page 350]) correspond to the classical distinction between schemes and tropes (Leech 1969). A figure in the schematic mode occurs when a text contains excessive order or regularity, while a figure in the tropic mode occurs when a text contains a deficiency of order or irregularities. Schemes and tropes thus encompass two distinct modes of formal deviation. Familiar examples of schematic figures include rhyme and alliteration, while metaphors and puns are familiar examples of tropic figures.

The deviations that constitute schemes and tropes can be understood in part through the linguistic distinction between combination and selection constraints, respectively (Leech 1969).[4] A combination constraint limits how signs can be combined into sentences, while a selection constraint limits which signs can fill certain positions (e.g., subject, object, verb) in a sentence. Schemes can be understood as deviant combinations, as in the headline, "Now Stouffers makes a real fast real mean Lean Cuisine." This headline is excessively regular because of its repetition of sounds and words. It violates the convention that sounds are generally irrelevant to the sense of an utterance; that is, it violates the expectation held by receivers that the distribution of sounds through an utterance will be essentially unordered except by the grammatical and semantic constraints required to make a well-formed sentence. Sound play can be used to build up meaning in a wide variety of ways (Ross 1991; van Peer 1986).

Many tropes, particularly metaphors and puns effected in a single word, can be understood as deviant selections. Thus, in the Jergens skin care headline (Table 20.2) "Science you can touch," there is a figurative metaphor, because "touch" does not belong to the set of verbs that can take as their object an abstract collective endeavor such as science. However, not all tropes are effected in a single word, so that tropes such as rhetorical question or paradox must be explained with the aid of the more general semiotic distinction between under-and overcoded texts (Eco 1979). In overcoding there are more possible organizations of information than are necessary for message reception, while in under-coding the readily available organizations of information are insufficient. Schemes thus fit a model of overcoding, while tropes fit a model of undercoding.

In addition to being qualitatively distinct from tropes, schemes are also quantitatively distinct. Specifically, a depth-of-processing perspective argues that, on average, schemes will be less deviant than tropes. This is because excess regularity is obtained via rearrangements of the surface of the text; it occurs at a sensory level, as when one repeats sounds to achieve a rhyme or inverts the order of words to create an antimetabole. By contrast, rhetorical questions or puns are not sensorially apparent features of

Table 20.1 Examples of Nonfigurative (Literal) Headlines in Magazine Advertisements

		Recent instances	
Type of headline	Brief description	Text	Brand, product, and ad source
Direct linkage of product and attribute	Claims some property for the product or brand	Dual airbags, antilock brakes, traction control . . . it's even supercharged	Pontiac auto (CD2)
		The circuit that helps reduce background noise	Miracle Ear hearing aid (P2)
Direct linkage of product and situation	Associates the product with some desirable situation, action, or event	Everything you expect from a leader	BellSouth telecommunications (BW1)
News announcement	Indicates that something is new	The intelligent choice Introducing the new Virginia Slims 10-pack	Beltronics radar detector (CD1) Virginia Slims cigarettes (CD2)
Direct naming	Gives the brand (and possibly the product category) name	New Special Lights The Tire Rack The American College of Obstetricians and Gynecologists Balanced Fitness Workout	Camel cigarettes (P2) The Tire Rack store (CD2) Instructional video (GH2)
Direct titling	Introduces the subject matter of the ad	Some expert advice about wheel cleaning This week on HBO	Eagle One wheel cleaner (CD2) HBO cable television (P2)
Specific price information	Provides information about price or terms	20% off when you buy two Free with membership	Escort radar detector (CD2) Doubleday book club (GH2)

Note.—The source code indicates the magazine and the issue where the headline or tag line was located, as follows: BW = *Business Week*, 1 = 5/6/91, 2 = 4/5/93; CD = *Car & Driver*, 1 = 6/91, 2 = 4/93; CO = *Cosmopolitan*, 1 = 8/91, 2 = 4/93; GH = *Good Housekeeping*, 1 = 6/91, 2 = 4/93; P = *People*, 1 = 8/5/91, 2 = 4/5/93; SI = *Sports Illustrated*, 1 = 9/1/91, 2 = 4/5/93.

the headline but become manifest as the text is related to semantic and background knowledge (see Childers and Houston [1984] for an experimental instantiation of a depth of processing manipulation based on this sensory vs. semantic distinction). Deviation thus tends to be greater in the case of tropes because irregularity represents incongruity at a deeper, semantic level of processing.

Figurative Mode and Consumer Response

Both the qualitative and quantitative distinctions between modes of figuration have implications for consumer response. With regard to the qualitative distinction, although both schematic ad language and tropic ad language should be more memorable than literal ad language, the underlying process will differ as follows. Because they are overcoded, schemes add internal redundancy to advertising messages. Repetition in a text can be expected to enhance recall just as repetition of the entire text does. For example, a rhyme forges extra phonemic links among the headline elements. When reading that "Performax protects to the max," the consumer has several encoding possibilities available, including the propositional content, the phonemic equivalence (i.e., Performax = max), and the syllable node (other words ending in the syllable "ax"). In terms of a spreading activation model, these multiple encoding possibilities lead to multiple opportunities for subsequent retrieval of the headline (Mitchell 1983).

The memorability of tropes rests on a different mechanism. Because they are undercoded, tropes are incomplete in the sense of lacking closure. Tropes thus invite elaboration by the reader. For example, consider the Ford ad with the headline "Make fun of the road" (Table 20.2). "Road" is unexpectedly included in the set of things to mock or belittle. Via reinterpretation, the first meaning, to mock, takes on a more resurgent quality, namely that Ford will help the consumer to overcome the road. The second meaning, to enjoy, is also given an edge, so that it takes on the more triumphant quality of an achievement against obstacles. This tropic headline, whose resolution sets in motion a rich network of associations, may lead to multiple encodings and/or the strengthening of existing conceptual linkages in memory (involving, e.g., Ford, driving pleasures, driving challenges, and personal needs for achievement). Thus, the additional cognitive activity expended in the reinterpretation increases the number of associative pathways stored in memory (Mitchell 1983).

Overall then, figurative ad language should be more memorable than literal ad language. However, in view of the distinct processes involved, there are no grounds for expecting a main effect on ad recall between modes of figuration. Instead, a variety of moderating factors will determine whether schematic ad language or tropic ad language is more memorable in a given instance. A general view of the nature of these moderating factors can be derived from the distinction between undercoded and overcoded text. For instance, consider factors that tend to inhibit elaborative processing (e.g., distractions, lack of ability). When such factors are operating, the processing resources available to the consumer are minimized and the invitation to elaborate provided by a trope may not be accepted (cf. Anand and Sternthal 1990), leading to diminished memory for tropic language. In fact, in such cases the trope risks not being comprehended at all (see experiment 2 in McQuarrie and Mick [1992]). Under these same circumstances of restricted or limited resources, schemes will actually be advantaged because of their overcoded and redundant nature, leading to enhanced memorability relative to tropes.

Consider now the quantitative distinction between modes of figuration in terms of the greater deviation characteristic of tropes. Consistent with Berlyne's assertions (1971), the greater incongruity of tropes should lead to enhanced "stopping power" relative to schemes. This suggests that a main effect for tropes over schemes should be found for attention to ad language. Similarly, the aesthetic reward from successfully processing deviant text argues for a more positive A_{ad} in the case of tropes relative to schemes. However, we would expect the tropic advantage over schemes in terms of A_{ad} to be augmented or diminished as a function of moderating factors that make the successful resolution of tropic irregularity more or less likely. Thus, although the invitation posed by a trope may be sufficient to draw attention, that invitation must be accepted and followed through in order to enhance favorableness toward the ad.

Rhetorical Operations

This third level of the framework (Fig. 20.1 [page 350]) distinguishes simple from complex schemes and tropes to yield four rhetorical operations—repetition, reversal, substitution, and destabilization. These operations are the immediate sources of the excessive order or disorder that produces the deviation that constitutes a rhetorical figure. An important implication of the framework is that particular named rhetorical figures handed down by the classical tradition ought not to be considered as entities sui generis that have distinctive impacts on ad processing. In our framework individual rhetorical figures are not causal loci for explaining advertising effects but rather names that distinguish different applications of a rhetorical operation. Instead, it is artful deviation, irregularity, and complexity that explain the effects of a headline such as "Say hello to your child's new bodyguards," and not its assignment to the metaphor category. Nonetheless, we retain the old names because they serve as useful pointers to particular applications of the rhetorical operations and also provide a connection to the historical literature on rhetoric.

Repetition

The rhetorical operation of repetition combines multiple instances of some element of the expression without changing the meaning of that element. In advertising we find repetition applied to sounds so as to create the figures of rhyme, chime, and alliteration or assonance (Table 20.2). Repetition applied to words creates the figures known as anaphora (beginning words), epistrophe (ending words), epanalepsis (beginning and ending), and anadiplosis (ending and beginning). Repetition applied to phrase structure yields the figure of parison, as in Kmart's tag line: "The price you want. The quality you need." A limiting condition is that repeated words not shift their meaning with each repetition (such a shift would create the trope known as antanaclasis, described near the bottom of Table 20.2).

Reversal

The idea of excess regularity that is intrinsic to any scheme can be manifest in relatively simple or complex ways. Thinking in more general terms of parallelism (Jakobson 1967) rather than iteration alone indicates the possibility for a second kind of schematic figure, which would be produced via an operation that we have named "reversal." The rhetorical operation of reversal combines elements that are mirror images of one another in an expression. A characteristic of a mirror image, of course, is that it repeats

Table 20.2 Examples of Figurative Headlines Formed by Four Rhetorical Operations in Magazine Advertisements

Operation and formal element	Brief description	Text	Recent instances Brand, product, and ad source
Repetition: Sounds: Rhyme	Repetition of syllables at the end of words	KitchenAid. For the way it's made. Performax protects to the max.	KitchenAid refrigerator (GH2) Pennzoil motor oil (SI2)
Chime	Key words in a phrase begin with identical sounds or letters	A tradition of trust. The best in the business.	Merrill Lynch brokerage (BW2) AT&T telecommunication (BW2)
Assonance and alliteration	Three or more repetitions of a vowel or constant	No one knows the land like a Navajo. Now Stouffer's makes a real fast real mean Lean Cuisine.	Mazda four-wheel drive (CD1) Stouffer's frozen dinners (CO2)
Words: Anaphora	Repetition of words at the beginning of phrases	Early treatment. Early cure.	Gyne Lotrimin medicine (P1)
Epistrophe	Repetition of words at the end of phrases	Choose to be your most beautiful. Salon beautiful.	Salon Selectives hair products (CO2)
Epanalepsis	Repetition of a word toward the beginning and end of a phrase	Smart phone smarts.	AT&T telecommunications (BW1)
Anadiplosis	Repetition of a word toward the end of one phrase and the beginning of the next	Kleenex Ultra. Ultra softness is all you feel.	Kleenex facial tissue (GH2)
Phrase structure: Parison	Marked parallelism between successive phrases; often involves the use of one or more embedded repeated words	You never had it so easy. Your tires never had it so good. The quality you need. The price you want.	Notouch tire cleaner (CD1) Kmart Stores (SI1)
Reversal: Syntax: Antimetabole	Repetition of a pair of words in a phrase in reverse order	Stops static before static stops you.	Bounce fabric softener (GH2)
Semantic: Antithesis	Incorporation of binary opposites in a phrase	It says what it does. It does what it says. We got hot prices on cool stuff. Easy on eyes. Tough on tangles.	Listerine mouthwash (P1) Musicland stores (P2) Pert Plus shampoo (GH2)

(continued)

Table 20.2 Examples of Figurative Headlines Formed by Four Rhetorical Operations in Magazine Advertisements (continued)

Operation and formal element	Brief description	Text	Brand, product, and ad source	Recent instances
Substitution: Claim extremity: Hyperbole	Exaggerated or extreme claim	Experience color so rich you can feel it.	Cover Girl lipstick (CO2)	
		Laser beams move at the speed of light. Fortunately, our engineers move somewhat faster.	Uniden laser and radar detector (CD2)	
Assertive force: Rhetorical question	Asking a question so as to make an assertion	Are you protecting only half your dog from worms? Don't you have something better to do?	Interceptor pet medicine (GH1)	
			Hewlett-Packard plain paper fax (P2)	
Epanorthosis	Making an assertion so as to call it into question	Take away his writing, his philosophy and his music, and he was nothing but a country doctor. In his case, a whole country.	BellSouth telecommunications (BW1)	
		Chances are, you'll buy a Ranger for its value, economy and quality. Yeah, right.	Ford pickup truck (CD1)	
Presence or Absence: Ellipsis	A gap or omission that has to be completed	A lot of tires cost less than Michelin. That's because they should.	Michelin tires (BW1)	
		Everyday vehicles that aren't.	Suzuki four-wheel drive (CD1)	
Center or periphery: Metonym	Use of a portion, or any associated element, to represent the whole	You're looking at 2 slumber parties, 3 midnight raids, 5 unexpected guests, 1 late snooze and 1 Super Bowl.	Hormel frozen foods (GH2)	
		The imports are getting nervous.	Buick automobile (P1)	
Destabilization: Similarity: Metaphor	Substitution based on underlying resemblance	Say hello to your child's new bodyguards. Science you can touch.	Johnson & Johnson Band-Aids (GH1)	
Pun (general)	Substitution based on accidental similarity		Jergens skin care (CO2)	
Homonym	One word can be taken in two senses	Make fun of the road.	Ford automobile (CD2)	
		How to make a home <u>run</u>.	Whirlpool appliances (GH2)	
Antanaclasis	Repeating a word in two different senses	Today's Slims at a very slim *price*.	Misty ultralight cigarettes (CO2)	
		Nobody knows the athletes foot like the Athletes Foot.	The Athletes Foot shoe store (SI2)	

Operation and formal element	Brief description	Text	Brand, product, and ad source
Syllepsis	A verb takes on a different sense as clauses it modifies unfold	It's too bad other brands don't pad their shoes as much as their prices.	Keds shoes (GH2)
		Built to handle the years as well as the groceries.	Frigidaire refrigerator (GH2)
Resonance	A phrase is given a different meaning by its juxtaposition with a picture	Will bite when cornered (with a picture of car splashing up water as it makes a turn).	Goodyear tires (CD2)
		Success Rice brings out the ham in you (with a picture of ham pieces in sauce).	Hormel rice (GH2)
Opposition: Paradox	A self-contradictory, false, or impossible statement	This picture was taken by someone who didn't bring a camera.	Kodak film (P1)
		Mark McGwire hit 42 home runs last year. But we held the bat.	Franklin batting glove (SI2)
Irony	A statement that means the opposite of what is said	Just another wholesome family sitcom (with a picture of the male lead licking cream off thighs).	HBO cable TV (CO1)
		We spent years developing this incredibly comfortable contact lens, and this is how you treat it (with a picture of a finger flicking a lens away).	Accuvue disposable contacts (P1)

NOTE.—See note to Table 20.1 for an explanation of sources.

the original, but in reverse. Consider this tag line for Bounce fabric softener: "Stops static before static stops you." In the first part, the noun "static" is the object of the verb "stops," while in the second part the noun "static" functions as a subject for the verb "stops." The classical literature applied the term "antimetabole" to figures of this type (see Table 20.2). Note the marked alliteration that also characterizes the "stops static ..." tag line. Multiple rhetorical operations can be and often are integrated into a single expression.

The English language permits semantic as well as syntactic reversals, in the form of binary pairs in which one term may be thought of as the reverse or opposite of the other (i.e., high/low, easy/tough). When a message structure includes both members of such a pair, the figure known as antithesis results, as in this Pert Plus shampoo ad: "Easy on eyes. Tough on tangles." Note how, in this instance, the accompanying chime (e . . . e, t . . . t) provides additional parallelism, in a role similar to that played by alliteration in the previously discussed tag line for Bounce fabric softener.

Substitution

The rhetorical operation of substitution selects an expression that requires an adjustment by the message recipient in order to grasp the intended content. Although both of the tropic operations involve a turn such that an expression takes on an unexpected or unconventional meaning, simple tropes produced by substitution have a tightly constrained resolution, while complex tropes produced by destabilization have a loosely constrained resolution. Because tropes of substitution have a single resolution, we can speak of the recipient applying a correction to what the communicator offers (Fogelin 1988). The adjustments required by tropes of substitution always take place along a dimension or, more generally, in some kind of preestablished relationship. Four dimensions were pertinent to the analysis of our sample of advertisements: exaggerated/understated claims (e.g., hyperbole), absence/plenitude of expression elements (e.g., ellipsis), strong/weak assertive force (e.g., rhetorical question), and part/whole relations (e.g., metonym).

Hyperbole results when a statement makes a claim that strictly speaking is impossible. Consider this headline for a computer system: "Witness the destruction of an entire department" (i.e., because someone pressed the wrong button on a computer terminal).[5] Destruction here is an exaggeration, and what the message recipient has to do in response to this hyperbole is perform a correction of the following sort: "Yes, computer systems that lack fail-safe features certainly can cause problems." Note that a requirement for hyperbole is that the claim made must be literally impossible. An unduly positive portrayal of a brand, as in puffery, represents hype rather than hyperbole and need not be figurative.

The figure of ellipsis occurs when one substitutes a gap or lacuna for an explicit or complete statement, that is, an empty place which the recipient corrects by filling in the blank (Garnham and Oakhill 1992). A familiar example would be the slogan "You can take Salem out of the country, but you can't take the country out of ———." Note how in this instance the antimetabole facilitates comprehension of the ellipsis, showing again how multiple figures can be combined in a single headline. In our sample a simpler example of ellipsis is the Suzuki headline, "Everyday vehicles that aren't." Here the recipient must fill in the gap following the verb by supplying a particular sense of the word "everyday" (i.e., ordinary).

Substitution can also occur along the dimension of strong or weak assertive force, by altering the manner in which a claim is asserted. Consider the rhetorical question in this ad for Hewlett-Packard fax machines: "Don't you have something better to do?" Instead of asserting a claim straight out, one supplies an interrogative phrasing, thus treating the claim as open to doubt, whereas the intent is for it to be taken as certain. Epanorthosis can be thought of as the inverse of a rhetorical question.[6] Here one makes an assertion straight out with the purpose of rendering it uncertain or dubitable, as in this ad for a Ford truck: "Chances are you'll buy a Ranger for its value, economy and quality. Yeah, right." Like all tropes of substitution, rhetorical question and epanorthosis require the message recipient to correct the sense, replacing the meaning conventionally linked to the expression with a meaning that better accords with the context of interpretation.

Finally, substitution can also occur in a relationship of part to whole. A metonym makes use of the fact that objects and events in the world are represented mentally as complex schemata built up from molecular concepts. When Buick advertises that "the imports are getting nervous," a metonym is constructed: "being an import" is a constituent concept of Toyota, BMW, and the like. Using a part in place of the whole makes that part more salient. Any unconventional substitution of a part for the whole (or whole for the part, as in the Hormel ad in Table 20.2) functions as a metonym.[7]

Destabilization

The rhetorical operation of destabilization selects an expression such that the initial context renders its meaning indeterminate. By "indeterminate" we mean that multiple coexisting meanings are made available, no one of which offers a final resolution. Whereas in a trope of substitution, one says something other than what is meant and relies on the recipient to make the necessary correction, in a trope of destabilization, one means more than is said and relies on the recipient to develop the implications. Tropes of substitution make a switch, while tropes of destabilization unsettle.

In order to render multiple meanings tenable, destabilization may make use of relationships involving either opposition or similarity. The figure of irony capitalizes on opposition. Consider this headline for Range Rover: "The British have always driven on the wrong side of the road," accompanied by a picture of the automobile driven on a steep slope off to one side of the road.[8] To understand this headline, the consumer must be aware that the British drive on the left side of the road (here, as is so often the case, a rhetorical figure draws on a specific body of preexisting sociocultural knowledge) and that the left side is the correct side in Britain, even though it seems wrong to those accustomed to the alternative. The message recipient may then further reflect that for a four-wheel drive vehicle, the "wrong" side of the road (i.e., off the road altogether) is the "right" side. Further reflections may also ensue about how it is wrong for an auto to leave the road but right (pleasurable, advantageous) not to be bound to the road.

The point is not that each message recipient will make all of these inferences but that the advertiser's choice of a message that signifies the opposite of what it at first appears to signify has a destabilizing effect that liberates a variety of meanings for consideration.

In the rhetorical figure of paradox, a statement is made that cannot be true as given but that can nonetheless be made true by reinterpretation, as in this headline by Kodak: "This picture was taken by someone who didn't bring a camera." This statement appears to contradict itself: a photograph by definition requires a camera. It can be made meaningful only by reinterpreting some aspect of it—in this case, by assimilating the concept of a disposable camera that can be bought on the spot. As a result of the paradox, a concept conventionally part of the understanding of "camera" (i.e., something that has to be brought along before a photo can be taken) has been destabilized.

Just as irony and paradox both capitalize on a relation of opposition, we can likewise link and distinguish metaphor and pun as two different fashions of using a relation of similarity for purposes of destabilization. A metaphor takes advantage of a conceptual similarity: with respect to our earlier example, Band-Aids are associated with the concept of protection, as are bodyguards. Hence, a metaphor asserts a substantial or fundamental resemblance between two terms that one does not expect to see associated and does so in a way that opens up new implications. A pun, by contrast, rests on a superficial or accidental similarity: two words that sound the same or one word that happens to have two separate meanings. The nature of puns in advertising is nicely captured by Attridge (1988, p. 141): "The pun is the product of a context deliberately constructed to *enforce* an ambiguity, to render impossible the choice between meanings, to leave the reader or hearer endlessly oscillating in semantic space." We observe, consistent with analyses reported by Leigh (1994) and McQuarrie and Mick (1992), that puns of various kinds (see Table 20.2) appear with greater frequency in headlines than almost any other single figure (see Redfern 1985; Tanaka 1992).

Rhetorical Operations and Consumer Response

The importance of distinguishing the four rhetorical operations can be understood from a resource-matching perspective (Anand and Sternthal 1990), which argues that persuasion attempts will be most successful when the processing demands placed on the message recipient match the processing resources that the recipient has available. Messages that place too few demands are as likely to fail as those that demand too much. In this connection we expect complexity and deviation (incongruity) to have additive effects, consistent with Ber-lyne (1971), in that both act to increase demands on processing. Thus, more complex figures, whether scheme or trope, should be more difficult to comprehend than their simpler counterparts. However, it is also the case that effortfully processed information is more readily retrieved from memory than less effortfully processed information (Greenwald and Leavitt 1984). Hence, if comprehended, the more cognitively demanding complex figures should also be more memorable than their simpler counterparts, parallel to the argument developed earlier with respect to the greater degree of deviance that distinguishes tropes from schemes.

Table 20.3 Validation Data for the Taxonomy of Rhetorical Figures

			\multicolumn{4}{c}{Figurative statements}	
Data collection	N	Literal statements	Schemes Repetition	Reversal	Tropes Substitution	Destabilization
Initial	67	1.95 (1.04)	3.63 (1.09)	4.58 (1.29)	4.10 (1.04)	4.89 (.92)
Replication	64	1.86 (1.29)	3.62 (1.29)	4.66 (1.53)	4.25 (1.18)	4.98 (.99)
Extension	64		3.25 (1.26)			4.39 (1.11)

Note.—Values shown are means with standard deviations in parentheses. Higher values indicate the statement was perceived as more artful or clever. The literal statements are from Table 20.1. For the initial and replication studies, the figurative statements are from Table 20.2; for the extension, they consist of eight repetition and eight destabilization headlines found in published experiments (see nn. 1, 10). The replication and extension data were collected from the same 64 subjects.

In sum, the fourfold categorization produced by differentiating schemes from tropes and simple from complex rhetorical operations makes it possible for the advertiser to vary the degree of processing demand over a substantial range. That is, schemes in general are less demanding to process than tropes because excess regularity is less deviant than irregular usage. Moreover, rhyme and other figures of repetition represent the simplest and least demanding type of scheme. A similar pattern holds for tropes, making figures of destabilization such as pun and paradox the most complex and demanding of all rhetorical operations. Taken together, the four rhetorical operations allow the advertiser to accommodate audiences whose resources for processing may differ while continuing to draw the benefits of an artfully deviant message.

Validation of the Taxonomy

It might be questioned whether the distinctions in the taxonomy are phenomenologically real to consumers. We collected data to address the issue of whether naive subjects would give different ratings to simple versus complex and less versus more deviant rhetorical figures in line with the proposed taxonomy. Of course, these data do not test the causal relations that constitute the larger framework linking rhetorical structure to consumer responses; we leave this to future research. For the initial data collection, 67 undergraduates from a psychology course were recruited to rate the headlines reproduced in Tables 20.1 and 20.2. To capture the characteristics of both complexity and deviation, a contrast between "clever, artful" and "plain, matter-of-fact" was implemented as a 10-point rating scale. In the rating form each headline was preceded by a boldface label indicating the product category it concerned (e.g., "AUTO"). Headlines reflecting different rhetorical operations were interspersed, and three different orders of presentation were used.

Paired-sample *t*-tests showed that headlines comprising each of the four rhetorical operations were judged significantly more artful and clever than the literal headlines (all *p*-values < .001). A repeated-measures MANOVA was then used to compare schematic with tropic and simple with complex figures. Tropes were judged more artful and complex than schemes, and complex figures (reversal plus destabilization) were judged more artful and clever than simple figures (repetition plus substitution), with all *p*-values < .001.[9]

In a second data collection, 64 undergraduates rated the same headlines (Tables 20.1 and 20.2). This replication yielded very similar results (Table 20.3), with all comparisons significant as before. To extend the results we also included figures from a new source: repetition schemes and destabilization tropes drawn from published experiments.[10] Paired-sample *t*-tests showed that these new sets of figurative headlines were judged significantly more artful and clever than the literal headlines in Table 20.1 and that the new set of tropes was judged significantly more artful and clever than the new schemes (all *p*'s < .001).

Taken together, these results suggest that consumer judgments are sensitive to differences in the rhetorical structure of advertising. Moreover, the findings support the pattern of distinctions between schemes and tropes and among the four rhetorical operations proposed in the framework.

Discussion

We have made salient a largely unacknowledged and undifferentiated aspect of advertising language. We described how a wide variety of rhetorical figures could be integrated conceptually and related to common consumer responses, and offered an explanation for the pervasiveness of rhetorical figures in print advertising in terms of the beneficial effects associated with artful deviation.

Understanding the structure and function of rhetorical figures in advertising requires a text- and reader-aware approach, and our effort builds on prior work, especially McQuarrie and Mick (1992) and Scott (1994a, 1994b). We would argue that in the absence of appropriate text-centered terminology (e.g., scheme, trope), and without access to the necessary conceptual tools (e.g., deviation), the longstanding and widespread use of rhetorical figures in advertising has simply been overlooked in consumer research. Text-centered approaches to advertising help to direct attention to the causal power that text structure may possess. The underlying assumption is that a rhetorical figure performs a function that makes a difference in how an ad is received. In fact, from the standpoint of text-centered approaches, a notable omission in historical models of advertising response is precisely the lack of a sophisticated system of categories for theorizing about executional aspects of advertising.[11] Our particular contribution in the spectrum of text-centered approaches lies in coupling vocabulary and distinctions inherited from classical rhetoric to modern consumer research concepts. Whereas our analysis of cause is text based, our suggestions concerning possible effects lie squarely in the mainstream of consumer research and build on such familiar concepts as attention, ad liking, and ad recall.

Most advertising texts must perform their function under circumstances in which the consumer is free not to process them at all. Here lies perhaps the most fundamental contribution of this article to consumer research: its explanation of how rhetorical figures function as a useful adaptation to field conditions of advertising exposure. If consumers do not have to read an ad, then one had best motivate that reading. If consumers will only skim an ad, then one must make it memorable at a glance. Rhetoric integrates and explains stylistic devices that may be used to accomplish these and related goals.

Limitations

An important limitation of this article when viewed in the context of the rhetorical tradition is a focus that is simultaneously too narrow and too broad. On the one hand, there is much more to the rhetorical tradition than a discussion of figures (see, e.g., Hart 1990), and both Corbett (1990) and Nash (1989) provide examples of how to conduct a nonfigurative but rhetorical analysis of individual advertisements. On the other hand, the goal of a relatively comprehensive taxonomy in conjunction with article length restrictions has left our treatment of individual rhetorical figures rather brief. Note that in the case of metaphor alone, the literature is massive (Noppen 1990).

For tractability and parsimony during the construction of the framework, we restricted our compass to headlines and tag lines in magazine advertisements. This restriction should not be read as an assertion that rhetorical figures are absent or insignificant in other components of magazine ads (e.g., body copy), other modalities (e.g., pictures), or other media (e.g., billboards, television). For example, Procter and Gamble has just introduced a new pain reliever with a tag line, used across diverse media, that reads "All day strong/All day long"—an example that combines the schemes of anaphora, parison, and rhyme.

Future Research

Crucial to any future research on the framework will be experimental designs that differ from those conventionally used with print ads. As a first step we recommend adopting procedures that create more realistic low-involvement conditions, that do not force exposure, and that embed the ad in other material. There is preliminary experimental evidence that at least some figures produce pleasure when processed (McQuarrie and Mick 1992) and that both schemes and tropes facilitate recall (see Rubin and Wallace [1989] on rhyme and McQuarrie and Mick [1992] on resonant puns). The proposed framework can be used to guide future research toward comparing and distinguishing the effects of different figures rather than focusing on an individual figure in isolation from the rest. It will also be important to examine moderating variables that heighten or limit the persuasiveness of rhetorical figures. These may include individual difference variables such as the need for cognition, tolerance for ambiguity, optimal stimulation level, or even a more specific propensity to respond to figurative language (Yarbrough 1991). In addition, the consumer's level of knowledge or product involvement at the time of ad encounter may be important, in that low levels of knowledge or involvement may favor schemes, while higher levels may favor tropes. These moderator variables can in turn be integrated under a resource-matching perspective (Anand and Sternthal 1990), as suggested earlier.

It might also be useful to consider a more purely cultural and interpretive extension of this work. For instance, Roberts and Kreuz (1994) showed that different figures were perceived by subjects as instrumental to quite distinct communication goals (cf. Fernandez 1991; Stern 1990). This suggests that individual figures may have a personality or create an ambiance apart from the meanings they convey in context. For example, if the very fact of using irony conveys an additional meaning, then figures of irony may be included in ads to support a brand's personality or call out to a particular target audience.

The most interesting extensions of the taxonomy may come from setting aside verbal materials altogether and examining the visual component of ads for instances of figuration, along lines originally suggested by Durand (1987; see also Forceville 1994 and Kaplan 1992). Ads do not always use pictures in the manner of straightforward copies of reality; instead, pictorial elements may be fragmented, combined, or altered for rhetorical purposes, and some of these manipulations will possess the patterned deviance that is characteristic of figuration (Scott 1994b). Figure 20.2[†] provides two examples: the ad for California almonds makes use of visual antithesis (a scheme) in its presentation of sad and happy croissants, while the Dramamine ad can be thought of as a visual metaphor (a trope) that brings the idea of seat belt protection and nausea protection into unexpected juxtaposition. Similarly, the Peracchio and Meyers-Levy (1994) study, which included ambiguous visual images created by photographic cropping, might be reinterpreted in our framework as a study of visual ellipsis. These examples show how the basic principles of figuration proposed in our framework might be extrapolated from language to pictures. More generally, rhetorical structure appears to hold considerable promise as a fundamental idea for organizing a broad range of text phenomena in advertising.

[*Received November 1994. Revised September 1995.*
Brian Sternthal served as editor and John F. Sherry, Jr.,
served as associate editor for this article.]

Notes

[†] To view this figure, please view this essay at www.jstor.org, "Figures of Rhetoric in Advertising Language," by Edward F. McQuarrie and David Glen Mick, in the *Journal of Consumer Research*, Vol. 22, No. 4 (March, 1996), pp. 424–438.

[*] Edward F. McQuarrie is associate professor of marketing at the Leavey School of Business, Santa Clara University, Santa Clara, CA 95053. David Glen Mick is assistant professor of marketing at the University of Wisconsin, Madison, WI 53706. The authors, each of whom contributed substantially to the project, gratefully acknowledge the comments of Jacques Delacroix, James Leigh, Christine Moorman, Michael Rothschild, Linda Scott, and Mark Seabright on earlier versions of this article.

1 A search of the literature uncovered numerous instances of rhetorical figures across all categories of the framework developed in this article. A list of sources can be obtained by writing the authors.

2 In a pilot phase we perused ads appearing in 20 different magazines during 1990–1991. We then selected six magazines from among the 50 with the highest ad revenues to reflect a range of

editorial content and audiences (*People, Business Week, Car and Driver, Sports Illustrated, Cosmopolitan,* and *Good Housekeeping*). One issue of each was randomly sampled during 1991, and a second issue during April 1993, Of the 621 ads in the sample, 57 percent of the headlines and 46 percent of the tag lines contained one or more identifiable rhetorical figures (31 percent of the ads contained no recognizable rhetorical figure). Table 20.1 lists some of the headlines in which no rhetorical figure was identified. These are included to offer a comparison and contrast for the figurative headlines in Table 20.2.

3 This ceteris paribus restriction applies to all the predicted effects to be discussed subsequently, inasmuch as it will always be possible to find a nonequivalent literal statement (e.g., one that addresses a more important brand attribute) that is superior to some specific figurative statement.
4 In Saussurean semiotics, these would be labeled as syntagmatic and paradigmatic axes, respectively.
5 This headline appeared in the pilot sample in the November 12, 1990, *Business Week*. Here and in the case of irony, we use examples drawn from the pilot study because their brevity, clarity, or interpretability was superior to anything in the main sample. Hyperbole and irony were not very common in either sample.
6 Note that in the classical tradition both hyperbole and ellipsis also had logical complements or inverses (litotes, i.e., understatement, and periphrasis, i.e., superfluity of words). For whatever reason, we found no clear instances of either in our sample.
7 Some authors wish to reserve the term "synecdoche" for figures based on the distinction between part and whole. We follow Eco (1984) in eschewing the distinction between synecdoche and metonym.
8 This ad appeared in the December 1990 *Car and Driver*.
9 Note that the Table 20.2 entries were selected before the collection of data was even contemplated (the need to collect data emerged after the first round of reviews). Because the Table 20.2 entries were initially chosen solely on the basis of the clarity with which they exhibited different types of rhetorical figure, it is less plausible that a biased selection of schemes and tropes from the larger set described in n. 2 can explain the results.
10 See n. 1; there were too few published instances of reversal and substitution to provide meaningful comparisons. For this extension data set we used a near census of the repetition schemes and destabilization tropes available from published experiments, which again makes it less likely that a biased selection process can explain the results.
11 For a nonrhetorical alternative to our framework, see the response-centered approach of MacInnis, Moorman, and Jaworski (1991).

References

Anand, Punam and Brian Sternthal (1990), "Ease of Message Processing as a Moderator of Repetition Effects in Advertising," *Journal of Marketing Research,* 27 (August), 345–353.

Attridge, Derek (1988), "Unpacking the Portmanteau, or Who's Afraid of *Finnegan's Wake,*" in *On Puns: The Foundation of Letters,* ed. Jonathan Culler, New York: Blackwell, 140–155.

Barthes, Roland ([1970] 1988), "The Old Rhetoric: An Aide-Memoire," in *The Semiotic Challenge,* trans. Richard Howard, New York: Hill & Wang, 11–93.

——(1985), "The Rhetoric of the Image," in *The Responsibility of Forms,* New York: Hill & Wang, 21–40.

Berlyne, Daniel E. (1971), *Aesthetics and Psychobiology,* New York: Appleton.

Burke, Kenneth (1950), *A Rhetoric of Motives,* New York: Prentice Hall.

Childers, Terry and Michael J. Houston (1984), "Conditions for a Picture Superiority Effect on Consumer Memory," *Journal of Consumer Research,* 11 (September), 643–654.

Cohen, Jean (1982), "A Theory of the Figure," in *French Literary Theory Today: A Reader,* ed. Tzvetan Todorov, New York: Cambridge University Press.

Corbett, Edward P. J. (1990), *Classical Rhetoric for the Modern Student,* New York: Oxford University Press.

Deighton, John (1985), "Rhetorical Strategies in Advertising," in *Advances in Consumer Research*, Vol. 12, ed. Morris Holbrook and Elizabeth Hirschman, Ann Arbor, MI: Association for Consumer Research, 432–436.

Dubois, Jacques, Francis Edeline, Joan-Marie Klinkenberg, Philippe Minguet, F. Pire, and H. Trinon (1970), *A General Rhetoric*, Baltimore: Johns Hopkins University Press.

Durand, Jacques (1987), "Rhetorical Figures in the Advertising Image," in *Marketing and Semiotics: New Directions in the Study of Signs for Sale*, ed. Jean Umiker-Sebeok, New York: de Gruyter, 295–318.

Eco, Umberto (1979), *The Role of the Reader*, Bloomington: Indiana University Press.

—— (1984), *Semiotics and the Philosophy of Language*, Bloomington: Indiana University Press.

Fernandez, James W. (1991), *Beyond Metaphor: The Theory of Tropes in Anthropology*, Stanford, CA: Stanford University Press.

Fogelin, Robert J. (1988), *Figuratively Speaking*, New Haven, CT: Yale University Press.

Forceville, Charles (1994), *Pictorial Metaphor in Advertising*, Wageningen: Ponsen & Looijen.

Garnham, Alan and Jane Oakhill (1992), "Aberrant Ellipsis: Advertisers Do, but Why?" *English Today*, 8 (January), 37–40.

Genette, Gerard (1982), *Figures of Literary Discourse*, trans. Alan Sheridan, New York: Columbia University Press.

Gibbs, Raymond W. (1993), "Process and Products in Making Sense of Tropes," in *Metaphor and Thought*, ed. Andrew Ortony, New York: Cambridge University Press, 252–276.

Greenwald, Anthony G. and Clark Leavitt (1984), "Audience Involvement in Advertising: Four Levels," *Journal of Consumer Research*, 11 (June), 581–592.

Grice, Herbert P. (1989), *Studies in the Way of Words*, Cambridge, MA: Harvard University Press.

Hart, Roderick P. (1990), *Modern Rhetorical Criticism*, Glenview, IL: Scott Foresman.

Hirschman, Elizabeth C. and Morris B. Holbrook (1992), *Postmodern Consumer Research: The Study of Consumption as Text*, Newbury Park, CA: Sage.

Jakobson, Roman (1967), "Linguistics and Poetics," in *Essays on the Language of Literature*, ed. Seymour Chatman and Samuel Levin, Boston: Houghton Mifflin, 296–322.

——and Morris Halle (1956), *Fundamentals of Language*, The Hague: Mouton.

Kaplan, Stuart J. (1992), "A Conceptual Analysis of Form and Content in Visual Metaphors," *Communication*, 13 (December), 197–209.

Kreuz, Robert J. and R. M. Roberts (1993), "The Empirical Study of Figurative Language in Literature," *Poetics*, 22 (September), 151.

Leech, Geoffrey N. (1969), *A Linguistic Guide to English Poetry*, London: Longman.

Leigh, James H. (1994), "The Use of Figures of Speech in Print Ad Headlines," *Journal of Advertising*, 23 (June), 17–34.

MacInnis, Deborah J., Christine Moorman, and Bernard J. Jaworski (1991), "Enhancing and Measuring Consumers' Motivation, Opportunity and Ability to Process Brand Information from Ads," *Journal of Marketing*, 55 (October), 32–53.

McCracken, Grant (1987), "Advertising: Meaning or Information?" in *Advances in Consumer Research*, Vol. 14, ed. Melanie Wallendorf and Paul Anderson, Provo, UT: Association for Consumer Research, 121–124.

McQuarrie, Edward F. and David Glen Mick (1992), "On Resonance: A Critical Pluralistic Inquiry into Advertising Rhetoric," *Journal of Consumer Research*, 19 (September), 180–197.

Mick, David Glen (1986), "Consumer Research and Semiotics: Exploring the Morphology of Signs, Symbols and Significance," *Journal of Consumer Research,* 13 (September), 196–214.

Mitchell, Andrew A. (1983), "Cognitive Processes Initiated by Exposure to Advertising," in *Information Processing Research in Advertising,* ed. Richard J. Harris, Hillsdale, NJ:Erlbaum, 13–42.

Mukarovsky, Jan (1964), "Standard Language and Poetic Language," in *A Prague School Reader on Esthetics, Literary Structure, and Style,* ed. Paul L. Garvin, Washington, DC: Georgetown University Press.

Nash, Walter (1989), *Rhetoric: The Wit of Persuasion,* Cambridge: Blackwell.

Noppen, Jean Pierre van (1990), *Metaphor II,* Amsterdam: Benjamins.

Peracchio, Laura and Joan Meyers-Levy (1994), "How Ambiguous Cropped Objects in Ad Photos Can Affect Product Evaluations," *Journal of Consumer Research,* 21 (June), 190–204.

Pollio, Howard R., Michael K. Smith and Marilyn R. Pollio (1990), "Figurative Language and Cognitive Psychology," *Language and Cognitive Processes,* 5 (2), 141–167.

Redfern, Walter (1985), *Puns,* New York: Blackwell.

Roberts, Richard M. and Roger J. Kreuz (1994), "Why Do People Use Figurative Language?" *Psychological Science,* 5 (May), 159–163.

Ross, Haj (1991), "Fog Cat Fog," in *Cognition and the Symbolic Processes: Applied and Ecological Perspectives,* ed. Robert R. Hoffman and David S. Palermo, Hillsdale, NJ: Erlbaum, 187–205.

Rubin, David C. and Wanda T. Wallace (1989), "Rhyme and Reason: Analyses of Dual Retrieval Cues," *Journal of Experimental Psychology: Learning, Memory and Cognition,* 15 (July), 698–709.

Scott, Linda M. (1990), "Understanding Jingles and Needledrop: A Rhetorical Approach to Music in Advertising," *Journal of Consumer Research,* 17 (September), 223–236.

—— (1994a), "The Bridge from Text to Mind: Adapting Reader Response Theory to Consumer Research," *Journal of Consumer Research,* 21 (December), 461–480.

—— (1994b), "Images in Advertising: The Need for a Theory of Visual Rhetoric," *Journal of Consumer Research,* 21 (September), 252–273.

Sherry, John F. (1987), "Advertising as a Cultural System," in *Marketing and Semiotics: New Directions in the Study of Signs for Sale,* ed. Jean Umiker-Sebeok, New York: de Gruyter.

—— (1991), "Postmodern Alternatives: The Interpretive Turn in Consumer Research," in *Handbook of Consumer Behavior,* ed. Thomas Robertson and Harold H. Kassarjian, Englewood Cliffs, NJ: Prentice-Hall, 548–591.

Sperber, Dan and Deidre Wilson (1986), *Relevance: Communication and Cognition,* Cambridge, MA: Harvard University Press.

Stern, Barbara B. (1988), "How Does an Ad Mean? Language in Services Advertising," *Journal of Advertising,* 17 (Summer), 3–14.

—— (1990), "Pleasure and Persuasion in Advertising: Rhetorical Irony as a Humor Technique," *Current Issues and Research in Advertising,* Vol. 12, Ann Arbor, MI: Division of Research, Graduate School of Business Administration, University of Michigan, 25–42.

Swasy, John L. and James M. Munch (1985), "Examining the Target of Receiver Elaborations: Rhetorical Question Effects on Source Processing and Persuasion," *Journal of Consumer Research,* 11 (March), 877–886.

Tanaka, Keiko (1992), "The Pun in Advertising: A Pragmatic Approach," *Lingua*, 87 (June), 91–102.
Todorov, Tzvetan (1982), *Theories of the Symbol*, Ithaca, NY: Cornell University Press.
van Peer, Willie (1986), *Stylistics and Psychology: Investigations on Foregrounding*, London: Croom Helm.
Vickers, Brian (1989), *In Defence of Rhetoric*, Oxford: Clarendon.
Wells, William D. (1988), "Lectures and Dramas," in *Cognitive and Affective Responses to Advertising*, ed. Patricia Cafferata and Alice Tybout, Lexington, MA: Lexington.
Wenzel, Peter (1990), "Rhetoric and Semiotics," in *Semiotics in the Individual Sciences*, Vol. 2, ed. Walter A. Koch, Bochum: Brockmeyer, 558–551.
Yarbrough, Donald B. (1991), "The Reliability and Validity of a Measure of Reported Affinity for Figurative Language," *Creativity Research Journal*, 4 (4), 317–335.

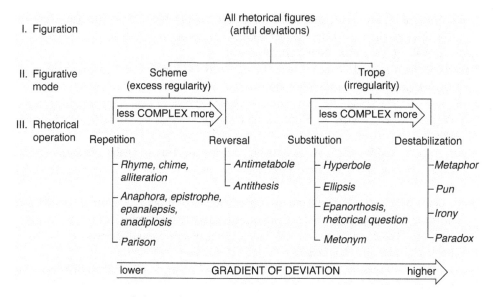

Figure 20.1 A Taxonomy of Rhetorical Figures in Advertising

21.
THE RHETORIC OF VISUAL ARGUMENTS
J. Anthony Blair

Visual Arguments Versus Other Types of Persuasion

If it is correct to distinguish visual persuasion from visual argument, presumably visual argument is one type of visual persuasion among others. The question then becomes, what distinguishes visual argument from other types of visual persuasion?

My suggestion is that what differentiates visual argument is the same as what differentiates argument in general. To be an argument, what is communicated by one party to another or others, whatever the medium of communication might be, must constitute some factor that can be considered a reason for accepting or believing some proposition, for taking some other attitude[1] or for performing some action. A test of whether such a factor is present is whether it would be possible to construct from what is communicated visually a verbal argument that is consistent with the visual presentation. This verbal construction would in no way be the equivalent of the visual argument, precisely because it could never adequately capture the evocative power of the visual element in the original presentation of the argument. However, it would abstract from the visual presentation the component that constitutes a reason for the claim being advanced.

Some of the best examples of visual arguments are the political advertisements made for television. One of the classics is the Democrats' anti-Goldwater spot run during the Presidential race between Lyndon Johnson and Barry Goldwater in 1964. Here is a description of what became known as "The Daisy Ad" (available on the Internet at www.cnn.com/ALLPOLITICS/1996/candidates/ad.archive/daisy_long.mov).

> This chilling ad begins with a little girl in a field picking petals off a daisy, counting. When the count reaches ten, her image is frozen and a male voice commences a militaristic countdown. Upon the countdown reaching zero, we see a nuclear explosion and hear President Johnson's voice: "These are the stakes, to make a world in which all God's children can live, or to go into the darkness. Either we must love each other or we must die." Fade to black. White lettering. "On November 3rd vote for President Johnson."

The purpose of the ad—remember, this was at the height of the Cold War—was to suggest that Goldwater was trigger-happy about the use of the H-bomb, and thus that to elect him would be to place the nation in grave peril. The ad did not mention

---

Blair, J. Anthony "The Rhetoric of Visual Arguments." In: Charles A. Hill and Marguerite Helmers (eds.), *Defining Visual Rhetorics*, Mahwah, NJ: Lawrence Erlbaum, 2004: 41–62.

Goldwater. It was thus a kind of visual enthymeme, requiring the viewing public to supply Goldwater as the alternative to Johnson. Never mind that the ad was an indefensible slur on Goldwater; it was brilliant. It conveyed the impression that Goldwater might, on something as arbitrary as a whim (the mere chance of which petal was plucked last), engage the nation in a nuclear holocaust, thus causing the destruction of everyone, including the innocent children who pluck daisies playing "s/he loves me; s/he loves me not." The inference that it would be a danger to the national interest to elect Goldwater follows straightforwardly.

I have just expressed in verbal form the *reasoning* of the ad, but to be clear let me set it out even more explicitly.

> Goldwater might, on something as arbitrary as a whim, launch a nuclear holocaust.
>
> Such a holocaust would cause unspeakable horror for everyone, including innocent children.
>
> Hence, it would endanger the national interest to elect Goldwater.

To repeat, I do not for a minute suggest that this verbal expression of the argument is equivalent to the visual argument. For one thing, a number of equally plausible alternative verbal renditions of the argument are available. For another, and more importantly, this verbal extraction leaves out completely the enormously evocative power of the visual imagery and symbolism of the actual visuals making up the ad. For instance, the juxtaposition of the child in its innocence and the nuclear mushroom cloud has huge pathetic force that words cannot capture. However, what the verbal construction does succeed in doing is identifying how the visual ad contained within it a reason for not voting for Goldwater. And that, I contend, is what made the Democrats' attack ad an argument.

If this account is correct, then visual arguments constitute the species of visual persuasion in which the visual elements overlie, accentuate, render vivid and immediate, and otherwise elevate in forcefulness a reason or set of reasons offered for modifying a belief, an attitude or one's conduct. What distinguishes visual arguments from other forms of visual persuasion is that in the case of the former it is possible to enunciate reasons given to support a claim, whereas in the case of the latter no such element is present. Thus we can see that the "Daisy" ad was conveying an argument against supporting Goldwater.

The Visual Difference

The advantage of visual arguments over print or spoken arguments lies in their evocative power. Part of this power is due to the enormously high number of images that can be conveyed in a short time. Television commercials today show between one and four *dozen* different moving visual images in a 30-second spot. We have no trouble processing that much visual information, whereas it would be impossible to express 30 different propositions verbally in 30 seconds, and even if it were not, it would be far beyond normal human capacity to process them. Visual images can thus be used to convey a narrative in a short time. Recall the Coca Cola commercial shown during the 2002 Winter Olympics in Utah, in which an awkward youth wins the heart of an elegant female figure skater against the competition of several older handsome young men by giving her a Coke at the end of her program. The story is told with ingredients of poignancy, sexiness and humor—all in 30 seconds—and although (I would argue) this commercial is not an argument, it does illustrate the narrative capacity of the visual.

Another factor is the sense of realism that the visual conveys. My students, for example, year in and year out tell me that television news is better than print news in the respect that with television news they can see for themselves what happened whereas with print news they are told by a reporter, and so have only second-hand access to the events depicted. I believe that this impression is quite mistaken. A lot of TV news pictures are file footage, but even video of the actual event being reported is limited to a small number of camera vantage points and angles, and a very few seconds of footage, and the video is packaged with voice over and cut aways. Besides that, each TV news "item" on network news programs, and often on local news programs too, is a carefully crafted "story." It is deliberately assembled with a beginning (a problem or question), a middle (information, opinions) and an end (resolution of the problem or answer to the question, followed by dénouement, the outcome). The result is that the "reality" is a selected perspective presented in a highly structured or filtered way. Nevertheless, my students are under the impression that the visual gives them direct access to what is visually portrayed in a way that print does not, and their impressions are what matter so far as the power of the visual is concerned.

The visual element in visual arguments is most significantly a *rhetorical* dimension, rather than *logical* or *dialectical*. Understanding the dialectical dimension of arguments to be the process of interaction between the arguer and interlocutors who raise questions or objections, we can see that visual arguments lack this dialectical aspect. The visual makes an argument in the sense of adducing a few reasons in a forceful way. It might contain or present a *didactic narrative*—a story that supports a point. But it does not permit the complexity of such dialectical moves as the raising of objections in order to refute or otherwise answer them. This is a serious deficiency in what Ralph H. Johnson has called the "manifest rationality" that ought, ideally, to characterize argumentation. Johnson's suggestion is that when we try to convince others using arguments, we ought to mention the objections to our views that we know about and explain how we would answer these objections. There should be no suppressed problems with our case. Johnson is calling for a kind of "truth in arguing"—a "full disclosure" policy. If his ideal is one we ought to try to meet, and if visual arguments cannot, as it seems they cannot, incorporate this "dialectical" dimension of challenge and response, then visual arguments will always fall short of dialectical rationality.

Understanding the logical dimension of arguments to be the support that the reason(s) offered provide for the viewpoint that is supported by them, we can see that visual arguments supply simple, minimalist support. The verbal expression of the argument will have one or two premises, tending to be more or less syllogistic in structure. The logic of the argument will not be complicated or subtle.

Understanding the rhetorical dimension of arguments to consist of the various facets of its situatedness, it is plain that the visual is above all rhetorical. To be effective, the visual properties of a visual argument must resonate with the audience on the occasion and in the circumstances. The visual symbolism must register immediately, whether consciously or not. The arguer must know and relate not only to the beliefs and attitudes of the intended audience, but also to the visual imagery that is meaningful to it. The arguer needs also to be sensitive to the surrounding argumentative "space" of the audience, because so much of the argument must remain tacit or unexpressed. Visual arguments are typically *enthymemes*—arguments with gaps left to be filled in by the participation of the audience. The anti-Goldwater "Daisy" ad is a clear example, with Goldwater the clear target of the ad but never mentioned in it. So the arguer has to be able to predict the nature of the audience's participation. Given the vagueness of much visual imagery, the visual arguer must be particular astute in reading the audience. Thus in a variety of ways, visual arguments rely particularly on the rhetorical astuteness of the arguer for their success. We may say, then, that visual arguments are distinguished by their rhetorical power. What makes visual arguments distinctive is how much greater is their potential for rhetorical power than that of purely verbal arguments.

Why Argue Visually?

One reason for using visual arguments is that there is no alternative way of giving the argument permanence. In a largely oral culture with little literacy, verbal arguments have only as much endurance as their currency in the oral tradition. Thus we see the didactic visual arguments chiseled in the granite "decorations" of the great European medieval cathedrals. A striking example is the sculpture of the damned going to hell and the saved going to heaven to be found in the tympanum over the south transept door of the high gothic cathedral. The damned are depicted in graphic detail, being led or herded naked down to the right, their bodies twisted in grotesque contortions, their faces distorted and their open mouths screaming in pain. They are shackled, flames lick at them, devils prod them with pitchforks, and some are tossed into great cauldrons of boiling liquid. The saved, on the other hand, troupe triumphantly upward to the left, clad in gowns, their faces smiling with delight, with those at the top being welcomed to heaven. The message is clear: These are the fates awaiting the virtuous and the vicious upon their respective deaths. The obvious implicit premise is that no one would want the fate of the damned and anyone would want the fate of the saved. The tacit conclusion follows straightforwardly: Be virtuous and refrain from vice. Many of these depictions of the argument have so far lasted, unmodified except by the weather, for over 700 years. They are fixed in stone no less effectively than had they been fixed in print.

Besides giving this moral argument a permanence, its visual expression communicates something unavailable to the verbal version, whether it is communicated orally or in writing. No words can convey the horrible fate of the damned or the ecstatic beatitude of the saved as dramatically, forcefully and realistically as do the stone carvings. It is one thing to hear a description of these respective fates; it is quite another, far more vivid and immediate, to *see* them with your own eyes. So here is another reason for conveying an argument visually: one can communicate visually with much more force and immediacy than verbal communication allows.

I think there are two related reasons for the greater force and immediacy of the visual. First, visual communication can be more efficient than verbal communication. In order to convey and evoke emotions or attitudes, the verbal arguer must rely on his or her oratorical powers to cause the audience to exercise its sympathetic imagination. There are three opportunities for failure in such communications: The arguer can fail to be effectively evocative, the audience can refuse to cooperate in the imaginative exercise, and the audience can, even if trying, fail in its imaginative task. In the case of visual arguments, these three chances to misfire reduce to one. The creator of the visual expression of the argument can fail to give adequate or appropriate visual expression to the feelings or attitudes to be conveyed, and in that case, the advantages of the visual expression of the argument are lost. However, should the visual expression succeed—as the medieval cathedral tympanum sculptures do so marvelously—then the audience cannot help but become involved, and in just the way the arguer intends. Hence the arguer does not have to rely on either the cooperation of the audience or its powers of sympathetic imagination. In this respect, then, visual argument is likely to be more efficient than its verbal counterpart.

What takes the need for the cooperation and competence of the audience out of the visual argument equation—and this is the second reason for the greater force and immediacy of the visual—is the power of visual imagery to evoke involuntary reactions—reactions that must be consciously countered by the recipient if their power is to be at all defused. Evidence of this power is today found most pervasively in movies and in television commercials. The power of visual imagery in commercials is actually confirmed empirically, at least for national TV advertising campaigns, though movies are increasingly also tested on focus groups prior to their release. The effects of various symbols are well-known and much exploited. For instance, images of young children and young animals evoke immediate sympathy in adults. Several years ago Pepsi ran a commercial that consisted of nothing else than two little boys (clearly twins, maybe 3-year-olds) and three or four puppies from the same litter at their ungainly stage of locomotion, frolicking together across a slightly sloping lawn. The puppies were jumping up to lick the boys' faces, the little boys were giggling with delight, and both the boys and puppies were tumbling together and getting up and running down the slope. The kids and the puppies were utterly adorable, and any adult viewer who wasn't a sociopath couldn't help smiling and responding, "Ohhh, they're so cute!" What the commercial had to do with choosing Pepsi is not my point at the moment. The point is that this imagery, however it might be explained, evoked a powerful involuntary response in the normal viewer.

It seems plausible that there is an evolutionary advantage to having the caring and protective responses of the adults of most species that are triggered by the young of their own or even other species biologically hard-wired in them. The hard-wiring seems indisputable. I have seen a pair of robins hatch and feed a starling nestling along with their own, and cowbirds are notorious for taking advantage of this response by laying their eggs in other birds' nests and having them raised by those other birds. We have all heard of nursing mothers of various mammal species taking on the nurture and care either of other offspring of their own species or the offspring of other species. Notice how advertisers often rely on this response by showing cute babies, both human and those of other animals, in commercials in which there is no plausible connection between the baby and the product. (Such appeals are *pathetic appeals*—appeals to the sympathy or emotional responses of an audience.)

Other kinds of symbolism, such as the authority of the physician or scientists used in pain-killer or indigestion-remedy commercials that is conveyed by actors dressed in white lab coats with a stethoscope around their necks, clearly have learned, conventional associations. (This is an *appeal to ethos*—an appeal to the character or stature of a person or a role to lend credibility to what is portrayed.) Yet others are mixtures of learned and biological responses, such as heterosexual responses to the appearance of members of the opposite sex considered beautiful. Sexual attraction is presumably at least partly hard-wired, although there are clearly social factors in sexual attraction that are culturally variable. Lean or stout, short or tall, tattooed or clear-skinned, pierced or unadorned—these are variations in sexual attractiveness that any student of other cultures, or indeed of our own, are bound to notice. The point is that our responses—learned, innate, or a combination of the two—are used by advertisers, and their effectiveness in advertising is well tested.

Thus, the use of such symbolism in visual arguments can almost guarantee the ethotic and pathetic rhetorical influences that the arguer intends. And all it takes to accomplish these rhetorical effects is the flash of a series of visual images.

For as long as we have had near-universal literacy and a tradition of print, verbal arguments have been as permanent as we might wish them to be, and in fact have greater permanency than the evanescent television screen or the movie. So the motivation for visual arguments has not in our time been the advantage of fixing the argument in a stable medium. The evocative power of visual means of communication, especially television (but also movies, pictures in magazines, and posters or billboards) is what has recommended the visual as a medium of argument.

Genres of Visual Argument

Traditional rhetoric as applied to arguments was concerned with the means of giving the greatest possible persuasive power to the written or spoken word. It did not seek to replace the propositional content of argument, but to position it so as to be maximally forceful. The same goes for rhetoric as applied to visual arguments. My contention is that visual persuasive communication cannot ignore or set aside prepositional content and continue to count as argument. Argument requires the giving and receiving of reasons. However, visual media offer rich means for generating forcefulness for arguments expressed visually. Let us consider briefly some of the different genres of visual argument, and some of their tools and deficiencies.

I have already given an example of a political cartoon used to make a visual argument. Cartoons are distinctive because they permit an explicitness and precision of meaning found in few other visual genres. The convention that allows for labeling, and the abilities of cartoonists to capture the distinctive visual traits of well-known public figures, and the opportunity that caricature provides for exaggeration, all enable their messages to be unambiguous. To be sure, a great deal more than that is going on in cartoons, as Janice Edwards in her chapter on the visual rhetoric of cartoons (chapter 8, this volume [sic]) makes clear. The multilayered meanings and associations of various visual cultural icons generate powerful resonances around simple pen-and-ink drawings. When the cartoonist is making an argument (and not every cartoon is intended as an argument), the points asserted visually have a particular forcefulness and credibility when such iconic imagery is used, and the means used can be analytically identified, as Edwards (chapter 8, this volume [sic]) shows in applying Perlmutter's (1998) list of ten characteristics of photographs of outrage that can give them iconic status.

Films empower arguments visually largely by means of the construction of credible narratives. When a movie is making an argument (and by no means is every film intended as an argument), it tells a story that makes the argument's cogency seem inevitable. Oliver Stone's *JFK* made the case that there was a conspiracy to assassinate President Kennedy and to cover up the conspiracy. In telling that story, it made the characters who believed in a conspiracy highly credible, and those who denied it highly unbelievable. The film made the argument forcefully by presenting a narrative in which that conclusion was the most plausible interpretation of the events portrayed. *Black Hawk Down* is a more current example. It makes the case that the U.S. attempt to capture a local warlord in Mogadishu during the Somalia intervention was an ill-conceived plan by portraying dramatically the horrible consequences that snowballed from just one thing going wrong (a soldier falling out of a helicopter during the initial attack). The idea of narratives functioning as arguments is familiar to us all. To give just one example, our countries often justify their foreign policies in terms of narratives, the only plausible resolution of which is the policy being defended. Thus the "Communist conspiracy" was a narrative that justified Cold War policies. More recently, the Muslim fundamentalist threat epitomized by the attacks on the World Trade Center and the Pentagon on September 11, 2001, were woven into a narrative that justified the Bush administration's "war on terrorism." To call these arguments narratives is not to call them fictions or to challenge their legitimacy, although they might be open to such challenges. The point is, rather, that as narratives they tell stories that have "logical" resolutions, and hence function as arguments. Because pictures, and especially films, both fictional and documentary, are wonderfully suited to telling believable stories, they provide an excellent medium for visual argument by means of narrative construction.

What the visual element adds to film or video, over, say, a novel or short story, or over documentary prose alone, is that with film or video, we don't just imagine the narrative, we "see" it unfolding before our eyes. Seeing is believing, even if what we are watching is invented, exaggerated, half-truths or lies.

The third and last type of visual argument that I want to discuss is advertising, and television advertising in particular. For the most part, we watch TV to relax, as a diversion from our working lives. Television commercials thus invade our private space and time and reach us when we tend not to be alert and vigilant. Although we can control which programs we view, we cannot control which advertisements accompany those programs and it takes an effort to "mute" the commercials. Moreover, advertisers can and do predict with a high degree of accuracy the demographics of the audiences of any program, and so they design their messages to exploit the vulnerabilities of the members of that demographic group. Combine with these factors the huge influence of repetition, and the attraction of the visual as the medium of influencing choice becomes obvious.

My view of whether TV ads are visual arguments is not widely shared. My initial point was to emphasize the evocative power of visual communication. This power is thus available for visual arguments, whether static (print) or dynamic (television). But that does not imply that all uses of visuals in persuasion are cases of visual arguments. It strikes me that although magazine and television visual advertising often presents itself as more or less rational persuasion aimed at influencing our preferences and actions, what is in fact going on in the most effective ads is that the actual influence is accomplished behind this façade of rationality.

Whether or not even to call it persuasion strikes me as moot, because it is not clear that we have the capacity to reject the influence. When I think of a rich custard cream sauce or creamy chocolate mousse, foods I adore, I cannot help but salivate. (I am salivating as I write this description! Try thinking about tastes you love without having your mouth water.) The only way to avoid it is not to think of these foods. It might be that especially television advertising is for most of us what chocolate mousse is for me—something whose influence can be avoided only if we avoid exposure to it. If that is true, it is more like the surgeon's brain implant than even the robber's gun. And then it is not persuasion, but unconscious causation, and so not rational persuasion, and so not argument, visual or otherwise.[9]

The Pepsi commercial with the giggling children and frolicking puppies was, I want to argue, not a visual argument at all. It merely evoked feelings of warmth and empathy, which were then associated with the brand. The objective of the advertiser, I expect, was to cause the audience to feel good about the commercial, and then transfer that good feeling to the brand. Presumably the hope (and probably it was an empirically confirmed conviction) was that the good feeling about the brand would cause shoppers to reach for Pepsi on the supermarket shelf when buying soda for their families. There was no reason of any kind offered for preferring Pepsi to alternative colas or other types of soda. To insist that this commercial be understood as an argument strikes me as to be in the grip of a dogma, the dogma that all influence on attitudes or action *must* be at least persuasion if not its subspecies, argumentation. What premises could possibly be reconstructed from the advertisement? That drinking Pepsi causes little kids and puppies to be cute? Absurd. That Pepsi, like you and I, thinks little kids and puppies are cute and so we, the consumers, should favor Pepsi over other cola brands or types of soda, which don't think kids and puppies are cute? Far-fetched. Stupid as we consumers might be, we are not complete idiots. Given the choice between interpreting this commercial as a completely stupid argument, on one hand, and as not an argument at all but an attempt to influence us via our psychological associations with young children and puppies, on the other, any principle of interpretive charity points to the second alternative as by far the more plausible.

By the way, this sort of visual influence through association and the power of visual symbols is not restricted to advertising. Consider another, more mundane, example.

Every evening on network television news broadcasts, when the broadcast turns to federal political news from Washington, a reporter stands against the backdrop of the White House or the Capitol and reads his or her report (with cutaways edited in, to be sure). The White House and the Capitol are not just buildings. They are powerful symbols, conveying the immense authority and prestige of the institutions of the Presidency and the Congress. Thus these visual images lend to the television reporter, by association, some of the authority of those political institutions, thereby adding to his or her credibility. These backdrops are visual rhetorical devices that render the message conveyed more believable or persuasive. They lend *ethos* to the reporter. However they are not arguments. No argument is offered to show that the reporter is credible or authoritative. If the reporter were to say, "I am standing in front of the White House, and it follows from this fact that you should take my report or opinions seriously," we would on that basis *not* take him or her seriously. The symbols do their work precisely by making contact with our unconsciously held, symbol-interpreting apparatus, not by engaging our capacity to assess reasons and their implications.

What typically happens in TV commercials and other visual advertising is that there is a surface "argument," usually supplied by the accompanying verbal text or voiceover. This argument is usually thin, offering little by way of reasons for preferring the product in question to similar products sold by competitors, or for liking that brand name. What does the influencing is the psychological appeal. Charles Revson, the founder of Revlon, is reported to have once said, "I don't sell cosmetics; I sell dreams." Advertising agencies use social science research (or do their own) into the current values and aspirations, the dreams and fantasies, *of their target markets*. What's hip? What's cool? What's *bad*? Their ads then use actors or celebrities dressed and behaving in ways that embody those values, aspirations, dreams and fantasies. We viewers transfer our identifications with the commercials to the brand or product. We want this brand or product because we think of ourselves as like the person in the commercial, doing the kinds of things done in the commercial. No reasoning occurs here at all. Think of the old Marlboro cigarette ads. A billboard with a picture of a cowboy with a tattoo on a horse smoking a cigarette. Visual influence? Absolutely. Visual argument? None.

So my view is that although TV commercials and other kinds of visual advertising might seem to represent the epitome of visual argument, in reality they constitute a poor case for their existence. I cannot claim that no TV commercial can reasonably be construed as an argument. On the contrary, I construed the Democrats' "Daisy" political ad against Goldwater as a visual argument. But "visual" plus "influence" does not add up to "argument" in every case.

Conclusion

It is time to sum up. Are visual arguments possible? It might seem not, since argument is paradigmatically verbal and essentially propositional, and visual images are often vague or ambiguous. However, we saw that vagueness and ambiguity can be managed in verbal argument, and so are in principle manageable in visual communication;

moreover not all visual communication is vague or ambiguous. As well, propositions can be expressed visually no less than verbally. Argument in the traditional sense consists of supplying grounds for beliefs, attitudes or actions, and we saw that pictures can equally be the medium for such communication. Argument, in the traditional sense, can readily be visual.

It does not follow that visual argument is a mere substitute for verbal argument. The spoken word can be far more dramatic and compelling than the written word, but the visual brings to arguments another dimension entirely. It adds drama and force of a much greater order. Beyond that it can use such devices as references to cultural icons and other kinds of symbolism, dramatization and narrative to make a powerfully compelling case for its conclusion. The visual has an immediacy, a verisimilitude, and a concreteness that help influence acceptance and that are not available to the verbal.

While granting the persuasiveness of visual argument, we saw that in logical terms, its structure and content tends to be relatively simple. The complications of the dialectical perspective are not easily conveyed visually, and the result is that visual argument tends to be one-sided, presenting the case for or the case against, but not both together. Qualifications and objections are not readily expressed. Where visual argument excels is in the rhetorical dimension.

Rhetoric as related to argument, we saw, is the use of the best means available to make the logic of the argument persuasive to its audience. In communicating arguments visually, we need to attend particularly to the situation of the audience. What is the setting, and how does it introduce constraints and opportunities? What visual imagery will the audience understand and respond to? What historical and cultural modes of visual understanding does the audience bring to the situation? Visual arguers will answer these questions in creating their visual enthymemes, thus drawing the viewer to participate in completing the construction of the argument and so in its own persuasion. When argument is visual, it is, above all, visual rhetoric.

Notes

1. I say, some "other" attitude, because it has become widely agreed among philosophers analyzing the concept of *belief* that beliefs are a kind of attitude themselves (a type of "propositional attitude").
2. I am setting aside for purposes of this discussion the enormous influence of music in television advertising. From the perspective of a study of persuasion, the role of music must be given a central place.

Works Cited

Aristotle. *Rhetoric.* Trans. W. Rhys Roberts. *The Complete Works of Aristotle.* Ed. Jonathan Barnes. Princeton: Princeton UP, 1984.

Birdsell, David S., and Leo Groarke. "Toward a Theory of Visual Argument." *Argumentation and Advocacy* 33 (1996): 1–10.

Blair, J. Anthony. "The Possibility and Actuality of Visual Argument." *Argumentation and Advocacy* 33 (1996): 23–39.

Engel, S. Morris. *Analyzing Informal Fallacies.* Englewood Cliffs, NJ: Prentice-Hall, 1980.

Fleming, David. "Can Pictures be Arguments?" *Argumentation and Advocacy* 33 (1996): 11–22.

Foss, Sonja K., Karen A. Foss, and Robert Trapp. *Contemporary Perspectives on Rhetoric*. Prospect Heights, IL: Waveland P, 1985.

Groarke, Leo. "Logic, Art and Argument." *Informal Logic 18* (1996): 105–129.

Jacobs, Scott. "Rhetoric and Dialectic from the Standpoint of Normative Pragmatics." *Argumentation* 14 (2000): 261–286.

Johnson, Ralph H. *Manifest Rationality: A Pragmatic Theory of Argument*. Mahwah, NJ: Lawrence Erlbaum Associates, 2000.

Perlmutter, David D. *Photojournalism and Foreign Policy: Icons of Outrage in International Crisis*. Westport, CT: Praeger, 1998.

Reboul, Olivier. *Introduction à la Rhétoric* [*Intoduction to Rhetoric*]. Paris: PUF, 1991.

Tindale, Christopher W. *Acts of Arguing, A Rhetorical Model of Argument*. Albany, NY: State U of New York P, 1999.

Music

22.
RHETORIC AND MUSIC
George J. Buelow

Rhetoric and music. The connections between rhetoric and music have often been extremely close, notably in the Baroque period. The influence of the principles of rhetoric profoundly affected the basic elements of music. (*See also* ANALYSIS, §11, 1.)

1. Introduction. 2. Musical-rhetorical concepts. 3. Musical figures. 4. The Affections. 5. Conclusion.

1. INTRODUCTION. Interrelationships between music and the spoken arts – *artes dicendi* (grammar, rhetoric, dialectic) – are at once obvious and unclear. Until fairly late in the history of Western civilization, music was predominantly vocal and thus bound to words. Composers have therefore generally been influenced to some degree by rhetorical doctrines governing the setting of texts to music, and even after the growth of independent instrumental music, rhetorical principles continued for some time to be used not only for vocal music but for instrumental works too. What still remains to be fully explained is how these critical interrelationships often controlled the craft of composition, at least until well into the 18th century. These developments are unclear partly because modem musicians and scholars are untrained in the rhetorical disciplines, which since the beginning of the 19th century have largely disappeared from most educational and philosophical systems.

All rhetorically related musical concepts originated in the extensive literature on oratory and rhetoric by ancient Greek and Roman writers, especially Aristotle, Cicero and Quintilian. The rediscovery in 1416 of Quintilian's *Institutio oratoria* provided one of the primary sources on which the growing union between rhetoric and music was based in the 16th century. Quintilian, like Aristotle before him, stressed the similarities between music and oratory. The goal of his work and all other studies of oratory since antiquity was the same: to instruct the orator in the means of controlling and directing the emotional responses of his audience or, in the language of classical rhetoric and also later music treatises, to enable the orator (i.e. the composer or even the performer) to move the 'Affections' (i.e. the emotions) of his listeners (see §4 below).

While early Christian sacred music has not been adequately studied to consider the potential influence on it of rhetorical concepts, it appears certain that Gregorian chant itself displays frequent and varied reflections of rhetorical expression. There is some evidence (see Flotzinger) for believing that a similar influence was exerted on early

---

Buelow, George J. "Rhetoric and Music." In: Vol. XV, Stanley Sadie (ed.), *The New Grove Dictionary of Music and Musicians*. London: Macmillan, 1980: 793–803.

polyphony. The direct impact of classical rhetorical thought on music first became unmistakable, however, with the advent of Renaissance humanism in the late 15th century. It was then that classical as well as contemporary books on rhetoric became the basis of an important part of European educational curricula. This development occurred both in Catholic countries as well as in those regions that became Protestant after the Reformation. Elementary Latin schools and universities placed similar emphasis on the study of oratory and rhetoric, and every educated man was a skilled rhetorician. This universal development had a profound impact on composers* attitudes to text-bound music, sacred as well as secular, and led to new musical styles and forms of which the madrigal and opera are only the most obvious products.

These dramatic changes in music, which can in general be traced to humanist influences, confronted music theorists with problems foreign to all traditional music theory. Music, which since antiquity had belonged, with arithmetic, geometry and astronomy, to the Quadrivium – the mathematical disciplines – of the Seven Liberal Arts, was forced to adopt new theoretical values if it were to embrace these new rhetorically orientated musical styles. While music remained closely allied to mathematics up to the 18th century, it was German theorists in particular who raised musical composition to a science based on the relationship of words to music. As early as 1537 Listenius introduced a broad new division of music theory, which he called *musica poetica*, into the former Boethian duality of *musica theoretica* and *musica practica*. Another German, Joachim Burmeister, first proposed a systematic musical-rhetorical basis for such a *musica poetica* in his *Hypomnematum musicae* (1599) and its later versions, *Musica autoschediastikē* (1601) and *Musica poetica* (1606). His theory included the significant new idea of musical figures, which were analogous to the rhetorical figures found since antiquity in treatises on rhetoric (see §3 below). Johannes Lippius suggested in his *Synopsis musices* (1612) that rhetorical doctrine was not only the basis for an effective musical setting of words but also for the basis of the *forma* or structure of a composition. It is particularly revealing that many German theorists of this period observed that rhetorical expression occurred in the music of many Renaissance composers. Johannes Nucius, in his *Musices practicae* (1613), for example, considered Dunstable first among the composers belonging to a new tradition of rhetorically expressive music, a tradition in which he also included Binchois, Busnois, Clemens non Papa, Crecquillon, Isaac, Josquin, Ockeghem and Verdelot. Lassus, however, was the composer whom theorists most often singled out as a master of musical rhetoric.

Not until the Baroque period did rhetoric and oratory furnish so many of the essential rational concepts that lie at the heart of most compositional theory and practice. Beginning in the 17th century, analogies between rhetoric and music permeated every level of musical thought, whether involving definitions of styles, forms, expression and compositional methods, or various questions of performing practice. Baroque music in general aimed for a musical expression of words comparable to impassioned rhetoric or a *musica pathetica*. The union of music with rhetorical principles is one of the most distinctive characteristics of Baroque musical rationalism and gave shape to the progressive elements in the music theory and aesthetics of the period. Since the preponderantly rhetorical orientation of Baroque music evolved out of the Renaissance preoccupation with the impact of musical styles on the meaning and intelligibility of words (as for example in the theoretical discussions of the Florentine Camerata), nearly all the elements of music that can be considered typically Baroque, whether the music be Italian, German, French or English, are tied, either directly or indirectly, to rhetorical concepts.

2. MUSICAL-RHETORICAL CONCEPTS. As early as 1563, in a manuscript entitled *Praecepta musicae poeticae,* Gallus Dressier referred to a formal organization of music that would adopt the divisions of an oration into *exordium* (opening), *medium* and *finis*. A similar structural plan appears in Burmeister's treatise of 1606. In both instances rhetorical terminology was raised to the level of defining compositional structure, and such a viewpoint remained valid until well into the 18th century. In 1739, in *Der vollkommene Capellmeister,* Mattheson laid out a fully organized, rational plan of musical composition borrowed from those sections of rhetorical theory concerned with finding and presenting arguments: *inventio* (invention of an idea), *dispositio* (arrangement of the idea into the parts of an oration), *decoratio* (the elaboration or decoration of the idea) – called *elaboratio* or *elocutio* by other writers – and *pronuntiatio* (the performance or delivery of the oration). Dressler's structure *of exordium, medium* and *finis* was only a simplified version of the more usual sixfold division of the *dispositio,* which in classical rhetoric as well as in Mattheson consisted of *exordium, narratio* (statement of facts), *divisio* or *propositio* (forecast of main points in a speaker's favour), *confirmatio* (affirmative proof), *confutaio* (refutation or rebuttal) and *peroratio* or *conclusio* (conclusion).

While neither Mattheson nor any other Baroque theorist would have applied these rhetorical prescriptions rigidly to every musical composition, it is clear that such concepts not only aided composers to a varying degree but were self-evident to them as routine techniques in the compositional process. Nor was rhetorical structure limited to German music theory. Mersenne, for example, in his *Harmonie universelle* (1636–7) emphasized that musicians were orators who must compose melodies as if they were orations, including all of the sections, divisions and periods appropriate to an oration. Kircher, writing in Rome, gave the title 'Musurgja rhetorica' to one section of his highly influential encyclopedia of the theory and practice of music, *Musurgia universalis* (1650); in it he also emphasized the analogy between rhetoric and music in the common divisions of the creative process into *inventio, dispositio* and *elocutio.*

The vitality of such concepts is evident throughout the Baroque period and even later. Just as an orator had first to invent an idea (*inventio*) before he could develop his oration, so the Baroque composer had to invent a musical idea that was a suitable basis for construction and development. Since each musical idea must express an inherent or sometimes an imposed affective element of the text to which it was joined, composers often required aids to stimulate their musical imagination. Not every poetic text possessed an affective idea suitable for musical invention, but again rhetoric provided the means to assist the *ars inveniendi*. In *Der General-Bass in der Composition* (1728), Heimchen extended the analogy with rhetoric to include the *loci topici,* the standard rhetorical devices available to help the orator uncover topics – i.e. ideas – for a formal discourse. The *loci topici* are rationalized categories of topics from which suitable ideas for invention could be drawn. Quintilian described them as 'sedes argumentorum'

– sources of argument. On the most elementary level they were symbolized by the well-known questions that he posed for any legal dispute: whether a thing is (*an sit*), what it is (*quid sit*) and of what kind it is (*quale sit*). Heinichen (see Buelow, 1966) employed the *locus circumslanliarum,* namely the use of a textual antecedent, concomitant or consequent – i.e. a preceding recitative, the first (*A*) section of an aria, and the second (*B*) section or a subsequent recitative – as sources of musical ideas for aria texts. In *Der vollkommene Capellmeister* Mattheson criticized him for limiting himself to only the *loci* of circumstance and urged the full employment of several other *loci* commonly used by rhetoricians, such as the *locus descriptionis, locus notationis* and *locus causae materialis*. It is not unimportant that both Heinichen and Mattheson were practical theorists with long and distinguished careers as composers, during which they wrote vocal music for the opera house as well as for the church.

3. Musical figures. The most complex and systematic transformation of rhetorical concepts into musical equivalents originates in the *decoratio* of rhetorical theory. In oratory every speaker relied on his command of the rules and techniques of the *decoratio* in order to embellish his ideas with rhetorical imagery and to infuse his speech with passionate language. The means to this end was the broad concept of figures of speech. As early as Renaissance music, both sacred and secular, there is ample evidence that composers employed various musical-rhetorical means to illustrate or emphasize words and ideas in the text. Indeed the whole musical literature of the madrigal unequivocally depends on this use of musical rhetoric. In recent discussions, some authors (e.g. Palisca) have connected the late 16th-century practice of musical rhetoric to the definition of a musical 'mannerism', suggesting that this particular approach to composing may well be the explanation of the obscure term 'musica reservata'. Of all the late Renaissance composers, Lassus was undoubtedly the greatest musical orator, as was frequently recognized by his contemporaries, and in the first treatise attempting to codify musical-rhetorical practices, by Burmeister, one of his motets, *In me transierunt,* was analysed according to its rhetorical structure and its employment of musical figures. For more than a century a number of German writers, following Burmeister, also borrowed rhetorical terminology for musical figures, with both Greek and Latin names, but they also invented new musical figures by analogy with rhetoric but unknown to it. In this basically German theory of musical figures there are thus numerous conflicts in terminology and definition among the various writers, and there is clearly no one systematic doctrine of musical Figures for Baroque and later music, notwithstanding frequent references to such a system by Schweitzer, Kretzschmar, Schering, Bukofzer and others. The most detailed catalogue of musical figures (in Unger) lists approximately 160 different forms, taken from definitions and descriptions of varying degrees of exactness in many 17th- and 18th-century treatises, among the most important of which are J. Burmeister: *Musica autoschediastikē* (Rostock, 1601), expanded as *Musica poetica* (Rostock, 1606); J. Lippius: *Synopsis musicae nova* (Strasbourg, 1612); J. Nudus: *Musices practicae* (Neisse, 1613); J. Thuringus: *Opusculum bipartitum* (Berlin, 1624); J. A. Herbst: *Musica moderna prattica* (Frankfurt am Main, 2/1653) and *Musica poetica* (Nuremberg, 1643); A. Kircher: *Musurgia universalis*

(Rome, 1650); C. Bernhard: *Troctatus compositionis augmentatus* (MS); J. G. Ahle: *Musikalisches Frühlings-, Sommer-, Herbst-, und Winter-Gespräche* (Mühlhausen, 1695–1701); T. B. Janovka: *Clavis ad thesaurum magnae artis musicae* (Prague, 1701); J. G. Walther: *Praecepta der musicalischen Composition* (MS, 1708) and *Musikalisches Lexicon* (Leipzig, 1732); M. J. Vogt: *Conclave thesauri magnae artis musicae* (Prague, 1719); J. A. Scheibe: *Der critische Musikus* (Leipzig, 2/1745); M. Spiess: *Tractalus musicus compositorio-practicus* (Augsburg, 1745); and J. N. Forkel: *Allgemeine Geschichte der Musik* (Leipzig, 1788–1801).

Attempts by writers such as Brandes, Unger and Schmitz to organize the multitude of musical figures into a few categories have not proved successful. The following list aims only to give the most frequently cited musical figures in an equally arbitrary but somewhat broader group of seven categories: (A) Figures of melodic repetition, (B) Figures based on fugal imitation, (C) Figures formed by dissonance structures, (D) Interval figures, (E) Hypotyposis figures, (F) Sound figures, (G) Figures formed by silence. No effort has been made to enumerate all of the many variant names under which some of these figures appear in the literature, and the indication of a theorist's name following the figure gives only one of often several sources in which the term is defined and discussed (see Unger for a more complete list of figures and sources).

A. FIGURES OF MELODIC REPETITION

1. Anadiplosis (Vogt). The repetition of a closing melody at the beginning of a new section, but see also no.55.

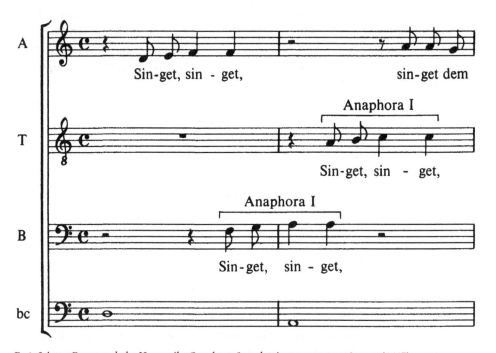

Ex.1 Schütz: *Freuet euch des Herren, ihr Gerechten; Symphoniarum sacrarum 2a pars* (1647)

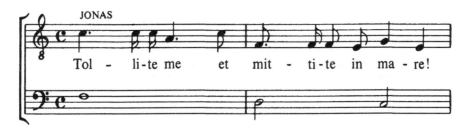

Ex.2 Carissimi: *Jonas*, 'Miserunt ergo sortem'

2. *Anaphora* (Kircher) = *Repetitio*(Nucius). The repetition of a melodic statement on different notes in different parts (see ex.1). Thuringus, however, limited it in his definition to the repetition of a bass part only (see ex.5).

3. *Auxesis.* See no.4.

Ex.3 Bach: Cantata no.78, *Jesu der du meine Seele*, 'Wir eilen mit schwachen, doch emsigen Schritten'

Ex.4 Viadana: *Exaudi me, Domine; Cento concerti ecclesiastici* (Venice, 1602)

Ex.5 Schütz: *Nun komm, der Heiden Heiland*; *Kleine geistliche Concerte, i* (1636)

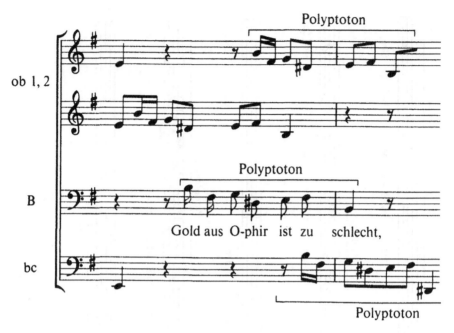

Ex.6 Bach: Cantata no.65, *Sie werden aus Saba alle kommen.* 'Gold aus Ophir ist zu schlecht'

4. *Climax* (Nucius) = Auxesis (Burmeister). The repetition of a melody in the same part a 2nd higher (see ex.2), which is a special case of *Synonymie* (no. 17). As *Gradatio* (no. 9) (Burmeister), a continuing *Climax* in sequence (see ex.3).

5. *Complexio* (Nucius) = *Symploce* (Kireher) = *Epanalepsis* (Gottsched) = *Epanadiplosis* (Vogt).The repetition at the endo of a melody or a whole musical section from the beginning.

6. *Epanadiplosis.* See no. 5.

7. *Epanalepsis.* See no. 5.

8. *Epistrophe.* See no. 10.

9. *Gradatio.* See no.4.

10. *Homoioptoton* (Kircher) = *Epistrophe* (Scheibe). The repetition of a closing section at the end of other sections.

11. *Hyperbaton* (Scheibe). The removal of a note or musical idea from the expected order for underlining of the text.

12. *Paronomasia* (Scheibe). The repetition of a musical idea on the same notes but with new additions or alterations for emphasis (see exx. 4–5).

13. *Palillogia* (Burmeister). The repetition of a melodic idea on the same notes and in the same part (see ex.5).

14. *Polyptoton* (Vogt). The repetition of a melodic idea in a different register or different part (see exx.5–6).

15. *Repetitio,* See no. 2.

16. *Symploce,* See no. 5.

17. *Synonymia* (Walther). The repetition of a melodic idea on different notes in the same part (see ex.7).

Rhetoric and Music

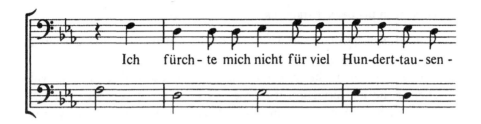

Ex.7 Schütz: *Ich liege und schlafe; Kleine geistliche Concerte, i* (1636)

B. FIGURES BASED ON FUGAL IMITATION (ALL FROM BURMEISTER)

18. *Anaphora.* A form of fugue in which a subject is repeated in some but not all of the parts. See also no. 2.
19. *Apocope.* Fugal imitation in which the repetition of the subject is incomplete in one part.
20. *Fuga imaginaria.* Canon.
21. *Fuga realis.* Regular fugal imitation.
22. *Hypallage.* Fugal imitation in contrary motion,
23. *Metalepsis.* Fugue with two subjects.

C. FIGURES FORMED BY DISSONANCE STRUCTURES

24. *Cadentiae duriusculae* (Bernhard). Unusual dissonances occurring before the final notes of a cadence (see ex. 8).
25. *Ellipsis* (Bernhard). The omission of an otherwise essential consonance which alters the normal formation of a suspension or passing note passage (see ex. 9). More generally (Scheibe), an unexpected new direction taken by a passage that has led up to an expected conclusion.
26. *Heterolepsis* (Bernhard). A leap or stepwise movement into a dissonance from a consonance; in effect the adoption of the note of a second voice part that would have arrived on the same note as a passing note (see ex. 10).
27. *Pleonasmus* (Burmeister). An abundance or piling up of harmonies that in the formation of a cadence, between preparation and resolution, is made up of *Symblemas* (see no. 34) and *Syncopes* (see no. 29), over two, three or more half-bars (see ex. 11).
28. *Prolongatio* (Bernhard). The extension of the normal value of a dissonance, whether a suspension or a passing note (see ex.12).
29. *Syncope* (Burmeister). An ordinary suspension.

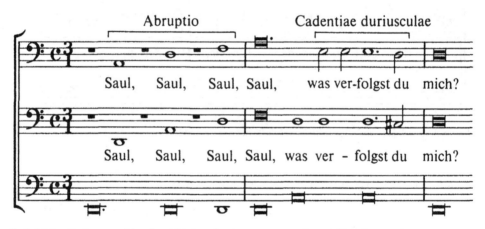

Ex.8 Schütz: *Saul, was verfolgst du mich?*; *Symphoniarum sacrarum 3a pars* (Dresden 1650)

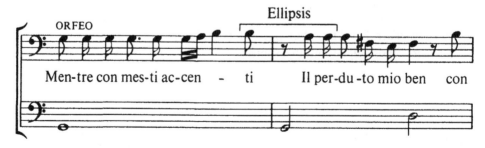

Ex.9 Peri: *Euridice*, 'Funeste piaggi'

Rhetoric and Music

30. *Syncopatio catachrestica* (Bernhard). This occurs when a suspension fails to resolve according to the rules (i.e. down a 2nd) but instead (*a*) resolves down a second but to another dissonance, (*b*) is prepared on a dissonance or (*c*) resolves by some other form of melodic movement (see ex.13).

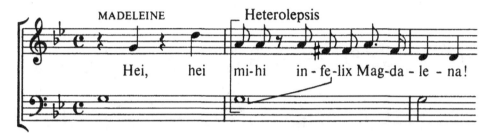

Ex.10 M.A. Charpentier: *Dialogue entre Madeleine et Jésus*

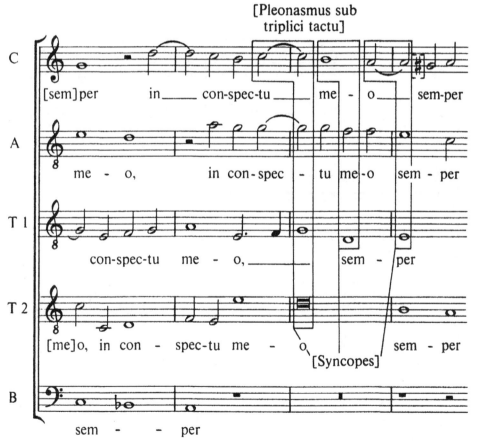

Ex.11 Lassus: *In me transierunt,* from Burmeister: *Musica poetica* (Rostock, 1606)

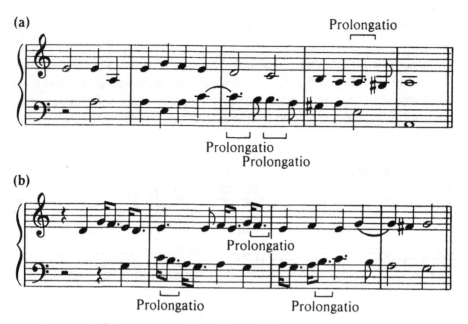

Ex.12 from Bernhard: *Tractatus compositionis* (MS, see Hilse)

Ex.13 from Bernhard: *Tractatus compositionis augmentatus* (MS, see Hilse)

Rhetoric and Music

D. INTERVAL FIGURES

31. *Exclamatio* (Walther). A melodic leap up by a minor 6th. In general practice, however, any leap up or down by intervals larger than 3rds and either consonant or dissonant, depending on the character of the exclamation. As a dissonant leap sometimes called *Saltus duriusculus* (see exx. 14–15).

Ex.14 Bach: Cantata no.155. *Mein Gott, wie lang, ach lange*

Ex.15 Bach: Cantata no. 1, *Wie schön leuchtet der Morgenstern*

32. *Inchoatio imperfecta* (Bernhard). An initial harmonic interval that is other than perfect.
33. *Interrogatio* (Scheibe). A musical question, a melodic ending or entire harmonic passage ending a 2nd or some other interval higher than the previous note or notes (see ex.16); also a Phrygian cadence.
34. *Parrhesia* (Kircher). A false relation, a stark dissonance, especially a tritone between parts (see ex, 15). More specifically, according to Burmeister, a mixture among other consonances of a single dissonance half the value of a tactus. In this sense *Parrhesia* is a special case of *Maius symblema*, a dissonance on the second half of a half-bar to the value of a minim.

Ex.16 Schütz: *St Matthew Passion*

Rhetoric and Music

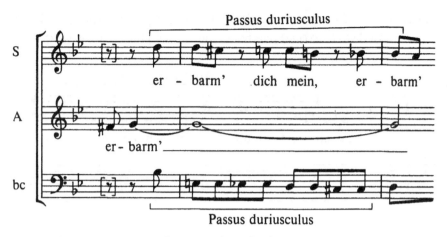

Ex. 17 Bach: Cantata no.23, *Du wahrer Gott und Davids Sohn*

35. *Passus duriusculus* (Bernhard). This occurs (*a*) when a part ascends or descends by a minor 2nd and (b), more generally, when a part moves by an interval too large or too small for the scale (see ex.17).
36. *Pathopoeia* (Burmeister). Movement through semitone steps outside a harmony or scale to express affections such as sadness, fear and terror.
37. *Salius duriusculus*. See no.31.

E. HYPOTYPOSIS FIGURES

38. *Hypotyposis* (Burmeister). A large class of musical-rhetorical figures, many without specific names, all serving to illustrate words or poetic ideas and frequently stressing the pictorial nature of the words. The rhetorical term is more accurate than the commoner expressions 'madrigalism' and 'word-painting'. All of the following figures in this section are in the *Hypotyposis* class.
39. *Anabasis* (Kircher). This occurs when a voice part or musical passage reflects the textual connotation of 'ascending' (see ex.18).
40. *Catabasis* (Kircher). The opposite of *Anabasis* (see ex.19).
41. *Circulatio* (Kircher). The musical description of circular or crossing-over motion (see ex. 20).
42. *Fuga* (Kircher). In the sense of 'flight', not as fugal imitation, a melodic figure illustrating flight, escape etc. (see ex.21).
43. *Hyperbole, Hypobole* (Burmeister). A melodic passage that exceeds the normal ambitus of a mode either above or below.
44. *Metabasis* (Spiess) = *Transgressus* (Bernhard). The crossing of one part by another.
45. *Passaggio*. See no. 47.
46. *Transgressus*. See no. 44.
47. *Variatio* (Bernhard) = *Passaggio* (Walther). A passage of vocal embellishment emphasizing the text, it can include forms of melodic ornamentation such as

accenio, cercar delta nota, tremolo, trillo, bombo, groppo, circolo mezzo and *tirata mezza*. Walther (*Praecepia*) referred to musical 'amplification' of a text.

Ex. 18 Bach: Cantata no.31. *Der Himmel lacht, die Erde jubilieret*

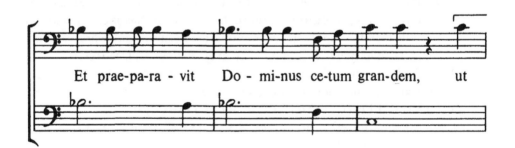

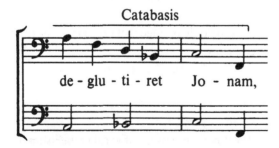

Ex. 19 Carissimi: *Jonas*, 'Miserunt ergo sortem'

Rhetoric and Music

Ex.20 Bach: Cantata no.131, *Aus der Tiefe rufe ich, Herr, zu dir*

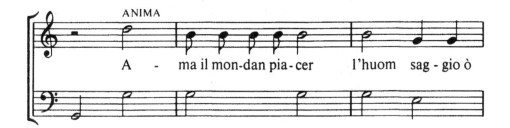

Ex.21 Cavalieri: *Rappresentatione di Anima, et di Corpo*

F. SOUND FIGURES

48. *Antitheton* (Kircher) A musical contrast, to express things contrary and opposite, occurring successively or simultaneously. It can be characterized by contrasting registers in a voice part, contrasting thematic ideas in a contrapuntal texture, contrasting musical textures etc.
49. *Congeries* (Burmeister). This occurs when a 5–3 chord moves to a 6–3 chord, which then moves back to a 5–3 chord, up and down. Burmeister defined the figure as 'an accumulation of perfect and imperfect consonances, the movement of which is permitted [by the rules of counterpoint]'.
50. *Fauxbourdon* (Burmeister). Parallel motion between parts in 3rds and 6ths.
51. *Mutatio toni* (Bernhard).The sudden shifting of mode for expressive reasons (see ex. 22).

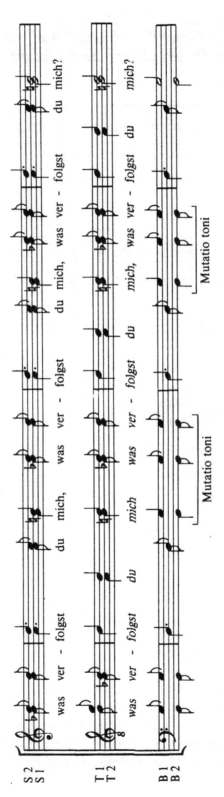

Ex.22 Schütz: *Saul, was verfolgst du mich?; Symphoniarum sacrarum 3a pars* (1650)

52. *Noema* (Burmeister). A purely homophonic section, usually consonant, within polyphony, for textual emphasis. Four special types can be distinguished:
53. *Analepsis.* Two immediately adjacent *Noenms* (see no.52).
54. Two successive *Noemas* (see no.52), the second of which is at a different pitch.
55. *Anadiplosis.* A double *Mimesis* (no.54), but see also no. 1.
56. *Anaploce.* A repetition of a *Noema* (no.52) heard in chorus A by chorus B while chorus A is silent.

G. FIGURES FORMED BY SILENCE (RESTS)

57. *Abruptio* (Bernhard) = *Aposiopesis* (Burmeister) = *Homoioteleuton* (Nucius) = *Tmesis* (Janovka). A general pause or silence within a musical texture where silence is not expected (see ex.8).
58. *Aposiopesis.* See no. 57.
59. *Homoioteleuton.* See no.57.
60. *Suspiratio* (Kircher). Usually the breaking up of a melody by rests to illustrate the text (see ex.23); it is closely related to all the other musical-rhetorical figures in this class.
61. *Tmesis.* See no.57.

Many of the musical figures, especially those from the earlier sources such as Burmeister and Bernhard, originated in attempts to explain or justify irregular, if not incorrect, contrapuntal writing. Although proceeding contrary to the rules of counterpoint, such passages were found to be suitable for dramatizing affective expression of the texts. Another large group of figures, the *Hypotyposis* class, have often been called madrigalisms (see under no. 38 above) because they occur so frequently in Italian madrigals of the 16th century and later; word-painting occurs in music as early as medieval plainchant and continues unabated in the music of today. Finally, it should be stressed that while German theorists were almost solely responsible for the terminology of musical figures, this is not to say that similar figurative guidelines were not followed by composers in other countries in the 17th and 18th centuries (see, for example, the detailed analysis in Massenkeil, 1952, of musical figures in the oratorios of Carissimi). What German theorists rationalized was a natural and common element in the craft of every composer. Whether or not composers of other countries made such precise terminological associations between rhetorical figures and musical equivalents cannot be established, but that such musical-rhetorical emphases exist in their music cannot be questioned.

4. THE AFFECTIONS. As a result of its intricate interrelationships with rhetorical doctrines, Baroque music assumed as its primary aesthetic goal the achieving of stylistic unity based on emotional abstractions called the Affections. An affection ('Affekt' in German, from the Greek 'pathos' and the Latin 'affectas', consists of a rationalized emotional state or passion. Beginning in antiquity the purpose of rhetoric and subsequently, therefore, all rhetorically inspired music, was to imitate human passions.

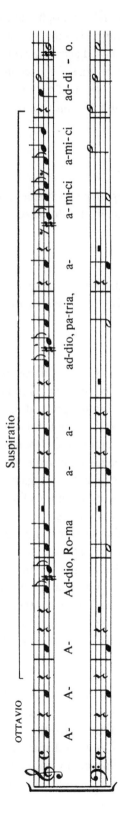

Ex.23 Monteverdi: *L'incoronazione di Poppea*. Act 3 scene vi

The extent to which Renaissance composers were influenced by rhetorical principles related to the Affections remains unclear, but theorists as early as Cochlaeus (1511) and throughout the 16th century (see Ruhnke) had connected rhetoric with musical expression. Zarlino (*Le istitutioni harmoniche,* 1558) urged composers to 'muover l'animo & disporlo a varij affetti'. After 1600, however, the representation of the Affections became the aesthetic necessity of most Baroque composers, whatever their nationality, and the fundamental basis of numerous treatises. During the Baroque period the composer was obliged, like the orator, to arouse in the listener idealized emotional states – sadness, hate, love, joy, anger, doubt and so on – and every aspect of musical composition reflected this affective purpose. While it was easier to appreciate it in music associated with a text, the aim in instrumental music was the same. It needs to be stressed, however, that to compose music with a stylistic and expressive unity based on an affection was a rational, objective concept, not a compositional practice equatable with 19th-century concerns for spontaneous emotional creativity and equally spontaneous emotional responses on the part of an audience. The Baroque composer planned the affective content of each work, or section or movement of a work, with all the devices of his craft, and he expected the response of his audience to be based on an equally rational insight into the meaning of his music. All the elements of music – scales, rhythm, harmonic structure, tonality, melodic range, forms, instrumental colour etc – were interpreted affectively. The styles, forms and compositional techniques of Baroque music were therefore always the result of this concept of the Affections.

Since the 19th century, writings on Baroque music have often referred to a so-called DOCTRINE OF THE AFFECTIONS (or 'Affektenlehre' in its commoner German equivalent), though in fact no one comprehensive, organized doctrine of how the Affections were to be achieved in music was ever established in Baroque theory. It has been assumed incorrectly, especially by writers such as Pirro and Schweitzer and those influenced by them, that composers worked with stereotyped musical-rhetorical figures – analogous to the Wagnerian leitmotif – in order to create a predetermined form of tone-painting. Other writers including Bukofzer continued to believe that such a stereotyped set of musical figures was an essential aspect of a Baroque Affektenlehre. More recent research has clearly shown that a concept of stereotyped musical figures with specific affective connotations never existed in the Baroque composer's mind or in theoretical explanations. Musical-rhetorical figures were devices meant only to decorate and elaborate on a basic affective representation and to add dramatic musical stress to words and poetic concepts. They functioned in music just as figures of speech function in oratory – as part of the *decoratio*.

The concept of the Affections was at least partly shaped by the writings of 17th-century philosophers of such diverse national backgrounds as Descartes, Francis Bacon and Leibniz. In an ever-growing stream of natural-philosophical studies in the 17th century, Descartes' *Les passions de l'âme* (1649) became perhaps the most decisive in its influence on the art of music. This resulted from the belief that he had discovered a rational, scientific explanation for the physiological nature of the passions and the objective nature of emotion. Nor was music unique, for a similar concern for the Affections dominated all the arts in the 17th century. The attempt to understand the passions lies deeply buried

Ex.24 Pages 62–3 from J. Burmeister's 'Musica poetica' (Rostock, 1606; the expanded edition of 'Musica autoschediastikē', 1601)

in the history of Western art long before Descartes, however. The connection with the ancient concept of the four temperaments or humours should not be overlooked, and the ancient Greeks wrote at great length about the control of human emotions. They believed that music possessed an ethical force, or ethos, that was bound together with the modes. The Renaissance witnessed a convergence of the Attic philosophy of Ethos, the theory of the temperaments and a developing theory of the Affections, for example in the numerous definitions of the modes according to their affective nature. In later treatises these ideas ultimately became doctrines of affections associated with keys, the best known of which was Mattheson's in his *Neu-eröffnete Orchestre* (1713).

The association of rhetoric with the concept of the Affections can be found almost continuously in the history of music from at least the end of the 15th century. It is explored in most of the major treatises on Baroque music (see Buelow, 1973–4, for a selective bibliography). By the turn of the 17th century, for example in Caccini's preface to his *Le nuove musiche* (1601/2), the musical goal of the singer became the moving of the affections of the soul ('di muovere l'affetto dell'animo'). The German theorist Michael Praetorius, in *Syntagma musicum*, iii (1618), warned that a singer must not simply sing but must perform in an artful and graceful manner so as to move the heart of the listener and to move the affections. An Italian theorist, Cesare Crivellati, in *Discorsi musicali* (1624), devoted a chapter to 'Come con la musica si possa movere diversi affetti' (chap. 11), and the English writer Charles Butler, in *The Principles of Musik* (1636), gave the purpose of music as 'the art of modulating notes in voice or instrument. De wie, having a great power over de affections of de minde, by its various Modes produces in de hearers various effects'. Among the many works contributing definitions of the Affections in the 17th century is Kircher's *Musurgia universalis*, an extraordinarily big work, full of valuable information, where a theory of intervals as related to the affections was proposed for the first time (see Scharlau). Of equal value are the several treatises of Werckmeister, who attempted to combine the rationality of mathematics with the rhetorical concepts of the Affections, providing a definition of particular value to an understanding of German late Baroque music.

In 1706 the German writer Johann Neidhardt, in his work on the tuning of a monochord, *Beste und leichteste Temperatur des Monochordi*, asserted that 'the goal of music is to make felt all the affections through the simple tones and the rhythms of the notes, like the best orator', and this remained the aesthetic credo of writers on music for much of the 18th century. Perhaps the most succinct and effective statement regarding the role of the affections in music was made by Mattheson (in *Der vollkommene Capellmeister*): 'everything that occurs without praiseworthy affections [in music] can be considered nothing, does nothing and means nothing'.

5. CONCLUSION. Musical-rhetorical concepts continued to figure prominently in music theory and terminology after 1730–40, when Baroque style was fading away. Even though the vitality of rhetorical doctrines weakened progressively during the course of the 18th century, a rhetorical viewpoint continued to influence the music aesthetics of the *galant* style and of early, as well as advanced, stages of Classicism. As late as 1770 J. F. Daube, a German theorist living in Vienna, continued to urge composers 'to

consider carefully the rules of oratory' (*Der musikalische Dilettant*). For many writers on music, among whom C. P. E. Bach, Quantz and Leopold Mozart were the most prominent, it was that part of rhetorical theory concerning execution or delivery – the *pronuntiatio* – that received new emphasis. Performers were reminded that music was an oration in sound and that the singer or instrumentalist must, like the orator, employ the techniques of good delivery: distinctiveness, pleasing variety of tone, contrasts of emphasis and a comprehension and expression of the affections in an appropriate style (see, for example, Quantz's *Versuch einer Anweisung die Flöte traverslere zu spielen,* 1752, chap. 11), Forkel, however, in his *Allgemeine Geschichte der* Musik (1788–1801), thought that much of the important knowledge formerly associated with musical rhetoric had already been forgotten. To restore it he published an outline of musical rhetoric which in many of its details returned to concepts that had been set out in the works of Mattheson, Scheibe and other Baroque theorists.

Although the writers of the later 18th century constantly reaffirmed the continuing validity of the affections as the primary aesthetic force governing musical styles and expression, their definitions of them showed subtle changes (see Dammann, chap,6). The affections lost their objective quality as rationalized emotional states that acted as unifying forces in every work. After 1750 they frequently became identified instead with subjective, personal emotions originating within the composer. There were conservative theorists who still proposed a basic affection for each work or section of a work, but there were other authors who advocated contrasting affections within the bounds of a single work, and it is clear that the old unity of the affections gradually lost its relevance to composers of the late 18th century.

While some of the terminology as well as the basic ideas about rhetoric remained part of compositional technique until well into the 19th century, the understanding of rhetorical expression was almost entirely forgotten. It was only early in the present century that music historians, beginning with Kretzschmar, Gold-schmidt and Schering, rediscovered the importance of rhetoric as the basis of aesthetic and theoretical concepts in earlier music. An entire discipline that had once been the common property of every educated man has had to be rediscovered and reconstructed during the intervening decades, and only now is it beginning to be understood how much Western art music depended on rhetorical concepts at least until the beginning of the 19th century.

Bibliography

B. F. Richter: 'Eine Abhandlung Johann Kuhnaus', *MMg,* xxiv (1902), 147

A. Schering: 'Die Lehre von den musikalischen Figuren im 17. und 18. Jahrhundert', *KJb,* xxi (1908), 106

H. Kretzschmar: 'Allgemeines und Besonderes zur Affektenlehre', *JbMP 1911,* 63; *JbMP 1911,* 65

H. Goldschmidt: *Die Musikästhetik des 18. Jahrhunderts* (Zurich, 1915/R1968)

J. M. Müller-Blattau: 'Zum Verhältnis von Wort und Ton im 17. Jahrhundert', *Kongressbericht; Basel 1924,* 270

G. Frotscher: 'Bachs Themenbildung unter dem Einfluss der Affektenlehre', *Kongressbericht: Leipzig 1925,* 436

A. Schering: 'Geschichtliches zur "Ars inveniendi" in der Musik', *JbMP 1925*, 25

——: 'Bach und das Symbol, inbesondere die Symbolik seines Kanons', *BJb*, xxii (1925), 40; xxv (1928), 119

G. Frotscher: 'Die Affektenlehre als geistige Grundlage der Themenbildung J. S. Bachs', *BJb*, xxiii (1926), 90

J. M. Müller-Biattau: *Die Kompositionslehre Heinrich Schützens in der Fassung seines Schülers Christoph Bernhard* (Leipzig, 1926, 2/1963)

F. Stege: 'Die deutsche Musikkritik des 18. Jahrhunderts unter dem Einfluss der Affektenlehre'. *ZMw*, x (1927–8), 23

W. Serauky: *Die musikalische Nachahmungsästhetik im Zeitraum von 1700–1850* (Münster, 1929)

K. Ziebler: 'Zur Aesthetik der Lehre von den musikalischen Figuren im 18. Jahrhundert', *ZMw*, xv (1932–3), 289

H. Brandes: *Studien zur musikalischen Figurenlehre im 16. Jahrhundert* (Berlin, 1935)

H.-H. Unger: *Die Beziehungen zwischen Musik und Rhetorik im 16–18. Jahrhundert* (Würzburg, 1941/R1969)

W. Gurlitt: 'Musik und Rhetorik', *Helicon*, v (1944), 67

A. Schmitz: *Die Bildlichkeit in der wortgebundenen Musik J. S. Bachs* (Mainz, 1950)

——: 'Die oratorische Kunst J. S. Bachs – Grundfragen und Grundlagen', *GfMKB. Lüneburg 1950*, 33

G. Toussaint: *Die Anwendung der musikalisch-rhetorischen Figuren in den Werken von Heinrich Schütz* (diss., U. of Mainz, 1950)

G. Massenkeil: *Die oratorische Kunst in den lateinischen Historien und Oratorien Giacomo Carissimis* (diss., U, of Mainz, 1952)

H. Federhofer: 'Die Figurenlehre nach Christoph Bernhard und die Dissonanzbehandlung in Werken von Heinrich Schütz', *GfMKB, Bamberg 1953*, 132

F. Feldmann: 'Untersuchungen zum Wort–Ton Verhältnis in den Gloria-Credo Sätzen von Dufay bis Josquin', *MD*, ix (1954), 141

M. Ruhnke; *Joachim Burmeister: ein Beitrag zur Musiklehre um 1600* (Kassel, 1955)

H. H. Eggebrecht: 'Zum Wort–Ton-Verhältnis in der 'Musica poetica' von 1. A. Herbst', *GfMKB, Hamburg 1956*, 77

F. Feldmann: 'Divergierende Überlieferungen in Isaacs "Petrucci-Messen", als Beitrag zum Wort–Ton Verhältnis um 1500', *CHM*, ü (1956), 203

——: 'Mattheson und die Rhetorik', *GfMKB, Hamburg 1956*, 99

G. Massenkeil: 'Zur Frage der Dissonanzbehandlung in der Musik des 17, Jahrhunderts', *Le Baroque musical: Wégimont IV 1957*, 151

F. Feldmann: 'Das "Opusculum bipartitum" des Joachim Thuringas (162S) besonders in seinen Beziehungen zu Joh. Nucius (1613)', *AMw*, xv (1958), 123

H. Lenneberg: 'Johann Mattheson on Affect and Rhetoric in Music', *JMT*, ii (1958), 47, 193

H. H. Eggebrecht: 'Zum Figur-Begriff der Musica poetica', *AMw*, xvi (1959), 57

H. Leuchtmann: *Die musikalischen Wortausdeutungen in den Motetten des 'Magnus Opus Musicum' von Orlando di Lasso* (Strasbourg and Baden-Baden, 1959)

K. Darenberg: *Studien zur englischen Musikaesthetik des 18. Jahrhunderts* (Hamburg, 1960)

F. A. Gallo: 'Pronunciatio: ricerche sulla storia di un termine retorico-musicale', *AcM*, xxxv (1963), 38

G. J. Buelow: 'The "Loci topici" and Affect in Late Baroque Music; Heinichen's Practical Demonstration', *MR*, xxvii (1966), 161

R. Dammann: *Der Musikbegriff im deutschen Barock* (Cologne, 1967)

U. Scharlau: *Athanasius Kircher (1601–1680) als Musikschriftsteller* (Marburg, 1969)

C.V. Palisca: '*Ut oratoria musica:* the Rhetorical Basis of Musical Mannerism', *The Meaning of Mannerism*, ed. F. W. Robinson and S. G. Nichols (Hanover, New Hampshire, 1972), 37

W. Hilse, trans.: 'The Treatises of Christoph Bernhard', *Music Forum*, iii (1973), 1

G. J. Buelow: 'Music, Rhetoric and the Concept of the Affections: a Selective Bibliography', *Notes*, xxx (1973–4), 250

R. Flotzinger: 'Vorstufen den musikalisch-rhetorischen Tradition im Notre-Dame Repertoire?', *De ratione in musica: Festschrift Erich Schenk* (Kassel, 1975), 1

W. Pass: 'Jacob Vaets und Georg Prenners Vertonungen des "Salve regina" in Joanellus' Sammelwerk von 1568', *De ratione in musica: Festschrift Erich Schenk* (Kassel, 1975), 29

K. Schnürl: 'Musikalische Figuren in den vierstimmigen "Harmoniae morales" des Jacobus Gallus', *De ratione in musica: Festschrift Erich Schenk* (Kassel, 1975), 50

G. G. Butler: 'Music and Rhetoric in Early Seventeenth-century English Sources', *MQ*, lxvi (1980), 53

INDEX

abstraction 32, 45, 128, 129, 138, 143, 191, 194, 235, 313, 381
abusio see catechresis
accumulation (*frequentatio*) 4, 22, 35, 53, 121, 379
ad Herennium 1–3, 11, 12, 17–24, 28–32, 34, 37, 43, 48–50, 54, 56, 62, 63, 65, 75–82, 84, 86, 88, 169, 184, 273, 276, 284, 314–315, 326
ad hominem 214, 217, 219, 223
addition (*quadripartita ratio adiectio*) 3, 64, 76, 85, 326
adiunctio see adjunction
adjunction (*adiunctio*) 19, 35
adnominatio see paronomasia
advertising viii, 328–331, 335–336, 342, 344, 346–350, 355–360
Agricola, Rodolphus 5, 12, 15
Alexander of Villa-Dei 1
allegory (*permutatio*) 21, 35, 40, 41, 78–81, 83, 85, 188, 195, 197, 298
allusion 57, 84, 164, 214, 238, 241, 243, 298
amplification 3–5, 12, 17, 20, 46, 48, 68, 70–72, 80–82, 85–87, 145, 150, 156, 169, 172, 173, 180, 185, 248, 272, 274, 289, 318, 378
anastrophe (*perversio*) 21, 208, 209
anthropomorphism 9, 192
antimetabole 56, 57, 64, 80, 88, 173, 208, 313, 328, 333, 337, 340
anti-rhetoric 6, 15
antistrophe (*conversio*) 17, 19, 34, 76, 173
antithesis (*contentio*) 3, 8, 11, 17, 18, 23, 31, 34, 35, 41, 46, 59, 67, 80, 170, 171, 202, 205, 208, 214, 219, 220, 254, 261, 265, 269, 313, 317, 323, 337, 340, 346
antonomasia or pronominado (*pronominatio*) 20, 35, 67, 80, 81, 175, 176, 316
aposiopesis (*praecisio*) 20, 24, 35, 46, 47, 49, 56, 59, 62, 76, 80, 81, 83, 88, 381

apostrophe 17, 34, 41, 52, 76, 83, 84, 89, 171, 180, 181
appropriateness 46, 67, 107, 207 226, 267, 292
Aquinas, Thomas 238
Arbusow, Leonid 32
Arderne, James 295
argument 1, 2, 5, 6, 9, 10, 17, 18, 20, 28, 30, 31, 33, 34, 36, 45, 49, 51, 56, 58, 64, 71–74, 82, 86, 89, 109, 112, 113, 115–118, 124, 125, 150, 151, 153, 156–159, 162, 180, 184, 189–191, 197, 201, 212–215, 217–221, 229, 231–243, 247–249, 255, 273, 277, 278, 291, 293, 296, 304, 314–319, 322, 323, 332, 364, 365; logical 39; political 263, 264, 269, 270; verbal 351, 352, 354, 356, 359, 360; visual viii, 351–360
Aristotle 1, 5, 6, 11, 18, 20, 28–31, 33, 37, 38, 40, 44, 46, 47, 49, 50, 52, 60, 62, 65, 67, 69, 71–73, 87, 102, 161, 162, 165, 184, 201, 202, 225, 275–277, 285, 292, 310, 327, 328, 360, 362
arrangement (*dispositio*) 2, 4, 12, 24, 29, 37, 48, 53, 98, 104, 144, 150, 158, 162, 163, 218, 235, 332, 333
Ars grammatica 27, 28
articulus see comma or phrase
asyndeton (*dissolutum*) 3, 11, 20, 24, 35, 46, 48, 51, 52, 55, 59, 63, 64, 67, 88, 208
Augustine 15, 38, 166, 187, 238

Bach, C.P.E. 368, 370, 375, 377–379
Bacon, Francis 5–8, 66, 287–290, 292–296, 298, 301, 302, 307–312, 383
Baroque 2, 13, 126, 362–365, 380, 383, 385, 386
Barthes, Roland 8, 13, 103, 109, 194, 328, 332, 347
Bede 1, 11, 31, 37, 77
behaviorist 94

belles lettres 2, 8, 38, 164, 165 see also literary criticism
Bernard de Chartres 6
Bible (biblical) 8, 77, 175, 207, 261, 269, 281
Blair, Anthony J. viii, 2, 7–9, 13, 351
Boethius, Manilius Severinus 15, 30, 31, 37, 38
Bossuet, Jacques-Bénigne 141
Brandt, William 9, 10, 13
brevitas see conciseness
Brutus 51, 131, 282–284
Buelow, George viii, 362
Bunyan, John 236, 238, 300, 309
Burke, Kenneth vii, 13, 91, 141–152, 155, 158, 160, 161, 164, 165, 329, 347

cadence 146, 207, 241, 248, 372, 376
Caesar, Julius 51, 84, 131, 282, 283, 316
canon(s) 16, 29, 149, 169, 371
Capella, Martianus 28, 39, 62, 102
Carter, Jimmy 136
cartoon 127, 136, 330, 356, 357
catechresis (*abusio*) 21, 35
Caussin, Nicolas 85–87, 90
character delineation (*notatio*) 23, 36
Charteris-Black, Jonathan viii, 250
chiasmus 64, 194, 254
Chinnery, George 8
Christian 27, 30, 38, 39, 168, 175, 230, 233, 235, 236, 238, 240, 243, 265, 268, 269, 278, 279, 285, 289, 309, 362
Churchill, Winston viii, 250–271
Cicero 1–3, 9–11, 13, 15, 20, 27–32, 36, 37, 40, 49–51, 56, 61, 65, 67, 68, 73, 76, 78–81, 84, 87, 88, 103, 141, 146, 168, 169, 179, 180, 183, 184, 186, 201, 202, 273, 274, 278, 283, 286, 292, 306, 315, 326, 362
circumitio see periphrasis
civil rights movement 231
Clark, D.L. 42, 66, 184
Clarke, M.L. 43, 49, 50, 66
climax (*gradatio*) 3, 19, 35, 41, 47, 51, 53, 80, 83, 84, 85, 90, 164, 183, 209, 219, 221, 242, 243, 312, 366
Cold War 250, 351, 357
Colin Clout vii, 168–185
colon or clause (*membrum*) 18
comma or phrase (*articulus*) 4, 18, 48, 55
commoratio see dwelling on the point
commutatio see reciprocal change

comparison (*similitudo*) 3, 4, 12, 14, 21–23, 30, 31, 36, 37, 69, 72, 76, 81, 83, 102, 106–110, 145, 155, 156, 159, 169, 175, 177, 178, 184, 186, 205, 249, 255, 257, 272, 290, 344, 347
complexio see interlacement
conciseness (*brevitas*) 24, 36
conclusion (*conclusio*) 3, 12, 18–20, 23, 32, 35, 37, 73, 82, 99, 120, 185, 188, 195, 211, 214–216, 219, 239, 241, 278, 295, 354, 357, 360, 362, 364, 372
conclusio see conclusion
conduplicatio see reduplication
conformatio see personification
conjunctio see conjunction
conjunction (*conjunctio*) 3, 4, 19, 20, 35, 71, 72, 76, 78, 205, 206, 208, 240, 259
Connors, Robert J. vii, 198
conpar see isocolon
contentio see antithesis
continuatio see period
contraries 3, 17, 18, 23, 31, 34, 36, 49, 57, 72, 277
contrarium see reasoning by contraries
conversio see antistrophe
Corbett, Edward P.J. vii, 11, 14, 64, 66, 198, 329, 330, 345, 347
correctio see correction
correction (*correctio*) 19, 35, 142, 246, 289, 313, 340, 341
criticism: literary vii, 8, 13, 41, 52, 93, 141, 160–165, 184, 300 see also *belles lettres*; modern 42, 163, 168, 348; rhetorical 157, 160, 161, 163–165, 348
Croce, Benedetto 63, 298
culture (cultural) 7, 8, 27, 98, 112–114, 118–122, 127, 134, 135, 138, 278, 319–321, 325, 326, 328, 354, 356
Curtius, Ernst Robert 32, 38, 109, 187

Darwin, Charles 10, 165, 318, 323
Day, Angel 68, 274, 276, 278
decoratio see elocution
de facto 103
de jure 103
de Man, Paul vii, 187
definitio see definition
definition (*definitio*) 1–4, 10, 11, 13, 19, 23, 27, 29, 32, 33, 35–37, 43, 49, 68, 69, 71, 72, 77–79, 82–84, 86, 99, 122, 161, 180, 185, 195,

Index   **391**

219, 236, 237, 243, 255, 278, 284, 292, 293, 315–317, 323, 330, 332, 342, 363, 365, 367, 385, 386
Deguy, Michel 9, 102, 108
deliberative 3, 4, 11, 102, 179, 202, 247
delivery (*pronuntiatio*) 22, 24, 29, 37, 154–158, 163, 209, 364, 386
democracy 142, 276
demonstratio see ocular demonstration
Demosthenes 47–49, 52, 53, 56, 103, 141
denominatio see metonymy
Descartes, René 297, 300, 385
descriptio see vivid description
Despauterius, Johannes 78–80, 82, 85, 87–89
detractio see subtraction
deviation/deviate 40, 47, 68, 232, 328, 330–336, 342–344
dialogue (*sermocinatio*) 23, 36, 85
dialogues 1, 8, 12, 22, 27, 64, 97, 99, 109, 177, 184, 276, 375
diction vii, 2, 17, 20, 23, 29, 43, 66, 79, 81, 89, 144, 155, 158, 163, 173, 185, 207, 210, 244, 304, 332
diminutio see understatement
Dionysian 194, 197
disjunction (*disjunctum*) 19, 35, 44
disjunctum see disjunction
disposition see arrangement
dissolutum see asyndeton
distributio see distribution
distribution (*distributio*) 3, 22, 35, 37, 72, 80, 229, 320, 333
divisio see division
division (*divisio*) 3, 12, 19, 22, 29, 30, 34, 35, 37, 40, 68–70, 72, 77–86, 100, 104, 110, 15, 172, 185, 213, 215, 218, 293, 316, 319, 349, 363, 364
Donatus, Aelius 1, 27, 28, 77, 78
Douglas, Stephen A. 212–214, 216, 217, 219, 221, 224, 227, 228
Dryden, John 61, 63, 65, 146, 309
Dumarsais, César 2, 103–105, 109
dubitatio see indecision
Dupriez, Bernard 7, 11, 14
dwelling on the point (*commoratio*) 23, 35

effictio see portrayal
elaboratio see elocution
elimination (*expeditio*) 20, 35, 104
Eliot, T.S. 98, 99, 238

ellipsis 62, 71, 107, 108, 209, 338, 340, 341, 346–348, 372
Elizabethan 12, 15, 42, 44, 45, 52, 53, 56, 58, 60, 73, 74, 87, 169, 177, 183–186, 277, 284, 312
elocutio see elocution
elocution (*elocutio*, also *decoratio, elaboratio*) vii, 2, 8, 9, 67, 71, 72, 87, 102, 103, 109, 272, 274, 284, 364, 365, 383
emotion 2, 4, 11, 39, 40, 44–55, 57–65, 71–73, 76, 84–86, 93, 117, 118, 120, 130, 131, 134, 147, 162, 172, 179–182, 189, 201, 202, 210, 213, 215, 219, 220, 221, 226, 237–239, 243, 257, 260, 326, 355, 356, 362, 381, 383, 385, 386 see also pathos
emphasis (*significatio*) 9, 11, 24, 36, 51, 71, 82, 93, 109, 141, 142, 157, 160, 161, 168, 184, 185, 201, 206, 208, 215, 248, 262, 263, 276, 314, 315, 363, 370, 381, 386
enargeia see vividness
enthymemes 28, 29, 33, 235, 354, 360 see also logos
epanaphora (*repetitio*) 3, 17, 19, 29, 34
epicheirema 73
epideictic 3, 4, 16
Erasmus of Rotterdam, Desiderius 5, 7, 12, 15, 79, 80–83, 86–87, 177
ethos 3, 4, 11, 12, 69, 71, 72, 106, 202, 212, 223, 237, 238, 269, 356, 359, 385 see also figures of ethos
Evrard of Behune 1
exclamation 3, 12, 50, 55–57, 61, 63, 71, 80, 99, 180, 375
expeditio see elimination
expolitio see refining

faculty 27, 150, 161
Fahnestock, Jeanne vii, viii, 7, 10, 14, 246, 313
Falstaff 100, 101, 280, 281, 283, 284
Ferguson, Robert 295
figurae 1, 28, 31, 32, 40, 41 see also figures
figurae sententiarum or *sententiarum exornationes* see figures of thought
figurae verborum or *verborum exornationes* see figures of speech
figurative 42, 51, 58, 63, 68, 91, 103–105, 116, 126, 127, 138, 169, 175, 183, 186, 188, 215, 295, 296, 319, 328, 330–335, 337, 338, 340, 343–345, 347–350, 381

figures see also *figurae*: and topics of invention 2, 3, 4, 12, 28, 31, 68, 69, 72, 80; Gorgian 11, 225, 228; of amplification 3, 4, 12, 68, 85, 272; of analogy 107, 108, 110; of argument 49, 318; of collection 72; of comparison 72; of conjunction 71; of description 12, 72; of diction vii, 2, 17–24, 29, 79; of exclamation 12, 55; of ethos 4, 11, 71; of figures 9, 57, 108, 193; of grammar 6, 71; of locution 79; of logos 4, 11, 69; of omission 85; of pathos 4, 11, 71; of question 10, 182; of rhetoric 2, 15, 45, 52, 56, 62, 83, 168–183, 328; of repetition 4, 10, 39, 55, 57, 59, 68, 69, 71, 85, 208, 314, 315, 343, 366; of sentences 4, 12, 55, 68, 180 see also figures of thought; of separation 3, 4, 72; of speech (*verborum exornationes* or *figurae verborum*) 1, 18, 31, 32, 35, 41, 46, 67, 70, 76, 79, 81– 83, 85, 168, 188, 193, 195, 202, 205, 207, 209, 210, 270, 278, 281, 298, 313, 328, 383, 385 see also figures of words; of thought *sententiarum exornationes* or *figurae sententiarum* 2, 3, 17–24, 29, 31, 35, 41, 49, 50, 68, 69, 72, 73, 76, 77, 79–81, 83, 86, 87, 103 see also figures of sentences; of words (*figurae verborum*) 4, 12, 68, 72, 76, 77, 84–86 see also figures of speech

Fontanier, Pierre 2, 103, 104, 109
frankness of speech (*licentia*) 21, 35
frequentatio see accumulation
Freud, Sigmund 57, 105, 109
Frye, Northrop 7, 14
Fulkerson, Richard P. vii, 229

Galileo, Galilei 5, 7, 13, 14, 16
Galton, Francis 323, 326, 327
Genette, Gérard vii, 2, 9, 13, 14, 102, 330, 331, 348
genre 79, 102, 173, 175, 212, 213, 268, 296, 299, 356
Gesner, Conrad 7
Gladstone, William 141, 155–159, 166, 167
Glanvill, Joseph 296–298, 304, 309–312
Gloucester, Richard 224, 279
God 33, 34, 39, 84, 92, 98, 99, 122, 171, 175, 177, 179, 180, 186, 198, 200, 233, 236, 252, 259, 261, 288, 317, 351
Gorgias (Gorgian) vii, 1, 8, 10, 11, 18, 31, 39, 67, 77, 225–228

gradatio see climax
Graecismum 1
grammar 1, 6, 7, 11–15, 27, 28, 32, 38, 42, 69, 71, 72, 75–79, 82–87, 103, 110, 253, 290, 301, 305, 332, 362
Greek 11, 30–32, 37, 38, 42, 43, 47, 51, 59, 61, 65, 70, 71, 75, 77–79, 81, 82, 84, 85, 90, 172, 186, 197, 200, 206, 272, 275, 276, 301, 303, 304, 310, 315, 316, 362, 365, 381, 385
grief 17, 51, 63, 171
Grimald, Nicholas 39

Hebrew(s) 63, 71
Herennius 24
Hermogenes 73
Hitler, Adolf 237, 251, 252, 255, 257–259, 266, 268, 270, 316
homoeoptoton (*similiter cadens*) 11, 18, 76
homoeoteleuton (*similiter desinens*) 11, 18, 76
Horace 52, 63, 168, 226, 295
Hoskins, John 2, 4, 57–60, 64, 65, 181, 322, 327
Howell, W.S. 43, 66, 170, 184, 185
hyperbaton (*transgressio*) 21, 35, 41, 53, 64, 78, 79, 84, 171, 370
hyperbole (*superlatio*) 21, 24, 35, 41, 46, 50, 62, 81, 83, 105, 252–254, 266, 269, 328, 338, 340, 347, 377
hypophora (*subiectio*) 19, 35, 49, 76

illustration 6, 42, 56, 71, 74, 77, 118, 155, 157–159, 172, 176, 274, 275, 317, 321, 330
imagination 6, 45, 97, 111, 130, 143, 144, 146–149, 155, 157, 158, 161, 162, 288, 290–292, 294, 299, 309, 310, 355, 364
imago see simile
immutatio see permutation
incantation 39
indecision (*dubitatio*) 20, 35
indignation 5, 17, 43, 80, 88, 180, 288
intellectio see synecdoche
interpretatio see synonymy or interpretation
interrogatio see interrogation
interrogation (*interrogatio*) 17, 34, 61, 71, 89
inventio see invention
invention (*inventio*) 3, 4, 6, 11, 12, 15, 19, 24, 29–31, 33, 36, 37, 42, 49, 68, 69, 78, 80, 92, 144, 165, 219, 244, 292, 295, 305, 364 see also topics of invention

Index

irony 9, 13, 41, 52, 74, 80, 81, 83, 85, 91, 97–101, 104, 105, 144, 146, 188, 195, 196, 232, 233, 339, 342, 346, 347, 349
isocolon (*conpar*) 11, 18, 35, 41, 67
interlacement (*complexio*) 17, 19, 34, 370

Jew(ish) 230, 237, 238
John of Salisbury 6, 27
Johnson, Mark vii, 111, 265, 271
Johnson, Lyndon 353
Johnson, Samuel 141, 142
Jones, R.F. 288, 291–303, 308, 309
Jonson, Ben 40, 61, 65
Joseph, Sister Miriam vii, 14, 44, 66, 67
judicial 3, 102, 148–150, 160, 161

Kant, Immanuel 8, 189, 298
Keckermann, Bartholomäus 85, 90
Kennedy, George 13, 14, 29, 38, 43, 47, 64, 66, 88, 329
Kennedy, John F. vii, 198, 200–210, 357
King Jr., Martin Luther vii, 229, 244, 315
Koch, Robert 319–322, 324, 325, 326, 327

Lakoff, George vii, 111, 261, 265, 268, 270, 271
Lamy, Bernard 2, 8, 109
Latin 1, 7, 14, 15, 28, 30, 32, 37, 38, 41, 42, 44, 50, 61, 71, 75–77, 79, 82, 84, 86–90, 109, 172, 184, 185, 206, 247, 275, 276, 277, 285, 291, 301–310, 312, 315, 363, 365, 381
Lausberg, Heinrich 3, 11, 14, 32, 38, 87, 309
Leff, Michael C. vii, 10, 12, 15, 38, 211
lexis (style, Aristotle) 28, 103
Liberal Arts 6, 13, 16, 40, 57, 60, 185, 200, 365
licentia see frankness of speech
Lincoln, Abraham vii, 10, 141, 143, 145, 146, 148, 150, 152, 207, 210, 211–224, 225–228, 236
Locke, John 8, 165, 297, 298, 309
loci 30–32, 36, 62, 74, 336, 364, 365, 387 see also *locus*, topics
locus 30–32, 36, 367 see also *loci*, topics
logos 2–4, 11, 12, 69, 71, 72, 237, 238 see also figures of logos, reasoning by contraries, reasoning by question and answer
Longinus 11, 50, 52–55, 57–59, 61–63, 65, 145
lore 172, 175, 314, 326
lucidity 67, 73, 157, 159
Lupus, Rutilius 77, 82, 88, 272, 284

Mack, Peter vii, 3, 6, 11–13, 15, 75
Mancinelli, Antonio 77–82, 87, 88, 274, 275, 284
Mann, Thomas 99, 195
maxim (*sententia*) 18, 34, 64, 144, 254, 255, 323
McQuarrie, Edward F. viii, 328
Melanchthon, Philip 2–5, 7, 9–12, 14, 72, 74, 79–82, 85–89
membrum see colon or clause
memorability 334, 337
memory 15, 24, 27, 29, 30, 37, 42, 268, 337, 344
metalepsis 80, 81, 104, 188, 190, 194, 371
metaphor (*translatio*) 21, 35; conceptual vii, 111–138, 259, 260, 265, 269; conventional 111, 117, 133, 270; extended 41, 173, 175; literal 126, 128; novel 127, 133, 134, 137; spatialization 120
metaphysics (metaphysical) 66, 93, 94, 96, 183–185, 190–192, 261, 309, 329
metonymy (*denominatio*) 9, 14, 15, 21, 35, 41, 74, 76, 78–85, 91, 93–95, 104–106, 109, 188, 190, 191, 194, 252
Meyer, Sam vii, 168
Mick, David Glen viii, 330
Middle Ages 6, 13, 15, 16, 28, 32, 37, 38, 44, 54, 67, 77, 102, 109
Milton, John 39, 60, 184, 291, 306
Mohrmann, Gerald P. vii, 10, 211
Morley, John 141, 144, 155–160, 164
Mosellanus, Petrus 1, 77, 79, 81, 84, 88–90
Mozart, Leopold 387
Murphy, James ii, vii, 1, 11, 15, 27, 38
music viii, 2, 9, 13, 16, 41, 149, 194, 197, 245, 297, 300, 316, 338, 349, 360, 362–386
myth (heroic) viii, 173, 175, 177, 179, 186, 211, 222, 233, 234, 241, 250–255, 257–261, 263, 267, 269, 270, 290

narratio see narrative
narrative (*narratio*) 3, 6, 95, 157, 162, 181, 196, 197, 234, 251, 256, 265, 269, 270, 287, 353, 357, 360
Neoclassic 62, 290, 309
Nietzsche, Friedrich vii, 9, 15, 187–197
nominatio see onomatopoeia
Norden, Eduard 31, 38
notatio see character delineation

occultatio see paralipsis
octo partes orationis 27

Index

reduplication (*conduplication*) 20, 35
refining (*expolitio*) 22, 35, 40
refutation 37, 216, 217, 223, 231, 232, 234–237, 242, 243, 292, 294, 318, 319, 364
relativism 97, 98
Renaissance 1–3, 5, 7–15, 28, 43–45, 49, 54, 55, 58, 60, 67, 68, 71, 72–77, 86, 87, 168, 169, 172, 173, 179, 180, 183–186, 272, 274–276, 284, 290, 308–310, 314, 315, 326, 363, 365, 383, 385
repetition 3, 4, 10, 19, 39, 41, 47–51, 54, 55, 57–60, 68, 69, 71, 72, 75, 80, 85, 86, 172, 181, 183, 195, 196, 207, 208, 215, 252–254, 256, 269, 313–324, 328, 333, 335, 336, 337, 343, 344, 347, 358, 366, 367, 370, 371, 381
repetitio see epanaphora
rhetoric: as means of persuasion (pathos, logos, ethos) 2–4, 69, 161; as species/genres of rhetoric/branches of oratory/types of speeches (deliberative, judiciary, epideictic) 2–4, 102; as organic whole 2, 9, 12; as deceit and fraudulent discourse 8, 193–195; and *belles lettres*/literary criticism see *belles lettres* and literary criticism; and "five canons" (invention, arrangement, style, memory, and delivery) 29; and topics see invention, topics of invention, figures and topics of invention; critique of 8, 9, 10, 13, 43, 45; decline of 8, 9, 13; exercises see *progymnasmata*
Reusch, Johannes 81, 89
rhyme 328, 333, 335–337, 343, 345
rhythm 9, 10, 21, 31, 41, 46, 48, 67, 71, 83, 145, 151, 157, 202, 208, 241, 242, 310, 383, 385
Richards, I.A. 8, 15, 93, 107
Roman 1, 3, 28–33, 40, 50, 79, 200, 272, 274–276, 303, 362
Romanus, Aquila 77, 82, 84
Roosevelt, Franklin D. 246–248
Royal Society viii, 5, 6, 14, 16, 287–289, 291–312, 323
Rufinianus, Julius 77, 81, 82, 84, 89

Saintsbury, G.E.B. 146, 150–152, 159, 160, 162
Salter, Elizabeth 45, 66
salto mortale 144
sarcasm 80, 159, 214
Scaliger, Julius Caesar 84–86, 89, 90, 315
Schade, Peter 79, 80, 82, 85–87

schematum/schemata see scheme(s) and *figurae*
scheme(s) 1, 2, 4, 33, 40, 43, 44, 53, 68, 69, 70, 72, 77–79, 81, 82, 138, 163, 168, 171, 172, 180, 185, 189–191, 193, 205, 206–209, 274, 302, 314–316, 324, 328, 332, 333, 335, 336, 342–347
Schlegel, Friedrich 189, 195
sententia see maxim
sententiarum exornationes or *figurae sententiarum* see figures of thought
separation 3, 4, 28, 72, 73, 193, 240
sermocinatio see dialogue
Seward, William A. 212, 216, 219, 221, 224
Shakespeare 10, 14, 44, 45, 53, 59, 60, 65, 67, 71, 74, 98, 279, 280, 282, 283, 286, 326
Sherry, Richard 2, 4, 68, 70, 73, 284
significatio see emphasis
simile (*imago*) 23, 36, 67, 151, 185, 290
similiter cadens see homoeoptoton
similiter desinens see homoeoteleuton
similitudo see comparison
Skinner, Quentin viii, 10, 15, 272
Smiley, Charles N. vii, 225
Smith, Adam 8
Socrates 1, 8, 27, 99, 200, 238
Socratic 97, 194
Sojcher, Jacques 9, 102, 108
Sonnino, Lee 11–13, 15, 42, 66, 87, 309, 316, 327
Sophists 27
spiritual 93, 94, 122, 198, 241, 265
Sprat, Thomas 5–7, 10, 287–291, 294, 296, 298, 299, 305, 308, 311
Stone, P.W.K. 63, 64, 66
Suarez, Cipriano 5, 12
subiectio see hypophora
subtraction (*quadripartita ratio detractio*) 3, 326
superlatio see hyperbole
surrender (*permissio*) 20, 35, 99, 253
Susenbrotus, Joannes 2, 3, 11, 54, 70, 81–85, 87–89, 172, 180, 185, 274–276, 278–279, 281, 285–286, 315
syllogism 12, 69, 84, 235, 293, 298
synecdoche (*intellectio*) 9, 21, 31, 35, 41, 42, 67, 74, 80–85, 89, 91, 94, 95, 104–106, 109, 188, 209, 347
synonymy or interpretation (*interpretatio*) 20
syntax 41, 47, 48, 215, 219, 241–244, 337

Talon, Omer 83, 84, 86, 87, 89
Terence 51, 76, 84